PEOPLES AND CULTURES
OF THE MIDDLE EAST

CONSULTING EDITOR:

ANTHONY F. C. WALLACE　*University of Pennsylvania*

PEOPLES AND CULTURES
OF THE *Middle East*

EDITED BY AILON SHILOH

University of Pittsburgh

RANDOM HOUSE   New York

To my wife, Cynthia

CONTRIBUTORS

HAMED AMMAR, Professor.

GABRIEL BAER, Professor in the History of Islamic Countries, Hebrew University, Jerusalem.

FREDRIK BARTH, Professor of Social Anthropology, University of Bergen.

MORROE BERGER, Professor of Sociology, Princeton University.

CARLETON S. COON, Research Curator in General Anthropology, University Museum, University of Pennsylvania; Research Associate in General Ethnology, Harvard University.

H. R. P. DICKSON †

ANNE H. FULLER, Center of Middle East Studies, Harvard.

JOHN GULICK, Professor of Anthropology, University of North Carolina.

ANN K. S. LAMBTON, Professor of Persian, School of Oriental and African Studies, University of London.

DANIEL LERNER, Massachusetts Institute of Technology.

BERNARD LEWIS, Professor of the History of the Near and Middle East, University of London.

GEORGE A. LIPSKY, Professor of Political Science and Geography, Wabash College.

MAHMUT MAKAL, Former Turkish schoolteacher.

M. KAMEL NAHAS, Dean of Teachers College, Abbasia, Cairo.

A. H. J. PRINS, Director, Instituut voor Culturele Antropologie, Rijksuniversiteit, Groningen.

EDWIN TERRY PROTHRO, Professor of Anthropology, The American University, Beirut.

S. M. SALIM, Iraqi Ambassador to Sudan.

AILON SHILOH, Associate Professor of Anthropology, University of Pittsburgh.

MELFORD E. SPIRO, Chairman, Department of Anthropology, University of California, San Diego.

LOUISE E. SWEET, Associate Professor of Anthropology, State University of New York at Binghamton.

HERBERT H. VREELAND, Director, Foreign Area Research Program, Human Sciences Research Inc.

ALEX WEINGROD, Professor of Anthropology, Brandeis University.

MOSHE ZELTZER, Professor of Middle Eastern Studies, University of Saskatchewan.

† 1881–1959

Foreword

CARLETON S. COON

Fifteen years ago, while a Ph.D. candidate at Dropsie College, Ailon Shiloh crossed Philadelphia once a week to take my course on the Middle East at the University of Pennsylvania. I felt that he knew considerably more about parts of it than I did, but he was very polite about it and always friendly and lighthearted. When he returned to Philadelphia four years later, after extensive sojourns in North Africa, Israel, and London, and with considerable experience behind him, he had not changed at all, nor seems he to have changed since.

In his forty-three years he has fought with the U.S. Marines on Iwo Jima, earned degrees from three institutions, done field work on southwestern and Great Lakes Indians, North African peoples, Hausas, and the crazy-quilt population of Israel. He has worked in physical anthropology, archaeology, social anthropology, serology, growth, geriatrics, and pathology. He has written some thirty-four books and articles on most of these subjects, plus the sociology of the possible inhabitants of outer space, and has finally touched earth again at the University of Pittsburgh in a position that embraces most of his interests—public health.

This book comprises an introduction by Ailon Shiloh and a selection of twenty-five chapters written by twenty-three authors, including two each by the author-editor and H. R. P. Dickson. Geographically, these chapters cover the West Asian Arabic-speaking countries, Egypt, Israel, Turkey, and Iran. The subject matter ranges from parental child-beating in Lebanon to the structure of the Egyptian army and public-health problems in Saudi Arabia, especially at the time of the pilgrimage.

Shiloh's own introduction is a capsule history of the region, from the time of Mount Carmel man to that of the First Arab-Israeli War, incidentally containing background material for the genesis of the repeat performance in 1967.   In attempting to define "an Arab," Bernard Lewis surveys Arab history.   Moshe Zeltzer presents a detailed list and description of the numerous ethnic groups in Iraq and Syria, Ailon Shiloh does the same for Israel, and Herbert Vreeland for Iran.

We are given four chapters on village life, including Anne Fuller's perceptive paper on the peasant's view of time and space.   Space, to the villager, is everything within his view from the heights behind the village, related to events in time, that is, King Solomon built Baalbek and Noah's Ark landed on Mount Knisseh.   Four other chapters cover nomadic life, and I am glad to see again Fredrik Barth's explanation of why some nomads have so little ritual.   They don't need it.   Their whole life is a formal procession, a circumambulation.

Spiro's account of teen-age life in a kibbutz is a riot.   It also reveals a fundamental truth about human relations—boys and girls who for years have slept in the same room and taken showers together develop an incest taboo like that of siblings.   On the other hand, Hamed Ammar's chapter shows how amorous Egyptian first cousins can be in a society where women are veiled and secluded.

This beautifully chosen collection of what are mostly essays in no way competes with my *Caravan*, from which one chapter was taken, and it may be read with profit by anyone—doctor, lawyer, vice-consul, oilman, and archaeologist—interested in the Middle East or indeed in what goes on in this turbulent world.

C. S. C.
West Gloucester, Massachusetts

Preface

The purpose of this volume has been to provide original, first-hand data concerning behavioral processes among contemporary peoples and cultures of the Middle East. In the pursuit of this goal I have attempted to include as wide a representation as possible of authorities studying and publishing material on the subject in this culture area. To emphasize the essential contemporary scene, I have limited the source of publications to approximately the last twenty years—no publications were called upon preceding 1945. Despite certain problems, I have, where possible, attempted to utilize the publications of native Middle Eastern students in preference to foreign authorities. So far as I am aware, all the authorities here called upon have personally conducted field work in the Middle East, and the majority of the included material represents aspects of the field work.

The problems of transliterating Semitic words into English are well known. In all quotations I have, of course, retained the spelling of the author; my own spelling has tended toward orthographic conservatism—for example, Muhammed, Muslim, kibbutz.

Acknowledgments

The University of Pittsburgh, and in particular the Graduate School of Public Health, provided me with the positive support necessary for the development and completion of this volume. Professor Ray Elling, Director of the Social Science Unit at the School, and Professor David Landy, Chairman of the Department of Anthropology at the University, offered direct interest and continuing encouragement. Anthony F. C. Wallace of the University of Pennsylvania and Theodore Caris, Editor in the College Department of Random House, provided a series of critical evaluations and suggestions during the development of the work. Prompt and positive secretarial assistance was provided by Mary Lou Budziszewski, Connie Papeaka, Annette Simek, and Ingeborg Herman. Patricia Devroude was an invaluable secretary, proofreader and general editor. Mrs. Ida Selavan of Dropsie College, Professor Emrys Peters of the University of Manchester, and Professor Richard Cottam of the University of Pittsburgh read portions of this volume in manuscript form, and their corrections and comments are gratefully acknowledged. Elaine Rosenberg of Random House is particularly thanked for her invaluable responsibility in directing this manuscript through its stages of production.

Contents

Foreword *vii*

Preface *ix*

Acknowledgments *xi*

INTRODUCTION
The Culture History of the Middle East, AILON SHILOH *xv*

PART I *The Distribution of Peoples*

1. What Is an Arab? BERNARD LEWIS *3*
2. Minorities in Iraq and Syria, MOSHE ZELTZER *10*
3. Ethnic Groups and Languages of Iran, HERBERT H. VREELAND *51*
4. Ethnic Groups of Israel, AILON SHILOH *68*

PART II *Cultures and Subcultures*

5. The Material Base of a Lebanese Village, JOHN GULICK *79*
6. A Day in a Syrian Peasant Household, LOUISE E. SWEET *99*
7. Personal Servitude and Dues in Persia, ANN K. S. LAMBTON *105*
8. The Peasant World of Time and Space, ANNE H. FULLER *112*
9. The Camp in the Desert, CARLETON S. COON *119*
10. The Tent and Its Furnishings, H. R. P. DICKSON *136*
11. The Ritual Life of the Basseri, FREDRIK BARTH *153*
12. The Sulubba of the Desert, H. R. P. DICKSON *170*

13. Social Stratification in the Middle East   *174*
14. Traditional Stratification Among the Marsh Dwellers, s. m. salim   *205*

PART III   *Population Dynamics*

15. Public Health and Welfare in Saudi Arabia, george a. lipsky   *219*
16. The Family in the Arab World, m. k. nahas   *233*
17. Adolescence and Marriage in an Egyptian Village, hamed ammar   *247*
18. Child Rearing in the Lebanon, edwin terry prothro   *270*
19. Adolescent Personality in the Kibbutz, melford e. spiro   *290*

PART IV   *Culture Change and Conservatism*

20. The Social Setting of the Egyptian Civil Service, morroe berger   *317*
21. Iran in a Bipolar World, daniel lerner   *331*
22. The Interaction of the Middle Eastern and Western Systems of Medicine, ailon shiloh   *372*
23. Reciprocal Change at Oren, alex weingrod   *387*
24. The Syrian Schooner: Problem Formulation in Maritime Culture Change, a. h. j. prins   *404*

PART V   *The Schoolteacher as Anthropologist*

25. A Village in Anatolia, mahmut makal   *427*

Bibliography   *439*

Index   *445*

Introduction

The Culture History of The Middle East
AILON SHILOH

TERMINOLOGY AND ECOLOGY

During the twentieth century this area of the world has been known by a variety of spatial terms. "Fertile Crescent," "Ottoman Empire," "Levant," "Near East," "Southwest Asia," and "Middle East" have been perhaps the most common appellations. The present terminology was rather decided upon during World War II when the British government designated one area from Libya to Iran as the Military Zone of the Middle East. The huge Middle East Supply Center subsequently established by the Allies in Cairo provided wide and official dissemination of the new term.

For the purposes of this volume, the Middle East is defined as the region

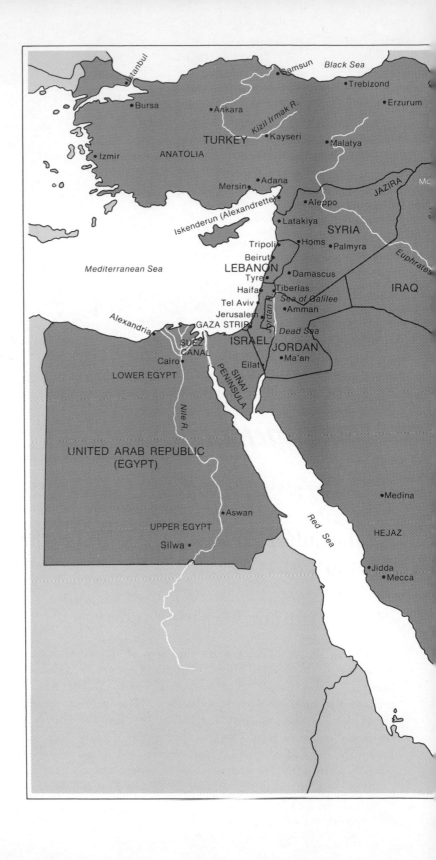

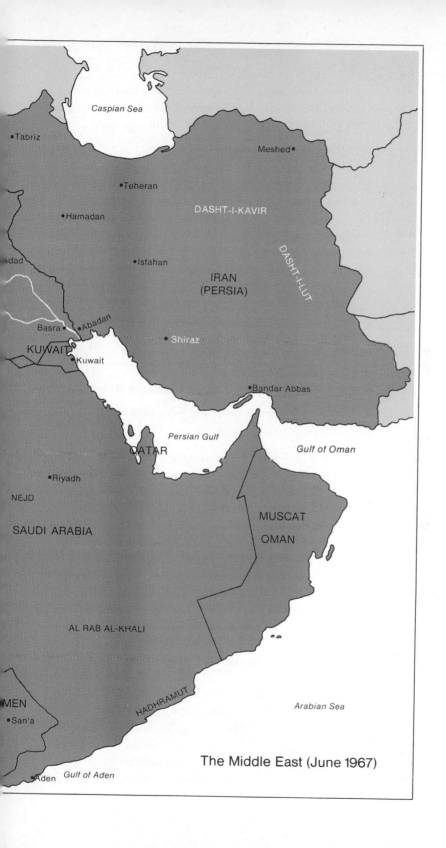

The Middle East (June 1967)

extending from Egypt on the west through Iran on the east. Countries included in this region, their land sizes, and population estimates are noted in Table 1. The total land of the Middle East is some 2.6 million square miles, and the total estimated population is more than 116 million people.

Table 1.   ESTIMATED AS OF JUNE 1, 1967*

Country	Total Area in Square Miles*	Population*
Arabian Peninsula	1,000,000	12,600,000†
Egypt (United Arab Republic)	386,200	30,053,861
Iran (Persia)	628,000	22,000,000
Iraq	175,000	8,261,527
Israel	7,993	2,580,000
Jordan	36,715	1,900,000
Lebanon	4,000	2,152,000
Syria	72,000	5,467,135
Turkey	300,000	31,392,000

* Data abstracted from *The Middle East and North Africa: 1966–67* (13th ed.; London, 1966) ; and *The Middle East: A Political and Economic Survey*, Reader Bullard, ed. (3rd ed.; London, 1958).
† Including Saudi Arabia (6 million) ; Yemen (5 million) ; Aden (1.25 million) ; and the Persian Gulf states (353,000).

In the north are Turkey and Iran, both essentially huge inner plateaus ringed by mountain ranges. The Anatolian Plateau of Turkey rises 3,000 to 3,500 feet above sea level; the plateau in Iran, occupying about half the total area, rises from 1,000 to 3,000 feet. Anatolia is bounded on the south by the Taurus and Anti-Taurus mountain ranges, and Iran is fronted on the north by the Elburz Mountains and on the west and south by the Zagros Massif. These mountain ranges drain off much of the moisture of the westerly rain clouds. Turkey, more favorably located, has some ten to seventeen inches of annual rainfall in the plateau, but in Iran, to the east, whole sections are arid and barren. On both plateaus the climate is one of relatively extreme cold in the winter and extreme heat in the summer. The average January temperature in central Anatolia is 30° F., rising to an average of 86° F. in July. In Teheran, the capital of Iran, it is 35° F. in January and 85° F. in July.

The Arabian Peninsula is also essentially a great plateau, reaching a height of 2,000 to 3,000 feet but dipping dramatically as it extends eastward. This highland is fronted by mountain heights rising 9,000 feet in the Hejaz, the Holy Land of Islam, to an estimated 14,000 feet in Yemen. These mountain ranges successfully tap and drain off almost all the available rains brought in by the westerlies. Except for the Nejd, a pastoral tableland in the north, the very western coastline, which receives about ten inches of rainfall annually, and Yemen in the southwest, where there is sufficient periodic rainfall to permit systematic cultivation, the Arabian Peninsula is a huge and barren land relieved by occasional oases. The south central portion, an area of some 40,000 square miles, is known locally as *al Rab al-Khali* ("the empty quarter"). The average summer temperature in Dhahran, headquarters of the Arabian American Oil Company (Aramco) is 118° F., reaching 165° F. in the sun.

Despite the prominence of these ranges, plateaus, and deserts, perhaps the outstanding geographic phenomenon of the Middle East is the Fertile Crescent, stretching in an arc from Egypt through present-day Israel, Jordan, Lebanon, and Syria into Iraq.

At each horn of the Fertile Crescent there is a fertile river valley—to the east that of the Tigris and Euphrates Rivers and to the west that of the Nile. The river valleys are made up of rich and fertile masses of alluvium deposited year after year on a substratum of sand or rock. In Egypt the rich deposit is almost forty feet deep. As they are annually replenished, these valleys continue to be refertilized and available for tillage. Furthermore, in these arid, almost rainless countries, it is the rivers that also provide the irrigation and drinking water.

In both Iraq and Egypt, spring and autumn are short transitional periods between long hot summers (in Cairo the mean July temperature is 84° F.) and short mild winters (Cairo's mean January temperature is 53° F.). Average rainfall does not exceed eight inches in Egypt and occurs mainly along the coast, whereas Baghdad in Iraq receives an average rainfall of 5.5 inches. (Mosul in the mountainous north receives about thirteen inches.)

Between these two horns of the Fertile Crescent lie Syria, Lebanon, Israel, and Jordan, an area often referred to—particularly by the French—as "the Levant." Syria and Lebanon are characterized by a narrow coastline (known historically as "the King's Highway") fronting on high mountain ranges (some 11,000 feet in the Maronite district of Lebanon). East of the Lebanon Range lies the Anti-Lebanon range of mountains culminating in Mount Hermon, 9,200 feet above sea level. Between these two ranges lies the Bekaa —a long valley generally fertile except in the extreme north toward Syria.

Toward the south, the Lebanon Range becomes less imposing and passes into the Galilee highlands of Israel; average heights are 1,000 to 2,000 feet, although a few peaks top 3,000 feet. This whole "Lebano-Galilean" massif comes to an abrupt end at the Jezree Valley—now a fertile valley extending from the Mediterranean seacoast near Haifa across Israel down to the Jordan Valley.

South of the Esdraelon Valley the highland is again resumed with the Judean Hills—including the Carmel Ridge in the north—leading into the Negev highland in the south. West of these hills lies the Shephelah—an intermediate zone below the uplands of the Judean Hills—and the coastal plain, known in the Bible as "the Plain of Sharon."

Due east of the Judean hills lies the Jordan Valley—a rift extending for 250 miles from the Israel-Lebanon border to the Gulf of Aqaba. The floor of the depression reaches its lowest in the region of the northern Dead Sea, where the lake bottom is 2,598 feet below sea level. East of these mountains and valleys, from Syria through Jordan, begins "the vast platform of Arabia."

One of the largest rivers in the Levant is the Orontes, which begins in the northern Bekaa and flows northward through Syria. The Litani River begins close by the Orontes but flows southward through Lebanon. The Jordan River flows southward from Lebanon forming the Huleh and the Sea of Galilee as it follows the Jordan Rift into the Dead Sea. The Yarqon, which enters the Mediterranean just north of Tel Aviv, is the most southerly of the rivers that flow all year round.

The Lebanon and Israel mountain ranges of the Levant coast catch most of the precipitation from the maritime winds, leaving little for the Syrian and Jordanian hinterland. Beirut receives an annual rainfall of almost thirty-six inches, more than parts of Great Britain, but all of it is normally crowded into the months from November through March. Damascus, behind the double screen of the Lebanon, receives only ten inches.

THE CULTURE HISTORY OF THE MIDDLE EAST

Skeletal evidence in Persia and Palestine indicate that some forms of pre-*Homo sapiens* lived and evolved in this area of the world. The origin and evolution of *Homo sapiens* occurred perhaps in a belt extending from East Africa through East Asia, and the Middle East apparently operated as the critical connecting land bridge.

Whatever the uncertainties about the origin and evolution of *Homo sapiens* and his Stone Age cultural levels, it does now appear rather definite that the Neolithic Period—the domestication of plants and animals—occurred earliest somewhere in the highlands of the Middle East, perhaps by 6000 B.C.

The Horns of the Fertile Crescent

By 4000 B.C. in the river valleys of both Egypt and Mesopotamia (the Iraqi river valley) agriculture was being practiced—wheat grown, vineyards cultivated—pottery was being made and fired, the wheel had been invented, and copper and bronze were being used.

By perhaps 3000 B.C. temple accounts in Mesopotamia were being kept in Sumerian cuneiform writing, and Egyptian hieroglyphic writing soon followed the Sumerian practice.

During the third millennium in Lower Mesopotamia powerful cities had annexed weaker ones, and compacts and unions were being made to form larger ones; by 2300 B.C. one ruler of Uruk claimed to have annexed all the city-states under his power.

The same process took place in Egypt as well, although the unification process seems to have occurred earlier and been more permanent. At that time Egypt was populated by Hamites or Mediterraneans—longheaded brunettes, relatively slender and of moderate stature.

The Sumerians of Mesopotamia are believed to have been of an Armenoid physical type—round-headed, of moderate height, and of heavy build —who spoke a language with some agglutinative features similar to the Mongolian family of languages.

Such additional peoples in the area as Akkadians, Babylonians, Assyrians, Amorites of North Syria, Aramaeans of Inner Syria, Canaanites of the coast, Hebrews, and Arabs are generally called "Semites"—not because they necessarily reflected any differences in physical makeup but because they all spoke languages assigned to the Semitic family and are believed to have originated in the Arabian Peninsula. (As far as we are aware, the Mediterranean peoples were indigenous to the area; the Sumerians were a very early intrusive population, as were such later Indo-European peoples as Hittites, Philistines, Persians, Greeks, Romans, and the much later Mongoloid Turks.)

Semitic hegemony in the Lower Mesopotamian valley was established by Sargon, the builder of Akkad, around 2350 B.C. For more than a thousand years previously, nomads from the Syrian-Arabian Desert had been infiltrating into the valley in the east, absorbing the high culture of the Sumerians until, under Sargon, they assumed control. Later Babylonian and Assyrian empires expanded this initial Semitic conquest.

The Levant: 1500–500 B.C.

The Amorites, of whom the Canaanites formed the southern branch, occupied the bulk of what is today Syria and Lebanon. Hemmed in between the mighty empires of Mesopotamia and Egypt, threatened to the north by the Hittites in Anatolia, and occupying a land fragmented by mountains, they never succeeded in establishing a strong unified state.

The Aramaeans were an inland Semitic population centered in northeastern Syria near Haran, but later they moved south and settled around and controlled Damascus.

The Hebrews may have entered the land of Canaan in a number of major if ill-defined movements. One was connected with Aramaean movements southward from Haran, and another was out of Egypt in the late thirteenth century. They encountered a formidable adversary—beside the Canaanites—in the Philistines, an Indo-European sea people that had just established itself along the Palestine coast, and it was not until the time of David that the Canaanite and Philistine grip on the land was loosened.

Such petty states as those of the Canaanites (Phoenicians), Aramaeans, and Israelites (northern and southern kingdoms) could exist only during the intervals when the expansive Egyptian and Mesopotamian empires were weak or occupied elsewhere, as was the case in the centuries immediately preceding and succeeding 1000 B.C.

The Assyrians were building up their war machine, and in 732 B.C. Tiglath Pileser overthrew Damascus, center of the Aramaeans. His successor, Shalmaneser V, overran Phoenicia and, in 722, conquered the northern kingdom of Israel. The southern kingdom of Judah was forced to become a vassal of Assyria until 586, when the Neo-Babylonian Nebuchadnezzar swept over the kingdom, devastated Jerusalem, and deported its leaders to his capital.

The Persians under Cyrus brought Neo-Babylonia under their empire and, in 538, Cyrus permitted the Jews to return to and rebuild Jerusalem.

Despite the end of the Aramaean political entity, the language continued to survive as the language of the countryside and as the *lingua franca* of commerce and trade.

From Hellenism to Byzantium: 500 B.C.–A.D. 500

The intrusion of Greek thought and language into the Middle East was a direct result of the conquests of Alexander the Great. In the spring of 334 B.C., this twenty-one-year-old Macedonian crossed the Hellespont (the Dardanelles) and began a series of conquests that ushered the Middle East into the European sphere of political and cultural influence—Macedonian-Greek (Hellenistic), Roman, and Byzantine—where it remained until the rise of Islam a thousand years later.

Alexander was particularly concerned with spreading his Hellenistic culture—a fusion of Hellenic and Near Eastern values and behavior—and this spread continued and developed even after his death in Babylon in 323 B.C.

One of his generals, Ptolemy, took control of Egypt; and another, Seleucus, took control of Persia, Mesopotamia, and later Syria and Asia Minor.

It was Antiochus, ruler of the later empire of Seleucus, who encouraged the identification of Zeus with Jehovah that led to the revolt of the Jews under the Maccabeans. The Jews attained religious freedom in 164 and political independence in 140. The Maccabean dynasty of priest-kings lasted until the advent of the Romans about eighty years later.

Beginning during the middle of the first century B.C., Rome conquered the Middle East: Syria from the Seleucids, Egypt from the Ptolemies, and the Pontic kingdom of Asia Minor from Mithridates. Rome also came to terms with the newly emergent Parthian kingdom extending from Mesopotamia to India.

Under the Hellenists towns and cities had been renamed and developed and others newly built, in order to spread the Greek language and the Hellenistic way of life more easily and quickly. The Romans continued this tradition and made the towns the focal military, political, and economic centers, often staffed largely with members of nonindigenous populations, who resided in separate quarters. In the countryside, however, older Semitic traditions persisted, particularly in religion and language.

A few outlying east-west caravan centers remained to be conquered—the Nabataean Empire whose capital was in Jordanian Petra (A.D. 106) and the Syrian empire of Palmyra, under its last famous queen, Zenobia, (A.D. 272).

Herod, an Edomite, ruled over Judea—the name given to Roman Palestine—for thirty-three years ending with his death in 4 B.C., *circa* the birth of Christ. Herod promoted irrigation, agriculture, industry, and commerce; refortified Jerusalem and rebuilt its temple; established new towns like Caesarea; and fortified such desert locations as Masada.

According to Philip K. Hitti, "Of all the multitudinous peoples who constituted the Roman world, the Jews—due to their nationalistic and religious peculiarities—were undoubtedly the most difficult for the Romans to govern."[1]

Herod repressed the outbreaks against his authority with bloody force. After Herod's death, the Jews remained restive and in A.D. 67 Vespasian moved against them with 50,000 troops. His son Titus carried on the operations against Jerusalem, and, after a few months' siege, the capital was starved into surrender (A.D. 70). The last remnant of that Jewish revolt was broken at Masada in A.D. 73.

It was during the period of these events in Palestine that Jesus Christ was born, lived, and died. (Jesus, whose name is a Hellenized form of the Hebrew name Yeshu or Yehoshua, was also known as "Christ," a translation of the Hebrew word for "anointed," *meshiach*, which led to the word "messiah.")

Under Paul, himself a Hellenized convert from Judaism, the teachings of Jesus began to be organized into a separate religion. Paul moved the teachings out of Judaism and established them as the religion of Christ, Christianity. As a monotheistic religion, Christianity could not tolerate the polytheism of the Romans, and already by A.D. 64 Nero was instituting severe persecutions of its followers. The Christians, still often confused with the Jews, continued to be persecuted by the Romans until A.D. 313, when Constantine was formally converted to the new religion.

During those early centuries, Christianity developed further as a religion. The Judaism of the Roman Empire, the neo-Platonic reasonings of the Alexandrian school of theology, traditional Middle Eastern beliefs and practices, and the then very popular mystery cult of Mithra all played a role in the early development of Christianity.

In 324 Emperor Constantine chose the site of an old Greek colony, Byzantium, in which to found his new city, Constantinople ("the city of Constantine," renamed Istanbul in 1923).

In an attempt to unify the divergent views and beliefs of the new religion, the early Christian Church was organized into four provinces, each province headed by a patriarch. Yet within a short time the increasing divergence in doctrine and ritual led to a complete separation of the four provinces. In Constantinople arose the Greek Orthodox Church, in Rome the Roman Catholic or Latin Church, in Alexandria the Coptic Church, and in Antioch the Syrian or Jacobite Church.

By the fourth century the Armenian (Gregorian) Church had come into existence, as well as the Nestorian (Chaldean or Assyrian) Church. Somewhat later the Maronite sect was established. (It was these eastern Christian sects that bore the full brunt of the later Muslim conquests. With their religion under attack and the majority of the population killed or converted, they soon dwindled to their present weak position.)

Politically, the Byzantine Empire was strongest in Asia Minor. Egypt and the Levant were never completely Hellenized, and neither the Greek language nor the Christian religion was fully adopted by the masses. In those countries there was political, religious, and linguistic hostility to the Orthodox, Greek-speaking central government in Constantinople.

The Arabs and Islam: A.D. 500–1500

By the fifth century the Arabs of the Arabian Peninsula had become traditionally divided into two main groups—the northern and the southern —which differed profoundly in language and culture.

The southern Arabian language was different from that of the north; it even possessed a different alphabet. Furthermore, the Arabs of the southern region were sedentary agriculturists who had developed such kingdoms as Saba (Sheba?) in the tenth century B.C., built the famous Ma'rib Dam around 750 B.C., established commercial links with Africa, colonized extensively in Africa, and even founded a kingdom in Abyssinia, whose name comes from Habashat, the name of a southwestern Arabian people.

During the Classical Period, southern Arabia was an important center along the trade routes to India and an agricultural source of cereals, myrrh, incense, and other spices—the *Arabia Felix* of the Romans.

The central and northern Arabian peoples were nomads who from time to time moved north into the Fertile Crescent or set up border states of varying size, strength, and duration. The dominant feature of these people was their nomadic, tribal existence. The social unit was the blood descent in the male line; the livelihood of the tribe depended on its flocks and herds and on raiding the neighboring settled countries. The head of the tribe was a *sayyid* or *sheikh,* an elected leader usually from one traditional family, and he was advised by a council of elders called a *majlis.* / The life of the tribe was regulated by custom, the *Sunna* or practices of the ancestors, and the *sheikh* was expected to heed the *majlis,* rather than to lead it. /

Certain gods transcended purely tribal cults. The three most important were Manat, Uzza, and Allat; all three were usually subordinated to a higher deity called Allah.

The desert oases provided a more permanent version of this tribal life, particularly Mecca in the Hejaz, which possessed a collection of sacred stones in one central shrine, the Ka'aba.

Christian and Jewish colonies were well established throughout the area; their religions, literatures, and cultures were well known, particularly in the towns where conversions were not uncommon. Two Byzantine border Arab states, Ghassan and Hira, were Christian—the former Monophysite and the latter Nestorian.

Muhammed ("most highly praised") was born sometime around A.D. 570 into the family of the Bani Hashim, a reputable family of the Quraish, the leading tribe in Mecca. His father, Abdullah, a camel driver, had died before his birth, and his mother died when he was six. He was brought up as a poor orphan, probably by his grandfather. He engaged in trade but acquired wealth and position in his middle twenties by marrying Khadija, the widow of a rich merchant.

In 610, sometime around his fortieth year, in a cave on Mount Hira, a barren hill outside Mecca, Muhammed received "The Call" from the voice of Gabriel to serve as messenger (*rasul*) and prophet (*nabi*) of Allah.

At first Muhammed won little support and that mainly from among the poor and the slaves. Among his first converts were his wife Khadija and his cousin Ali, later to become the fourth caliph.

Despite pronounced Arab opposition, Islam, as Muhammed's faith was called, continued to gain such new adherents as Abu Bakr, Umar, and Uthman of the Umayya house, one of the dominant families of Mecca. In the summer of 622, 200 of Muhammed's followers fled to Medina; soon after he followed them. This flight, the Hijra, is the turning point in the religion of Islam; it is the starting point of the Muslim calendar. In Mecca Muhammed had been a private citizen; in Medina he became the ruler, able to develop and practice his religion as well as to preach it.

Gradually he broke with Judaism, Christianity, and Arab paganism. He replaced the Sabbath with Friday, substituted the muezzin call to prayer for the sound of gongs or clappers, changed the direction of prayer from Jerusalem to Mecca, increased the number of daily prayers from three to five, sanctioned the pilgrimage to the Ka'aba, and abolished wine-drinking and gambling.

Toward the end of January 630, Muhammed and his followers entered Mecca and established Islam. This religion is primarily derived from the Koran (*al quran*, "reading" or "recitation")—the word of God as dictated in Arabic by the messenger-angel Gabriel to Muhammed.

The Koran derives much from early Judaism and Christianity. Abraham, Muhammed's ideal predecessor, is cited seventy times in twenty-five chapters, and his name titles Chapter 14; Joseph is the title of Chapter 12 where his story is told; the name of Moses occurs in thirty-four different chapters; the story of the creation and the fall of man is cited five times and that of the flood eight times.

From Christianity, Zachariah, John the Baptist, Jesus ('Isa), and Mary are mentioned. The virgin birth of Jesus is accepted, as are such noncanonical miracles as Jesus' preaching while still in the cradle and his creating birds out of clay. Jerusalem, and especially the Temple of Solomon, acquired special sanctity as the spot from which Muhammed was once transported to heaven.

The religious duties of a Muslim can be summed up under the five categories known as the Five Pillars of Islam: the profession of faith; prayer five times a day; almsgiving; the observance of fasting during the month of Ramadan; and the pilgrimage to Mecca.

A sixth pillar, *jihad* ("holy war"), has sometimes been added. As the world is believed to be divided into that of Islam, *dar al-Islam*, and that of war, *dar al-harb*, it becomes the duty of a devout Muslim to attack the latter. Death on the battlefield in a holy war is martyrdom and ensures special privileges in Paradise for the victim. To this institution, Islam owes much of its early expansion.

When Muhammed died, in 632, the problem arose as to who would be his successor (caliph). The bitter disagreement that attended such decisions led to many of the later dissensions and divisions of Islam. The essential struggle for power was the traditional one between the early followers of Muhammed (represented by Ali, his son-in-law and husband to Fatimah, the only surviving daughter of Muhammed) and the powerful Meccan families (represented by Uthman of the Umayya). Matters were brought to a head when Uthman, the third caliph, was killed by fellow Muslims and Ali was proclaimed fourth caliph. Aisha, the youngest widow of Muhammed, united with Muawiyah, the nephew of Uthman, to implicate Ali in the assassination and demand that he abdicate.

Ali was out-maneuvered, abdicated, and was later assassinated (in 661). One of Ali's sons, Hasan, was bribed to give up his claim and apparently was later poisoned; the other son, Husayn, fought and was defeated and beheaded.

One of the great schisms of Islam developed from these events. The Shiites (from *shiatu Ali,* "the party of Ali") elevated Ali and his son Husayn to sainthood. Ali's burial place at Najaf and that of Husayn at Karbala, both in Iraq, became and are still holy shrines to the Shiites equal to Medina and even Mecca of the Sunnites—the orthodox or traditionalist Muslims.

Politically, the death of Ali marked the end of the simple patriarchal Orthodox Caliphate of the Hejaz (632–661) and the beginning of the monarchial and worldly, anchored-in-Damascus, Umayyad Caliphate (661–750).

It was during this period that the Arab military conquests were at their peak. Begun originally as the wars of the *riddah*—"bringing back by force into the fold of Islam" the many tribes all over the peninsula who had seceded on the death of Muhammed and refused to pay alms—they soon spread to areas beyond that of the original converted tribes of Arabia. Muhammed died in 632. By 635 Damascus and the border states had been conquered, and in 636 on the banks of the Yarmuk, a tributary of the Jordan, the Byzantine army was defeated. By the time of the Battle of Tours in 732, 100 years after the death of the Prophet, the Arabs had conquered a kingdom extending from southern France through Spain, North Africa, Egypt, Syria, the Arabian Peninsula, Iraq, parts of eastern Anatolia (Constantinople was then under siege but not yet conquered), Persia, Afghanistan, and into central Asia as far as Bokhara, Baluchistan, and the southern Punjab.

In the early conquest, bedouin furnished the rank and file of the troops under Meccan and Medinese leadership. Shortly thereafter, however, the army began to be composed of Christian, Jewish, Persian, and Berber neo-Muslims. Certain of the military leaders also came from these newly converted populations.

Under the Umayyads there were four major social classes: the Amsar (the ruling Arabian Muslim aristocracy and its descendants); the Mawali (the Christians, Jews, Persians, Aramaeans, Egyptians, Berbers, and other non-Arab neoconverts to Islam, who were in theory equal but in practice second-class Muslims); the Dhimmi (the professors of the revealed religions of Christianity and Judaism, who, because they were the "People of the Book," were tolerated but were subject to special taxation and social disabilities); and the slaves (during the century of the conquests literally thousands of slaves were taken; some of whom achieved meritorious rank in Islam).

Abu al-Abbas, a descendent of al-Abbas, a paternal uncle of the Prophet, sought to unite Mawali dissatisfaction, Shiite dissidence, Sunnite disapproval of the "ungodly" Umayyad, and a traditional Persian unity and sense of superiority over the Arabs to end the Umayyad Caliphate. The black banner of the Abbasids was raised against the white banner of the Umayyads in 747, and the revolt was successful by 750, when the last Umayyad caliph was caught hiding in Egypt and decapitated.

The Abbasids soon established, in Baghdad, an Islamic economic empire in which the arts and sciences flourished. Much of the romance and glory of Islam of this period (during the "Dark Ages" in Europe), was centered around the Caliph Haroun al-Rashid (ruled 786–809). Morally, there was open drinking, excessive concubinage, and lax sexual morality—particularly homosexuality and eunuchism.

Political and religious reactions to the Abbasids developed quickly. Spain, under a surviving Umayyad, became the first lost province. Dissident Shiites set up independent kingdoms in Morocco and later in Tunisia. Afghanistan and northern India were also won by independent Muslim rulers; and Persia, whose inhabitants never were fully converted to Islam or Arabic, operated all but independently. A Shiite sect, the Qarmatians, carved out an independent empire on the western shore of the Persian Gulf, seized Oman, raided Mecca and removed the sacred Black Stone, the *Ka'aba*. Another Shiite sect established the independent Fatimid dynasty in Egypt and Syria. In addition, Sufism, a mystical monastic sect of Islam—with saints, rosary, and spiritual excitement, which subsequently profoundly affected the traditional Islamic religion—was developing and being persecuted as heresy during this period.

Two temporary invasions and one permanent invasion scarred these troubled times. The Crusaders landed in Asia Minor in 1097 and the coastal area of the Levant, from Cilicia to central Palestine, was under their domination. A century later, in 1187, in the Battle of Hittim, above the Sea of Galilee, the Crusaders' army was almost wiped out and Jerusalem lost. The resulting Third Crusade, with its armistice between Richard and the Kurdish Muslim, Salah al-Din of the Ayyubid, merely delayed the ultimate Arab reconquest of the coastal strip, completed with the fall of Acre in 1291.

Much more devastating to the Arabs were the Mongol invasions from the East that wreaked extensive destruction. During the early thirteenth century the armies of Jenghis Khan, led by his grandson Hulagu, devastated Persia. In 1258 they destroyed Baghdad; devastated the countryside in Iraq, particularly the irrigation works; and extinguished the Abbasid Caliphate. A century later the Mongol armies of Timur advanced into Syria, burning Aleppo, Homs, and Damascus before they were defeated near Nazareth by the Mamluk Baybars.

The third invasion into the Middle East, and the only permanent one, was that of the Turks. The Arabs had first met the Turks in central Asia and had for some time been importing them as slaves. These slaves were especially trained for military and administrative purposes, and were later known as *mamluk* ("slave," "owned") to distinguish them from the domestic slaves. The Turkish warriors were famed for their superior mounted bowmen and cavalry speed. They soon came to be used as mercenary soldiers and as the private bodyguard of the Abbasid caliphs.

One group of these Turks emigrated as a tribe, around 970, and converted to Sunni Islam. They became known as the Seljuqs, conquered much of Persia, and in 1055 entered Baghdad and incorporated Iraq into the Seljuq realm. In a few years they conquered Syria and Palestine from local rulers and the declining Fatimids; then, under the leadership of Alp Arslan, they succeeded where the Arabs had failed, defeating the Byzantines at Manzikart in 1071 and taking the Byzantine emperor, Diogenus, prisoner. Turkish tribes poured into the area, and the Turkification of Asia Minor began.

Seljuq rule in Egypt was superseded by the Kurd Salah al-Din, and the Ayyubid dynasty, when, upon the confusion after the death of the last Ayyubid, a Turk named Baybars became sultan (1260–1277). He checked the Mongol invasions into Palestine and attacked and conquered most of the Crusader fort-towns remaining there. Later known as the Mamluk Sultanate, these Turks ruled Egypt, Palestine, and Syria until 1517.

Despite early Mamluk strength, later avaricious Mamluk rulers—in an area weakened by Christian and Mongol invasions and frequent bedouin depredations—regularly raised the taxes of the trade between Europe and India and China. In 1498 Vasco da Gama opened a new route to the Farther East, a cheaper and safer route than the Middle Eastern land route, by sailing around the Cape of Good Hope. The Mamluks lost their great source of revenue and fell, an easy prey, before the rising Ottoman power.

The Ottoman Empire: 1500–World War I

The Ottomans were another of the Turkish tribes that flowed out of central Asia into the Middle East. As a result of attacks from Mongols and Byzantines, Seljuq power in Anatolia decayed and they were absorbed by the Ottomans who, under Uthman (*c.* 1300), fought and defeated them. The Ottomans began a series of conquests in Anatolia and the Balkans (where they learned the effective use of firearms); finally, in 1453, they took Constantinople. The Turks then moved against the Persians and the Mamluks (1517). By the time of Suleiman the Magnificent (1520–1560), Ottoman power was at its zenith; the Ottomans had a powerful navy and army, headed by the Janissaries (from *yeni-cheri*, "new troops"), and they ruled North Africa (the Barbary States), Egypt, Palestine, Syria, the Hejaz, Yemen, Mesopotamia, Armenia, western Persia, Anatolia, and Balkan Europe, almost to Vienna.

The empire was ruled by a Turkish royalty, maintained by a military-administrative force (originally composed of Christian slaves, later of Turkish Muslims), with religion controlled by an *ulema* headed by the *shaykh al-Islam* ("Leader of Islam').

Social stratification followed religious lines. In Turkey the religious grouping was termed *millet*. The two major millets were Islam and Rūm (Roman and Greek Orthodox Christians). Armenians and Jews also constituted millets. The religious head of the millet was officially recognized by the government as the administrator of laws pertaining to personal status within the community (marriage, divorce, inheritance, and adoption). The millet system was later extended to European residents in the empire in the form of capitulations (extraterritorial rights).

The aim of Ottoman provincial administration was to provide the central government with taxes for its treasury and manpower for its army and to maintain internal provincial security. The taxation system offered fertile ground for abuse, corruption, dissensions, and rebellion. By the twentieth century, much of Ottoman Europe was independent, whereas North Africa and Egypt were European-ruled; central and southern Arabia had evolved into more or less independent states; the Levant and Iraq had become poverty-stricken, and Turkish peasants in Anatolia were little better off. Turkey, once the terror of Europe, had become the "sick man of Europe."

By 1900 Germany, with its *Drang nach Osten* ("drive to the east"), had replaced England and France as the key influence in Constantinople. Kaiser Wilhelm visited Constantinople, Damascus, Beirut, and Jerusalem; acquired the concession for the Berlin-Baghdad Railway; assumed responsibility for the Syria-Hejaz Railroad; and sent military missions to train the Turkish Army.

In the meantime liberal-intellectual forces within Turkey were slowly developing. In 1826 the Sultan had had the Janissaries exterminated. Despite the long and reactionary regime of Sultan Abdul Hamid (ruled 1876–1909), civilian and military liberals and reformists grew in strength. Finally, in 1908 a corps of young officers in the Turkish army (the "Young Turks") forced Hamid to accept a Western-type constitution for the Turkish Empire. The following year the Sultan was caught intriguing and was deposed, and the Young Turks assumed the rule of the Ottoman Empire.

World War I to the Present

On the eve of World War I, the "sick man" was in a dubious position. Much of the Barbary Coast was already under French, Italian, and Spanish control; the British were in Egypt, Aden, and along the Persian Gulf; and virtually all of Ottoman Europe had been annexed or declared independent. The Ottoman government itself had a national debt of some $740 million, which was administered by an international committee sitting in Constantinople.

Only Asia Minor and the Levant—perhaps the "heartland" of the Ottoman Empire—remained outside foreign political control. Russia, France, and England, however, were involved with religious minorities in the Levant; Arab nationalist movements were being organized in Damascus and Beirut; and Jews were immigrating into Palestine in increasing numbers as part of the Zionist nationalist movement.

War in Europe began on August 2, 1914, and Turkey signed a secret alliance with Germany on that day. The British reopened secret talks they had begun, early in 1914, with Abdullah, second son of Sharif Hussein of Mecca, on the feasibility of a revolt by the Ottoman Arabs against the Ottoman Turks. This possibility became particularly relevant when the Sultan-Caliph in Constantinople proclaimed a *jihad* against the Allies.

An exchange of correspondence between Sharif Hussein and Sir Henry McMahon, the British High Commissioner, ensued, and the Arab revolt began in June 1916.

On October 30, 1918, Turkey signed an armistice with the Allies, and in August 1920, in the peace agreement of Sèvres, it agreed to renounce all claims to non-Turkish territories.

The Arabs and others now expected the fulfillment of promises made, or understood to have been made, by Britain and her allies. Important documents include the McMahon correspondence, the Sykes-Picot Agreement (that there should be an international zone in Palestine, a British zone in Iraq, a French zone in Syria, and an independent Arab state, under Allied influence, between the zones, that is, Transjordan), and the Balfour Declaration (that "His Majesty's Government views with favor the establishment in Palestine of a National Home for the Jewish people . . .").

The problems raised by these apparently contradictory promises, agreements, and understandings have still to be resolved. At the conference of the victors at San Remo in 1920, France received the mandate for Syria and Lebanon; England received the mandate for Palestine, including Transjordan, "with the obligation to carry out the policy of the Balfour Declaration."[2] The results of these arbitrary decisions still plague the region.

In 1919 Greek troops landed in Izmir in order to annex much of western Anatolia, an action that precipitated widespread Turkish nationalist resistance. Under the leadership of Mustafa Kemal, the Greeks were defeated, and the Allies were forced to recognize the full sovereignty of Turkey.

Mustafa Kemal then proceeded to work toward the establishment of Turkey as a modern Western state. The sultanate was abolished in 1922, Turkey was proclaimed a republic in 1923, and the caliphate was abolished in 1924. In 1925 the fez was forbidden and replaced by the wearing of European hats and caps; in 1926 use of the Gregorian calendar became compulsory, and a new legal code was adopted; in 1928 the state became officially secular, a Latin-based alphabet was introduced, and the use of Arabic letters became illegal; in 1934 women were given the right to vote and stand for office; and in 1935 the use of surnames on the European model was introduced.

Mustafa Kemal took the name of Ataturk ("Father of Turkey") and, until his death in 1938, was effecting unique culture changes at the national level.

Between the two world wars, France maintained an uneasy rule over Syria and Lebanon; Britain established Transjordan as an entity separate from Palestine, with Abdullah, the second son of Sharif Hussein, as its ruler; Jewish immigration into Palestine continued at a low rate with limitations being imposed as Arab unrest, disorders, and riots increased.

Britain had originally been allotted a mandate for Iraq; Emir Feisal, son of Sharif Hussein, was chosen to be its king, and Iraq achieved independence in 1932. In Egypt the British Declaration of 1924 handed over control of the bulk of Egyptian affairs to Egyptian political leaders.

During the early nineteenth century, Iran suffered a series of disastrous defeats at the hands of the Russians. It lost much of its northern territory, and since then, as a limited military power, it has adroitly balanced between British (and later Western) and Russian power interests. During World War I, Iran was ostensibly neutral, but both warring sides fought on its territory. An ex-army officer, Reza Khan, effected a coup d'état in 1921 and in 1925 became the Shah of Iran. Like Mustafa Kemal in Turkey, he attempted to consummate positive Westernization.

In the Arabian Peninsula Abdul Aziz Ibn Saud, leader of a small Islamic religious sect, the Wahhabi, organized his forces to challenge Sharif Hussein successfully for the leadership of Arabia. In 1925 he defeated the Sharif, who retired to Cyprus, and for the first time in many centuries the interior of Arabia was united under a single ruler. Such coastal units as Yemen, Aden, Muscat and Oman, the Trucial States, Bahrain, and Kuwait continue to exist as independent or protected entities.

During World War II various Middle Eastern states were involved in Fascist activities, but the Allies, particularly the British, were able to curtail their growth so effectively that the Middle East, and in particular Cairo, served as a key base in the war against Germany.

Even before the end of World War II, victims and survivors of the Nazi concentration camps made it clear that the status quo could not continue in Palestine. Arab and Jewish terrorist activities intensified the problem. The British government referred the problem to the newly formed United Nations, declaring that, if no settlement acceptable to both Jews and Arabs could be found, it would withdraw from Palestine. On November 29, 1947, the United Nations plan for the partition of Palestine was approved and on May 14, 1948, the British mandate was abandoned and the State of Israel proclaimed. The armies of five Arab states invaded Israel and were repulsed; armistice agreements were signed in 1949.

CONTEMPORARY PEOPLES
AND CULTURES

The culture history of much of the region continues to be one of limited social and economic development.

The Middle Eastern economy is still termed the "Cadillac-camel" economy. A small number of wealthy landowners own a large proportion of the land and there are thousands of dwarf-holders, tenants, and landless laborers. "The annual income per head in Turkey and Lebanon is less than one quarter that in Great Britain; in Egypt and Syria it approaches one fifth; while in Saudi Arabia it is less than one tenth."[3]

The majority of the population are poor, illiterate, slum-dwelling rural or newly urbanized peasants. Despite the potential increased food supply through known techniques of soil and water improvement, only some 5 to 6 per cent of the land is cultivated, and masses of the population exist on inadequate diets. Morbidity and mortality rates continue to run high even though, with a birth rate ranging from 25 to 60 per 1,000 (cf. United Kingdom 15, United States 17), the population is increasing at an annual average rate of about 20 per 1,000, a rate which doubles the population in thirty-five years.[4]

The goal of providing a selection of original field-work studies detailing critical aspects of the contemporary peoples and cultures of the Middle East is recognized as being difficult and subjective. Authorities may question not only the actual subjects selected but also the authors of these selections and, perhaps more important, the wide variety of subjects and studies omitted.

Whatever the criteria an editor uses in making his final decisions, he is confronted constantly with the realities of limited and questionable data. It has been argued that the Middle East possesses two veils—the first being lack of data, the second the questionable validity of the data.

An example of this problem is the apparently simple assessment of population dynamics. Despite accepted published figures, it is difficult to provide precise demographic data for the Middle East. Egypt had an excellent tradition of ten-year censuses, dating back to 1897, but the 1957 census was omitted for political reasons. The first census in Iraq, however, was taken in 1947 and in Jordan in 1961. The most recent census in Lebanon was in 1932, and in Syria no population count took place between 1922 and 1960. Population counts in the huge Arabian peninsula have occurred only in the tiny enclaves of Aden, Bahrain, and Kuwait—and there only since 1955. For the remainder of the vast peninsula, including Saudi Arabia and Yemen, there are only generally accepted estimates.

These limitations in the Middle East, like those in other underdeveloped regions of the world, are understandable for a variety of reasons. They include, first, the nomadic existence of the bedouin population, which does not lend itself to accurate census taking or even to estimates; second, the enormous rate of illiteracy among the rural and nomad populations may result in inaccurate or false figures designed to satisfy census takers rather than to reflect accurate demography (this problem is particularly apparent in age breakdowns when ages are often provided in "round" figures) ; third, particularly among the fellaheen, the past experiences of the population make them reluctant to provide correct information to government authorities, who might then use the data for taxation or military purposes; fourth, the figures may be reduced during military or taxation periods but raised in times of rationing; and, fifth, the traditional cultural factors that conflict with federal, objective census taking may result in inaccurate reporting. Examples of the last problem are failure to report newborn children or reporting sons as daughters because of fear of the evil eye; the view that the number of wives a man has is considered a private matter and the fact that the census taker may not enter the women's quarters to check reliability of reports; exaggeration of the number of family members for purposes of prestige, or neglect to mention girls because they are not important, or disguising the presence of unmarried daughters of eligible age, which may be considered shameful; and, finally, possible bedouin resentment of interference in their personal affairs so that census taking among the nomads may be reduced to tent counting.

Another complicating factor of the Middle Eastern scene is the existence of numerous and distinct ethnic, religious, and linguistic population groups. Coon has called the Middle East a "mosaic" of peoples; a simple example of this mosaic may be seen in Syria.

> Although 85 percent of the population is Muslim, every fifth Muslim belongs to a schismatic sect, such as the Alawis (Nusayries), Druses, Ismailis, Shiites, or Yazidis. Even more fragmented are the eleven Christian denominations, including Greek Orthodox, Syrian Orthodox, Armenian Gregorians, Greek Catholics, Syrian Catholics, Chaldean Catholics, Armenian Catholics, Maronites, Nestorians, and various Protestants. There are also non-Arabic-speaking subminorities, such as the Sunni Muslim Kurds, the Turkomans, and the Circassians, each with its own language, culture, and distinctive social, and often political, orientation. They constitute nearly 10 percent of the population. Nearly half a million bedouin and seminomads roam the vast desert in the eastern two thirds of Syria. Although only 10 percent of the total population, they are a major divisive factor. Sectionalism is still another centrifugal force weakening the State's central authority. Competing social, economic, and political interests have grouped around each of the four major cities—Damascus, Homs, Hama, and Aleppo.[5]

This mosaic has been developing and expanding for millennia. The Middle East has the longest culture history of any region in the world; it was the birthplace of human civilization; three monotheistic religions originated there and developed numerous schisms and sects; the land bridge connecting Africa, Asia, and Europe, has been traversed by numerous peoples and cultures, many of whom have left remnants in the region; and, finally, its cultural evolution has been such that, until recently, minority groups were permitted to maintain separate and distinct identifications.

There are not only indigenous Jewish populations in the region but also Samaritans and Karaites—early offshoots from the mainstream of Judaism. Christianity is represented by communities of both indigenous early Christian groups such as the Copts, Armenian Orthodox, and Greek Orthodox and the numerous varieties of later Catholicism and Protestantism.

Although the main population of the region is Muslim, it is not mainly Arab. The Turks, Persians, Kurds, Armenians, Turkomans, and Circassians reflect Indo-European and Asiatic large-scale population movements. There is still disagreement over what precisely an Arab is, although many authorities might agree with H. A. R. Gibb's reasoning that an Arab is an Arabic-speaking Muslim who cherishes the cultural heritage of the Arab empire. Christian Arabs, however, might be dismayed by this definition, and Don Peretz therefore adds the proviso that an Arab also identifies with "Arab" problems.

Not only are all Arabs not Muslims, but most Muslims are not Arabs. It has been estimated that there are some 400 million Muslims in the world, of whom only about one-sixth are Arabs.

Islam as a religion has reflected numerous religious schisms. Tradition has it that Muhammed himself predicted that there would be ninety-nine sects in Islam. One of the earliest schisms occurred at the very death of the Prophet, when the followers of his son-in-law Ali were dismayed to see the role of caliph awarded to three others before it was given to Ali. Out of this resentment and the subsequent suspicious deaths of Ali and his sons developed the profound schism in Islam between the Sunni (the "tradition" followers) and the Shia (the followers of Ali who claim that the succession passed directly from Muhammed to Ali and thence to a varying number of imams).

Today while both Sunni and Shia followers are found throughout the Middle East, relationships are not necessarily peaceful. There are profound emotional and religious differences separating the two groups, and mutual mistrust still exists. The annual observance in Karbala in southern Iraq of the anniversary of the tragic death of Ali's son Husayn is a dramatic and emotional re-enactment of the slaying that helps to maintain and reinforce these passionate differences.

Iraq reflects these religious differences well. Sunnite and Shiite Muslim Arabs constitute some 75 per cent of the total population. The Sunnites form the majority of the economic, political, and social elite of Iraq and have been the traditional leaders of the country; they are found largely in central Iraq. The Shiites, however, although in lesser positions, constitute a slight majority over the Sunnites; they are concentrated mainly in southern Iraq.

Northern Iraq, however, is inhabited by Kurds who constitute some 15 to 20 per cent of Iraq's population. Although they are also Sunnite Muslims, they have their own Kurdish language and culture and do not identify nationalistically or culturally with the Muslim Arabs.

Despite the rifts between the Sunni Muslim Arabs and the Shia Muslim Arabs, they are forced to unite to fight the Sunni Muslim Kurds in the north, who have demanded greater political independence, even though the Sunni Muslim Arabs might prefer to unite with the Sunni Muslim Kurds to constitute a sound religious majority over the Shia Muslim Arabs.

The Shia division of Islam has itself been split into many sects, three of which are still very important: the Imami (or "twelvers," as they recognize twelve imams) have been the state religion of Iran since 1499 and are also found in southern Iraq and along the Arabian seacoast; the Ismailis (or "seveners," as they recognize Ismail as the rightful seventh and last imam), established the Fatimid Caliphate in Egypt and are presently led by Aga Khan III, today live mainly in Pakistan, India, and the Hama province of Syria; and the Zaydis (or "three'ers," who branch off at the third imam), who are found today mainly in the Yemen. The rulers of Yemen, like Imam Yahya, who was murdered in 1948, are of this Zaydi dynasty.

These three Shia sects have also split into further subgroupings. A distinct subdivision of the Imami is the Matawili of Lebanon. Totaling perhaps a quarter-million, they constitute approximately one-fifth of the population of that country. Located primarily in Tyre, Sidon, and the Baalbek Valley, some of them are, according to Coon, "so fanatical" that they carry packets of Persian soil (a token of the homeland) and smash the pottery out of which Sunnis or Christians have eaten.

The Ismailis, who early gave rise to the "Assassins" (a hashish-using terrorist sect active during the eleventh and twelfth centuries), later gave rise to two extremist branches—the Alawi and the Druze—both of which are considered by some authorities to have moved almost completely out of the Islamic framework. The Alawi, also known as the Nusairi, live chiefly in the Syrian province of Latakia, where they constitute some 60 per cent of the inhabitants; the Druze are located mainly in the Jabal ad-Druze region of Lebanon, Syria, and Israel. Both religions are secret, revealed only gradually to the select; in each great importance is attached to the number seven (reflecting perhaps the original Ismaili influence). The Alawi are believed to have incorporated pagan Syrian nature elements into their religion, whereas the Druze are noted for their practice of *taqiya* (concealment)—it is legitimate for them to pretend to belong to another religion when this subterfuge is considered necessary. All three of these Shia subsects, the Matawili, Alawi, and Druze, maintain uneasy relations with their Shia as well as Sunni Muslim Arab neighbors.

The Wahhabi movement is a recent development from Sunni Islam. It is a puritanical movement calling for a return to the original Islam of the

Koran and Sunna. The Wahhabi are noted for their opposition to saint-worship, mysticism, magical beliefs, and emphatic rejection of wine drinking and for their insistence on wearing the traditional Arab garb. The movement began during the eighteenth century among the bedouin of the Nejd, and it was expanded into a politico-military force by the family of Saud. The first Wahhabi-Saud empire was smashed by the Egyptian forces of Muhammed Ali on the orders of the Turkish Sultan. A subsequent revival of the Wahhabi-Saud combination led to the eventual conquest of most of the Arabian peninsula. The political rulers of Saudi Arabia are also the religious heads of the Wahhabi movement, and these leaders are still unable to reconcile themselves to essential differences in Egyptian religion and political activities.

The Kurds are one of the larger non-Arab minorities in the Middle East. Linguistically they are related to the Indo-European Shia Persians, but religiously they are nearly all Sunni Muslims. In addition to a common language and culture, they also manifest a series of physical characteristics that distinguish them from their neighbors.

One estimate has it that there are perhaps 8.5 million Kurds, of whom perhaps 4 million live in Turkey, 2.5 million in Iran, 1.5 million in Iraq, and .5 million in Syria and Russia Transcaucasia.

So strong is the "national" sentiment among this people that, after World War I, the Allies agreed to carve out from the disintegrated Ottoman Empire a national territory for the Kurds. Although this promise was never fulfilled, Kurdish nationalist tendencies continue to run so high that in Turkey, Iraq, and Iran, where they constitute large minorities, their frequent political controversies over independence have resulted in revolt and guerilla warfare.

Such differences in language, religion, history, and culture, constitute one of the major problems in the present-day Middle East and complicate the development of nationalism. Although Iraq has been cited as one example of national Muslim heterogeneity, the Kurds represent a cross-national Muslim minority bloc. Egypt and Lebanon are examples of Christian-Muslim national patterns.

In Egypt more than 90 per cent of the inhabitants are Arabic-speaking Sunni Muslims. The single large minority is the Copts—the original, indigenous Egyptians who converted to Christianity. At the beginning of this century and during the British rule over the land, the Copts, who had a generally higher level of education and literacy, constituted 45 per cent of the Egyptian civil-service force and 97.8 per cent of the tax collectors. This occupational and educationl composition has since altered rapidly. More than half the Coptic population presently earns its living from agriculture, and, already by World War II, less than 10 per cent of all Egyptian civil-service personnel were Copts. The current pronounced socioeconomic similarities between Egyptian Muslims and Copts are also reflected in laws and customs. Many Copts do not eat pork, they circumcise their sons, and the women wear veils in places where their Muslim neighbors observe the practice. Coptic marriage and funeral ceremonies are similar to those of the Muslims, and both Copts and Muslims worship at similar saints' tombs. The younger generation of Copts does not differ significantly from that of their Muslim neighbors in physical appearance or dress, and it has been advanced that as the pronounced nationalistic homogeneous values increase, the Copts may disappear as a meaningful entity in Egypt.

Egypt's striking ethnic homogeneity is in contrast to Lebanon where Christians are officially half the population. Lebanese Christians, however, are divided mainly into the Maronites, who constitute about 30 per cent of the total Lebanese population and are concentrated in the north; the Greek Catholics, who are concentrated mainly in the south and east; the Greek Orthodox, who are scattered mainly in Beirut and the north; and the Armenians, who settled in the Beirut region after World War I.

The Muslims are divided primarily into the Sunni, concentrated largely in the coastal cities; the Shia, concentrated largely in rural southern Lebanon and the poor quarters of the coastal cities; and the Druze, in distinct rural communities in the southern part of Mount Lebanon.

It is unofficially accepted that widespread Christian Lebanese emigration to the Americas and consistently higher Muslim fertility have changed the traditional proportions of Christians and Muslims on which intercommunity equilibrium is based. No census has been taken in Lebanon since 1932, and the lack of a new census has served as an effective means of preserving an apparently fictitious balance.

The governmental structure also maintains this community equilibrium. Positions in the government and in the parliament are reserved for specific communities. Lebanon's President is a Christian Maronite, the Prime Minister a Sunni Muslim, and the President of the Chamber of Deputies a Shiite Muslim. Foreign affairs are traditionally a Christian preserve, and defense usually is managed by a Muslim or Druze. Furthermore, the different communities have the right to proportional representation in public administrative positions as well.

Although Lebanon is the only country in the Arab League that does not have a Muslim majority, it is also the only country in which no single community, Christian or Muslim, has a majority. The essential tensions inherent in maintaining this sensitive balance have been exacerbated by recent nationalist movements and identifications. The 1958 civil war, when American troops were brought in to establish order, was one indication of the complexities in compromising traditional ethnic heterogeneity with modern political nationalism.

Although an introduction to present-day peoples of the Middle East may involve a résumé bristling with difficult-to-pronounce names and confusing places and dates, that is the reality of the contemporary scene. To ignore this reality, or to attempt glibly to oversimplify it, is naïvely to compound misunderstanding of a region sorely in need of objective understanding.

Part I of the present selection of studies is intended to provide some knowledge of the range and complexity of the population mosaic. Bernard Lewis's trenchant analysis of the Arab people, Moshe Zeltzer's intensive and detailed survey of minorities in Arab Iraq and Syria, and Herbert H. Vreeland's and this editor's descriptions of ethnic groups in specific Middle Eastern countries where there are not Arab majorities are all designed to provide necessary data for understanding this mosaic.

The way of life in the Middle East presents a series of three essential groupings. In addition to their community identifications, the populations are divided among nomads, agriculturists, or townspeople. Part II of this volume presents a range of critical articles dealing with the subcultures of each.

The fellah, the Arab peasant, is still the predominant factor in the Middle East. Two-thirds to three-fourths of the total population continues to make its living by varieties of precarious subsistence agriculture. These argricultural practices have a long and deep tradition. The average Middle Eastern peasant lives not on a farm but in a village near or in the midst of his fields. For generations his family may have lived in this village and tilled the same plot of land. His life cycle is determined, as theirs was, by the sun, the rains, the agricultural seasons, customs, and religion. Numerous authorities have commented on the continuity in the practices and technology of the Middle Eastern peasant. Biblical literature and Pharaonic temple murals have detailed the essential contemporary fellah implements—the short-handled hoe; the long, pointed wooden plow; the simple rectangular, flat-topped homes built of mud or stone around a courtyard; the crowding inside of the extended family and its domestic animals; the outdoor conical mud ovens; and the simple furniture, clothing, and diet of the peasant. Even the methods of obtaining water for irrigation, from Iran to Egypt, may date back to antiquity.

This agricultural continuity of the Middle Eastern fellah has often been romantically idealized as the good life of the simple farmer. An astringent antidote to this approach is offered by Doreen Warriner, who opened her study of land tenure in the Middle East with these words, "Near starvation, pestilence, high death rates, soil erosion, economic exploitation—this is the pattern of life for the mass of the rural population in the Middle East."[6]

Land is the critical factor determining the economic and social life of the farmer—and few of the fellaheen own the land they work. It has been argued that the essential nomadic influences on the region have created in the fellah a contempt for land and agricultural activities. A more useful explanation, however, is to be found in the study of the land-tenure system.

Land tenure in the Middle East, like so much else of the culture, has a long tradition. Early Muslim conquests and apportionment of land and property, as well as later Ottoman tax farming, all contributed to development of a system of wealthy landowners, who reside in urban centers and are supported by a mass of landless or tenant farmers. There are presently perhaps five categories of land registration in the region:

mulk land, in absolute freehold ownership
miri land whose absolute ownership belongs to the state but usufruct to the individual
waqf land, dedicated to or reserved for religious purposes
matruka land, reserved for such public purposes as marketplaces or village threshing floors
mawat land, "dead," desert, or empty land

Despite ostensible reforms by the later Ottoman government and the post-World War I, newly-emerging, semi-independent states, much ownership of the land in most of the countries of the Middle East became concentrated in the hands of a limited number of large landowners. According to Gabriel Baer,[7] in this century more and more land has passed into the hands of large landowners in all the countries of the Arab Middle East. During the same period the small landowner's plots have been split up and dispersed. Much of his land has been seized for failure to pay debts or to pay the interest on debts; some small landowners registered their land through city notables or village authorities and then saw their land lost legally. Throughout the Middle East these landless fellaheen till the land of rich, city-dwelling absentee landlords.

Since World War II agrarian reform has been a keynote of the revolutionary movements. Except perhaps in Lebanon and Turkey, where the situation was not as drastic, one of the hallmarks of revolution in the Middle East has been promised redistribution of land. To what extent these programs are genuine and successful may well determine the future of the Middle East. To date, the agrarian-reform movements have made only limited progress.

The indictment of the fellaheen of Syria by the French scholar J. Weulersse is still valid:

Paradoxical, in our Western eyes even shocking, is the existence of a peasant population in the East which lacks all peasant atavism; here are people of the land who have no feeling for the land or respect for it, farmers who despise farming, tillers of the land who loathe the plough, villagers who disavow their village in order to remain faithful to their tribe. The peasant masses of the Middle East exist in a state of self-rejection. This is quite unique, an almost pathological situation among farmers in the whole world.[8]

John Gulick's article provides a thorough foundation for understanding the essential ethnography of a Lebanese village. Louise Sweet graphically portrays the routine of Syrian farm life, and Ann Lambton spells out the heavy obligations of a Persian peasant. Anne Fuller presents a broad philosophical explanation of the concepts of time and space in the Middle Eastern fellah—concepts that have profound cross-cultural implications for the administrator seeking to accelerate effective acculturation.

The nomad continues to be the stereotype of the Middle Eastern man, despite the fact that nomadism has always been a distinctly minority way of life there. Even today nomads constitute no more than 15 per cent of the total population, and the proportion is declining annually as thousands become settled agriculturists or seek permanent urban employment.

The nomadic way of life and its traditions may conflict sharply with the orderly administration of a modern, nationalistic state, and this century has witnessed growing governmental restrictions on the nomads. Since World War I the airplane and machine gun have been effective means of controlling traditional nomad raids and incursions on the villagers, and the governmental settlement of many tribes, particularly in Saudi Arabia, Egypt, and Iraq, has hastened the process of enforced peace and settlement.

General urban and specific industrial development since 1945 have led to the voluntary urbanization and industrialization of additional tribesmen. In particular this has been the case of the Saudi Arabian bedouin and the exploitation of Arabian oil resources. The automobile and radio, like soap and Christianity of an earlier generation, have been effective means for exposing traditionally isolated nomads to technology and Westernization values and nationalism.

In general nomads occupy semiarid lands between the barren desert and the agricultural lands. Nomadic life is pastoral and based upon raising sheep and goats and the exchange of their by-products—milk, butter, cheese, wool, animals—in villages and towns for such traditional commodities as coffee, sugar, and bullets.

"Horizontal" nomads, like the Arab bedouin, are concentrated in the dry plateau of central Arabia, which extends into Jordan, Israel's Negev, the Sinai Peninsula, Syria, Lebanon, and Iraq. During the summer, these nomads must seek camp sites near permanent water supplies, the oases; during the winter rains, the grass lands are extended, and flocks and herds can graze more widely.

"Vertical" nomads live in or near such mountainous regions as those in eastern Turkey and western Iran. They live on the lower plains during the winter and in the spring follow the vegetation up the mountains. In the autumn the migration is reversed. Kurds and some Persian tribes are among the main groups of vertical nomads in the Middle East.

Carleton Coon has provided a comprehensive view of the nomadic way of life in the Middle East, and H. R. P. Dickson has targeted in on the ethnography of the classic Arabian bedouin tent and its furnishings. Fredrik Barth has written an excellent study of the ritual life of one of the vertical nomadic tribes of Persia—the Basseri—whereas Dickson has provided carefully gathered material on one of the smaller nomadic subcultures in the Arabian Desert.

These selections certainly are not intended to present an exhaustive survey or ethnography of the Middle Eastern nomad; they are intended, however, to present sound data toward an understanding of the variety of nomadic subcultures, as well as certain details on the nomads' material and social patterns.

There is at least one other critical factor in comprehending the cultures and subcultures of the contemporary Middle East—social stratification. There have been few sound and specific studies of this very real problem, and those that do exist are too often of a general nature dutifully inserted into studies with other orientations. Even sociological studies of the Middle East have been remiss in not providing direct investigations of this profound social reality.

S. M. Salim's study of ech-Chibayish in the marshlands of southern Iraq and the formation of class differentiation based upon economics is one of the few sound studies of this problem in the entire region, and Gabriel Baer's analysis of social stratification in the Middle East is virtually unique as a serious attempt to provide careful data covering the broader scene. Both these papers should be read and studied by every serious student of the contemporary Middle East. As the region moves more and more into the Western twentieth century, social stratification will emerge more clearly as one of the critical factors it is.

The wealthy Middle Easterner who banks his money in Lebanon or Switzerland and vacations in Europe; the regional businessman seeking to expand his industrial or commercial enterprises and to safeguard his investments; the factory worker fighting for labor rights and salary raises in inflationary settings; the university-educated population concerned with intellectual freedom and professional standards; the rapidly urbanizing slum-dwelling, illiterate, unskilled, and unemployed peasant masses swelling the cities—all of these can be better understood through cross-cultural social-stratification studies. Already these classes may have as much in common with their counterparts in other nations as they have with their own fellow citizens.

It seems clear that social stratification is another critical factor to be added to the mosaic of peoples and cultures of the contemporary Middle East and it is to be hoped that further volumes on the Middle East will offer sound studies of this topic.

It has been argued that man differs from all other animals in the possession of culture—learned behavior common to a group of socially interacting human beings—and that culture can and does exert a profound influence on the expression and development of the human life cycle. As members of the species *Homo sapiens*—the one species to which all living persons belong— Middle Easterners share a life cycle common to all human beings but influenced and determined by their particular culture patterns.

Part III, population dynamics, reflects the study of the life process among Middle Easterners. The emphasis here is primarily on how the Middle Eastern culture influences the formative years, which have been demonstrated to be critical determiners of adult behavior.

To evaluate properly this period in the human life cycle, however, it is essential to comprehend the realities of human health and welfare. Health and welfare are essential to any population; without them, human beings are a sick and weak population prey to the rapacity and whims, goals and ideals, of local and foreign exploiters. Essential group survival may be threatened.

The majority of the people in the contemporary Middle East, as in the rest of the underdeveloped world, are in a sorry condition of health and welfare. Reference has already been made to Warriner's portrayal of the plight of the fellaheen—the main population group in the Middle East; even in her later, more optimistic study, she could only state that "Poverty still exists in the Middle Eastern countries," but "the abolition of poverty is within the bounds of possibility, as ten years ago it was not."[9]

The French team Jean and Simonne Lacouture devoted an entire volume to modern, developing Egypt, whose population they characterized as subdued by "reverence, humiliation and exploitation."[10] In the section entitled "Men That Man Has Forgotten,"[11] the Lacoutures spell out certain of the realities of health for the Egyptian fellaheen—a group that constitutes almost four-fifths of the total Egyptian population.

Egyptian agriculture is based upon year-round irrigation, and the fellah accordingly spends much of his day with his feet and often part of his upper body in water and mud. The water in the ditches, canals, and even the Nile shallows is infested with the parasite bilharzia—a tiny mollusc whose larvae enter the human body through the skin. The parasite attacks the bladder and the kidneys, causes ulcers and fistulas, and upsets the intestines. Contaminated feces from bilharzia victims are returned to the water, and the cycle of disease is complete. It is estimated that this endemic disease affects some 95 per cent of the Egyptian fellaheen. Its victims do not necessarily suffer acute pain so much as a gradual wasting away.

In addition to this water parasite, the fellah may also be a victim of ancylostomiasis, an earth parasite. Its larvae are transmitted through the feces of already infected human beings. They multiply in the wet soil and enter the human body through the soles of the naked feet, to attack the intestines. Subsequent fecal discharges from the victims complete the cycle.

Victims suffering from these two diseases may spend their entire adult lives in a state of exhaustion and anemia.

Vitiating malaria is still widespread among the fellaheen in the Nile Delta rice fields, despite intensive World Health Organization efforts to curb the disease.

Diseases of the eyes and their attendant problems of impaired vision or blindness are another kind of affliction suffered by the Egyptian fellah. The rapid spread of such infections is particularly tragic. "We did not see a single child with perfectly healthy eyes, in any of the villages we visited between Damietta and the Sudanese frontier," wrote the Lacoutures.[12]

Chronic malnutrition and resulting evils are perhaps the Egyptians' worst affliction. Virtually the entire peasant population is suffering from deficiency diseases that so debilitate the individual that he becomes easily susceptible to a variety of communicable diseases and chronic disorders. Adolescents between the ages of fourteen and nineteen years are rated as the healthiest of the fellaheen, but 80 per cent of the men have to be rejected as unfit for military service.

The population dynamics of Egypt do not necessarily lend themselves to simple solutions to these problems of human health and welfare. Despite the inroads of the debilitating endemic diseases recorded here, acute widespread epidemics have been virtually eliminated. Much of the population accordingly survives into the breeding and propagating years. During this century the population has increased fivefold, while little new land has been developed. Two children are born every minute in Egypt—more than 3,000 a day, two-thirds of whom survive. Egypt is shrinking in proportion to its population. Even the effects of the Aswan Dam program, it has been argued, may be neutralized by the population growth during its planning and completion. By 1975, when the full benefits of the Aswan Dam may be realized, Egypt's available land will have increased by 40 per cent. But by the same year—unless the present birth rate falls—the population will have risen 50 per cent.

Egypt has been selected as an example of population dynamics in the Middle East, but it is not unique. The Human Relations Area Files report on public health and welfare in Saudi Arabia demonstrates that, even when morbidity and mortality may be widespread, availability of funds does not guarantee that the necessary positive health services will be provided. There are cultural factors that profoundly affect the health services provided and thus the optimum life cycle of a population.

The article by K. Nahas on the family in the Arab world and the three subsequent articles on childhood and adolescence in an Egyptian village, Lebanese towns, and an Israeli kibbutz, provide foundations for a better understanding of population dynamics in the Middle East. Contemporary adult values and behavior, it is clear, are instilled in children during their formative years, and attempts to develop change or understand conservatism must program for their study.

Culture change, programmed and otherwise, is the norm in the contemporary Middle East, as in the rest of the "underdeveloped" world. The nations are moving along a continuum of change toward industrialization and modernization. Fundamental changes are being wrought in the Middle Eastern culture, and the contemporary period reflects the disruptions and crises accompanying the profound upheavals of this transitional period. It is also necessary to evaluate, however, the conservative forces that operate to slow or modify change. Complete culture change is rarely met with complete equanimity by all the affected population. Although technology and its benefits may be eagerly sought, the social implications may at first be only dimly perceived. When they become more apparent, there may be a determined effort to reject or restrict cultural innovation or, ideally, to modify the innovation so as to provide maximum benefits while necessitating minimum changes in traditional behavior. Culture change, furthermore, is rarely a one-way process: Both influencer and recipient are affected by the interaction.

Anthropology is replete with demonstrations of these concepts of culture change, and the purpose of Part Four of this volume is to provide material on the essential dynamics of Middle Eastern culture change and conservatism.[13]

Morroe Berger has prepared an excellent description of the forces of conservatism in the Egyptian civil service, and Daniel Lerner has outlined the complexity of the emotions operating in a nation like Iran, with its strong bipolarization of conservative and modernizing forces. This editor has studied one specific aspect of this culture-change phenomenon—the interaction between Middle Eastern and Western systems of medicine—and Alex Weingrod has analyzed the reciprocal nature of culture change in the adjustment of Moroccan immigrants to an agricultural settlement in Israel. Finally, A. H. J. Prins has described the Syrian schooner and analyzed it as a problem in maritime culture change.

Still to be developed are adequate studies of one phenomenon that is common to most underdeveloped countries of the world—rapid, unplanned, and uncontrolled urbanization. The Middle East is no stranger to this phenomenon.

In a report prepared for the Bureau of Social Affairs of the United Nations, Miss Isis Ragheb[14] has outlined certain causes of urbanization in the Middle East. They are, first, the 3 per cent annual rate of population growth (the population of the region is growing faster than that of any other major region in the world except Latin America), which has caused great pressure on the land; second, growing difficulty in finding additional land for cultivation, along with modern agricultural policies which make much of the rural labor force even more redundant (mechanization of agriculture in Turkey between 1948 and 1957, for example, displaced approximately 1 million people, three-quarters of whom moved to urban areas). In addition to these "push" factors, certain "pull" factors are operating. They include, third, increased accessibility to the towns, which has been accelerated through improved roads and motor transportation; fourth, increased communications, which have spread the attraction of cities as centers of education, health, employment, recreation, and a totally different way of life; fifth, discovery and exploitation of oil resources, which have brought thousands of workers into the new urban settlements in search of employment; and, sixth, the flow of capital from oil revenues, which has made a direct impact on the rate of growth of the cities in these and nearby countries (Lebanon, particularly Beirut, has been an outstanding beneficiary of Kuwait's annual oil income of $150 million).

An International Labour Office study published in 1960 illustrates well these "push" and "pull" factors as they operate in Iraq. The fellaheen were living at a subsistence agricultural level by reason of low farm yields, and much of what they did raise was claimed as rent by the landowners. Health conditions were extremely bad, and the majority of the fellaheen suffered from diseases related to acute malnutrition.

Contrasted with this negative environment was the attraction of the towns for the peasants. Although the oil industry in Iraq itself employed only small numbers, "the volume of employment created by new public expenditure was large; most of the new employment was on construction, water control projects, roads and urban building"[15]—all of which may call upon masses of unskilled laborers.

It is no surprise, accordingly, to record the accelerated pace of Middle Eastern urbanization. At one extreme, Israel has the dubious honor of holding third place in the world in ratios of urban population to total population (75.9 per cent). In Kuwait 50.6 per cent of the total population lives in towns of 100,000 and more inhabitants, in Lebanon 33.2 per cent; and in Syria 28.9 per cent.

This large-scale urbanization has been a movement primarily of this century and in particular of the past generation. Turkey's urban population, distributed among its six largest cities, has more than doubled in less than thirty years. The population of Aleppo, Syria, has undergone a similar transformation. A large proportion of Lebanon's inhabitants (perhaps one-third of the total population), already live in the one metropolitan area of Beirut, and it is estimated that by 1978 the urban population will constitute 75 per cent of the total population in Lebanon.

The population of the Middle East is not only becoming more urban;

it is also becoming concentrated in specific areas. By 1961 the Amman district, for example, already contained 26 per cent of the total Jordanian population. By 1959 the Baghdad Liwa (province) contained one-sixth of Iraq's total population. Iraq's four main cities (Baghdad, Mosul, Basrah, and Kirkuk) contain almost half the urban population of the whole country.

This rapid and for the most part unplanned urbanization has resulted in a series of physical changes and problems. "The uncontrolled growth of what were for the most part medieval towns has led to their mushrooming over surrounding areas at a rapacious rate."[16]

Most cities have doubled in size within the past few decades, and some, like Beirut, have incorporated surrounding towns. "Greater" Baghdad and Kuwait have spilled beyond their city walls. In Israel almost the entire coastal plain from Haifa to below Tel Aviv is gradually evolving into a single metropolitan area. "Megalopolis," as well as "metropolis," is becoming a significant term in the Middle East.

As in many other regions of the world, acute urban problems have accompanied this movement. Land speculation, the "real estate craze," has dominated the economic scene of the last two decades. Traffic in urban land and building for quick speculative profit have become major economic activities and serve to modify greatly traditional values and behavior. Ragheb estimates that one-third of downtown Beirut is in the hands of speculators from Islamic Waqf and Christian religious foundations.[17] Land prices in Ankara have boomed under the manipulation of profit seekers. In an upper-class urban section of Ankara prices rose from 10 lire per square meter in 1952 to 150 lire in 1958. A similar process has occurred in some areas of Kuwait where in 1961 the United States government paid $261,000 to acquire plots of land for the accommodation of public toilets and a small transformer station.

Housing for the poor has been one of the most obvious victims of this type of speculation. Slums and shantytowns have become hallmarks of metropolitan growth in underdeveloped countries. In the Middle East rural migrants build simple, quick, and inexpensive one-room shacks. These shacks are crowded together without sanitary facilities, and quickly deteriorate into unhealthy and unsightly slums.

Sections of Greater Baghdad are surrounded by strips of slum dwellings reaching sometimes a width of 5 kilometers. These dwellings are mainly of the *sarifa* type. The *sarifa* is a one-room house constructed mainly of reed matting. Family members themselves can assemble, dismantle, and move such a structure. It is estimated that there are 44,000 *sarifas* in Greater Baghdad, nearly 45 per cent of the total number of houses. Their inhabitants are estimated at 250,000—more than a quarter of the total population of the city.[18]

Supplying pure water for these mushrooming towns is a growing problem, and slum areas are often served only by community hydrants. Sewage disposal is even more critical. Ankara's and Istanbul's garbage-disposal and sewage systems are described as "hopelessly inadequate," and Baghdad's only open sewage canal has become the headquarters of one of the city's biggest slums.[19] Metropolitan coastal cities like Beirut and Tel Aviv have contaminated their seacoast with sewage runoff; Amman basically has no system at all.

Many Middle Eastern cities are divided into "new" and "old" towns. The old towns still reflect the traditional Middle Eastern arrangement of ethnic quarters. The two most prominent buildings are the great mosque and the citadel or palace of the ruler. That most secular of all Middle Eastern institutions, the *suq* (marketplace or bazaar), dominates a large area of the old town. It is the center where all commercial transactions take place. The market is often nearly roofed in by overhanging houses, and it may be covered with fabric. The streets are narrow and winding, and the numerous workshops, often grouped by craft, produce many of the goods required by the local population.

Traffic in the narrow and winding streets of these medieval "old" towns, although exotic to visiting tourists, creates severe problems for industrial motor movement. Attempts to clear rights of way often flounder when it becomes necessary to destroy cherished religious shrines or ancient classical ruins.

An appreciation of the need for concerted planning and action in the problem has only recently developed. At the first international seminar on "The New Metropolis in the Arab World," sponsored by the Egyptian Society of Engineers and the Congress for Cultural Freedom and held in Cairo in December 1960, the invited authorities could conclude only that "This seminar has proved to be a fruitful beginning for the understanding of the New Metropolis in the Arab World. This interest must be maintained."[20]

As grim as these urban problems are, however, there is an even more serious social problem. The reality of a large and rapidly growing unskilled—and therefore often underemployed or unemployed—illiterate, and unhealthy peasant population in the towns may create a new version of the *Lumpenproletariat*. With little to lose and much to gain, these people may profoundly and radically alter traditional religious and familial values and behavior. Juvenile delinquency, petty thievery, prostitution, and mob violence may reflect certain of the disorders accompanying this social disorganization. Violence, of course, may be aggravated by political figures: Acute xenophobia, particularly directed at traditional "imperialist" powers, and the brutal manhandling of incumbent leaders are two of the more obvious by-products. (During the July 1958 revolution in Iraq, street mobs ran amok in Baghdad, pillaging and burning at will. Scores were slaughtered, including King Faisal II and Prime Minister Nuri al-Said.)

The army, often foreign-trained and foreign-armed, may then appear to be the one stable center in a rapidly disintegrating social structure. Furthermore, as the army is generally staffed by local members of the middle class, it may appear to be one of the few institutions representing the indigenous population and its national identity. Army dissatisfaction with obvious political ineptitude and corruption may lead to popularly supported military revolutions—such as the military coups in Syria, Lebanon, Turkey, Egypt and Iraq.

Critical studies of the anthropology of these complex phenomena are still virtually nonexistent. As with social stratification, it is hoped that later volumes on the peoples and cultures of the Middle East will be able to include relevant articles on the subject of local urbanization and its consequences.

June 1967

* * *

Since the date when the preceding section was prepared, the Arabs and Israelis have engaged in yet another round of conflict. Termed variously the "Six-Day war" and the "Third Arab-Israel war," firing began on the morning of Monday, June 5, 1967, and was curtailed on the afternoon of Saturday, June 10.

The armies of Egypt, Jordan, Syria, and Israel were directly involved on a large scale. During the war, Israeli troops occupied the Gaza Strip and the Sinai Peninsula; the old City of Jerusalem and the entire West Bank of what was formerly Palestine, up to the Jordan River; and the Golan Heights above the Sea of Galilee. As of December 31, 1968, they continue to occupy these regions.

Much has been made of the supposed David-and-Goliath pattern of this conflict, wherein vastly outnumbered Israel fought and defeated the massive armies of surrounding Arab states. In reality, the numerical disproportions and the results of this recent conflict are not to be considered a sudden, unique phenomenon. There were only 80,000 Jews in Palestine when Britain took the Mandate from the League of Nations in 1922, and, although their number increased to 450,000 by 1939, the Jews were still less than one-third of the total population of Palestine. Despite these early, constant, and pronounced numerical limitations, the Jews held their own during the riots of 1929 and those from 1936 to 1939. The numerical odds against the Israelis during their 1947–1948 War of Independence were even more pronounced, and they were only slightly improved during the 1956 Sinai war.

A clear understanding of what is occurring between Israel and her Arab neighbors in the Middle East cannot be achieved by mere head counting. Factors far more fundamental may have to be evaluated.

One such factor, it is suggested, is the deliberate revitalization process upon which the Jews of Israel have embarked. The Jewish national revival of the nineteenth and twentieth centuries has been a modern expression of identification with the past and the desire by a revitalized people to build a new culture. Theodor Herzl, the founder of political Zionism, expressly developed this theme in his work *Altneuland*, a later and lesser-known document than his clarion *The Jewish State*.

Even before the Balfour Declaration of 1917, waves of Jews were going up (*aliya*) to the Holy Land, then part of the Ottoman Empire, specifically to rebuild the Jewish homeland and to be rebuilt in the process. The implications of the carefully planned and executed mass murders of men, women, and children carried out by the Germans during World War II intensified this revitalization process, and the constantly reiterated threats of Arab leaders to "drive the Jews into the sea" merely reinforced the original motivation and impetus.

This revitalization process entailed the deliberate evaluation and rejection of a variety of aspects of *galut* (Diaspora) Jewish life and the deliberate appraisal and assumption of a series of specific new values and roles. Self-defense, the assumption of the military role on the part of all able-bodied citizens, and the acceptance of specific values of the military mentality became some of the earliest tenets of the developing Haganah (the army of the Jews of Palestine) and the later Israel Defense Forces.

Self-labor was another early tenet. The Zionists were convinced that the Jews would develop a new state only if they fulfilled functional roles in all the occupational strata. Manual labor was assigned a value equivalent to that of intellectual pursuits, and bus drivers were assigned a status comparable to physicians.

A return to the land—farming as an economic livelihood—was a third of the early role assumptions. It was considered that the Jews could truly rebuild the Holy Land only if they lived and worked on it. The idealization of Jewish youth living on farms and working in their own fields of wheat, fruit, and vegetables was perceived as a direct means of achieving this goal. The *kibbutz*—the collective agricultural settlement—was one system that developed out of this farmer role assumption.

Influencing all of these role and value developments, however, was one constant fundamental principle: The revitalization process could be accomplished only if the Jews looked forward and utilized the most recent developments in science and technology. Herzl emphasized the critical role that these would play in the development of the modern Jewish state, and the succeeding events of each generation tested and demonstrated the validity of his belief.

The way of life of the Ottoman Turks and the Arabs was examined and rejected, and there began the constant, deliberate incorporation of developing science and technology into the revitalization process. This modernization process quickly became one of Westernization, and the Israelis developed a culture incorporating the values of nineteenth-century Europe and the technology of twentieth-century America.

As two recent authorities have written, "The Israelis, more than any indigenous Middle Eastern people, display the qualities of hard work, technical expertise, and self-confidence which historians once mistakenly associated with the Protestant religion and the spirit of capitalism."[21]

These are certain of the political, social, and economic realities of the Middle East two-thirds of the way through the twentieth century. This volume is intended to contribute toward the strengthening of existing constructive factors in the Middle East and the positive solution of current problems.

December 1968

NOTES

1. Philip K. Hitti, *The Near East in History: A 5,000 Year Story* (New York, 1961), pp. 149–50.
2. Reader Bullard, ed., *The Middle East: A Political and Economic Survey* (3rd ed.; London, 1958), p. 16.
3. Arthur Mills, "Present-day Economic and Social Conditions" in George E. Kirk's *A Short History of the Middle East* (New York, 1957), p. 231. Cf. also pp. 231–48.
4. *Ibid.*, pp. 234–5.
5. Don Peretz, *The Middle East Today* (New York, 1963), pp. 342–3.
6. Doreen Warriner, *Land and Poverty in the Middle East* (London, 1948), p. 1.
7. Gabriel Baer, *Population and Society in the Arab East,* trans. Hanna Szoke (New York, 1964), p. 145.
8. J. Weulersse, *Paysans de Syrie et du Proche-Orient* (Paris, 1946), p. 66, as quoted by Baer, *op. cit.,* p. 137.
9. Doreen Warriner, *Land Reform and Development in the Middle East: A Study of Egypt, Syria and Iraq* (2nd ed.; London, 1962), p. 1.
10. Jean and Simonne Lacouture, *Egypt in Transition,* trans. Francis Scarfe (Eng. ed; London, 1958), p. 28.
11. *Ibid.*, pp. 324–7.
12. *Ibid.*, p. 326.
13. See Raphael Patai, *Golden River to Golden Road* (Philadelphia, 1967), Chapter XIV: "Resistance to Westernization" (pp. 386–406), for an intelligent evaluation of the dangers in Middle Eastern "superficial Westernization."
14. Isis Ragheb, "Patterns of Urban Growth in the Middle East" (Bureau of Social Affairs, United Nations [66–47105]).

15. *Ibid.*, p. 66.
16. *Ibid.*, p. 12.
17. *Ibid.*, p. 30.
18. Kahtan A. J. al-Madfai, "Baghdad," *The New Metropolis in the Arab World*, ed. Morroe Berger (New Delhi, 1963), p. 59.
19. In her 1962 work (cited earlier) Doreen Warriner has described one of the slums of Baghdad. "There is much trachoma and dysentery, but not bilharzia or malaria, because the water is too polluted for snails and mosquitos. . . . On the adjacent dumps dogs with rabies dig in the sewage, and the slum-dwellers pack it for resale as garden manure." (*Land Reform and Development in the Middle East*, pp. 181–2.)
20. *Ibid.*, p. 234.
21. Michael Howard and Robert Hunter, *Israel and the Arab World: The Crisis of 1967* (Adelphi Papers, No. 41; London, 1967), p. 41.

PART I

The Distribution of Peoples

*"The peoples of the Middle East are many and varied," as Coon so
felicitously phrased it. The region is characterized by such a wide variety
of peoples and cultures that it has been termed by some an
anthropological mosaic. Serving as a landbridge between Asia, Africa,
and Europe, the Middle East has witnessed the movements of vast
population groups and cultural developments, whose remnants and
residues may still be found in the area. In addition, the fact that the
Middle East is the oldest culture area in the world has merely
served to deepen and intensify the process.*

*In reply to his question concerning the largest population group
in the region, Bernard Lewis—who is the Professor of the History of the
Near and Middle East at the University of London—has provided
the reader with a careful and documented analysis and approach toward
an objective reply. His scholarly discussion possesses sound temporal
and spatial perspective.*

1

◇◇◇

What Is an Arab?

BERNARD LEWIS

What is an Arab? Ethnic terms are notoriously difficult to define, and
Arab is not among the easiest. One possible definition may be set aside at
once. The Arabs may be a nation; they are not as yet a nationality in the
legal sense. A man who calls himself an Arab may be described in his
passport as of Syrian or Lebanese, Jordanian or Egyptian, Iraqi or Saʻūdī-
Arabian nationality, but not Arab. There are Arab states, and indeed a
League of Arab states, but as yet no single Arab State, of which all Arabs
are nationals.

But if Arabism has no legal content, it is none the less real. The pride
of the Arab in his Arabdom, his consciousness of the bonds that bind him to
other Arabs past and present, are no less intense. Is the unifying factor then

From *The Arabs in History*, third edition (1956), pp. 9–17; reprinted by permission of
Hutchinson University Library.

one of language—is an Arab simply one who speaks Arabic as his mother tongue?   It is a simple and at first sight a satisfying answer—yet there are difficulties.   Is the Arabic-speaking Jew of Iraq or the Yemen or the Arabic-speaking Christian of Egypt or Lebanon an Arab?   The enquirer could receive different answers amongst these people themselves and among their Muslim neighbours.   Is even the Arabic-speaking Muslim of Egypt an Arab? Many consider themselves such, but not all, and the term Arab is still used colloquially in both Egypt and Iraq to distinguish the Bedouin of the surrounding deserts from the indigenous peasantry of the great river valleys.   In some quarters the repellent word Arabophone is used to distinguish those who merely speak Arabic from those who are truly Arabs.

A gathering of Arab leaders some years ago defined an Arab in these words: "Whoever lives in our country, speaks our language, is brought up in our culture and takes pride in our glory is one of us."   We may compare with this a definition from a well-qualified Western source, Professor Gibb of Harvard: "All those are Arabs for whom the central fact of history is the mission of Muḥammad and the memory of the Arab Empire and who in addition cherish the Arabic tongue and its cultural heritage as their common possession."   Neither definition, it will be noted, is purely linguistic.   Both add a cultural, one at least a religious, qualification.   Both must be interpreted historically, for it is only through the history of the peoples called Arab that we can hope to understand the meaning of the term from its primitive restricted use in ancient times to its vast but vaguely delimited extent of meaning today. As we shall see, through this long period the significance of the word Arab has been steadily changing, and as the change has been slow, complex and extensive, we shall find that the term may be used in several different senses at one and the same time and that a standard general definition of its content has rarely been possible.

The origin of the word Arab is still obscure, though philologists have offered explanations of varying plausibility.   For some, the word is derived from a Semitic root meaning "west," and was first applied by the inhabitants of Mesopotamia to the peoples to the west of the Euphrates valley.   This etymology is questionable on purely linguistic grounds and is also open to the objection that the term was used by the Arabs themselves and that a people is not likely to describe itself by a word indicating its position relative to another.   More profitable are the attempts to link the word with the concept of nomadism.   This has been done in various ways; by connecting it with the Hebrew " *'Arābhā*"—dark land, or steppe land; with the Hebrew " *'Erebh*"—mixed and hence unorganised, as opposed to the organised and ordered life of the sedentary communities, rejected and despised by the nomads; with the root " *'Abhar*"—to move or pass—from which our word Hebrew is probably derived.   The association with nomadism is borne out by the fact that the Arabs themselves seem to have used the word at an early date to distinguish the Bedouin from the Arabic-speaking town and village dwellers and indeed continue to do so to some extent at the present day. The traditional Arab etymology deriving the name from a verb meaning "to express" or "enunciate" is almost certainly a reversal of the historic process. A parallel case may be found in the connexion between German "deuten"— "to make clear to the people," and "deutsch"—originally "of the people."

The earliest account that has come down to us of Arabia and the Arabs is that of the tenth chapter of Genesis, where many of the peoples and districts of the peninsula are mentioned by name. The word Arab, however, does not occur in this text and makes its first appearance in an Assyrian inscription of 853 B.C. in which King Shalmaneser III records the defeat by the Assyrian forces of a conspiracy of rebellious princelings; one of them was "Gindibu the Aribi" who appropriately contributed 1,000 camels to the forces of the confederacy. From that time until the sixth century B.C. there are frequent references in Assyrian and Babylonian inscriptions to Aribi, Arabu, and Urbi. These inscriptions record the receipt of tribute from Aribi rulers, usually including camels and other items indicative of a desert origin, and occasionally tell of military expeditions into Aribi land. Some of the later inscriptions are accompanied by illustrations of the Aribi and their camels. These campaigns against the Aribi were clearly not wars of conquest but punitive expeditions intended to recall the erring nomads to their duties as Assyrian vassals. They served the general purpose of securing the Assyrian borderlands and lines of communication. The Aribi of the inscriptions are a nomadic people living in the far north of Arabia, probably in the Syro-Arabian desert. They do not include the flourishing sedentary civilisation of south-western Arabia which is separately mentioned in Assyrian records. They may be identified with the Arabs of the later books of the Old Testament. Towards 530 B.C. the term Arabaya begins to appear in Persian cuneiform documents.

The earliest classical reference is in Aeschylus, who in "Prometheus" mentions Arabia as a remote land whence come warriors with sharp-pointed spears. The "Magos Arabos" mentioned in the "Persians" as one of the commanders of Xerxes' army may possibly also be an Arab. It is in Greek writings that we find for the first time the place-name Arabia, formed on the analogy of Italia, etc. Herodotus and after him most other Greek and Latin writers extend the terms Arabia and Arab to the entire peninsula and all its inhabitants including the southern Arabians, and even the eastern desert of Egypt between the Nile and the Red Sea. The term at this time thus seems to cover all the desert areas of the Near and Middle East inhabited by semitic-speaking peoples. It is in Greek literature, too, that the term "Saracen" first becomes common. This word first appears in the ancient inscriptions and seems to be the name of a single desert tribe in the Sinai area. In Greek, Latin and Talmudic literature it is used of the nomads generally, and in Byzantium and the mediaeval West was later applied to all Muslim peoples.

The first Arabian use of the word occurs in the ancient southern Arabian inscriptions, those relics of the flourishing civilisation set up in the Yemen by the southern branch of the Arab peoples and dating from the late pre-Christian and early Christian centuries. In these, Arab means Bedouin, often raider, and is applied to the nomadic as distinct from the sedentary population. The first occurrence in the north is in the early fourth-century A.D. Namāra Epitaph, one of the oldest surviving records in the north-Arabian language which later became classical Arabic. This inscription, written in Arabic but in the Nabatean Aramaic script, records the death and achievements of Imru'l-Qais, "King of all the Arabs," in terms which suggest that the sovereignty claimed did not extend far beyond the nomads of northern and central Arabia.

It is not until the rise of Islam early in the seventh century that we have any real information as to the use of the word in central and northern Arabia. For Muḥammad and his contemporaries the Arabs were the Bedouin of the desert, and in the Qur'ān the term is used exclusively in this sense and never of the townsfolk of Mecca, Medina and other cities. On the other hand, the language of these towns and of the Qur'ān itself is described as Arabic. Here we find already the germ of the idea prevalent in later times that the purest form of Arabic is that of the Bedouin, who have preserved more faithfully than any others the original Arab way of life and speech.

The great waves of conquest that followed the death of Muḥammad and the establishment of the Caliphate by his successors in the headship of the new Islamic community wrote the name Arab large across the three continents of Asia, Africa and Europe, and placed it in the heading of a vital though not lengthy chapter in the history of human thought and endeavour. The Arabic-speaking peoples of Arabia, nomad and settled folk alike, founded a vast empire stretching from central Asia across the Middle East and North Africa to the Atlantic. With Islam as their national religion and war-cry, and the new empire as their booty, the Arabs found themselves living among a vast variety of peoples differing in race, language and religion, among whom they formed a ruling minority of conquerors and masters. The ethnic distinctions between tribe and tribe and the social distinctions between townsfolk and desertfolk became for a while less significant than the difference between the masters of the new empire and the diverse peoples they had conquered. During this first period in Islamic history, when Islam was purely an Arab religion and the Caliphate an Arab kingdom, the term Arab came to be applied to those who spoke Arabic, were full members by descent of an Arab tribe and who, either in person or through their ancestors, had originated in Arabia. It served to mark them off from the mass of Persians, Syrians, Egyptians and others, whom the great conquests had brought under Arab rule, and as a convenient label for the new imperial people among others outside the "House of Islam." The early classical Arab dictionaries give us two forms of the word Arab—" '*Arab*" and "*A'rāb*" in Arabic—and tell us that the latter meant "Bedouin," while the former was used in the wider sense described above. This distinction, if it is authentic—and there is much in the early dictionaries that has a purely lexicographical validity—must date from this period. There is no sign of it earlier. It does not appear to have survived for long.

From the eighth century, the Caliphate was gradually transformed from an Arabic to an Islamic Empire in which membership of the ruling caste was determined by faith rather than by origin. As ever-increasing numbers of the conquered peoples converted to Islam, the religion ceased to be the national or tribal cult of the Arab conquerors and acquired the universal character that it has retained ever since. The development of economic life and the cessation of the wars of conquest which had been the main productive activity of the Arabs produced a new governing class of administrators and traders, heterogeneous in race and language, which ousted the Arab military aristocracy created by the conquests. This change was reflected in the organisation and personnel of government.

Arabic remained the sole official language and the main language of administration, commerce and culture. The rich and diverse civilisation of the Caliphate, produced by men of many nations and faiths, was Arabic in language and to a large extent also in tone. The use of the adjective Arab to describe the various facets of this civilisation has often been challenged on the grounds that the contribution to "Arab medicine," "Arab philosophy," etc. of those who were of Arab descent was relatively small. Even the use of the word Muslim is criticised, since so many of the architects of this culture were Christians and Jews, and the term "Islamic," as possessing a cultural rather than a purely religious or national connotation, is suggested as preferable. The authentically Arab characteristics of the civilisation of the Caliphate are, however, greater than the mere examination of the racial origins of its individual creators would suggest, and the use of the term is justified provided a clear distinction is drawn between its cultural and ethnic connotations. Another important point is that in the collective consciousness of the Arabs today it is the Arab civilisation of the Caliphate in this wider sense that is their common heritage and the formative influence in their cultural life.

Meanwhile the ethnic content of the word Arab itself was also changing. The spread of Islam among the conquered peoples was accompanied by the spread of Arabic. This process was accelerated by the settlement of numbers of Arabians in the provinces, and from the tenth century onwards by the arrival of a new ruling race, the Turks, in common subjection to whom the distinction between the descendants of the Arab conquerors and the Arabised natives ceased to be significant. In almost all the provinces west of Persia the old native languages died out and Arabic became the chief spoken language. From late 'Abbāsid times onwards the word Arab reverts to its earlier meaning of Bedouin or nomad, becoming in effect a social rather than an ethnic term. In many of the Western chronicles of the Crusades it is used only for Bedouin, while the mass of the Muslim population of the Near East are called Saracens. It is certainly in this sense that in the sixteenth century Tasso speaks of

"altri Arabi poi, che di soggiorno,
certo non sono stabili abitanti;"
(Gerusalemme Liberata, XVII 21.)

The fourteenth-century Arabic historian Ibn Khaldūn, himself a townsman of Arab descent, uses the word commonly in this sense.

The main criterion of classification in these times was religious. The various minority faiths were organised as religio-political communities, each under its own leaders and laws. The majority belonged to the *Ummat al-Islām,* the community or nation of Islam. Its members thought of themselves primarily as Muslims. When further classification was necessary, it might be territorial—Egyptian, Syrian, Iraqi—or social—townsman, peasant, nomad. It is to this last that the term Arab belongs. So little had it retained of its ethnic meaning that we even find it applied at times to non-Arab nomads of Kurdish or Turkoman extraction. When the dominant social class within the *Ummat al-Islām* was mainly Turkish—as was the case for many centuries in the Near East—we sometimes find the term "Sons or Children of the Arabs"—*Abnā al-'Arab* or *Awlād al-'Arab* applied to the Arabic-speaking townspeople and peasantry to distinguish them from the Turkish ruling class on the one hand and the nomads or Arabs proper on the other.

In colloquial Arabic this situation has remained substantially unchanged to the present day, though others have replaced the Turks as the dominant class. But among the intellectuals of the Arabic-speaking countries a change of far-reaching significance has taken place. The rapid growth of European activity and influence in these lands brought with it the European idea of the nation as a group of people with a common homeland, language, character, and political aspiration. Since 1517 the Ottoman Empire had ruled most of the Arabic-speaking peoples of the Near and Middle East. The impact of the national idea on a people in the throes of the violent social change brought about by the entry of Western Imperialism produced the first beginnings of an Arab revival and an Arab national movement aiming at the creation of an independent state or states. The movement began in Syria and its first leaders seem to have thought in terms only of that country. Soon it spread to Iraq and in recent years has developed closer relations with the local nationalist movements in Egypt and even in the Arabic-speaking countries of North Africa.

For the theorists of Arab nationalism the Arabs are a nation in the European sense, including all those within certain boundaries who speak Arabic and cherish the memory of bygone Arab glory. There are different views as to where these boundaries are. For some they include only the Arabic-speaking countries of south-west Asia. Others add Egypt—though here there is a conflict of opinion with the many Egyptians who conceive of their nationalism in purely Egyptian terms. Many include the entire Arabic-speaking world from Morocco to the borders of Persia and Turkey. The social barrier between sedentary and nomad has ceased to be significant from this point of view, despite its survival in the colloquial use of "Arab" for Bedouin. The religious barrier in a society long dominated by a theocratic faith is less easily set aside. Though few of the spokesmen of the movement will admit it, many Arabs still exclude those who, though they speak Arabic, reject the Arabian faith and therefore much of the civilisation that it fostered.

To sum up then: the term Arab is first encountered in the ninth century B.C., describing the Bedouin of the north Arabian steppe. It remained in use for several centuries in this sense among the settled peoples of the neighbouring countries. In Greek and Roman usage it was for the first time extended to cover the whole peninsula, including the settled people of the oases and the relatively advanced civilisation of the south-west. In Arabia itself it seems still to have been limited to the nomads although the common language of sedentary and nomad Arabians was called Arabic. After the Islamic conquests and during the period of the Arab Empire it marked off the Arabic-speaking ruling class of conquerors of Arabian origin from the mass of the conquered peoples. As the Arab kingdom was transformed into a cosmopolitan Islamic Empire it came to denote—in external rather than in internal usage—the variegated culture of that Empire, produced by men of many races and religions, but in the Arabic language and conditioned by Arab taste and tradition. With the fusion of the Arab conquerors and the Arabised conquered and their common subjection to other ruling elements it gradually lost its national content and became a social term applied only to the nomads who had preserved more faithfully than any others the original Arabian way of life and language. The Arabic-speaking peoples of the settled countries were usually classed simply as Muslims, sometimes as "sons or children of the Arabs," to distinguish them from Muslims using other languages. While all these different usages have survived in certain contexts to the present day, a new one born of the impact of the West has in the last fifty years become increasingly important. It is that which regards the Arabic-speaking peoples as a nation or group of sister nations in the European sense, united by a common territory, language and culture and a common aspiration to political independence.

*Moshe Zeltzer has analyzed the mosaic of the Middle East by targeting
in on the peoples of two specific countries—Iraq and Syria.
Demonstrating a sophisticated usage of political science and economics,
in addition to the traditional tools of linguistics, religion, history,
and anthropology, he has prepared an excellent analysis of contemporary
human interaction in these two countries.*

    *Zeltzer's own background has prepared him well for this cultural
sensitivity and thoroughness. Born in Russia, he studied at the
University of Vienna and later in England, and he has lived in Israel,
where he edited a monthly publication on the Middle East. Presently
he is in Canada, a faculty member at the University of Saskatchewan.*

2

◇◇◇

Minorities in Iraq and Syria

MOSHE ZELTZER

No hard and exhaustive rules can be set forth for distinguishing minorities in this region.[1] Even in the West, opinions differ about exactly what
constitutes a national entity, and with the establishment of multilingual and
multiracial India, Pakistan, and Indonesia, the criteria have become much
more confused. Successive waves of immigration, caused by invasions and
infiltrations, and religious ferment, have left behind them both national and
confessional or sectarian minorities. These minorities differ from one another
both in their bonds of unity and the strength of these bonds, that is, in the degree of their historical consciousness or of their attachment to a particular language. Some of them occupy an intermediary stage between nation and
community. They also differ in their trends of development. The following

From *Aspects of Near East Society* (1962), pp. 15–59; reprinted by permission of Bookman Associates.

classification, therefore, will do no more than throw a certain light on this matter.

1. National, linguistic, and territorial minorities: Kurds (Iraq and Syria), Turkomans (Iraq), Circassians (Syria).
2. Religious, linguistic, and territorial minorities: Yazīdis.
3. National, religious, and linguistic minorities: Armenians.
4. Religious and territorial minorities: 'Alawis, Druzes.
5. Confessional and linguistic minorities: Syrian Orthodox, Syrian Catholics and Chaldeans (that is, those sections that still use an Aramaic dialect).
6. Confessional minorities: Greek Orthodox, Greek Catholics, Syrian Orthodox, Syrian Catholics, Protestants, etc.

There are at least four main factors which have brought about this great split of the population.

1. Ever since the Christian faith became dominant on the east coast of the Mediterranean until the rise of Islam, this region has been the scene of constant religious strife. The Nestorians, in order to escape from the Byzantine emperors, removed from Syria, after the schism at about A.D. 498, to the other side of the Euphrates and farther away. Most of the Syrian Orthodox were also squeezed out of Syria to the other side of the Euphrates, and only in the last century, especially after World War I, did thousands of them reach the Jazīra from Turkish Kurdistan. In the seventeenth century the Jesuits commenced to work in the Near East; and with other orders that followed them, they succeeded in winning over sections of the Eastern Churches to the Roman Catholic Church. The activity of the Protestants commenced in the first half of the last century.

2. The identity of three secretive communities—Ismā'īlis, Druzes, and 'Alawis—may have been preserved also by their isolation in the mountains. In some degree these three extreme offshoots of Shī'ism may be theologically related. Some scholars are inclined to see in Ismā'īlism, the oldest of them, traces of a national and racial revolt of Persia against Semitic Islam. Others again lay more stress on its social elements, seeing in revolutionary Shī'ism "the natural expression, in a theocratic milieu, of the revolt of the depressed classes, Persian and Semite alike."[2]

3. The dualist tradition of the early Christian Gnostics and Manichaeans (opposition of Light and Darkness, divine abstractions beneath God, initiation and consequently division of the adepts into select and simple) may have left a residue in other sects, too (Yazīdis, Mandaeans). Manichaeism spread from Turkestan to North Africa and was still powerful in eastern Turkestan in A.D. 1000.[3]

4. Mass migrations.

a. Migration of Turkish peoples from the eleventh century onward, especially from the time of the Mongolian irruptions. During the Ottoman period, Turks were transferred to the territories of Iraq and Syria to protect communications.

b. The penetration of Kurds from Kurdistan southward. This movement had already taken place in the days of Saladin and has not ceased to this day. For security reasons, Kurdish settlements were established in Syria by the Ottoman government.

c. Tranfer of segments of Caucasian peoples, and to a lesser degree groups from the Balkans, from the 1860's and 1870's.

d. After World War I, Syria and Lebanon became, through their mandatory government, an asylum for refugees from Christian and other communities fleeing from Turkey,[4] and to some extent from Iraq.

KURDS

Among the minorities the Kurds stand out most clearly as a national entity. In claiming self-determination, they point to the following:

1. A distinct ethnic group, one of the oldest within the human race. The question of their origin, as yet unresolved, has no relevance whatsoever to their claim.

2. Common fundamental characteristics of the dialects.[5] They have a vast folklore, a number of classical works and the beginnings of modern literature.[6]

3. Community of religion. Within Sunni Islam, mysticism embodied in orders, notably *naqshbandi* and *qādiri,* is the main characteristic. Outside it, a number of heterodox sects thrive among the Kurds.[7]

4. Almost unbroken territorial contiguity of the Kurdish settlements: from close to Marash in Turkey to the boundary of Iran, that is, on both sides of the Syrian-Turkish frontier, and then northward to Erzerum and Kars; in Iraq from the Iraqi-Turkish border southward to Mandalī; and in Iran from Maku on the border of Soviet Armenia to Kirmanshah. This contiguity is also confirmed by tribal ties across the frontiers. Large confederations of tribes live in or migrate between Iraq and Iran (Jāf, Bilbas, Kalhur, Harki) and between Iraq and Turkey (Mazuri).[8]

5. National self-consciousness combines with a centuries-old tradition of rule of Kurdish principalities, some of which still existed in the first half of the last century. The last century witnessed social revolts there and risings of Kurdish feudals against centralization of government in Turkey and Iran. After 1908 the first shoots of a national movement emerged, in the form of a club and a literary society. After World War I, the Kurdish problem had been raised on an international plane for the first time. The Treaty of Sèvres provided for local autonomy in the Kurdish areas and acknowledged,

under certain conditions, the possibility of independence "if the majority of the population desired it." A new and more advanced phase started in 1927 with the setting up of Hoybun (National Committee) in Syria which initiated cultural activities.[9] The outcome of World War II seemed to be favorable to the national cause, but the resulting cold war prevented the upsetting of the status quo in the Middle East.

6. All the national and social characteristics that entitle a people to statehood are found in them. It is the conflict of interests in this "seething cauldron" which facilitates, by means of negligence or support, a policy of oppression towards the Kurds. Power politics after the two world wars helped to establish states for peoples or tribal conglomerations far less fit for independence.

The main reasons against Kurdish statehood are given as follows: the isolation of the mountain districts and the consequent difficulties of communication among the three parts of Kurdistan; backwardness of the Kurds; particularism of the tribes; and mutliplicity of dialects. But these and similar reasons can be applied, to a far greater degree, to all the states recently established in Asia.[10]

The problems concerning the position of the Kurds in Iraq and Syria are in many respects inseparable from those of the Kurds in Iran, Turkey, and the Soviet Union.

Turkey

In Turkey, where nearly half of the Kurdish people live, the policy adopted towards them since the end of World War I has been one of forcible assimilation, that is, "absorption in the Turkish nation." Officially, there is no Kurdish question and the Kurds are regarded as "mountain Turks." Since 1923 the Turkish government has had to cope with rebellions, particularly in the years 1925, 1927, and 1937. Various methods of Turkification have been used: enrollment of the men in labor squads in distant camps, and, as during 1914–1918, deportation; transference from the mountains to the plains; ban on the Kurdish language in office and school; and denial of facilities for cultural and social activities. Steps calculated to destroy the tribal organization were also taken. After World War II, a more conciliatory attitude toward the Kurds was adopted, but the basic policy remained unchanged.[11]

Iran

In Iran, Riza Shah tried to settle the Kurdish question in his own way —by disarming the Kurds, by carrying off tribal leaders to Teheran as hostages, by forcing tribes to settle without providing the means, and by splitting up tribes and scattering some of them in remote districts. In the years between the two world wars, Kurdish revolts took place, and in 1932, during the uprising of Jalali in the region of Maku, many villages were laid waste. Conditions after World War II favored the emergence of a Kurdish republic in the Soviet-occupied part of their territory (end of 1945 to the end of 1946). Its government initiated social reforms, and it consequently became the center of Kurdish national aspirations. It was crushed by the Iranian government, and its leaders were put to death.[12] The republic of Mahabad was a combined attempt of representatives of different classes—tribal chiefs, religious leaders, and town dwellers. It was the first Kurdish movement preponderately urban.

The Kurds in Iran are regarded as Iranians and consequently are forbidden to carry on cultural work in their own language. It is open to question how far it is a means to an intended gradual absorption.[13] The authorities are not strong enough to destroy the tribal organization of the Kurds.

U.S.S.R.

The 120,000 Kurds in Armenia, Azerbaijan, and Turkmenistan enjoy, speaking in Soviet terms, cultural autonomy. Yerevan has become their intellectual center.[14] They have a network of elementary and secondary schools, and a pedagogical institute. A Latin alphabet, adopted in 1929, was replaced, in 1945, by the Russian alphabet supplemented by some Latin signs. Studies in the Kurdish language have been pursued with tangible results. Broadcasts in Kurdish are also designed to impress Kurds beyond the border.

Iraq

There are over a million Kurds in Iraq, forming at least 20 percent of the population.[15] Most of them live in the northeastern mountain range— the liwās of Sulaymāni, Arbil, Kirkuk and in the four northern districts of Mosul. Two of the four districts of Diyāla liwā—Khanāqīn and Mandalī —are to a large degree Kurdish. They are also found in Kūt and Baghdad liwās.

Kurdish society in Iraq is basically tribal. The continuous process of detribalization has been accelerated by closer control of the central authorities, by modern communications, and in a great degree by land settlement which, as in the whole of Iraq, tended to fix property rights in favor of tribal chiefs and other men of power. This could not but result in the transition from a tribal to a feudal pattern of society. The oil fields and the recently executed damming projects contribute their share to detribalization. The national movement, nowadays chiefly directed from the town, brings about a shift of loyalties from the tribal hierarchy and from the nontribal, merely residential associations, to the nation as a whole. If one may generalize, one might say that the mountain areas still are, in the main, tribally organized (Ruwandiz area in Arbil, areas of Pushdir and Halebja in Sulaymāni). In the lower parts, the nontribal groups of tenant farmers (Garmian area in Kirkuk liwā, the area around Qizil Rubat in Diyāla liwā, the valley around Sulaymāni) predominate. They owe much allegiance to landlords, mostly absentees, and their agents. In many cases they work as tenants on their old tribal land. Distinct social groups are subtenants and laborers, and in certain areas nontribal serf groups.

The once powerful seminomadic tribes (Harki, especially Jāf) are rapidly losing their nomadic character.

The town dwellers, also partly descended from tribes, are nontribal. In most towns the Kurdish element is predominant, but ethnically they show a great diversity (various Christian denominations, Turks, Arabs, and, until recently, Jews).[16]

The position of the Kurds in Iraq is in some respects far more tolerable than in Turkey and Iran, but there they have had the misfortune of being subjected, a second time in our own days, to the rule of a foreign people which like themselves has been subordinate to the Turks. The Kurdish question with all its implications was acute as early as 1918.[17] On account of the oil-bearing region, the British government threw all its weight onto the scale so that it was joined to Iraq in 1925. The R.A.F. played a decisive part in subduing Kurdish revolts against the government in 1922–23, 1927, 1930–31.[18] In 1930, on the eve of the abolition of the mandate, Kurdish leaders pressed their petitions on the League of Nations for the establishment of a "Kurdish government under the supervision of the League of Nations." In 1925 and in 1932 the Iraqi government pledged itself before the League of Nations to guarantee the use of Kurdish in school and office, and employment of Kurdish officials in Kurdish areas. At the same time it continued to foment dissension among Kurdish tribes.[19]

In the 1940's the main complaints of the Kurds were:

1. The Kurdish community in Iraq has no political existence because any political activity in a national framework is forbidden to it. By contrast, national feeling among the Arabs has reached its peak. There are two principal peoples in Iraq, but both domestic and foreign policy represent the Arab section alone. The ties between the Kurds of Iraq and those of Turkey and Iran are not different from the ties between the Arabs of Iraq and Syria. The policy of Turkey and Iran is to disintegrate the Kurds, and yet Iraq has entered with them into the Treaty of Saadabad, one of the purposes of

which is to coordinate the suppression of the Kurdish aspirations by all of them.

2. The administration is inefficient throughout the country, but the districts of the Kurds have been deliberately neglected.

3. On paper, Kurdish is recognized as one of the official languages in Kurdish districts, but in fact the law is not carried out even in the Sulaymāni liwā. Of the few schools in the area, only a small portion are Kurdish. The curricula and the history books do not deal with the Kurdish people, and printed matter in Kurdish is scarce.

4. The authorities dismiss or remove beyond the Kurdish boundaries those local officials who have any attachment to Kurdish nationalism.[20]

The answer to complaints about the economic plight was expulsion from the area or imprisonment. Power seekers, eager to pose before the public as heroes, exploited the situation by provoking racial and communal dissensions.[21]

After the revolt of the Barzani tribes in 1930, their leaders Mulla Mustafa and his brother Ahmad were removed to the south, and from there to Sulaymāni, where they were forcibly detained for about thirteen years. In June 1943, Mustafa escaped and joined his fellow tribesmen, and affrays involving bloodshed took place. In consequence of defeats at the hands of the rebels and desertion of Kurdish policemen and soldiers, the authorities decided, on the advice of the British, to open negotiations with the rebels. The Kurdish deputy Majid Mustafa associated some Kurdish officers with the negotiations. The Kurds assert that the following agreement was then arrived at:

1. All the Barzanis in detention should be released.
2. The Barzanis should retain their arms.
3. Foodstuffs should be equitably distributed in the Arab and Kurdish districts.
4. The Arab officials in the Kurdish districts should be replaced by Kurds.
5. Proper cultural autonomy should be guaranteed in Iraqi Kurdistan, and Kurdish schools and hospitals should be established.

Nūrī al-Saʿīd accepted these terms, but a majority in parliament rejected them. In consequence, Nūrī al-Saʿīd resigned in June 1944.[22]

The government of al-Pāchachī renewed the negotiations with Mulla Mustafa. In July 1945, the government troops suffered a severe defeat, and it was only after the air force hurriedly intervened that the rebels withdrew into the mountains. Finally thousands crossed the frontier of Iran. The Barzanis were joined by members of other tribes, officers, some of them of high rank, soldiers, civil servants, and teachers.[23] About 800 of them proceeded to Soviet Armenia.

The movement in Barzan had three aspects: local, national, and international. The district was one of the most neglected, and the inhabitants lived on chestnut bread and some fruit. The pick of the young men were imprisoned and removed on the pretext that they were busying themselves with the Kurdish question. The inhabitants complained of economic unfairness, particularly in the handling of the tobacco monopoly.

Government of the country appeared to rest on a constitutional basis, but in fact the constitution was a dead letter. Unscrupulous men sought to attain office by exaggerating differences of race and community.[23]

On the international side, the interests of the great powers prevented the Kurdish question from making itself heard in the world. The Kurds knew that as long as their aspirations for independence did not fit in with the prevailing trends of world politics, they had no hope of sovereignty.[24] Toward the end of World War II, the course of events seemed to be favorable to them. In the zone of Soviet occupation in Iran they were greatly encouraged. During the war, the British authorities evinced a certain sympathy towards them. American envoys also displayed interest in the Kurds in Iran, and after the war they counseled the authorities in Turkey to show patience. The Kurds thought that the time had come to call attention to the Kurdish question.

In the Iraqi parliament at that time, various attitudes on this question were voiced. Some denied its communal or national character. What people wanted was justice and fair treatment. The causes of the revolt were corruption, hardship, and official ineptitude. A state with many communities could not be united unless each community received its share of the benefits from reforms. Others again laid the blame on too great leniency in dealing with the rebels. One deputy pointed out that fifteen years earlier the government had brought forward a bill equivalent to an amnesty for the Barzanis, which was a proof that the causes which had produced the revolt were still operative.

There were two deputies who tried to get to the root of the matter. Sālim Namīq saw in the amnesty only a palliative. It was necessary to investigate the psychological and material causes of the revolt; moreover, it was necessary to examine the question in the light of the international situation. The latest events had reached a new stage, and it was only through the prompt action on the part of the government in sending a punitive expedition, and through the cooperation of a number of Kurdish leaders and their tribes, that a disaster had been averted. Comprehensive reforms were to be introduced in the zone. "The Kurds were a portion of the kingdom and in serving their interests we should serve the kingdom."

The deputy Uzrī called for a "philosophical and historical examination of the problem." Reforms were of secondary importance. "We must make clear to our Kurdish brethren, both by word and deed, that it is not our desire to subject them to exploitation." The Iraqi state was based on two

large nations and some smaller ones, all of which had one fatherland. The
Arabs would remain Arabs; they would work for the cultivation of their
language and their nationality, and would link themselves with the Arabs of
other countries; and they wished that the Kurds would also have success in
cultivating their language and their nationality. Switzerland and Canada had
shown how differences between peoples could be reconciled.[25]

The uprising of the Barzanis signaled a turning point in the Kurdish
national movement. In some respects tribal organization offered many advantages. It helped to preserve a tradition of unity. Unlike the Arab tribes,
Kurdish tribes are not, at least for the most part, based on traditions of
consanguinity, but are nevertheless organic and territorial units headed by a
nobility. Moreover, these units are associated with religious orders, so that
the sheikhs sometimes combine hereditary temporal and spiritual power.
On the other hand, dervish brotherhoods may encompass parts of various
tribes. All this, however, is counterbalanced and even outweighed by the fact
that the state possesses means for stirring up dissension among the tribes
or taking advantage of existing feuds among them. In the last revolt of
the Barzanis, the towns already took part so far as to provide it with political
support. The Kurdish town resorted to the usual *modus operandi* of the Arab
town—students' strikes, demonstrations, leaflets, side by side with negotiations.

The Kurdish society in Iraq has already reached a stage in which detribalization on account of economic development does not imply weakening
of national bonds. On the contrary, the loss in cohesion is being offset by a
broader outlook and closer attachment to the urban centers. We witness a
shift of the center of gravity from landed aristocracy to socially more advanced associations.

Syria

The immigration of Kurds into Syria has been going on for centuries,
and the increase in their numbers is already noted by Bazily.[26] Seminomadic, they used to go down with their flocks from Kurdistan to the pashalik
of Aleppo. Since the eighteenth century, Kurds had been charged with
the task of protecting the pilgrims on their way to Mecca, and immigrants
followed in the wake of the protectors. Kurds settled in the towns as bodyguards for the Pashas, and as horsemen in the service of the government or
some powerful faction. In Bazily's day there were about a thousand Kurdish families in Damascus.

In various parts of the country, especially in the west and in Hawrān,
and also in Lebanon, Upper Galilee, and across the Jordan, there are scattered Arabicized islands of Kurds. In some cases some remembrance of

their origin is preserved in the name of a tribe or a place: Jabal Akrād in the northeastern slope of Jabal Ansāriyya; to the south of this mountain Krak des Chevaliers, which formerly was called Hisn al-Akrād; Akrād Ibrā-hīm, Akrād ʻUthmāni, on the west of it; Hārat al-Akrād in Safed. Arabicized families took an active part in the civil and military life of the country (al-Barāzī, a family from the Euphrates region owning many villages in the districts of Hamā and Masyāf; Būzū, and others). There are tribes or large families in the east of the country, the origins of which are uncertain; some of them claim Arab origin although their Kurdish background is still re-membered or they still speak Kurdish. A kind of symbiosis is represented by the Kurdish-Arab confederation of Millī, which is mostly Kurdish. At the beginning of the twentieth century they were in the service of the Turkish government (Hamidiyye cavalry, dissolved by the Young Turks).[27]

Alongside the Turkish frontier there are three Kurdish belts.

1. In the Upper Jazīra, Tigris-region, sedentary Kurdish tribes are pre-dominant. They are interspersed with Arab, Turkoman and Yazīdi elements. Since 1926 they have been joined by Kurdish groups from Turkey. In the Khabur area some thousands from the Millī confederation who crossed over from Turkey are settled. Here, too, they were joined by Yazīdis, Armenians, and Jacobites from Turkey. The new town of Qamishli is a kind of capital for the Kurds.

2. Kurdish tribes in the Euphrates belt make up a part of the population of the districts of Jarablus and Manbij, Bāb and Aʻzāz in the province of Aleppo.

3. A large Kurdish group is to be found in the district of Kurd Dag (Mountain of the Kurds). Its center is the townlet ʻAfrīn. Although its tribal formation has been almost completely broken up, the influence of the sheikhs is still considerable.[28]

In the Sālhiyye quarter of Damascus, there are about 20,000 Kurds. They still retain their language and customs, partly because of the influx of fellow Kurds from the north.

After World War I, the Kurds of Syria enjoyed a spell of comparatively liberal treatment. The immigration from Turkey strengthened the Kurdish element in the Jazīra to such an extent that, with the Christians, the Kurds formed the majority of the population.

Although the voice of the Kurds is not heard in the peoples' assemblies, the Kurdish question is one of grave importance in the Middle East. Their claims for self-determination were not supported after World War II either. On the other hand, the Kurdish national movement has now reached a stage where partial concessions, such as language rights and a certain share in the administration, are likely to stimulate rather than curb it.[29]

Within a few months, in 1958, the Kurdish question became a factor in world politics. As far back as 1957, it could still be stated that Iraq "seems to have solved the Kurdish question," and that the Kurds "docilely accept the rule of Baghdad."[30] The reason was seen in the appeasement policy of Nūrī Saʿīd's government through an increased share of the Kurds in the development program and in government posts. The situation improved also in the field of education. As in the case of Iraq as a whole, it was a race with a mounting tide of discontent.

The Provisional Constitution of the new republic sees in Iraq "a part of the Arab nation" (art. 2), but considers Arabs and Kurds "partners in this homeland," and "provides for their national rights within Iraqi unity" (art. 3). Thus the policy of assimilation is explicitly abandoned. An abortive Council of Sovereignty was formed with one Shīʿi Arab, one Sunni Arab, and one Kurd. A member of the first government was Baba ʿAli, son of Sheikh Mahmud from Sulaymāni, since 1918 a rallying point of the Kurdish movement.

Mustafa Barzani, who led the Kurdish revolt in 1944–45, returned from his exile in Soviet Armenia and was acclaimed a national hero. Kurdish tribes helped to crush the rebellion in Mosul in March 1959. The Kurdish position became even stronger with the resignation of the pan-Arab Baʿth and Istiqlāl members from the government. In a greater Arab unity the Kurds would be reduced to a relatively small minority. Recently their impact on the government has lessened.

Repercussions of the changes in Iraq are felt in Iran. Prior to the upheaval in Iraq, Egypt espoused the Kurdish cause and inaugurated a broadcasting service in Kurdish. Its targets were the Baghdad Pact and Nūrī Saʿīd's regime. As in the case of the Negro south in the Sudan, it was a self-defeating undertaking. The Iranian government "retaliated" with broadcasting in Kurdish and allocations for the development of Kurdish areas. The Kurds are being assured that they are no match for Arabs. For the first time since 1946, a Kurdish weekly appeared in Iran, in June 1959.[31]

LURS

Linguists differ in the classification of their language, some considering it a Kurdish dialect and others claiming that it is closer to the Persian dialects of the Fars province. They are thought to be Shīʿis; some of them are ʿAlī-Ilāhis. For the most part workers, they are to be found in villages of the eastern part of the country (ʿAmāra and Kūt) as well as in Baghdad and Basra. Some of them take part in the Kurdish national movement. The last word as to kinship and allegiance should be theirs.

NUSAYRIS

They are an offshoot of extreme Shīʻism, secretive since the ninth century. One version traces the origin of Nusayri to Ibn Nusayr, the "gate" of the eleventh *imām* at the end of the ninth century. Being believers in the divinity of ʻAlī, they are also called ʻAlawis. Problems of their relation to Islam, particularly to Ismāʻīlism, and of the origin of syncretic elements in their faith, undoubtedly including ancient Semitic, Iranian, as well as Byzantine and perhaps crusaders' practices, remain to be cleared.

There are about 375,000 Nusayris in Syria, of whom 87 percent are in the Latakiya province, that is Jabal Ansāriyya, which in 1920 was extended by the French authorities towards the south and renamed the province of the ʻAlawis.

This is a tribal community. In their province they are linked, mainly, in five confederations (Haddād, Khayyāt, Metāwira, Kalbī, and Haydarī, the last seemingly representing a kind of *madhhab*, persuasion). Owing to migrations and feuds, the first three are not geographically compact, and since, in addition, they are sedentary, the stature of the tribes as social units is constantly diminishing.

Broadly speaking, the tribal bond, epitomized in allegiance to chiefs (*raʼīs* or *muqaddam*), is outweighed by the zonal bond, that is, the bond between tribes or parts of tribes living next to one another. Still more important is the personal bond which leads certain groups to form around a prominent and wealthy family which is able to afford them protection. These groups grow larger or smaller according to circumstances and to the leader's success.

The ʻAlawis constitute the majority in the province—over 70 percent— and if the towns are excluded, over 80 percent. Of the towns, some are Sunni islands (Haffa, Ruʼād, Jabala); others Sunni with a considerable Christian minority (Latakiya, Tartūs), or inconsiderable (Bānyās); and one is Christian with a considerable ʻAlawi minority (Sāfītā).

This community is preponderantly an agricultural proletariat—laborers, shepherds and foresters. There are comparatively few big landlords in it. Large estates are the rule in the east of the province, where towns are very few, and also eastward of the boundary toward Homs and Hamā, in the area overspread by ʻAlawi tenants who are being brought over by Sunni and some Christian landlords. In the northern part of the mountain, medium and small ownership is predominant, but even here the peasant is oppressed by his dependence on the sheikhs and the middlemen who market the tobacco.[32]

DRUZES

The eviction of Christian and Muslim elements by Druzes coming from Lebanon to Jabal al-Durūz began as early as the eighteenth century, but it assumed large proportions only in the last century, especially after the war-like feuds between the Druzes and the Maronites in 1860. By the middle of the last century, the Druze settlement in Jabal A'lā of the Aleppo province, at one time the strongest, still provided a refuge for war victims. From here, too, many emigrated to Hawrān.[33]

Other groups of Druzes are in Damascus (town and province), and in Homs and its environs.

The great majority of the 120-odd villages in Jabal al-Durūz are inhabited by Druzes only, the rest of them by Druzes mixed with either Christians or Muslims or both.

Less than a third of the cultivated area belongs to large proprietors, and about 38 percent are medium-size holdings. As in most parts of Syria, the share-cropping system is prevalent. Seasonal workers are employed under contract.[34]

Although the 'Alawis have been settled in their province for probably seven to eight centuries, whereas most of the Druzes removed to Jabal al-Durūz only about a century ago, they have many features in common. Their numbers are large enough to inspire a certain self-respect. They have a recent tradition of struggle for autonomy, and they have followed similar lines of political evolution under the mandate.

Various attempts to confer autonomy on them were made by the French authorities, from the État du Jebel Druze and the État des Alaouites in 1920, to the *gouvernements* of these territories, in May 1930, which were a kind of tentative arrangement. In all these experiments they remained under direct control of the French. However, in view of the treaty of 1936, they were included as ordinary provinces in the state of Syria, at the same time being promised a special administrative and financial regime. The treaty was not ratified, but it was put into practice, on a trial basis, in regard to the two provinces. At the beginning of World War II, matters returned to the *status quo ante*. In January 1942 the union of the two provinces to Syria was proclaimed. In 1944 their administrative and financial autonomy was withdrawn.

The differences between the two areas are as follows:

1. In the degree of confessional homogeneity. Of the inhabitants of Jabal al-Durūz about 90 percent are Druzes, while of the seven minorities only three are represented among them considerably—Greek Orthodox, Greek Catholics, and Sunnis. In the region of the 'Alawis at least seven minorities

stand out—Greek Orthodox, Sunni Arabs, Maronites, Ismāʿīlis, Turks, Armenian Orthodox, and Greek Catholics.

2. Economically, and therefore politically, the town has almost no advantage over the village in Jabal al-Durūz. Its three district towns are Druze in character. By contrast, Sunnis and the Greek Orthodox are dominant in the towns and in the coastal areas of the Latakiya province. And since the ruling class in the towns lives principally on the product of the villagers' labor —officeholders, landlords, and produce merchants—it is easy to see that from the political and social point of view the ʿAlawis are nothing more than a minority to the dominant groups of the province.

3. The two communities differ in their geographical distribution. Adjoining the Jabal al-Durūz, there are 88,000 Druzes living in Lebanon. What is more, their position in Lebanon is that of a state-community, that is, of a partner in the government. They also have as neighbors the 18,000 Druzes in Israel, who form a compact group, politically and socially advanced.

By contrast, there are only some 46,000 ʿAlawis close to the Latakiya province, those in the provinces of Homs and Hamā, which are now their chief field of expansion. About 70,000 ʿAlawis lived in the region of Alexandretta before 1939, while about 80,000 live farther north, in the neighborhood of Adana. Socially and economically these are better off than their brethren in the mountain, and some of them are town dwellers; but efforts of Turkification, especially by means of education and military service, are weakening their ties to the community. At any rate, the ʿAlawis in the mountain cannot draw any communal sustenance from them.

A few thousand ʿAlawis are to be found in the lowlands of ʿAkkār (Lebanon).

4. Unlike the ʿAlawis, the Druzes have not preserved tribal ties. They are usually grouped on a territorial basis, around a ruling family or a clan with a tradition of leadership and form a kind of party named for it (Atrash, ʿAmir, Dervish, etc.).

5. The Druze community made a notable contribution to the revival of the Arabic language and literature and to the political movement among the Arabs. The younger generation also gave its share to the Arab interterritorial organizations (League of National Action, Syrian National Party). The more advanced state of the Druzes and their proximity to Damascus and Beirut helped them to a better political standing.

During the whole period of the mandate, the leaders of the two communities argued with the leading Arab circles—the National Bloc on one side and, on the other, the al-hayʾa al-shaʿbiyya, popularly called Shahbandariyya, after Shahbandar, their gifted leader who was murdered by his adversaries in 1940. To some extent, political affiliation or estrangement is founded on mistrust and considerations of personal gain. Political tergiversation, or sitting on the sidelines, is not considered reprehensible. Party affiliation may be decided by the relationships between the leading families in the community, by those between branches in the family, between houses in the branch, and sometimes between individuals in the household. These relationships spring from fear of the majority and yearnings for autonomy, from a desire for position in the government, and from land disputes. The confusion has naturally been increased by outside factors.

Any prominent Druze could not but adopt an attitude toward the mandatory authorities, toward the rival blocs in Syria, and toward the British and Transjordan. On the whole, Atrash, the leading family since 1850, inclined toward the British—following a long-standing tradition among the Druzes— and toward the Popular Bloc. The ambitions of King 'Abdullah also acted as a kind of stimulant on this family. Varying considerations also gave it a certain leaning toward the French, and, especially among the inferior branches of the family, toward the National Bloc. Of the other principal families, some supported Atrash while some—among others, al-Halabī and al-'Asalī—sought to undermine them. The common feature was that practically all of them were split internally, even the few Bedouin tribes in the Jabal who tended the flocks of the Druzes.

In 1947, the dissensions in Jabal al-Durūz almost assumed the proportions of a civil war, revolving around the representation of the community in the Chamber of Deputies. Sultān Atrash took offense at the abolition of representation of the Druzes in the government by a minister, at the neglect of the Jabal in fields of education and communications, and at the alleged barring of members of the community from government service. Other complaints concerned withholding of grants from the family, and, most of all, the support by Damascus of the opposition in the Jabal. There can be no doubt that at that time high hopes were pinned on a union with Transjordan, because in it the Jabal would have a recognized place of its own.[35]

The rivals of Atrash at that time formed a so-called Popular Party. They complained that the Atrash family fell in with the plan for a large Syria and the schemes of 'Abdullah, that they were opposed to family domination based on "divine inheritance" and not on popular choice, to "medieval tyranny and feudalism."[36] They demanded that the separate administration of the Jabal should be abolished and that the government offices in it should be redistributed.

In Jabal Ansāriyya the relations between the 'Alawis and Damascus were affected by those between its various communities. Most of the leading families in the Sunni community were attached to the National Bloc, though some of them threw in their lot with the Popular Bloc. The 'Alawi leaders also took sides in the quarrels between and within the ruling families in the minorities.

Feuds for influence went on at various levels among the 'Alawis: between or within leading families of the confederations (Raslān from Kalbī; al-'Abbās from Khayyāt; Hawwāsh from Metāwira and Kinj from Haddād); between them and the religious leaders, though in many cases temporal and spiritual powers were exercised by one person. The feuds sprang from claims to authority in the community or the tribe, or to positions in the government service, from attempts to lure portions of another tribe away from allegiance to their leaders, and from land disputes. Parts of some tribes even owed their allegiance to Sunni landowners. Even the attitude to Islam is sometimes colored by political considerations.

In this atmosphere of intrigue, a sort of internecine war on one side, with the ignorant masses of share-croppers completely under the heel of the landowners on the other, the way was open for land expropriation and misuse of government authority for private gain. This was stimulated by the fact that religion has been compensating the 'Alawi community for an actual condition of subservience as a minority by a sense of superiority and election, and that oppressed masses incline to attach themselves to adventurous leaders who claim to perform miracles. The yearning for Messianic deliverance found satisfaction in Sulaymān Murshid. In the end, an enthusiastic mass movement sprang up around him.

This movement of Murshid contained a certain communal reaction against wiping out the traces of autonomy. 'Alawi leaders—among them Ibrāhīm al-Kinj and Munīr al-'Abbās—called upon the government to add an 'Alawi minister, to appoint an 'Alawi governor in the province, and to act free the group of Murshid. Otherwise, they said, the province would seek to attach itself to Lebanon.[37] 'Alawi leaders were also in contact with adherents of 'Abdullah.[38] The advocate of Murshid stated at that time that nearly all the leaders of the 'Alawis wanted to secede from Syria because they saw in independence the only means of extricating the province from its low status.[39]

The French in Syria were undoubtedly motivated by an urge to support the cause of minorities. On the other hand, there was the necessity of leaning on them so as to mitigate the pressure of the majority. No new stimuli were provided for the instinct of self-preservation such as might have raised it to the level of a communal consciousness as a positive force. Communal identity cannot be ensured for a long time by means of topographical isolation or of an obsolete social structure. It has not been provided with any new social basis and eo ipso a new élite, which might, by means of new values, compensate for communal confinement and counteract the temptations to join the majority.

The leaders of these self-centered communities themselves circumscribed the opportunities to make their political unity a reality. Nowadays the communities have to face a government which seeks to see their identity fade.

How the relations of the majority and the communities would evolve when
the country reaches a higher level of social advancement, and when the religious tradition fades, is uncertain.

YAZĪDIS

They form a self-contained community, Kurdish by origin and language.
There are many versions of the origin of their name, one of them being the
Persian Izād (God, angel). The current version among the Yazīdis is that
it is derived from the caliph Yazīd ibn Muʿāwiya, and it is therefore presumed
that a political movement in favor of the house of Umayya gained a lasting
foothold in Kurdistan.

According to some scholars, Yazīdism originated in Islam in the thirteenth century, but Persian beliefs and superstitions prevailed in it. Traces
of Islam almost disappeared from it, and the Yazīdis do not consider themselves Muslims. To others, Yazīdism is to be traced in the religion practiced
in Kurdish paganism. Similarly, there are questions as to how far other
contacts are discernible in it: Semitic, especially its relations with Mandaeism,
Christian, and others.

The Yazīdis are usually called Devil worshipers, and here again opinions
differ on whether the much-revered Peacock Angel—Taʾūs-é-Melek—em-
bodies the Devil as a representative of God, or whether it is purely a defama-
tory name.[40] This Devil worship does not necessarily involve a denial of
the principle of good in God. On the contrary, trust in the good may impel
appeasement of evil in order to induce it to do good. They believe that the
spirit of evil, originally good, is merely separated from God, and will ultimately arrive at a reconciliation with Him.

Yazīdism is distinguished by having a hierarchy of partly hereditary
castes. The grand sheikh—*ikhtiyār*—is a kind of patriarch. Endowed with
supernatural gifts, he exercises absolute power in religious matters, including
excommunication. Some families of sheikhs are authorities on doctrine and
ritual. The *pirs*—like the sheikhs hereditary descendants of Sheikh ʿAdi,
a twelfth-century Sūfi—perform similar religious functions. The sheikhs
and pirs are supported by a tax. There are also *qewwāls* (reciters), a kind of
itinerant missionaries and collectors of offerings, who live in two villages in
Shaykhān, and *faqīran,* ascetics of the sect, alongside with *küchaks,* vision-
aries and healers who live on gifts. Every Yazīdi is attached, as a *murīd*
(disciple), to a definite sheikh and pir. Some of the clergy, especially the
first two castes, are wealthy. Sometimes they compete with tribal chiefs for
political influence.

There are about 70,000 Yazīdis scattered over five countries. Most of
them (up to 40,000) live in the province of Mosul. The Yazīdis in Turkey,

in the region of Diarbekr and elsewhere, joined the revolt of the Kurds in 1927, and most of them escaped to Sinjār, to the Jazīra, and even to the Soviet Union. The rest of them are living in Syria (about 5,000), in Persian Azerbaijan (the mountains around Maku), and in the Soviet Union (Tiflis, Azerbaijan, and Soviet Armenia). Their centers in Iraq are as follows:

Jabal Sinjār, a lonely mountain range, is 100 miles west of Mosul. There are about fifty villages wholly inhabited by Yazīdis; and only in Balad, the capital of the district, are there some Christians and Muslims.

The Yazīdis in Jabal Sinjār are grouped in tribes, some of them almost sedentary and others seminomadic. In the early days of the last century they may have numbered about 150,000, but they suffered at the hands of Kurdish *begs* and Turkish *walis*, and were considerably reduced in numbers, especially in 1830–44 and 1892. During World War I they refused to hand over to the Turkish authorities Armenians who had escaped from Deyr el-Zor, and in 1932 they also gave refuge to Assyrians. After World War I they again gathered some strength, but factional strife over claims to the position of hereditary chief (*mir, amīr al-umarā'*) has weakened them considerably. The revolt of 1935 against compulsory military service failed because some tribes refused to take part in it and even supported the government. In this revolt the most important of the tribes—Mihirkan—was ruined and the back of the community was broken.

In the districts of Shaykhān and Mosul there are about fifty-eight Yazīdi villages. Eight of these have a mixed population—Christians or Muslims as well as Yazīdis, or all three.[41] Ba'adhrī, about forty miles north of Mosul, is the residence of the *mir*. Nominally he is the secular head of the community and as such levies a tax on it. North of Ba'adhrī lies the grave of Sheikh 'Adi, a sanctuary and a place of annual pilgrimage. 'Adi is said to have lived in seclusion in Hakkiari. If the assumption that he is the founder of Yazīdism is true, the religious structure of the Yazīdi society may have been patterned on a Sūfi order founded by him. But the tribal structure also may offer a clue to it.

In Syria about half of the Yazīdis live in villages around 'Amūda in the Jazīra. Since the eighteenth century, they have been attached to the confederation Millī. In 1927 Yazīdis joined the Kurds in their exodus to Syria. With the expansion of mechanized farming they have been shifted by the landowners from place to place and tend to submerge as an ethnic group.

The Yazīdis in Jabal Sim'ān and the valley of 'Afrīn have long been sedentary. Practically all form an agricultural proletariat. The stony soil provides a scanty sustenance for the flocks of the mountain folk. The dwellers in the lowland grow corn and cotton. Most of the land is the property of Muslims from Aleppo and 'Afrīn.

The Yazīdis here seem doomed to disappear. They are not recognized as a religious community but only as a Muslim faction. They try to conceal their religious practices from outsiders, and they are also reluctant to defend their rights. Members of the community, especially landowners, are going over to Islam in such numbers that in most of the villages they have already been reduced to a minority.[42]

A characteristic feature of the Kurdish society is the dervish brotherhoods within the Sunni faith. Secret ritual and fervent allegiance seem to serve as a sublimated means by which the underprivileged raise their moral and social status. Secret sects related to extreme Shīʻism—*ghulāt*—or Yazīdism represent a higher degree of cohesion. Al-ʻAzzāwī stresses the affinity of their beliefs.[43]

Kakāʼiyya, the largest brotherhood, which became a kind of sect, comprises town dwellers (Baghdad, Mosul, Sulaymānī) and tribes, or tribal segments. Groups of their villages are to be found in Kirkuk and Diyāla liwās.[44]

The *Shabak,* a community of 10–15,000 souls, live in about twenty villages of their own or in mixed ones (Bajorān, Kurds, Turkomans, Arabs). Like the Bajorān they speak a language that is a mixture of Persian, Kurdish, Arabic, and Turkish. In one breath they mention Allāh, Muhammad and ʻAlī. Shīʻi elements are easily discernible in their creed. Their head (*pir, baba*) exercises immense power over them. He is the forgiver of sins.[45] They are close to the Yazīdis and have their shrines in common.

PERSIANS

They number about 140,000. For centuries Persians have made a yearly pilgrimage to the Shīʻi shrines in Iraq. They are numerous in Kerbelā. Najaf, on the other hand, is more Arabic in character, but there are also various elements—Persian, Indian, Pakistani, and Turkish. Students from the Shīʻi countries attend the numerous colleges in these towns. Here and in Kāzimayn the great theologians, *mijtahids,* reside, some of whom are of Persian origin, and whose influence extends beyond the borders of Iraq. In Baghdad and Basra the Persians are dealers in carpets, textiles, and tea.

BAHĀʼIS

Their religion developed away from Bābism, which emerged in Persia in the first half of the last century as a kind of protest against the Shīʻi clergy and the social conditions. Its founder escaped to Baghdad in 1852. Bahāʼism represents a universal religion holding to humanism and pacifism. It has neither clergy nor ceremony.   As in Persia, the small Bahā'i community in Baghdad is to a great extent underground.   It gained some foothold in the United States.   Its center is in Haifa, Israel.

ARMENIANS

Armenians have been settled in Syria and Lebanon from ancient times, notably in some villages in the north of the 'Alawi mountains.   Owing to massacres in 1894, Armenians moved there from Turkey, and before 1914 they numbered about 5,000.   Because of massacres and deportations during 1915–1918, a large part of the Armenian nation perished (estimates range up to over a million).

Three waves of Armenian immigration into Syria and Lebanon are to be noted:

1. The survivors of 1914–1918, who had returned and settled in Cilicia, left this region with the departure of the French in 1921.
2. Armenian refugees who settled in Iran, Iraq, and Greece gradually moved to Lebanon.
3. During 1938–39, when the region of Alexandretta was ceded to Turkey.

Of the 100,000 Armenians in Syria, 73,000 are Gregorians, 20,000 Catholics, and 6,000 Protestants.   Their main centers are Aleppo (70,000), Damascus (6,500), Qamishli (9,300), Latakia (950).   Armenian settlements are scattered over the three northern provinces, notably in the Jazīra.

The sixty-eight primary and secondary schools are attended by 16,850 pupils.

The Armenians in Lebanon and Syria are divided into two major political groups.   The Armenian Revolutionary Federation (Tashnag) advocates complete independence of Armenia and, in consequence, pursues an anti-Soviet policy.   The other faction, mindful of past experience and present world conflicts, sees the nation's survival in the protection given to the small republic by the U.S.S.R.; but ideologically they are not Communists.   This faction is composed of the Armenian Democratic League (Ramgavar), the Huntchag Party, the Progressive Party and non-partisans.   It represents the majority of the Armenians in the Diaspora.

Armenians had been living in Iraq before 1914.   Most of them, however, came there during World War I and after it.   Of the 15,000 Armenians in the great refugee camp in Ba'qūba, a part returned at the time to Iran or were transported by boat to Batum.   They are estimated to number about 24,000, including 2,000 Catholics and an Evangelical congregation.   Their main centers are: Baghdad (8,000), Basra (3,000), Kirkuk (2,200), Mosul (2,000),

Sulaymāni (1,200), Zakho (950). As elsewhere, church and school are the mainstay of the community.

After World War II a movement to return to the Armenian republic in the Soviet Union started among the 300,000 Armenians in the Middle East. About 20–25,000 migrated from Syria and Lebanon alone.

CIRCASSIANS[48]

In the 1860's and 1870's Muslim refugees from the Caucasus reached northern Mesopotamia. Chachans settled alongside Rās al-'Ayn in the Jazīra, but their numbers were greatly reduced by malaria and pressure of the Bedouin. At present a small Chachan tribe is encamped there.[49]

After the Russo-Turkish war of 1877–78 Circassians settled in Jawlān (Damascus) and in the district of Manbij (Aleppo);[50] also some in the Latakiya province.[51] Qunaytra in Jawlān, then a deserted village near the ruins of a Roman town, was rebuilt by them. The Circassian community was enlarged as a result of the Franco-Turkish agreement of 1921, by which the Turkish frontier with Syria was moved southward. Circassian groups were at that time enrolled in the French army. Before 1939 Circassians still lived in tents in the area of Upper Khabur.[52] On the whole, there are some forty villages scattered over the country, with about 35,000 inhabitants.

The future of this community, which is a national minority in every respect, is problematical. Apart from close settlements in Jawlān and to a certain extent in Jordan (about 12,000 souls),[53] there are only a few isolated islands left in this region, two of them in Israel; and of these some have become Arabicized.

Settled for political reasons, the Circassians were assigned the task of maintaining order as gendarmes and officials of the Sultan. In the revolt of 1925 they fought vigorously for the French. Throughout the period of the mandate, they took a prominent part in local security units. The freedom they enjoyed stimulated in them the sense of national separateness, and in the 1930's they went so far as to demand autonomy for the district of Jawlān and representation in the parliament as a national minority. They also became conscious of the bonds they had with other fragments of their community in the Middle East. On the other hand, some of them inclined to assimilation. The Daghestanis and the Chachans became absorbed politically, and mixed marriages occur between them and the Arabs.

Most of them are small landowners; there are very few traders among them. The tribal bond is still strongly in evidence in the way in which they herd in villages and in the assemblies of the elders. Unlike the Arab tribes, the elders practice no economic or social exploitation. Nevertheless, the influence of the leading families is considerable.

Various factors help to preserve their particularism in Syria—common language, customs, an urge for independence, connections with their brethren in Jordan, Turkey, and Egypt, where they have attained to wealth and influence. Some factors work in the opposite direction—a weakening of attachment to their language, which in spite of all efforts remains a spoken tongue only, education in Arab schools, lack of opportunities for the young people in a small community.[54] With the abolition of the mandate, their hopes for national self-assertion waned. Statistically, they are regarded as a part of the Sunni majority.

TURKS AND TURKOMANS

Their settlements are scattered over a line stretching from northwest (the predominantly Turkish Tall 'Afar, 47 miles west of Mosul, and a dozen villages adjoining it in the Mosul liwā, where traces of tribal structure are still to be found) to southeast (Altun Köprü and Tuz Khurmatu in the Kirkuk liwā and the Khanāqīn district, where there are some Turkoman tribes). Qizil Rubat and Khanāqīn, Kirkuk, and Arbil are predominantly Kurdish-Turkoman towns.

Turkoman settlements were established by the Turks at strategic points as a defense against Persians and Kurds. In a way this is a kind of enclave separating the Arab from the Kurdish zone. In 1947 they numbered 108,000. They are mostly Sunnis and partly adherents of secretive Shī'ī sects.[55]

In Syria Turkomans are concentrated in villages in the districts of Latakiya, Tall Kalakh, and Sāfītā, 13,350 in all. They have preserved their language and to some extent their tribal grouping.

Remnants of Turkoman tribes are also found in the Jazīra, where they had been nearly decimated by the Kurdish and Shammar tribes at the beginning of the last century, and in the Euphrates province (Jarablus). Turks are found in the towns of Syria, and some of them have extensive estates in the northern area.

As in Iraq, Turkoman settlements were established here to protect the traffic routes. In the interior they have become more or less Arabicized. There are three large villages of Turkoman origin south of the 'Alawi mountain, around Krak des Chevaliers, and five in the south of the Hamā district; also some in the subdistrict of Qunaytra. They are estimated to number 75,000.

JEWS

Before the great exodus to Israel in the years 1950–51, about 130,000
Jews were living in Iraq: 90,000 in Baghdad, 10,000 in Basra, and 16,000 in
the northern districts. They were divided roughly into three classes. A small
wealthy class was almost dominant in some branches of commerce, especially
in export and import trade, and in banking. Then there was a professional
class—lawyers, physicians, teachers, government officials, and business managers. Lastly, there was the great majority of very poor people engaged in
petty trading and handicrafts. A special class was formed by some thousand
Kurdish Jews in the north, mostly manual workers (woodchoppers, tanners,
dyers, weavers, porters, also silversmiths and peddlers). In the highlands
they were scattered in agricultural groups under the protection of Kurdish
aghas. Their vernacular is *targum* interspersed with Kurdish, Arabic, or
Turkish elements.

The Jews in Iraq have passed through many vicissitudes. In 1921–30,
they were comparatively well off politically. Owing to the personal influence
of Faysal, the British control and the policy of appeasing the minorities in
order to prove fitness for independence, as well as lack of training among the
Arabs, opportunities were thrown open to Jews in the government service and
in commerce. A feeling of confidence strengthened the attachment of the
Jewish intelligentsia to Arabic culture, and this attachment even found expression in literary activity. This is the first and only attempt that has been
made in our day at conscious assimilation.

In the 1930's, a decisive change took place in the position of the Jews,
due to the attainment of political independence by Iraq, the impact of fascism
on Arab nationalism, and the Palestine problem. The Jews were driven out
of government posts, educational establishments, and business situations, although no legal sanction was given to this discrimination. On the other side,
the authorities sought to sever the ties which bound the Jews to Palestine
and the Hebrew language. Even teaching of Jewish history was forbidden.
This period reached its climax with the massacres of May 1941.

Between 1941 and 1945, when the British army was encamped in Iraq, the
confidence of the Jews revived, but they did not recover their former social
position. In spite of an official ban, migration to Palestine continued.

After the war, tension because of the Palestine issue increased and spread
fear among the Jews. From November 29, 1947, and still more from May 15,
1948, a policy of persecution against the Jews, which also had legal sanction,
began. It took the form of mass imprisonment, maltreatment, and economic
exactions.

At the beginning of 1950 permission was given to the Jews to emigrate
to Israel. Whereas between 1919 and June 1950 about 19,000 Jews had gone

to Palestine, by the end of 1951 the number had risen to about a hundred thousand. Several thousand Jews went to Europe, the United States, and India. Only a few thousand remained.[56]

In the early 1940's there were about 30,000 Jews in Syria, for the most part town dwellers (Aleppo, Damascus, Homs, Latakiya). Of these some 18,000 were Sephardis, mostly engaged in petty commerce and trade, some 4,000 indigenous and extremely poor, the rest Kurdish Jews, fellahin and some peddlers in the Jazīra, and Ashkenazis, mostly professionals. Large-scale immigration into Palestine, to a lesser degree to Lebanon and Europe, started in the 1930's, and increased in the war years and after 1948. Of the remaining Jews some 2,000, mostly refugees, are confined to two narrow streets in the Jewish quarter; some 2,000 are less restricted in Aleppo; and some hundreds of families are in Qamishli. Stripped of their property, they are denied elementary rights. It is a slow death of starvation and degradation.[57]

ISMĀ'ĪLIS

Their name is taken from the shī'i imām Ismā'īl (d. about 760), seventh in the line of the imāms descending from 'Alī by Fātima. By the end of the ninth century, they represented a strong politico-religious movement involved in a fierce struggle with the Baghdad Caliphate, and its successors. By means of highly refined propaganda they built up strong centers in Persia, Yemen, North Africa, and Salamīya, southeast of Hamā. The great Ismā'īli dynasty in Egypt—the Fātimis—reigned over a large part of Islamic territories for more than 150 years. At the end of the eleventh century, a related movement of Nizāris—named after Nizār, who was murdered by his brother after the death of his father, the Fātimi caliph Mustansir (d. 1094)—issued from Alamut in Northern Persia, through the medium of the order of assassins (hashshāshin) and in fight with the Sunni Saldjuqs and the crusaders, and spread terror for more than 150 years.[58] By the middle of the twelfth century the Ismā'īlis were still scattered over all Syria, but their mainstays were a few centers in the 'Alawi mountains (region of Qadmūs and Masyāf). According to their own tradition, they dispersed from Salamiya in the wake of the invasion of Tamerlane. In 1843, they started to move from the mountains to the then derelict area of Salamiya, and the process of colonization still goes on.

Under the French mandate, the Ismā'īlis were recognized as a community with a personal status, but they took little advantage of this, so as not to expose their tenets. Similarly they refrained from taking part in politics. Most of their leaders were emirs owning large estates, and some of them have held religious offices, too. These represented the community with the authorities, and they were also entrusted with government posts.

The Ismā'īlis have two centers in Syria. In Salamiya and in about thirty villages east of it, they number over 30,000. In the 'Alawi mountains, there are about thirty small villages on both sides of the river Ismāʻīliyya and a few encampments with about 10,000 souls. Urban settlements are found in Qadmūs and especially in Masyāf (about 2,000). The Ismāʻīlis in the mountain region are very backward, and because of the pressure of the neighboring 'Alawis some of them cross over to the zone of Salamiya either permanently or for seasonal labor. Some of their settlements are becoming depopulated or mixed with an influx of 'Alawis. On the other hand, in the towns, through the very fact of their being a minority requiring coherence, they have managed to set themselves up in trade and moneylending, and in consequence, they have become landowners also.

The Ismāʻīlis in the zone of Salamiya differ from the others in several respects. They are Nizāris, pay allegiance to the offspring of Agha Khan as descendant of the Nizāri imāms, and turn to him for assistance in religious and educational matters. This connection with a kind of world movement helps to keep alive in them a spirit of independence. Their position is distinctly better, another reason being the fertility of the irrigable land.

And yet, World War II threatened the existence of the Ismāʻīlis in this region. The opportunities for trade and employment opened up by the presence of Allied forces brought abundance of money and a spirit of enterprise into the community, and this accelerated the transition from dry farming to irrigated crops. The authority of the emirs weakened more and more, and with it the dependence of the share-croppers on them. With the introduction of motor-pumps, some of the large estates are being broken up. A new middle class of officials and traders is gradually displacing the feudal families from their positions in the community and in government offices. Some have even left the community. With the independence of Syria a shift in the political loyalties of the leading men took place. The economic and social intercourse with the majority brings with it a danger of extinction.[59]

MANDAEANS

The original home of this ancient community is still a matter of controversy (the Hawrān plateau in the west or the highlands in Media), and it remains to be answered how they moved to Khuzistan in Persia and to lower Iraq. European travellers since the first half of the seventeenth century called them, erroneously, "Christians of John the Baptist." They themselves referred to him as their prophet, probably in order to keep in touch with the Christians. Their faith seems to have been subject, directly or indirectly, to Babylonian, Hebrew, Nestorian, and Islamic influences. Recently, more and more attention is drawn to Persian elements in their beliefs, ritual, and language. No answer has yet been found to the question of how far the common element in Manichaeism, Mandaeism, and Christian Gnosis are coincidences or could be traced to common sources.[60]

The core of their faith is worship of the principles of life and fertility, with rushing water as its symbol. An elaborate system of baptisms and ritual meals serves to ensure purity. To the Mandaeans, the celestial and infernal realms of the world are peopled with male and female beings of different ranks—spirits of light dispensing health, virtue, and justice as against spirits of darkness and evil. Health of the body is to be combined with health of mind and with upright conduct.

They practice certain crafts with artistic distinction. They are well known as goldsmiths and silversmiths, especially providing tribal jewelry, armorers, carpenters, ironworkers, boat-builders. The priests supply charms.

This community, persecuted down through the ages, is threatened with extinction. Their ceremonial language is Mandaean, an ancient Aramaic dialect, but the spoken Mandaean (ratna) is falling into disuse, and Arabic is spoken by all members of the community. Under the British mandate, they were inclined to emphasize their identity, but in face of rising nationalism, they have to be very guarded. The younger generation is adjusting itself to the environment; they attend general schools, in defiance of their precepts, and serve in the army. Even the priestly caste is dwindling because their sons who should inherit the office are deviating from the tradition. Mixed marriages are also diminishing the community.

They are scattered in towns and villages of southern Iraq (Muntafiq, Basra, and 'Amāra, especially in Qal'at Sālih, Sūq al-Shuyūkh). They are also found in Baghdad and Mosul. In 1949 they numbered 6,597. There are a few groups in Muhammera and Ahwaz in Khuzistan, and some individuals live in Damascus, Beirut, and Alexandria.[61]

COMMUNITIES OF
THE EASTERN CHURCHES

These communities are the Assyrian Nestorians (Church of the Orient), the Chaldean Catholics (Uniate Eastern Church), the Jacobites (Syrian Orthodox Church) and the Syrian Catholics. In many respects they constitute small nations. Each has its spoken Aramaic dialect, or memories of it (with a liturgical Aramaic), its own church, a tradition of self-governing entities (millet), and a measure of historical conscience. For centuries they have been oppressed by neighbors and invaders. Before World War I, they were mainly concentrated in the Turkish vilayets of Mardin and Mosul up to Lake Van, and in Persia, in the lowlands of Urmiya. Eastern Aramaic dialects were then spoken by the Nestorians and the Chaldeans, and Western by the Jacobites in Tūr 'Abdīn (vilayet Mardin), in the Jazīra and in Aleppo, and also in three villages in central Syria (two Muslim and one mixed). Cognate dialects were spoken by the Jews (*targum* in Kurdistan, and the dialect of the Jews in Salmas, northwest of Lake Urmiya). Through the pressure of the environment the dialects received an infusion of foreign elements, Turkish or Kurdish, Persian or Arabic, and in many places they were entirely driven out.[62] At present, members of these communities, insofar as they still cling to their own dialect, are often bilingual, all according to their contact with neighbors and the route of their wanderings.

Assyrians

At the turn of the tenth century, Nestorian congregations were scattered over a large territory, from Basra to Nisibis in the Jazīra. In the following centuries the community shrank more and more, and its center shifted to Mosul. By the middle of the fifteenth century the leadership of the community, secular and religious alike, passed to a militant family—Shim'ōn. The Church, hitherto interterritorial, became more and more a millet, a kind of church-bound coalition of tribes.[63]

Owing to its closely knit character, the Assyrian community comes nearest of all these communities to the concept of a nation. It stands out by memories of religious expansion, by its social structure, and by a stronger political consciousness. Most Assyrians speak their dialect (*soureth*) and understand Arabic, or Kurdish, or Persian. Before World War I, most of them, about a dozen tribes, were grouped together in the midst of Kurds and Armenians, on the heights of Hakkiari, northeastward of Iraq, in an area assigned in 1925 by the frontier commission of the League of Nations to Turkey. About a quarter of them lived in valleys on the west of Urmiya. Their numbers were then variously estimated at between 100,000 and 200,000.

In 1916, after they joined the Allies, they were forced to leave Hakkiari, and those who had not starved to death or been killed by Turkish or Kurdish bullets reached Urmiya. In 1917, when the Russians retreated, they had to seek refuge once more. About 70,000 set out from Urmiya and less than two thirds reached Hamadan. In 1918 about 35,000 were transferred by the British to the camp of Ba'qūba, northeast of Baghdad. Thousands moved to the Caucasus.

Great Britain recognized them as allies in this war. In 1919, and later on, they were employed in the pacification of the Kurdish districts in Iraq. In 1922, when an invasion of the north of Iraq by the forces of Kemal Pasha was imminent, two thousand of them enrolled within three weeks and helped to foil the Turkish plans. Later, Assyrian levies served at the British bases in Iraq. A number of factors combined to frustrate the aspirations of the Assyrians. They had no leadership worthy of the name to which the fate of the community could be entrusted, and what leaders they had were at variance with one another. The refugees from Urmiya wanted to return, and some of them actually did return to their former homes. In 1920, a plan was hatched among them to occupy an area on the borders of Turkey, Persia, and Iraq and to set up a state in it. The British authorities, it would seem, desired to consolidate the community in one area, but they were not determined enough to take risks. An attempt was made to settle them in scattered groups, chiefly in Mosul liwā, thus causing friction between them and the Kurds. Several thousands moved to Baghdad, Mosul, and Basra. Their cause was already killed in the years 1925–1928, in the course of a futile argument between the League of Nations, Turkey, and Great Britain.

The problem of settling the Assyrians occupied the attention of the British up to the cessation of the mandate. The Iraqis saw them as tools of a foreign power. But even without this it was clear from the first that an Arab government would do everything in its power to suppress any idea of a close settlement, and still more, that it would have no intention to further administrative autonomy. In the autumn of 1931 the Assyrians appealed to the League of Nations with a request to be transferred to Syria or to some European country. The Assyrian units gave up their service and asked that the Assyrians should be recognized as a millet and their Patriarch as its temporal and spiritual leader. If there was no possibility of annexing Hakkiari to Iraq, a national home for all the Assyrians in the world should be established in Iraq, for which an area was proposed in the province of Mosul. The authorities of Iraq succeeded in inducing a section of the Assyrian leaders, mostly from among the old established villages, to demonstrate their loyalty by a counter petition. Attempts were made also to divert the antipathy of the Kurds to the Assyrians. The tension reached its climax in July 1933, when eight hundred Assyrians crossed the border to Syria. They were induced by the French authorities to return. Part of them returned. Those who were not caught and shot by Iraqi guards dispersed to their villages. These events culminated in massacres perpetrated by the Iraqi army in the village Sumayl. Assyrian villages were devastated and hundreds of persons were murdered.[64]

After these events, up to nine thousand Assyrians were settled in 30-35 villages, under the auspices of the League of Nations, on both sides of the upper Khabur in the Jazīra. A few scattered over Syria and Lebanon. In these villages they preserved their own modes of life; every village contains one subtribe and has its own *malik*, whose influence varies, and clergymen.

As in Iraq, they did not cease to dream of returning to their native country and at the same time looked for a country to which they might immigrate—even casting eyes on Brazil.

In Iraq there are still 23,000 Assyrians. Some of them are in the towns (Mosul, Kirkuk), others are employed in the Iraq Petroleum Company works or until recently at the British air bases, and the rest live in villages in the Mosul area. Of these, some are in ancient settlements (Barwar) while others have settled on their own land or as serfs.

Assyrians are found in the Soviet Union, and some 15–20,000 of them in the United States. In all, they may number 80,000. The community is diminishing owing to a sizable conversion to the Catholic Chaldean faith in the Jazīra and in Iran.

This ancient community is still striving, under an exiled patriarch who resides in Chicago, to preserve its identity. The Iraqi authorities are on the watch to prevent any contacts between the Assyrians in Iraq and other branches of their church. Their excellent service in both world wars has availed them nothing. The Western Powers have not been able to secure a home for them.[65]

Chaldeans

This community has about 170,000 members in the Middle East (145,000 in Iraq, 11,500 in Iran, 5,500 in Syria [diocese of Aleppo-Jazīra], and the rest in Lebanon, Egypt, Turkey). The Chaldean Church in the region of Mosul was definitely established under Dominican guidance in 1750, but organized attempts to secede from the Nestorian Church go as far back as 1553. In 1845 the Chaldeans were recognized by the Ottoman government as a millet. The Patriarch of Babylon resides in Mosul.

Their chief center is the Mosul plain. There they have some dozens of villages, among them Tell Keif with a population of several thousands, Batnai, Alqōsh and Tell Uskūf. During World War I, thousands of them escaped from the south of Turkey to these places and also to the Jazīra. The rest of their centers are Baghdad with 15,000 souls, Basra with 10,000 and Kirkuk with 8,000. They are of enterprising spirit and are also represented in the government service. A few thousands of them have migrated to North and South America. Their centers in Syria are the Jazīra, Homs and Aleppo.[66]

Jacobites

The Syrian Orthodox (Jacobite) Church takes its name from Jacob Baradai (d. 577) who helped to reorganize and consolidate it. It originated from a fifth-century schism. During the period of its renaissance (1150–1300), Jacobites were scattered in compact groups comprising a large area; suffice it to mention Tabriz, Mardin, Urmiya, Mosul, Damascus, Jerusalem and Cyprus.[67] Despite persecutions at the hands of Turks and Kurds, they may have numbered 200,000 by the middle of the last century. Their center was Tūr 'Abdīn with 150-200 villages. Nowadays there are about 23,000 in Iraq, most of them in Mosul and, together with Syrian Catholics, in some villages within this province (Baʻshiqa, Bartelli, Karaqōsh); also in Baghdad and Basra.

Most of the 50,000 Jacobites in Syria live in the Jazīra, Homs, and Aleppo. After World War I the seat of the Syrian Patriarch of Antioch was transferred from Zaʻfaran near Mardin to Homs. They have congregations in Lebanon (5,000), Jerusalem and Cairo (3,000), Turkey (Tür ʻAbdīn 20,000, other regions 10,000), North and South America (25,000).

Syrian Catholics

These are the Jacobites who have joined the Roman Catholic Church since the seventeenth century, especially at the end of the eighteenth century. Within the jurisdiction of the Patriarch of Antioch of the Syrians, who resides in Beirut (the former Ottoman Empire and Egypt), they number about 70,000: 35,000 in Iraq (Mosul and villages within the province, Baghdad, Basra), about 20,000 in Syria, chiefly in Damascus, Aleppo, Homs, and the Jazīra. Many of them fled after World War I from Turkish Kurdistan. There are some 18,000 Syrian Catholics in the United States, South America, France and other countries.

The disintegration of these communities, especially since World War I, is closely bound up with the gradual displacement and disuse of the Aramaic dialects. As far back as the 1830's, missionaries who found their way to Urmiya (Presbyterians in 1835, Lazarists in 1840) fixed a script for a basic Aramaic and began to collect and publish educational and religious literature in it. Scholarly interest in these dialects arose in Europe, too. This literary work was not carried on regularly, so that traces of changes in these dialects have been lost. It came to an end with the outbreak of World War I.[68]

In the 1880's Aramaic dialects were still spoken in a large area bounded roughly by Lake Urmiya to the east, the lower Great Zāb to the point of its confluence with the Tigris to the south, the Jazīra, the north area of Van, and pashalik Diarbekr as far as Mardin. One may assume that despite conversion and massacres there were then some 300,000 Aramaic-speaking Christians in this area.

At the end of the last century, Aramaic was little spoken in Mosul, having been supplanted by Arabic. In the plain of Solduz south of Urmiya, Azerbaijan-Turkish elements found their way into Aramaic, and in many villages it had almost been displaced by Turkish. In the mountains Aramaic had been affected by Kurdish and in the plains westward by Arabic. The same applies to *fellīhi* (dialect of fellahin) which had been spoken to the west of the Tigris and in Mosul.[69] The dialects were preserved, mainly, in village centers.

These peoples defended themselves for centuries, and it was just in the period which raised the standard of self-determination that they were condemned to dispersal and decay. What was left by famine and massacres during World War I was liable to fall a victim to the policies of the one-nation state. They are far from identifying themselves nationally with the majority; but against this the desire for self-preservation works toward assimilation.[70]

ARABIC-SPEAKING CHRISTIAN COMMUNITIES

These communities—the Greek Orthodox, and the Greek Catholic (Melkites)—are a tiny minority in Iraq. In Syria, the Greek Orthodox are the largest of the Christian communities, numbering about 174,000 of whom about 72,000 are in the province of Latakiya, while the rest are in Damascus, in the districts of Homs and Hamā, and in Aleppo. The Greek Catholics are fewer in numbers—about 58,000—in the province of Damascus, in Aleppo, in Hawrān, and elsewhere. A considerable part of these communities live in villages, or even groups of villages, and in small towns. The groups are found in the 'Alawi province, especially in the southern part of it, around Hamā, and in the south of the Ghāb valley on both sides of the Orontes.[71]

With the exception of a few Russians and Greeks, all the members of the Greek Orthodox community in these two countries speak Arabic. At the end of the last century, the Greek Orthodox Church secured autonomy with the assistance of the Pravoslav Church, which before World War I had succeeded in gaining the hegemony of the Orthodox Church.[72] The Greek Catholics, who at the beginning of the eighteenth century acknowledged the supremacy of Rome, retain, too, a certain measure of independence. Their patriarch ordinarily resides in Damascus.

Various factors molded the characteristics of these communities. Their superior education, derived from the activity of missionaries, has opened up to them more opportunities in the fields of commerce and civil service. Both the regime of the capitulations and that of the mandate benefited them in many respects. The community controls a large part of the individual's life from birth to death, and of his attachment to the society (education, mutual assistance, representation). Each community has maintained relations with outside bodies, and this has given it a sense of ease, in the main imaginary, and inculcated a dangerous feeling of lasting security.

On the other side, the Christian minorities are affected by the social conditions in the country as a whole. The affairs of the community have largely been in the hands of families of distinction. The interfamilial—sometimes intrafamilial—dissensions, frequently on questions of office in the church itself, decided political affiliations or links with external elements. The deeply ingrained habit of camouflage, which is a powerful force in the life of the

country, assumes a communal coloring and maintains itself toward the majority. The members of the community oscillate between an urge to throw in
their lot with the rest of the inhabitants, and fear for their autonomous framework which in any case may be a shield against encroachment from the
majority.

Two further factors:

1. Emigration. It assumed large dimensions about 1890, with the migration to America, and grew even more after World War I.[73] This, on the one
hand, weakened the communities by markedly depleting the Christian villages
and urban groups, while on the other hand it helped to improve their cultural
and moral status.

2. The future of the community is bound up with its demographic trends.
The improvement of education and living standards tends to upset the equilibrium in natural increase which is conditioned by the birth and death rates,
and especially by the infant mortality, by the age and frequency of marriage,
and the frequency of divorce. Experience shows that in a period of transition
from a backward to a higher stage of social development, the decline of the
death rate is greater than that of the birth rate. The proportion of the Christian communities in the population (at present about 14 percent in Syria)
tends to decline.[74]

The differences in the social and cultural status of the two communities
spring in part from the fact that the Greek Catholic Church kept uninterrupted
contact with the West, whereas the Greek Orthodox Church renewed its contact with the Pravoslav Church after a break of about thirty years.

The Orthodox Church sees itself threatened by an expansionist activity on
the part of the Catholic Church with its greater resources, world-wide connections, especially in North America, its schools and philanthrophic establishments, and, moreover, with its acute sense of vocation and devotion to
work in villages. At the beginning of this century, the Greek Catholics in
Syria and Lebanon numbered 60–70,000 members and nowadays about 140,-
000. Being given to one authority, there is a wider scope for interconfessional
activity in it, especially through its lay organizations (Action Catholique).
In contrast, the Greek Orthodox Church, the largest Christian minority in the
Middle East, is rent by rivalries within the hierarchy. It even knew local and
regional splits with a double hierarchy. The connections with the Hellenic
Church are weak and are affected by those with the Russian Church.

Nowadays a new *modus vivendi* seems indispensable. Despite the sad
experience of the past and the present-day hardships due to discrimination
in government service, educational policy, etc., Christians are called upon to
discard the "minority psychosis," the perpetual search for protection, and to
assert themselves in the life of the country. Not that they have to give up
their ties with the West or their function as link between East and West.

Being culturally more advanced, they have a mission to fulfill within the majority, especially within the weaker layers in it. After World War I, they seemed sheltered under the mandate and therefore withdrew into themselves. They have to revive their interest, once keen and creative, in the social renascence of the majority.[75]

It is a grave decision to make. The prerogatives of the Greek and Armenian Patriarchs are traced to 1453. Eastern Christian communities were recognized as millets in the first half of the last century. Their institutions became, to a varying degree, focal points of loyalty to the members, and with the deterioration of the state, the political standing of their leaders became stronger and stronger. The Patriarch is still the representative and shield of the community. Oddly, European nationalism, itself born of speech-bound entities, made these mostly creed-bound groups equate millet with Nation.[76] It is open to question whether the current authoritarian trends within the majority can encourage a development toward integration.

OTHER CHRISTIAN MINORITIES

Maronites

There are about 18,000 of them in Syria, roughly a half in the Latakiya province, some of them in villages close to the borders of Lebanon, and about a quarter in Aleppo. In Iraq there are only a few.

Protestants

Some of them have come from the Orthodox communities in Syria. They have a good social position on account of their education and cultural advantages derived from links with missionary institutions. They number about 13,000 in Syria, and about 3,500 in Iraq.

Latins

These are the western branch of the Roman Catholic Church in the Middle East. Most of them, or the ancestors of most of them, came from Europe. They are about 7,000 in Syria. They, too, enjoy a good social and economic position. In Iraq they may number 1,300.

In regard to the proportion of the Muslim Arabs to the total population, Syria does not differ much from Iraq; it is estimated at 66 to 70 percent. The Muslim Arabs of Syria, however, with the exception of the 15,000 Shī'is, most of whom live in the province of Aleppo, are Sunnis. Of the Arabs in Iraq, on the other hand, a large majority are Shī'is. In the 1930's the Shī'is in Iraq still felt discrimination in the government service. The royal house was Sunni, and around it had been gathered Sunnis from the entourage of Faysal. Since the power of the state was mainly in the hands of this tiny group, members of their families had the first claim to high positions in the state. In spite of this, the share of the Shī'is in the administration has been growing.

Evidently the problem of the minorities is also different in the two countries. In Iraq it is mainly centered in the North, where an autonomous basis is being claimed by a national community, while in Syria it has other aspects. Most of the provinces of Syria are a kind of ethnic and religious mosaic. Only Jabal al-Durūz and Hawrān are near-homogeneous.

Throughout the period of the mandate, the French and the British policies vied with regard to the minorities. Previously the Christian communities had been accustomed to view foreign protection as a kind of favor. Now they enjoyed protection of a Western power as a right, and all the minorities, including the non-Christian, gained self-confidence. But when the era of promises was over and the workday period of the mandate arrived, dimmed as it was through the 1920 and 1925 insurrections, Great Britain adopted a well-designed policy not to encourage autonomous leanings of the minorities. Through Great Britain's influence, the Sunni kingdom in Iraq was established, and the Shī'i South was attached to it. The interests of the British Empire were declared to lie in the stability of Iraq, and this was regarded as being bound up with the unification of the country. No due regard was paid to the consideration that factors making for national self-assertion cannot be forcibly and permanently subdued, and that the stability of the state depended on its social and economic soundness.

The French policy was at first one of federation and of preserving the identity of the minorities. But the autonomist impetus shrank more and more, no doubt also on account of pressure by the majority. All the same, during the whole period of the mandate the administrative autonomy of Jabal al-Durūz and Jabal Ansāriyya continued. French policy also resulted in the opening of the mandated territories to waves of refugees, Christians and Muslims, from Turkey and from Iraq. Of course, this may partly be ascribed to motives of expediency, to the necessity of mitigating the pressure of the majority. But at the same time the mother country behaved in the same way to refugees from all parts of the world. Another point, too, is that political motives do not lessen the value of humanitarian action. On its administrative side the French policy was harsher than the British, especially in times of crisis. The British and the French left a lasting imprint in the civil administration; the former in the judicial system, too. The French left behind a valuable legacy in the shape of the brilliant research of such observers as Weulersse, Lescot, Savaget, Charles, Thoumin, Rondot, and others in the field of "géographie humaine."

The march of events frustrated both policies. For whatever reasons, the British view had to acquiesce in the authoritarian approach of the ruling circles, and in the deficiencies of a regime which could not assure elementary rights even to the majority. The French system was not calculated to give a proper social and cultural basis to the cohesion of the communities and so to enable them to hold their ground against the majority. Thus the opportunity of securing autonomy for the communities was missed.

With the cessation of the mandate these communities entered into a new phase. Arab nationalism in these countries had been centralist and legalistic, and practically identified with a social system based on large landownership. The first and foremost object of the governing class was to increase its social and political power. Just as it was not capable of a constructive approach in the social field, so it was incapable of dealing constructively with minorities. This kind of nationalism possesses no such social and economic dynamism as would enable it to absorb the minority politically and culturally.

The Arab state does not see itself under any obligation to change its attitude. Present-day circumstances seem to leave no room for international discussion of the problem. Still, if one is not prepared to accept disappearance or decay tamely, it is imperative to examine some possibilities. There is no question that the existing social order is also anchored in the structure of the communities. Let us assume that an enlightened regime should enable the communities to do away with the domination of leading families, whose leanings toward isolation or assimilation are also determined by considerations of personal advantage. The sources for political exploitation of confessional particularism would be cut off. The remnants of tribal structure, which help preserve the separateness of the community, would pass away. Further, some of the asocial elements in the secretive religions for which there is no more room, would cease to exert any influence. What shape would the aspirations of the communities then take?

No doubt, the identity of the communities would be sapped by modes of life that cut across old loyalties. Hence there are possibilities in both directions—either for absorption or for a kind of regeneration. Formerly the desire of self-preservation drew strength from the very oppression by the majority and from distrust of its intentions. In the new conditions it would not have to feed mainly on assessment of the merits or demerits of the majority.

In any case it is out of the question that an enlightened policy would seek to uproot the language of any people or to hamper its progress. It is humanly possible that the lot of a minority should be determined not by the interests, genuine or fancied, of a ruling oligarchy, but by social and cultural needs of human groups. A community which has been formed by historical causes should be treated with respect for its traditions and its identity. Various fruitful plans to deal with the needs of minorities have been tried by Switzerland, by Sweden, and by Canada.

NOTES

1. Even the reports of the mandatory government in Syria did not mention Kurds, Turkomans, and Circassians. Presumably they were included among the Sunnis, that is, Arabs.

   A. Hourani (*Minorities in the Arab World*, 1947, pp. 1–2) classifies them according to religion and spoken language. J. Weulersse ("La Question de minorités en Syrie," *Politique Étrangère*, Feb. 1936, pp. 28–39) puts a few of them into a category of *minorités mourantes* (linguistic: Circassians; religious: Ismā'īlis).

   Attachment to a language does not always imply identity of ethnic origin. Some Turkoman tribes in Iraq, particularly in the Diyāla province (Qara Ulus, Bajlan) are Kurdish-speaking; al-Kird in the Diwāniyya province speak Arabic. See al-'Azzāwī, *'Ashā'ir 'Irāq* (Baghdad, 1947), II, 182, 183–84, 187–88.

2. B. Lewis, *The Origins of Ismā'īlism* (Cambridge, 1940), pp. 91–92.

3. See Steven Runciman, *The Medieval Manichee* (Cambridge, 1947), pp. 5–25.

4. On the composition of the population in the southeast area of Asia Minor, see Arnold J. Toynbee, "A Summary of Armenian History Up To and Including the Year 1915," in *The Treatment of Armenians in the Ottoman Empire, 1915–16 (Documents presented to Viscount Grey . . .)* by Viscount Bryce (London, 1916), pp. 611–16.

5. Of the two main dialects, *sorenî*, spoken in Sulaymāni region, is close to the major dialect of Iranian Kurdistan; *kurmancî* is spoken in Mosul region, in Turkish Kurdistan and by Syrian and Soviet Kurds. Most of the publications in Iraqi Kurdistan have been written in *soreni*. At present the question of fusing the two dialects is being discussed. See Nêveran, "Notes sur la presse kurde d'Irak," *Orient*, No. 10, 1959, pp. 139–48. Cf. C. J. Edmonds, *Kurds, Turks and Arabs* (London, 1957), pp. 10–11; Kamuran Ali Bedr Khan, "The Kurdish Problem," *JRCAS*, XXXVI (1949), 240; C. J. Edmonds, "A Bibliography of Southern Kurdish, 1920–36," *JRCAS*, XXIV (1937), 487–89; *ibid.*, "A Bibliography of Southern Kurdish, 1937–1944," *JRCAS*, XXXII (1945), 187.

6. For a survey of Kurdish literature, especially in 1920–1955, see Thomas Bois, "Coup d'œil sur la littérature kurde," *al-Mashriq*, XLIX (1955), 201–39. On recent literary activity and folklore in Iraq, Syria, and U.S.S.R., see Thomas Bois, "Les Kurdes," *ibid.*, LIII (1959), 128–41, 266–99.

7. B. Nikitine, *Les Kurdes* (Paris, 1956), pp. 210–19; Edmonds, *Kurds, Turks and Arabs*, p. 63.

8. Edmonds, *op. cit.*, pp. 141–42; al-'Azzāwī, *op. cit.*, II, 28–29, 101, 134, 197–98, 207.

9. Nikitine, *op. cit.*, pp. 191–97; also Edmonds, *op. cit.*, p. 143.

10. Cf. H. M. Burton, "The Kurds," *JRCAS*, XXXI (1944), 70–72; W. G. Elphingston, "Kurds and the Kurdish Question," *ibid.*, XXXV (1948), 48–49; Malcolm Burr, "A Note on the Kurds," *ibid.*, XXXIII (1946), 289–92.

11. W. L. Westermann, "Kurdish Independence and Russian Expansion," *Foreign Affairs*, XXIV (1946), 681–82; *New Statesman and Nation*, Jan. 26, 1946; Philips Price, "Soviet Azerbaijan," *JRCAS*, XXXIII (1946), 194.

12. Archie Roosevelt Jr., "The Kurdish Republic of Mahabad," *MEJ*, I (1947), 247–69.

13. P. Rondot, "L'Expérience de Mahabad et le problème social Kurde," *En Terre d'Islam*, May–June 1948, pp. 179, 182–83; P. R., "Où va la question kurde?" *L'Afrique et L'Asie*, 1949, 2 trim., pp. 51–55; P. Price, "The Present Situation in Persia," *JRCAS*, XXXVIII (1951), p. 109.

14. Price, *op. cit.*, pp. 193–94; Kurdoyev, "The Kurdish Literature Across the Border" (in Russian), *Učënye Zapiski*, No. 128, (University of Leningrad, 1952), pp. 136–39.

15. According to the census of 1947, 17 percent of 4,799,500. Kurdish circles contend that nomadic tribes are not included in these numbers.
    According to Shākir Khozbak, *Al-Kurd wa-'l-mas'ala al-kurdiyya*, 1959, p. 41, they make up in the liwās Sulaymāni, Arbil, Kirkuk, and Mosul, respectively, 100, 91, 52.5, and 35 percent of the population.

16. See F. Barth, *Principles of Social Organization in Southern Kurdistan*, Universitetets Etnografiske Museum Bulletin, No. 7, Oslo, 1953; E. R. Leach, *Social and Economic Organization of the Rowanduz Kurds*, London, 1940.

17. See Gertrude Bell, *Revue of the Civil Administration of Mesopotamia* (London, 1920), pp. 57–74.

18. ". . . it is no exaggeration to say that but for the British air cooperation Kurdistan today would not be administered by an Arab government in Baghdad." See Ernst Main, *Iraq from Mandate to Independence* (London, 1935), pp. 117, 136–38.
    "The British desire to control the sources of oil in the Vilayet of Mosul resulted not only in the incorporation, thanks entirely to British diplomacy, of that province into the Arab State, but also in effective Anglo-Iraqi cooperation towards the solution of the Kurdish problem." G. Antonius, *The Arab Awakening* (New York, 1946), p. 367. See also W. L. E., "Iraqi Kurdistan," *The World Today*, XII (1956), 419.

19. *Special Report . . . on the progress of Iraq during the period 1920–31* (London, 1931), pp. 252–64; *Survey of International Affairs: 1925*, I, 471–528; *1934*, pp. 122–34.

20. Dr. 'Abd al-Karīm, *al-Siyāsa*, July 12, 1946.

21. Majid Mustafa in the Chamber of Deputies, *al-Zamān*, Jan. 23, 25, 28, 29, 1946; Sawt al-Ahālī, Jan. 30, 1946.

22. See *Mémorandum sur la situation des kurds et leurs revendications*, presented to Mr. Trygve Lie, Paris, 1948, pp. 28–30; see also Rambout, *Les Kurds et le droit* (Paris, 1947), pp. 71, 77.

23. Majid Mustafa in the Chamber of Deputies, *Sawt al-Ahālī*, Jan. 2, 1945; Amin Zaki in the Senate, *ibid.*, April 22, 1946.

24. Majid Mustafa, *op. cit.*, April 22, 1946; see also his statement in *al-Balad* (Damascus), March 21, 1946.

25. See *al-Zamān*, Jan. 11, 1946; *al-Bilād*, Jan. 13, 1946; *al-Sā'a*, Jan. 10, 11, 1946. See also *Sawt al-Ahālī*, April 12, 22, 1945.

26. *Siria, Palestina pod tureckim pravitel'stvom* (Odessa, 1875), II, 128–29.

27. Oppenheim, *Die Beduinen* (Leipzig, 1939), I, 25–26, 54, 233–34.

28. Rondot, "Les Kurds de Syrie," *La France Méditerranéenne*, 1939, pp. 81–126; Oppenheim, pp. 233–34.

29. For the historical background of the problem, see Nikitine, "Problème Kurde," *Politique Étrangère*, XI (1946), 250–60.

Other sources: Arshak Safrastian, *Kurds and Kurdistan* (London, 1948); Edmonds, "The Kurds of Iraq," *MEJ*, XI (1957), 52–62; *ibid.*, "The Place of the Kurds in the Middle Eastern Scene," *JRCAS*, XLV (1958), 141–53; *Bulletin du Centre d'Études Kurdes*, Paris, 1948–50, Nos. 1–13; W. L. E., "Iraqi Kurdistan," *op. cit.*; Elphingston, "The Kurdish Question," *International Affairs*, XXII (1946), 91–103.

30. Homer Bigart, *New York Times*, May 26, 1957.

31. See "Chronique de sociologie kurde," *L'Afrique et L'Asie*, No. 40, 1957; Nos. 43, 44, 1958.

32. J. Weulersse, *Les Pays des Alaouites* (Tours, 1940), pp. 47, 64, 66, 126; R. Strothman, "Festkalender der Nusairier," *Der Islam*, XXVII (1946), 1–14; *ibid.*, "Die Nusairi im heutigen Syrien," *Nachrichten der Akademie der Wissenschaften in Göttingen* I, 1950, No. 4; E. J. Jurji, "The 'Alids of North Syria," *The Moslem World*, XXIX (1939), 329–41; É. de Vaumas, "Le Djebel Ansarieh," *Revue de Géographie Alpine*, XLVIII (1960), 266–311.

33. J. Wortabet, *Research into the Religions of Syria* (London, 1860), p. 289.

34. See Bouron, *Les Druzes* (Paris, 1930) pp. 411–13; F. Désidéri, "Au Djebel Druze," *L'Asie Française*, April 1932, pp. 133–35; Kurd 'Alī, al-Rifā'ī, *Jaghrafiyyat al-bilād al-'arabiyya* (Damascus, 1950), p. 121; Haim Blanc, "Druze Particularism," *Middle Eastern Affairs*, III (1952), 320.

For their origin, see N. M. Izzedin, *The Racial Origins of the Druzes* (The University of Chicago Press, 1944).

35. The government newspapers did not conceal their affection for the adversaries of Atrash (*al-Qabs*, July 7, 1947). The opposition papers, however, accused the government of stirring up trouble (*al-Ahrār*, June 27, 1947; *al-Nidāl*, Nov. 12, 1947). According to *Alif Bā'* (Sept. 25, 1947) and *al-Ittihād al-Lubnānī* (Sept. 19, 1947), the great majority of the Jabal favored Sultān Atrash, but the government was seeking to overthrow his rule, so as to undermine the autonomy of the Jabal.

36. *al-Balad*, July 2, 1947; *al-Inshā'*, August 17, 1947. In respect to landed property, the accusation of feudalism leveled at one side does not correspond to facts, since both sides contained wealthy proprietors, followed by small owners.

37. *al-Hadaf*, April 23, 1946.

38. *al-Baradā*, April 27, 1946.

39. *al-Nasr*, Dec. 9, 1946.

40. Cf. the conflicting views of Menzel in EI and of F. Maier, "Der Name der Yazīdi's" in *Westöstliche Abhandlungen* (Wiesbaden, 1954), pp. 244–57. Maier holds to the probability of the derivation from Yazīd and of devil worship.

41. See the list of their villages in al-'Azzāwī, *Ta'rīkh al-yazīdiyya* (Baghdad, 1935), pp. 99–109.

42. Other sources: Lescot, *Enquête sur les Yezidis de Syrie et du Djebel Sindjar* (Beyrouth, 1938); Empson, *The Cult of the Peacock Angel* (London, 1928); Nikitine, *op. cit.*, pp. 226–29. A few different data are given in Sebri, Osman & Wikander, Stig: "Un témoignage sur les Yézidis du Djebel Sind-

jar," *Orientalia Suecana*, II (Uppsala, 1953), 112–18; *Report on the Administration of Iraq . . . for the Period January to October 1932* (London),
pp. 5–6.

For somewhat different views see the exhaustive study by Thomas Bois,
al-Mashriq, LV (1961), 109–20, 190–244. To him, "it is not easy to deny the
Islamic origin of Yazīdism, although nothing of the Islamic religion is preserved in it" (p. 244).

43. *al-Kakā'iyya fi'l-ta'rīkh* (Baghdad, 1949), pp. 30, 35, 95–98.
44. According to Edmonds, *Kurds, Turks, Arabs*, pp. 182, 190, 194–96, Kakai
are known in western Persia as 'Ali-Ilāhi (*ahl i-haqq*, people of truth),
although their latter name may denote other sects. In Iraq they "remain
on the Sunni rather than on the Shi'a side of the border." They feel themselves Kurds.
45. Ahmad Hāmid al-Sarrāf, *al-Shabak, min firaq al-ghulāt fi 'l-'Irāq* (Baghdad,
1954), pp. 2, 92, 99, 121.

Sarli, a sect to be found in some villages, claim to belong to Kakai. See
Minorsky, EI, Shabak.

Bajorān, who live in several villages, reverence the prophet Ishmael.

Minorsky stresses the attachment of these sects to Shī'i imāms and the
syncretic tendencies of their faiths.
46. For the position of the Armenian Church in the Middle East and the hold
of the pro-Soviet faction of the community on it, see S. Atamian, *The
Armenian Community* (New York, 1955), pp. 440–70.
47. Louise Nalbandian, "Armenians in the Middle East," *The Armenian Review*,
VIII (1955), 76–79; Vahe A. Sarafian "Armenian Population Statistics . . . ,"
ibid., XI (1958), 83.
48. Caucasian peoples of different origin are generally called Circassians
(Chachans, Daghestanis, etc.).
49. Oppenheim, *Vom Mittelmeer zum Persischen Golf* (Berlin, 1900), II, 69, 70.
50. Weulersse, *op. cit.*, pp. 47, 64, 66, 126.
51. *Ibid.*, p. 221, n. 1.
52. Oppenheim, *Die Beduinen*, I, 52.
53. Here they take an active part in political life. They are represented in
the government and in the parliament and are a reliable element in the army.
54. The above is based mainly on a paper by Mlle. Proux, "Les Tcherkesses,"
La France Méditerranéenne et Africaine, 1938. See also: "La Situation
actuelle des Tcherkesses en Syrie," *L'Asie Française*, Mars 1933, pp. 94–95.
55. Edmonds, *op. cit.*, pp. 267–69, 275.
56. See Enzo Sireni, "Ba'ayat Yehudei Iraq," *Yalqut Hamizrah Hatikhon*, Jan.
1949, pp. 10–17; W. J. Fischel, "The Jews of Kurdistan," *Commentary*,
VIII (1949), 554–59; Dr. Hayim Shushkes, *Hadoar*, March 3, 1961.
57. *Hapoel Hatza'ir*, June 25, 1957.
58. For the Nizāri Ismā'īlis and their predecessors, see M. G. S. Hodgson, *The
Order of the Assassins* (Hague, 1956).
59. Sources: W. Ivanov, *Studies in Early Persian Ismailism* (Leiden, 1948),
pp. 1–31; *ibid.*, *Ismā'īliya*, EI; Weulersse, *op. cit.*, pp. 61–64, 341; N. N.
Lewis: "Malaria, Irrigation and Soil Erosion in Central Syria," *The Geographical Review*, XXXIX (1949), 284–86; "The Isma'ilis of Syria Today,"

JRCAS, XXXIX (1952), 69–77; "The Frontier of Settlement in Syria, 1800–1950," *International Affairs*, XXXI (1955), 57–58.

60. Widengren, *Mesopotamian Elements in Manichaeism*, Uppsala Universitets Årsscrift, 1946: 3, pp. 175–79.

61. Sources: E. S. Drower, *The Mandeans of Iraq and Iran* (Oxford, 1937), pp. xv–xxi, 1–16; Lady Drower, "Marsh People of South 'Iraq," *JRCAS*, XXXIV (1947), pp. 88–89; Oppenheim, *Vom Mittelmeer zum Persischen Golf*, II, 290; Alfred Loisy, *Le Mandéisme et les origines chrétiennes* (Paris, 1934); *Divan Abatur or Progress through the Purgatories* (text with translations by E. S. Drower), *Biblioteca Apostolica Vaticana*, 1950, p. iv.

62. S. Reich, *Études sur les villages araméens du L'Anti-Liban*, (Institut Français de Damas, 1937).

 A. J. Maclean, *Grammar of the Dialects of Vernacular Syriac . . .* (Cambridge, 1895), pp. ix–xv; *ibid.*, *A Dictionary of the Dialects of Vernacular Syriac* (Oxford, 1901), pp. ix–xii.

 According to A. v. Kremer, *Mittelsyrien und Damascus* (Wien, 1853), p. 196, the inhabitants of the village Qaryaten on the way to Tadmor, Christians and Muslims alike, belonged to the tribe Qarāwina—"a collective name given to a certain sector of the rural population, perhaps originating from the ancient Syrian community." Many of the fellahin in Qaryaten spoke Aramaic along with Arabic.

 In the 1870's Aramaic was said to have been spoken in Syria in 30 to 40 villages. See Prym, Socim, *Der Neu-Aramäische Dialect des Tûr 'Abdîn*, (Göttingen, 1881), I, vii.

63. For the vicissitudes of this church, see P. Kawerau, "Die nestorianischen Patriarchate in der neueren Zeit," *Zeitschrift für Kirchengeschichte*, LXVII (1955/6), 119–31; Wigram, *The Assyrians and Their Neighbours* (London, 1929).

64. *Report on 'Iraq Administration, October 1920 to March 1922*, pp. 102–10; *Special Report on the Progress of 'Iraq: 1920–1931*, pp. 267–74; *Report . . . for January to October 1932*, pp. 6–10; S. A. Morrison, "Religious Liberty in Iraq," *The Moslem World*, XXV (1935), 118–22. See also *Survey of International Affairs*, 1934, pp. 134–74; R. S. Stafford, *The Tragedy of the Assyrians* (London, 1935).

65. J. Rowlands, "The Khabur Valley," *JRCAS*, XXXIV (1947), 147, 144–49; H. B. Mar Eshai Shimun, "Assyrians in the Middle East," *JRCAS*, XL (1953), 151–56.

66. For the early patriarchates, see R. Strothmann, "Heutiges Orientchristentum und Schicksal der Assyrer," *Zeitschrift für Kirchengeschichte*, LV (1936), 36–39. For some statistical data I am indebted to Raymond Etteldorf, *The Catholic Church in the Middle East* (New York, 1959). See also G. Khouri-Sarkis, "Les églises de langue syriaque," *L'Orient Syrien*, I (1956), 9–22.

67. Kawerau, *"Die Jakobitische Kirche im Zeitalter der Syrischen Renaissance* (Berlin, 1950), pp. 97–100; R. Strothmann, "Ein orientalischer Patriarch der Gegenwart. Mar Ignatius Aphrem I Barsaum," *Zeitschrift für Kirchengeschichte*, LXIV (1952/3), 292–98.

68. L. Yaure, "A Poem in the Neo-Aramaic Dialect of Urmia," *JNES*, XVI (1957), 73.

69. Sources: F. Rosenthal, *Die aramäistische Forschung seit Nöldeke's Veröffent-lichungen* (Leiden, 1939), pp. 254–69; A. Socin, *Die neuaramäischen Dialecte von Urmia bis Mosul* (Tübingen, 1882), pp. v–viii; Nöldeke, *Grammatik der neusyrischen Sprache am Urmia See und in Kurdistan* (Leipzig, 1868), pp. xxiv–xxvii; Ed. Sachau, *Skizze des Fellihi-Dialects von Mosul* (Berlin, 1895), pp. 3–4; Guidi, *Beiträge zur Kenntniss des neu-aramäischen fellihi-dialectes, ZDMG*, XXXVII (1883), 294–95; L. Yaure, *op. cit.*, pp. 76–79.

70. As far back as the 1830's, the Kurds served as a tool of the Ottoman government in assisting to eliminate the Aramaic-speaking Christians, and in massacres of Armenians in 1875 and 1915, a policy initiated by Abdul Hamid and continued by the Young Turks. The fate of the Kurds during 1914–17 at the hands of the government was not different from that of the Christians. In addition the Armenians retaliated under the cover of the Russians. See E. W. C. Noel, *On Special Duty in Kurdistan, July 1919* (Baghdad: Office of Civil Commissioner of Mesopotamia, 1919), pp. 4–15; Strothmann, "Heutiges Orientchristentum und Schicksal der Assyrer," *op. cit.*, pp. 41–42.

71. Weulersse, *op. cit.*, pp. 67, 70–71, 368–69.

72. In Palestine, with its larger Greek colony, the struggle between the high Greek hierarchy and the lower Arab clergy continued during all the period of the mandate. Prior to the 1948 war, the Orthodox community numbered 40,000, and in Transjordan, 10,000.

73. For the Christians in Central Syria, see R. Thoumin, *Géographie humaine de la Syrie Centrale* (Paris, 1936), pp. 213–14, 261–67, 332–33.

74. Weulersse, "Influences confessionnelles sur la démographie du Proche-Orient," *Cong. int. de la population* (Paris, 1937), VI, 23–26.

75. See N. Edelby, "Notre vocation de Chrétiens d'Orient," *Proche-Orient Chrétien*, III, (1953), pp. 201–17.

76. See Lootfy Levonia, "The Millet system in the Middle East," *The Muslim World*, XLII (1952), 90–96; Sir Harry Luke, *The Old Turkey and the New* (London, 1955), pp. 66–101.

   I am much indebted to the following sources: R. Janin, *Églises orientales et rites orientaux* (Paris, 1955); P. Rondot, *Les Chrétiens d'Orient* (Paris, 1955); P. H. Musset, *Christianisme, spécialement en Orient* (Harissa-Liban, 1949), Vol. III.

*The volume on Iran, from which this selection is taken, was
prepared by three successive interdisciplinary teams at the Washington
office of the Human Relations Area Files. Represented disciplines included
anthropology, economics, geography, history, international relations,
jurisprudence, political science, social psychology, and military science.
Work began in 1955; the volume was completed in 1956 and published
in 1957.*

*The authors indicate as one of their goals the presentation of the
Persian, not as the Westerner thinks he should be, but as the Persian
sees himself, his culture, his world. While it is not clear that this
commendable goal has always operated, the authors have succeeded
in presenting a concise and up-to-date report on the ethnic groups and
languages of one specific Middle Eastern nation—Iran.*

3

Ethnic Groups and Languages of Iran

HERBERT H. VREELAND

ETHNIC GROUPS

In Iran, as elsewhere, language is the most important single element
dividing the peoples of a nation into component ethnic groups. People within
a given nation who speak a common language tend to share their other attitudes
and ways of life to a substantially greater extent than those who do not.
More than half of the people of Iran speak some dialect of Persian. There
are dialects (Mazanderani for example) which are not understood readily
by speakers of the standard Persian of Teheran, but most speakers of such
dialects also understand and can make themselves understood in the standard
Persian. Many other languages are spoken in Iran: four language families

From Herbert H. Vreeland, ed., *Iran* (1957), pp. 37–55; reprinted by permission of
Human Relations Area Files.

are represented and the speakers of each tend to have other important distinctive attitudes and ways of life.

As elsewhere, the cities are the centers of complex governmental organizations, contain many distinct occupational specialists, and are storehouses of wealth and of accumulated knowledge and scholarship.

Access to the advantages of city life depends upon a person's ability to visit a city, or to communicate with people in it by message. It depends upon a person's speaking the language, knowing his way around, knowing what is available, whom to see to get it, and how to approach him; and it depends upon a person's having money or personal influence. A typical Persian village or nomadic tribe is made up largely of people who seldom visit a city and who lack access to many of its advantages. But there is a

Fig. 1. *Ethnic groups of Iran. Major Persian groups are in upper case; non-Persian groups are in lower case; pastoral groups are in italics.*

crucial difference between the peasant village and tribal peoples of Iran and those of some other parts of the world.   All the people of a typical "primitive" village or tribe of Brazil or New Guinea are isolated from the world's cities and from the wealth, power, and knowledge gathered there.   They can deal with people of the outside world only through foreigners whom they neither understand nor trust; such dealings are few and likely to be unsatisfactory to them.   But the landlord of an Iranian village, the khan of an Iranian tribe is likely to be a man at home in Teheran or some other large city, a man who knows his way around there, who has "connections" and influence with important officials.   Often he is a man who has studied in Europe or America and hence can read French, English, or German and can deal directly with people in New York, London, or Paris.

Historically, almost all the ethnic groups in Iran today trace their origin to a pastoral tribe or tribal confederation that invaded Iran at some time in the past.   The tribal type of organization has persisted among herding peoples of the mountain areas to this day.   Tribesmen in Iran usually think of one another as kinfolk and have strong loyalties to their tribal leaders.   Consequently, even when herding tribes settle down as peasant villagers, tribal traditions and attitudes may persist for centuries, especially where the tribesmen speak a language other than Persian.

The tribesmen almost all live in one of the mountain ranges that rim the central bowl of the Persian plateau: along the Zagros chain to the west and southwest, along the Elburz to the north, and along the lesser ranges which divide Iran from Afghanistan.   Most of the Persians proper live inside the bowl of the plateau, most of the settled non-Persians outside.

People in Iran think that they can often tell a person's ethnic group membership from his physical appearance.   Color of skin, shape of nose and lips, general physique are often used as criteria.   There has, however, been much mixing in Iran, as everywhere, so that such physical identifications are often misleading.   Some of the groups wear distinctive clothes, however, especially men's hats, and identification is really based on these as often as on physical type.

The Persians

The Persian-speaking inhabitants of Iran comprise an enormous ethnic group embracing more than two-thirds of the population of about fifteen million people.   Their language is the official language of the kingdom, and since the coming of Reza Shah it has been taught in all the schools.   It is also the language of all significant Iranian literature, and of almost all newspapers and radio broadcasts.   In music, poetry, and art the Persians consider themselves (and are generally considered by other groups) as the leaders of the country.   This is strengthened by a consciousness of an herioc past; but it will be seen that other groups consider that they also are the heirs of ancient Persian glory. The upper class and more highly educated Persians fill the bulk of government posts and are the most subject to Western influences. The majority of Iranians abroad belong to this group.

Among the Persians, the physical ideal is to be found in Persian art. Large black almond eyes, black wavy hair, oval face with pale olive complexion, and a slender build appear to be ideals for both sexes.

Although in urban areas many male Persians now go clean shaven, a mustache is more usual, especially among villagers. Beards are a prestige symbol and are worn chiefly by old men, dervishes, and mullas. The chins of most villagers are likely to be covered with a short stubble. Costume is various. Western dress is standard in urban areas and is increasing, though in very shabby form, in an increasing number of villages. Still to be seen are baggy trousers, fastened at the waist with a sash and caught at the ankles. Round caps are familiar village headgear, while mullas are still distinguished by robe and turban.

Among women the veil was discouraged by Reza Shah; but village women still wear a shawl over the head which they often draw across the face, either in modesty or to inspire the curiosity of the male. Their dresses, in public at least, are long and full.

The vast majority of the Persians belong to the Shi'a branch of Islam, the official religion of Iran, but their way of life is still conditioned to some extent by their pre-Islamic Zoroastrian faith. A few thousand Persians, many of them in the area of Yazd, in the very center of the country, still practice Zoroastrianism.

Outside the northern rim of the central plateau, in the warm wet plains south of the Caspian live other Persians, in the provinces of Mazanderan and Gilan. They speak dialects which people from Teheran cannot understand, but most Mazanderani and Gilani also are able to speak and understand the standard Persian of Teheran. Many of them live by fishing for caviar in the Caspian Sea. Important crops include rice and citrus fruits.

The Persians from the plateau regard these northerners as a distinct variety of Persians, an attitude not unlike the sectional differences found in other countries. In Teheran, people say that the Gilani tend to be sharp-tongued and critical of outsiders; in contrast, they speak of the Mazanderani as meek and downtrodden.

The Tribal Peoples

Around the rim of Persia are found group after group of people who are organized into pastoral tribes. Many of them live near settled folk who speak their language and often have a tradition of having formerly been tribesmen themselves. Such an ethnic group is likely to be dominated by the tribesmen rather than the settled folk even though the latter are more numerous. The tribesmen are better organized for war and hence have more political influence.

A Specimen Pastoral Tribe: The Bakhtiari ◆ All along the Zagros mountain range from Azerbaijan to the Arabian Sea, pastoral tribes move with their herds back and forth every year over the spine of the mountains between summer ranges in the high valleys of the east and winter ranges in the low foothills of the west. A segment of the Zagros about 150 miles long and centered due west of Isfahan is the homeland of the Bakhtiari tribe.

Most Bakhtiari tribesmen speak a Persian dialect: it is not recorded how much difficulty speakers of the Teheran dialect have in understanding or making themselves understood among speakers of the Bakhtiari. Some Bakhtiari tribesmen speak a dialect containing many words of Arab origin not found in other Persian dialects; others speak a Turkish dialect differing little if any from that of the neighboring Qashqa'i tribesmen.

The Bakhtiari were until 1924 an autonomous political unit; they still have a common tradition of unity; and they reveal their feeling of belonging together in legends of a common origin. One legend asserts that all Bakhtiari are descendants in the male line of a Mongol noble named Bakhtyar, who came into Persia in ancient times and founded a lineage that maintained its independence in the mountains until subdued by the founder of the Sassanid dynasty, Ardashir. Bakhtiari who believe this legend consider themselves all distant relatives.

In recent centuries, the Bakhtiari have been a powerful political confederation of about a dozen main bands. The bands are grouped into two main branches of the tribe, the Haft Lang and the Chahar Lang. Typically, each band considers itself descendants in the male line of a single progenitor; according to one legend, Bakhtyar, the founder of the tribe, had two wives, by whom he had seven (*haft*) and four (*chahar*) sons, respectively.

In 1924, the Haft Lang branch was ruled by a single family, each band headed by one of the descendants of Jafar Quli Khan. Jafar had gained control of the Bakhtiari tribe about 1850, establishing his sons and grandsons as leaders of the Haft Lang bands, but permitting a rival leader, Muhammad Taki Khan, to keep control of the Chahar Lang branch, and those bands in 1924 were ruled by his descendants. Thus each of the two main Bakhtiari branches is controlled by a single ruling family, whose political power is buttressed by substantial wealth in herds and arable lands. From about 1850 until 1924, the khan of the Haft Lang branch was also the *il-khan*, the leader of the entire Bakhtiari tribe.

The members of the ruling Bakhtiari families are at home in Teheran as well as in the Zagros. They own landed estates like other wealthy people in the heartland of Iran; the peasants who farm these estates are not fellow

Bakhtiari tribesmen who owe them political loyalty, but only tenants who owe them rents.   Like other wealthy Iranians, the ruling families of the Bakhtiari often send their young men abroad for an education; in 1949, the daughter of a Bakhtiari khan was a student at the University of California. Another daughter of a Bakhtiari khan was the wife of Muhammad Reza Shah, the present ruler of Iran.

The major cohesive force in Bakhtiari social structure is the need of the tribesmen to band together to maintain control of their pasture lands. The power of the Teheran government to enforce its laws and collect taxes among the Zagros tribesmen has rarely been effective.   Pasture rights are normally gained and maintained by the rifles of the tribesmen.   Cattle raids and blood feuds between neighboring tribes are common.   The Bakhtiari then are a confederation of bands of herding people who combine to defend their lands, herds, and persons against outsiders.   They think of themselves as distant relatives and, in fact, the bands of the two main branches are controlled and led by a single family each.

The main support of the Bakhtiari tribesmen is their herds of cattle and sheep; and the wealthier men pride themselves on their fine riding horses.   Many Bakhtiari also raise crops of wheat and barley.   Some sow two crops a year: one crop in the uplands in autumn just before they leave, which they reap when they return; and a second in the lowlands in winter, for which they leave some men behind to harvest when the main body of the tribe leaves in the spring.

The semiannual trek over the Zagros crest is a journey of seventy-five or a hundred miles on difficult mountain trails.   Tents and household goods are packed on mule-back.   Women and children may likewise ride, but many women make the difficult journey on foot carrying their infants in wooden cradles on their backs.   Driving the pack animals often falls to the women also and theirs is the major labor of loading and unloading.   The men do the difficult and dangerous work: they float the animals across raging mountain torrents, cut a path through mountain snow fields, scout for rival tribes, and if need be, fight them for pasturage.   The journey takes five or six weeks each way. Thus, in all, the people spend nearly three months a year on the move.

The Bakhtiari make their own clothes, tents, and carpets.   The women of each household do its weaving and dyeing.   Among the men are expert specialists including blacksmiths, carpenters, and armorers (whose most important job is the repair of rifles).

Within the household, Bakhtiari family life is substantially like that of the Persians proper. . . .

Although the Bakhtiari are nominally Shi'a Muslims, no mullas are recorded among them and it may be that like many other nominally Muslim tribes of Southwest Asia, they have special non-Islamic rites, ceremonies, and supernatural experts.

The Kurds ♦ In all, about three million Kurds live in an area that runs from the Euphrates River in eastern Turkey to the Zagros Mountains in Iran; fewer than one million live within the borders of Iran. A short-lived "Kurdish Republic," supplied with Russian arms, was swiftly eradicated by Iranian troops in 1947 by the hanging of about twenty Kurdish leaders in Kermanshah.

The language of the Kurds is quite closely related to Persian. In religion, they follow the Sunnite branch of Islam, an important difference which sets them off from most of the remaining population of Iran. On the whole, however, linguistic affinity may have been a greater force than religious differences in the relation between the two peoples. The Iranians seem to have had less trouble with the Kurds than have their Sunnite neighbors, the Turks and Iraqi. However, the Kurds have been a difficult element in Iranian history. In the seventeenth century, Shah Abbas found it necessary to move a part of the tribe to Khurasan, partly to defend the area against Turkmen raiders, but partly also to break up a dangerously concentrated force in the west.

The Kurdish communities of today vary from highly nomadic tribal groups to settled town life. The Kurds are organized in a tight system of kinship, binding together large units of several hundred households, which band together to form tribes. Despite the close kinship alliances, there is no consistent hierarchy among kin, and power rivalries often lead to violence. For this reason, the head of a family likes to have on call a group of riflemen, bound by blood or marriage, who will defend his interests in time of need.

The Kurdish tribes are aggressive and warlike. They used to make frequent raids on caravans and settled villages. A tribe would capture a village and reduce the villagers to the status of tenants. The villagers, who are gradually moving toward the way of life of their Persian neighbors, have a rather ambivalent attitude toward the banditry of the tribes. They naturally do not relish being subjected; but if tribal violence does not affect them directly, they are likely to regard the tribesmen much as Robin Hood is supposed to have been regarded by the English yeomen of his day.

The Lurs ♦ South of the Kurds in the Zagros chain, the Lurs still pursue a largely tribal existence. Together with the closely associated Bakhtiari, they are said to number somewhat less than half a million. Their language is a dialect of Persian and they are Shiites by religion. Among the settled Iranians they have the reputation of being great hunters, wild but wary like the animals they hunt. They are a proud people, who tend to look down on Kurds and other tribes.

The Arabs ♦ Several Arab tribes are found in the Zagros and many settled Arab villages and towns are found along the coast of the Persian Gulf, whose people often live by fishing or fruit-growing. Like the Kurds, they are Sunnites. Their ties and interests lie less with the Persian cities of the plateau than with the Arab cities of neighboring Iraq and of Arabia across the Persian Gulf.

There are about two hundred thousand Arabs in Iran, many of whom have become mixed with Persian and other groups. Although the Arabs are a minority in Iran, they know that they represent a dominant group in the Middle East. The Arabs in Iran are segmented into many small groups, and count for little as a political force. If outside powers should attack, it is probable that they would join in resisting; but much would depend on the immediate interest of each particular Arab tribal group. They have no sense of loyalty to the Iranian state or the Iranian past; but at the same time they do not look on themselves as an oppressed minority.

The Qashqa'i ♦ The Qashqa'i are primarily a Turkic-speaking group, though a few Arab and perhaps even some Persian-speaking bands have allied themselves to the group. They are reported to have about thirty-three thousand families in the area of Fars, though their numbers may have been much reduced lately by defection to other groups. Their annual migration from winter to summer pasturage is the longest in Iran, extending almost from Isfahan to the Gulf. They follow the Shi'a branch of Islam. Their costume is distinguished chiefly by a felt cap, with flaps often worn turned up. In recent years they have been very active politically. Their resistance to Reza Shah's efforts to disarm them led to the imprisonment and death of their chief.

The Baluchi ♦ The Baluchi of Iran are part of the larger group which form the major part of the population of Baluchistan in West Pakistan. They speak an Aryan language akin to Persian and are quite conscious of bonds with Iran. However, they are Sunnites by religion (though with several Shiite modifications). They may number as many as a million in Iran, in an area stretching from near the Gulf of Oman to Seistan on the Afghan border. In ways of life they vary from the tribal to the village pattern, from sheep-raising to fishing and fruit-growing.

The Brahui ♦ The Brahui in Iran represent a very small fragment, under one hundred thousand, of a much larger group in Pakistan and Afghanistan. They live in the neighborhood of Seistan and speak a Dravidian language, unrelated to any other language in Iran.

The Turkmen ♦ Historically, Iran has been much troubled by the nomadic, raiding Turkmen, who have crossed and recrossed the Russian border for many centuries, wreaking havoc on the Persian inhabitants of the area. With rather broad heads, Mongoloid eye folds, and straight hair, not always dark, they present a markedly different appearance from other Iranians. In dress their long, fur-lined coats are notable, as in the *khala'at*, a bright-colored, light gown for warmer weather. Their embroidered skull caps and light fur caps have lately been at least partly supplanted by visored caps like an American golf cap, probably from across the Russian border. Westernization of costume is taking place here as elsewhere.

It was partly to combat the marauding Turkmen that Kurds were sent to Khurasan in the seventeenth century, but now the border area has been tightened, and the Turkmen are beginning to adopt a more settled way of life. No accurate figures are available on their numbers; their distribution is through most of northern Khurasan and down into the eastern part of Mazanderan.

Other Turkic Tribes of Mazanderan and Gilan ♦ Several other Turkic-speaking tribes have settled along the Elburz in Mazanderan and Gilan. Among them are the Qajars, who produced the dynasty of shahs which ruled Iran from 1796 to 1926. Tribal organization in these two provinces is less important than in most other mountain regions of Iran and, in recent generations, most of the herding people have settled down as farmers.

Tribes of Azerbaijan ♦ In earlier, tribal days some of the tribes of Azerbaijan gave considerable trouble to the central government. Particularly difficult were the Qizilbash tribes (a Turkic group), whose warlike habits were alternately a boon and a bane to the government of the shahs. Another group, the Shah Savan, were set up as a sort of military tribe in the area to protect the shah's interests.

Other Ethnic Groups

Peoples of the Northwest ♦ The northwest corner of Iran is a potential trouble spot because of its proximity to Turkey and Russia. This largely mountainous area is know as Azerbaijan, and before the nineteenth century it included what is now the Soviet Republic of Azerbaijan in the USSR. The dominant people are called Azeri or Azerbaijani. A small part of the area, near the Turkish border, is inhabited by Assyrians. The Azeri are a Turkic-speaking group, numbering about two million, identical in language and probable origin with the inhabitants of the Soviet Republic of Azerbaijan, immediately across the Russian border. This fact the Russians have tried to exploit; immediately after World War II, a separate republic of Azerbaijan was set up under Russian occupation. It is reported that some Azeri were attracted by large promises, but after the Russians withdrew their forces there was no difficulty in reintegrating the Azeri into the Iranian nation. The term Azerbai'ijan *aziz* (dear) has been like a slogan in Iran, welcoming the Azeri back to the fold.

The Azeri are largely employed in agriculture and cattle raising. They follow the Shi'a branch of Islam, and their village life does not appear to differ markedly from that of the Persians.

Although they jealously preserve their language, Persian has been taught in the schools since the days of Reza Shah; but knowledge of that language still seems to be limited to the educated classes, chiefly in the city of Tabriz.

The Assyrians ♦ The Christian Assyrians live chiefly in the neighborhood of Lake Urmia, numbering about twenty thousand. Their language, of the Semitic group, is distantly related to Arabic; their religion, of the Nestorian branch of Christianity, provides a great cohesive force.

The Assyrians are mountaineers, with a reputation as fierce, aggressive fighters. As Christians, with most of their number across the border in Iraq, they are regarded by the Iranians as rather dangerous outsiders, especially as many Assyrians were used by the British in World War I (though they were later disappointed in their hopes for the foundation of an Assyrian nation). In their main area they have taken to farming; but many are employed in mechanical work in the major cities.

The Armenians ♦ Some Armenians, as we have mentioned, live in northwestern Iran, near the borders of their traditional native land. Others were settled by Shah Abbas across the river from Isfahan where they engaged their skills in the production of brocades and rugs in the royal factories. Still others live in Teheran and other major cities. Their total number is probably about sixty thousand. In costume, being chiefly urban, they have generally adopted Western garb.

The Armenians are Christians of their own sect, whose patriarch is in the Armenian SSR. Iranian Armenians are predominantly Dazhmaks, strong advocates of an independent Armenian state. Their language is of the Indo-European group, but not at all closely related to Persian; and they write in a Greek-derived alphabet of their own.

Armenians in Iran are generally literate and comparatively well-educated. Persians show some resentment against these "outsiders" who do well in business and industry. They resent especially the European and American use of Armenians as interpreters, regarding it as a slur that they should be approached through these "foreign" intermediaries, and suspecting that religious affiliations may have something to do with it. Armenians in Iran usually know several languages and are most active in international trade.

The Jews ◆ The Jews have been in Persia since ancient times. Their mother tongue today is Persian; but most of them jealously preserve their ethnic group integrity (including religion) through inbreeding and segregation. In appearance, there is little to distinguish them from other Iranians. Some have been converted to the Baha'i religion, but very few indeed have accepted Islam. They are occupied largely as merchants and importers and in moneylending. The latter occupation has caused some tension between them and other Iranians. In general, however, there is much less anti-Jewish feeling in Iran than in the Arab countries. Jews in Iran number perhaps seventy-five thousand with the greatest concentration in Teheran, Hamadan (for them a holy city), Isfahan, and Tabriz. Another Jewish shrine is the grave of Daniel near Ahvāz.

LANGUAGES

Persian is the official national language of Iran, spoken by a majority of the population. The Persian speakers naturally regard their language as one of great beauty. They love to listen to the verses of the poets of many centuries ago. The language is a tie with their past and a force which binds the nation together. Even the linguistic minorities, jealously though they guard their own speech, seem to share this reverence for the national language.

For the non-Persian speaking groups, however, the most effective communication is by means of their own particular language.

Every Iranian is flattered when an outsider has gone to the trouble of learning his particular language. According to the report of an Azeri from Tabriz, two American agricultural experts were sent to Azerbaijan to work close with the villagers. On the advice of Persians in Teheran, they were taught Persian only. The Azeri villagers were amused but somewhat resentful to discover that the Americans were apparently unaware that a different language was spoken in Azerbaijan.

Arabic, a number of Turkic dialects, and a few other languages are spoken in Iran, in addition to Persian, which is, of course, the most important language. (See Fig. 2.) Spoken by more than half the people, it is also, as the official language of the country, known in one way or another by most of the other inhabitants. By law, Persian must be taught in all the schools, and is the language of almost all newspapers. Radio broadcasts, however, are made in Kurdish, Azeri, Arabic, French, and English, as well as in Persian.

Distribution of Languages

Persian and Its Related Languages ◆ Persian is a member of the Indo-European family of languages, which includes languages as diverse as English and Albanian. Persian words similar to English such as *berader* (brother) and *pedar* (father) give us some idea of the relationship. Persian belongs to the Indo-Iranian branch of this family.

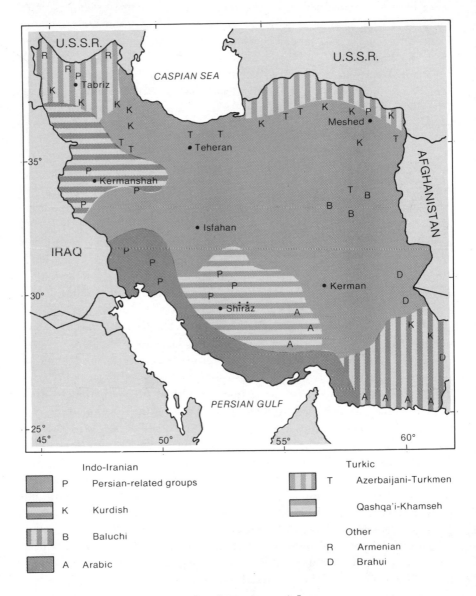

Fig. 2. *Languages of Iran*

Inhabitants of various cities can be identified by minor variations in pronunciation and choice of words. Most Persians believe that the "purest" Persian is spoken in Shīrāz. These regional differences do not seriously affect mutual understanding. North of the Elburz Mountains, however, the speech of the Gilani and Mazanderani is far enough from standard Persian as to be almost incomprehensible to a Persian. To a lesser extent, this is also true of the Lurs and the Bakhtiari tribesmen, whose language has been described by one Persian as comprehensible though "it has the wrong music." The Afghans in Iran generally speak Persian, rather than their native Pushtu, which is related. Two other languages, that of the Kurds on the west and the Baluchi on the east, are related languages of the Indo-European group, close enough to Persian to be more or less comprehensible. As a matter of fact, comprehensibility in the case of these related dialects and languages is rather a one-way proposition. Persian having the greater prestige, officially and culturally, it is the Persian who is to be understood; and even the Kurd acknowledges the Persian language as a richer cousin.

Arabic ◆ The Arabic dialects spoken by some two million people in Khuzistan and along the south coast of Iran are modern variants of the same older Arabic that formed the base of the classical literary language and all the dialects from Morocco to India. Arabic is a Semitic language, related to Hebrew, Syriac, and Ethiopic. There is thus no relationship of linguistic family between Arabic and Persian, but conquest and the legacy of Islamic religion and culture have resulted in an enormous infiltration of Arabic words into Persian. Arabic is still the language of the mosques; and many children, even in the villages, learn to read the Qur'ān, though without understanding it. Arabic words actually incorporated into Persian have been modified to fit the Persian sound pattern. Persians of the south coast often learn Arabic for commercial reasons.

Turkic Dialects ◆ The Turkic languages, unrelated to Arabic or Persian, belong to the Uralic-Altaic family, which includes languages spoken as far west as the European shores of the Bosphorus and east to Mongolia. Turkic dialects are spoken by about four million people in Iran: the Azeri in the northwest; various tribes, including the Qashqa'i and Khamseh, in the south; and the Turkmen in the northeast. These languages are not written to any extent in Iran. In Azerbaijan, however, the language is written as well as spoken, and though the educated classes understand Persian, they prefer to be addressed in their own language. Many Turkic words have been incorporated into Persian, and vice versa.

Other Languages ◆ The Assyrians around Lake Urmia speak Aramaic dialects related to the older Syriac. With their religion, this is a great binding force, which unites them with the Assyrians of Iraq, and makes them a foreign minority in both countries. Armenian is an Indo-European language, but is entirely incomprehensible to a Persian. Almost all Armenians in Iran speak Persian in addition to their native tongue; and many also know at least one Western language. Finally, the Brahui of the eastern border speak a Dravidian language, unrelated to any other language of Iran.

Foreign Languages ◆ Among Western languages, French was for many decades the one most widely learned among the upper classes in Iran. Not only was it the language of diplomacy, but also it appeared on postage stamps and paper currency. French language and culture provides the main link with the West. In the last thirty years, however, English has gradually been replacing French in diplomacy and commerce. Educated Persians today will generally have English rather than French for their first foreign language. German has been important for the military, and for several reasons, including proximity, some Persians have learned Russian. Westernized Iranians in the cities are rapidly learning the English and French terms for many of the Western concepts and objects of material culture that are being introduced.

Persian Usage and Style

Structure of the Language ◆ Persian is a fairly simple language for an American to learn to speak. Verbs are inflected with great regularity, and nouns lack gender and case distinctions. Prepositions are much used, and word order is important. Many words have their primary stress on the last syllable, but other stress patterns also occur. The pitch pattern or intonations are much like those of English, and the "tone of voice" phenomena used in Persia will often express the same emotion.

The Persian language has lacked technological expressions, and in recent years has borrowed much from the West. Under Reza Shah a movement to "purify" the language by eliminating Arabic and Western words resulted in the creation of whole new vocabularies, such as those associated with administration (military and political terms). This movement is not very active now. The language has been the vehicle for a fine body of literature, especially poetry, and has a rich vocabulary for emotional and philosophic expression.

Language and Class ◆ Education and social position make a difference in the use of the language, but there seems to be little sharp differentiation in the overall patterns of speaking. Deference and formality call for flowery speech. Women are supposed to be especially deferent.

Literacy in Iran

The Writing System ◆ Persian is written in the Arabic alphabet, modified by adding some special letters (ordinary letters with extra diacritical marks) for Persian sounds not found in Arabic. The spelling system is traditional and is based on Arabic practices: short vowels are not written, the marks intended for that purpose being omitted except in schoolbooks or the like. Long vowels and diphthongs are represented in a not wholly consistent way. Consonants are distinguished by separate letters for each sound. There are several instances of two or more letters which originally represented different sounds in Arabic being pronounced with the same sound in Persian. As is true for practically all writing systems, stress and intonation are not shown, even punctuation being little used. The Western punctuation marks are of recent introduction in Arabic-alphabet regions.

The Turkic languages used in Iran are also still written in the Arabic alphabet, though in Turkey the Latin alphabet is used and in the USSR the Cyrillic. Arabic, of course, is written in its classical, literary form only. Armenian has its own alphabet. The various Iranian dialects and Brahui are usually not written at all, though Arabic-letter orthographies have been devised for Kurdish.

There is no single accepted standard transliteration of Persian into Latin letters, and Iranians write their names for Western use in any manner that suits their fancy, often following French spelling habits.

Extent of Literacy ◆ Iranians placed a high value on the written as well as the spoken word; but the writing is difficult to learn. Schools are by no means the rule in Iranian villages, and what schooling there has been beyond the recitation of Arabic lines from the Qur'ān is extremely limited. Literacy among Iranians is the exception rather than the rule. Steps are being taken to correct this situation, such as the government decree that every employer must set up classes in his factory to teach his workers to read and write.

In the cities the rate of literacy has already risen considerably, but it is still true that in an Iranian village there are not likely to be more than one or two literate people, generally including the mulla, who serve as scribes and readers for the rest of the population. Among minorities the situation is even worse. It has been said of the Azeri that "they speak in Turkish, write in Persian, and pray in Arabic." In fact, few Iranians are accustomed to read and write their own language or any other, for that matter. Most Iranians learn by the spoken word . . . and the written word so important in Western societies is quite secondary as a means of conveying the general culture. An Iranian orator loses his audience if he reads his speech. But if he gives it "out of his heart" his chances of being regarded as convincing are greatly enhanced.

Gestures

Gesture and facial expression in Iran are used in situations where Americans would reduce them to a minimum. An Iranian regularly makes more use of his hands, his face, his whole body, to supplement his words than does an American. He is likely to consider an Englishman or American discussing similar subjects as unnaturally calm and unemotional. Moreover, many gestures are different from those used by Westerners, and familiar ones may have different meanings. Some understanding of the situation is necessary for satisfactory communication with an Iranian.

Deference ◆ When an Iranian is confronted by someone whom he considers his superior, he stands before him at a distance of five or six feet, with head down and hands folded before him. He keeps his voice low and shows as little expression as possible. In the presence of the shah, an Iranian stands with his arms folded across his chest. A peasant before his landlord can show dissatisfaction only in the subtlest way. If the landlord has given him five tomans for some service calling for more money, the dissatisfied peasant may simply say "Thank you." Some nuance of intonation indicates to the landlord that the peasant is not satisfied. He will ask, "What's the matter? Isn't that enough?" "Oh, yes, thank you. God bless you," the peasant will persist. But a perceptive landlord understands that the peasant had expected more.

Friendship ◆ Friends greet each other by kissing and embracing. Handshaking is virtually unknown among peasants, who look with amusement at this strange "foreign" custom. Among city dwellers, however, handshaking has now become the rule and, following European custom, is much more frequently employed than in America. Sometimes young men friends hold hands, or fingers, while walking. A city dweller is likely to clasp his friend by the shoulder. In conversation Persian friends stand within about two feet of each other.

Righteous Anger ◆ Righteous anger is an emotion highly regarded, the state in which the Iranian is at his peak of excellence in expression. However, it may not be shown before superiors. The angry man flushes, narrows his eyes, laughs sarcastically, and expresses himself in carefully chosen words spoken rapidly and in a high tone. It is a disgrace not to show righteous anger when one's honor is involved. In the Majlis members often express their finest thoughts in a state of righteous anger. One who never shows such anger is considered spineless.

Other Emotions ◆ Happiness, valor, carefree nonchalance, depression, gloom, love, hate, and various other emotions are shown by expression and gestures that would, in general, be comprehensible to a Westerner, but almost invariably, the Persian is more consciously dramatic than the Westerner in such expression.   It is not that he is more emotional; he simply follows, consciously or otherwise, certain traditional patterns of expression.   A Persian can describe in detail, for instance, how a man looks when he's in financial straits: "He will walk with his head down and his hands behind his back; he wants to be sure not to break any pots he can't pay for."

Miscellaneous Gestures ◆ There are a few hand gestures common throughout the Middle East, which differ markedly from Western custom.   To express admiration, a man will raise his cupped hand, fingers joined and pointing toward his mouth.   If he kisses the fingers tips, the admiration expressed is still stronger.   To express disgust, he will snap his thumb from behind his upper teeth, or shake the lapel of his coat.   For farewell, he will hold his hand forward, palm out, as if in benediction.

The population of Israel has been characterized by large-scale immigration growth within a very short period of time. Over one million persons have emigrated to Israel, many of them from surrounding Middle Eastern countries of origin. The purpose of this chapter is to spell out certain of the historical, geographical, and linguistic criteria determining and distinguishing the present-day population of Israel.

4

◇◇

Ethnic Groups of Israel

AILON SHILOH

Since Israel's Declaration of Independence in May 1948, over 1 million individuals from more than sixty different countries have immigrated into the country. During the entire Mandate period of thirty years, fewer than 500,000 Jews entered the land; after Israel was declared a free and independent state, more than 500,000 Jews immigrated within two and a half years. Within three and a half years of its birth the population of Israel doubled, and by the end of 1957 it had tripled.

By May 1958, on the tenth anniversary of the foundation of the state, six out of every ten Israeli Jews were foreign-born—three from the continents of Asia and Africa and three from the continents of Europe and America.

From Gertrude Kallner, ed., *Cancer Mortality and Morbidity in Israel, 1950–1961*, Part II, pp. 10–19; reprinted by permission of the World Health Organization.

One of the most common techniques for distinguishing among elements in the rapidly developing Israeli population is through the use of the term "ethnic group." This term has never been clearly defined and includes a variety of meanings, mainly of a historical, geographic and religious nature.

I

The wide geographic dispersion of the Jews has a long history. The history of the Jews begins with Abraham, who, around 2000 B.C., went up from Ur of the Chaldees, in the southern Iraq of today, and migrated into the land of Canaan, part of which is today's Israel. The Hebrews of Abraham, his son Isaac, and his grandson Jacob settled in Canaan, and it was back to Canaan that Moses, some 400 years later, led the children of Israel.

II

Subsequent centuries were taken up with the slow settlement and development of the land by the Israelites until the Assyrians, in 722 B.C., conquered the ten tribes of northern Israel and exiled them to distant and uncertain corners of the empire. The southern kingdom of Judeah survived for 136 more years, until 586 B.C., when Nebuchadnezzar destroyed the first temple and led the population of Judea into captivity. Five-sixths of the people of Israel had vanished and the people of Judea were in exile. Technically, the Jewish Diaspora had begun.

III

Despite the fact that some of these Jews later returned to Jerusalem and rebuilt the temple, there still remained large Jewish centers in Babylon (near present-day Baghdad) and Persia.

Post-Babylon Jewish independence was determined by Persian domination, which was succeeded by Hellenistic rule starting with the conquest by Alexander the Great in 332 B.C. The revolt of the Jews led by the Maccabees succeeded in obtaining a brief interlude of independence for the Jews before the Romans invaded and added Judea to their growing empire.

As a result of two bitter revolts against Roman hegemony, the second temple was destroyed (A.D. 70), the temple area was plowed over, the name of Jerusalem was stricken from the map, and Jews were banished from Judea (A.D. 135). Exiled once again, the Jews were dispersed from the Mediterranean basin throughout the world.

Two millennia later, an independent Israel was able to welcome home many descendants of these Jews, but by then they reflected striking differences in physical characteristics, language, dress, diet, behavior in illness and in health, and numerous other cultural manifestations. These differences had developed over the centuries in the Diaspora.

During these 2,000 years, persecution and isolation had alternated with relative freedom and intermingling with host peoples. Numerous Jews converted, willingly or by force, to other religions, and the reverse had also occurred. The Jews today do not constitute a distinct physical racial type, and there is no evidence that they ever did. However, there is much evidence to indicate that over the centuries the Jews have taken on certain physical characteristics of their host populations. Precise genetic studies remain necessary to ascertain the full significance of these centuries of conversions, fraternization, and intermarriages.

On the cultural level, the evidence is clearer, particularly that derived from geographic considerations. One large group of exiled Jews moved east from Israel. Iraq and Persia and the smaller countries of present-day Lebanon and Syria (particularly Aleppo) had long supported small communities of Jews; they were now augmented and became (particularly Babylon and Persia) great Jewish religious and intellectual centers. Furthermore, the Jews from these two large centers continued to move north and east as far as India and China.

Kurdistan, comprising parts of northern Iraq, eastern Turkey, and Western Persia, has been the home of a distinct Jewish population since perhaps the destruction of the second temple. These Kurdish Jews speak Aramaic, an early Semitic language common during the period of Jesus; they settled in numerous isolated mountain villages, and in and around Mosul in northern Iraq.

Georgia, north of Persia and Kurdistan along the southern border of Russia by the Black Sea, was the home of a small and distinct Georgian-speaking Jewish community; in Turkistan, north of Persia along the Caspian Sea, there was a small community of mountain Jews who spoke Tat (a Persian dialect spiced with Turkish and Hebrew words and written with Hebrew characters) and followed the religious and cultural lead of the Jews from Iraq; and in Bokhara, just north of central Persia, a small isolated Jewish community, which had acquired the striking physical and cultural characteristics of its neighbors, learned by accident, in 1802, that there were other Jews in the world. Despite their long separation and isolation, these Jews, Kurds and Bokharians in particular, were among the early settlers of the new Jerusalem.

Afghanistan, east of Persia, has a population of Muslims who claim that they are of Jewish origin, descendants of the tribe of Benjamin, and that Afghana, their legendary founder, was a son of King Saul. Despite this supposed heritage, the *bona fide* practicing Jews of Afghanistan suffered severe persecution, and few managed to flee into neighboring Persia and India.

Although it is possible that Jews lived in Cochin, on the very south-western coast of India, since the Hellenistic period, it seems certain at least that during the early centuries of the first millennium Jews from Babylon and Persia provided the main body of immigrants. These Jews of Cochin were well to do, influential, and an important element in the armies of the local princes.

The arrival of Christian Europeans, particularly the Portuguese, in India early in the sixteenth century, radically altered the life of the Jews there. The Inquisition was imported at the very time when some Spanish Jewish refugees were arriving in India.

Over the previous centuries the indigenous Jews of Cochin had lost much of their knowledge of the Jewish religion and had acquired a skin color similar to that of the other inhabitants of India, mainly through conversion and intermarriage. Despite problems, the Jewish refugees from Spain kept themselves aloof from these indigenous Jews because of their own greater knowledge of the Jewish religion and of the differences in skin color. Further-more, in caste-structured India, the indigenous Jews began to be called the "black" Jews of Cochin.

The Bnei Israel ("Sons of Israel") are also indigenous Jews of India but resident in and around the province of Bombay, in west central India. Like their Cochin brothers, the Bnei Israel had lost much of their knowledge of Judaism and had acquired the skin color of their Indian neighbors, again probably through conversion and intermarriage.

The occupation of India by the British brought in a fourth group of Jews, particularly from Baghdad, many of whom entered the educated and in-fluential strata of India.

China had colonies of Jews in the European sectors of such ports as Shanghai, Hong Kong, and Tientsin by 1900; these communities and in particular that of Harbin, the city nearest Russia, were later greatly augmented by refugees coming from Russia after World War I and from Germany during the 1930s.

The colony of indigenous Jews in China, however, dates back to the first centuries of the Roman Empire, and was apparently founded in connection with the silk trade. The Muslim conquests in the seventh century put a temporary end to the normal caravan trade and disrupted communications between these Chinese Jews and their western brothers.

Christian missionaries in the sixteenth century were the first to report the existence of Jews in the interior of China, particularly in Kai-feng fu in Honan province. By 1850, when the interior could be visited more frequently, it was found that these indigenous Jews had almost disappeared: they had no religious leaders; the sole recognizable synagogue was in ruins, and the remaining books and scrolls were virtually meaningless and available for sale.

When this author was in China in 1945 and 1946, he was unable to find any evidence of the continued existence or whereabouts of these indigenous Chinese Jews—despite a century of intermittent offers of help by Western Jews and Christian missionaries.

Another large part of the Jewish exodus took a southerly direction. There are reports that before the second temple, Jewish trading settlements already existed all the way from Judea, down the Arabian Peninsula through Mecca, and on to the very southwestern tip of the Red Sea into Yemen; but Muhammed and his followers expelled all Jews who refused to convert to Islam, and only in Yemen were they permitted to remain as protected people.

The Jews of Yemen, unlike their Indian and Chinese coreligionists, never lost contact with their fellow Jews; nor did they ever lose their knowledge of Hebrew or of the Jewish religion. Despite centuries of forced conversion and persecution, these Yemenite Jews retained strong community; early in the twentieth century considerable numbers of them emigrated from Yemen to the Holy Land via British-ruled Aden, where a number of them remained.

The Hadhramaut, close to Yemen, had a small Jewish population, similar in many respects to that in Yemen and living in tall, fortresslike apartment buildings. With the establishment of the State of Israel, many of these Jews also immigrated.

The most important westward movement of the Jews was into Egypt and along the coast of North Africa. Although Abraham and his descendants knew Egypt well, it was during the Hellenistic period that such towns as Alexandria hosted large and thriving Jewish communities with an active intellectual and religious life.

During the war against the Romans, the Jews of Egypt and of neighboring Cyprus and Cyrene (in present-day Libya) were massacred; the survivors were further decimated by Christian persecutions. Under Muslim Arab rule, the Jews of Egypt enjoyed occasional periods of freedom, which allowed the intellectual development represented by, for example, Maimonides.

Under the Ottoman Turks, the position of the Jews in Egypt improved considerably, and their numbers were increased by refugees from Spain and Portugal. When England gained control of Egypt in the nineteenth century, a considerable immigration of European Jews strengthened the Jewish communities of Alexandria and Cairo.

South of Egypt below the Sudan lies Ethiopia (then Abyssinia), the home of the Falasha Jews. The Falasha Jews may possibly be traced back to approximately 600 B.C., for contemporary records indicate that the Babylonians who had just conquered Egypt, hired Jewish soldiers to defend the southern border of their new vassal state against invasion by the Ethiopians. In later centuries some of these Jews and perhaps others from Egypt and Yemen settled in Ethiopia and converted many members of the local population to their faith.   During the destructive wars of the sixteenth century, the Jews lost many of their own adherents to the Christianity and Islam of their neighbors and became—and remain—a small and isolated segment within the total Ethiopian population.   Like other long-isolated Jewish communities, the Falasha Jews closely resemble their Ethiopian neighbors in physical makeup and way of life, and when discovered were found to have lost or never to have acquired much of later rabbinical lore.

Although individual Israelites may have lived along the coast of North Africa from the time of King Solomon on, in the numerous Phoenician trading centers, large-scale and widespread Jewish settlement dates from the exile, that is, from the time following the destruction of the first temple.   North African Jews first settled in the coastal urban centers of Cyrene and, later, spread gradually into Tunisia, Algeria, and Morocco (then Mauretania).

Many of the local inhabitants, particularly the indigenous Berbers, converted to Judaism, and the Jews lived in relative peace and security until the arrival of the Muslim Arab armies in the seventh century.   Many Jews and most Berbers were forced to convert to Islam; others fled into the Atlas Mountains and the Sahara Desert.

During the long centuries of Muslim rule, the Jews of North Africa, particularly from the middle of the eleventh century on, suffered intense religious persecution and economic oppression, and were forced to live in ghettos (the *mellah* or *hara*) and to wear derogatory identifying clothing.

The occupation of North Africa by the French beginning in the nineteenth century, first in Algeria, then in Tunisia, and finally in Morocco, led to the emancipation of the North African Jews and their gradual "Frenchification."   This process was most pronounced in Algeria, where the Jews after a century of freedom, considered themselves equal to continental Frenchmen, and least pronounced in Morocco where, during this author's investigation in 1954, the majority of the Jews still lived inside ghettos and led lives of political insecurity and grinding poverty.

In addition to these North African Jews, primarily coastal and urban, there were the Jews of the Atlas Mountains, who closely resembled their Berber neighbors in physical makeup and way of life; the Jews of Djerba— a small island off the coast of Tunisia; the isolated and poverty-stricken Jews along the northern Sahara caravan routes; and their neighbors, both historically and culturally, the cave-dwelling Jews in western Libya (southern Tripolitania).

The fourth great migration of the Jews was to the north.   Although there was some Jewish emigration into Asia Minor (present-day Turkey) and southern European port towns in the Hellenistic period, the great movement of the Jews into Europe began during the first century A.D.   Exiled from Judea by the Romans, the Jews were often moved into the Roman Empire of western Europe—Italy, France and western Germany (Gaul), and Spain.

During the first millennium, under relatively peaceful Roman and Christian rule, the Jews spread throughout continental western Europe and England, intermingling and intermarrying.

Spanish Jewry, after a century of physical and religious slavery under the last of the Visigoths, was freed by the Moorish conquerors of Spain and developed a brilliant culture, particularly reflected in religious thought, poetry, and philosophy.

The onset of the Crusades in 1096 marked the end of a millennium of relatively peaceful Jewish-Christian coexistence. The second millennium, ushered in by the Crusaders, was characterized by fierce Christian persecution and exile from the western and central countries of Europe south into North Africa and east into Poland and Russia. As a result of the centuries of sexual relations and intermarriage, it was no longer easy to distinguish a Jew from a Christian, and therefore identifiable derogatory dress was made obligatory for the Jews, and they were forced to live in special Jewish quarters—the ghettos.

In Spain, as the Christians gradually conquered the country, the Jews were given the choice of conversion or exile. Of those Jews who accepted conversion to Christianity there were many Marranos—continuing but secret adherents of Judaism. On August 2, 1492, the day on which Columbus set sail from Cádiz, all Jews were expelled from Spain. Many of them fled to North Africa; some continued on to Italy, Egypt, the Turkish Empire of the Balkans (particularly Salonika), and Asia Minor, replenishing and revitalizing the indigenous, long standing, local Jewish communities in those areas. In later centuries the Marranos fled to France and Holland and west to the New World.

The Jews expelled from England, France, and Germany were gradually being pushed eastward into the kingdoms of Hungary, Poland, Lithuania, and Russia. From the fourteenth century on, the center of European Jewry shifted to these eastern European countries, from the Baltic down to the Adriatic and Black Seas.

The following six centuries saw the gradual development of a Jewish population and culture in eastern Europe, despite accelerating restrictions and pogroms (anti-Jewish riots aimed at property and persons), which culminated in the Nazi sickness of the twentieth century. During these centuries, there was a gradual and growing movement of Jews back to western Europe and into America, South Africa and the Pacific lands. The world-wide dispersion of the Jews had been accomplished.

I V

To recapitulate, present-day Israeli Jews can trace their ancestry back to the Hebrews of 2000 B.C., the Israelites from 1400 B.C., and the Jews from the fifth century B.C. All the present ethnic groups in Israel descend from the widely scattered communities established by the last group, particularly as the result of the Roman invasions in the early centuries A.D.

These Jews strongly reflect the physical makeup and cultural behavior developed in the Diaspora. The Jewish religion has also been affected by these peregrinations. Just as the religion of Hebrews was further developed by the Israelites, so the Jews have further developed the religion of the Israelites, particularly as a result of the destruction of the second temple and exile from the Holy Land.

In the State of Israel, it must be clear, there are many Israelis who are not of the Jewish religion. The population of Israel comprises a number of religious communities—the Jews constitute only 89 per cent of the total Israeli population. Other religious communities in Israel include Muslims, Christians, Baha'is, Druze, and Samaritans. Sometimes called "minorities" and occasionally "ethnic groups" (although this term is applied generally to the Jewish community alone), they are the non-Jewish religious communities of Israel.

The Jewish community of Israel can be broadly divided today among Ashkenazim, Sephardim, and Karaim, all derived from differences in the developing Jewish religion.

The smallest group, the Karaim (also Karaites), dates back to Iraq in the eighth century A.D. Originally, the Karaim were purists who argued that only the Bible was essential to the Jewish religion and that later rabbinical commentaries and laws were human and fallible. The duty of the true Jew, accordingly, was to study the Bible and to be his own authority on its meaning. The Karaim, by adopting this extreme stand, removed themselves from the mainstream of the Jewish religion, which continued to be modified and expanded by rabbinical commentators and interpreters.

The terms "Ashkenazim" and "Sephardim" were used at least as far back as the eleventh century in Europe, where a clear cultural division was already apparent between the Jews resident in France and Germany and those in Spain and Portugal. The terms are derived from the Bible: Spain was called "Sepharad," and the Jewish residents of that country "Sephardim;" the term "Ashkenazim" referred to those Jews resident in France and Germany.

These geographic and cultural differences were later enhanced by language differences as well. Whereas the Sephardim spoke Ladino (a derivation of fifteenth-century Spanish), the Ashkenazim spoke Yiddish (a derivation of medieval German). Both Ladino and Yiddish also contained Hebrew words, and both were also written with Hebrew letters.

The basis of the religious distinction between Sephardim and Ashkenazim dates back to Joseph Karo, who was born in Toledo in 1488 and died in Safed in 1575. Karo, one of the greatest religious scholars of Safed, wrote the *Shulchan Aruch (Prepared Table)* for the religious lay Jew to follow in his everyday life. As Karo was of Sephardic origin, his book drew on the religious customs of the Sephardic Jews. The Polish rabbi Moshe Isserles (1530–1572) then carefully, and in detail, described where the Ashkenazi tradition and religious customs differed from those set forth by Karo.

Technically, today adherents of the religious code of Joseph Karo are Sephardim, and adherents of the amended version by Moshe Isserles are Ashkenazim. In fact, however, this essential religious distinction has been blurred by the pronounced historical, geographical, linguistic, and cultural differences between the two groups.

To complicate this terminology slightly, when the Sephardim were exiled from Spain and migrated to North Africa, Egypt, Turkey, and the Balkans, they came into contact with the rooted local Jewish populations. Despite the fact that all these Jews also followed the *Shulchan Aruch* of Karo and hence were also technically Sephardim, it became common to limit the term "Sephardim" to those Jews who actually trace their heritage back to the Iberian peninsula.

Those Jews who follow the Sephardic *Shulchan Aruch* but who do not trace their heritage back to Spain are called Mizrachim, "oriental" or "eastern" Jews. Oriental Jews generally speak dialects of Arabic or Persian.

To pursue the matter still further, there are oriental Jewish groups that prefer, because of particular historical, geographical, or religious characteristics, to distinguish themselves more precisely by such terms as Chalabim (the Jews from the town of Aleppo in Syria), Bavlim (the descendants of the Jewish inhabitants of ancient Babylon), Urfalim (from a region in southern Turkey), Kurdim (from the region of Kurdistan), and Mughrabim (the "westerners," referring to North Africa), to name only a few.

Furthermore, the western movement of Sephardic Jews, from Spain into France, Holland, and England or from Spain to the New World brought many Sephardim into new or developing Ashkenazi communities, where they have remained to this day separate and distinct religious groups.

In summary, the ethnic groups of Israel are manifold, their characteristics determined by a series of historical, geographic, and religious criteria, all of which may operate in a critical and meaningful manner. Furthermore, inasmuch as the majority of the world's Jews still live outside Israel (there are still more Jews in New York City than in the entire State of Israel), it is clear that recognizing and distinguishing among the various groups continues to be relevant and functional.

PART II

Cultures and Subcultures

Following on the previous papers, which have dealt with the Middle East's distribution of peoples, it is relevant to now target in on specific subcultural groups. The fellah, the Arab peasant, is the mainstay of the Middle East. His subculture still dominates and characterizes the region.

In 1952, while teaching at the American University in Beirut, John Gulick did a field study of a Christian village in Lebanon. The essay reprinted here is topical, thorough, and clearly written. Dr. Gulick visited the village again in 1961–1962 and found that in the intervening ten years the village had changed in several important ways: "These changes included the installation of electrical power and piped water, the considerable growth of Hilwi, and an increased dependence on ready-made bread bought in Jbayl rather than made locally."

5

The Material Base of a Lebanese Village

JOHN GULICK

The Physical Pattern of the Village

As a physical site, al-Munṣif has five parts. . . . The hamlet of Ḥilwi; the three saints' shrines each of which has been, at one time or another, the nucleus of a small house-cluster, and the village proper. The territory which belongs to the village is roughly triangular in shape. The apex of this triangle is at the eastern extremity of the village proper, the sides extend from the apex to the seashore which forms the base. The paths which lead from the village proper to the shore, via Mar Maama and Mar Mukhail, run along ridge crests. The boundaries of the village lie in the *wadis* (dry stream-beds) which are immediately adjacent to these crests, to the south and the

From *Social Structure and Culture Changes in a Lebanese Village* (Viking Fund Publications in Anthropology, No. 21), pp. 29–46; reprinted by permission of Wenner-Gren Foundations for Anthropological Research, Inc.

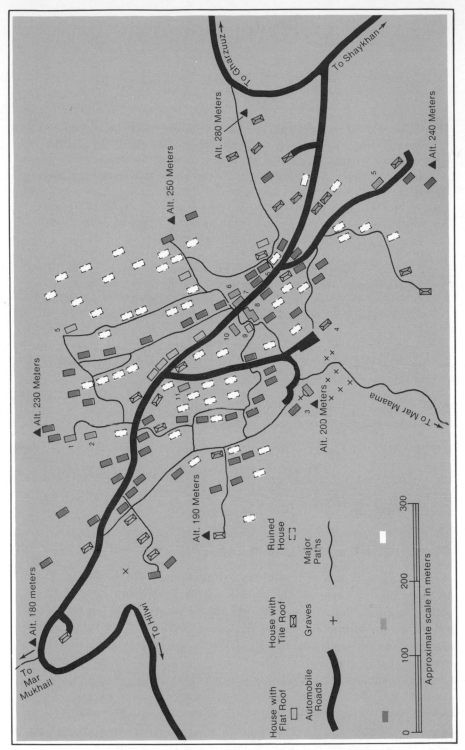

Fig. 1. *Al-Munṣif: institutional structures*

north of them, respectively. All of the real property within the area thus defined belongs to the citizens of the village.

Ḥilwi owes its existence to its location on a main highway, near a small, sheltered cove. . . . Ḥilwi has the most extensive fig orchards in the village, and, in a small building which is used as a store in summer, there is a public telephone. This is the only electrical appliance of any kind, dependent upon a central public power system, in the entire village.

. . . Of the three [shrines], only Mar Mukhail has recently had any significance as a residence site. At present, one family of outsiders lives there in the winter. It will be noted that the site has a special name, Arqbi, besides that of the shrine.

The village proper (see map, Fig. 1) is built, as has been noted before, on the flank of a crest, extending in a northwest-southeast direction for the greater part of one kilometer and steadily decreasing in altitude from 280 meters above sea level in the southeast to 180 meters in the northwest. The highest houses in the southeast are virtually on the top of the crest. As the map and figures indicate, the village is also sharply tilted in a northeast-southwest direction. For the most part, the houses, as well as the terraces, are oriented longitudinally along the contours of the ridge. In the section of the village which lies to the south of the main road there is a very full distribution of functioning terraces, but in most of the northern part, terraces are either entirely absent or (except in the eastern extremity) fallen into ruins. In its essential details, this settlement pattern belongs to a type which is commonplace in Lebanon (Thoumin, 1936, p. 283).

Most of the territory of the village is divided into a large number of sections each of which has its own name. The map (Fig. 2) indicates the sections—*Ḥayy*—in the village proper. Most of these names are evidently very old, and those in the village proper were translated as follows: "fig place," "lowland" (i.e., the *wadi* which abuts it to the north), "infertile" (mostly bare rock), "surrounded" (connotation obscure), "lemon place" (no citrus plants are grown in the village), "little head" (a secondary crest, see Fig. 2, . . .), "graves," "center of town" (*saḥa*), "small green fertile place," "place of small olive press" (no longer so), and "priest's shrine" (obscure). Translations could not be obtained for a few others. Just outside the village proper there are two sections of whose names no one could even guess the meaning. They are probably not of Arabic origin. No particular name is given to some sections of the village proper especially in the central portion. The word *saḥa* has been applied to part of this central portion for at least fifty years but apparently not much earlier than that. This suggests that the present concentration of commercial establishments (see map, Fig. 1) is relatively recent, for in general *saḥa* means the part of a village where the stores are located.

Those portions within the settlement which do not have specific names

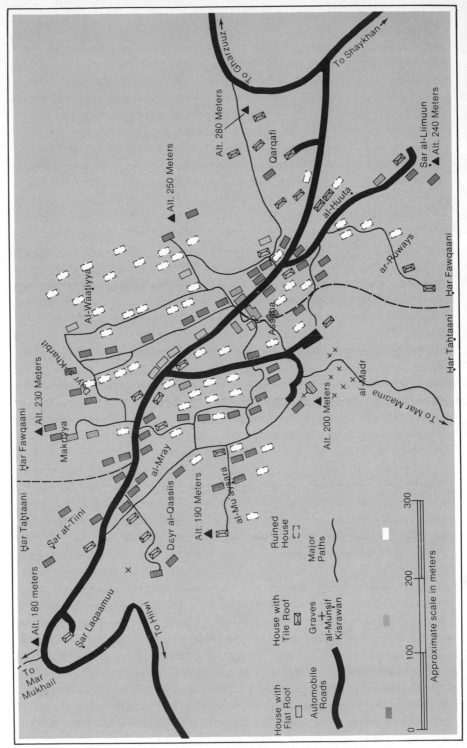

Fig. 2. *Al-Munṣif: named sections*

are generally referred to as *jdaar,* which means the deep fertile soil which is usually devoted to the growing of vegetables. This is a generic term for this particular soil-type. Others in use in the village are *sahl* (plain—land without trees), *saliikh* (land with trees), and *mulk* (orchards). Of these, the last is of particular interest. *Mulk* really means "land held in fee simple." In Munṣif, nearly all the land is held in fee simple, and orchards are the most valuable property. *Sahl* is incorporated into some of the section names, but *saliikh* and *mulk* are not, as far as could be determined.

On either side of the road leading to Ḥilwi (the old path which it superseded was called *tariiq al-maaliha*—"road to the brackish spring"), there are eight named sections. Similarly, along the path which leads to Ḥilwi via Mar Maama (*tariiq al-Ḥilwi*—"road to the fresh-water spring"), there are twelve. In all, then, thirty-four named sections were recorded, and there are unquestionably a good many more. The names, in general, refer to physical characteristics of the land in question or to past owners or associated events; or their meaning is obscure or unknown. As far as could be determined, the named sections have no social significance except that they make it possible to specify exactly different parts of the village. This is very helpful in a situation where the individual's landholdings are usually widely scattered.

The map (Fig. 2) also indicates the division of the village into two halves: *ḥar fawqaani,* "the upper part," and *ḥar taḥtaani,* "the lower part." This division *does,* or at least did, have social significance. It was stated that up to about eighty years ago, the upper part was completely dominated by Maximal Lineage A, the lower part by Maximal Lineage C. . . .

Buildings, Houses, and House-Types

The map (Fig. 1) indicates the location of the institutional buildings in the village proper. Four of the six shops (sing. *dikkaan,* plur. *dakakiin*) are concentrated in the *saḥa.* Actually, building 9 was not open during the period of study, but building 6 is partitioned into halves in each of which there is an independent shop. Building 10 is also partitioned, one half being devoted to a shop whose proprietor is also a butcher. The other half is open when the need arises, being the place of business of one of the two barbers. Building 11, an old house, is occupied by the fifth shop, open only at times, which specializes in cloth. The sixth shop, also not of the "general-store" type, is located in the house of its proprietor, farther down the main road. The two schools are rather widely separated, but this is probably accidental since the location of the private school is determined by the fact that it occupies the lower floor of the master's own house. Similarly the two bakeries, one in the *saḥa,* are immediately adjacent to the houses of their respective owners, one of whom is the private school master. Building 5 is the only one in the village which is entirely devoted to an olive press. There are, however, two other presses in the village proper (one in the lower part of the one remaining occupied house in the al-Waaṭiyya section, the other in the lower part of a house near the meeting point of the Sar at-Tiini and Dayr al-Qassiis sections); there is a third under construction in the eastern end of the *saḥa*, and a fourth at Ḥilwi. Two of these presses are specialized for the reduction of carob pods to a mash from which *dibs*, a kind of jam, is made. There is also a mill, operated by a German-made gasoline engine, which is part of the store in building 8. The upper story, and part of the lower story, of building 8 is occupied by one of the Affiliate Families . . . of the village.

It has been noted that the long axis of most of the houses is parallel to the contours of the ridge, often flush with terrace walls. Not infrequently the paths between the houses are, in fact, the tops of wide terrace walls, and sometimes these are two or three feet higher than the earth which they support.

The great majority of the houses have two levels. In some cases these are directly superimposed. In many others, they are staggered, so that the roof of the lower level forms a very useful terrace which is flush with the floor of the upper level. There are invariably separate entrances to the upper and lower levels. The writer is aware of not a single instance of interior staircases leading from one level to another. Probably the reason for this is that staircases would take up a great deal of room which cannot be afforded. Frequently, the pitch of the ground is such that one can simply walk onto the roof of a house directly or by a very short flight of steps. More frequently, however, one must climb onto roofs, either on a wooden ladder or by an ascending series of stones projecting from the wall of the building.

The flat roofs are used extensively in the sunny part of the year. Apricots, almonds, and grapes are set out on them to dry. Many householders ornament them with potted plants and receive guests on them. In the heat of midsummer, the interiors of the houses tend to be stuffy at night since the gentle breezes do not penetrate inside. Consequently, all who can, sleep on the roof (or terrace) under a brush shelter called *khaymi* ("tent").

Although no two houses are exactly the same, it is legitimate to classify all of them into a number of types, which are indices of successive eras in construction and design.

The first, which still has the greatest number of examples, has two subtypes. By far the most numerous of these has one room on the upper level, few windows, but often more than one door, and a flat earth roof. The lower level (*qabl*) is designed as a stable and storeroom and frequently consists of a long, low barrel-vault. The roof of the upper level (living quarters for the family) may or may not be supported on masonry pillars and arches, in addition to the outer walls. The walls are usually very thick, often exceeding three feet, for the old style of construction was two (dry-laid) stone walls with a rubble fill between them. The roof of the old-style house is constructed as follows: round or semi-round beams are laid from the top of one wall to the opposite one at right angles to the long axis of the house. A layer of shorter, thick sticks is placed across the beams, and then a layer of finer sticks is added. Finally, a layer of earth about a foot thick is packed down as hard as possible on top. To prevent leaking, the roof must be packed down several times each winter; for this purpose every old-style house is equipped with a stone roller (*maḥji*), weighing about a hundred pounds. These houses are dark inside because of the paucity of windows which are unglazed and closed by solid wooden shutters. To counteract this, the inside plastered walls are either whitewashed or painted very pale blue. There is every reason to suppose that this style of house is very ancient indeed. However, none of the existing examples of it in Munṣif is probably more than a hundred and fifty years old, and some are probably as little as sixty years old. Repairs—sometimes amounting to rebuilding—and alterations have always been a matter of course. However, no houses of this type have been built since the early 1890's. Weulersse (1946, p. 267) says that this traditional Lebanese house is well adapted to its environment. It provides insulation against the chilly blasts of winter and against the heat of summer as effectively as any essentially primitive construction could.

The second subtype of old-style house has only two examples in the village. The construction is essentially the same as the foregoing, but the following features are added: two or more distinctly separate rooms in the upper level; sculptured ornamentation, including fully round columns, around the windows; and glazed ornamental windows, with rather elaborate designs formed by the lead mullions, usually in a row of three rounded or pointed arches. These were evidently the dwellings of people of some affluence, although no stories were related about this. The houses are evidently eighty to ninety years old.

The second house-type is the tile-roof style which was typical of the period 1890 to 1914. It was stated that all the tile-roof houses in the village were built with funds earned by emigrants in, or returned from, America. By and large, this is probably true. For Lebanon as a whole, Thoumin (1936, p. 295) makes the same statement. Weulersse (1946, p. 238) points out that this style of house, which is very common in Lebanon, is a symbol of prestige and wealth. Févret (1949, p. 163), commenting on this statement, says that actually this is no longer true, for now it is the even more European-style villa (*fiilla*) which the rich and influential build for themselves—not in ordinary villages, but in the luxurious suburbs and mountain resorts. At any rate, the tile-roof house, in Munṣif as elsewhere, is one of the earliest and most conspicuous items in the process of material acculturation. The tiles are flat and grooved, mostly made in France—rather different from the semi-cylindrical Spanish and Italian tiles.

A map in Thoumin (1936, p. 220) indicates that Munṣif is an area of relatively high frequency of tile roofs. Somewhat less than a third of the village's houses now have them.

There are two subtypes of the tile-roof house. The first is very like the old-style house in that it has only one room above, and a storage room or stable below. The major differences are the roof style, the fact that the masonry courses tend to be more even and are frequently wet-laid and the fact that there are more windows, mostly still unglazed.

The second subtype of the tile roof house is more elaborate. The triple arch, in glazed windows—which sometimes have some panes of colored glass—or in arcades, is a conspicuous feature of these houses. There is usually an ornamental cornice just below the roof, and just below the cornice there frequently are small round windows. These appear high up on the interior walls, which are often as much as twenty feet high, from floor to ceiling. The ornamental windows are invariably glazed, and others usually are. The panes of a window are set in double, wooden casements which open inward. In addition, there are solid wooden shutters outside. The doors and shutters of houses of all types usually have simple rectangular panels, and the doors have big iron locks with keys to match them in size. Some of the large tile-roof houses, however, have rather elaborate doors, somewhat baroque in style.

The interior floor plan of the large tile-roof house consists essentially of a large central salon (maq'ad—"seat") off which open perhaps two rooms on each side. The ornamental windows occupy a third wall of the maq'ad, with the front door in the opposite, fourth, wall. Assuming that this idealized pattern forms a rectangular plan, we can add that it is often modified into a shallow U-shape by building additional rooms on either side of the front door. The kitchen very often occupies one of these rooms, and perhaps the other is a wash room. The cistern is likely to be enclosed by one or the other of them.

Many of the tile-roof houses have the thick old-style walls, but some do not. Limestone, often fossiliferous, is the universal building material. The floors are of cement, or stone flags, or both.

After the era of great prosperity which ended with the start of the First World War, there appears to have been no building to speak of until the 1930's.

Of the modern houses, there are six which are essentially additions to older structures, either second stories or side-by-side with, and connected to, the old. Three more are entirely new. These nine conform to older patterns in their limestone masonry, rectangular plan, and room arrangement. The walls are, however, relatively thin, and cement is used much more liberally than of old to hold the stones together.   Projecting porches, supported by cylindrical concrete pillars, are a new feature, but the most outstanding innovation is the flat, concrete roof.

There are two more modern houses each of which is in a class by itself. One is the highest house in the village, and at first glance it does not seem unusual.   It is built of limestone and has a tile roof.   On closer inspection, however, a number of unusual features become evident.   There is an extensive ell and a projecting porch in back.   A sort of garden path leads to the front door on each side of which there is a trellis.   The windows are large, and, of course, glazed.   This house is somewhat in the style of the villas which can be seen in Lebanese mountain resorts.   Its builder and owner is a man who works and lives in Tripoli, except in the summer.

The other modern house of special note represents the most radical departure from the old patterns.   It is not yet completed, consisting only of the frame which is made of reinforced concrete and concrete blocks.   (The old-type construction does not require a frame.)   Probably it will have a limestone facing, including some curved surfaces, when it is finished, and it will conform in design and construction to a modernistic European style which is frequently seen elsewhere in Lebanon.   This house, also, is being built by a summer resident.

The great increase in the use of concrete is worthy of comment, for cement is one of the few important non-agricultural products of modern Lebanon.   Consequently, it is relatively inexpensive.   In addition to this, there is its admirable property of plasticity.   However, its use in roofs is, in the writer's opinion, a poor environmental adaptation.   In winter, concrete roofs make cold, damp ceilings.   In summer, they radiate a great deal of heat, and the rooms which have them usually become very hot.

The significance of the ruined houses (*khirbi*) is much more of a social than a material nature.   Many ruined houses are used as latrines for there are few specially constructed privies in the village; at least one has its floor plowed up, and this is planted to onions.   Otherwise, the ruins have no function whatever.   It might be thought that the stones of which they are built would be removed and used in new constructions.   This is not the case— at least, it is not to an observable degree.   All the stones used in new building in the village are freshly quarried.   Perhaps the reason for this is that nearly all the ruins have recognized owners, nearly all of whom are emigrants or their descendants.   Even the villagers now admit that "they will never come back," but their property rights are still maintained, either because the older emigrants hesitate to relinquish their claims or because their American-born children are uninterested, both of which prevent local disposition of the property.   However, most of the now ruined houses were of the old style, whose roofs would naturally go to pieces if not tended. Consequently, the roofs were removed so that the very valuable timbers in them could be used for other purposes. This hastened the partial collapse of many of the buildings' walls.

Household Arrangement and Furnishings

Nearly every house has its own cistern (*biir*), either within the building or just outside it. The water is entirely winter rain water drawn from the roof of the house and conducted to the cistern, nowadays, by sheet-iron pipes. This is much more efficient than the older method of letting the water flow down a shallow vertical trough on the outside of the wall of the building. The cisterns have circular openings raised off the ground or floor on a stone or concrete curbing. The opening is fitted, more or less tightly, with a wooden cover.

It is one of the women's jobs to draw water from the cistern by means of a sheet-iron, European-made, bucket attached to a chain or rope. The water needed for the day is stored in large, two-handled, pointed-bottom jars (*jarra*), of porous earthenware, which stand in wooden frames in the kitchen corner, or the kitchen room if there is one. From the *jarra*, water is transferred to cooking utensils, to the spouted pottery or glass drinking jars (*ibriiq*), and to the two to three gallon, semi-cylindrical metal tanks in which washing water is stored. These hang against an outside wall or in the wash room if there is one. The tanks are called *ḥanafiyyi*, a term primarily applied to the small brass spigots with which they are fitted. The term is derived from the Ḥanafi school of Muslim jurisprudence which decided that the use of spigots was not a violation of the provisions of the Koran. Near the *ḥanafiyyi* one usually finds a dish for soap and a towel-rack. A few houses are equipped with hand-pumps, a raised tank, and a limited system of pipes and spigots. This, however, is unusual.

The interior arrangement of the one-room house is essentially the same in every case, although of course there are many minor variations. The following description is composite. On entering the front door, one will observe that the room is divided into two sections, front and back. The division is effected by tall cabinets, with doors and drawers, placed across the room. These are used for keeping clothes, dishes, and so on. This means of division may be supplemented by a curtain. In the front section, a long wooden seat, really a bench with a back and arms at the ends, extends around the walls. This is fitted with hard, flat cushions which are upholstered in some very light color —often plain white. Very likely a set of modern, reclining chairs, with stiff cane backs and bottoms, will be set formally around a table in the center of the room. Here and there, there will be rather rough wooden stools with soft cane seats. At one side, there will be a large rectangular dining table with a cloth or plastic cover. In some houses, fully upholstered modern easy-chairs will be found.

The walls are devoid of ornamentation, with one exception which is conspicuous in the houses which have it. This is a concentrated mass of photographs, some yellowed with age, some brand new, of various members of the owner's family, including emigrants who are fondly remembered. Sometimes, among the family photographs, there will also be one or two postcard-sized pictures of saints or members of the Holy Family. However, as far as the writer is aware, there are no houses which have anything resembling a household shrine, and many have no religious symbols whatever.

Especially in the older houses, there are recesses in the walls, often closed with wooden doors. These are used for storage—for example, large jars for the year's supply of olive oil.

Only a close friend of the family will ordinarily be given the opportunity to go from the *maq'ad*, or front section, to the rear. Here are the sleeping quarters of the family, and cooking equipment will be found in one corner also—unless there is an additional room for this purpose, as is the case with several essentially one-room houses.

Every house is wholly or mostly equipped with metal bedsteads, springs, mattresses, pillows, pillowcases, sheets and blankets, all of European manufacture and/or design. Sixty years ago everyone slept on the floor on sheepskins wrapped in blankets or quilted puffs. Only suggestions of this practice are now to be found in a few houses.

The traditional type of stove was a masonry oven with apertures in the top, in which the chief fuel was brushwood. Very few such stoves are now used. Rather, nearly every house is equipped with at least one "Primus" stove, a small, portable appliance, made in Sweden, which operates on the principle of the ignition of kerosene which has been vaporized by heat and pressure. Basic instructions for its operation are etched on the side of its brass fuel tank in Arabic, Hindustani, and Chinese, and we might say that this is an item in a process which might be called "deliberate diffusion." It is inexpensive to buy and operate and is quite efficient except for the fact that there is only one burner per stove.

A minimal assortment of cooking utensils would include: a teakettle; a set, in graduated sizes, of long-handled metal beakers (for boiling coffee); a cylindrical brass coffee grinder; pots, bowls, and platters of various sizes and shapes, made of metal or pottery; and a stone mortar and pestle. Hardware would include a ladle, knives of various sizes, and long-handled serving forks and spoons. Food is served on china platters and/or round plates. If necessary, everyone is provided with knives, forks, and spoons, but napkins are not ordinarily used. Cups and demitasses are provided for tea and coffee, respectively. (The only kind of coffee which is consumed in the village is "Turkish" coffee.) Wine is drunk from small glasses. The only acceptable way to drink water, however, is directly from the spouted jug called *ibriiq*. This is definitely an acquired skill which children are taught as early as possible. For this purpose, a small *ibriiq*, usually made of glass, is provided. With the exception of the coffee grinder, usually the coffee beakers, the pestle and mortar, and the *ibriiq*, all these items are of European manufacture and/or design.

Although kerosene heaters are readily available in Beirut, the standard means of heating houses in the village is by small, round, charcoal braziers which sit low on the floor. If a social group in one room of a multi-room house moves to another, the brazier around which the group has sat will be picked up and carried along. The idea, in other words, is to keep the people warm rather than to heat the room. The European and American kerosene heaters are undoubtedly more efficient, but they are a great deal more expensive to buy and operate. Besides, the charcoal braziers can also be used for boiling coffee and broiling meat on skewers.

Oil lamps, with glass chimneys, of European manufacture and of the same type which is still sometimes seen in rural areas of the United States, are used in many houses. Everyone keeps a supply of candles in case of emergency. But the most widely used type of illumination is provided by a kerosene pressure lantern. This gives a very strong light and is frequently suspended on an iron rod from the ceiling of the room.

Nearly every individual who is adolescent or older has a flashlight and uses it. On moonless or cloudy nights, the village is enveloped in pitch blackness, with only a few undiffused lights showing here and there from doors or windows.

Floor-covering is provided either by small "oriental" rugs or straw mats. Such ornamental or luxury items as elaborately inlaid boxes and furniture, engraved brass or copper trays, and painted pottery, are rare.

Diet

The villagers regularly eat three meals a day, of which the evening meal is ordinarily the largest, except on Sundays. Breakfast is likely to include the leftovers from the preceding evening meal. Bread is eaten at, and coffee served after, every meal. Lunch tends to be small, and the family is apt to be incomplete at lunch, for men or boys working in the fields usually take their lunches with them—a couple of loaves of bread, some olives, and perhaps an onion or cucumber or two, and a jug of water.

The villagers say that in summer they have more to eat than in winter. In effect, what they mean is that fresh fruits and vegetables supplement the year-round staples, all, except citrus fruits, in the summer. The staples, which are either constantly obtainable or can be locally preserved and stored, are the following:

Wheat (mostly imported)
Rice (imported)
Mutton (mostly bought on the hoof from outsiders)
Hens' eggs (locally produced)
Olives (locally produced)
Figs (locally produced)
Fresh fish (caught locally)
Potatoes and turnips (imported and produced locally)

Onions and garlic (imported and produced locally)
A variety of legumes (imported and produced locally)
Milk (locally produced)
Salt (locally produced)
Sugar (imported)
Coffee and tea (imported)

This base is supplemented in summer by the following items, most of which are produced locally: apricots, fresh figs, grapes, tomatoes, cucumbers, green and yellow squashes, peppers, lettuce, and almonds.

It is clear that the village is heavily dependent upon the outside for food staples. Among the forms in which these staples are eaten are the following:

Bread ♦ Americans, among whom bread is now a food of secondary importance and generally of poor nutritive value, will at once recognize the significance of "daily bread" when they observe its use among present-day Semitic-speaking peoples. Although it would be an exaggeration to say that it is *the* staff of life, it is certainly the most important single item of food—important both in regard to its nutritive value and the attitudes toward it of its eaters. Bread-making is an important social as well as economic function. . . . The loaf is a disk about one foot or more in diameter and about a third of an inch thick. Tannous (1944, p. 534) says that every adult eats from one to two pounds of it a day and takes it at every meal. Although no attitudes toward it of a religious nature were encountered in Munṣif, its importance was indicated by such remarks as: "A meal is not a meal if there is no bread"; "If there is nothing else, bread is enough"; "If you do not eat bread, you will always be hungry"; and "If you drink too much water at a meal, you will not be able to eat enough bread." The average adult in the village eats about two loaves per meal, which is consistent with Tannous' statement.

Bread can be eaten alone, but usually it is not. The eater tears it into pieces about three inches square. With this between fingers and thumb (usually, but not exclusively, of the right hand), he reaches out to a common dish and takes a piece of food. The morsel is then conveyed to the mouth as is, or after that which has been taken from the dish has been more thoroughly wrapped up in the bread. For eating semiliquid foods, the piece of bread is made into the shape of a small, crude shovel. Virtually the entire meal can be, and frequently is, eaten, associatively and instrumentally, with bread.

Bread (*khubz*) is not the only wheat product which is made in the bakery and eaten. There is also holy bread (*qurbaan*). . . . And a special treat is *manquushi* ("fingered"). This starts as a disk of unleavened dough which looks very much like an unbaked loaf of bread. But a rim is pinched up around the edge and the maker may punch herringbone or crosshatch designs in the center with her fingers. The center is then covered liberally with olive oil and on this sugar and sesame seeds are sprinkled. It is preferably eaten as soon as possible after it has been baked. It is sweet and filling. None of the very sweet, flaky pastries, which can be bought in Middle Eastern restaurants, was encountered in the village.

Meat ◆ Sheep are killed ordinarily only on Sundays, and the meat is bought and most of it eaten immediately. There appears to be a sort of folk hygiene connected with this practice. One of the few complaints about city life voiced by a young person was that it was not a good idea to buy meat in the city because one didn't know how long it had been hanging in the butcher shop, completely exposed to flies and the dust of the street. Beef, a prime source of tapeworm, is not eaten at all, nor is pork.

The main dish of the standard Sunday dinner, taken at noon, is raw *kibbi*, perhaps the most famous Lebanese dish. It consists of raw meat and cracked wheat ground up together in the stone mortar and served as a smooth mound on a platter. It is washed down with another famous item, *'araq*, a distilled grape liquor, flavored with anis, which is clear and colorless when it comes from the bottle but turns milky white when water is added to it, as it usually is. The villagers buy *'araq* which is made in the city, although they would undoubtedly make their own if they had to. The intake of alcohol is very moderate. It is never drunk alone but always as part of a meal. Four small glasses of *'araq* mixed with water are considered enough, if not too much. The writer is reasonably certain that there is no cultural pattern for getting really drunk for its own sake. A little wine is made locally, but not very much.

Raw meat is also eaten in small chunks, taken in bread and dipped in the rough salt which is obtained locally from the sea. Most of the specialized organs, such as liver, kidneys, testicles, and lungs, are eaten in this manner.

What is left over from the raw *kibbi* is cooked, either in the form of a flat disk or in individual patties. This cooked *kibbi* will appear on Monday's, and perhaps Tuesday's, menu. *Laḥm mishwi* ("broiled meat"—on skewers) another regional specialty, is an alternative.

Roast chicken is sometimes served but usually only on special occasions, such as the saint's-day feasts at which certain families entertain the priest.

Olives ◆ All the olives which are consumed in the village are local produce. Some are cured in brine and stored for eating throughout the year. A dish of them appears at every meal. But most of a year's harvest is reduced, locally, to oil which is used in nearly every phase of cooking.

Sweet Preserves ◆ Figs and apricots (which are also eaten raw in season) are made into very sweet jams which are eaten throughout the year. Grapes (extensively eaten raw in season) and carob pods are made into another type of preserve, called *dibs,* which has the consistency of molasses.

A preserve of a rather special type, *ḥalaawi* ("sweet"), is obtained from the city in returnable cans. It comes in a hard cake which flakes when cut. Its essential ingredients are sugar and *ṭiḥiini* (mashed sesame seeds). *Ḥalaawi* is very sweet and "rich," and is considered to be a great delicacy which is eaten, alone or with bread, at the close of the meal.

Milk Products ◆ Milk is not usually taken raw, although there is one dish, *laban?immu,* which consists of hot milk in which float pastry balls which are stuffed with rice and/or meat. Rather, milk is preferred in three fermented forms: white cheese (from goat's milk), *laban* ("sour" milk, known in America as "yoghurt"), and *labni* (drained *laban,* which has the consistency of cream cheese). Of the three, *laban* is the most extensively used. It appears at every meal and is the preferred sauce with which to eat cooked *kibbi.*

Eggs are sometimes eaten hard boiled, but they are preferred when included in a dish which is a combination of omelette and meat loaf. Potatoes and turnips, also, are usually included in a larger combination. "French fried" potatoes are known, but not by that name.

Onions and garlic are eaten cooked or raw, alone or in combination with other things; rice is used for stuffing or is served as a dish, boiled, and covered with onions.

Tea (*shayy*) is taken very sweet, but milk is never added. As with coffee, the sugar is boiled along with the main ingredient. The common occidental notion, however, that "Turkish" coffee (*qahwi*) really isn't Turkish coffee unless it is sirupy sweet is not necessarily founded on fact. Some prefer it with little sugar or none at all, and the guest is usually asked if he prefers it very sweet, sweet, or bitter. The only requirements are that it be thick and very hot.

Of the summer products which have not been considered so far, squash is the only one which appears in cooked form, frequently stuffed with rice and/or meat (*kuusa maḥshi*). (There is a general notion that cool foods are preferable in hot weather, hot foods in cold weather, but this not rigidly followed in practice.)

Sliced cucumbers and tomatoes, in olive oil, are served in summer, but these, and other vegetables, are preferred when included in two larger dishes. One of these is a very delicious salad (*ṣalaṭa*) consisting of lettuce, tomato, cucumber, parsley, mint, onion, and garlic. The dressing is a mixture of lemon juice and olive oil. The other is *tabbuuli*. This has nearly the same ingredients as the salad, but they are chopped up very fine and mixed with cracked wheat which has been soaked in water. Like raw *kibbi*, *tabbuuli* is served in the form of a mound, and its eating is associated with the drinking of *'araq*.

Legumes are not too commonly eaten alone without further preparation than cooking. There is a cooked bean mash (*mujaddara*), but this is not considered to be very tasty. However, chick peas, mashed, are mixed with *ṭiḥiini* to form a very popular and filling "sauce" called *ḥumuṣ biṭḥiini*. This is served as a substitute for, or in addition to, *laban*.

Foreign foods are very rare. The most important is spaghetti, whose eating requires the use of a fork. Scandinavian canned tuna, also, supplements the local fish supply which is rather meager, although in summer, sea urchins are consumed in large quantities, as well as squids and octopi.

In conclusion, it should be pointed out that diet is one of the most conservative and least acculturated aspects of the material culture. Cooking and serving utensils, it is true, have been heavily influenced, but this has been a process of substitution, for purposes of efficiency, rather than of innovation.

Clothing

To some degree, the clothing worn by the villagers varies in style according to the age of the wearer. Among males, the elderly are definitely conservative, the middle-aged vary, the young men and boys wear European-style clothes almost without exception. A similar gradation among the females is a little less obvious, probably primarily because the women's traditional costume, unlike the men's, is not particularly distinctive to Western eyes.

Men ♦ The second oldest man in the village is the only one who wears the *ghumbaaz*, a long, long-sleeved, tubular gown, of white, striped cotton-backed silk. This costume is frequently seen in the heterogeneous city populations, often on younger men. Weulersse (1946, p. 244) says that it is of Bedu origin.

More typical of the older men is the traditional *shirwal* (tremendously baggy trousers with short, tight legs), open-necked, or collarless shirt, and European jacket. Headgear is the cylindrical *ṭarbuush*, maroon felt with a black tassel. Especially in winter, a cloth or scarf may be wrapped around the *ṭarbuush*. One man in the village wears a tall conical brown felt cap, called *libbaadi*, which is often seen elsewhere.

A few middle-aged men wear the complete traditional costume, but more of them have adopted European (*franji*) clothes. For work, they wear nondescript, but European, trousers, shirt, sweater if needed, socks and shoes. On more or less formal occasions, however, a complete suit, with tie, is worn. This tendency is even more pronounced among the young men. No one ordinarily goes unshod except small boys and girls in summer. Sport shirts —preferably plain white—are worn in summer.

Those working in the fields frequently wear pith helmets and jodhpur-like trousers which bear a superficial resemblance to the *shirwal* which were not observed on any man under about fifty. Quite a number of middle-aged men who have given up the *shirwal*, nevertheless retain the *ṭarbuush* which, however, is not worn by any man younger than about forty. The European hat with a brim (*birnayta*) is unusual; only two or three men wear them regularly, although others wear them on occasion. Thus, it can be deduced that a good many men, especially young adults and adolescents, ordinarily go hatless, and this is a rather singular practice in a culture where headgear has practical and symbolic significance. The writer believes that the prevailing hatlessness in the younger generation is an aspect, and rather an apt symbol, of the cultural situation in which they find themselves. He believes that if systematic questioning were undertaken on this topic, it would reveal that the younger generation has more or less consciously rejected the old style— which it associates with peasant life—and at the same time is often hesitant to accept the new which represents foreign influence. The European brimmed hat obviously provides better protection than the *ṭarbuush* against the sun, which is the reason, stated by young and old alike, why one should always wear a hat.

Women ◆ The costume of the older, middle-aged, and many of the village-dwelling younger women consists basically of a rather formless, full-skirted black dress (cotton or wool) supplemented by sweater or jacket. A scarf is very often worn over the head, but it is secured under the back hair rather than under the chin. In winter, woolen stockings are worn. There is no elaborate jewelry. The younger women, especially those who work in the city, follow modern European styles.

However, the Western practice of women or girls wearing slacks or shorts has been completely rejected. For this there are at least two reasons. One is that the men regard the practice as a usurpation of a symbol of masculine status. The second is that women who wear slacks or shorts are assumed to be of loose morals. This is because the wearing of these garments by women in the area is associated with the "artistes" (who are mostly European women) who are entertainers in the numerous Western-style nightclubs in Beirut and are generally assumed to be available for other purposes after hours.

For the most part, those who wear European clothes regularly are careful to appear in well-pressed and clean garments. This means more inconvenience and expense than the maintenance of the traditional costume did. Dodd (1940, p. 686) remarks that the relative tightness of Western clothes is not well adapted to summer weather, and certainly the *shirwal* are better and more comfortably adapted to male anatomy than European trousers are.

Tools and Miscellaneous Equipment

It has already been mentioned that the flashlight is a widely distributed item of personal equipment. Another is the wrist watch. Certainly a majority of the villagers who have attained any degree of responsible age have them. Traditional village life required no accurate chronometry, and there was none. The villagers still rise with the sun, although they go to bed after dark. On the whole, there is no specific horological time for meals. However, the village schools operate on a definite time schedule, and this affects quite a large proportion of the resident population—the teachers and their families, the children, and their mothers, who prepare their lunches. Of course, those who are, or have been, working in the city, are quite thoroughly conditioned to clock-schedules. A good deal of apparently unnecessary reference to and synchronization of watches was observed in the village. On the whole, however, it can be said that future plans which involve exact hours are made and fulfilled in a casual manner. Perhaps a valid generalization would be that the average individual regards his watch as a symbol of prosperity, an instrument, on occasion, of practical value, and an interesting toy—all in about equal measure.

Combs, toilet soap, safety and straight razors, shaving lotion, etc. (all of European or American manufacture), are universally distributed. Some people have and use toothbrushes. The women do not appear to use cosmetics to any great extent.

A variety of containers have already been described, but several more must be added. The rectangular five-gallon gasoline can, with its top cut out and fitted with a wooden handle, is widely used for carrying water, cement and other bulk materials. Various sizes of coiled baskets, cylindrical with large handles over the top, are used for carrying food. Large, flat wicker trays are used for carrying such things as bread and laundry and for the display of vegetables in the stores. Formerly, silk worm coccoons were set out on them.

Carpenter's and mason's tools—hammers, saws, planes, levels, drills, screwdrivers, chisels, and trowels—appear to be the same in form as they are in the West. Probably most of the items now used are western-made, but most of the forms are very old in the Middle East.

Agricultural tools are conservative and of very ancient form. There are no horses in the village (the Arabs use them for riding rather than for traction), and the ox is the chief draft animal. The plow consists of a wooden shaft (in several segments) to which a round iron spike is set at an angle. The thresher is a heavy sledge into whose bottom sharp volcanic stones (from the Akkar) are set. (See Thoumin, 1936, pp. 134–36, for illustrations.) Grain is winnowed by tossing it up into the air with a rather crude fork made entirely of wood. Small saws and hand-clippers (the only recent foreign element in the toolkit) are used for pruning. The last item is an iron spade, which is, if possible, manipulated by two or three men. One man grasps the handle and shaft in the usual manner, and, in effect, pushes the spade. One or two other men pull the spade by means of cords attached to the shaft just above the shoulders of the blade.

The traditional means of communication were donkeys, horses, and human backs and legs, traveling over rough stone paths. To this, can be added a nonmaterial means, which is still used a great deal—shouting from one section of the village to another. The horse and the donkey have given way to the automobile, the bus, the truck, and the paved roads which they require. Two automobiles are stationed in the village, and a number of them are owned by villagers who live in the city. Those in the village are at least fifteen years old. One of the owners operates a regular (about three times a day) taxi service to Jbayl. The Beirut-Tripoli buses regularly stop at Ḥilwi, but the railroad trains never do. No one in the village owns a truck, but it is not difficult to hire one from Jbayl if necessary.

In terms of message communication, there are two new elements in the village. One is the public telephone at Ḥilwi. This does not seem to play a very important part in the life of the community. It is simply one apparatus in the network of telephones which the French Mandatory Government installed along the main highways. The other is the radio. There is one at Ḥilwi and one in the village proper, both in private houses. A third, portable one was purchased during the period of study. There would doubtless be more if it were not necessary to run them on batteries. However, the villagers keep up to date on the news very efficiently. Every day several people go to and return from Jbayl in whose shops radios blare away constantly.

In the field of communication, foreign influence has been of profound importance.

REFERENCES

Dodd, S. C. *Social Relations in the Near East*, Second edition. (Beirut, 1940).

Févret, M. "Paysans de Syrie et du Proche-Orient," *Revue de Géographie de Lyon*, Vol. 14, No. 2 (1949).

Tannous, A. I. "The Arab Village Community of the Middle East," *Annual Report for 1943, Smithsonian Institution*, (Washington, 1944).

Thoumin, R. *Géographie humaine de la Syrie centrale*. (Paris, 1936).

Weulersse, J. *Paysans de Syrie et du Proche-Orient*. (Tours, 1946).

Louise Sweet studied a small Muslim Arab village in northwestern Syria. She lived there during the year 1954 when she was a member of the Aleppo Field Session of 1953–1954 of the Department of Near East Studies, the University of Michigan. Full-length studies of the villages of this region are still rare and even rarer are such studies having been conducted by women (Hilma Granqvist's earlier field work stands out as a pioneering effort).

Louise Sweet's volume follows a traditional anthropological presentation; of particular value is her section on the routine of the day.

6

<figure>◇◇◇</figure>

A Day in a Syrian Peasant Household

LOUISE E. SWEET

In mid-March in Tell Ṭoqaan, when the young lambs, kids, and calves have begun to graze, when the heaviest rains of late winter are over, when the wheat is well up and seedling beds and vegetable gardens are being planted, when the days are long and pleasant with mild weather, warm sun, and scattered showers, before insects have begun to multiply and the dust of summer to blow and drift, life in a peasant household is at its most agreeable. To narrate the day's routine in a peasant compound at this time is to give some idea of the pace and concerns of daily living at its "best." What the Tell Ṭoqaaniis remember as "best" from past years, of course, are the unusual and outstanding events, the great feasts and celebrations, the special

From *Tell Ṭoqaan: A Syrian Village* (Anthropological Papers, No. 14), pp. 136–179; reprinted by permission of Anthropological Papers, Museum of Anthropology, University of Michigan.

favors from Allah or from the wealthy and powerful, and the seasons of unusual harvests. Here the "best" is conceived of as a typical good day, when the
weather is clear, the work is accomplished without mishap, minor problems
are solved or settled, hopeful plans are made, and no unusual events mark the
day.

In the early darkness just before dawn the household begins to stir; the
father and head of the household is heard reciting the first prayer of the day
in the courtyard. Shortly afterward he and his eldest son release the animals
from the stables—the two mules and the young horse, the cow and her calf
from their small stable at the end of the far courtyard, and the seven black
nanny goats and their seven kids from the former dwelling room, now assigned
to animals, which opens off the near courtyard. Around this space the reception room, dwelling room, and kitchen room are also, and here most of the
social life of the day takes place, in the sun or in the shadow given by the
walls, as comfort demands. In the kitchen room the wife spends a few
minutes mixing bread dough for baking later in the morning. The two mules
nibble at the remains of green barley lying in the mangers along one wall
of the courtyard; the eldest son and his father throw the light halters over the
mules' heads and the collars around their necks. Then, the youth, with a bag
of bread for lunch tied to his belt, drives the team out to plow. He will begin
where he left off the day before, the place marked by his plow slanted back
on the handle, plow beam high in the air, and the yoke supporting it. He
is working on a fallow plot near the tell, plowing it for the third time since
January. And he carries a couple of homemade bird traps to set, for spring
has brought many birds to the village lands. Other plowmen of the village
are moving out to neighboring plots and elsewhere on the fallow lands, and
call greetings to each other.

The second son, a boy of thirteen or fourteen, follows the cow, calf, and
young horse out of the courtyard, watching sleepily until he sees that they
join the village herd of similar animals which is moving under the care of
the village herdsman's sons slowly toward the grazing on the far slope of the
great tell near the border of the marsh. The seven nanny goats are separated
from their kids by the mother and her youngest son and the adult animals are
driven out of the compound to join those of the carpenter's family with which
this houshold co-operates in herding their small flock of product animals. The
combined flock of the two households number 17 nanny goats, 16 of which
are giving milk, two bucks, and a ewe giving milk. The carpenter's second
son leads the small flock in the direction of the low limestone ridge on
the southwest side of the village where he and the shepherd for the local
tribal Shayx will graze the animals of their flocks near each other. Far along
the ridge which encircles the village, the shepherds of the two major lineages
of the village are moving with their flocks to the day's grazing.

After the goats and the ewe are well on their way the carpenter's ten-year-old daughter and her small brother arrive in an erratic and disorderly rush with the flock of kids; the seven kids of the peasant household are shooed out to join them. The young animals are just learning to graze a little, but most of the day they will lead the two children a chase from the field borders where they nibble a little, cluster in a group to sleep briefly in the sun, then are up and away through the village, leaping and clambering by way of half-ruined walls to the roofs of stable compounds. Then nearby adults must go to the rescue of both children and animals. "They are little devils."

Once the animals are taken care of, the remaining members of the household breakfast quickly on tea and bread and leftovers from supper the night before. The two younger boys set out for school, held in a room the Shayx has taken in the compound, across the village, of an old shepherd partner of Shayx Nuuri. The father of the household begins to clean the mule-stable floor; his wife carries out the dung and straw in loads on a broad round tray to the spot outside the compound and among the storage bins where previous loads have been dumped. Between trips she complains to her husband that their client's wife, who is supposed to come every other day to help her around the compound, rarely comes more than twice in a week. When their client is home in the village, she tells him, he sees to it that his wife comes regularly, but now that he is away for a while she never turns up, just like all the Hadiidiin women from Tell Qelbi—no brains for their obligations. This morning, she goes on, she expects one of the widows in the village to come and help her instead. Her husband listens and grunts in more or less agreement.

When the widow arrives she is put to work rolling the churning bag of laban and water. She squats on a mat in the chill shadow of the compound wall and as she churns the laban the two women carry on a conversation that begins with formal greetings, the widow respectfully addressing the peasant and his wife Abu Adnaan and Umm Adnaan after their eldest son. The conversation continues with brief comments, and when the husband leaves, warms slowly to a cautious exchange of gossip and information between the two women. In the sixteen years each has been in the village (their two eldest children are nearly the same age), the widow has visited this compound only half a dozen times, for medications for herself or her children for earache, in the treatment of which the peasant has some special reputation. The peasant's wife has never been in the widow's house, for the two women are of different tribal groups, but more significantly, the widow is a Bu Layl who lives to some extent on the generosity of Shayx Nuuri, since her only boy is still a child of five. The peasant's wife, on the other hand, came to Tell Ṭoqaan from Saraaqab, a much larger village. She is a member of a large and powerful family there, a poor branch of it, but nevertheless, a member; and her husband is a grandson of the founder of Tell Toqaan, perhaps, it has been rumored, an illegitimate son, but in any event locally recognized as a descendant of the founder and acknowledged by his cousins, the legitimate descendants, as a kinsman. And the cousins are urban landlords, educated men, effendiis, who own automobiles, tractors, and residences in Aleppo. In part, the conversation of the two women skirts these subjects and alludes to these facts and rumors; together they get the work done. The peasant's wife hears that the widow's daughter does not know how to make peasant bread since they do not have a peasant oven, but she has learned to sew well. It is generally known that of the four or five marriageable girls in the village, her daughter is regarded as one of the best in comportment and ability. The widow hears that, yes, the peasant's oldest son is interested in finding a wife, but has not settled on anyone yet. The laban is churned, the compound is swept, the peasant's wife shakes out the sleeping mattresses and quilts, folds and stacks them on the rack above the wooden bride's chest at the end of the long dwelling room. The widow sweeps the room and shakes the mat in the courtyard while midmorning tea is brewed.

The husband, who had gone out to watch once more the way the old mule worked at the plow, scarcely able to finish a furrow, returns for tea. The mule won't last, he comments. Already all he wants to do is to lie down at the end of a furrow; he might go on a while if he could rest and eat grass every other day, but the plow must work every day to get even half their land cultivated. One of the men in the village whose property is in sheep and who has no land to cultivate has a white mare that is pregnant. She might be a good buy and Allah might bring them a mare, a horse, or at least a strong mule. The peasant leaves for the carpenter's shop or the small store next to the mosque; the man who owns the white mare will be in either place. His wife asks the widow to pick over some lentils while she bakes the bread. A fire of coarse chopped straw is started at the base of the big oven jar and, while the fire burns down to a bank of coals, the peasant's wife prepares the working space and dough. The widow sits outside the door of the small domed room in which the oven is located; while the two continue working and talking a young girl strides gracefully into the courtyard bearing a tinned copper pan filled with freshly collected and peeled down thistle stalks, a favorite green eaten raw or cooked in laban. At the instruction of the peasant's wife she tips the greens, nearly half a bushel, out on a tray in the kitchen room and leaves. The widow asks why the girl had brought the greens, but the wife declares that indeed she doesn't know. Probably her husband bought them. However, both of them know the girl is the muxtaar's daughter, the next to the eldest and another of the eligible. After the breadmaking is finished it is approaching noon and time to go out to the first milking. The widow's work is finished, so the peasant's wife pours several handfuls of the dry lentils into a small pan the widow brought with her and adds over them a generous portion of the greens. She picks up the wooden container for the milk, locks dwelling room door and compound gate, as they leave together.

The trip out to and back from the place on the ridge where the goats are grazing takes nearly an hour; as she moves across the village she is joined by the wives of several employees of Shayx Nuuri, who will milk the sheep of his flock, and the carpenter's wife and oldest daughter. When they return to the village the carpenter's wife and the peasant's wife take their milk to the compound where the cheesemaker's agent, who comes each day to buy their milk, has his containers and measuring utensils arranged. The peasant's wife returns alone to her compound, pausing at the house of their client to ask the client's wife why she had not come to work on the days she is expected. The client's wife says she will come the next day certainly, but she had heard that her husband and oldest son were returning from their trip and she wanted to have her husband's small shop freshly white-washed for him. The peasant's wife, on her return to the compound, puts out bread, onions, and laban for her husband and two youngest sons for lunch. She mentions to her husband that their client's wife says she will come tomorrow. The youngest son comes first from school and tells his mother that his brother was beaten on the soles of his feet by the Shayx because he did not know his lesson, but his brother denies the whole event and is evidently in a bad mood for he throws clods of dirt at the young dog. After lunch there is time for the peasant to take a brief nap in the sun in the courtyard and for his wife to chat with an old shepherd while she adds another layer of mud to the new beehive she is making. He has come in to ask if they could use a little green fodder he would glean for them. Perhaps tomorrow, she puts him off. About midafternoon the oldest son returns from plowing with the team; he unharnesses them, waters them at the stone trough in the stable courtyard, and leaves the animals in the courtyard. The second son returns from school soon and takes the plow team out to graze near the spring until sunset. The oldest son eats, then changes his plowman's gown and heavy boots for the striped gown and long coat of a peasant farmer, and goes to join his friends at one of the shops.

The peasant's wife starts the kettle of burghul for the evening meal simmering soon after her eldest son returns from the fields. Sewing, repairing a broken basket occupy her for an hour or so. Villagers may come in to talk, some to ask what to do about a sore that is not healing, or perhaps a girl of pastoralist background who is learning to embroider a gown in the pattern like that the peasant woman wears.

Late in the afternoon the peasant's wife again goes out to milk the goats grazing west of the village. Along the way she meets again the group of women who went out together at noon. After the milking the women, shepherds, and the flocks move slowly back toward the village together. The lambs and kids have been brought part way from the village and held behind a rise of ground until called for. When they are turned loose within sight of the mother animals, there is a brief pandemonium as the two groups of animals come together and parent seeks offspring, and the young take the last milk that was left for them. It is just sunset as the people and animals slowly re-enter the village. From the hillock in front of the mosque the shopkeeper, as muezzin, chants the evening call to prayer. The animals of the village herd are walking slowly toward their owner's compounds, finding their own ways from the edge of the village.

In the compound, after all the animals have been stabled by the boys, the members of the family go in to eat in the dwelling room. The father of the household has brought a friend who came to the village this day, an itinerant shoemaker returning with a caravan from selling his services among the shepherds nomadizing in the eastern grazing steppe. Two or three times each season, when the caravan returns to its starting point at Idlib, he drops out at Tell Ṭoqaan to visit this household, as his father did before him. He has been among the Harraamshii shepherds, who will return after reaping, to camp at Tell Ṭoqaan and pasture their flocks on the fallow fields during the dry summer, and he has seen the shepherd who cares for the two young ewes which the peasant owns. He relays greetings from the shepherd and assurances that the animals are well. After performing the sunset prayer the men and sons of the peasant gather around the supper tray. They are served bread, burghul, the fresh greens brought that day, fresh green onions, and sugared fresh butter from the morning's churning. After the meal the men smoke, drink sweet tea, talk and play a few games of cards. The visitor fits a pair of sandals to the youngest son's feet. He will leave them as a gift the next morning. Two or three men who usually work for the peasant come in for the evening's talk. News heard on the shopkeeper's radio is repeated, news from the grazing areas, the condition of the barley growing in the vicinity of the ridge is reported by the wife. The peasant speculates on the possibility of borrowing money to buy an irrigation wheel this year. And where he will place it and how he will lay out the garden around it. His wife prepares the evening's milk production for the next day's laban while the men talk.

Late in the evening, when the callers are gone, the family retires one by one. The mattresses are placed in a line along the floor. The one nearest the door is occupied by the head of the household; next is his wife. Her youngest son sleeps beside her, then the second son. The eldest son, who must be up and plowing again at dawn, long since retired on the far mattress while the men were still talking. Before retiring, stable doors, compound gate, and dwelling-room door are securely locked. Just before he comes in for the last time, the father of the household scans the sky and predicts the next day's weather to be fair, if God is willing.

Ann Lambton has highlighted graphically certain of the responsibilities of the Persian peasant. She has carefully and in detailed fashion documented peasant obligations of personal servitude and dues. Data of this nature are essential for a correct understanding of the subculture of the Middle East's agricultural population.

Material for this presentation was collected by Dr. Lambton in Persia mainly during 1948 and 1949, although she had begun to study the problem during her earlier visits to Persia in 1936–1937 and 1939–1945.

Her work was stimulated and supported by such authorities as H. A. R. Gibb, Doreen Warriner, and Sir Reader Bullard of the Royal Institute of International Affairs.

7

Personal Servitude and Dues in Persia

ANN K. S. LAMBTON

The peasant, in addition to the share of the crop or the rent which he pays to the landowner or lessee, is, in many areas, liable to various dues, which may be regarded, in part at least, as personal servitudes. The number of these and the rate at which they are levied varies from place to place. One of the most common is the liability of the peasant to transport the landowner or lessee's share of the harvest from the threshing-floor to the granary. Thus in Āẕarbāyjān the transport both of the landlord's share from the fields to his granaries and of the grain which the landlord delivers to the state granaries by way of taxation is commonly a charge upon the peasant. This is also the case in Kurdistān, Kirmān, and in the vicinity of Kāshmar. In Souj Bulāgh and

From *Landlord and Peasant in Persia* (1953), pp. 330–336; reprinted by permission of Oxford University Press under the auspices of the Royal Institute of International Affairs.

Shahrīār in the neighbourhood of Tehrān the landlord takes delivery of his share of the harvest at the granaries in the villages, and the cost of transport from the fields to the granaries falls upon the peasant; in the nearby area of Khwār and Varāmīn, however, the peasant is not responsible for the delivery of the landlord's share to the granaries.

The most onerous of the personal servitudes is probably labour service, or *bīgārī*. The performance of such service or the provision of so many men for labour service was a normal obligation upon those who held land in Ṣafavid and Qājār times and probably in earlier times also. One of the most common immunities granted to those in receipt of royal favour was immunity from such service. Clearly, therefore, it was regarded as a service to be rendered to the ruler by those who held land grants or who owned land. It was presumably performed by those who actually tilled the soil, but in so far as rights over the land, whether of ownership or merely of jurisdiction, were granted to a third person, the obligation to provide men for the performance of labour service, unless special immunity had been granted, was a charge upon the grantee or the owner. But, in so far as the grantee was in effect often the local governor, he would in many cases have levied labour service on the population in the area under his jurisdiction in his capacity as the local representative of the government. In the course of time many of the dues levied on behalf of the government by those holding grants of land came to be regarded by the grantees, as they were transformed into ordinary landowners, as services due to them. When the status and nature of the landowning class began to change at the beginning of the twentieth century, and the custom of paying officials by grants of land or its revenue was abolished, and public services such as road-making were taken over by the central government and were no longer a charge upon the local landholder in the person of the *tuyūldār* or grantee, labour service died out in some areas; in others the landlord continued to levy it on his own behalf.

At the present day, although labour service is no longer demanded in all parts of the country, and its incidence, where it is levied, is less than was the case formerly, it still survives in many areas, notably Kurdistān, Āzarbāyjān, Khūzistān, parts of Fārs, Kirmān, and in east Persia.

It is levied in a variety of ways: on each household, plough-land, or share of water, or, occasionally, upon the male peasant population, and consists of so many days of free labour by a peasant or the provision of an ass for free labour on so many days of the year.[1] In the latter case the asses are used, for example, for the transport of the landowner's produce from the village to the town, or for the transport of building materials, etc. The labour service of the peasants usually takes the form of labour on the construction of buildings, irrigation works and road-building, or agricultural labour in the fields which the landowner cultivates himself, i.e., those fields not worked on a crop-sharing basis or leased, or in his gardens.

So many days' labour service of men and asses per *juft* per annum is exacted in the landlord areas of Kurdistān. In Hasanābād (near Sanandaj) the levy is made per *juft* and amounts to seven days' free labour of a peasant and four days' free labour of an ass per annum.[2] In addition the peasants have to dig the landowner's garden in spring, providing two free days' labour per household. In Dabbāgh seven free days' labour per *juft* are taken; in Dālān four free days' labour of a peasant and two free days' labour of an ass. Similar levies are made in the neighbouring villages. In the Saqqiz area also each *juft* has to provide several free days' labour in men and asses. In addition to this, agricultural labour has to be performed for the landowner whenever required. Thus, if the landowner wants his land ploughed, or the harvest reaped, or any other agricultural work performed, it is done by corvée. Food is provided for those taking part but no other payment is made. This levy, which is taken in certain other parts of Kurdistān also, is known as *gal*, and is in addition to the peasant's liability to perform free labour on a fixed number of days per annum. It differs from *bīgārī*, in that the latter, in Kurdistān, is levied not mainly for agricultural work but for building and road-making, etc. In certain areas it would appear that *gal* also takes the form of mutual self-help and is performed not only for the landowner, but also for peasants or small landowners when necessary to help them get in their crops.

In Āzarbāyjān also *bīgārī* is commonly levied by the landowners. For example, in Varzaqān in Uzum Dil, four days' free labour in men and asses is levied per *pānzdah*.

Similarly in Khūzistān *bīgārī* is levied in some areas, but the rate is rather less heavy, being usually one day's labour a year per plough-land. In certain areas it is the practice for the holder of a plough-land to be required also to plant, reap, and thresh a certain amount of grain free in the land which that landowner reserves for himself, i.e., land excepted from that distributed among the crop-sharing peasants or tenants. For this the landowner provides the seed.[3]

In Fārs, in the Mamasanī, *bīgārī* is levied. In Shāpūr also every peasant is bound to give one day's labour in the rice fields per annum. In Nūrābād, however, free agricultural labour is not usually levied, but the holder of each plough-land is required to sow and reap for the landowner without payment a small quantity of rice.

Bīgārī, known locally as *qalūn*, is common in most areas in the province of Kirmān, though it is alleged to be less heavy than was formerly the case. It usually takes the form of corvées levied for the performance of some project or other which the landowner wishes to undertake. It is said to be the heaviest in those areas where the rule of the old-fashioned *khāns* survives. In Shahdād it is less common than around Kirmān; in Rafsinjān it is no longer demanded.

In Khurāsān in the more remote areas *bīgārī* is still common.   In Turbati Ḥaydarī it is taken from all crop-sharing peasants and landless peasants but not from the *sālār*, i.e., the peasant in charge of an agricultural unit. . . . In Zāveh this form of labour service has taken on a somewhat different guise: attached to each *ṣaḥrā* there is an individual known as the *bīgāreh*; he is paid by the peasants who work the *ṣaḥrā* but is in effect the servant of the landlord.

Until relatively recent times labour service in men and asses was taken in Qā'ināt.   The late Shoukat ul-Mulk abolished it.

A special form of labour service known as *hashar* is levied in Sīstān for the making, cleaning, and repairing of irrigation channels.   Since most of the land in Sīstān is *khāliṣeh*, this labour service is levied by the government. Originally *hashar* may conceivably have been performed in part at least as a kind of public service and to have been a form of "self-help."   Whatever may have been the position in the past, however, no such conception attaches to it at the present day.   It has become a source of oppression, an occasion for bribery and corruption, an important factor in the prevailing decay in the area, and a cause of great discontent.   It is levied by government officials not only for irrigation works but also for the performance of all kinds of work including road-building, both in Sīstān and Balūchistān.[4]   Men have to be provided for this labour service by those who have the right to a share of the water, in proportion to the number of their shares, whenever called upon to do so by the officials of the government (see also below).

Another form of labour service is the duty to provide a certain number of loads of firewood, or camel-thorn.   This levy, which only survives in a few areas including parts of Āẕarbāyjān, is made upon the holder of a plough-land.

In certain areas, notably west Persia and Āẕarbāyjān, it is the common practice of landowners to levy per plough-land or per share of water (where the village land is divided in this way) a due payable in clarified butter (*roughan*) or in cash or in both.   This due is known as *sar juftī*.   The sum varies somewhat from village to village.   Collection is made on behalf of the landowner by the *kadkhudā* or by a collector (*ẕābiṭ*).   On a given day a crier is sent out to announce that the holders of plough-lands should bring their clarified butter on such and such a day.   In Dastjird and Sulaymānābād, near Hamadān, *sar juftī* consists of a cash payment and two loads of lucerne, one dry and one fresh, per annum.   In Asadābād, near Hamadān, it was levied in 1945 at the rate of 50–100 rs. (approx. 5s. 10d.–11s. 9d.), and 5–6 *manni tabrīz* (approx. 32 lb., 12 oz.–39 lb.) of clarified butter per annum.   In the Pushti Kūh area of Kangāvar *sar juftī* was levied in the same year at the rate of some 1 *manni tabrīz* (approx. 6 lb., 9 oz.) clarified butter, three hens, and 200 rs. (approx. £1. 3s. 6d.) per annum. In Kullīā'ī the rate was some 50 rs. in some properties; in others owned by the old-fashioned type of *khān* higher rates were taken.   For example, in 1945 it was alleged that there were cases of *sar juftī* being levied at the rate of 1,000 rs. (approx. £5. 17s. 6d.). In Kurdistān also a number of dues are levied in various areas, such as ½ *mann* (approx. 3 lb., 4½ oz.) clarified butter per plough-land, a number of hens and eggs, and a quantity of *dūgh* (a kind of whey) and butter, etc. In Hasanābād (near Sanandaj) three to four hens, ½ *manni tabrīz* (approx. 3 lb., 4½ oz.) clarified butter, and 100 rs. are levied per plough-land. In Dabbāgh, near Dīvān Darreh, the levy is five hens, 100 rs., and 1 *manni kurdistān* (approx. 5 lb.) clarified butter. In Dālān in the same area it is 35 rs. (approx. 4s. 1d.) and four hens. Similar dues are paid in the neighbouring villages. In Saqqiz some 50 rs., 1 *manni tabrīz* clarified butter, and one sheep are taken per plough-land. In the Kirmānshāh area *sar juftī* usually amounts to some five to ten hens, 1 *manni tabrīz* clarified butter, and some fuel. In Āzarbāyjān a number of dues were, and to a lesser extent still are, levied per plough-land or per share of water, as in parts of Qarājeh Dāgh. These include cheese, clarified butter, hens, eggs, lambs, kids, and money. In Hashtrūd a sum in cash is levied upon the peasant according to the area of land he occupies, or so much per head of livestock. The peasants in this area are of two kinds, *zāri'* and *gharībeh*. The latter, who are landless peasants, pay more per head of livestock than the former, who are crop-sharing peasants or tenants.

In the Kirmān area it is usual to provide one or two loads of firewood or camel-thorn a year and occasionally a number of hens per *juft*.

A poll tax[5] was formerly levied in most areas. It has now largely died out, but is still found in Āzarbāyjān.[6]

The entertainment of government officials and travellers in former times was a charge upon the inhabitants of the country through which they passed. In some areas a due is still levied by the landowner for this purpose. This is known in Āzarbāyjān as *qunāghliq*. A similar due is also levied in parts of Kurdistān and parts of Fārs. Elsewhere it survives only in isolated instances. For example, in Āb Shīrīn, a small place on the Qumm–Kāshān road, the proceeds of two *āb mīān*[7] were still set aside in 1945 to meet the expenses of government servants, visiting officials, and the *kadkhudā*.

Various other dues are still found in isolated areas. For example, in Kilaybar in Qarājeh Dāgh in one village the peasants provide the landowner with an annual due in partridges, which are caught in winter in the snow. In some parts of Kurdistān a due known as *sūrāneh* is still levied. This is a payment which the peasant makes to the landowner for permission to marry. This due illustrates the essentially personal nature of the link between the landlord and the peasant.

Formerly at the Persian New Year a due known as *nourūzī* was levied. This has been abolished in many areas, but in the more remote places and especially in the tribal areas, "presents" of sheep, hens, eggs, clarified butter, etc., are given to the landowner by the peasant according to their means. Occasionally a return of equal or greater value is given. In some of the more remote districts similar presents are expected on other occasions, such, for example, as the birth of an heir to the landowner.

In certain areas where the affairs of the landowner are looked after by a bailiff, usually known as the *mubāshir*, as distinct from the *kadkhudā*, he is often paid in part by the peasants. For example, in Hashtrūd a levy known as *takhteh* was formerly made for the *mubāshir*. It is now seldom made. Similarly when the landowner sends a collector (*ẓābiṭ*) at harvest time to a village to collect his share of the harvest, the collector usually lives on the country. This, in Sārī Chaman in Qarājeh Dāgh, the landowner's *mubāshir* visits the village at harvest time. His entertainment is a charge on the villagers, who also pay him a certain quantity of *roughan* and a number of hens. These, however, were stated to be the only extra dues levied on the villagers in that village. From the landowner the *mubāshir* received 1 *kharvār* (approx. 5 cwt., 95 lb.) grain. In Havīzeh 4 *manni havīzeh* (approx. 3 cwt., 85 lb.) is deducted from the total harvest on irrigated crops and 2 *manni havīzeh* (approx. 1 cwt., 84 lb.) on unirrigated crops for the *mubāshir*, where there is one.

Until recently in Sīstān there were *mubāshirs* representing the Ministry of Finance. Although they had no function after the distribution of *khāliṣeh*, they nevertheless lingered on for a period, receiving 6 per cent of the total harvest. In the *khāliṣeh* of Bampūr the *mubāshir* receives a small payment in cash from the government or the lessee; his main income derives from the plough-lands which he works himself and on which he does not pay the landlord's share.

In many areas the *mubāshir* and *ẓābiṭ* are paid entirely by the landowner. In Kirmān the *mubāshir* usually receives 10 per cent of the owner's share. In certain properties in Qā'ināt the *mubāshir* also gets 10 per cent of the landowner's share, or in the more prosperous properties, 5 per cent. In Gīv the *mubāshir* shares the 5 per cent with an official known as the *taḥvīldār*, who is virtually his assistant. At harvest time, further, a *ẓābiṭ* comes on behalf of the landowner to collect the crop in many areas in Qā'ināt. In Kāshmar in certain districts a *ẓābiṭ* is employed by the landowner for three to four months to collect the harvest. His wage is deducted from the total harvest.

The various dues mentioned in this chapter will give the reader an idea of the variety of practice which prevails. In many cases the actual amount of these dues is not heavy, but they reflect the continuance of a certain attitude of mind and of the survival of a certain type of social organization. Indeed, it is perhaps in the field of personal servitudes that the survival of medieval customs and even more of a medieval attitude of mind is most striking. Other aspects of land tenure, such, for example, as the crop-sharing system, may perhaps be partly justified on the grounds that the economic and social conditions which engendered them still persist. For personal servitudes there can be no such defence. The system of labour service was originally designed to meet political and social needs which no longer prevail and cannot be regarded as anything but an anomaly, while the special form which labour service takes in Sīstān is an enormity which may well make life intolerable for those upon whom it is imposed.

NOTES

1. In some areas this is known as *khari sīāh.*
2. In other words it is stipulated in the contract (which is usually a verbal one between the landowner and the peasant) that the latter shall give in addition to a share of the crop seven days' free labour, known as *haft nafar,* and four days' free labour of an ass, known as *chahār ulāgh.*
3. This is known as *gārā* in Dizfūf, and *shikarteh* in the Arab areas.
4. The argument put forward in support of, or rather to excuse the levy of, *hashar* by the government for public works, that the capital expenditure on such works is prohibitive, and that only in this way can they be carried out, can hardly be regarded as relevant.
5. Known as *sarāneh.*
6. The Democrats during the regime of Pīshehvarī (1945–6) forbade the levying of this and other dues. In fact, however, many of them have been reimposed and continue to be levied.
7. That is, a share of the water and the land irrigated by it set aside for a special purpose.

Buarij is a small, poor, and isolated Arab Muslim village, located near the crest of the eastern slope of the Lebanon Mountains. This inland village faces eastward toward Syria, and it overlooks that elevated tableland, the Bekaa. In one sense, perhaps, Buarij is an extreme example of the Middle Eastern fellah village, a situation aggravated due to the fact that the data for this report was collected mostly in 1937–1938 (although a brief visit was effected in 1945).

Anne Fuller has attempted, however, a unique approach to the temporal and spatial world of the fellah.. Few other scholars have employed such a technique, and her presentation is marked by a mature and sophisticated handling of raw field data.

Despite the changes that may be wrought in the life of the Middle Eastern peasant, Anne Fuller has established a certain philosophical foundation essential to the understanding of his subculture.

The Peasant World of Time and Space

ANNE H. FULLER

Time to the peasants of Buarij is conceived in qualitative and personal terms rather than in quantitative and abstract terms. Time is thought of not so much in fine-drawn lineal dimensions as in a vague conglomerate of which outstanding events are a part and of its essence, while the notion of time in itself as an isolated abstract entity has little significance. Since time is not conceived of primarily as lineal, entailing a notion of progress or change, the peasants in their general attitude towards life possess a peculiar patience or capacity to wait, believing that things will be revealed within the body of time, since events characterize and are part of time rather than that events can be forced through human endeavor. Certain periods of time or certain days are considered to be auspicious or unauspicious for the undertaking of or abstinence from specific events, or for personal welfare. Accordingly the character of time or its segments is conceived of as bearing influence on man, rather than he giving to it its pattern.

Past time in the peasants' minds fades off beyond the boundaries of their own memories. For three or four generations back, events are kept in fair chronological order. As time recedes, passing beyond the founding of the village, it tends to fall into the general category of "long ago," while the far past takes on the aspect of a golden age interpreted in terms of persons. It is the time of King Solomon and Alexander the Great, both outstanding heroes in Arab lore. These two figures are placed in the same general chronological epoch. Among the peasants it is not so much the quantitative divisions of time that are of significance as its qualitative and emotionally impregnated character. Towards the use of numbers the peasants have a similar qualitative and emotional, rather than a quantitative and analytical, approach. Figures in regard to persons, possessions, and cash are loosely used, except when accuracy benefits the peasant, conveying primarily an emotional reaction rather than any degree of exactitude. Accurate count, moreover, is connected with the demands of the tax collector, an unpopular intruder from the outside world.

The current passage of time among the villagers tends to be defined in terms of the objective world of persons, nature, and local events, which set a rhythm to village activity. Seasons are referred to more often than months in setting a date for outstanding festivals of the Muslim religious calendar or for specific village activities that have a definite time of occurrence, such as the grape harvest. The Christian calendar as well as the Muslim is recognized, its major feast days likewise establishing points of reference, since the peasants in their dealings with the outer world are inevitably brought in contact with Christians. If designating months, the peasants rely on the Christian calendar rather than the Muslim, since the Christian solar count coincides with the seasons or with the basic and visible rhythm of the peasants' agricultural life, while the Muslim calendar in contrast, based upon a lunar count, annually falls eleven days behind the solar year. The Christian calendar, moreover, is the recognized official calendar for business transactions, particularly in dealings with the outer world, its use promoted through French mandate control and through Christian predominance in larger business affairs.

Among the peasants, the age of a child is seldom given in years but is said to be similar to that of a kinsman or neighboring child. The day is rarely broken into the abstraction of numerical hours, but its divisions are designated in terms of the passage of the sun or the moving of shadows thrown by the mountains on the plain below. Or the call to prayer from the village mosque is used as a mark of temporal reference. Watches and clocks are possessed by only a few households and are primarily a symbol of the owner having been to the city. They are regarded more as an ornament similar to a ring or piece of household adornment than as a mechanical means of designating time. When used, they are most often handled in the traditional Muslim and Byzantine manner—each evening reset at the point of twelve to coincide with the moment of sundown, time being conceived of as related to natural order and natural phenomena rather than as a numerical abstraction.

Space likewise is conceived of largely in organic and personal terms rather than in numerical abstractions, and receives its most clear-cut definition within the rimmed world with which the peasants have visual and firsthand personal experience. As firsthand familiarity with the spatial world fades off, so in direct ratio does any exactitude of measurable spatial concepts. Spatial measurements, furthermore, are largely given in terms of human activity entailing time duration, although the official metric system is known and referred to by those persons most familiar with the outer world and its marked routes and highways.

The spatial world with which the peasants are most familiar is that rimmed world which they view from village slopes. Within this rimmed world of space, outstanding past temporal events are given fixed locations. Noah's Ark is said to have landed on top of Mt. Knisseh on whose slope the village lies. King Solomon is said to have built the Roman temples of Baalbek situated to the north upon the plain. At the foot of Mt. Hermon across the plain lies a buried treasure of Alexander the Great. Thus the era of the golden past is drawn closer at hand by fixing it within known spatial surroundings.

This fusion of past temporal events with known spatial dimensions tends to reinforce lore by localizing it. It gives the past a living background, so making it the more vivid. It brings the past closer to daily experience, for as the peasant feels more at home within his own community, so he feels closer to past temporal events if given spatial setting within the orbit of his own visible horizon. By drawing the noose tighter about time and space the peasant himself secures a firmer place within the flux of events. Like the boundaries of his own village, which give him security, he also finds boundaries to space and time. The very fact that it is difficult to conceive of space and time apart from village existence and tradition acts, moreover, as a cohesive factor relating the peasant more closely to his environment and establishing the commnunity as a center of gravity. To the peasant the village is the measure of life. Although a small military airport lies upon the plain below the village and although aircraft can be seen making their descents or ascents, no villager has visited the air base, a two-and-a-half-hour walk from the mountain home, since curiosity is seldom evinced towards matters that bear no relation to village ways.

The peasant's notions of time and space, personal rather than abstract, qualitative rather than quantitative, and the habit of locating outstanding temporal events in familiar settings bear relation to similar temporal and spatial concepts common to the ancient Near East. And it would appear that this way of conceiving of time and space is a strand from a remoter period of thought which has persisted through the centuries and still persists among the peasant population.[1]

Yet the peasants of Buarij, despite a habit of personalizing time and space concepts, are not without a knowledge of the larger world and its occurrences. There is the shadowy mysterious story of the sinking of the Titanic and the mountain of ice. There is the tragedy of the Czar of the Muscovites and his innocent children. There is political knowledge drawn from the personal experience of soldiering. There is the current knowledge of political events in Beirut and Damascus and a general sense of the main trend of events in neighboring countries, although these tend to be reported and viewed chiefly in terms of leading personalities. There is an interest in district elections in which the adult men participate. Here again the interest is in personalities rather than in broader issues. There is the local district paper that comes to the village store. There are the moving pictures witnessed by the men in the larger towns. There are the radios in town coffeehouses.

Yet despite this broader horizon, traditional and local lore continues to lie at the roots of peasant life and plays the more intimate role, giving shape to and preserving the village pattern. Because much of this tradition is localized in a time-space configuration, it is the better ingested and kept alive, while other events in contrast tend to be ephemeral or less concrete in character.

About one-third of the adult village men are literate. But since the accomplishment is not commonly utilized it often falls into atrophy. Only one adult woman can read. She has been lame since early womanhood and her resort to literacy, a late accomplishment, is in part a compensation for her handicap. Village children of the present generation presumably attend the village school up until adolescence. Instruction is extremely rudimentary and attendance irregular. The few girls who attend drop out within a year or two since forms of formal education are not considered to benefit a woman's life. The schoolhouse is a simple one-room building, its wooden benches and sloping ink-stained desks signifying the preoccupation with letters; for according to the villagers every occupation has its proper tools, the two intimately related.

Reading matter, despite the presence of a local newspaper and simple school texts, with short paragraphs on Edison and Lindbergh, remains primarily traditional and sacred. Although school children learn that "the world is round like an apple," chanting it in unison from their school texts, it is the Koran and its context that remains the book of books. Folk tales and legends of early Arab heroes are also popular. A literate member of the community may read aloud to village members on a winter's evening; or the holy writ and hero tales are recited from memory. There is also the common body of village lore handed down orally from one generation to another—the story of the cruel winter when wolves came down from the mountain heights and invaded the village. This has become exaggerated until it is told that a village hero rode off on a wolf's back throttling it with his own hands. Then there is the tale of the sheep thieves from the outer world. And the recitation of the years of starvation following the First World War, when women weakened by hunger crawled on all fours, searching the slopes for wild greens for their dying children. Lesser stories of sprites and spirits, some encountered by the villagers themselves, are recounted, along with folk sayings, riddles, and the singing or reciting of village or local folk songs and verses. Despite possible means of access to a larger body of literature, the peasants prefer to draw upon that which has been and is part of their local tradition, is most related to their own way of life, and which serves to strengthen and support it. In so doing the peasants' minds are continually nourished by an order that has already been established.

Although the world that lies within village boundaries and which can be viewed from village slopes is that with which the peasants are most familiar, the village inhabitants are not without firsthand knowledge of the world that lies beyond the visible horizon. Older men served in the First World War in various parts of the then Ottoman Empire. There are the few men who spent some years in South America. Aside from the men who as sharecroppers work on the landed estates on the plain below the village, there are those who leave the community in the slack of the agricultural season to find work elsewhere on the coastal plain or in other regions. Village herdsmen, moreover, must take the flocks across the range to the warmer Mediterranean coastal area for winter grazing. All these persons, however, return to the village or are expected to return. A wife with grown children still awaits the return of her husband who went over twenty years ago to Argentina. It is primarily because of economic reasons that men leave home in order to augment family incomes. It is primarily because of sentiment that they return.

This deep-rooted sentiment stems from the feeling that whatever may be the momentary economic advantages of the larger world, ultimate security, not necessarily dominated by economic forces, exists and persists within the village orbit. For here there are always kinsmen and people of one's own blood to whom the peasant may turn. Here is the plot of land enduring through generations. Here is the familiar world which, through lore and tradition, has nourished the peasant since childhood. Here within the village is an emotional form of security not found elsewhere. The village is conceived of as the ultimate place to which the peasant belongs.

Village women have far less experience with the outer world than men. The spatial orbit of their lives is primarily confined to village homes and fields. Occasionally a young girl previous to marriage goes into domestic service for a short time in Beirut. But this is regarded as unfortunate and usually pertains to a widow's daughter. Twice a year or so women may go in groups, or accompanied by their men, to buy necessary household supplies at the town of Zahle, the district center, a three-hours' walk.   A small minority have travelled the sixty miles east of Damascus, by bus or train, usually to buy wedding furnishings.   Almost all adult women have gone at least once to Beirut, an hour's distance by bus.   Certain of the women follow their kinsmen or husbands to the coast for winter grazing.   Women, however, never leave the village boundaries unaccompanied, except to the nearest foothill settlements. These missions always involve some necessary task such as obtaining medicine from a foothill pharmacy or transporting grain on donkey back to the foothill water mill for grinding.   The missions are never excursions of frivolous pleasure or sightseeing.

Women themselves have little interest in mingling and mixing with the larger world.   They complain of headaches from the noise and confusion on return from visits to the towns.   They feel ill at ease outside village boundaries, for since childhood a woman has had instilled within her that her place is at home.   Here surrounded by kinsmen, especially her father and brother, a woman is sure of protection.   In her own community a woman has status and security; outside its boundaries, unaccompanied and alone, she can be certain of neither.

Because women are more closely identified with the spatial and personal boundaries of the community, it is their sex which is the most familiar with the details of village lore and village gossip.   It is likewise their sex which is the main repository and transmitter of village tradition and lore.   Since women play the greater role in child-rearing it is they who most affect the education of the child, transmitting and impressing upon it a traditional view of life. Women are the conservative factor in the village influencing the overall tone of the community.   It is their sex which tends most to promote the feeling and concept of the village as a world in itself.   Since they do not leave the community freely and only rarely accompany their men on the latter's longer sojourns from home, their confinement to the village is in itself a strong influence in drawing men back to the community and in maintaining the village as the permanent focal point.

Men are inevitably affected by their participation in the larger world. Their conversation, in contrast to women's, includes far greater reference to the outer orbit, its political happenings, the general state of the crops, the chances of employment, and news of any unusual event.   Yet on return to the village from beyond its borders men easily fall back into the general pattern of village ways.   Even the men who have spent several years in South America fall back quickly into the village pattern.   With their earnings they may enlarge an orchard or vineyard or build a new house.   But their lives in no way appear to be perceptibly altered by their sojourn abroad.   Only the watch that no longer runs, a batch of colored postal cards, or an out-dated picture calendar are tangible evidence of their years in foreign parts.

Since childhood, persons have sensed that the village is its own world. Conformity to village ways brings approbation, while without group or kinship approval personal security diminishes. Thus the peasant on returning home falls into the village picture in order that he may be provided with the forms of security the village affords. Yet it is through men's contact with the larger world that changes in the village most readily accrue. New types of dress or tools are introduced. New ideas sift down. Nevertheless, the weight of tradition tends to stand against sudden or radical change.

Concepts of time and space—and the manner of regarding both in personal rather than in abstract terms—relate to the general outlook of the peasants which is primarily personal. Interest in temporal events, past and present, is selective and personal in accordance with the peasants' body of general knowledge and experience. Excursions into the larger world are of limited influence, since the peasants judge the outer world by the personal standards of their own village. The village itself is a personal world, its tradition and lore handed down orally from one generation to another, with its people, related by blood or marriage or a combination of the two, laying emphasis primarily on the personal ties that link peasant to peasant. Within this known world of persons the peasant feels most at home.

NOTES

1. For so Pedersen has pointed out the qualitative rather than the quantitative aspects of time among the ancient Hebrews, where "time is charged with substance . . .; time is the development of the very events." (Johanes Pedersen, *Israel, Its Life and Culture*, I–II [London, 1926], p. 487.) Frankfort, in referring to concepts of space in the ancient Near East, has observed that ". . . primitive thought cannot abstract 'space' from its experience of space." (Henri Frankfort *et al.*, *Before Philosophy, the Intellectual Adventure of Ancient Man* [Penguin ed.; London, 1949], p. 30.) The mythopoeic mode of mind permeating early Near East thought still lingers among the villagers and in terms of primary orientations towards the surrounding world.

"Nomads," according to Professor Coon, "like cowboys, are more glamorous than numerous." Except for Saudi Arabia they form a minority in every Middle Eastern country. The ecology of the Middle East is such that perhaps 90 per cent of the land is arid, barren, and largely unpopulated. The primary population groups that do exist in this expanse are nomadic herdsmen. Carleton Coon, an outstanding physical anthropologist, archaeologist, ethnologist, and Middle East authority, has provided a clear and concise description of selected nomadic populations and their way of life.

9

◇◇

The Camp in the Desert

CARLETON S. COON

We have seen how important geography is in determining the location of villages, their spacing, and the ways in which their inhabitants are able to trade with urban centers. This exercise can be carried further; we can divide the entire Middle East into three principal geographical components on the basis of the suitability of each for occupation. These are the lands suitable for sedentary village and urban life, the lands unfit for human occupation on any basis, and those in between, where human life can be supported if the inhabitants are equipped to move around, either seasonally or at the whim of the rain, or both.

The in-between lands again fall into three categories: the habitable portions of deserts, of mountain pastures, and of steppes. In each case the

From *Caravan* (1958), pp. 191–210; reprinted by permission of Holt, Rinehart and Winston, Inc.

transition from village land to pasture is gradual, and consequently transitional economic systems are also encountered in each. The animals available to the nomads of these three kinds of terrain are the same: the camel, the horse, the ass, the ox, the water buffalo, the sheep, and the goat. These are the same animals available to the villagers, and except for the camel and water buffalo, they go back far into Middle Eastern antiquity.

The nomadic peoples of each of the three kinds of terrain have found different combinations of these seven animal species to be best suited to their purposes. Their experience has been based on the interplay of a number of considerations, aside from the value of the animal as a source of wool or hair, milk, and meat. These are its feeding requirements, its resistance to thirst, its resistance to cold, its traveling speed, its tractability, and the amount of load it can carry. The camel is thus the animal par excellence of the open desert, and the horse of the steppe. The sheep, favorite of the villages, is also suitable for slow nomads on the edges of cultivation in both desert and steppe, and for mountain pastoralists who make but two shifts a year, between the chill upland meadows and the warmer plain.

The deserts of the Middle East belong to two separate categories. The Sahara and the Arabian deserts are of the Plateau and Dune type, while the deserts of the Iranian plateau are of the Mountain and Bolson variety. In the former the landscape consists of plateaus of varying height, with some mountains and many deeply eroded, dry valleys. Part of the desert is covered by huge stones and other parts with sand, but most of it is merely rubble. During the winter months rain falls on the desert in varying amounts and with great seasonal variability. The higher plateaus and mountains usually receive more rain than the lowlands, all else equal, but in the parts of the deserts between the westerly and monsoon storm tracks, the rainfall is negligible, regardless of altitude. The Libyan desert and the Rubʻ al-Khāli are the two driest places. Elsewhere thunderstorms scatter moisture erratically, and the dry wadis run with flash floods. In the wadi bottoms the underground water table is often high enough to be reached by the roots of date palms, and wells furnish water for camels as well as for some patches of irrigation. At one time or another, large sections of the Sahara and Arabian deserts support the animals of nomads.

The Mountain and Bolson type of desert is far less hospitable. The Iranian plateau, including most of Iran and Afghanistan, consists of a rim of mountains enclosing a series of basins, and in the hollow center of each basin is a desert, the Dasht-i-Kavir, Dasht-i-Lut, and Dasht-i-Margo. These basins get no rain whatever. Water from the westerlies descends on the crests of the surrounding mountains. That which falls on the outer slopes runs off in short streams to the oceans and seas, but the share of the inner slopes drains into the desert basins, where it becomes saline and alkaline and unfit for drinking, even by camels. Hence land suitable for nomads is scarce and limited to southeastern portions of the outer rim of the plateau (except for the Indus gap, this country joins onto the Thar Desert of Pakistan, which is of the Plateau and Dune category), where the rainfall is too scant for agriculture, and to the country around the Helmand mouth.

In the three separate parts of the Middle East which will support them, we find three different aggregations of camel nomads: the Baluchi and some of the Brahui in Baluchistan; the Bedawin in Arabia; and the Berber-speaking Tuareg, along with other Bedawin from Arabia, in the Sahara.[1] As might be expected, all of these possess a number of traits in common, and these traits distinguish them sharply from most villagers.

The village has an optimum size, which remains constant from season to season and from year to year. The camp of nomads, however, has not one but several optimum sizes which vary greatly by seasons and may even vary in the same season of different years. Both the villager and the nomad lead hard, healthy, out-of-door lives, but the activities of the villager are repetitive and cyclical while those of the nomad are erratic. The villager knows what is going to happen each season, each day, and each hour; his calendar has been prearranged for hundreds of years. The nomad does not, and consequently he must be more alert.

Unless he is a mountain tribesman and his home has natural defenses, the villager does not like to fight. Even if he lives on flat, open country he will defend his home bitterly if the need arises, but he finds it easier to pay tax or tribute than to suffer the loss of his crops and livestock, for he is extremely vulnerable. On the other hand, vagaries of weather throw nomads into fierce competition with each other and survival depends on warfare. The nomad is a warrior, with all the pride and aristocratic bearing that this profession denotes.

The village has a simple organization. Areas of conflict have long since been defined by custom, and leadership is loose and informal. The camp has a more complex system because it includes several categories of people, and leadership must be firm and decisive because life depends upon it. The warriors, particularly those of leading families, develop a pride of race and a concern for the purity of their breeding, a matter of relative indifference in the village.

The amount of ethnographic information available on the nomads of these three areas varies greatly. We have more on the Bedawin than on any other people in the Middle East, and four excellent monographs on the Tuareg, but on the Baluchis and nomadic Brahuis very little indeed. This is a pity, since these last-mentioned peoples very likely were the first to develop a camel culture in the desert. What we know about them refers chiefly to a period a hundred years ago and more, when the British, who were worried about them, sent out a number of army officers to investigate.

Brahuis and Baluchis may be considered equivalent peoples, in that each

maintained political independence until within the last century, and each consists of a number of tribes, graded into more and less noble categories on the
basis of birth order within their traditional genealogies. In each the leading or
most aristocratic tribe refuses to give its daughters in marriage to outsiders.
The tribes are divided in *kaums*, or camps, each with its local chief, who may
or may not have a fixed headquarters in some fortified place furnished with
permanent water.

Each kaum has its regular territory and its seasonal camping places where
its members pasture their animals. They live in black tents, said to be covered in some cases with felt,[2] although the ones I have seen were made of
woven goathair, like those of Bedawin. No one would think of making a black
tent for use in a northern latitude, because black is supposed to absorb the
heat. But the nomads of the Middle East all use black tents. Why? The answer is that they move about much by night and like to sleep or sit under cover
by day. They pitch their tents in such a way that it gets the maximum of
ventilation needed. Whatever else is wrong with the desert, it usually has a
breeze. Being loosely woven, the goathair cloth allows air to pass through,
and becomes tight and rainproof when wet. The air in the tent moves, and
hence absorbed heat is no problem. Light, however, is a problem, particularly
ultraviolet rays. The thick, black material of the tent keeps out all light, and
the nomad, his wives, and children can rest in the shade, which is actually
cooler than outside, and much cooler than the interior of a translucent, breeze-
choking tent made for the camping trade.

Those Baluchis who are still nomadic (in the Indus Valley and India
many have settled down as landlords, landlords' agents, and mercenary soldiers) make two principal moves a year, to the higher country of the interior
in summer and to the lower coastal regions in winter. In the late autumn they
butcher a number of animals and preserve the meat by sun-drying and smoking over fires of green wood. They also convert milk into cheese and ghee,
which like the meat will keep through the lean season. Their women convert
surplus wool into rugs, blankets, and felt carpets for sale.

Each of the Baluchi tribes was headed by an amīr who, while holding
executive authority in time of war, served as the moderator of a tribal council,
in which all freemen were entitled to speak. The camps into which the tribe
was divided for purposes of pasture each had its *sirdar*, or leader, who decided
when and where to shift, and on the conduct of *chapaos*, or raids. The sirdar
had his guest tent in which he entertained travelers, at common expense.

Aside from stockbreeding the Baluchis protected the villages of Persian-
speaking farmers for which they were responsible and raided those for which
they were not. They conducted merchants through their individual territories
as guides and guards, for a fee, and under their protection caravans had little
trouble. Their raiding grounds reached west to Yezd, east to the Indus, and

north to the Helmand. Their favorite weapons are the rifle and the sword; a hundred years ago their amīrs would send emissaries as far as Istanbul to buy sword blades and matchlock barrels, although good ones were made locally. The warrior wore a shield of rhinoceros hide between his shoulder-blades, and he might even carry a bow and a quiver of blunt arrows, for hunting birds. Between raids the warriors exercised with martial games, and by hunting. One sport was for the horseman, at full gallop, to pierce a stake lightly driven into the ground with the tip of his lance, and carry it away. They also coursed salukis after gazelles, and a good saluki would sell for three camels or even more. Hawking was another of their pastimes.

The warriors of a camp would spend much time planning a chapao down to the last detail. Under the command of their chief they would set out on camels, leading baggage camels and mares for the final dash, and leaving their stallions to avoid whinnying. They took rations of dates, cheese and bread, and water in leather bags. Riding to the neighborhood of the victim village, they would halt in a thicket or lonely canyon to rest the camels, and as soon as the inhabitants were believed to be asleep, they would dash in, burning, destroying, and carrying off whatever they could find. They would keep this up, moving from village to village, riding eighty or ninety miles a day, until the baggage camels were loaded, ten or twelve to a man, and then they would return home via a different route.

This was dangerous work. Some were killed, others caught and mutilated, while still others died of fatigue. Some of their camels might be lost, others might die of overexertion. Sometimes the victims would be alerted and waiting for them, but now and then they struck it rich, and each man would get several thousands of rupees and a number of slaves.

These slaves were of both sexes. Once captured, they would be blindfolded and tied on the camels, so that they could not tell where they were taken. The raiders shaved off the women's hair and the men's beards and rubbed the scalp and beard skin with a quicklime preparation to kill the follicles, and thus to discourage the slaves from wishing to go home. Many of these slaves were sold to the north and east, while a few were kept around the camp as workers. The Baluchis themselves were thus able to concentrate on their martial exercises and hunting.

Among the Baluchis we now see a dual division of labor, in the first place between the tribesmen and their subject villagers, which provided vegetable foodstuffs in return for protection, and in the second between the warriors in the camp and their slaves, who did the routine work. A third is between the warriors and the trading caravans, which they protected for a fee, and a fourth between the Baluchis and various kinds of specialists whom they considered beneath them socially and hence not to be harmed. These were the Hindu traders, who brought the products of the cities, and the Loris or Dōms, a gypsy-like people who served in the camps as blacksmiths, tinkers, musicians, and serving maids. Having a safe-conduct and the entree to the women's quarters in the camps, the female Dōms acted as go-betweens in the initial prospecting for marital partners for the sons of their masters.

A fifth arrangement was with the holy men who formed settlements of their own and traveled about with the camps, always ready to be called on to officiate at a funeral or to write an amulet for a sufferer. Many of these claimed the rank of sayyid, or descendant of the Prophet through 'Alī and Fāṭima. When a particularly holy one died, his clients would build a tomb over him, and he thus became a pīr. As time went on, his reputation would increase. If his tomb were beside a spring, then he was believed to have brought that spring forth from the rock with a stroke of his lance. Litigants would travel to his tomb to swear oaths over his grave, and so great was their fear of his retributive power if an oath should be false, that each party would be satisfied with the other's truthfulness.

This is a complex social system, and nothing could illustrate better the ethnic mosaic of the Middle East. Being situated between large centers of population which in themselves are varied, the Baluchis had many sources from which to draw. The Bedawin, however, have achieved an equal complexity from a smaller ethnic pool. This in itself demonstrates that the complexity is a matter not of chance but of necessity.

Bedawin occupy most of the Arabian peninsula, except for the Rub 'al-Khāli and its northward finger of the Nafūd, the agricultural lands of the Yemen, 'Asīr, Ḥaḍramaut, and Oman, the cities of Ḥijāz, and the palm orchards and shipping centers of Kuwait and al-Ḥasa. The Bedawin discussed here are those living north and west of the Empty Quarter. Those between Ḥaḍramaut and the sea, and in the Qara hills, are a different people with their own culture. The northern Arabian desert lands occupied by the Bedawin with whom we are concerned stretch across the pipeline where Jordan and 'Iraq join wings, into Syrian territory. Damascus and Baghdad and the semi-circle of cities between them all stand on the edge of Bedawin territory, and owe part of their prosperity to trade with these nomads.

In the world of the Bedawin permanent water may be obtained on the banks of rivers, particularly the Euphrates, and from wells. Some of these wells are in the open desert, while others support oases. During the rainy season, from October to March, local showers may create pools which will remain for a week or two, and in the wadi bottoms it is often possible to reach water for several months after these rains by digging shallow pits. During the summer, from the first of June until the end of September, everyone who lives in the desert is obliged to camp near permanent water, for in this season camels must be watered every day because of the lack of moisture in the tinder-dry perennials which form their fodder and because of the heat. After the rains fall, succulent annuals grow rapidly, and the desert air is filled with the sweet perfume of their flowers. Camels need water only once in five days in the fall, and at much rarer intervals in the full flowering of the springtime. Then the Bedawin can move their camps farther and farther from the wells, since only they need daily water, and expeditions of a few men can be sent several days' journey to fetch it.

The storms which bring the rain do not distribute it evenly. Watching a thundercloud and the flashes of distant lightning, the Bedawin will send scouts to locate the rainfall, and then race to reach it. If the only livestock in the camp are camels and horses, he will attain his goal. If encumbered with sheep, however, he might fail, although he could afford to keep sheep if he were content to stay on the edges of the desert or in a few favored places where the rain is sure. Like the Persian villager in Baluchi territory, the shepherd is a fat but sitting duck.

These environmental considerations provide one of the axes on which the Arab of the desert bases his complex classification of his fellows, whom he divides into two broad categories, sedentaries and nomads. By sedentaries he means both the full-time agriculturalists and traders who live in the oases and along the rivers, and the transhumants. The transhumants are people who own or rent tillage and houses, plant cereal crops with the first rain, and then drive their sheep a little way into the desert for the winter. In April or May they come home for the harvest and pasture their sheep on the stubble.

The nomads he further divides three ways, into the *Badw* or *A'rāb*, the *'Arab ud-Dār*, and the *Shawaiya*. The *Badāwi* or *A'rābi* (singular of the words given above) is a camelman. Since sheep would hinder his mobility, he does without them. He spends the summer months camped about his wells or near the bank of a stream, and the rest of the year out on the desert. These people are the true Bedawīn (a word used only by non-Arabs) about whom many books have been written. The *'Arabi ud-Dār* (literally "House Arab") is a man who owns sheep as well as camels. In the fall he leads his flocks out into the desert after the fashion of the transhumant, from whom he differs in that he does no planting.[3] His summer camp is located near a town or city, where he can avail himself of its permanent water; he may also own a town house which he occupies during the season, and visits at other times.

The Shawaiya, who are the shepherd tribes proper, are highly specialized people. In the northwest they include principally the Shararāt; in the northeast Colonel Dickson identifies three separate groups, belonging to the Muntafiq confederation.[4] The shepherd tribes spend the summer at permanent water and in winter take their sheep to the usual places, riding mostly on asses. They are quite expert at their work and serve other tribes and townsmen in two ways: by taking out other people's sheep on contract and by acting as individually hired shepherds with tribes such as the 'Arab ud-Dār.

The second axis of the Badāwi's classificatory system is kinship. He divides all desert tribes into two groups: *'Asīlīn,* of pure origin and blood, descended from the patriarchs Qaḥtan and Ishmael; and all others. The pure of blood themselves represent two lines, the *'Arab al-'Araba* (Arab of the Arabs)[5] who go back to Yarab ibn Qaḥtan, who lived before Abraham, and the *'Arab al-Musta'riba* (Arabs by Having Become Arabs), relative upstarts descended from Ishmael, son of Abraham and Hagar, the daughter of a king of Ḥijāz. The 'Arab al-Musta'riba include the tribe of Quraish, and hence the lineage of Muḥammad. About eighteen tribes or tribal confederations belong to this closed circle of 'Asīlīn and these include the 'Anaza with their famous branch the Ruwalla, the Shammar, the Āl Murra of the borders of the Empty Quarter, and the Bani Khālid.

As the inclusion of the Quraish indicates, desert residence and pure camel nomadism are not necessary qualifications. Most of the 'Asīlīn are desert Bedawin because, away from the towns, it has been easier for these to keep their lines pure and because the concept of the pure family line is essential to their way of life. The townsman can be a success without a pure lineage—or can hire someone to fabricate it for him. Hundreds of thousands of Middle Eastern Muslims speak Arabic who are not, in this sense, Arabs.

The A'rab marries his father's brother's daughter, and if no such first cousin is available he will make sure that his wife is of equal status. Although the Badāwi marries and divorces several women either in a series or simultaneously or both, and a woman can expect to have several husbands, all mates are members of this closed corporation.

The 'Arab ud-Dār are not excluded from it, if they belong to the right tribes. In fact, in Kuwait if not elsewhere, it is common practice for well-to-do members of this group to receive their desert cousins in their town houses and to take the latter shopping, as well as to introduce them to the higher society of the city. Some of the permanently city-dwelling Arabs who hold high offices in the various governments also belong to the elite, as do most if not all Arab kings, and they are extremely proud of it. As a physical anthropologist I have been called upon a number of times, in cities, to comment on the Bedawin-like features of my hosts and associates.

Arabs who are beyond the pale and who cannot mix genes with these aristocrats are much more numerous and as a rule worry as much or as little about it as do we Americans whose ancestors may not have come over on the *Mayflower*. These non-aristocratic people are far from homogeneous. They include every category based on occupation which we have so far mentioned— camel nomads, shepherd tribes, 'Arab ud-Dār, transhumants, farmers, and traders. They also include three classes of people whom those just named would themselves refuse in marriage, Ṣulaba,[6] smiths, and slaves.

The Ṣulaba are members of a small ethnic community, living scattered in groups of one or two families usually attached to a camp of camel nomads. The Sulaba ride on asses and pitch small, threadbare tents just outside the camp. They serve as desert guides and are skilled hunters. They are also coppersmiths, repairing the Bedawin's vessels; woodworkers, charged with making wooden bowls and repairing well pulleys, saddles, and the like; and leatherworkers. Their women dance publicly and are said to be not above prostitution. (There is a story that in the summer, when the Bedawin are crowded about their wells and river banks, the Ṣulaba head for the open desert where they uncover secret sources of water and hold high jinks and a merry time. I cannot vouch for its truth.) Many Arabs are convinced that these people are descendants of the Crusaders, because some are said to be blond; to the anthropologist they and the shepherd tribes look like the oldest inhabitants of the desert.

The smith (*Ṣunnaʿ*) are a group of ironworkers, who have their own kin and are reputed to be of partly Negro origin, although this is not always evident. A family of smiths is attached to each noble tribe, and calls itself Ṣunnaʿ al-Muṭair, or Smiths of the Muṭair, etc., just as some of the gypsy tinkers in England took the name of their protector and became Lees. They act as farriers, swordsmiths, and gunsmiths—shoeing the mares, repairing the weapons, beating out the tent stakes of their hosts and thus sparing the latter a trip to the town, and making it possible for them to keep on fighting in a critical moment. To the Badāwi at war, the smith is a vital member of his company.

The slaves are Negroes brought from Africa, and their descendants. Every princely household and the chief of every tribe have them. The slave wears fine clothing, is fed of the best, even when his master goes hungry. He will fight for his master bravely and has much to do with the upbringing of his master's sons. He also is chief of protocol in the guest house or tent; the visitor from foreign parts will do well to keep in with the slaves. His master may set him free, and he may marry among the freedmen group in the towns, or the daughter of a smith.

The Badāwi splits his human world on still a third axis: whether or not the man and his group will fight. All of the ʿasīlīn tribes fall into the fighting class; if they fell out of it and became tribute payers to their erstwhile peers,[7] their blood would not avail them, and the chances are that it would soon be found in some way impure. Some of the non-ʿasīlīn Badw tribes are also fighters, as for example the Rashaida, hereditary retainers of the shaikhs of Kuwait and bitter foes of the Saʿūdi family. The wars between Rashīdi and Saʿūdi were unusually bloody, because the rules of chivalry which are followed in combats between two aristocratic outfits do not hold when one or both sides are outside the blood particular.

The nonaristocratic camel breeders who pay tribute instead of fighting perform a special service in the complex desert economy. They hire themselves out to the fighters as camel herders, leading the flock out to pasture, bringing it back, milking the she-camels, and going after water. Being noncombatants, no one will touch them, and their employers and the employers' slaves can spend their time guarding the flocks if danger is expected, guarding the animals sent for water, guarding the camp, and scouting for new pasture and for enemies.

The first-class Badāwi is thus more of a soldier and a policeman than a camel breeder. He has two other obligations of this order. One is protecting refugees from other tribes—those refugees who come to him in a prescribed ritual manner and who need shelter until they can get to safety outside the desert, or until compensation for their disturbance has been arranged and they can go home again. The other is giving travelers safe-conduct across the tribal territory, from border to border.

Both these obligations operate on the conceptual basis of *wejh* (face). A man's face is his honor. If his honor is clear and unquestioned, his face is white. If someone dishonors him, his face has been blackened and he must take steps to restore its color. The more important a free, fighting man, the greater his face. Weaker individuals or strangers who, though strong elsewhere, find themselves outside their home territory, have the privilege of demanding protection under the face of a great man, and were he to refuse it, no matter what the circumstances, his face would darken several shades. A traveler must ask permission to cross tribal territory. The shaikh who grants it assigns to the stranger an *akh* (brother), who accompanies him from border to border. The penalty for violation of protection, once granted, is death. The guest is sacred. This concept is of great importance in the development of caravan routes and trade. Without them, indeed, the deserts could not be crossed.

As to who will and will not fight, some of the sheepowners and shepherds fall in either category. Those who have driven their flocks down to Kuwait and Sa'ūdi territory in the fall from their homes in 'Iraq buy protection from ordinary raiding, but if war comes, weakening the authority of their protectors, the shepherds will drive their flocks back again out of season, provided they receive warning. If caught unawares, or warned too late, they will fight as desperately as anyone else, and they are armed with good rifles and carbines. The 'Arab ud-Dār sheepowners similarly try to avoid trouble, but they will fight to defend both their own property and that of their masters, the shaikhs of the towns where they live in summer.

Nor are all of the sedentary people pacifists. Some form parts of tribes which have settled on the land, and although they may not be sought out as bridegrooms for the camel nomads' daughters, they still retain their tribal organization and obey their shaikhs. If the desert tribes raid them, they will fight back, often with success. They count some noble blood, including that of the Sha'lān, paramount chiefs of the Ruwalla. If the settled people live in a small oasis, however, they have little chance of resistance and usually become tributary to some camel-raising chief. If the oasis is larger the chief may establish his court there, and if he conquers other tribes he may establish himself there as a king.

It will be remembered that the sedentaries include merchants as well as farmers. We have already noted that in Oman merchants go out into the palm groves in season, to sell to the pickers. The same kind of enterprise is shown toward the camel breeders. The Badāwi cannot be expected to leave camp during the height of the season merely to ride back to the city on a shopping trip, nor can he be certain of buying a full season's supply each summer—during his visits to town, or from the dozens of tents set up near his camp by enterprising shopkeepers who pay for the privilege.

A certain class of shopkeepers even go out to the winter camps. These are the Kubaisāt, named after the town of al-Kubais on the Euphrates, whether they come from it or not. The Kubaisi leads a couple of camels, laden with merchandise, to a winter camp far out on the desert. He sets up a round white tent, easily distinguished (in case of trouble) from the black tents of the camp members. He pays the shaikh for the privilege of trading in the camp, and his gift may amount to one complete change of clothing. He sells small objects: bolts of cloth, braid, candles, sugar, and hardware, and will give the Bedawin credit at the modest rate of twenty-five per cent interest. The shaikh sees to it that debts are paid, for he does not want to lose his handy shop in the desert.

A much more high-powered kind of merchant is the 'Aqaili, the agent of one of the three or more big business houses, with offices in Baghdad, Basra, Damascus, Cairo, and elsewhere, who buys up camel futures. He is called an 'Aqaili because he is usually a member of the tribe of 'Aqail and comes from the town of al-Qāsim. He too comes out on the desert with his baggage animals, bringing cash and rifles as his stock-in-trade and taking in return priorities in camels. He too is protected by the shaikh, who gets a fee for every camel purchased. The 'Aqaili also pays off another clan member, whom he calls "brother." This brother is responsible for the care of the camels bought by the 'Aqaili, and their delivery at the beginning of summer. The 'Aqaili brands each camel bought with the mark of his firm and then moves on to the next camp.

Both the Kubaisi and the 'Aqaili belong to non'asīlīn tribes, and both are noncombatants. The same is true of the heads of the export-import houses for which the 'Aqailis work, who may send their sons to the American University of Beirut and to Oxford and who could buy out several shaikhs many times over. Of the people who may be found in a Bedawin camp, five classes —camel herds, Kubaisis, 'Aqailis, Ṣulaba, and smiths—are noncombatants. If a rival band raids a Bedawin camp early in the morning, only the shaikh, his male kin, and their slaves, are in danger, for they alone are fighters. The women will not be touched, nor the children. The smith will pound his anvil louder than ever, to make sure that no raider mistakes him, and the Ṣulabi camped in the nearby draw will come out cringing to offer his services to a new master. The Kubaisi will prepare his tent for the next stand, and if an 'Aqaili is present he will locate the brother who represents his firm among the raiding party, to make sure that of the captured camels about to be driven away, those with his company's brand will be delivered as previously contracted.

Thus life goes on, and the free Badāwi who follows the noblest of the professions—camel breeding, who belongs to the cream of the land, genealogically speaking, and who crowns his nobility by his willingness to fight with his peers over pasture and camels, pursues his stirring, eventful, and often brief career. His may seem a simple life, and in a sense it is, but it is also the keystone to a complicated arch, each stone of which may be equally simple.

In a country where nature itself has made life difficult and travel dangerous, the order of values placed upon human skills, competences, and specializations reflect these perils. Most honored of all is the possession of the best means of transport, the camel and the pampered mare, along with the ability to produce more of the same and the courage to fight off rivals and to protect travelers and the members of vital professions. No man can be a craftsman or trader, and a fighter too, else he would lose his immunity and his life, and the Badāwi his services and goods. The Badāwi is willing to risk his own life in battle to preserve a system which gives him a chance to survive. He is unwilling, however, to risk the lives of others whose absence would render his own life on the desert impossible. This delicate balance between the classes of people who make up the desert population, this system of calculated risks and laissez-faire, with glory to the brave and safety in humility, is the key to the social structure of the Middle East as a whole, which it mirrors on a smaller scale.

The third and largest piece of desert suitable for camel nomadism is the Sahara, and our third example of a nomad society is that of the People of the Veil, the Tuareg. Until 1920[8] when the French finally took this duty away from them, they policed the desert. Breeding camels and selling them to the caravan men, providing desert guides, fighting off rival bands, defending the caravans which paid for this service against their rivals, and providing forage for the merchants' camels, they made trade possible between the Sudan and North Africa.[9] To maintain themselves as specialists they too had to have a complicated set of service institutions protected by a number of fixed social attitudes governing their mutual relations, as in the case of the Bedawin.

West of the Tibesti, which houses another kind of people, the Sahara contains four principal plateaus: the Azjer, Ahaggar, and Adrar Ahnet (reading from east to west), and in the south, the Aïr. Each of these contains sources of permanent water. The Adrar Ahnet, which is the driest, has exactly thirty-three such sources. Each of the other three contains patches of land capable of cultivation, while the nearby oasis of Belassa provides the Adrar Ahnet people with cereals. Wheat, barley, and millet are the principal crops of these small but fruitful areas, along with onions, gourds, melons, and a few figs and grapes. Each of these four natural ecological areas also contains one or more uninhabited oases where the Tuareg go in season to harvest dates.

The domestic animals of this area are principally camels, asses, sheep, and goats, with some long-horned cattle in the Ahnet, and very few horses. The Tuareg seem even more skillful at camel riding than the Bedawin. They have developed a special breed of riding animals, and mounted on the females, they can maneuver them well enough to attack with lances. While the Arab is accustomed to leap from camel to mare, and to fight with a saber on horseback, the Tuareg's special manner of fighting is to jump to the ground and duel on foot, clad in mail, protected also by a huge, rectangular bull-hide shield, and fighting with a long, straight, two-handed and two-edged sword of Crusader type. The warriors practice this style of combat interminably. With their lean muscular bodies, and spider-long arms and legs, they develop great speed, mobility, and skill.

Each of these four natural regions is the home of a separate Tuareg confederation. A confederation is a group of noble tribes with their various dependents and protégés. Each tribe has its own government which, Berber style, consists of a council, ruled by a chief, the *amghar*. The paramount chief of the confederation is known by the title *amenokal;* his authority does not prevent the tribes under him from mutual raiding in times when no danger threatens all. As with the Bedawin, the amenokal must come from a certain family and be of pure noble blood.

On the north the Tuareg are separated from the fertile regions of North Africa by mountains and by relatively barren stretches of desert. The Atlas ranges are steep and dry on their southeastern faces. Contact with sedentary Berbers and Arabs, then, is inhibited by geography and is limited to the inhabitants of oases, like Ghardaia, Tuat, and Tidikelt, which are too large to raid—beside which plundering them would be killing the golden goose. On the south, the desert gradually shifts to grassland, and the grassland to park land, and eventually forest.

This is the Sudan. It is rich in grain, rich in cattle, and rich in people. The latter are mainly Hausa Negroes, some Muslim and some pagan. In their country there are several cities in which Arabs also dwell, and the Negroes are organized into a number of kingdoms. The rulers of these kingdoms tax their subjects and raid the more distant tribes for goods and for slaves. Here the great trans-Saharan caravans are organized, and here the Tuareg come to trade. They also come to raid in the open villages between cities—or so it was at the time the Tuareg were still functioning, up to the latter part of the nineteenth century.

The eyes of the Tuareg, then, were turned to the rich and open south, and their backs toward the land of their closest kin, the Senhajan Berbers of the Middle Atlas. Being warriors, the Tuareg had no time for handicrafts. They outfitted themselves almost entirely with the products of the Sudan— blue cloth for their clothing; the skillfully woven black veils worn, like the Arab's kufīya, to protect their lungs from fine particles of sand; all kinds of metalwork and leatherwork, including lances, swords, daggers, shields, saddles, and bags; wooden boxes; cereals including durra and rice; salt and dried cheeses. From the northern oases their purchases were limited mostly to dates, tobacco, tea, and sugar, with now and then fine weapons. Firearms, of course, also came from the north.

In return for these products the Tuareg gave livestock, ghee, and trade objects from the opposite side of the desert, including, of course, goods received as fees for their services, and cash. While the Tuareg used slaves and sold a few, they were not primarily in the slave business. Their trading in human as in other forms of merchandise was essentially for their own consumption, and they did not compete with the merchants whose caravans they protected.

The Tuareg themselves are divided into two hereditary classes, *Ihaggaren*, or Nobles, and *Imghad*, or Vassals.[10] This division is as old as the camel nomad heritage of the Tuareg themselves—sixteen centuries at the most. The Ihaggaren trace their descent from a woman named Tin Hinan, who came from Tafilelt and was buried at the confluence of the Wad Tefift and the Wad Abalessa, in the Ahaggar.[11] The Imghad go back to Takamat, Tin Hinan's serving-woman, who first came with her and was buried beside her. Both were Tuareg, both were white Berbers. The Ihaggaren, to whom it is particularly important, have memorized their genealogies and can recite them, like the noble tribesmen in Arabia. They trace their descent through their mothers, for theirs is a matrilineal society. The Tuareg women, who have little work to do because of the abundance of domestic help, amuse themselves by singing and reciting poetry and by writing the same in *tifinagh*, their curious archaic alphabet, a relic of the old Libyan unciform script. These noble dames take great pains to raise their children to have good manners and to teach them, especially the girls, to make music and to read and write.

The relationship between the noble tribe and its vassals is not quite the same as that in Arabia between warrior and tributary tribes, nor is it identical among all Tuaregs. The Imghad, who are much more numerous than their masters, are encouraged to pasture their camels on the best land; their masters want them to get rich. In the tribes of the Ahaggar confederation, apparently each noble has his individual vassals within the opposite number of his tribe's Imghad, and the tribute is paid from person to person.

Apparently the reason for this difference is that the Ihaggaren see their Imghad at close quarters twice a year. In the winter the nobles are out on the caravan road, at their stations. In the summer they are living in the high plateaus, feeding off their agricultural tenants. In fall and spring they camp among their Imghad and consume the products of their herds, while replacing their riding and baggage camels with new stock.

Among the Adrar Ahnet tribes, which seem atypical in a number of other ways as well, an elder of the noble tribe collects from the Imghad tribe as a whole. Each tent of Imghad pays one unit of dates per year to the nobles collectively, and if they have been unable to send their yearly caravan to the oasis that year to harvest the dates, the entire tribe pays a fee of twelve camels, or ten Negro slaves.

Ordinarily the Imghad do not initiate warfare on their own, but have been known to raid when placed in tempting situations. Their primary job is one of supply, but they too have slaves to do much of the detailed work. The Ihaggaren take Imghad with them to fight on big expeditions, and the nobles are obliged to protect their vassals at the cost of their own lives. The Imghad, however, will not sit meekly by; they also know how to defend themselves.

Also requiring protection are the agricultural serfs who provide vegetable food for their masters and for the Imghad. These people are Negro *Ḥarātīn*, part of the general oasis population of the Sahara, brought to the plateau by the Tuareg landowners and lodged in adobe houses and straw beehive huts. Like the hired help among the Berbers to the north, they receive a fifth share of the produce for themselves. Some of them are also skilled welldiggers, whom the Tuareg employ to maintain the permanent water supply.

In the Ahnet country a further complication is caused by the presence of two small tribes of Arabs, specialists in caravan work, who pay the nobles a small fee in dates and cloth. This permits them to camp among the Ahnet, who will defend them, and it gives them full protection on the caravan road which the warriors of this confederation police. In the eastern confederations specialists of another kind receive protection from all tribes, for no one will harm them. These are the families of *murabiṭīn,* or holy men, whose ancestors had obtained their hereditary *baraka,* or magical power, in some miraculous way. The murabiṭīn can read and write Arabic and recite the Qur'ān. They draw around them small companies of junior murabiṭīn, who travel with them, studying whatever branches of medieval Arab learning the master can teach. These men go from camp to camp, teaching the children the elementary knowledge usual in the Muslim *kuttāb* elsewhere, writing charms, healing, and conducting ritual. They are the equivalents of the sayyids among the Baluchis. No one will lay a hand on their holy persons, and when trouble arises between tribes and confederations, they hie to the tents of the leaders and to the councils, to offer their advice and services as peacemakers. (According to our authorities, their efforts at times were successful.)

So far we have discussed Ihaggaren, Imghad,[12] agricultural serfs, Arab tribes, and holy men. Two other categories remain, slaves and smiths. The Tuareg were in an excellent position to select the best slaves that passed through their hands for their own use. Each noble woman had one or more female slaves for the drudgery of cooking and cleaning, fetching water, baby sitting, and collecting wild vegetable food. They waited on their mistresses hand and foot. Male slaves tended the flocks for nobles and Imghad alike and served as guards in the camp. Each noble usually had one favorite slave in whom he placed full confidence, sending him out as messenger, arming him, and taking him into battle. Such slaves usually repaid this attention by great loyalty and ferocity in combat.[13]

From among the available female slaves the young noble would pick one notable for her comeliness, strength, and good disposition. She would become his concubine, traveling with him wherever he went on the long and weary expeditions and offering him the comfort of her "cool" black skin. Sooner or later he would marry a woman of his own class and hue and would give her the children needed to perpetuate her line. This, however, was an expensive undertaking, and under the circumstances it could wait until the young noble reached his late twenties or even thirties, when he could afford to spend longer intervals in the home encampment. Meanwhile any children born to his concubine would rate as slaves, for "the belly holds the child," as the Tuareg say. He might set them free, but they would have no rank.

The blacksmiths hold exactly the same position among the Tuareg as in Arabia. They set up their movable anvils and forges in the camp of noble or Imghad, collect their due, and move on when they wish to serve a new client. They are partly Negroid, but not black like the slaves. They will not fight, nor will any one harm them. They marry their own kind, and no one else wants their daughters. At Tamanghasset the traveler can see a large cemetery of ancient tombs, and these are said to be those of a tribe of smiths, massacred or wiped out by starvation.

The Tuareg system is just as complicated as those of Baluchi and Bedawin, but different from both, just as the two first described differ from each other in emphasis and detail. In all three, however, we find a noble, dashing group, whose members spend their time in martial games, the chase, and war, protecting their sources of food and equipment and raiding each other's, relegating to slaves and servants the drudgery of material existence, and policing the roads. Each in his own fashion provides for the perpetuation of his own inbred and highly specialized branch of the Mediterranean race. One detail in particular is common to all three. The maker and mender of arms and tools, the basic artifacts on which both warfare and all material culture depend, has an international passport. He is so low in popular esteem that no one will touch him, and his reward is bare subsistence. But he does his job as well, in his own cultural situation, as the lords of steel in ours, who sit at high table in the banquet of the West.

NOTES

1. The Sahara also contains Beja and their subgroups, the Bisharin and Heden-doa, Kushite-speaking "Fuzzy-Wuzzies," who live between the Upper Nile, south of Aswan, and the Red Sea. Being Sudanese and Ethiopian in cultural affiliation, they fall outside the range of this work.
2. Pottinger, *Travels in Beloochistan and Sinde*, p. 61.
3. There seems to be a little confusion between Musil and Dickson in the classification of sheep raisers. Musil used the word Shawaiya to designate the kind of people Dickson calls 'Arabdar (properly al-'Arab ud-Dār), and classifies the shepherd tribes, such as the Shararat, as Bedawin of inferior status. See Musil, *Manners and Customs of the Rwala Bedouins*, Monographs of the American Geographical Society, No. 6 (New York, 1928), pp. 603–605, and Dickson, *The Arab of the Desert*, pp. 108–113. Some if not all of this difficulty may be explained by the fact that Musil wrote about the northwestern nomadic area. Dickson's highly informal Arabic transliteration has been changed to conform with George Rentz' corrections in his review of Col. Dickson's book in *The Muslim World*, XLI, No. 1 (1951), 49–64.
4. These are the Albū Ṣalāh, the Ajwād, and the Beni Malik. Dickson, *op. cit.*, p. 545.
5. Also known as *ul-'Arabā* and *ul-'Arabuyya*.
6. This plural is also rendered as *Sulubba* and *Slaib*.
7. Most or all have paid taxes at one time or another to one or more governments. This presumably does not count. Ibn Sa'ūd, by calling his tax zakā, saves the tribesmen under his control the humiliation of tribute.
8. Henri Lhote, *Les Touaregs du Hoggar* (Paris, 1944), p. 337.
9. E. W. Bovill, *Caravans of the Old Sahara* (London, 1933), p. 25.
10. A much more accurate translation than the usually rendered serf.
11. This historic monument was dug up by an "archaeological" expedition in the 1920's and the bones of Tin Hinan removed.
12. There were also a few small tribes of *Irajenaten* of half-noble, half-Imghad origin, exempt from tribute but shorn of a voice in the government. These are only casually mentioned and were not essential to the system; if anything, the reverse.
13. The French, who have replaced the Tuareg, used their Senegalese troops for the same purpose.

This section on the Arab tent is characterized by careful detail and accuracy.. H. R. P. Dickson comes to this task unusually well prepared. He was born in Beirut in 1881 and, as an infant, was taken to Damascus where his mother's milk failed early. A bedouin girl from the 'Anizah tribe was volunteered to serve as his wet nurse or foster mother. To drink a woman's milk in the desert is to become a child of the foster mother and, as Dickson records, "This fact has been of assistance to me in my dealing with the Badawin of the high desert and around Kuwait."

10

◇◇◇

The Tent and Its Furnishings

H. R. P. DICKSON

A Badawin tent or *bait al sha'ar* is made up of strips of black or brown coarse cloth known as *fala'ij* (plural: *filján*). These are woven from goats' hair or from sheep's wool, never from camel hair, so that the name "camel hair tents" is a misnomer. The length of each strip used, and the number of such strips, naturally depends on the importance and circumstances of the owner. An average shaikh, for instance, will have a tent of, say, six extra-broad strips, each seventy feet long and supported by four poles, while a poor man may have cheap narrow strips to his tent, each twenty-five feet long, with only two poles, possibly with one.

The true Badawin shaikh does not go in for bigger tents than the one described, as his movements from camp to camp would be hampered thereby.

From *The Arabs of the Desert*, pp. 66–83; reprinted by permission of George Allen and Unwin, Ltd.

Among the leading Shaikhs of the 'Anizah and Northern Shammar, such as ibn Sha'alan, ibn Hathal, Ajil al Yarwar and also among Arabian princes like the Al Sa'ud, the Shaikhs of Bahrain, Kuwait and Qatar, tents of enormous size are the fashion.   These, however, are practically used only when the owners are going out for the spring months to certain standing camps, from which they will sally forth and hunt gazelle, or hawk *hubara*.   They would never be used for migration purposes.

To return to the tent: the strips are all sewn together so as to form one long rectangular whole, and are then raised up on the tent poles (*'amdán*) and the sides stretched taut by means of tent ropes (*atnáb*).

The tent is then divided, usually by two or three long and gaily decorated curtains, known as *qáta* (pronounced *gáta*), which hang on the tent poles inside the tent to a height of some six feet from the ground.   They have their ends attached to the roof at the back of the tent, and to the roof and the tent ropes on the open side respectively.

Each *qáta* has one of its ends especially gaily decorated. . . . This decorated end must face outwards on the side of the tent which is open. If the wind changes, and the reverse side of the tent is used, the *qáta* must be taken down, turned round and refixed.

The number of tent ropes which support a tent in front and rear depend on the number of poles the tent has.   Opposite each pole there will be two ropes, one in front and one behind, so that a tent of three poles will have six ropes (three on either side).   Apart from these front and rear ropes, the two ends of the tents are kept stretched out taut by six other ropes, three at each end.

On the reverse side of each tent and stretching well round so as to shut in the two open ends, and with enough material to spare to close them at night from the front, are two long stretches of cloth known as *ruag*, made up of four narrow strips each, which join in the centre of the reverse side of the tent; these are attached to the tent sides by a series of bodkins known as *khillal*.   The whole then hangs down in the form of a heavy curtain which, where it meets the earth, is buried in the sand for its whole length, or pegged down if the ground is hard.

The lowest strip which always is covered or buried in sand is of inferior material, as it gets most wear and damage from white ants and rain.

We thus have in the completed pitched tent the following main parts:

(*a*) The roof of the *bait al sha'ar* consisting of six strips *filján* (singular: *fala'ij*) joined together.

(*b*) The poles *'amdán* (singular: *'amúd*).

(*c*) The partition curtains *qáta*.

(*d*) The two rear curtains *ruag* joined together at centre of the back of the tent and stretching round the two ends.

(*e*) The tent ropes *atnáb* (singular: *tanb*).

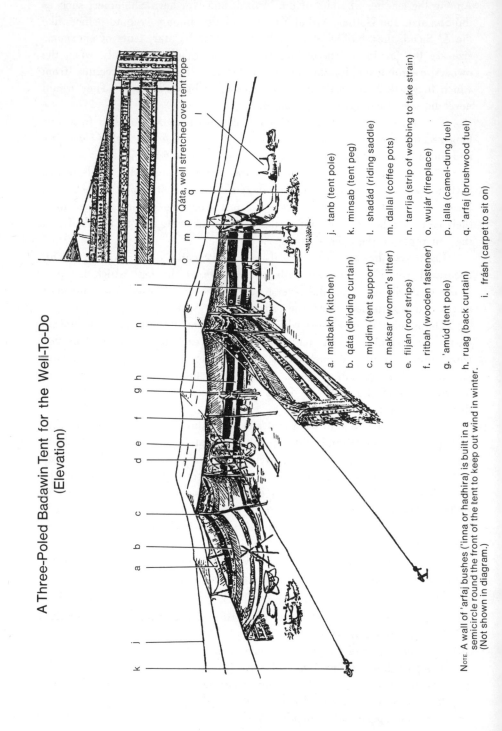

A Three-Poled Badawin Tent for the Well-To-Do
(Elevation)

Qáta, well stretched over tent rope

a. matbakh (kitchen)
b. qáta (dividing curtain)
c. mijdim (tent support)
d. maksar (women's litter)
e. filján (roof strips)
f. ritbah (wooden fastener)
g. 'amúd (tent pole)
h. ruag (back curtain)

i. frásh (carpet to sit on)

j. tamb (tent pole)
k. minsab (tent peg)
l. shadád (riding saddle)
m. dallal (coffee pots)
n. tarrija (strip of webbing to take strain)
o. wujár (fireplace)
p. jalla (camel-dung fuel)
q. 'arfaj (brushwood fuel)

NOTE. A wall of 'arfaj bushes ('inna or hadhira) is built in a semicircle round the front of the tent to keep out wind in winter. (Not shown in diagram.)

A Three-Poled Badawin Tent (Elevation)

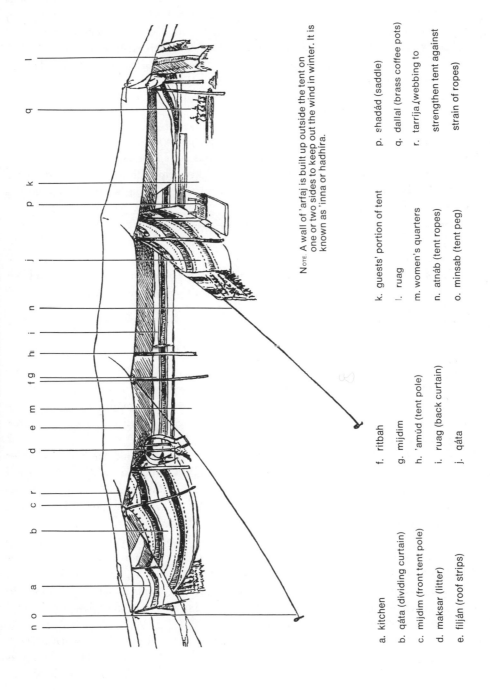

NOTE. A wall of 'arfaj is built up outside the tent on one or two sides to keep out the wind in winter. It is known as 'inna or hadhira.

a. kitchen

b. qáta (dividing curtain)

c. mijdim (front tent pole)

d. maksar (litter)

e. filján (roof strips)

f. ritbah

g. mijdim

h. 'amúd (tent pole)

i. ruag (back curtain)

j. qáta

k. guests' portion of tent

l. ruag

m. women's quarters

n. atnáb (tent ropes)

o. minsab (tent peg)

p. shadád (saddle)

q. dallal (brass coffee pots)

r. tarrija (webbing to strengthen tent against strain of ropes)

The Qáta or Dividing Curtain

Patterns commonly found on Mutair and 'Ajman *qátas*, or the curtains which divide the tent, together with the particular names under which they are known, are given below. Although the number and name of each strip always remain the same, the actual pattern on each strip varies according to the tribe, and the time that is given to the making of each strip. This in particular applies to strips (1), (2) and (3).

The *qáta* or divide is composed of four strips sewn together as under, and commencing from the top.

(1) The first strip or *saif* is all black with pattern (*a*) in the centre and pattern (*b*) above. Width: one span plus four fingers.
(2) The second strip or *al ghadir* is a white strip with a one-inch-wide black border in the centre of which is pattern (*a*). The width of *al ghadir* is two spans.
(3) The third strip or *al ba'ij* follows below *al ghadir*. Its upper half is black and lower half white with pattern (*c*) in the centre. Width: also two spans.
(4) The fourth and last strip is *al muta'ba*. This is the lowest piece and lies along the ground. Its upper half is white and its lower half light or dark brown. Width: two spans.

The Ruag (or Back Curtains of a Tent)

These consist of four strips sewn one on top of the other horizontally so as to form a long narrow curtain. Below is given a pattern very commonly used in the Kuwait and Hasa desert. The well-to-do-man goes in for handsome black and white *ruags*, while the poor man practically always confines himself to plain brown or black ones.

These four strips are sewn together and placed round the back and sides of the Badawin tent. The patterns vary slightly, some are without the second white strip. A coarse piece is woven and sewn along the bottom edge. This goes on the ground, and is usually covered with sand to weigh it down. The shade of brown varies according to the wool available.

The weaving of the tent material is largely done by the inhabitants of the towns and villages bordering on the desert, and both in Kuwait and the neighbouring hamlets of Jahrah and the Qusur a good trade is done in this commodity. This does not mean that this work is not largely done in the tribes themselves, but the best qualities and strongest materials for shaikhs' tents probably come from the towns.

Actually every humble tribal woman makes and renews the worn parts of her own tent, and only those with means go into the towns to buy. This was confirmed to me by Rifa'a, wife of Shaikh Thuwairan abu Sifra of the Mutair

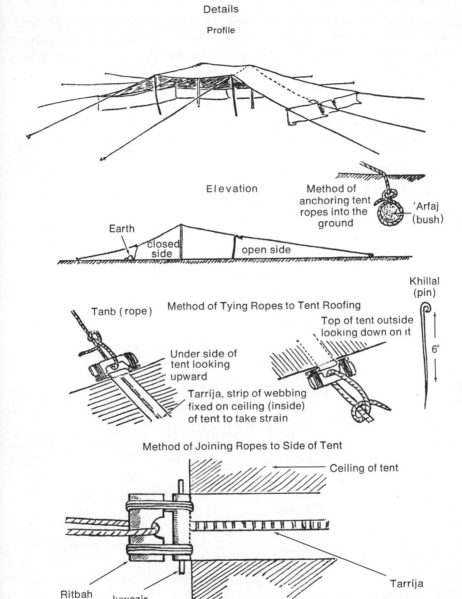

Details

Profile

Elevation

Method of anchoring tent ropes into the ground

'Arfaj (bush)

Earth

closed side

open side

Khillal (pin)

Tanb (rope)   Method of Tying Ropes to Tent Roofing

Top of tent outside looking down on it

6"

Under side of tent looking upward

Tarrija, strip of webbing fixed on ceiling (inside) of tent to take strain

Method of Joining Ropes to Side of Tent

Ceiling of tent

Ritbah   Juwazir

Tarrija

Ceiling of tent

in 1934, and by many other women. The best and most sought-after material is made of goats'* hair alone. It is jet black and is thicker than that made from sheep's wool. It also looks better. A good and favourite material is also of goats' hair and sheep's wool mixed. It has a streaky brown and black appearance and is handsome also. A noticeable feature are the tent ropes. They are made very long, on the principle of a ship's anchor, better to take the strain. These ropes are attached to the ground by wooden pegs if the ground is firm, but if the soil is sandy the practice is to dig a hole two feet deep, tie the end of the rope round a bundle of *'arfaj* and bury the whole in the earth. An excellent anchor is thus formed, and a rope so treated rarely comes away. When a man first buys a tent, he purchases the poles separately,

* Probably the best are made by the Bani Lam tribe near Amara in Iraq.

A Three-Poled Badawin Tent for the Well-To-Do

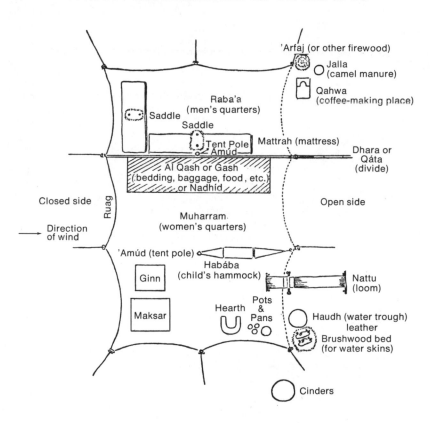

NOTE. In Eastern Arabia the Raba'a (the men's portion of the tent) is always at the eastern end. In a stone or mud house the men's portion is known as Al Diwániyah.

next the necessary rolls of tent strips of the lengths he requires, then the *qátas*, ropes, side poles, etc., and lastly the back curtains.

He then hands the tent strips to his women, who start sewing them together under the experienced eye of one of the older women. Much skill and care is needed to sew up a tent so that it stands straight and does not give way at any of the seams, which are carefully drawn together and sewn with extra-strong all-goats'-hair thread.

After the tent roof has been put together the *tarríja* (plural: *tara'ij*) has to be sewn on from side to side on the underside to support the poles and take the strain of the ropes. These are extra-strong white-and-black patterned strips 6 inches in width (like the Indian *nawar*). Immediately over the spot where the roof bears on the tent poles, two strips of wood are sewn into the tent roof, each 1½ feet long, so as to prevent the tops of the poles tearing open the roof. Each wooden strip is called a *gatba*. These wooden strips are not evident to the naked eye as they are rolled sausage fashion into the tent roof where the centre strips join. Each pole is placed exactly under the centre of the wood, and when in position does not damage the tent cloth. In the north proper holes are made for the tops of the poles in the tent ceiling, but not so among the tribes of Hasa and Nejd.

Lastly the *ritbah* (plural: *artáb*) or semicircular wood fasteners have to be sewn on to the ends of the *tarríja* on which the ropes are fastened to the tent sides. This is a very important operation, as there must be no weakness here. The ropes (always thick hempen ones) are now tied to the tent and everything is ready for pitching.

The pitching process is always done by the women, assisted by servants and slaves, occasionally also by a young son. It is supposed to be the women's particular job in life. The head of the family (*rai al bait*) directs the operation, and it is surprising to see how every person has a particular task allotted to him or her, knows it and sticks to it at every tent-pitching. The daughters of the house, for instance, usually do the hammering in of the pegs with the long stone instrument known as *al fihr*, while the menservants attend to the poles and supports, etc.

The following are the orders the owner of the tent gives to his women and servants in the form of a regular drill, addressing individuals by name. Of course they are accompanied by a lot of chat and talk which need not be detailed here.

(1) "Spread out the tent *ya 'aiyál*" (O my people) (from its rolled up position when taken off the camel's back).

(2) "Stretch out the ropes *ya auládi*" (O children) (so that they are at right angles to the tent).

(3) "Anchor the rope ends in the ground *ya fulan wa fulan*" (O So-and-So).

(4) or "Drive in the pegs and wind the ropes round them *ya Nasir* "

Diagram of the Qáta

First strip or saif

Width: 1 span
and 4 fingers
or
approximately: 12 inches

(b) Pattern

(a) Pattern

Second strip or al ghadir

2 spans
or
approximately
18 inches

(a) Pattern

Third strip or al ba'ij

2 spans
or
approximately
18 inches

(c) Pattern

Fourth strip or al muta'ba

2 spans
or
approximately
18 inches

4 inch
height

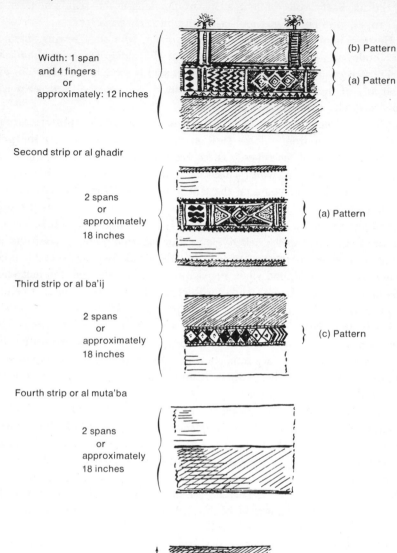
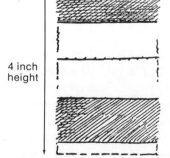

(5) "Tighten the ropes *ya Hussa, ya Wadha.*"

(6) "Take a pull on the end ropes *ya Marzuk, ya Nasir.*"

(7) "Affix the *majadím*" (frontside support-poles). This is done on the side away from wind.

(8) "Raise the centre poles"—the men's job.

(9) "Raise the back side poles and remaining end side poles."

(10) "Now lay to and take a pull at all the ropes once more."

(11) "Now *rawwagu al bait*," i.e., attach the *ruag* or back and side curtains, and cover the lower edges with sand to keep them down.

(12) "Now affix the *qáta* or partition curtains."

(13) Lastly, "Spread out the carpet and the *dawáshaks* and get ready the women's and men's portions of the tent." Women's quarters centre and left (*margad al harim*), men's quarters right (*margad al rijál*).

The tent is now fully pitched and the women place their treasures and stores in the centre portion of the tent, including their litters (*maksar, ginn,* etc.), sleeping gear, blankets, food, etc., and transfer to the end compartment the cooking pots, cooking utensils, etc., turning it into a sort of kitchen.

Men's Portion of the Tent

In the men's portion of the tent are then unrolled a well-worn carpet or two, the best *dawáshaks* (mattresses), to sit on, and the master's own camel saddle covered with white or black sheepskin. Pillows (*masanad*) are placed on both sides of this camel saddle, and also behind it for the guest's back to rest on, and generally the place is turned into a neat guest chamber for anyone who may come. The master now hangs up his rifle on a hook attached to the tent pole in the guest chamber, and prepares a fireplace to make coffee in the centre of the floor by digging out a shallow circular hole (*wujár*). This done, he gets out his row of three coffee pots (*dalla*), also a fourth "stock" pot, and lays them alongside the fireplace, together with the *mahmása* (coffee roaster) and *yed al mahmása* (coffee-berry stirrer). Last of all he places in position the *shat finajín* (brass case for coffee cups) alongside the *yed wal háwan* (brass pestle and mortar), the *mubarrad* (wooden slipper for cooling coffee beans), the *mukhbát* (wooden peg for stirring the hot coffee), the *lifa* (coir piece to stuff into the coffee-pot's spout), and finally the *makhbár* (incense burner). All is now ready to receive a guest, except that the actual coffee beans, the cardamum seed to mix with the coffee, the firewood (*'arfaj* bush) and the *jalla* camel manure (in place of coal) and the drinking water, is round in the women's part of the tent or outside it, and will have to be fetched.

As a guest is seen arriving these last necessities are brought and by the time he sits down, firewood, *jalla*, etc., all are ready to hand.

The scheme of things in a poor Badawin tent is the same, only everything is on a very much more modest scale—in fact, according to his purse.

A man leaning on the guest saddle is said to be *murtachi*; if he leans his back against a cushion (*masnad*), he is said to be *mutasannad*. If he tells a story he sits cross-legged; when eating he kneels on his left knee and sits on his left heel; his eating hand works outside his right upright knee; when he washes his hands he squats with knees wide apart.

A Three-Poled Badawin Tent

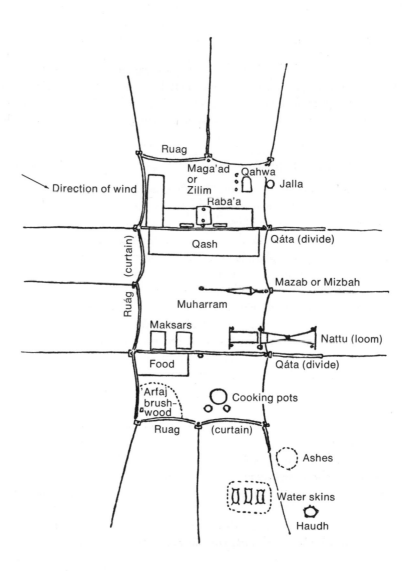

Women's Portion of the Tent

Women and servants (if any) carry all cooking utensils, etc., into the women's apartment and cooking portion of the tent, the heavy baggage and bags containing rice, flour, dates, salt, sugar are stored up against the *qáta* curtain dividing the women's from the men's apartments. The camel saddle-bags are then hung up on the tent poles, as well as other odds and ends, including the owner's spare rifle and ammunition. Red *laháfs* or quilts, which take the place of blankets, are then rolled up and placed on top of the stores, and the woman of the house and her daughter's decorated *maksars* (litters) are placed in a prominent position on the other side of the tent, so as to be seen by passersby.

Not the least important of the women's treasures are the spindles (*maghzal*), with which the womenfolk in their spare time spin camels' or sheep's wool. These they are forever whirring, whether on the march or on camel back; indeed, the *maghzal* would seem to be almost part of the *Bada-wiyah*. The method of spinning is as follows:

The spinner keeps the wool she is spinning under her right arm, or in her bosom, while with her left hand she prepares the wool to be spun some two feet in length, ties it to the lower end of the spindle pole, and thrusts it under the hook fixed to the top of the spindle head. Next she raises her left knee (she is sitting at the time) and, placing the lower end of the spindle pole on it, she sharply twists the spindle handle on her knee with an outward move of the palm of her hand. This causes it to spin sharply. Next moment she holds the spinning spindle aloft in her right hand by means of the wool. When this latter has got a sufficient twist on it, she winds the completed wool round the underside of the spindle head. The other most important article of the women's quarters is the hand loom (*nattu*) on which all the cloth parts of the tent are woven or replaced. Mother or daughter keeps the loom in constant action: they are never idle, these desert women. Treasures such as money, coffee beans, cardamum, sugar, salt, silks and special holiday attire are kept by the housewife locked up in a small tin or wooden box. The key of this she always keeps on her person, and tied to a portion of her head veil or *milfa*. This key is one of the first things that catch the European's eye when talking to a Badawin woman.

Close to, but outside the women's quarters, and away from the guest compartment, lie the filled water-skins (*garab*), which for coolness' sake are always placed on a thick mattress of *'arfaj* bush. Near these are kept:

(*a*) The small leather bucket and rope (*dallu*) for drawing water out of wells, with or without the cross-piece of wood in the centre to keep it open, and

(*b*) The large leather bucket or bath (*haudh*) standing on its curved wooden legs, from which camels and sheep drink. Both *dallu* and *haudh* are usually bought by the owner of the tent when he comes up to Kuwait or other town to do *musábilah*; in the same way he buys his goat water-skins which have to be renewed fairly frequently.

(c) The still larger camel water-skin or *ráwi* for conveying water from wells that may be distant.

Last, but not least, the *mirjahah* (or tripod) with goatskin hanging below it ready to make *leben* (sour milk) with, or, if necessary, to hang a sheep's carcass on, preparatory to skinning it.

Position of Tent with Regard to the Wind

Tents are always pitched with one of their long sides facing in the direction of the wind. Hence in the eastern and north-eastern part of Arabia, where there are two very common prevailing winds, the *Shamál* (north-west wind) and the *Kaus* (south-east wind), it is the general rule to see black tents pitched with their longer axis facing towards the north-west. This does not mean that tents are opened towards the side from which the wind is blowing—the contrary is the case, and the side of the tent is always closed in the direction from which the wind is blowing, and the sheltered side opened.

The side which is open is called *wejh al bait* (the face of the tent), the closed side *guffa al bait* (the back of the tent). Should the wind suddenly change, as often happens during the rainy season, it is necessary for the inhabitants of the tent to change the "face" of the tent at once. Otherwise the wind gets under the tent, billows it up, and if it does not carry it away, at least causes the tent poles to fall and lets the tent then collapse upon its occupants. A sudden change of wind therefore means confusion and lots of shouting. The owner's first and immediate orders are, "Change the back wall, my children, the wind has come," or in Arabic, *Jaina al hawa, dabbaru al bait ya awaladi*. The excited women and servants thereupon rush about, drop the front bamboo supports (facing the wind), quickly unpin the back curtains and carry them round to the side from which the wind is blowing, and again as quickly pin them on to the tent roof, and bury their bottom edges in the sand; the side poles are next put under the edge of the tent roof facing away from the wind, each under a rope, and lastly the tent partition curtains are taken down, reversed and fixed up again with the embroidered ends extending out of the tent and thrown back over the tent ropes. The whole process takes a surprisingly short time.

Of course, in very hot weather the Badawin wants to take advantage of the slightest breeze, so he rolls up the back curtain or unpins several yards of it so as to let portions of it lie on the ground: the breeze in this manner percolates into every part of the tent. If the sun is very strong, a locally woven carpet (usually some shade of orange) is hung up near the tent roof between poles and is pinned to the underside of the tent roof. This doubles the thickness of the tent and brings relief.

In very cold weather, on the other hand, the tent can be closed from the front by drawing inwards the embroidered ends of the *qáta* (which already extend several yards outside the tent) and by joining the ends near the middle of the tent side. The top edge is then pinned to the edge of the roof of the tent as is done in the case of the back curtain. This encloses the tent completely and gives great cosiness and warmth to the occupants. Similarly, the ends of the *ruag* are brought right round the guest quarters and the woman's cookhouse respectively, and turn those places into warm corners to sit in.

NOTE   The men's quarter of a tent or *raba'a* is always situated at the east end of the tent, irrespective of which way the tent is facing. This is the universal rule in eastern and north-eastern Arabia.

Similarly it is the rule for a tent to be pitched with its longer axis at right angles to the north-west wind (*Shamál*). In inner Najd, and especially among 'Utaiba tribe, the longer axis facing the north-west is the rule, and the tent is opened at its ends only. The *raba'a* here is at southern end.

The Tent Dogs

Every tent has its watch-dogs, and also (especially amongst the 'Ajman, 'Awazim and Mutair) a *salúqi* or two. The former are fierce, shaggy animals who usually have their ears cut off short to make them good fighters. Their heads are broad, rather like our bull-terrier type, and they are fierce and very powerfully built. These dogs guard the camels and sheep at night from wolves and strangers, and are trained to move round and round the tents all night in a large circle. The incoming or departing guest usually has a busy time keeping off these savage dogs, who bark at his heels in a most disconcerting manner, and are only kept back by a continual motion of his cane behind him, or by the shouts of the occupants of the tent. The watch-dog usually sleeps outside the women's apartments and is fed with little bits of rice, bread and dates that are left over from the meals. It is never allowed inside the tents, being unclean (*najis*). The *salúqis* (pronounced *salúqi*, plural: *salag*), on the other hand, are regarded as clean, especially by those Badawin following the Maliki tenets of Islam (who are in the majority in Hasa and Kuwait), and they are allowed to enter tents and sleep in the women's portion at will. They are valued for hunting purposes, and are taught to kill hare and gazelle for the pot. Great care is taken that there shall be no interbreeding between the tent watch-dogs and the *salúqi*, and when the female *salúqi* of the household is in heat one of her hind legs is attached by a leather thong to her collar, thus forcing her to sit down, which effectually prevents a heavy dog covering her.

A Stranger Arriving at a Tent

A stranger arriving must approach a Badawin tent from the front only. It is the worst of bad form to come up from the back. He must then approach the guest side of the tent and halt and make his camel kneel while some way off. This shows that he wants a night's rest or some food. He must never approach or halt his camel near the women's end of the tent (*muharram*). The purpose of this custom is to give the women time to adjust their *burqas* or veils whilst the visitor is some distance off. Were the visitor to come up from behind, he might come upon an unveiled woman attending to nature or washing her hair, or cleaning kitchen utensils.

Favourite Spots for Pitching Tents

In choosing a tent site the proximity of water is, of course, the first essential. Next, the nature of the grazing decides where a man will wish to pitch his tent. If he is migrating with the tribe or part of the tribe, the tent owner leaves the selection of the area to be camped on to the shaikh, but tries for the convenience of himself and his family to get as close as possible to a sandy nullah or dry water course with high banks. This is very important, for it allows the whole household, and especially the women, to attend to their toilet and other sanitary duties out of sight and in sandy surroundings which are ideally healthful. In this connection a Badawin (male or female) never unnecessarily soils the ground, but makes a point of digging a small hole in the sand, which he afterwards fills in. If water is scarce, as more often than not it is, sand may be used for the necessary ablutions in place of water. So the cleaner and more handy the sandy bed of the nullah, the happier are the occupants of the tent.

The phrase "proximity of water" is used in a relative sense only. In summer it must, of course, be close, within at most half a mile, but preferably much closer. In winter, however, when camels are not watered at all, and sheep and mares drink only once in four days, camps may be pitched twenty or thirty miles from any well. The household water is brought out on camel-back and in large and small skins, whilst sheep are sent off to drink at the wells, or in exceptional circumstances have water brought to them on camels.

Changing the Camping Ground

For sanitary reasons the camping ground is changed every eight or ten days, but especially to provide new grazing for the camels and sheep. An ordinary change of ground usually involves a march of ten or twelve miles, always provided water is handy. This is not in any sense a "migration." . . .

When it is time to move, tents are struck, and tents and other heavy material are loaded on to the male camels (*jamal*), which are stronger and more suited for the work than the females: lighter gear, spare water, etc., are placed on selected females, and of course the family themselves mount on riding camels, the women moving off sheltered in their *maksars* or *ginns*, the tops of which are canopied over with bright coloured woollen or cotton material, as a protection both from the eyes of men and from the sun. The men go before on their *dhalúls*. If an individual householder with half a dozen tents is changing ground, he himself heads the procession, while his sheep and milch camels either follow, grazing as they go on a flank or in the rear, or have already been sent on ahead. When nearing the new ground, the head of the house rides ahead, selects the site for the tents, makes his camel kneel *nauwakh al dhalúl* and declares this to be the new camping ground.

If a whole tribe is changing ground the fighting men move out first under their leader, all of them riding *dhalúls* and with mares and horses attached to their saddles by long leading ropes. Scouts (*sbúr*) have already gone ahead to spy out the land, the grazing and the water. Assuming that there is no enemy near or danger imminent, the baggage-camels and women folk follow fairly close on their heeels. After the women and camp gear, the herds of camels and sheep follow on a broad front, slowly grazing along till they reach their new camp. There they find everything ready and the tents pitched. A strong guard is, of course, left with the herds. As in the case of the individual tent owner, the shaikh decides on where the camp is to be, and on the spot where he kneels his camel and off-saddles, his own tent will be pitched.

A tribe in camp is not concertinaed up but scatters out over a wide space, each group of family tents being about two hundred yards from its neighbour if the ground is broken, and possibly four hundred yards apart in flat open ground. Hence a body of Badawin having, say, four hundred tents will cover a wide area when camped. This is the procedure in winter or spring when no enemy is about and likely to attack. In summer, on the other hand, when the tribe is camped on water, it literally surrounds the wells with tents, leaving only sufficient space for the camels and sheep to drink. Tents on such occasions are close together and generally in a series of lines, with tent ropes almost touching those of their neighbours. The widely scattered camp formation of winter may make it difficult for the fighting men to concentrate suddenly, but is ideal for passive defence. A sudden surprise raid cannot penetrate deeply into such a camp, as each tent becomes a small fort from which fire is directed on the intruders, who soon find themselves fired on from all sides. (The German pill-box system during the first Great War proved the efficacy of the method.)

NOTES

Assás—the man who goes ahead to look for best grazing ground.

Salláf—the leader of the tribe or head of family on the march. He always rides alone at head.

Makhúr—is name given to the family baggage-camels as opposed to *Al Aba'ir*, milch and loose camels on march.

Al Ghanam—the sheep on the march.

Al Baham—the lambs who march separate from the ewes.

*Material from which the following selection was taken was collected
by Fredrik Barth in Iran during 1957–1958, while he was engaged in
research on nomads and the problems of sedentarization under the Arid
Zone Major Project of UNESCO.. According to Barth, the Basseri are
a tribe of tent-dwelling pastoral nomads who migrate in the arid steppes
and mountains south, east, and north of Shiraz in Fars Province,
South Persia. The total population of the Basseri is estimated at
nearly 3,000 tents, or roughly 15,000 people.*

*There have been few recently published studies in English on the
nomads of southern Persia and Barth's publication is a most welcome
addition.*

11

The Ritual Life of the Basseri

FREDRIK BARTH

Only few references have been made to ritual in this account of the
Basseri—hardly any ceremonies have been described. and the behaviour patterns have been discussed in terms of the pragmatic systems of economics, or
politics, and hardly ever in terms of their meanings within a ritual system.
This has followed from the nature of the material itself, and is not merely a
reflection of the present field worker's interests or the analytic orientation
of this particular study. The Basseri show a poverty of ritual activities which
is quite striking in the field situation; what they have of ceremonies, avoidance
customs, and beliefs seems to influence or be expressed in, very few of their
actions. What is more, the different elements of ritual do not seem closely
connected or interrelated in a wider system of meanings; they give the

From *Nomads of South Persia* (1961), Appendix I; reprinted by permission of Oslo
University Press and Humanities Press.

impression of occurring without reference to each other, or to important features of the social structure. Perhaps for this reason, I have been unable to integrate many of my observations on ritual practices into the preceding description; and to make the descriptive picture of the Basseri more complete, and in a sense to correct the impression of ritual poverty, I shall therefore present these observations in the following section. It concludes with a brief discussion of the reasons for this apparent poverty in ritual idioms, and of the concept of ritual itself.

The Basseri, as Shiah Moslems, accept the general premises and proscriptions of Islam to the extent that they are familiar with them. On the other hand, they are aware of their own laxity in these matters, and are generally uninterested in religion as preached by Persian mullahs, and indifferent to metaphysical problems. The Il-e-Khas, who recently rejoined the tribe after having resided in the Isfahan area for 100 years, are a partial exception to this rule, and are today criticized and somewhat despised by other Basseri as being rigidly orthodox, miserly, and humourless.

There are no ritual officers of any kind in the tribe; but in some situations, mainly marriages, the Basseri call in a village mullah or other holy man to perform religious acts. The tribe is also visited by persons claiming sacred status, either as a *Sayyid*—Descendant of the Prophet—or as a *Darvesh* —an ascetic beggar. The latter sing and chant long song cycles on the death of Ali, while the former more frequently write amulets and promise blessings. Both categories are given small gifts of food and other produce, but are frequently ridiculed and abused even while the gifts are given. Everyone I spoke to, including the Sayyids and Darveshes, agreed, however, that this was a recent trend, and that up to 15 years ago people were consistently respectful, and to a great extent really fearful, particularly of the Sayyids. But even then, no members of the tribe were either Sayyids or Darveshes, nor did any such persons reside permanently with the tribe. Within the limits defined by the general tenets of Islam the Basseri are thus free to develop and elaborate their ceremonies and customs as an autonomous folk system. In the following, these are grouped in terms of their relevance to (I) the yearly cycle, (II) the life cycle, and (III) special practices and avoidances.

(I) The Basseri operate in a sense within three separate calendrical systems: the Islamic year, the Persian or solar year, and the yearly cycle of their own migrations, which brings them past the same series of localities in a regular succession. Each of these cycles is marked by a few ceremonies.[1]

There is much confusion among the Basseri with respect to the divisions and events of the Moslem year, though they are continually being reminded of them through their contacts with sedentary society; and even where they have the knowledge, there is great laxness in observing the prescribed customs. The nomads pray irregularly and always individually; even on Friday there is no communal gathering of worshippers within a camp or even within a tent. Islamic feast days are rarely celebrated, though a pious respect for them is often expressed when decisions on migration schedules are being made. . . . Even the fast of Ramadan and the feast of Moharram, of central importance to the surrounding Moslems, are observed and celebrated by few. Thus when we visited the market town of Jahron during Ramadan, the group of nomads I was with went to great trouble to get in by a back door to a shut restaurant and be served a meal, claiming dispensation from fast because we were travelling—which we were not that day. On the other hand, the Moslem calendar is thought to be important in questions of good and bad luck—thus the nomads will not divide a herd on a Friday, nor shear the sheep on a Moslem holiday.

The Persian, or solar, year is of greater importance to the Basseri, since it is in terms of it that the chief organizes and directs the migrations, and it defines the one universally observed feast day: that of *Nowruz*, the Persian New Year, at spring equinox. On this day everyone wears new clothes, or at least an item of new clothing; the women and girls colour their hair and hands with henna; friends and acquaintances greet each other formally, exchanging good wishes for the coming year; and there is much intervisiting and serving of food and tea in the tents of a camp, and between related and adjacent camps, and nomads and village friends. Nowruz falls at the beginnings of the main spring migration and therefore marks the beginning of a new year in a very real sense. None the less, the celebrations are not elaborate and time-consuming enough to prevent many groups from striking and moving camp also on that day.

Finally, the migrations themselves form a yearly cycle, and it is in terms of them that the average Basseri conceptualizes time and organizes his life. In the course of such a cycle, the nomad passes by a succession of localities, and many points along the way are marked with shrines (Imamzadeh/Ziarat) in the form of the graves of holy men. Few of these have any great significance to the nomads, but they usually pray or show respect as they pass by, though they often have no name, and rarely any myth about the actions of the Saint who was buried there. Nor do any of these shrines serve as centres around which larger groups congregate. Individuals may seek such shrines for prayers and special requests for help and support from the dead Saint; in the southern areas of winter dispersal are several shrines which are visited by nomads and villagers alike. A particularly famous and important shrine is that of Said Mohammed, located in the Kurdshuli summer pasture areas. It lies where three very large natural springs burst forth from the foot of the mountain, and is unique in being visited by larger groups of people, rather than separate individuals. Most of the camp groups which regularly pass close to the shrine make a practice of stopping over one day to visit it; men, women, and children dress in their best clothes and go there together, often several persons from each tent. Each household which is represented should give an animal in sacrifice by the shrine—though often several tents combine for a single sacrifice to save animals. When the animals have been slaughtered and while they are being cooked, most of the visitors enter the shrine itself, first all the women, then the men, though many remain outside. After this, those who have combined in a sacrifice join in a meal of meat and rice, and members of the same camp group mix while drinking tea. Similar groups of visitors from other camps, on the other hand, are ignored, whereas beggars and shrinekeepers who reside in a small village beside the shrine are given a share of the sacrifice and the cooked rice. Throughout, there is a general lack of ceremonial, and a gay and carefree feeling of a festive picnic prevails.

(II) Rituals connected with the life cycle are considerably more elaborated, and relate mainly to birth, marriage, and death.

Whereas pregnancy is associated with no particular rituals, birth is marked, especially in the case of the first child or the first son, by *khushhali* —happiness expressed by the giving of sweets, and shooting rifles into the air. Every day for the first three days of its life, and every subsequent Wednesday (*Charshambe*) for 40 days, the infant is cut on nose, neck and chest with razor blades, later also on the ears. This is to prevent the child's blood from becoming unclean later in life—a condition revealed by pimples in adolescence. Laceration in front of the ear and on the ear-lobes is also used later in childhood as a remedy against ear-ache.

Boys are circumcised, generally by a village barber or physician, before the age of two months. If circumstances prevent it being done so early, the parents generally wait till the boy is 6–7 years old, since otherwise he is very afraid when the operation is performed. There is no corresponding operation on girls, and no external mark to indicate maturity in either sex.

Usually around her 14th year, a girl will start being interested in boys, and may find a sweetheart whom she will meet and kiss in secret trysts. If they are surprised in this, her father will beat her; even when uninterrupted, such relations rarely develop into full-fledged liaisons. These relations have little relevance to future betrothals. In general, sexual abstention is the pattern for boys as well as for girls, in the case of the former perhaps largely because of the lack of opportunities in a small community largely composed of kin, where the girls are required to be virgins at marriage and strictly faithful to their husbands. Even elopements appear to be very rare, and such action was the cause of one of the two cases of homicide within the tribe which I was able to collect.

In the normal course of events, girls are betrothed some time after the age of 15, though not infrequently much later. The men are generally older, and may not be betrothed till the age of 30. Parents may make a promise long before the age appropriate for betrothal, but many prefer to remain uncommitted. The choice of spouse lies squarely in the hands of the parents; and even adult men, e.g., widowers, never negotiate their own marriages, but act through a senior relative.

Once a father and son have agreed to seek a betrothal, the son starts performing a sort of informal bride-service, helping his prospective father-in-law by fetching wood, serving tea, and assisting in tasks requiring the co-operation of several men, such as breaking in young horses for riding, or shearing sheep. Gifts for the girl are also offered to her father, the acceptance of which places him under a certain obligation, while the refusal or return of such gifts is a clear idiom of dismissal.

Finally, if a formal promise can be extracted from the girl's father, this is solemnized the next day in a betrothal ceremony (aghd-bandun = the tying of the contract). The crucial feature of this is the drawing up of a marriage contract, usually by a Sayyid or a mullah from a village. This document stipulates the size of the mahr, or deferred dowry, but not of the bride-price. The sum of the mahr is arrived at by bargaining in which a number of persons participate, and it ranges from 500–1,000 Tomans. The betrothal ceremony consists of a simple feast of rice and meat, given by the boy's father, to which the members of the camp are invited, and in which they partake after witnessing the document. The female guests bring presents of cloth to the future bride, taking care to arrive in a group to create the maximal effect. In a technical legal sense, it is the witnessed document of this betrothal ceremony that constitutes the legal Moslem marriage, the consummation of which is merely deferred.

The wedding itself (arosi) follows as soon as the necessary equipment for the future family has been collected and produced, and agreement has been reached on the bride-price, which usually has a value of c. 1,000 Tomans, and is paid partly in sheep, which the girl's father is expected in time to pass on to the young couple. A token gift of sugar is also presented to the bride's mother's senior brother by the groom. The wedding ceremony consists of a great feast, the central features of which are the conducting of the bride from her tent to her husband's tent, the joining of their hands by a person of authority, and the consummation of the marriage.

The whole feast, however, is considerably elaborated, and persons from neighboring camps, as well as from the camp or camps of the spouses, participate. The feast is given by the groom's parents, who hoist a green or red flag on their tentpole, erect a separate kitchen tent (ashpaz-khune) and preferably also a guest tent where they serve food and tea and cigarettes throughout the day. There is music where possible—professional musicians must be brought out from the villages—otherwise dancing by women to rhythmic handclaps, and stick-fights and horse-racing by the men. Guests are greeted by the women of the camp with a high trilling call, used otherwise only for distinguished visitors; everyone who can do so comes to the feast on horse-back, and people all dress in their best clothes.

The bride sits in seclusion in her tent with her female relatives, who help wash her, oiling and combing her head hair and removing body hair, colouring her palms and feet with henna, etc. Meanwhile, a very provisional tent is made by the groom's relatives, under the direction of a man who serves as "barber." It may consist of nothing more than a few gaily coloured blankets thrown over two churning tripods outside the groom's tent; this he enters, and there he is supplied with hot water for washing, and shaving of armpits and pubes. While he washes, his female relatives stand outside the tent, clapping their hands and chanting rhymes: "My brother is going to the bath to become sweet"—"Tie my brother's horse well away from his bath, for in it is a deep, deep well, and the horse might break its leg"—"Lowlands in winter, high mountains in summer; lowlands and mountains are good places for marriage." When the groom is clean, he emerges in his pyjamas and puts on new clothes which the barber has laid out for him on a rug outside; while he bathes and dresses, raisins (for blessing) and salt (against evil eye) are flung over him, the bath tent, and the spectators. When he is partly dressed, his face is shaved and his hair cut by the barber.

Male relatives of the groom thereupon erect a small nuptial tent, which he is then taken to inspect. When the word is received that the bride is ready, a group of men from the groom's family ride away to fetch her, bringing a spare horse for her to ride on, while the groom enters the nuptial tent and waits there. When the procession arrives at the girl's tent, her mother and father claim their *ru-aghdi* (on-the-wedding-contract) of 20–30 Tomans, and their *ba-ruzi* (for-the-day) of rice, sugar, and leg of lamb for a feast meal. Bride and bedding are then loaded on the free horse, and covered with a veil. Her father leads her horse, often holding a mirror behind its head, for luck and against evil eye. Dancing women and galloping men accompany and circle the procession. On reaching the vicinity of the nuptial tent, the bride's father generally stops and has to be coaxed on; when he comes close, the groom emerges from the tent, at which point the men try to catch him and beat him. Once he escapes back into the tent, he may come out again unmolested—the horse is brought to the tent opening and the groom emerges to lift the bride down. At this point her father intervenes again, claiming his *pa-ranjun* (foot-hand-journey, for bringing the bride), which he is then promised, usually in the form of an appropriate beast, such as a camel. The groom then lifts the bride down from her horse and carries her into the tent, at which point all the women enter and thereby drive him out, whereupon he stands around rather sheepishly, not participating in the festivities, or retreats from the camp.

At sunset he re-enters the nuptial tent, where his and the bride's hands are joined by a Sayyid, or a prominent man of the community, and then they are left. The only equipment in the tent is the bride's bedding and a clean white cloth for sleeping on, and perhaps some sweets or fruit for a breakfast. A male relative of the groom stands guard outside the tent; when the marriage has been consummated he shoots a gun into the air, and the women of the camp greet the news with their high-pitched trilling. Next morning the white sheet is inspected by both families together; if the girl was not a virgin, her husband may divorce her without giving her the *mahr* dowry and may even, if his family is strong, succeed in getting back the bride-price. The couple sleep in the nuptial tent for three nights; after that they usually reside in the groom's father's tent for a while before they establish an independent household.

Married status is often, though not always, marked by women by a change of hair style, whereby the hair is cut short and bobbed, instead of leaving it long and loosely tucked under the headcloth, in the fashion of unmarried girls. The use of eye make-up is also limited to married women.

According to Basseri informants, the wedding ceremony has changed its form somewhat during the last generation. It used to be that the groom himself went, with his relatives, to fetch the bride; he would help her up on her horse, then mount another horse and set off at full gallop across the plain, pursued by the men, both of his own and his bride's group. If they succeeded in catching him, they would all beat him. This has now been replaced by the smaller show of hostility and sexual jealousy when the groom emerges from the nuptial tent to meet the bride.

Even this milder form of ritual hostility is according to the Basseri now on the decline, and is replaced by a custom borrowed from the villages and towns, which I also saw in one of the Basseri weddings I witnessed.

According to it, the groom comes out of the nuptial tent unmolested, and meets his bride 100–200 meters away from the tent. He there lifts her off her horse and presents her with an orange, which she clasps in her hands and carries to the tent. People say an orange is used because it is a sweet thing, a good thing between friends; some interpret it as a pledge of good treatment, "like an oath on the Koran."

In comparison, death and burial are relatively little elaborated. The persons in the tent where a death has occurred spend the subsequent hours wailing and singing laments, joined at times by male and especially female visitors from other tents of the camp. The corpse is buried within a day of death; for this purpose it is always carried to a village cemetery, never buried out in the hills; prominent men are sometimes brought to the closest shrine for burial. The group within which the death has taken place always remains camped for a day or two to complete the funeral.

The body is washed by a close relative of the same sex, and laid out in orthodox Moslem fashion. No ritual specialist from the village is present; a group of male relatives, though usually not those most closely related to the dead person, such as parents or children, perform the whole ceremony alone. Since knowledge of the Koranic specifications for burial is incomplete, the digging and construction of the slab coffin, and the arrangement of the body in it, take much thought. A literate or quasi-literate person tries to chant the appropriate texts from the Koran, while after the corpse is laid into the grave, one man sits at the head of the grave holding a stick which touches the dead person's head, to maintain contact with him until all the earth is thrown over the grave. A slab of stone is erected at the head and one at the foot of the grave, and the piled earth is decorated with dry grass and weeds and the short thorny brush which grows on the sun-drenched hills of the cemetery, pathetically referred to by the bereaved as *gwul*—"flowers." Throughout, there is no great show of sorrow, only a quiet and serious attempt at doing everything properly.

The following evening or night, the women and closest male relatives go to the grave, light fires at its head and foot, weep and wail, and finally distribute sweets. Three days and seven days after the death, feasts should be given in honour of the dead by the relatives, even though they have probably moved on by then to new camp-sites; if the deceased was a prominent man, people from other camps throughout the tribe may come for these feasts, bringing gifts such as lambs. Exceptional love for the dead person is expressed by regular distributions of sweets every Friday for a period of time, sometimes even for several years.

Later on, the graves of close relatives are occasionally visited when the camp group passes through the neighbourhood. In cases where the death was considered particularly tragic, small groups of mourners may assemble for a visit to the grave every year; particularly the women maintain this practice. The group will approach the grave weeping and crying "Oh Mother, Oh Father, Oh Beloved!" and then sit around the grave crying and chanting laments. Often, they will knock at the stone slabs of the grave with pebbles, to call the attention of the dead to their laments; before leaving, they distribute sweets to the village children, who shamelessly congregate there to benefit from the pickings. Improvised laments are also chanted after conversations in the tent about close dead persons, or at other occasions of sorrow and despair—often when a child has been beaten by its parent, he or she will sit a short distance from the tent, wailing and chanting laments.

(III) A certain number of special proscriptions and avoidances are also observed which have no direct relation to the yearly cycle or the life cycle. These are generally associated with notions of good and bad luck, especially with respect to the flocks, and with witchcraft beliefs in the form of beliefs in the evil eye.

Most striking is the taboo on association of important animals in certain situations: thus a horse must not be permitted to approach the sheep while they are being sheared, or milked, while lambs, kids and foals should not enter a tent in which there is a new-born infant. Similarly, a man riding a horse, or a man who is very tired, should not approach the tent in which a new-born baby lies, likewise a woman wearing gold or yellow or white beads. In these cases, however, if the person stops a short distance from the tent and the baby is brought out to meet him or her, they can subsequently enter without causing harm.

More diffuse are the beliefs in the evil eye of envy (*nazar* or *cheshm-e-shur*), and in the means of protection against it. Though many people profess complete scepticism, the belief is widespread that evil eye and envious thoughts in any person have certain automatic effects which may at times cause illness and death. Though all people have it, some are much stronger than others, and particularly persons with blue eyes are suspect. Since illness and death are the consequences, only live objects, e.g., animals and children, may be the objects and victims of evil eye.

There is no cure or effective penance for the evil eye, but since its efficacy depends on the spontaneous nature of the envy, a number of simple protective devices may shield the animal or child. All of them are designed to make the spectator immediately aware of his thoughts: a string of blue beads, or rags, broken pottery, or other objects of striking contrast tied around the neck or leg of the animal or child. On the other hand, strong amulets *(taviz* = citations from the Koran) which may be obtained from Sayyids, may protect a person by their inherent power, without the knowledge of the envious spectator.

Again since it is the unconscious envy that harms, only friends, acquaintances and relatives *(khodeman* – one's own people) cast the evil eye, while declared enemies are impotent to do so. The effect of the evil eye may be to cause illness or one or a series of accidents; sometimes children or animals simply wither. In cases where strange behaviour or staring by someone causes suspicion which is confirmed by subsequent disaster (such as in one case I heard of, where the unexplained death of a 3-year-old boy followed within 24 hours of the visit of two men from a different camp to the tent where he lived), general indignation may lead to sanctions within the camp of the suspects, such as severe beating or even lynching.

In connection with joyful events or particular successes, e.g., in hunting, a person is expected to give sweets to the members of his community. This is explained as an effort to prevent envy and evil eye, and to express a feeling of friendship and good will towards all. The reciprocal of this is the habit of associating expressions of admiration with pious exclamations, rendering them incapable of harm, and expressions such as *dun ziat*—may the milk be plentiful—as greetings on approaching persons engaged in milking.

Finally, games and play may be regarded as a form of ritual behaviour. I have mentioned above the group dances by women, and stick-duel dancing by men. Small children also play at rhythmic word-games, chanting ditties to a simple 2:4 beat with sticks on the tent-cloth or a hollow object, to words such as: "The flock ran up on top of the mountain / my brother brought it down again." Men play backgammon and a type of whist. The only team game I ever saw was a rather brutal one between two teams of four young boys each, one group attacking, and the other defending four shallow pits according to special rules. Success in the attack gave the winning side the right to whip the defeated team, followed by a reversal of their positions as attackers and defenders. In this, as in cards, much time is taken up by attempts at, and accusations of, cheating.

The ritual idioms described above are largely very naive and simple, and they are not combined in larger complexes to communicate more subtle meanings. The use of sugar and sweets to express amity between persons, and thereby prevent ill-feelings and maintain literally sweetness in social relations; the use of salt and mirrors against evil eye, and of objects in striking contexts to create incongruity and awareness of evaluative thoughts in an observer; the custom of explicit well-wishing in situations where one might have been envious—all these idioms show an obvious association of their ritual meanings, and their characteristics or tangible properties; none of them are derivative from other complexes of meanings and beliefs, and all of them are consistent with the pragmatic and un-ritualistic attitude I have implied in my whole description of Basseri life. The one striking custom that seems to fall outside this pattern is the cutting and bleeding of infants, which incidentally is found also among Lur tribes of Fars. With the lack of elaboration of apparently similar themes, however, it seems methodologically hopeless to speculate on the possible connection of this practice with notions regarding sacrifice and blood, or circumcision. In general, I feel that the above attempt at an exhaustive description of the ceremonies and explicit ritual practices of the Basseri reveals a ritual life of unusual poverty.

To me this raises an inevitable question—can one isolate particular reasons, or explanations, for this apparent poverty? In the present case, I feel that some further analysis of the material may serve to modify, and in a sense correct, this picture.

In the above description, I have adopted a sort of "common sense" view of ritual, and compiled a list of those customs or actions which are explicitly non-technical, essentially those which the Basseri themselves classify in categories translatable as "ceremonies," "religion," and "magic." Greater sophistication in the definition of ritual might lead to an expansion of the field of inquiry.

In the literature of social anthropology, a number of different, but closely related, refinements of ritual and related concepts have been presented. The views expressed in Leach's (1954) discussion seem to me the clearest and most stimulating. In these terms, ritual may be defined as the symbolic aspect of non-verbal actions—those acts or aspects of acts which *say* something, in terms of shared values and meanings, rather than *do* something in terms of predictable material and economic consequences (*ibid.*, pp.

12–13). By isolating the symbolic *aspect* of actions, one avoids the difficulties inherent in Durkheim's absolute distinction between the sacred and the profane (*ibid.*, p. 12).

However, the dismissal of an absolute distinction between sacred and profane contexts raises certain problems, revealed in relation to the associated concept of myth. Myth is defined as the counterpart of ritual; myth as a statement in words "says" the same thing as ritual, regarded as a statement in action (*ibid.*, pp. 13–14). To this, most anthropologists would agree. But the above definition makes "ritual" of *all* symbolic aspects of acts, whereas no one would hold that all speech, because it has meaning, is "myth." If only because of the presence, apparently in all cultures, of concepts such as ceremony, religion, and magic, we need to be able to distinguish between rituals as systems of communication, and the mere fact that all actions, no matter how pragmatic, have "meanings" to the persons who observe them. Though Durkheim's dichotomy of sacred and profane is untenable, the feeling remains that rituals are actions especially pregnant with meaning, that they are at least in a relative sense set apart from other acts, for one thing because they are, in a sense, more important. Very tentatively, then, one might say that ritual is the symbolic aspect of acts in contexts vested with particular value.

Before returning to the material there is one further point I wish to make. Anthropologists often make the unnecessary and naive assumption that since the symbolic aspect and the technical aspect of actions may be separated by analysis, their correlates in the *form* of an act must also be separable. They seem to argue that technical requirements impose certain restrictions on the form of an act—therefore, its symbolic meanings must lie elsewhere, in those formal features that are technically superfluous or unnecessary. This does not follow. Clearly, there is no reason why the very forms of an act which reflect the technical imperatives may not *also* be vested with central and crucial meaning in a symbolic system or context.

We may now return to the material at hand, and look for further sets of acts, or aspects of acts, which carry and communicate meanings in contexts vested with particular value. It becomes overwhelmingly clear that the whole basic system of activities involved in the economic adaptation of the Basseri, of camping and herding and travelling, are pregnant with such meanings, and that the context in which they take place, that of the great migration, is vested with extreme value.

Let me try to show what this statement implies—firstly, the kinds of meanings of sociological relevance which these actions appear to have, and secondly, the value which is placed on their context, the migration, which warrants their classification with more conventional rituals. Some of the most explicit meanings associated with camping and travelling have been touched on already. . . . The camp itself, with its semicircle of fires, alone in an empty landscape, and constantly re-pitched in new localities in changing circumstances, serves as a clear expression of the social unity of the group which inhabits it, and of the mechanisms whereby that group is maintained. The caravan which travels the long way over steppes and through valleys and across passes cannot but become a procession: those at the head lead the way, they must decide which path to take, while those behind can have no active part in that decision; the aggregation in a camel and donkey train and the dispersal over a restricted plain for camping repeat daily the social facts of group allegiance and divisions; the sullen hostility of unfamiliar spectators wherever the caravan road goes through a village marks the caravan off as a group totally different from the sedentary communities. Finally, the scatter sometimes of a thousand tents over a single valley floor rich in pastures, the parallel movement over a plain of scores of caravans, visible as low lingering clouds of dust on the horizon—such occasions serve to dramatize the community of membership in tribe and confederacy, and their segmental structure.

These meanings, or symbolic aspects, of the activities are of the same logical order and partly of the same form as many of the ritual idioms of a religious ceremony, as these have been analyzed by anthropologists elsewhere. But they can only be compared to these if the context in which they take place is one of correspondingly predominant value. The context of these meanings is the cycle of migrations, which dominates the life and organizes most of the activities of the Basseri.

It is an economic necessity for the Basseri to move with their flocks in each season to where pastures can be found. But the migration has a value to them exceeding even this, as is apparent from the following considerations. Firstly, time and space alike are interpreted with reference to migration. Thus (as noted elsewhere, Barth 1960), when we passed through the Sarvestan valley in the beginning of April, the nomads collected a great supply of truffles which enlivened our diet for a week. When I asked them whether truffles appear only briefly in the begining of April, or perhaps are found only in the Sarvestan valley, the only answer I could obtain was "yes." My two alternatives were to them merely two ways of expressing the same experience: a season is a stretch of country, and *vice versa*—or rather, both are aspects of a unit within the migration cycle.

Other types of data also show the value placed on the migration itself. When internal Persian administration collapsed in 1941 the sanctions behind forced sedentarization were removed. All the Basseri expressed their reaction as one of resuming migrations—not as "becoming pastoralists again." As a matter of fact, most of them had very few animals, and some appear to have resumed migration entirely without stock—the supreme value to them lay in the freedom to migrate, not in the circumstances that make it economically advantageous.

Finally, if this is so, if the migration is a context vested by the Basseri with particularly great value, this should also be revealed in the emotional engagement of those who participate in it. The long journey of a great number of flocks and people from the low plains to the high mountains is in itself a highly dramatic set of events, utilized, e.g., in Cooper and Shodesack's book (1925) and film on the migrations of the Bakhtiari. If one can show that the Basseri react significantly to the inherent dramatic structure of their migrations, this is a measure of the value which they place on it as a context for activities.

When I joined the Darbar tent group, it was slowly moving from the broken mountains south of Harm towards the large plain of Mansurabad, which serves as an area of congregation before the large spring migration starts. The feeling of general excitement, the richness of "meaning" in the technical acts of coming under way and approaching this goal that is only a stage of a longer journey, was a strong subjective experience. In an attempt to devise a less subjective measure of this noticeable tension, excitement, or emotional involvement, I subsequently recorded the times of awakening, packing, and departure of the camp. The assumption was that, apart from the interference caused by random factors and changing natural obstacles, these times would reflect changes in the level of excitement or tension, and thus register the extent of the nomad's perception of, and subjective participation in, the migration as a drama, as an ordered and unique context. Rising tensions should be expressed in earlier awakening, more rapid packing, and earlier departures; a lack of reaction and involvement should give no, or random, variations in these times.

The resulting data are presented in Fig. 1. In spite of the multitude of disturbing variables—such as the fact that the beasts of burden are not tethered, and have to be found every morning, or the event of feasts or accidents or even births within the camp—in spite of all this, some clear and regular features are revealed. Tension—if indeed this is what is being measured—builds up progressively within shorter cycles of 3–6 days, before it is broken by a day or two of camping and rest, followed by a new cycle of build-up. The points at which these build-ups were broken, defining the cycles, were in part accidental, resulting from rainstorms, in part arbitrary, reflecting direct orders by the chief, or the need or desire to visit larger market towns. Only in one case did it depend on physical features and a climax of muscular exertion (5th of April), when the cycle was broken after the crossing of a major pass. Nor does early rising and departure correlate significantly with the length of the daily march—which is, in fact, unknown in advance, since it depends on chance circumstances of crop presence or absence and previous utilization and occupation at a number of possible alternative sites. The only deviant case of considerably *later* departure on the second day than the first day of a cycle (27th of April), followed one such

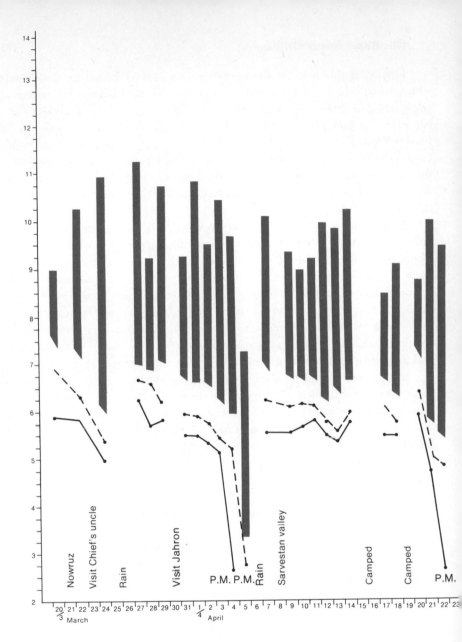

Fig. 1. *Time-chart for the Darbar camp's spring migration in 1958. Abscissa: calendar dates; ordinate: hours of the day. For each day of migration, the following are indicated: the time of striking tents in the morning, the time of starting to load the donkeys, the times of departure from the camp site (with span of time between first and last households to depart), and at the time of arrival at new camp site. The duration of each daily migration is thus indicated by the cross-hatched column. Lines have been drawn connecting the times of striking the tents (solid) and times of loading (stippled) on the consecutive days of each migratory cycle, showing the cyclical trend towards progressively earlier rising and departure.*

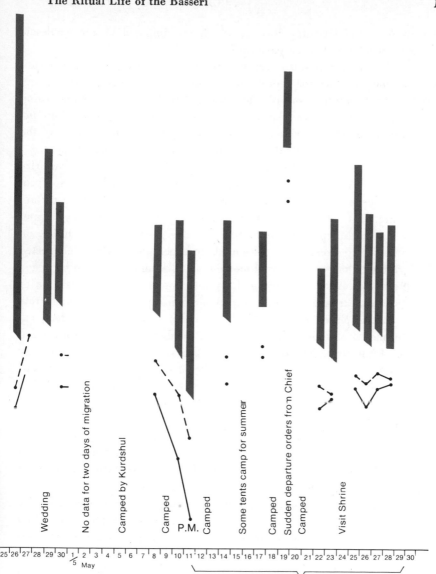

extremely long and fatiguing journey which was imposed by the wholesale encroachment of fields on the pastures.[2]

Once the summer pasture area was reached, the feeling of tension subsided, and the camp drifted more slowly, moving and camping without any marked cyclical patterns, towards the region in which that particular camp usually spends the summer. But when we topped the last pass, and saw before us the mountains for which we had been heading, all the women of the caravan broke out in song, for the first and only time on the whole trip.

I suggest, therefore, that the poverty which seemed to characterize Basseri ritual life is an artifact of the descriptive categories I have employed, and that it depends essentially on the naive assumption that *because* certain activities are of fundamental practical economic importance, they cannot *also* be vested with supreme ritual value. If one grants this possibility, on the other hand, it becomes very reasonable to expect the activities connected with migration to have a number of meanings to the nomads, and to be vested with value to the extent of making the whole migration the central rite of nomadic society. It is, admittedly, a methodological problem to demonstrate the value that is placed on migration, when this value is not, in fact, expressed by means of technically unnecessary symbolic acts and exotic paraphernalia. I have tried briefly to show that this value is revealed in the way the migration cycle is used as a primary schema for the conceptualization of time and space, in the fact that many nomads, after the external disturbance of enforced sedentarization, resumed migratory life in spite of economic costs, and finally, in the emotional engagement of the participants in the migration. The latter data show that the participants respond, not to the utilitarian aspects of the activities—to good pastures and potential butterfat—but to the movement and its dramatic form—to the *meanings* implicit in the sequence of activities.

This realization is important for the understanding of Basseri life—by it, the description contained in the preceding chapters is transformed from an external and objective description of the economic and social arrangements within a tribe to a description of central features of the culture of that tribe, the meanings and values which make up their life. Whereas this is usually achieved by an exploration of religious and ceremonial practices, in which these meanings and values are predominantly expressed, this could not, because of the nature of the material, be done here. The Basseri differ from many people in that they seem to vest their central values in, and express them through, the very activities most central to their ecologic adaptation. This is perhaps possible for them only because of the peculiar nature of that adaptation—because of the picturesque and dramatic character of the activities, which makes of their migrations an engrossing and satisfying experience.

NOTES

1. Only the period of March–June, or from the eighth to the eleventh Moslem month, were observed in the field; for the rest of the year I have only general and specific statements by informants.
2. The atypical curves for the period 7–14 April may be related to the fact that the group during this period passed *by* the town of Shiraz, at a distance, searching for a campsite where they could wait while I made a brief visit to Shiraz.

REFERENCES

Barth, F. "The Land Use Patterns of Migratory Tribes of South Persia," *Norsk Geografisk Tidsskrift* (1960).

Cooper, M. G. *Grass* (New York, 1925).

Leach, E. R. *Political Systems of Highland Burma* (London, 1954).

The Sulubba are, perhaps, a useful example of the numerous, smaller groups of peoples of the Middle East who contribute toward its general exotic mosaic. As the subcultures of such peoples may be at striking variance with those surrounding them, there have developed a series of beliefs, often rooted in certain historical phenomena, to explain their origins and present behavior. Dickson has incorporated behavioral and historical material to present a concise but clear summary of the Sulubba.

12

◇◇

The Sulubba of the Desert

H. R. P. DICKSON

The word *Sulubba* is a generic term. The singular of the name is *Sulubbi,* and the plural *Sulaib.*

Much has been written about this low-class tribe, or more properly community.

They are found all over the northern half of the Arabian Desert roughly from a line drawn east and west through Medina and Riyadh in the south, to another line drawn from Aleppo to Mosul.

In the south they are more despised and looked down on than in the north, and their worldly possessions are less.

Practically every tribe within the area described has a community of

From *The Arabs of the Desert* (1949), pp. 515–517; reprinted by permission of George Allen and Unwin, Ltd.

Sulubba living with it, as they are found useful as menders of pots and pans, hunters and trackers.

Chief among the Sulubba's characteristics is their uncanny knowledge of the secret water-holes of the country they live in. They are valued for this knowledge by the tribe which protects them, as it is a great asset in war, and most useful on long raids. Some Sulaib, for this reason, are nearly always taken with a raiding party.

Similarly a Sulubbi hunter is nearly always to be found in the entourage of a shaikh, as he usually knows better than others where gazelle and ostrich are to be found.

The Sulubba are said to be Muslims, but few pray properly, and it would probably be true to say that they possess no religion, except when it is diplomatic to appear to have one as in Najd and Kuwait.

The Sulubba men are in general a miserable fawning lot; they effect endearing and diminutive Arab terms of address, and are cringing in their manner.

Both men and women are good-looking above the average, especially the women, among whom there are often very pretty girls indeed. Their usually half-starved appearance is repellent, and gives colour to the Arab story that they eat offal and "animals they find dead."

In cast of countenance they would appear to be definitely non-Arab, and have none of the pronounced Semitic features of the latter.

In areas like Kuwait and Zubair, where they always maintain a large permanent camp outside the city walls, they are sometimes taken by Europeans for ordinary Badawin. This is a bad mistake and leads at times to awkward situations.

No Arab can marry a Sulubba girl. He would be killed by his people if he did, and she also. Nevertheless, I have heard it said that the Amir Fawaz of the Ruwala has no compunction in taking a pretty Sulubba maiden into the desert and keeping her as his mistress. For this he is roundly cursed by all good Badawin.

Most Sulubba settlements have their headmen, but where they are in strength among the major tribes of Arabia they have their shaikhs, some of whom own large flocks and herds of camels and are up to a point highly respected.

For instance:

Shaikh Hamad ibn Shennut is the Shaikh of the Mutair Sulubba.
Shaikh Mutallij al Safi is the Shaikh of the Shammar Sulubba.
Shaikh Muhammad ibn Jilad is the Shaikh of the Amarat Sulubba.
Shaikh Ma'aithif is the Shaikh of the Ruwala Sulubba.

The Sulubba women never veil and rarely wear a *milfa* over the lower part of their faces. Hence in Najd they are at once recognisable.

They are very fond of dancing, and on any feast day or at a marriage ceremony, the first thing they do is to organise a dance. This takes the form of men and women dancing together (a highly disgraceful and unseemly thing among Arabs), at which the men every now and then kiss their partners on the mouth and before the audience.

The Sulubba has among his ceremonies, dances, etc., the strange custom of hoisting a cross made from two pieces of wood tied together in the form of a Christian emblem. It may be called his tribal mark or standard.

Well-read Arabs, like Shaikh 'Abdullah Salim al Subah, cousin of the Shaikh of Kuwait, and others, say quite definitely that the Sulubba are descendants of the large number of Crusader camp followers, who were taken captive during the Crusade and Saracen wars; that vast numbers of these camp followers were taken in several great battles in which the Crusaders were worsted, and were carried off into slavery by the desert Arab, and that the present-day Sulubba are their descendants. Shaikh 'Abdullah will quote to prove his point,

a. The fact that the "cross" is the symbol of the Sulubba.
b. That the plural of their name "Sulaib" is clearly the same as the Arab name for the Christian cross which is known as *Salib*, the word *sulaib* being merely a diminutive form of *Salib*.

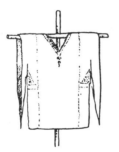 

There is perhaps something to say for the theory, but it would be dangerous to form conclusions pending the collection of more data about these interesting people. In particular it would be interesting to collect extensive anthropometric measurements.

The Sulubba women are accused of having (i) the power of casting the Evil Eye (*'ain*), (ii) special knowledge in preparing poisons and love potions for those who want them (*saqwa*), and (iii) above all of being versed in the devilish lore of witchcraft (*sahar*).

(i) The first accusation is probably due to the fact that many young Badawin men have lost their heads over pretty Sulubba girls and have had to flee their tribes. (ii) and (iii) are probably fairly true accusations, for they certainly claim to have the power of making one person love another, as well as of divination. On the other hand, they are a useful target for the public, if something evil happens to a prominent person. "It must be a Sulubba woman who has cast a spell on so-and-so," they say.

The Sulubba must not be confused with the Kauliyah or Gipsies. These latter are to be found all over Iraq and its borders, and are, I think, without a doubt one and the same as the Romany Gipsies of Europe and England. They dress like Badawin and live in small black tents, moving about by the aid of donkeys which seem to form their only visible means of support. These Iraq Kauliyahs are thieves, bad characters, fortune-tellers, are versed in the art of palmistry of sorts, and last but not least their women are in demand for performing the operation of "circumcision of female babies," a rite which is widely practised in Southern Iraq, and among the Muntafiq tribes of the Euphrates and Bani Tamim Arabs.

Too frequently the subcultures of the Middle East have been analyzed by traditional variables such as religion, language, or way of life. In reality, of course, social stratification is another meaningful variable— and growing in significance with the increasing of the urbanization and industrialization processes.

Gabriel Baer has prepared a topical description and analysis of the major social classes of the Middle East with particular emphasis on the dynamics of this class stratification. These data originated in lectures given at the Hebrew University in Jerusalem.. The 1963 English edition of his work is an enlarged and up-to-date version of his 1960 Hebrew publication.

13

◇◇

Social Stratification in the Middle East

GABRIEL BAER

Analysis of the class stratification of Arab society in the Middle East is hampered by the almost complete absence of research material in this field. There has not been a single attempt to investigate the stratification of a sector of Arab society using criteria such as power, status, or prestige. Even on more concrete criteria, such as wealth or economic function, there is only a very limited extent of information, since not one of the Arab countries has actually issued statistics on income. Statistics on distribution by occupation exist for Egypt alone, and even here they leave much to be desired. The following discussions can, then, only suggest general ideas which some future research may complement by filling in the details or correct on the basis of new material and new conclusions.

From *Population and Society in the Arab East* (1963), pp. 204–239; reprinted by permission of Routledge and Kegan Paul, Ltd. and Frederick A. Praeger, Inc.

Because of insufficient data, it is unwarranted to attempt to divide Arab society into a large number of well-defined classes. A more practical and realistic method, and that adopted here, is to analyse the special characteristics of economic and occupational groups within each of three main classes—upper, middle, and lower.

The "upper class" is taken to include groups in whose hands abundant possessions or great wealth are concentrated, the social power groups in most Arab villages and towns; these groups also held political sway until recent years (whenever foreigners were not in control). Apart from large land-owners and merchants, this class includes entrepreneurs and industrialists who have close ties to the former two groups (indeed, they are generally identical), and thus are not to be included among the "middle classes," as is the practice in the West.

In the "lower class" we include persons without property who are wage-earning labourers, or who are engaged in undefined work, as well as fellahs whose small landed property is insufficient for upkeep of the family, and who are therefore compelled to lease land from larger estate-owners or to work for a wage, while also farming their own plots. This class does not include persons whose earnings are gained from work involving any degree of education, since the differences in standard of living, way of life, social standing, and power between clerk and physical labourer are so much greater in the Middle East than in the West. Furthermore, the bureaucracy is mainly of higher-class origin.

The "middle class," embracing all groups not belonging to either of the other two classes, is very heterogeneous and diversified, including fellahs of limited means, professionals, small merchants, and army officers, among others. The middle class has remnants of a traditional society in the process of disintegration and new developing branches. Despite its variegation, the class is still much smaller than its counterpart in the West. True, as it is difficult to pinpoint the class in any precise fashion, its size cannot be determined accurately either; there are enormous discrepancies between the results of two recent attempts in this direction. Two authors tried to work out the number of gainfully occupied persons who may be said to belong to the urban middle class of Egypt, the only country which has issued any statistical information.[1] One arrived at the figure of 112,900 and the other at 499,164. Even assuming that the higher figure is an underestimate of the actual number of gainfully employed members of the middle class, it is still true that the middle class is relatively much smaller in Egypt than in the West. In all other Middle Eastern countries, except for Lebanon and possibly Syria, the urban middle class constitutes an even smaller percentage of the total population than in Egypt. The result is a great polarity of class stratification and marked class differences.

It is still more difficult to define the *rural* middle class and to estimate its scope. Here, statistics (again, for Egypt alone) are likely to be even more misleading. Indeed, the authors quoted earlier arrived at the figures of 620,395 and 134,562, respectively, for the rural gainfully employed members of the middle class. At any rate, it is clear that because of the existence of large-scale landed property, the middle class is relatively limited in the village, particularly in countries such as Iraq with its almost total absence of middle-sized estates. Nevertheless, there is no doubt that the middle class is steadily gaining ground in the Arab world, and its first intimations have been heard even from countries such as Saudi Arabia.

Before discussing the various strata and classes in any detail, two remarks are pertinent. Differentiation between groups does not signify that each occupies a well-defined and clearly distinguishable position. On the contrary, a basic characteristic of Middle Eastern society is the personal or familial identity of landowners and big businessmen, or even industrialists, and the ties between landowners and a large proportion of the educated classes and the bureaucracy. Furthermore, strata are not rigid, and it is common to find transitions from one to another and from class to class. This phenomenon of great social mobility is connected with the fact that Islam and Middle Eastern society in general has no exclusive nobility or aristocracy preserving marriage ties within its own close circle. Also quite foreign to Islam is the system of castes, prevalent in much of Asia. Hence also the cultural differences between classes are slight, and, for example, there are no class dialects such as are found in other countries.

This mobility has increased in the last generation as a result of urbanization, economic development, and spread of education, and as a result of the political upheavals which terminated the privileged political and social position of foreigners and local landowners. Abolition of the special status of these groups had its greatest impact on urban society. To take one example, the boundaries between the living-quarters of this former *élite* and those of other groups have blurred. The following statement, written of Khartoum, is more or less valid for other cities: "With the recently increasing social and political mobility, class segregation has become much less rigid than it was a few decades ago, when residential zoning was avowedly on a class and race basis."[2]

Upper Classes

The large landowners of the Middle East are generally town-dwellers, although their income derives from agriculture. This is no novelty peculiar to the twentieth century: throughout the history of the Arabs, the group which ruled the village generally lived in the city rather than on a rural estate. The class has undergone changes in keeping with political permutations, but its members have remained mostly in the cities. This is also one of the reasons why a real landed aristocracy has never been formed in the Middle East.[3] There are a few exceptions to this rule: for instance, some prominent families of certain minority groups living in mountainous regions which were autonomous during the period of the Ottoman Empire.

The large landowners of today are a new class, formed, as noted in the discussion of land tenure, in the nineteenth and twentieth centuries. Its manner of formation, discussed earlier, explains the urban nature of this class. Every one of the large landowners whose property was confiscated in Egypt (up to the end of 1955) lived in Cairo or Alexandria or both cities. (Occasionally, the city residence was additional to one on the estate or in a nearby provincial town.) In other Middle Eastern countries the situation is similar. The urban location of this class is due not only to the fact that many rich and prominent people of the city became landowners within the last hundred years; also beduin shaikhs and village notables who became landowners transferred to the cities in search of new fields of economic activity. Furthermore, cities were the centres of administrative and political influence, and when the Arab states won independence cities became the seats of parliaments in which these landowners acted as delegates.

Large landowners and their families fulfilled functions of primary importance in civic and national public life, and in many places their position has remained unaltered to this day. They themselves, their sons who studied law, or members of other prominent families related to them by marriage, had strong representation in the Government, the high bureaucracy, parliaments, municipalities, various committees, and all political parties (except those formed recently after the Western pattern). An investigation of the sources of income of Syrian Members of Parliament in 1937 disclosed that among those from whom details were elicited (60 out of 85 members), at least 20 were landowners. (Possibly a further 9 lawyers and 2 other persons, previously Ottoman officials, should be added to the list.) Similarly, an Egyptian newspaper found that among the 319 Egyptian Members of Parliament elected at the beginning of 1950, 115 owned land amounting to more than 100 feddans each, 45 owning at least 500 feddans of land. In the Lebanese Parliament of the early 1950s there were 21 landowners out of 44 delegates.[4] Even the Egyptian women's movement was headed by a member of the Sha'rawi family (one of the largest landowners of Egypt). In Egypt the rule of this layer took the form of high legislative and executive authority granted to the king, the largest of landowners. However, political rule by landowners has now been abolished in some of the more important Arab countries by the revolutions of recent years. As agrarian reform proceeds, the economic and social standing of landowners is also undermined.

As mentioned earlier, the group of large landowners is not exclusive or clear-cut. On the contrary, it is interwoven with the group of large-scale merchants, real-estate owners, contractors, and even industrialists.[5] At times landowners or members of their families have participated in all branches of urban activity. An outstanding example of this is Egypt in 1929–35, when an agricultural crisis and protective tariffs led many landowners (e.g., the Badrawi-'Ashur, Sultan, and Wisa families) to invest their capital in industry.[6] Similar examples may be found in Syria (the Mudarris family of Aleppo, for instance). On the other hand, there are large-scale merchants and contractors who have invested their profits in land, and some have become landowners by accumulating capital from moneylending or other means (the Ahmad 'Abbud family; cotton merchants such as Amin Yihya, Muhammad al-Maghazi, al-Wakil, and others; merchants of Homs and Hama; and so on). The amalgamation of merchants and landowners is one of the principal reasons why there is no sharp contrast in the Middle East between the urban bourgeoisie and the landed aristocracy, while that contrast is an essential feature of the history of some European countries at the dawn of the modern era.

A second group of the upper class, having strong ties with the large landowners, is that of large-scale merchants. Commerce, unlike agriculture, has always been an esteemed activity among Arabs. However, with the spread and development of trade with Europe, important positions in large-scale commerce were taken over by Europeans, and later by members of minority groups. The commercial activities of large-scale Muslim Arab merchants, which also spread in all countries of the Middle East, were concerned chiefly with internal trade and dealings in agricultural produce rather than industrial goods. These merchants have always engaged in moneylending and banking as well as commerce.

Over the last generation, the wealthy mercantile class has been the major source of a third group—the entrepreneur class of contractors and industrialists.[7] This group is still small, chiefly for the same reasons that held back development of industry in the Middle East: backwardness and a low standard of living in the village, and hence a limited domestic market for the young industry; lack of independent growth of the city, which was ruled by the same group as the village; retarded spread of education, and in particular, the low standard of technical skills; and finally, since the nineteenth century, obstruction of industrial advance because of trade relations with Europe, or even sometimes, because of the deliberate policy of European powers which were not interested in the growth of local industry. Possibly in the past the Islamic tradition of fatalism, prohibition of usury (*riba*) and risk (*maysir*) may also have obstructed the development of an entrepreneur class. However, even in the Middle Ages, Muslims used to circumvent these interdictions, and nowadays their influence is negligible.

Local industrialists derive their capital primarily from large-scale commerce, and to a lesser extent from the profits of large landownership. On the other hand, the new stratum was only to a small extent drawn from the group of artisans (its source in some European countries); the latter group lost its wealth as a result of the import of European goods, which outsold local produce. Furthermore, the class of artisans and medium-scale industrialists is altogether limited in the Middle East. More will be said of the structural polarity of Arab industry in the discussion of the working class.

Many of the new entrepreneurs were originally members of minority groups—Armenians and Arab Christians, Jews, Greeks, and other European minorities. But Islam does not preclude capitalistic or industrial enterprise; in Syria, for example, the majority of industrialists are Muslims, and so, too, in present-day Egypt and Iraq. Investment in Lebanese local industry was provided by merchants whose capital had been formed by brokerage, merchants dealing in inter-Arab trade, and financiers, as well as merchants who emigrated to America and Africa and amassed their capital there. Most Syrian industrialists were merchants (importers, representatives of foreign firms, etc., such as the owners of the *al-Khumasiya* firm, the Sahnawi group of Damascus, Hariri, and Shabarik of Aleppo). The new Syrian entrepreneurs, leasing land in Jazira from beduin shaikhs and cultivating it as large-scale capitalistic farms with mechanised agricultural equipment, were also formerly merchants (e.g., the Mamarbachi, Asfar, and Najjar families).

The Egyptian entrepreneur class, too, is mainly of mercantile origin, but it is more variegated than its counterpart in other Arab countries. There are large landowners, contractor engineers such as 'Abbud, professionals such as 'Afifi, and others. Many have continued to engage in their original occupations in addition to their activities in industry. This may explain one characteristic of the Middle Eastern upper class which has already been mentioned: the absence of internal economic and political conflict. As an example, we may consider the professional organisations within the class. In the cities of Lebanon there are combined chambers of commerce and industry; in Egypt (1958) these organisations were separate, but of the six executive officers of the Egyptian chamber of commerce in Alexandria, three were at the same time presidents of industrial organisations. In Syria there are separate chambers of commerce (formed before the First World War in Damascus and Aleppo) and industry (all formed within the past two decades). In Iraq and the Sudan there are no chambers of industry.[8]

Some claim that entrepreneurship in the Middle East is at the same stage of development as in the era of commercial capitalism in Europe, with all that that implies—absence of rational business practices, operation without visible records, direct management by the owner, etc. An outstanding characteristic of entrepreneurship in the Middle East is the persistence of the family firm. The social status of merchants is at least as estimable as that of industrial entrepreneurs, and generally it is regarded even more highly.[9]

Close ties are not limited to industrialists, entrepreneurs and large-scale merchants. Many persons of the upper class still prefer to invest their capital in immovables rather than in industry; industrialists, for their part, tend to invest in land, partly because of the social prestige which landowner-ship implies. This is one reason for the common vested interests of indus-trialists and landowners. A further reason concerns the newly emergent working class, engaged in a fierce struggle against industrialists. This, and the general social tension in the city, has checked the industrialists from open conflict with the rule of landowners. Thus, there was no Middle Eastern party representing industrialists which called for agrarian reform, for in-stance; in all traditional parties landowners and industrialists have gone hand in hand.

Even after the rule of landowners was abolished, following the military revolts in many Arab countries, private enterprise was not impelled towards a fresh spurt of industrial development. For various reasons the new régimes replaced private enterprise by government-sponsored enterprise, and even sup-pressed the efforts of private industrialists. Some of their reasons were the need for rapid development with the aid of loans and grants from abroad; disbelief in the capacity of private enterprise to turn to industrial development (capitalists displayed a trend towards investing in urban immovables or hoarding gold rather than investing in industry); a desire, in Egypt, to get rid of members of foreign minorities in high economic positions; fear of the creation of a new socio-political power which would not yield to the central rule; and the need and desire to carry out a social policy for the benefit of the lower classes without obstruction. In 1961 a series of laws was passed in Egypt whose object it was to restrict private enterprise and to place a large number of industrial concerns in government hands.

Consequently, in several Arab countires, especially in Egypt, a new type of entrepreneur-bureaucrat has appeared: "L'entrepreneur du moment, c'est l'activité bureaucratique."[10] Examples are the officials in charge of manage-ment of the Suez Canal when it was put into operation after nationalisation. Obviously, it is too early to assess the character of this new group.

Middle Classes

The middle classes in the Arab countries have not consolidated like the upper class, and they contain many highly diverse elements. It is the middle class which in fact bears the greatest burden of public activities in the city— religious and secular, social and political. This class has been the main source of active party members. (One of the outstanding expressions of the political struggle in these countries was the closing of shops and workshops, and demonstrations by students.) Although the middle class has also pro-duced its spokesmen, organisers, and even leaders, the main leadership has generally remained, until recently, in the hands of the upper class. Up to a few years ago the middle classes, unlike the upper class, played no independent role in social and political life.

> As a non-employing class, the middle class in the Arab world has little economic power, and has been, as a class, rather distant from the fount of all power in that area, the government. The other major component of the middle class, the civil servants, are of course closer to the seat of power, but are a rather pliant instrument in the hands of the real holders of political and economic power.[11]

Recently there have been changes, but it is still difficult to evaluate their character. At any rate, in some Arab states groups such as the army officers have emerged and come out openly against the formerly dominant upper class.

Of course, all this applies to the urban middle classes. The rural middle class is very small, and its members are scattered among thousands of villages, so that it lacks any power or activity as a group. It has indeed provided a good many of the political and spiritual leaders of the modern Arab states, particularly Egypt (Muhammad 'Abduh, Sa'd Zaghlul, 'Abd al-Nasir, and others). However, as a class, it has not participated in public affairs like the urban middle classes and has not actively contributed as they have to the changes of recent years.

The largest group among the urban middle classes is probably that of artisans and small tradesmen. This group, whose contact with Western influences and culture is slight, has suffered from the infiltration of Western merchandise. Outstanding in this respect is Syria, which before the First World War, was an important centre of traditional handicraft. The number of persons employed in the traditional crafts changed as follows (according to a survey by the Mandatory Government in 1937) :[12]

	1913	1937
Damascus	39,511	25,404
Aleppo	44,889	38,005
Homs	19,530	6,500
Hama	6,743	1,915
Total	110,673	71,824

The same survey indicates that, over a certain period, modern industries did not develop at a rate comparable to the decline of the traditional handicrafts, and thus could not absorb those workers who lost their jobs. Traditional small-scale commerce has also suffered as a result of competition with modern shops, which have increased in number as consumer tastes change. In various parts of the Arab East, particularly in Egypt, the appearance of department stores has seriously harmed the traditional sector of small tradesmen. (Most of the owners of the modern shops were foreigners or members of minority groups.)   As a result, artisans and small tradesmen in various parts of the Arab world have become vociferous in their opposition to and hatred of foreigners and Westernisation in general.

It should be noted that a decline in the absolute number of the artisan and tradesman group has not occurred in all parts of the Middle East.   The trend towards urbanisation over the past generation, and in particular the growth of new governmental and military centres, has created favourable conditions for increased numbers of shops, laundries, barbers, and other services required by the new government officials, labourers in the building trade, and in transport, etc.   Despite the lack of reliable statistics, it seems unlikely that in the long run this class has suffered a numerical decline.   On the other hand, social consolidation and organisation of the class have clearly been harmed as a result of the economic developments and Westernisation of the last few generations.   As late as the end of the nineteenth century, artisans and tradesmen were organised in corporations, each headed by a shaikh. They afforded their members considerable social security, and fulfilled other important functions in social and economic spheres.   At the end of the nineteenth and the beginning of the twentieth centuries the corporations disappeared, and they are no longer to be found in the cities of the Arab East.[13]   They have not been replaced, however, by new social bodies, and the group of artisans and small tradesmen is now amorphous, lacking any organised form.

Besides artisans and tradesmen, the middle classes are largely composed of various groups whose occupations demand some degree of education, that is, religious functionaries, the bureaucracy, professionals, and the educated class in general.   Among these groups there is much differentiation, between *muftis* and local *imams*, for example, or between the high officialdom and small clerks.   A small but important sector of this group definitely belong to the upper class by origin, income, influence, and attitudes; another larger part is proletarian in social standing.   However, the majority undoubtedly lies between these two groups—that is, in the middle classes.

The group having the longest tradition is that of religious functionaries. In theory there is in Islam no clergy who might claim to intervene between man and God.   However, as Islam assumed more rigid forms, a group of persons commanding social and religious authority and prestige similar in kind to that of the Christian clergy came into being.   They are collectively known as the *'ulama*—versed in law and theology and their interpretation. The group is composed of the following professions: *qadi* (judge); *mufti* (who expands on questions of law); teachers at all levels, from shaikh of the *kuttab* to professor at religious seminaries; the *imam* (leader in public worship); *khatib* (deliverer of the sermon in public worship); and *wa'iz* (preacher).   The group also includes other employees of religious institutions whose work does not require religious training, such as the position of the *mu'adhdhin* (who summons the believers to prayer) and a long list of officials and servants of the mosque. Also to be counted in the group are the heads of the *sharifs* (descendants of the family of the Prophet) and of the orders, which over the years have been joined by orthodox men of religion.

The gamut of religious functionaries is, then, most diverse. In Muslim history this class has been subject to many vicissitudes, and its state has differed from country to country. In general, however, it may be said that until the nineteenth century the class was one of the important elements of the old social structure of the Arab world. With the establishment of modern systems of rule in the Middle East its influence and power have dropped; none the less, it has maintained considerable authority among Muslims, as its members still pass judgement in all questions of personal status and related matters, such as inheritances, wills, etc. It is recognised as a body defending the interests of the Muslim masses. Religious functionaries are in direct contact with almost every individual of the urban (and rural) Muslim population, via the *imams*, *khatibs*, and shaikhs of the *kuttab*. An institution which helped them to retain their influence was the waqf, the income of which was an important source of revenue to charitable causes and religious or educational establishments, and which were in many cases managed by religious functionaries. In some countries the Sufi orders channelled contact and influence of the religious establishment to extensive sectors of the population, particularly to small-scale craftsmen and merchants. In the last generation, with the decline of the orders, a new form of middle-class organisation under religious direction has appeared—clubs and associations of Muslims with philanthropic, social, and political aims.

As against these factors, which tend to preserve the influence of the religious group, there are many developments of the nineteenth and twentieth centuries whose effect has been to weaken their position. First, their economic position has declined: previous to modern development many religious functionaries amassed capital as *multazims*. However, after tax-farming had been abolished few religious functionaries continued to be large land-owners. Furthermore, the institution which provided them with their most important source of income, the waqf, has considerably changed. The number of waqfs which were established in favour of religious bodies is small, and the supervision of religious functionaries was restricted when the management of waqfs was taken over by the State.

The social standing of the religious group has also been greatly affected. Earlier, it was mentioned that the standing of *sharifs* and *sayyids* has declined; so has the social importance of the orders. It is still too soon to assess the social function of religious clubs and political parties as substitutes for the orders, but there are indications that the importance of these organisations is less now than it was ten or fifteen years ago. The spread of education and literacy meant an end to the monopoly of religion in that sphere. The establishment of a secular school system also had much the same influence. Finally, there are some indications that religious functionaries are about to lose their juridical monopoly in matters of personal status also. Obviously the future position of religious functionaries depends more than anything else on the future of religion as an element of Arab society.

The rate at which religious functionaries are losing their hold varies, of course, from country to country; Egypt and Syria, in the throes of Westernisation, differ from conservative Saudi Arabia and Yemen. But it is not only the degree of Westernisation that counts. In Lebanon, for example, the influence of religious functionaries has been preserved more than might be expected of a country which is perhaps more Westernised than any other in the Arab East. The decisive factor here is Lebanon's unique political structure with strong communal representation. The standing of the religious establishment depends on other factors too, such as the deeply rooted tradition of the orders in the Sudan and Cyrenaica, or the strong representation of the Shi'a in Iraq, particularly its southern regions (the position of the Shi'i *mujtahid* being much stronger than that of the Sunni *'alim*).

It was mentioned earlier that, until recently, middle classes had no independent function in the Arab East, but were dependent on the upper class and supported that class. This is certainly true of the religious functionaries.[14] While their support seems to have been shaken somewhat since the Second World War, it is not they but rather the secular educated groups and the army-officer group which have challenged the old social order.

The group of religious functionaries is one of the oldest social groupings in the Arab city; the secular educated class is a young group, about a century old, which arose with the great extension of secular learning and its institutions. Most of the "educated" are officials, and especially government employees, and this is a profession highly esteemed among the Arabs. Actually, Berger, in his investigations of the high officialdom of Egypt, reached the conclusion that officials among themselves do not regard their profession so highly; but to the public, their prestige is as great as it ever was.[15] Other signs, too, indicate that much of the urban population regards the bureaucrat's position as superior and that education of sons has this occupation as its object. The sons of many upper-class families are engaged in clerical work, since family means are not sufficient to provide for all its members; also, it is hoped that the family may thus manage to gain influence among the public and with the authorities. Seventy per cent of all officials included in Berger's survey had private resources; nearly all derived some income from possessions to supplement their salary; and a large percentage of them were of landowning families.[16] Also among the middle classes, rural and urban, officialdom is a coveted occupation, freeing men from physical labour and raising them to a higher social rank.

The enormous expansion of the bureaucracy began mainly after the

establishment of independent governments. According to a former Iraqi
Minister of Finance, 'Ali Mumtaz ad-Daftari, the index of the number of
officials in government departments (based on 100 in 1936) was 130 in 1940,
159 in 1944, and 218 in 1947.[17] According to a civil service commission in
Egypt, the number of governmental posts rose by 61% between the years
1940–1 and 1954–5, reaching 381,615. The number of posts requiring at
least a primary education rose, in the same period, from 47,480 to 170,345
—that is, more than two and a half times. According to another survey of
the Egyptian civil service, the percentage of the total population engaged as
governmental employees was higher there than in Britain; expenditure on
bureaucracy, expressed in terms of the percentage of the total budget, was
again higher than in Britain, and has risen in recent years, reaching 46%
in 1952–3.[18]

Until the achievement of independence there was much competition for
these positions between local candidates and foreigners. Even after the
establishment of independent governments in some Arab countries the struggle
persisted between Muslim candidates and members of the minorities (Copts,
Armenians, and Syrians in Egypt, Christians in Syria), who held many
posts by virtue of their high level of education. This is one of the causes
of the nationalistic resentment common among both the educated classes
and those whose ambition it is to place their sons in clerical posts.

A group somewhat similar to the bureaucracy in character and occupation is that of teachers. This has never been so well regarded a profession
as the clerical. Many teachers are of middle-class origin, whereas more
officials derive from the upper class. With the spread of education, the
number of teachers has risen greatly: in Egypt, for example, there was a more
than twofold rise from 1913–14 to 1942–3 (to almost 50,000), and in the
ten succeeding years (to 1952) the number of teachers increased to 64,000.
In Iraq the number of teachers at government schools rose almost tenfold
between 1920 and 1941, in the following ten-year period it again doubled,
reaching 10,000 in 1951, and in 1960 it amounted to 24,367.[19]

The origin of many professionals, such as doctors, engineers, etc., is the
upper class. The number of doctors and engineers is as yet small in relation
to needs, but the number of lawyers is very great. Many families of the
upper class sent their sons to study law in order that they would later be able
to protect family business affairs and would enter the political arena as
family representatives. The increase of professionals in Egypt is well illustrated by the following table:[20]

	1937	1947
Doctors and Dentists	3,700	6,300
Pharmacists	1,200	1,600
Engineers	8,400	15,800
Writers and journalists	1,200	8,200

The last figure again indicates the definitive trend towards political activity.

Despite a notable increase in the number of positions filled by officials, teachers, agronomists, and lawyers, there is, of course, a limit to the capacity for absorbing these groups—a limit set by the general standard of living and by the government budgets. Thus, in some Arab countries the spread of education, particularly higher education, has surpassed the potentialities for absorbing professionals. Development of industry has been limited, and even where there was a lack of engineers, supervisors, and technicians, the educated classes were not prepared to take up those professions and saw no future in them. Among the educated of the Middle East, and particularly in Egypt, there is thus a problem of unemployment.[21] The problem is especially serious because of the contemptuous attitude to manual labour which prevails among most educated persons in the Arab world. For a long time it was customary in Iraq to send orphans (who have always been allotted the more despicable jobs) to the Kulliyat al-Handasa (Engineering College).[22]

There are other reasons, deriving from the present social structure of the Middle East, which underlie the frustration which is so typical of the contemporary Arab intellectual. Education and contact with the outer world have given him personal ambitions directed towards raising his standard of living, and idealistic ambitions to help his country towards rapid modernisation. But he is conscious of the enormous disparity between himself and the masses, which prevents any real mode of communication with most of his fellow countrymen. Furthermore, the existing social and economic structure prevents him from fulfilling either his personal or his national and social aspirations.[23]

In the face of the general social tension prevailing in the city there was much bitterness among intellectuals regarding the existing state of affairs, and this is undoubtedly one of the reasons for the lively political activity of students in the Arab countries. Another reason is that the universities and secondary schools are among the most important concentrations of large numbers of people (another such concentration being the factories), and for intellectual youth there is hardly any social activity other than politics. For example, it may be remembered that in the Sudan a congress of college graduates has been the nucleus for the formation of political parties in the past twenty years. When the army officers revolted against the old order they found that much of the educated class was their willing ally.

The last group to be included in the middle classes, small in scale but important in its function in Middle Eastern society, now as in the past, is the group of army officers. Throughout the modern history of the Middle East (since the nineteenth century), army officers have periodically seized power over the country in order to introduce fundamental social reform: 'Urabi in Egypt in 1881; the Young Turks in 1908; in Iraq between 1936 and 1941 and again in 1958; in Syria in 1949 and following years; and in Egypt in 1952.

What is the reason for the instability of army officers' loyalty to the ruling classes? Unlike most Western countries in the various stages of modern development, the Middle East has an army-officer group characterised by the following qualities:

a. Their origin is generally middle class rather than upper class (except for the highest ranks, where appointments were made on the basis of proximity to the ruling *élite,* that is, Isma'il Shirin, Faruq's brother-in-law, in pre-revolutionary Egypt, or General Taha al-Hashimi of Iraq). Many officers are members of the educated classes who despaired of a professional career. (Naguib, for example, studied law, and there are many other instances of lawyers and teachers.)

b. In some Arab countries the religious or ethnic community of army officers was also different from that of the ruling classes. The clash between Arab officers and the Turkish-Circassian ruling elements was part of the background of the 'Arabi rebellion of 1881; Bakr Sidqi, who headed the Iraq revolt of 1936, was of Kurdish descent; the Syrian Army of the 1940s, which was the heritage of French rule, had especially strong minority-group representation (Kurds, Circassians, 'Alawis); and even in the Egyptian revolution of 1952 the contrast between the insurrecting officer group of Arab origin and Muhammad 'Ali's family, of Turkish descent, was given great publicity.[24]

c. In the Middle East and other Eastern countries young army officers were the pioneers of Westernisation and social reform. The Army was the first body to be modelled on the Western pattern; it was an agent for the dissemination of Western influences, including concepts of social reform. Moreover, the blemishes of the old social order are openly reflected in army life. The ignorant and sick fellah is an inefficient soldier; retarded industry greatly harms the Army's capacity for technical performance; and the corruption affects fighting ability. The Army learnt of these consequences of the old social order from its experience in the Arab-Israeli war.

These characteristics of the new army-officer group in the Middle East go far to explain why it has assumed political rule with the object of bringing about social reform. There are, however, other reasons. Since the urban middle class was formerly always a small group, and remains fairly small even today, it has not constituted a broad foundation on which some form of democracy could develop, as in the West. Even those members of the class who earnestly strove for reform had no power to carry it through. Therefore the parliamentary system was applied in a way that actually left all the power in the hands of the upper class. At the same time, social differences grew greater; corruption spread; the helplessness of the upper class was disclosed in foreign affairs, both military (the Arab-Israel War) and diplomatic (relations between Egypt and Britain) ; and the internal rule of the class was undermined by increasing social and political tension (in Egypt, Black Saturday in January 1952, and the November demonstrations of Syria in 1948, during which the Army was summoned to save the old order). The Army's confidence in and loyalty to the upper class faltered and gave way. However, there was no other social body—group or class—with the power to change the state of affairs. The Army would thus assume power in order to carry out reform on its own and to maintain that social equilibrium which is in the interests of the middle class.

The Army, however, was unable to build up rapidly a broad intermediate stratum which would be capable of preserving equilibrium and maintaining the reform imposed, under conditions of democratic rule. Hence it was always compelled to institute military dictatorship, without wide public backing.

Lower Classes and Labour

The lower classes form the majority of the population of the Arab East. From the viewpoint of standard of living, it would be suitable to include much of the beduin population in their ranks, but because of its single economic function, beduin society cannot be split into classes. Even recalling that at its lowest rung, the social scale of beduins includes artisans and black slaves, these two groups together do not make up any significant proportion of beduin society.

In this connection, it must be stressed that in the Arabian Peninsula slavery still exists. True, it was abolished by law in the colony of Aden long ago, in Bahrain (1937), Kuwait (1947), and Qatar (1952), but for all that, slaves are still to be found, especially among household servants, in the Aden Protectorate, Trucial Oman (which has prohibited traffic in slaves), Yemen, and most of all in Saudia Arabia. Here the rulers prohibited the import of slaves in 1936, but they continue to ignore that regulation.[25] According to various witnesses, slave traffic is mainly from Africa, and there are some private markets. The offspring of slaves and Negro couples also contribute to the slave class. Sometimes freeborn Negroes, who are found in large numbers throughout Saudi Arabia and are generally regarded as of inferior social standing, sell their children into slavery because of financial straits. The impression is that economic prosperity and the high incomes of the upper classes of Saudi Arabia have resulted in an increased demand for slaves in the last generation and have preserved the institution of slavery. Slaves and slave girls are employed primarily for household labour. A few are bodyguards of personages in high administrative positions, and these slaves, like those of important shaikhs, sometimes gain considerable power for themselves. Slaves are not employed in agriculture (except for isolated cases in the large estates of Hijaz).[26] Use of slaves in the Army and bureaucracy, formerly very common all over the Middle East, ceased in the nineteenth century.

The largest group of the lower classes is made up of landless fellahs and fellahs whose plots are insufficient for their livelihood. Since large landowners are generally town-dwellers, and few middle-class folk live in the villages, it is obvious that an exceedingly high proportion of the rural population must be considered lower class. However, as we have noted, village class stratification according to occupation or economic standing is a recent phenomenon and one limited to certain areas; even where some differentiation has set in, the traditional social structure has usually remained intact.

From the viewpoint of income, some of the groups treated as middle class should really be included among the urban lower classes. However, since there is no information on the income of these classes, the division was of necessity based only on occupation and economic function. By these criteria, the urban lower classes may be divided into two main groups: (a) those lacking any fixed and definite livelihood; and (b) the class of urban wage-earners. The boundary between the two groups is by no means clear-cut.

The sector of those lacking a fixed and definite livelihood has reached quite a size in some cities of the Arab East. It came into being as a result of urbanisation, which is more rapid at times than the growth of potential sources of employment in the city. This group also contains persons of other class origin (such as artisans) who lost their livelihood. While the group is most extensive in all Middle Eastern cities, Baghdad being a typical example, it is particularly large in the two great cities of Egypt, Cairo and Alexandria. Some of its characteristics—impermanence of work; the search for jobs wherever they may be found, even if they involve crime (theft, robbery, smuggling, etc.); and the low level of education (most members are illiterate)—have made this group a convenient tool in the hands of powerful personages in the small towns or in town quarters of the cities, and of those who have political ambitions, particularly when the object of their attack is minority groups, foreigners, and their shops and stores. This lower-class sector, lacking as it does any opinion on public affairs and any concern over its leader's objects, is easily incited when there is some profit to be gained on the side.

The urban wage-earner class is a recent development, from the second quarter of the twentieth century only, in most Arab countries. Its precise dimensions are difficult to assess, because what data there are relate to all persons engaged in a certain occupation, both self-employed and wage-earners (population censuses) or cover only industrial workers (industrial censuses). The various attempts in the early 1950s to compute the number of Egyptian workers, on the basis of incomplete and inaccurate statistics, put the figure between 900,000 and 1,100,000 engaged in industry, construction, mining, transport, and communications, out of a total gainfully employed force of 7 to 8 millions. While these "workers" also include self-employed, there can be no doubt that the overwhelming majority were wage-earners. According to Husain ash-Shafi'i, Minister of Social Affairs, there were 725,000 workers in industry and construction in Egypt at the end of 1957.[27] Data for the Sudan are also incomplete. To the 25,000 persons employed in industry and crafts (including self-employed), most of the 25,000 railroad workers should be added, as well as an unknown number of other transport workers and mining and construction workers.[28]

In the Arabian Peninsula the only available figures are for workers employed by the oil companies; these workers, however, make up the bulk of the urban wage-earning class in these countries. Aramco employs 20,000, two-thirds of whom are Saudis; the Bahrain Petroleum Co. about 8,500, 6,000 of whom are Bahrainis; the Kuwait Oil Co. about 8,000, of whom 5,000 are Arabs; and several hundred persons are employed in Qatar and the Kuwait Neutral Zone.[29] In the refineries of Aden there are 1,700 workers, and many others are employed at the port. The 1956 industrial census of Bahrain found a total of 29,596 persons engaged in industry, construction, mining, commerce, transport, and services, of whom 12,203 were foreigners.[30]

The number of workers employed in industry and crafts in Iraq is estimated at 75,000 (among them 30,000 small craftsmen) and in transport, 45,000.[31] These figures apparently do not include construction workers, whose number has grown in recent years. Even without their contribution, a comparison of Iraq and Egypt indicates that in the former country there are relatively more workers in commerce and fewer in industry and communications. Indeed, without doubt the working class is greater, even relatively speaking, in Egypt than in Iraq.

According to official figures, Syria had 91,167 workers in 1953, including more than 8,000 in communications, 6,000 in oil installations, and 4,000 in building; some claim, however, that the figures are incomplete.[32] On the basis of several sources, Grunwald tenders the following estimate of industrial workers in Lebanon: "25,000 employed in 'modern' industries, 25,000 in the 'traditional' industries, either on a permanent or seasonal basis, and an unknown number in the oil industry."[33] If building and communication workers were added, Lebanon would have, relatively, a sizeable labour class. No reliable figures are available for Jordan and Libya; the number of labourers in the oil industry of Libya was 6,300 in 1960.[34]

It would thus appear that, in most of the Arab countries of the Middle East, the urban working class is larger than might be expected, considering how limited has been the development of private domestic industry. This is because workers are largely concentrated in transport (railways, railway workshops, ports, shipyards, etc.) and other public services (electricity, water supply) and oil installations—in other words, in enterprises established by foreign capital or by the Government. Railway and port workers in Basra, for instance, form a considerable part of the working class of Southern Iraq; oil-company workers and their dependents make up a third of the population of Kirkuk; in many other oil centres they form an even higher percentage. (In Saudi Arabia workers of the oil companies constitute 40% of all industrial workers.) Of the 40,000 inhabitants of 'Atbara in Sudan, 90% are railway workers and their families.[35] Similar trends are evident in Egypt and Syria, countries with some degree of private domestic industry.

These factors, which have contributed to the formation of a working class in the Arab East, also explain, at least partially, another characteristic of that class. Industry in the Middle East is composed of a large number of very small enterprises and a limited number of very large ones which employ thousands of workers; the medium-sized plant is rather rare. The largest employer in Sudan, the railway, has more workers than have several hundred small enterprises combined. It is learned of Bahrain in 1956 that 96.6% of all concerns engaged 0–10 labourers, accounting for 32.9% of the labour force, while at the other extreme of the scale were 0.5% of all concerns, each of which engaged over 200 workers, accounting for a further 46.9% of the labour force. According to the 1954 survey of industry in Baghdad, one-third of all workers were employed in enterprises of more than 500 workers, and another third in enterprises of less than nine workers. The three largest concerns together employed 20% of all workers. In the 1940s 93% of all enterprises in Egypt employed less than five workers, and the remaining 7% accounted for 72% of all workers. The two largest textile factories (*Misr* in al-Mahalla al-Kubra, and *Filature Nationale* in Alexandria) employed over 30% of all textile workers.[36]

Two additional factors influenced the uneven growth of the working class: (1) the late development of Arab industry. In order to meet the competition of advanced Western industry, it has tried to rationalise procedures by the establishment of large enterprises; and (2) the lack of capital and industrial credit, and a limited domestic market. These factors hindered or prevented entrepreneurs from setting up competing establishments; as the market grew, existing undertakings expanded.

A third characteristic of the working class in the Arab East is that it is concentrated in a few cities, usually no more than two—the capital and one other city (in some countries the port city). Seventy per cent of the industrial workers of Iraq are centered in Baghdad and the overwhelming majority of transport workers are to be found in Baghdad and Basra. In Syria most urban workers are in Damascus and Aleppo, although Latakia's share has apparently grown in recent years. Beirut and Tripoli in Lebanon occupy a similar position. Various censuses conducted in Egypt have shown that over 50% of all workers were employed in plants located in Cairo and Alexandria.[37]

Authors have put forward three explanations for this fact, in the case of Egypt (and they are largely true of the other countries as well) : (1) industry was not dependent on sources of raw materials and was built up near the centres of consumption. A large percentage of all the population, and especially of its urban sector, are to be found in the two main cities, and the purchasing power of that group is proportionately still higher; (2) the major cities are provided with more adeaquate transport networks, water supply, and gas and electricity facilities than other cities, and they are centres of skilled labour and possess repair and maintenance shops; (3) these cities were the seats of foreign capitalists and entrepreneurs from minority groups who pioneered the development of industry.

The working class in the Arab countries is young both in its own existence and in the age of its members. This is related in part to the generally low age-composition of the population in Arab countries; in part to the fact that villagers who come to the city to earn their living are young (and this factor tends to be self-sustaining, because village emigration still continues and older workers are constantly being replaced by newcomers) ; and finally, to the high percentage of child labour in Arab industry, because of defective labour legislation, poor implementation of the law, and weak trade unions. Industrial censuses conducted in Egypt and Iraq in the 1940s showed that children constituted 8% of all industrial workers, and the same percentage appeared in the 1937 census of modern industries in Syria and Lebanon. These censuses did not include small workshops, in which the percentage of child labour is much higher, as indicated also by the data on traditional industries of Syria and Lebanon in 1937 (13%). Some evidence seems to suggest that the percentage was actually still higher. In 1955-6 child labour in the Sudan made up more than 20% of the total labour force. There are indications, however, that child labour is on the decline.[38]

A further characteristic of the Arab working class is the relatively high proportion of unskilled workers, a characteristic of countries whose industries are young. As a consequence, until recently, and in many areas even at present, foreigners and various minority groups have provided the skilled and managerial man-power, though this may be the result of other factors as well: the contempt for manual labour and the inferior social status associated with it have led Arabs with any degree of education to aspire to an official or administrative position. A second reason for the preponderance of Arab unskilled labourers is that workers recently arrived from the villages and desert find it strange to conceive that the individual should strive to gain greater responsibility and rise above his fellow men. In their view, authority does not stem from skill, experience, and achievement, but from lineage and wealth. Finally, foreign firms, particularly the oil companies, have frequently followed a policy of employing foreigners in all grades above that of unskilled worker, in order to maintain full control over operations. These practices created wide gaps between the wages of unskilled workers and those of skilled workers and managers; as a result, the latter identified themselves with the employers rather than with the workers. There is an even greater gap between the incomes of worker and official; this is one of the reasons for the outstanding disparity between workers and members of the middle class in the Middle East—a disparity both social and economic in nature.[39]

Since the Arab working class is such a recent development, many of the early industrial workers were either villagers or members of tribes, and represented the first generation of workers in their families. A survey conducted in 1954 among port workers of Port Sudan showed that the fathers of only 11% were also port workers, while the fathers of 83% were engaged in agriculture or raised livestock. The percentage of workers of tribal or rural origin in Cairo, Alexandria, Aleppo, Beirut, and similar cities is probably lower. Many of the workers still maintain close ties with their villages, as is seen by the organisations on a tribal or village basis at places of work (investigated in Port Sudan, Aramco, and the "Misr" works of al-Mahalla al-Kubra).[40] Workers regard their employment in the city as temporary, and plan to return to their previous way of life as soon as they have earned a certain sum of money. Indeed, work in the city is frequently of very short duration, and many enterprises have a rapid turnover in their labour force. In Syrian textile mills absenteeism in summer months has reached 15%. In the I.P.C. and A.I.O.C. oil companies, the turnover during the Second World War was 21%, and in Aramco, at certain later periods, it was even greater, especially when expansion was under way. Naturally, the largest turnover of all was registered during periods of oil exploration, when the teams were mobile. One Egyptian economist reported an average annual turnover of 50–100%, and in the textile mills of al-Mahalla al-Kubra it was once 300%. One of the consequences of a high turnover is that a large proportion of the workers remains in low-wage brackets. This lack of permanence also stems in part from the seasonal character of the industries, particularly those based on agricultural raw materials.[41]

There are, however, certain indications pointing in the direction of greater stability of the labour class. As workers acquire a skill, they work more regularly, and more of them tend to remain on a permanent basis. The establishment of housing for workers also reduces the incidence of turnover. The Misr concern claimed that by building a "workers' city" it succeeded in reducing the percentage of workers who left their jobs from 35% in 1946 to 5% in 1949. Nevertheless, the prevailing lack of stability prevents the consolidation of Arab workers as a movement.

The characteristics of the Arab working class, as noted above, go far to explain the size, structure, and nature of the trade-union movement (*niqabat al-'ummal*) in Arab countries. Reliable data on trade unions are available for only a few of the countries. Over 900 trade unions, with a total membership of over 250,000, were registered in Egypt in the middle 1950's, but many of these unions existed on paper only, and the actual number of organised workers was estimated at less than 150,000. Since then, that number has undoubtedly risen, but the periodically published figures should be treated with some caution, as there is a great difference between paper unions and actual ones. At the end of 1956 there were 150 trade unions in the Sudan, whose members numbered at least 100,000; however, these figures also included organisations of clerks and employers. After the military revolt of late 1958 the activity of Sudanese workers' unions was outlawed. In February 1960, a new law on trade unions and labour disputes placed even greater restrictions on workers than the former legislation. Unions hitherto existing were dispersed, and the establishment of new unions was the subject of bitter conflict.[42]

Unions are also found in some countries of the Arabian Peninsula. In Aden there were 11,500 organised workers in 1957, and the Bahrain Federation of Labour claimed that its membership was 6,000 in 1956; but the federation was dissolved at the end of that year. In Saudi Arabia workers are forbidden to organise in trade unions.[43]

In Iraq there were quite a number of trade unions in the 1940s, but most were later outlawed, and the legal movement was very limited before the revolution. In January 1959, after the revolution, workers were again permitted to organise, and in late 1959 a General Federation of Iraqi Labour Unions was established. In Syria official figures mention 256 trade unions in 1956, with a membership of 32,943. Jordan had approximately 11,800 organised workers in 1957. The number of Lebanese unions was thirty-five to forty in the middle 1950s, and by their own estimation they had approximately 60,000 members. Thus, of all Arab countries, Lebanon and Sudan have the greatest percentage of organised labour. In 1956 an inter-Arab federation of trade unions (the "International Confederation of Arab Labour Unions") was established; it is mainly concerned with politics, and the scope of its activities depends largely on the political relations among the Arab countries.[44]

In terms of membership and geographical distribution, the trade unions naturally reflect the characteristics of the Arab working class, even to an exaggerated extent. Of the 146,000 Egyptian workers organised in 488 unions in 1951, 86,000 (59%) belong to the 255 unions (52%) of Cairo and Alexandria. In 1958 the provinces of Damascus and Aleppo claimed 53.5% of all Syrian trade unions and 67.5% of their total membership.[45]

The Arab trade-union movement consists of a few large unions and a very great number of small ones. According to official 1951 Egyptian figures, of 491 unions with a total membership of 149,424, twelve had 55,730 members and 392 (with less than 300 members each) had only 46,946 members. In 1947 about 30,000 workers were organised in the two unions at al-Mahalla al-Kubra and *Filature Nationale,* compared with 16,460 organised in 82 individual unions in the field of transport. In the Sudan one union (railroad workers), out of a total of 41, encompassed 45.7% of all organised workers in 1951, and even after the establishment of several dozen trade unions in subsequent years, this union with its 25,000 members, or a quarter of the total number organised, remained unrivalled in terms of size.

The large number of small trade unions may be explained by the manner in which Arab trade unions were organised. Each union included at first only the workers of a particular plant. This form of organisation prevails in the Sudan and Aden, and formerly in Egypt also. In Egypt, however, particularly in recent years, the trade unions in specific economic branches formed national organisations, while in a few cases the trade unions in a particular provincial town formed a general organisation. At the end of 1956 the General Federation of Egyptian Workers (*Ittihad 'Ummal Misr*), which included the most important trade unions and labour associations in the country, was formed. In June 1959 trade unions were organised in the two regions of the U.A.R. with the object of establishing a common organisation, divided into branches by trade; in practice, the scheme encountered some difficulties, and it was still incomplete at the time of the U.A.R. split. In the Sudan a general labour federation was established in 1949. Syria has many trade unions, each covering workers in a single trade or occupation in a given city; these in turn are associated with any one of three organisations, distinguishable from one another by the political leanings of their leadership and by geographical concentration. In Lebanon the differences among the four trade-union associations are also based on political orientation.

Wide fluctuations in size and composition of membership characterize the trade unions in the Arab countries. The chief reason for this is the instability of the working class itself. The organising of labourers who come to the city for short periods presents serious difficulties. But even the unions which are composed of permanent workers lack stability. In practice, only a small nucleus of active workers maintains contact with the union, and then only when a burning issue faces the movement. Even those workers who are registered in a trade union as permanent members do not pay regular dues, and their interest is largely determined by the immediate union benefits. Ordinarily, when no strike or negotiations for better conditions are taking place, they are apathetic towards the union.

The unions' poor financial situation and limited funds contribute further to the apathy, as well as being one of its results. Wages in Arab countries are low, many unions are small and fragmented, and they have no sources of revenue other than membership dues. They hesitate to press workers for

back dues lest they lose them altogether. One trade-union leader declared in
the 1940s that "the financial reserves of the most successful trade unions in
Egypt do not exceed fifty pounds."[46] Consequently, the services which the
unions can provide, such as assistance during a strike and in times of sickness,
or legal and medical help, are limited. Funds are often so scanty as to
prevent organising activity or the efficient administration of the union itself.
Badaoui has noted that many unions in Egypt did not have their own quarters
and held meetings at the president's home or in a café. The staffs of most
of them consisted of volunteers who engaged in union activity after working
hours. At the beginning of 1946, when the trade-union association in Lebanon had tens of thousands of members, no more than three or four union
officials were paid. The secretaries of the unions, including the secretary of
the 4,000-member railway workers' union, served as volunteers during the
evening hours. This situation prevailed in the trade unions of all the Arab
countries during the 1940s and 1950s.[47] It should be noted that the larger and
well-established unions naturally fare much better, and that financial support by various political elements has sometimes provided staff and facilities.

The poverty and ignorance of the majority of workers, as well as their
indifference, explain the character of the labour-movement leadership and its
attitude to union members. As a rule, the lower echelons of union officials
come from the ranks of the workers (skilled workers or those with some
education) ; the top leadership, which has contacts with the authorities,
organises labour associations and acts as liaison between the trade unions
and political groups, comes from the intelligentsia—teachers, officials and
other educated persons connected with political movement. Lawyers have
played a particularly significant part in the Egyptian trade-union movement.
Aware of their own limitations and inexperience, workers not infrequently
entrusted the protection of their interests to lawyers, who saw in this labour
activity a source of income as well as a stepping-stone to a political career,
or a means of strengthening their standing in the local or national political
arena. Lawyers played a prominent part in trade-union activity in the 1920s
and 1930s, and even more so in the early 1940s, when the Wafd attempted
to organise the trade-union movement on a large scale, on the basis of
"leagues" and "fronts." One of the leaders of the Egyptian trade-union
movement, Sawi Ahmad Sawi, is a lawyer by education. A member of the
royal household, Prince 'Abbas Halim, headed the Egyptian trade-union
movement for about twenty years. Similarly, some Lebanese trade unions
were directed in the 1950s by politicians and powerful notables, such as
Khalid al-Khuri, son of the Lebanese president at that time, and Henry
Pharaon, a rich businessman of Beirut. In some instances, however, workers
themselves have risen to positions of leadership (e.g., Muhammad-Yusuf
al-Mudarrik in Egypt in the 1940s and Subhi al-Khatib in Syria).

The social and educational gulf that exists between the leadership and the workers does not, naturally, provide a basis on which union democracy and workers' participation in the management of union affairs can develop. Trade unions in the various Arab countries have not lived up to their democratic constitutions. The provision calling for periodic general meetings has been completely overlooked, and all union affairs have been conducted by the leadership. Many trade unions are, in fact, under the control of employers. In Egypt this practice seems to be declining as a result of the strong links that have developed between the union leadership and the ruling army-officer group, which has imposed stringent controls on trade unions. In contrast to company-sponsored unions in Egypt, the prevalent form of labour organisation in Syria and Lebanon was a joint body of employers and workers (e.g., the transport association in Lebanon).

In spite of strong outside influences on the trade unions, the workers of the Arab East have for many years been waging a continuous struggle for their demands. In Egypt the first wave of strikes broke out immediately after the First World War (1919) in protest against the privations suffered during the war and as part of the national struggle against the British authorities (the workers' demands being in part social, in part political). Following a long period of quiet, a new wave of strikes broke out in the early 1930s in the wake of the world-wide depression. After smaller waves in 1936 and 1938, the Second World War brought full employment and an emergency régime, and there were no strikes

But at the end of the war the rise in the cost of living, coupled with lay-offs and unemployment, led to a new period of unrest. This was also in part due to the gathering political campaign of those years. The outcome was a series of strikes greater than any previous one and lasting three years, centered first in Cairo's industrial suburb, Shubra al-Khaima, and then spreading to other points, such as al-Mahalla al-Kubra (in September 1947). The Arab-Israel war, the resulting emergency régime, and the introduction of compulsory arbitration brought another pause which lasted until 1950. But the refusal of employers to abide by the Wafd administration's cost-of-living allowance law triggered a wave of strikes which aimed at forcing employers to carry out the provisions of the law. The closing down of many enterprises in 1951–2 because of export difficulties following on the Korean War, and the ensuing unemployment, contributed further to labour unrest. During this period the authors of a book on modernisation in the Middle East who were in contact with Egyptian workers reached the conclusion that these workers have developed a very strong class-consciousness.[48] The height of the crisis was the strike of Kafr ad-Dawar workers and the sympathetic strike of the Muharram Bey workers in Alexandria, in August 1952. The revolutionary régime has so far been generally successful in maintaining "industrial peace" in Egypt, through improving the lot of the workers, instituting a complex machinery for compulsory arbitration, exerting influence on labour leaders, and through sheer Army and police power.

The trade-union struggle in the Sudan reached its high point in 1947-8, when the railway workers declared two long strikes. Improvements in working conditions and unionisation ushered in a two-year period of peace, which came to an end in 1950, when there was a rise in the cost of living. A number of general strikes were at their most severe in 1952. In Saudi Arabia there was a large-scale strike at the Aramco concern in October 1953, and in consequence, working conditions were considerably improved; labour disputes continued until strikes were prohibited by a royal decree of 11 June 1956. In Bahrain, too, many strikes, some forming part of the national movement, broke out in the 1950s; in Aden waves of strikes swept the country in 1959 and 1960; in Iraq the oil industry workers' struggle reached a climax in July 1946 with large-scale strikes involving demonstrations, and again in December 1953.

In Syria the first wave of strikes swept the country in 1936-7 as the result of a decline in the value of the franc and rising prices. A second wave after the Second World War (1946-9) may be traced to inflation, to the adverse effects of the resumption of imports on the young Syrian industry, and to governmental instability. (There was a wave of strikes in Lebanon at the same time.) The military régimes attempted to improve labour conditions and suppress strikes, and it was not until the overthrow of Shishakli that another series of strikes erupted, three in number, each comprising some 20,000 workers, in 1954-6. A fresh wave of strikes hit Lebanon in 1960.

Several major features have characterised the labour struggle in the Arab world. Many strikes have broken out spontaneously, without prior organisation of any kind; the workers themselves walked out when conditions became intolerable. This lack of organisation has often led to inconsistency in policy and to the early termination of the strike if it did not immediately attain its objectives. The trade unions' weakness prevented a united, co-ordinated campaign. The numerous walk-outs which occurred in Egypt in 1950 all revolved around one basic demand—implementation of the cost-of-living allowance Bill—but they were entirely unco-ordinated. Even between two such closely associated groups as the port workers of Alexandria and Port Said, there was no co-operation.[49] However, the struggles were very intense. The living standard of the Arab worker is so low that any further deterioration as a result of increased living costs hits his essential needs, his very subsistence, and impels him to put up a desperate fight. But the bitterness of the struggle also stems from its form. Since the unskilled workers faced the unrelenting pressure of the rural and urban unemployed, who threatened to undermine the effectiveness of the strike, they frequently resorted to the sit-down strike. Employers' attempts to dislodge them from the factories, with the help of the police or armed forces, resulted in pitched battles and many casualties (mainly in Egypt, but also in Syria and other Middle Eastern countries).

The labour struggle was no doubt one of the factors chiefly responsible for the extensive labour legislation in the Middle Eastern countries which have a working class. The principal laws were enacted during periods in which agitation by the labour movement was strong. In Egypt two statutes (child and female labour, and working hours) were adopted in 1933 and 1936. The Wafd government promulgated several laws in the early 1940s, an arbitration law in 1948 following the wave of strikes in that year, and a whole series of laws in 1950 (sickness funds, accidents, social security, and collective agreements). In 1952 the revolutionary régime introduced a new set of labour laws (the individual labour contract, trade-union organisation, and an amendment to the arbitration law).

The principal labour legislation in the Sudan (trade unions, labour contracts and working conditions, arbitration, and health and accident compensation) was enacted in 1948 following on the first wave of strikes.[50] In pre-revolutionary Iraq there had been no new legislation since the 1939 law concerning safety and hygiene in factories, and the 1942 amendment to the 1936 labour law regulating working conditions, child labour, compensation, arbitration, and unionisation. After the revolution a new general law and various regulations on labour came into effect in 1958 and 1959. They deal with employment, trade unions, accident and illness insurance, compensation, and housing.[51] In Syria and Lebanon labour legislation was first introduced at the beginning of the Second World War; in both countries the main law—which covered working conditions (wages, hours, days off, holidays), work by women and children, arbitration, trade-union organisation, and other provisions—was enacted in 1946. The "Labour and Workman Regulations" of Saudi Arabia were enacted on 10 October 1947, and those of Bahrain on 1 January 1958. Labour legislation in Aden, including compulsory arbitration, was violently attacked by a congress of trade unions of the colony in August 1960.[52] On 5 April 1959 the U.A.R. issued a general labour law for Egypt and Syria. The law includes clauses on labour exchange, employment of the disabled and foreigners, apprenticeship, individual and collective labour contracts, working hours, employment of women and children, work in mines and quarries, wages, trade unions, and arbitration.[53]

While there are serious gaps in the laws themselves in some countries, the main problem is that many of the provisions of existing laws are not implemented. The reasons for this are not far to seek: ineffectual control over the many small dispersed plants; the influence of employers on the bureaucracy and on the Government itself; the weak status of the workers and the trade unions. The laws are, of course, most effectively implemented in the large plants, in the big cities, where strong unions exist, and in those countries where the régime is genuinely interested in carrying out the laws.

The lack of worker representation in the legislative bodies of the Arab countries may be another reason for the inadequate labour legislation and the poor implementation of the labour laws. Various attempts by workers' representatives to win a seat in the Egyptian Parliament ended in failure. Thus, in the January 1945 elections there were seven candidates supported by the trade unions and the Egyptian Labour Party which in all received 3,000 votes, but not a single candidate was elected. In the November 1949 Syrian elections the trade-union federation entered candidates in Damascus, Homs, and Aleppo, but they were all defeated. In the 1953 general elections in Sudan the 'Atbara workers voted almost unanimously for the sectarian leader, while the secretary of the railway workers' union, an outstanding labour leader, received only a negligible number of votes.[54]

The reason for these defeats does not necessarily lie in the greater prestige or position of the non-labour leader. There are many ways by which election results can be influenced. At any rate, the total result has been that not a single representative of the workers was elected to any parliament of the Arab countries prior to the military revolutions. In the new Congress of the Popular Force, which met in May 1962, there were 250 representatives of workers out of a total of 1,500.[55]

None the less, the trade unions are sufficiently strong and consolidated to be used by political parties and movements as an avenue through which they can extend their influence among the workers, and the parties use the unions in order to organise the workers and win their support. The liaison between workers and political groups is maintained by the union leadership, which is made up of skilled workers and educated persons who subscribe to certain political ideologies, mostly leftist, or who have connections with the parties and national movements (such as the organisations recently established by the army-officer group). While it cannot be said that the rank and file has been deeply penetrated by these political movements, the labour organisations as such have assumed considerable importance in the national political arena.

NOTES

1. Saaty, p. 57; Berger, *The Middle Classes*, pp. 63–64.
2. Hamdan, p. 33.
3. Arab names have no titles denoting nobility, like the French *de* or the German *von*.
4. *OM*, 1937, pp. 471–95; *Images* (illustrated weekly), 28 January 1950; Lerner and Pevsner, p. 454.
5. Many examples for Egypt are given in Baer, *History of Landownership*, pp. 140–2.

6. A. A. I. Gritly, "The Structure of Modern Industry in Egypt," *L'Égypte contemporaine*, November–December 1947, p. 376.

7. For detailed discussion see C. Issawi, "The Entrepreneur Class," in S. N. Fisher (ed.), *Social Forces in the Middle East*, New York, 1955.

8. *The Middle East 1958*, Europa Publications, London, 1958, pp. 127, 196, 283, 332, 363.

9. A. J. Meyer, *Middle East Capitalism*, Cambridge, Mass., 1959, pp. 34–9; cf. Berque, *Les Arabes*, pp. 106, 109.

10. Berque, *Les Arabes*, p. 118.

11. Berger, *The Middle Class*, p. 66.

12. Grunwald, p. 224.

13. Remnants of craft guilds are to be found in Yemen (Fayein, p. 102), and in Qatar among artisans and merchants of the lower classes, who keep up the traditional rites (oral information).

14. See Issawi, *Egypt at Mid-Century*, pp. 259–60, 264.

15. M. Berger, *Bureaucracy and Society in Modern Egypt*, Princeton, 1957, pp. 94–5 and Chapter 4.

16. Berger, *Bureaucracy*, pp. 45, 107.

17. *az-Zaman*, 3 May 1949.

18. Berger, *Bureaucracy*, pp. 82–3.

19. Matthews and Akawi, pp. 37, 140; Cohen, p. 189; *Directory of the Republic of Iraq*, 1960, p. 487.

20. Makarius, p. 31.

21. The problem of thousands of unemployed among graduates of agricultural schools was one of the concerns of the land reform committee. See, for instance, *al-Ahram*, 15 January 1955; cf. also Lerner and Pevsner, pp. 237–8, 276.

23. Cf. Lerner and Pevsner, pp. 92–3, 236–7, 277–9.

24. See G. Baer, "Egyptian Attitudes towards Land Reform," in W. Z. Laqueur (ed.), *The Middle East in Transition*, London, 1958, pp. 95–7.

25. Sir Reader Bullard (ed.), *The Middle East, A Political and Economic Survey*, third edition, London, 1958, pp. 74–5.

26. Lipsky, pp. 29–30, 67–8, 175–7, 210. For the Yemen see Fayein, pp. 163–4.

27. *al-Gumhuriya*, 14 February 1958.

28. Fawzi, *The Labour Movement in the Sudan*, pp. 9, 36.

29. D. Finnie, "Recruitment and Training of Labour—The Middle East Oil Industry," *MEJ*, Spring 1958, pp. 127–37.

30. W. A. Beling, "Recent Developments in Labor Relations in Bahrayn," *MEJ*, Spring 1959, p. 158.

31. IBRD, *The Economic Development of Iraq*, pp. 2, 129, 149; United Nations, *Economic Developments in the Middle East 1945–1954*, New York, 1955, p. 99.

32. Hadas, "Hapo'el hasuri," *Hamizrah Hehadash*, VII, p. 102.

33. Grunwald, p. 254.

34. Thomas, p. 266.

35. International Labour Organisation (ILO), *Social Conditions in the Petroleum Industry*, Geneva, 1950, pp. 10–11; G. Lenczowski, *Oil and State in the*

Middle East, New York, 1960, p. 254; Fawzi, *The Labour Movement in the Sudan,* p. 36.

36. Fawzi, *ibid.,* pp. 9, 36, 94; Beling, p. 159; UN, *Economic Developments 1945–54,* p. 99; Gritly, pp. 488–98.

37. *UN, ibid.;* IBRD, *Economic Development of Syria,* pp. 357–67; Gritly, pp. 469–76; UN, *The Development of Manufacturing Industry in Egypt, Israel, and Turkey,* New York, 1958, p. 59.

38. ILO, Regional Conference for the Near and Middle East 1951, *Manpower Problems,* Geneva, 1951, p. 17; Grunwald, p. 246; Issawi, *Egypt at Mid-Century,* p. 172; Fawzi, *Manpower Distribution in the Sudan,* p. 27.

39. Fawzi, *Labour Movement,* p. 10; Hadas, pp. 102–3; Issawi, *Egypt at Mid-Century,* p. 172; Finnie, passim; Thomas, pp. 272–3; Makarius, p. 36.

40. Fawzi, *Labour Movement,* pp. 10–11, 36–7, 101; T. B. Stauffer, "The Industrial Worker," in S. N. Fisher (ed.), *Social Forces in the Middle East,* pp. 89–92.

41. A. A. Allouni, "The Labour Movement in Syria," *MEJ,* Winter 1959, p. 71; Lenczowski, pp. 296–7; Thomas, p. 270; Stauffer, p. 89; Issawi, *Egypt at Mid-Century,* pp. 165–6; ILO, *Manpower Problems,* pp. 14–15.

42. *MER,* 1960, pp. 411–12.

43. *ME Aff,* March 1960, p. 89; Beling, pp. 161–3.

44. For details see Lenczowski, pp. 281 ff; Wheelock, pp. 266–8.

45. Issawi, *Egypt at Mid-Century,* p. 174; Europa Publications, *The Middle East 1958,* p. 363.

46. *al-Ba'th* (Cairo), 1 February 1946.

47. Z. Badaoui, *Les Problèmes du travail et les organisations ouvrières en Égypte,* Alexandria, 1948, pp. 118–22; A. Cohen, *Tenu'ath hapo'alim ha'uravith,* Tel-Aviv, 1947, p. 78. See also Hadas, p. 106; Fawzi, *Labour Movement,* pp. 99–100.

48. Lerner and Pevsner, pp. 229, 232–3, 260–1.

49. *al-Ahram,* 6 and 14 April 1950.

50. For detailed analysis see Fawzi, *Labour Movement,* Chapter 7.

51. Details in the *Directory of the Republic of Iraq,* 1960, pp. 572–3.

52. *al-Ahram,* 7–10 August 1960; *The Times,* 16 and 19 August 1960.

53. Law No. 91 of 1959, French translation of full text in *Cahiers de l'Orient contemporain,* XL, pp. 287–332.

54. Egyptian Press of December 1944 and January 1945; *Hamizrah Hehadash,* I, p. 163; Fawzi, *Labour Movement,* p. 101.

55. *OM,* 1962, pp. 244–6.

REFERENCES

Newspapers and Periodicals

(Abbreviations used in References and Notes are in parentheses.)

al-Ahram, Cairo, daily.
al-Ba'th, Cairo, weekly (appeared for a short period in 1946).
Annales Economies—Sociétés—Civilisations, Paris (*Annales*).
Cahiers de l'Orient contemporain, Paris.
al-Gumhuriya, Cairo, daily.
Hamizrah Hehadash, Jerusalem (Israel), quarterly.
Middle East Journal, Washington, D.C., quarterly (*MEJ*).
Middle Eastern Affairs, New York, monthly (*ME Aff*).
Oriente Moderno, Rome, monthly (*OM*).
az-Zaman, Baghdad, daily.

Yearbooks, Collective Publications, and Publications of International Bodies

Bullard, Sir Reader (ed.), *The Middle East, A Political and Economic Survey*, third ed., London, 1958.
Darwish, M. F., and others, *Directory of the Republic of Iraq* 1960 (in Arabic; Arabic title: *Dalil al-Jumhuriya al-Iraqiya*), Baghdad, 1961.
Europa Publications, *The Middle East 1958*, sixth edition, London, 1958.
International Bank for Reconstruction and Development (IBRD), *The Economic Development of Iraq*, Baltimore, 1952.
IBRD, *The Economic Development of Syria*, Baltimore, 1955.
ILO, Regional Conference for the Near and Middle East, Teheran, April 1951, *Manpower Problems*, Geneva, 1951.
United Nations (UN), Department of Economic and Social Affairs, *Review of Economic Conditions in the Middle East 1951–2*, New York, 1953.
Economic Developments in the Middle East 1945–54, New York, 1955.
The Development of Manufacturing Industry in Egypt, Israel, and Turkey, New York, 1958.

Books and Articles

Allouni, A. A., "The Labor Movement in Syria," *MEJ*, Winter 1959.
Baer, G., "Egyptian Attitudes towards Land Reform 1922–1955," in W. X. Laqueur (ed.), *The Middle East in Transition*, London, 1958.
———, *A History of Landownership in Modern Egypt 1800–1950*, London, 1962.
Beling, W. A., "Recent Development in Labor Relations in Bahrayn," *MEJ*, Spring 1959.
Berger, M., *Bureaucracy and Society in Modern Egypt*, Princeton, 1957.

————, "The Middle Class in the Arab World," in W. Z. Laqueur (ed.), *The Middle East in Transition*, London, 1958.

Berque, J., *Les Arabes d'hier à demain*, Paris, 1960.

Fawzi, S., *The Labour Movement in the Sudan 1946–1955*, London, 1957.

Fayein, C., *Hakima, Eineinhalb Jahre Ärztin im Jemen*, Wiesbaden, 1956.

Finnie, D., "Recruitment and Training of Labor—The Middle East Oil Industry," *MEJ*, Spring 1958.

Gritly, A. A. I., "The Structure of Modern Industry in Egypt," *L'Égypte contemporaine*, November–December 1947.

Grunwald, K., "Hati'us shel Surya ve-Halevanon," *Hamizrah Hehadash*, Vol. V, pp. 243–57.

Hadas, Y., "Hapo'el hasuri," *Hamizrah Hehadash*, Vol. VII, pp. 99–109.

Hamdan, G., "The Growth and Functional Structure of Khartoum," *GR*, January 1960.

Issawi, C., *Egypt at Mid-Century*, London, 1954.

————, "The Entrepreneur Class," in S. N. Fisher (ed.), *Social Forces in The Middle East*, Ithaca, N.Y., 1955.

Lenczowski, G., *Oil and State in the Middle East*, Ithaca, N.Y., 1960.

Lerner, D., and Pevsner, L., *The Passing of Traditional Society, Modernizing the Middle East*, Glencoe, Ill., 1958.

Lipsky, G. A., *et al.*, *Saudi Arabia, its People, its Society, its Culture*, New Haven, 1959.

Makarius, R., *La Jeunesse intellectuelle d'Égypte au lendemain de la deuxième guerre mondiale*, Paris, 1960.

Matthews, R. D., and Akrawi, M., *Education in Arab Countries of the Near East*, Washington, D. C., 1949.

Meyer, A. J., *Middle East Capitalism*, Cambridge, Mass., 1959.

el-Saaty, H., "The Middle Classes in Egypt," *L'Égypte contemporaine*, April, 1957.

Stauffer, T. B., "The Industrial Worker," in S. N. Fisher (ed.), *Social Forces in the Middle East*, Ithaca, N.Y., 1955.

Thomas, F. C., "The Libyan Oil Worker," *MEJ*, Summer 1961.

Wheelock, K., *Nasser's New Egypt*, London, 1960.

The Iraqi Marsh Dwellers occupy the low-lying country in the south basin of the Tigris and the Euphrates just above Basra. The marshland of southern Iraq is perhaps one of the largest in the world; Salim records that it has been estimated to cover as much as 20,000 square miles.

Dr. Salim prefers the specific term Marsh Dwellers over previously used terms such as the "Marsh Arabs" or "Ma'dan" and he suggests that these people are "partly descendants of the Sumerians and Babylonians, although their numbers have been augmented by immigration and intermarriages with the Persians on the east and the bedouins on the west."

Ech-Chibayish, the village wherein Dr. Salim conducted his field study in 1953, had a total of approximately 11,000 people and was rated by him as a "typical marsh-dwelling community."

Dr. Salim's selection is a relevant contribution toward an understanding of social stratification in the Middle East and his total work is a valuable study of a singular regional subculture.

14

Traditional Stratification Among the Marsh Dwellers

S. M. SALIM

In ech-Chibayish five social classes are traditionally recognized. First are the "holy men," second the ex-ruling clan, third the heads of commoner clans and lineages with other commoners, fourth the slaves and last the foreign Subba.

THE "HOLY MEN"

Is-sāda claim descent from Muhammad the Prophet. All are supposed to be descendants of one or another of the Imams through Fatima, the Prophet's

From *Marsh Dwellers of the Euphrates* (Monographs in Social Anthropology, No. 23), pp. 62–71; reprinted by permission of The Athlone Press.

daughter, and her husband, Ali Ibn Abu Talib, the Prophet's cousin, and thus hold a highly esteemed religious position.   There is no way of ascertaining whether a man is really a direct descendant of the Prophet, since there are no authentic records and the whole matter depends entirely on claim.   Many people in the marsh region and other communities pretend to be *sāda,* since such a claim confers a high social prestige, with possibilities of material gain. The only precaution taken is that the claimant sometimes changes his place of residence, so that his claim may not be examined too thoroughly.

Because these reputed "holy men" enjoy high prestige among the Shi'ah Marsh Dwellers, many of them have come to the marsh region.   They live, in general, by begging, and on whatever concession of land and crops the shaikhs may grant them.   They exploit the ignorant Marsh Dwellers by claiming supernatural powers to cure maladies or cause misfortunes; and they make a great deal of money by practising magic rites.

At ech-Chibayish there are eight families of "holy men" comprising altogether about 50 individuals.   Six of these families are known to have been living in the village for many generations.   The *sāda* of ech-Chibayish differ in many respects from the "holy men" of the other marsh communities.   None of them is known to have practised any magic or claimed supernatural power. This is probably connected with the unusual care and generosity shown to them by the shaikhs and with their consequent economic security.   Apart from their claimed descent and (in the case of one or two) the wearing of blue head-cloths,[1] the *sāda* of ech-Chibayish are quite ordinary individuals in their way of life.   Only two earn their living by begging.   The others are traders, cultivators or mat-weavers.

Two of the *sāda* families, those of Bait Sayid Khalaf, are by far the richest people in the village.   They are the main grain and mat-traders and are also the main moneylenders of ech-Chibayish.   Two other *sāda* families, Bait Sayid Baqir is-Sayid Ali and Bait Sayid Yousif is-Sayid Jabir, are mat-traders and shopkeepers, who come twelfth and thirteenth among the 20 rich men of the village.   Two of the remaining four *sāda* families live by cultivation and matweaving and the other two by hiring their labour or by occasional cultivation.

Like all the Shi'ah of Iraq, the inhabitants of ech-Chibayish look upon *is-sāda* as sacred people, "the sons of the Messenger of God" (*awlad rasūl allah*), so that respect and veneration are paid to them as a religious duty. Ahl ech-Chibayish take oaths by *is-sāda,* especially by one or two of them known to be scrupulous in their religion.   In matters such as betrothal, paying compensation for a crime, sending a delegation to soften the feelings of an injured man, it is preferably a *sayyid* who leads the delegation, because he is never refused if he makes a demand or request.   *Is-sāda* sit at the best places in the guest houses and are given priority wherever they go.   The clan heads do not take their share of the crop from *is-sāda* who cultivate their lands.

Being descendants of the Prophet, *is-sāda* are supposed to be very scrupulous in religious matters and far removed from the struggle for gain, more especially if this struggle involves usury, which is strongly condemned by Islam. In practice, four of the eight families of *is-sāda* at ech-Chibayish almost monopolize the business of moneylending. The other two *sāda* families do the same in connection with the mat trade. In fact, these four *sāda* families not only depart from the religious duties imposed on them as Moslems and their status as "Sons of Muhammad," but they seem to be using their religious status for material gain. People believe in them and never think of suing them in cases of dispute. At the mere mention of the oath, "By my grandfather, the Messenger of God," a tribesman has to believe what the *sayyid* claims, or otherwise he becomes an infidel. This oath, however, has always been used as a means of gain and cheating. But Ahl ech-Chibayish are quite aware of the *sāda* traders' attitude in business and, consequently, do not look upon them with the same respect as they do the non-business *sāda* who do not allow the lust for gain to get the better of them.

It should be stressed that *is-sāda* is not a caste, or a clan. This applies to every part of Iraq. The *sāda* of ech-Chibayish live scattered over the village; five families live with Ahl ish-Shaikh clan, two with Ahl Ghrīj, and one with Ahl Limabir. The eight families are attached to the clans with whom they live. There is no agnatic relationship among the *sāda* families, not even between *sāda* of the same clan. Nevertheless, the *sāda* tend to marry among themselves. There is no strict endogamy as a few cases of inter-marriage with non-*sāda* families have been recorded in the village; but they are rare.

Il-muwamna are the religious agents of *il-mujtahid,* the chief religious head of the Shi'ah sect at the holy city of in-Najaf. Such an agent, referred to locally as *mūman,* and addressed as *shaikh,* is *mukhawal shar'i,* religiously authorized to settle matters covered by Islamic law, such as marriage, divorce and inheritance. *Il-mūman* is supposed to be a graduate of one of the religious schools of in-Najaf and lives on what money people give him for his religious services. In addition, he has other important functions. He conducts the *qrāyat* mourning ceremonies performed throughout the first ten days of *Muḥarram* (an Arabic month) to commemorate the death of the Imam Husain and his kin and followers in the Battle of Karbala. *Il-muwamna* are paid for conducting such ceremonies from the communal contributions paid by the mourners, who do their utmost to pay as much as they can because they believe that the more they pay, the greater the religious reward.

At ech-Chibayish there is one *mūman* who is a graduate of a religious school and thus fully authorized in all religious matters. He is not a native of ech-Chibayish but is responsible as far as religious matters are concerned for ech-Chibayish and il-Midina, a village about ten miles down the river, and divides his time between the two. There is also a family whose late head

was an authorized *mūman*. After his death, two of his sons, though uneducated in religious affairs, began to perform some simple religious practices,
such as reading prayers or conducting *qrāyat* ceremonies, but neither enjoys
the same prestige as the authorized *mūman*. During the month of *Muḥarram*,
one or two of the numerous touring *muwamna* come to the village to conduct
the *qrāyat* ceremonies of which there are about 15.

   Il-muwamna, especially graduates of religious schools, are highly respected and classed with the *sāda*. They are usually entirely devoted to their
religious duties and do not take up any secular business. But some of them,
especially those who are unauthorised, practise begging, and exploit the ignorant Marsh Dwellers, particularly those of Amara region. The *mūman* of
ech-Chibayish, Shaikh Muhammad Ali Hmūzi, was devoted to his duties; he
enjoyed high prestige in the village because of his religious knowledge and
because he did not beg.

THE EX-RULING CLAN

   Ahl Khayūn are the noble clan of Beni Isad. They trace their descent to
one Dahla 13 generations back from the eldest living members of the clan.

   For four centuries Ahl Khayūn were the rulers of Beni Isad. Till the
abolition of the shaikhdom in 1924, they lived as a military aristocracy. They
exercised great power and treated all other members of the tribe as subjects,
or serfs. A tribesman was always supposed to be at the disposal of the noble
clan for any services that might be required of him. The shaikhs, the heads of
Ahl Khayūn, used fines and imprisonment in their mud fortresses as the usual
method of punishment. The shaikh and his kinsmen appropriated most of
the produce of the land and collected dues on date palms and cattle. The
shaikh used to share with the fathers even the brideprices of girls. The
Khayūni used to have the undisputed right to insult, beat or maltreat any
tribesman. Any member of the clan had the right to intervene in any dispute.
In travelling, or any kind of labour, the Khayūni could order any number of
Beni Isad to offer their services. If he needed money he would collect from the
tribe, because a Khayūni was not expected to work; his only task was to rule.

   When the Shaikhdom was abolished, and the government established a
strong administrative unit in the village, Ahl Khayūn found themselves in a
changed situation. They would not submit to the government and some of
them took to leading groups of outlaws and thieves to the Hor. They caused
much trouble before they were finally defeated and banished. Others left for
Amara and other districts hoping for a change of conditions but returned later
to ech-Chibayish. One or two of the wiser and more peace-loving men, such
as Abdil-Hadi Ahl Khayūn, remained in the village, and even helped and supported the government in its efforts to maintain law and order. Later the

government allotted salaries and rich lands outside ech-Chibayish to some of them.

To-day the great bulk of Ahl Khayūn, about 30 men, live at ech-Chibayish, but there are branches of the clan at Gurmat Ali and Amara, and the last shaikh divides his time between Baghdad, where he maintains a modern house, and his lands about 50 miles away in the Diyala Province. At ech-Chibayish, two families of Ahl Khayūn live on salaries received from the government as "banishment stipend," one lives on the salary of its head who is a government employee in the village, one lives on previous savings, whilst the remaining ten families live by land holding, trade and cultivation.

Ahl Khayūn are now in a state of transition from their previous high status to that of ordinary citizens. Some of them have begun, for the first time in the history of Ahl Khayūn, to cultivate land and tend cattle. Others have entered government service as clerks and soldiers, and some have taken up jobs which even the ordinary member of Beni Isad despise, such as running a motor launch service.

Except for a certain superficial respect, which is indeed only accorded to those who are really "good fellows," Beni Isad do not to-day allow Ahl Khayūn any of their previous privileges.

Ahl Khayūn, however, still maintain in general a higher standard of living. Except for one or two families, they live in better huts equipped with good furniture, such as chairs, wardrobes, boxes for keeping clothes, etc. They wear clothes of the same style as those of the natives but always more luxurious. Their women dress far better than the other women, using jewellery and cosmetics. They eat food which is nearer to that of the townspeople and better and richer than that of the rest of Ahl ech-Chibayish. In their homes they maintain certain traditions about which they are very particular. For example, the younger members of the clan, though younger only by a single day, must show respect by kissing the hand of the elder and rising in his presence in any public place. Women are permitted neither to eat with nor in the presence of men, and may not go to bed before them. No Khayūni should paddle or pole himself in a canoe. The majority of Ahl Khayūn are literate.

The strongest Ahl Khayūn tradition is that of clan endogamy which is strict in the case of their womenfolk and only occasionally broken in the case of their men. Since the days of Shaikh Hasan Ahl Khayūn, not a single Khayūniya woman has been given in marriage outside the clan. But Ahl Khayūn men do sometimes marry outside the clan. Nearly all Ahl Khayūn shaikhs were married to one or more non-Khayūniya women in addition to their Khayūniya wives. Although few men among the present younger generations of Ahl Khayūn are married to outsider wives as well, this tendency to out-marriage has given rise to a surplus of unmarried women in the clan. In 1953 there were six very old unmarried women of Ahl Khayūn and there were a number who were passing the marriageable age. Understandably Ahl Khayūn women resist strongly any attempt on the part of the men to marry wives from other clans.

HEADS OF COMMONER CLANS AND LINEAGES: THE AJAWĪD

The shaikhs of Beni Isad used to choose distinguished men, one from each clan, and appoint them as their agents in those clans. When the last shaikh was overthrown, the government wisely appointed all those who were agents at that time as ṣirkals, each in his own clan. Also, the government ratified the lineage headmen in their positions and made them mukhtārs.

Each clan contains a number of men who are members of large lineages and known to be "good fellows," helpful and peace-loving, with a good knowledge of tribal law and traditions and sound, trustworthy opinions. Such men are known as ajawīd it-tayfa. Together with the ṣirkals and mukhtārs, they constitute a subdivision of the third class of the ech-Chibayish community. They do not differ from the other commoners either in traditions or customs, nor do they intermarry to any extent. Except for the ṣirkals, who are relatively wealthy as a result of land holding and other dues, and who with the mukhtārs enjoy some political power, they differ little economically from the other commoners. Their rights and privileges derive from the respect they enjoy in the community and from the influence they exert.

OTHER COMMONERS

The commoners are the vast majority of Ahl ech-Chibayish. They live by mat-weaving, cultivation and seasonal labour migration. They keep cattle and most families have date palms on their dwelling islands. In general they are poor and the majority are heavily in debt either to mat traders or money-lenders.

It has already been mentioned that in the past the commoners suffered a great deal from exploitation by their shaikhs. But nowadays this is not possible. The government is there to check any abuse of power on the part of ṣirkals. The commoners have full freedom to follow any occupation, to cultivate anywhere they like and live in any part of the village. They can even change their lineage or clan by process of adoption. In their personal affairs, such as marriage, divorce, mortgage, sale and other similar matters, the commoners are quite free and the ṣirkals or the mukhtārs cannot legally intervene.

The commoners form one class equal in rights and obligations, but certain distinctions affect an individual's personal prestige. Thus it is more distinguished to belong to certain clans, or to follow certain occupations than others. A member of Ahl Ghrīj or Ahl Khatir clan is, for example, less respected in the community than a member of Ahl ish-Shaikh or Ahl Anaisi clan. According to tradition, some occupations count as beneath the dignity of a Beni Isad.

SLAVES (IL-'ABID)[2]

During the old days of the shaikhdom a distinctive feature of the shaikh's household was the large number of slaves employed as household servants, coffee men, paddlers, messengers and agents. All these were African Negroes imported from Arabia and sold in the slave markets of Basra and Baghdad during the old days of the slave trade. Though slaves were then treated as chattels, they were, at ech-Chibayish, monopolized by the shaikhs and Ahl Khayūn. Any slave outside Khayūni households had originally come from them.

In those days, when even the free tribesmen were serfs to their shaikhs, the slaves were without legal or social status. At ech-Chibayish they used to live in their masters' households "for the food of their bellies" and what clothes their masters cared to allow them. Their masters controlled their marriages. They could not own or inherit property. If a slave was involved in a criminal case, his master settled the case and paid or received his compensation. Their masters beat them, fettered them, and if any suspicions were aroused of sexual relations between them and their masters' womenfolk, they were killed.

The slave's main duties were either inside the shaikh's household, preparing and serving coffee at the guest house, bringing fodder for the cattle, paddling the shaikh's canoe and so on, or outside the household. Those employed outside acted as liaison officers between the shaikh and tribesmen, and were chosen from among the more faithful and intelligent. They were employed as messengers, to pass on the shaikh's orders, or as agents in the fields, to supervise cultivation and crop division. Those appointed to represent the shaikh in his widely scattered estates attained high authority and accumulated fortunes of their own. A few slaves enjoyed the full confidence of their masters, and consequently were second in command to them. Some even built guest houses, which were frequented by people seeking their favour. The personal servant of Shaikh Salim Ahl Khayūn, for example, used to dress like the shaikh himself and bathe in perfumed water, and paid a large sum of money as a brideprice for a "white" wife whom he brought from Baghdad.

When the shaikhdom was abolished, the slaves were suddenly left without masters. The shaikh was arrested, the majority of Ahl Khayūn were living as outlaws in the Hor, and the few Khayūni families who remained at ech-Chibayish were too poor even to maintain themselves. At that time there were at least 50 slave families. Some of them migrated to Basra and Baghdad to work and live as labourers or to join the newly formed army and police forces. Most of those who stayed in the village left their masters' households and began to earn a living as free men.

To-day there are only 22 families of slave origin (109 individuals) in ech-Chibayish. All of them have Negroid features. Only six of these families are still living as slaves in the old sense of the word: five families working in four Khayūni households, and one family in the household of a lineage head-man of Ahl Ghrīj clan. Every one of these six families had been compelled for various reasons to remain in their previous status. Two of those who remained in the village agreed to return to two Khayūni families as servants but not as slaves; they were paid monthly salaries and each maintained their own hut and household. Eight of the remaining 14 families of slaves are earn-ing their living by cultivation and mat-weaving, and six by living on salaries received from 12 of their members employed as soldiers and government employees.

The slaves, like their previous masters, have adjusted themselves to living as ordinary tribesmen. They speak of themselves now as "Beni Isad" and not " 'abīd Ahl Khayūn." The relation between them and Ahl Khayūn is that of fellow tribesmen, except in the case of those who are still living in their mas-ters' households. They earn their living freely and enjoy full rights in the community. In many tribal affairs, such as mourning ceremonies and com-pensation, they are treated as ordinary tribesmen, and have no extra obliga-tions in the community.

Though the six slave families living in their masters' households continue to live as their fathers did before them, they can enjoy full freedom if they wish. No master can now stop a slave from leaving him, and there is none of the former cruelty shown to the slave, because he can run away if mal-treated. Besides, owing to the full legal status now enjoyed by a slave, legal action can be taken against the master. In fact, these six slave families do enjoy considerable freedom in their personal affairs. The link between them and their masters is not of the old bondage of slavery but of loyalty to the families in whose service they have been living for so long. Moreover, such a life ensures the slaves an easy security. The masters need their service and keep them because it is not possible to find servants at ech-Chibayish. The real situation of these ex-slaves and their masters is quasi slavery or voluntarily suspended freedom.

But there is no intermarriage between ex-slaves and the rest of Ahl ech-Chibayish. There have been rare cases when masters fell in love with their female slaves and married them; but the offspring, called "half-breed," though free, cannot get "white" wives; and they usually marry either slaves or half-breeds like themselves. It has not been known in the village for a freewoman to be given in marriage to a slave.   The case of Shaikh Salim's personal servant, referred to previously, was the only case in which a slave was married to a freewoman and, as has been stated, she was a townswoman from Baghdad.   In a case of elopement which concerned il-Hadadiyīn and Ahl Wnais clans many years ago, the eloping girl's kin demanded exceptionally high compensation because the lover had some slave traits in his features and it was therefore believed that his mother had borne him illegitimately through liaison with a slave.   It was a double disgrace that a man suspected of being a half-breed should have eloped with their free-born daughter.

IS-ṢUBBA (THE MANDAEANS)[3]

The Ṣubba are a religious minority living in southern Iraq, mainly near the marshes and on the river banks because water is so important to them for ceremonial ablutions.   They claim to be followers of St. John the Baptist, and have certain holy books written by hand in a language akin to Syriac and Aramaic, called Mandaean.   Their chief rite is ceremonial ablution. Water, they hold, is the element which gives life to body and soul; they practise ablution as often as they can, and everything eaten must be washed in running water.   Their priests slaughter the animals which they eat and perform marriage and funeral ceremonies.   They have certain feasts and days of fasting.   They never intermarry with non-Ṣubba and avoid close contact with those of different faith.   They number about 4,000 souls in Iraq and are mainly occupied as blacksmiths, silversmiths and canoe- and boat-builders.

The two main centres of Ṣubba in Iraq are Amara and Sūg ish-Shyūkh regions.   Until 40 years ago about 170 Ṣubba families used to live at ech-Chibayish, but all migrated gradually to il-Gurna and Sūg ish-Shyūkh, because during the period of political instability from 1914 to 1924 they were frequently violated and plundered by Ahl Khayūn.   All the boats and the canoes used by Ahl ech-Chibayish used to be locally built by Ṣubba, but owing to their growing outside contacts, Ahl ech-Chibayish have now begun to buy their canoes and boats from il-Hwair, a marshy village about 15 miles down the river.

There are now only three Ṣubba families living at ech-Chibayish and these consist of only 13 individuals.   All three families are blacksmiths and manufacture fishing-spears, sickles, reed-splitters, spades, nails and so on. They never practise cultivation or mat-weaving, but they keep cattle.

Being non-Moslems, the Ṣubba are considered religiously polluted.   The people of ech-Chibayish do not eat with them nor drink from receptacles they have used.   No question of intermarriage ever arises.   The one known exception at ech-Chibayish was an elopement between a slave and a Ṣubbiya girl. In this case the girl's kin made great efforts to arrest the eloping couple and

subsequently refused to accept compensation according to the tribal law because they did not want to give their daughter in marriage, as the law required, to a man who was a Moslem and a slave as well.

As a result of the constant plunder and injuries they suffered in the past,
the three families who chose to remain at ech-Chibayish obtained adoption
into Ahl Awaiti lineage of Ahl ish-Shaikh clan, who were then notorious
plunderers and thieves, so that they might enjoy greater security. In spite of
this adoption and residence, and though they share the compensations with all
other members of the tribe, the Ṣubba, nevertheless, neither settle their cases
through the ṣirkal of the clan into which they are adopted, nor participate in
any of the tribe's activities. For protection and justice they depend entirely
on the government.

As I have tried to show, social stratification among the Beni Isad is
entirely determined by birth in the case of the five traditional classes, is-sāda,
Ahl Khayūn, the commoners, il-'abīd and the Ṣubba. In the case of the two
subdivisions of the commoner class, however, the determinants are not inherited but acquired—wealth, good conduct, knowledge of tribal traditions
and law. A commoner can become a member of the ajawīd, a head of his
lineage, or a ṣirkal, and conversely one of the ajawīd may lose his prestige
and be counted as an ordinary commoner, and a ṣirkal or mukhtār can be
dismissed from his position. In the case of the appointment of ṣirkals, however, heredity is taken into consideration. Mobility is possible only between
these two subdivisions.

The class structure cuts across the lineage and clan system in the case of
the classes of "holy men," commoners and slaves, since members of these
classes can exist in any lineage or clan. But Ahl Khayūn form a distinct clan,
and the Ṣubba, though adopted into Ahl ish-Shaikh clan, are in fact not
counted as clansmen.

Barriers between social classes were more rigid before the abolition of
the shaikhdom than they are now. Both Ahl Khayūn and the slaves now mix
with the rest of the tribe—Ahl Khayūn losing most of their old privileges and
rights, and the slaves gaining new ones. After 30 years of such drastic
political, economic and social change, Ahl Khayūn are a distinct social class
only by virtue of their history and birth, and this is also the case with the
slaves. Though the hereditary barrier is still in operation for the "holy men,"
the fact that all of them began to earn their living in various ways immediately after the abolition of the shaikhdom, has destroyed a great deal of the
old character of this class. Four families of "holy men" practise usury; two
individuals even beg for their living; none of the sayyids at ech-Chibayish live
nowadays on a generous income accruing to them directly from their hereditary
religious status, as they used to before the abolition of the shaikhdom. No-
one is there to-day to give them "the fifth of their grandfather."[4]

Contact among the various classes is quite free and not restricted by any rules or traditions, except in connection with the Ṣubba where it does not go beyond talking and touching. The "holy-men," Ahl Khayūn, the *ṣirkals* and other commoners, and former slaves, sit down together, deal and talk freely with one another. The rule of endogamy is strict only where the Ṣubba are concerned, though normally Beni Isad do not intermarry with former slaves. This is mainly because of an ideal or racial purity, the slaves being of Negro descent. Ahl Khayūn also practise a restricted form of clan endogamy, but only where their women are concerned, and it is doubtful whether now, owing to the surplus of unmarried women in the clan and to the gradual weakening of Ahl Khayūn's traditions, this custom will be long preserved.

Occupational distinctions are used by Beni Isad to distinguish themselves from outsiders . . . but they are now less important than formerly for the differentiation of status within the tribe; nor is there now a clear correlation between social status and economic advantage. For example, among the "holy men," the highest social class, there are land holders, shopkeepers, employees, cultivators and beggars. Similarly, slaves are shopkeepers, cultivators and mat-weavers, and this is the case with the other classes. No man is banned from any occupation by reason of his social class; and wealth and poverty in themselves do not determine social standing.

NOTES

1. The *sāda* of Iraq distinguish themselves by wearing either black, blue or green turbans, or blue head cloths according to the *imam* from whom they claim descent.
2. *'Abīd* in colloquial Arabic means "slaves", and indicates "lack of freedom", "inferiority in status", but does not indicate "chattel". If the latter meaning is to be implied the word *'abīd* should be followed by the word *mamlūk*, which means "owned."
3. On the Mandeans, see the works of E. S. Drower (E. S. Stevens), particularly *The Mandeans of Iraq and Iran*, Oxford, 1957.
4. According to the Shi'ah doctrine, *is-sāda* have a claim of one-fifth of all the property of Shi'ah Moslems. At ech-Chibayish the shaikhs used to get this from the tribesmen and paid it to *is-sāda*, but now none of Ahl ech-Chibayish pay this fifth except when a tribesman wants to go on a pilgrimage to Mecca, when it is believed to be a necessary pre-requisite. Even in this case the fifth is paid for the cash property only and at in-Najaf, the religious centre of the Shi'ah, where it is distributed according to a certain system among all the *sāda* of the country or used for other religious purposes.

PART III

$\diamond$

Population Dynamics

Unless it is accompanied by economic development and land reform, population growth can hinder and even negate health and educational improvement. Furthermore, the existence of desired natural resources and even hard currency in themselves are no guarantee of programmed national social or economic development. A case example of this complex of disorders may be taken from Saudi Arabia where, at least since 1933 when the concession to exploit Saudi oil was granted to California Arabian Standard Oil Company and later to Aramco (Arabian American Oil Company), some 85 per cent of the government revenues and some 90 per cent of the country's foreign exchange come in the form of hard currency. What improvements this has brought to the health and well-being of the local population is simply and clearly summarized by an editorial staff from the Human Relations Area Files—a nonprofit research corporation affiliated with Yale University and sponsored and supported by sixteen member universities.

15

<><><><><><><><><><><><><><><><><><><><><><><><><><><><><><><><><><><><><><><><>

Public Health and Welfare in Saudi Arabia

GEORGE A. LIPSKY

Government in Arabia has traditionally played a relatively minor role in dispensing charity and improving living conditions. As elsewhere in the Middle East, the primary welfare agency has always been the family or larger kinship group. Those few unfortunates who either lacked relatives or belonged to a destitute kin group were provided for by religious foundations or by private almsgiving—an obligation of every good Moslem. In the past only when these sources of assistance proved inadequate was the individual likely to seek relief from the government. Despite a considerable economic and social upheaval created by the establishment of the oil industry, this traditional welfare system continues to function and in many parts of the country provides the only available welfare facilities.

From George A. Lipsky, ed., *Saudia Arabia* (1959), pp. 262–276; reprinted by permission of Human Relations Area Files.

In recent years, however, government has entered more directly into welfare work, and incipient public welfare programs, particularly in the sphere of preventive medicine, are under way. More elaborate welfare projects remain in the blueprint stage and are often handicapped by lack of trained personnel to implement them. In these endeavors the government has been greatly aided by foreign technical advice and assistance, especially that provided by the Arabian American Oil Company. Aramco has also set an example for other business enterprises and the government by making available many modern educational, medical, housing, and other facilities not only to Aramco employees and their families but to the general public in the oil-producing region and in the vicinity of Trans-Arabian Pipe Line Company (Tapline) operations. The government has relied increasingly on Aramco to supply welfare services in the Eastern Province and has periodically exerted pressure on Aramco officials to expand its services and to assist in developmental projects affecting other parts of the country.

Although the government has no extensive welfare programs currently in operation, considerable sums of money from oil revenues have been allocated to various development schemes in some degree related to the public welfare. Projects undertaken by the government with foreign technical assistance include the building of modern hospitals, clinics, and schools; the establishment of experimental farms; the construction of dams; and the drilling of wells. Except for some constructive projects in the sphere of public health, such specifically welfare work as is undertaken by the government is directed almost entirely to the relief of misfortune rather than to its prevention.

In past emergencies, such as drought and famine, the government has provided direct relief. Today, numbers of bedouins throughout the country are being supported by the government, partly as a result of widespread drought in recent years. At ar-Riyadh alone thousands of destitute tribesmen are camped on the outskirts of the city; every day men, women, and children enter the capital to draw rations of rice and, occasionally, meat from the royal storehouses.

Although Aramco employs only a minute percentage of the total population, the company has established in the oil towns of the Eastern Province a number of welfare facilities which directly or indirectly benefit a wide circle of Saudis in addition to the employees and their families. The standard of living enjoyed by inhabitants of the oil region is substantially higher than that of the country as a whole.

At the outset of its operations, Aramco set out to increase the efficiency of its Arab workers through an extensive program of community development on the American model, providing modern housing equipped with electricity, running water, air coolers, and sanitary facilities. Industrial safety measures were enforced, recreation facilities were provided, mosques were built, and a workman's compensation fund was set up to provide assistance in cases of death or injury. . . . Schools, hospitals, and clinics were opened for the general public as well as for Aramco workers and their families; the company cooperated with the government in preventive medicine and pest control schemes.

By December 1953 the company had provided accommodations for 14,568 employees in housing developments at Dhahran, Ras at-Tanura, and Abqaiq. Housing projects have since been greatly expanded in all the oil communities. Aramco's Employee Housing Loan Plan made it possible for Saudi employees to purchase their houses, and Saudi contractors were given technical advice and interest-free loans for construction projects. The company's city-planning service is not limited to the oil area but is available to any community in Saudi Arabia which requests technical assistance.

In the interests of maintaining high standards of health and efficiency, Aramco provides employees on the job with a substantial and balanced diet. The local markets of the oil towns are inspected by company officials, and employees and their families are given instruction in hygiene and preventive measures to reduce the incidence of disease. Extensive as are Aramco's welfare services, they directly benefit only a small proportion of the Saudi population. Welfare problems of the country as a whole have yet to be tackled in any fundamental way.

The age-old factors contributing to poverty, illiteracy, malnutrition, and disease are still present, and the standard of living of the majority of Saudis has improved but little as a result of the vast oil revenues flowing into the country. The new wealth through its highly uneven distribution among various segments of the population, has in fact greatly exaggerated long-standing disparities between economic levels, and the increasing consumption of Western luxuries by privileged groups has given rise to resentments and dissatisfactions not previously in evidence. Moreover, the inflation which has accompanied the country's largely oil-derived prosperity has had its most acute adverse effects on the underprivileged bulk of the population, which was already living barely above a subsistence level. . . .

Environmental factors, long isolation, and poverty have all contributed to the health situation that probably has changed little since early times. Despite recent advances in preventive medicine, infant mortality remains high, the average life expectancy is short, and numerous endemic diseases continue to plague the country. Food and water shortages threaten nomadic tribesmen and settled villagers alike, and health problems are aggravated by intense heat, sudden changes of weather, and an abundance of animal-transmitted parasites, which thrive in unsanitary conditions. Each year thousands of pilgrims from all over the Moslem world enter the country, often bringing disease in their wake and creating special problems of sanitation. Superstition, ignorance, and the persistence of harmful traditional practices are serious obstacles to improvement in standards of personal hygiene and to the widespread application of techniques of preventive medicine.

Bad as the total picture appears, health problems in Saudi Arabia are not as acute as in some of the more congested parts of Asia. The Saudi government does not have to contend with overpopulation, and it is receiving substantial assistance from the World Health Organization (WHO) and Aramco in establishing modern medical facilities and in training personnel. Medical services now available do not begin to meet the needs of the population as a whole, but an increasing percentage of the country's oil revenues is being used to remedy health problems.

TRADITIONAL MEASURES

Welfare and social security are built into Saudi society through the ancient extended family pattern. The unemployed, the aged, the chronically ill, the mentally and physically handicapped, the divorced, the widowed, and the orphaned are usually cared for as a matter of course by more fortunate family members. An individual in need of economic help or protection is expected to turn to his kinsmen to whom he is bound by a network of mutual obligation. Islam superimposed on this traditional pattern a concept of a broader responsibility of the good Moslem in the community of the faithful. Although Moslems accepted inequalities of talent and wealth as ordained by God, they insisted on the moral obligation of the wealthier members of the community to assist the poor. Almsgiving, which represents the direct application of a religious ideal, was originally conceived of not as gratuitous generosity but as the duty of the donor and the right of the recipient.

In time alms came to be collected by the authorities as an annual tax (Zakat). The proceeds of the alms tax, assessed at 2.5 percent of a person's income, were to be used partly for charitable or religious purposes. (An individual is expected to pay 1.25 percent to the collector and contribute to charity a further 1.25 percent.) Since the government began to receive large revenues from oil, the alms tax has not been so rigorously collected as in the past. Indeed, many peasants and bedouins have come to expect aid from the government as their right without recognizing any obligation to pay taxes. This attitude stems partly from a tradition of royal largess and concern for the needy and partly from the custom established by the late king, Ibn Saud—and perpetuated by his son, Saud—of giving subsidies to tribal sheikhs to ensure their allegiance to the central authority. . . . Although these sums of money were not viewed as payments for welfare purposes, varying amounts generally reached the followers of the sheikhs, who have always assumed a certain responsibility for the well-being of their people.

Another traditional source of charity is the institution of the religious or family trust (wakf). Trusts typically have taken the form of endowments of land left by the donor in perpetuity to his heirs or to charity. Property held in the trust cannot be sold or otherwise alienated; only its yield may be used by the beneficiaries. A bequest in the form of a trust frequently carried the stipulation that the income could not be used for charitable purposes until the donor's line had become extinct. Although the religious and family trusts have made a contribution to public welfare, they benefit only a small segment of the population.

THE STANDARD OF LIVING

The largely oil-derived wealth accruing to a small proportion of Saudis presents a picture in sharp contrast to the poverty of the bulk of the population. Although oil revenues and accompanying prosperity have raised the annual per capita income to $80, wealth is in fact very unevenly distributed among regions and occupational groups, and the average Saudi's standard of living is lower than that in neighboring countries.

The inflation which followed World War II brought special hardships to nomads, villagers, and the poorer town dwellers. Merchants, contractors, and oil workers, on the other hand, were little affected because their rapidly increasing incomes kept pace with rising prices. These urban groups tend to be increasingly strident in their complaints, but their dissatisfaction generally stems more from political frustration than from actual economic hardship. The extent of discontent among the largely inarticulate, poorer groups in both the towns and the countryside is difficult to gauge. It seems apparent, however, that more resentment is aroused among poorer Saudis by ostentatious display by privileged groups of such Western luxuries as air conditioning and automobiles than by such traditional marks of elite status as fine clothing and housing.

Nomads

The nomads and seminomads, who comprise 66 percent of the population, include both destitute herdsmen, who live on a bare subsistence level, and wealthy sheikhs, who possess large camel herds, own townhouses and date groves, and drive automobiles. Whether rich or poor, however, nomads are faced with the age-old problems of scarcity of water, extremes of climate, and frequent droughts. Even at its best, nomadic life offers less security and comfort than does life in the villages and towns.

Most bedouins continue to live in the traditional black hair tents which their womenfolk can quickly set up and take down. Whereas a great sheikh may live in a magnificent pavilion richly furnished with cushions, carpets, and chests, a lowly hunter or tinker generally lives in a miserable lean-to equipped with only a few essential cooking utensils. Clothing varies widely from the finely woven robes and headcloths of the wealthy sheikh to the single, coarse shirt and plain headcloth of the average bedouin. All but the poorest, however, possess boots made of wool and leather for cold days.

In recent years numerous attempts have been made to settle the nomads. The government offers homesteads and farm equipment on the basis of long-term loans as an inducement to them to become settled cultivators. The transition, which involves problems of adjustment to new methods of work and sources of income, also creates new welfare problems, and many recently settled tribesmen have either returned to pastoralism or have drifted to the cities.

Villagers

Settled cultivators comprise about 12 percent of the population. Most of them live in ancient villages where tribal customs and farming practices have changed but little over the years. Except for a few landowners and the more prosperous traders, poverty is the common lot of villagers, and unsanitary living conditions, the contamination of water supplies, and malnutrition contribute to the prevalence of disease.

The typical village is a cluster of flat-roofed, simple houses of mud-brick or stone close to gardens and fields. Frequently, domestic animals are given shelter in a room adjacent to the living quarters. House furnishings consist of little more than a few mats, chests, and cooking utensils. Electricity is a luxury restricted to the wealthier townspeople; candles and oil lamps provide light in village dwellings.

The cultivator generally consumes a large proportion of what he produces. Although more substantial than the typical bedouin diet, the diet of villagers is also deficient in proteins and calories. The small yearly income from the sale of surplus crops is spent on bare essentials, and little is left for such luxuries as coffee, incense, or an occasional wedding feast. Clothing is similar to that of the bedouins, but shoes are generally worn only on special occasions. Although increasing quantities of imported goods are reaching the villages, continuing inflationary pressures keep their prices high.

Townspeople

About 22 percent of the total population is concentrated in the towns, and this percentage is increasing as more and more nomads and villagers seek employment or government relief in urban areas. Many of the more rapidly growing towns have changed radically in the last twenty years. While the old, congested quarters of the poorer people, centered around the bazaars and mosques, remain much the same, new and spacious suburbs, occupied by the more prosperous, are springing up on the outskirts of towns. Only the wealthy enjoy electricity, air conditioning, modern plumbing, and sewage facilities. The influx of nomads and villagers to urban areas in recent years has created a severe housing shortage in many towns, and the attendant overcrowding has aggravated the unsanitary conditions in which the majority of townspeople live.

The average, poor townsman has a more varied and better balanced diet than has his counterpart in the desert or the village, but the imported foods consumed by the wealthy are beyond his means. Many of the newly prosperous urban dwellers have adopted Western dress. The poorer people, as well as conservative Moslems at all economic levels, tend to dress in traditional fashion. Western imports popular with the wealthy range from food, radios, and house furnishings to new Cadillacs.

SANITATION

The scarcity of water in Saudi Arabia is a factor contributing to the unsanitary living conditions of the majority of the population. In many localities the water supply is not only inadequate but highly contaminated with human and animal wastes, which spread disease; it is often also made unfit for drinking by a high mineral salt content. Only in the oil communities and a few urban centers is water purified for drinking purposes. Chlorinated water is piped to the houses of Saudi residents of Dhahran. In Jidda, Mecca, and a few other towns, spring water is conveyed to houses by underground conduits.

In connection with the pilgrimage the Moslem custom of sacrificing livestock at the outskirts of Mecca has created a special sanitation problem for the city. It is estimated that from 100,000 to 500,000 head of livestock are slaughtered annually by pilgrims, and most of the carcasses are left in the hot sun to decompose; about 20 percent of the meat is consumed by the *takarinah*, laborers who came to Arabia originally as pilgrims from Africa. Alarmed by the wasteful depletion of meat supplies and the unsanitary conditions created by the slaughtering of the animals, the government in 1951 sought and received the sanction of religious authorities at al-Azhar University in Cairo to make plans for the preservation of the meat. No information is available on the extent to which this project has been implemented.

Except for modern systems at Aramco and a few government installations and in the wealthiest areas, such sewage and sanitary facilities as exist are poor by modern, Western standards and are entirely inadequate in crowded urban areas. The problem is aggravated in Jidda and the holy cities of Mecca and Medina at the time of the annual influx of pilgrims.

The nomads are casual in their disposal of waste. Whenever a camp site becomes too filthy, they pull up stakes and move to a new area in the desert. Cesspits and pit privies are used in towns and villages, while surface privies are common in the huts on the outskirts of towns.

Recent measures undertaken by the government to improve health conditions include purification of water supplies in a number of towns, quarantining of pilgrims, and cooperation with Aramco and WHO in the control of disease and expansion of medical facilities.

NUTRITION

Chronic food shortage is a serious problem in Saudi Arabia and the diet of most of the population is inadequate in vitamins, proteins, and total calories by modern, Western standards. Because of transportation problems, produce grown in many areas reaches only the local markets, and surplus foods often spoil before they can be consumed. . . . Meanwhile, the country must rely on imports for much of its food needs.

The nomads have a better balanced diet than most settled cultivators, but their total caloric intake is lower than that of the latter. Townsmen, except for the destitute, generally have a more varied menu than do the rural people as a whole. In the past the towns, dependent on the countryside for food, often faced famine conditions during bad crop years. Today, imported foods from the United States and Middle Eastern countries are available in the larger towns and coastal seaports for those who can afford them.

The diet of nomads consists mainly of milk and milk products from goats, sheep, or camels, together with dates, rice, or less frequently, wheat. Milk is drunk fresh or curdled into yoghurt or cheese. Coffee and tea are the favorite beverages among nomads as among other Saudis. A guest is served a cup of coffee, then a glass of tea, and finally another cup of coffee. Meat is eaten only on special occasions when an animal is slaughtered or when wild game is available. Locusts are also consumed. Nomads eat fresh fruits and vegetables when they visit the villages of settled cultivators. Despite his meager diet, the average bedouin generally has considerable physical endurance. In nomadic families the husband and adult sons are better nourished than the women and children, who must content themselves with leftovers after the men have finished their meal. The nomads take little food during the day, and the main meal is in the evening.

Although the diet of the average cultivator is more substantial than that of the nomad, it is more deficient in proteins and fats. The staple food of this group is millet, supplemented by rice, barley, and wheat, when they are obtainable. These cereals are cooked into a gruel, and wheat and barley are made into bread. Fruits, especially dates, and vegetables are eaten regularly; meat only occasionally.

Although goats and camels are eaten, the main source of meat for those who can afford it in all groups is sheep. Cattle are not numerous and are used mainly as beasts of burden. The consumption of pork is forbidden to Moslems and the slaughtering of other animals is governed by Islamic ritual prescriptions. Fish is becoming more available but is not widely eaten.

INCIDENCE OF DISEASE

Among the diseases most prevalent in Saudi Arabia are malaria, tuberculosis, trachoma, dysentery, rickets, scurvy, and venereal and parasitic infections. Because of the lack of medical statistics and the number of cases of illness which are never reported, precise information on disease is scanty.

Malaria is endemic in Saudi Arabia, and it has been estimated that virtually all Saudis suffer from the disease at one time or another. The incidence of malaria is especially high in the valleys of Asir, the Tihamah region, the irrigated areas of the Eastern Province, and the Khaybar and Jabrin oases, where it matches that in any other part of the world. Malarial conditions in fact force the abandonment of certain areas for part of the year. Malaria control programs sponsored by WHO and Aramco in cooperation with the government are in operation, but they benefit only a relatively small percentage of the population, largely in the Eastern Province and in Asir.

Tuberculosis is prevalent throughout the country. The Ministry of Health has constructed a number of hospitals and clinics in the major cities for the isolation and treatment of this disease. In 1956 WHO conducted a survey in preparation for the establishment of a tuberculosis control service. In addition, Aramco provides wards in company hospitals for the treatment of the disease and offers courses in home care.

The high incidence of trachoma and conjunctivitis is related to unsanitary living conditions and aggravated by frequent sand storms. It is estimated that 95 percent of the population suffer to some degree from eye ailments, and many Saudis have been blinded by untreated trachoma. Aramco, in cooperation with the Harvard University School of Public Health, has begun a trachoma research project in an effort to discover a vaccine for the prevention of the disease.

Amoebic and bacillary dysentery and other enteric disorders occur throughout the country but are especially prevalent among the bedouins and villagers. The unsanitary habits of the people, the abundance of flies, the drinking of contaminated water, and the use of human excrement as a fertilizer —all contribute to the high incidence of these diseases. Diarrhea and enteritis are extremely widespread among infants and are believed responsible for half of all infant deaths.

Of the diseases related to malnutrition, scurvy is frequently found among nomads, and rickets among townspeople. Pellagra reportedly occurs only sporadically. Widespread as these diseases are, their impact is less severe than that of the general weakening of the system caused by chronic malnutrition, especially among children, which results in low resistance to tuberculosis and other diseases. The chewing of *qat* (narcotic leaves which produce mild stupefaction) is believed to contribute to malnutrition in Asir by dulling the appetite; it is forbidden elsewhere in the kingdom.

Syphilis and gonorrhea, which are most common in the coastal towns and villages, are estimated to affect about 25 to 30 percent of the population in all age groups. Bejel, a disease caused by a spirochete, has apparently long been endemic in most of the Arabian peninsula. Because its transmission is nonsexual, it incurs no stigma in the popular view, whereas syphilis and gonorrhea tend to be regarded as shameful. The government, with the assistance of WHO, has established a Venereal Disease Control Demonstration Center at Mecca and diagnostic laboratories at Medina and elsewhere.

Parasitic infections account for another group of ailments commonly found in Saudi Arabia. Chief among them, bilharziasis (schistosomiasis) spreads primarily through the passing of human wastes into slow-moving water channels, where snails, the intermediate hosts for the parasites, breed. Intestinal roundworms are estimated to infect about half the population. Other worms infecting humans are pinworms, beef tapeworms, fish tapeworms, and Guinea worms.

Smallpox, a traditional killer in Saudi Arabia, nowadays occurs only in localized outbreaks, even though vaccination for smallpox was carried out only on a small scale until 1957, when, because of a threatened smallpox epidemic, the government initiated a program to encourage mass vaccination. All government employees and military personnel were ordered to be vaccinated and all persons entering or leaving the country have to be vaccinated. Aramco and Tapline facilities were used to further this project. Leprosy, once seen throughout the country, is now restricted to a few communities. Bubonic plague has not been reported in recent years, and typhus, cholera, and relapsing fever are only occasionally encountered. Along the coasts dengue fever is prevalent. The childhood diseases familiar in the West are also found in Saudi Arabia.

Of the diseases of animals which may be transmitted to man, a disease of goats is the most common; it is transmitted to humans through milk products. Anthrax also occasionally affects humans, and rabies occurs in isolated outbreaks.

The annual Moslem pilgrimage to the holy cities of Saudi Arabia aggravates the country's health problems. It is estimated that between 150,000 and 250,000 pilgrims come to Mecca and Medina every year. Poverty obliges many of the pilgrims to walk all or part of the way, and even for the strongest the pilgrimage imposes a severe strain. The mortality rate among pilgrims is high, and they tend to be subject to serious epidemics, particularly on the return journey after exposure to contagion carried by their fellows from all parts of the Islamic world. The outbreaks of cholera and smallpox among pilgrims have given rise to an international agreement to enforce supervision over standards of sanitation in the areas visited by pilgrims. These controls have been incorporated into a code of International Sanitary Regulations. Today, all pilgrims journeying to Mecca are obliged to be vaccinated against smallpox and inoculated against cholera and yellow fever. The Saudi government has assumed the responsibility of caring for sick pilgrims; facilities for pilgrims in Mecca have been expanded; a hospital has been established; and improved standards of hygiene have been enforced. In Jidda the government, with assistance from WHO, has built a quarantine station which has a hospital and an isolation area. Supplementing these arrangements are medical missions sent by many of the Moslem countries to accompany their pilgrims.

MEDICAL ORGANIZATION

Public health services in Saudi Arabia are of recent origin and are still largely in the organizational stage. The government established a Ministry of Health in 1951. As reorganized in 1955, the Ministry of Health consists mainly of a technical, advisory staff concerned with projects and planning and an administrative staff. Supplementing the work of these staffs are three sections directly under the Minister of Health and headed by an Inspector General, a Director of the Pharmaceutical Division, and a Director of Storehouses respectively.

The activities of the ministry are conducted through five regional health districts: the region of Mecca and Pilgrimage Affairs, with headquarters in Mecca; the western coastal region, with headquarters in Mecca; the Eastern Province with headquarters in ad-Dammam; the region of ar-Riyadh, with headquarters in ar-Riyadh; and the region of Asir, with headquarters in Abha.

Information is not available on the current activities of these regional units. The government has drawn up elaborate plans for the future, however, and it is projected that each unit, under the direction of a medical officer, will be responsible for the functioning of a health center, quarantine units, pharmacies, teams to combat disease, nursing schools, and mobile health

units, and for the construction of additional health facilities. The mobile
health units are to provide preventive medical services as well as treatment
until more hospitals and clinics are established. Such medical facilities as
are currently available are concentrated mainly in the larger towns.

Military hospitals are located at ar-Riyadh, at-Taif, ad-Damman, and
al-Kharj. The military hospital at al-Kharj, which was established in 1954,
has 600 beds and the latest German medical equipment.

Almost the only private medical facilities in the country are those provided by Aramco. The company maintains an active public health program
with modern hospitals and free medical facilities available not only to its
employees and their families but also to the local Saudi population in the
oil-producing region and, in the vicinity of Tapline operations. The Saudi
government has looked more and more to Aramco for help in treating Saudi
citizens, and the company has increased its medical services by 300 percent
to take care of some of the country's needs. It is reported that 28 percent
of Aramco's clinical facilities are available for use by the general public.
Medical service is free for those who are too poor to pay for treatment.

Aramco operates three modern hospitals, located at Dhahran, Ras at-
Tanura, and Abqaiq respectively. These hospitals have recorded an average
of 9,000 hospital admissions per year and many thousands more out-patient
visits. Aramco also operates three mobile clinics which travel to the various
company installations. A research and diagnostic laboratory is located at
Aramco's Dhahran Medical Center. Every Tapline pump station has an
infirmary with a resident physician. The Badanah pump station has a small
hospital, the only one in the Emirate of the Northern Frontiers. . . .

Apart from the hospitals, the government's medical facilities are currently limited to a few mobile dispensaries and clinics, health centers along
the pilgrim route, several vaccination and quarantine units, an eye clinic, a
blood bank, and a few laboratories, established with the assistance of WHO,
which is also undertaking studies of communicable diseases, the control of
water supplies, foodstuffs and drugs, and the treatment of epidemics in Saudi
Arabia.

Personnel and Training

One of the most serious problems facing the Saudi medical authorities
is the shortage of trained personnel. In 1955 the Ministry of Health had
on its staff fewer than 200 doctors, nearly all of whom were foreigners. The
Saudi Arabian army does not have one Saudi doctor on its medical staff,
which is made up of Germans, Palestinians, and other nationals, who are
hired on a contract basis. A number of German doctors also serve in the
Ministry of Health. Like government medical personnel, the few physicians
in private practice tend to be concentrated in the larger towns.

In 1957 Aramco's medical staff consisted of 62 doctors, 7 surgeons, 231 nurses, 71 technicians, 9 dentists, and 64 midwives and nurse's aides.

Young Saudis are beginning to seek medical training, and the government provides numerous scholarships for qualified students to study medicine in Egypt and at the American University of Beirut. Several local schools of nursing were organized in 1950 through the cooperative effort of the government and Aramco, and in 1952 eight more schools were opened by the government for the training of nurses and health workers.

Aramco also provides nursing training for male students at the Dhahran Medical Center and a nurse's aide program at Ras at-Tanura Hospital. In addition, WHO provides fellowships for specialized medical training abroad for Saudi Arabians.

Because of the seclusion of most women in Saudi Arabia, there are almost no Saudi female nurses or doctors. There are midwives who function in the tradition of folk practitioners. The treatment of female patients at present poses difficulties, however, since many Saudis object to having their womenfolk examined by male doctors.

ATTITUDES TOWARD
MEDICAL TREATMENT

Like other Middle Easterners, Saudi Arabians have traditionally regarded illness as a manifestation of God's will or as the work of evil spirits. Although the divine will was regarded as unchangeable, evil spirits could be propitiated or warded off by charms or the remedies of folk practitioners. Before the introduction of modern medicine into Arabia, people depended upon practitioners whose lore represented a mixture of practical folk remedies, magic, and quasi-religious interventions. Today, as in the past, almost every bazaar and market place has its peddlers of folk medicines. Many of these remedies, made from herbs and minerals, have actual therapeutic value. Examples are senna as a purgative, copper sulfate crystals for the treatment of trachoma, and mercury for syphilis. Most folk practitioners also know how to set broken bones with splints and how to operate on eyelids afflicted with trichiasis.

Although sorcerers are not numerous, in many parts of the country disease is thought to be caused by witchcraft. Tribesmen, particularly in the more remote areas, wear charms and amulets to ward off the evil eye, and belief in jinn, who can bring good or bad luck, and in the spirits of the dead is prevalent.

Many tribal customs constitute health hazards. Some tribesmen of Asir and Nejd practice female circumcision and the flaying of the skin of the abdomen and thighs of adolescent males; occasionally young people die from infections resulting from these wounds. Branding is universally employed by the nomads to relieve pain and in the treatment of wounds. Other practices are the insertion of salt or sand in the vagina after childbirth, the reliance on camel urine as an almost universal remedy, and the use of kohl by women to darken the eyelids.

Townsmen in general are apt to be better informed about the real causes and proper treatment of disease than are the nomads and villagers and less inclined than they to accept illness and death with resignation as part of the natural order of things. Faith in modern medicine is becoming more widespread, however, as medical facilities become increasingly available and as the efficacy of new techniques is demonstrated. So far, only a beginning has been made in this direction; the majority of the people living in remote areas of the country do not yet have access to modern medicine. Except among the more educated people living in towns, personal hygiene and knowledge of the importance of cleanliness as a preventative of disease are all but lacking. Although ritual cleanliness before prayer is required by Moslem doctrine, unsanitary habits abound.

*There is no lack of articles describing the traditional extended family
of the Muslim Middle East, in particular that of the Arabs, and the
material is often used in cross-cultural studies of lineage structure.
The overwhelming majority of the these articles, however, have been
written by extranationals to the area.*

*It is good, therefore, when a Muslim Arab such as Dr. Nahas,
then Dean of the Teachers College, Abbasia, Cairo, prepares a
critical study of the family in the Arab world utilizing both descriptive
and demographic data. Writing as a participant within the culture
pattern he is describing, his is a work characterized by a utilization
of demographic data to corroborate and delineate his generalizations.*

16

<hr />

The Family in the Arab World

M. K. NAHAS

The countries of the Arab world are located in both Africa and Asia;
some are politically independent, while others are occupied by foreign powers.
There have been both internal and external revolts, and these no doubt have
influenced the more educated young people to revolt against the autocratic
authority of their parents. This social revolution is increasingly affecting
family relations. Particularly in Egypt, following the revolution of 1952,
many important changes aiming toward social justice have been taking place.
Farm laborers are becoming emancipated from the old feudalism; landlords
are no longer highly venerated; women are gaining equality with men; young
people are obtaining freedom from the authoritarian family head.

The Arab countries are *Egypt, Libya*, Tunisia, Algeria, Morocco in
Africa and *Saudi Arabia, Yemen, Palestine, Lebanon, Syria, Transjordan,
Iraq* and Kuwait in Asia. There are small Arab Protectorates south of Saudi
Arabia, such as Aden. (Those in italics are members of the Arab League.)
Unfortunately, some of these countries have not yet started a census which
would help in giving a clear picture of family life. We could not find statistics

From *Journal of Marriage and the Family* (November 1954), Vol. 16, No. 4, pp. 293–
300; reprinted by permission.

related to this topic in Saudi Arabia, Yemen and Libya. Some other countries started a census a few years ago. One must be very cautious with some of the figures given; the only reliable census is that of Egypt.

POPULATION

The approximate populations in 1954 of the Arab countries which are members of the Arab League are as follows (in millions): Egypt, 22; Iraq, 5; Lebanon, 1.3; Libya, 1.5; Saudi Arabia, 8; Syria, 3.8; Transjordan and Arab Palestine, 1.5; Yemen, 5.

Excess of Females

In each Arab country the number of females is more than that of males, except in Lebanon and Syria. One would have expected that there would be more females than males in Lebanon in comparison with other Arab countries because Lebanese men tend to emigrate. One may suggest that there is some fault in the statistics of both Lebanon and Syria.

Table 1.   EXCESS OF FEMALES OR MALES IN ARAB COUNTRIES

Country	Excess of Females or Males	Population	(Census Date)
Egypt	183,844 females	19,021,840	1947
Iraq	301,495 females	4,816,185	1947
Transjordan	21,229 females	1,330,021	1952
Syria	42,018 males	3,006,028	1946
Lebanon	22,112 males	1,165,208	1946

Average Age

We have no exact figures for the average age of men and women. In Egypt it is estimated that it is thirty-one for men and thirty-two or thirty-three for women. The average ages for the other Arab countries must be less than this figure except in Lebanon, for which we have no figures. The most important reasons for these low ages are: (1) Education is still backward in all the Arab countries, excluding Lebanon. Health goes hand in hand with education. Egypt, which is a more educated country, has about 70 per cent illiteracy. (2) The majority of people are poverty stricken, resulting in widespread malnutrition. (3) Health care is still backward; especially in the rural districts in which the majority of the people live (in Egypt about 70 per cent of the whole population live in the country).

Religion

The majority of the population of the Arab countries are Moslems, except in Lebanon, as shown below:

Table 2. PER CENT OF RELIGIOUS GROUPS BY COUNTRY

Country	(Census)	Moslems	Christians	Other Religions
Egypt	1947	91.7	7.9	.4
Iraq	1947	94.0	3.0	3.0
Syria	1945	83.2	14.1	2.7
Lebanon	1945	46.2	52.7	1.1
Transjordan	1952	95.0	5.0	–
Saudi Arabia	1952	100.0	–	–

This is very important, as Islam sets many social rules, some closely connected with family living and having a strong influence upon the ties in the family and the upbringing of children, such as polygyny, easy divorce, and rules for inheritance. Besides Islam and Christianity, we find other religions in many of these countries, such as Judaism, Bahaism, Yazidi, Sabai and Alawy.

Age Distribution by Sex

We have no figures of age distribution except from Egypt and Iraq, as shown in the following table:

Table 3. AGE DISTRIBUTION BY SEX IN EGYPT AND IRAQ
(*According to 1947 Census*)

Age	EGYPT		IRAQ	
	Male	Female	Male	Female
	Per Cent		Per Cent	
Under 5	13.6	13.6	19.3	17.6
5–9	12.8	12.5	15.8	16.3
10–19	22.7	20.8	15.0	17.1
20–29	14.5	15.6	9.5	11.7
30–39	13.5	14.0	11.8	12.4
40–49	10.6	10.2	11.8	9.6
50–59	6.3	6.5	7.0	5.9
Above 60	5.5	6.4	9.8	9.4
Unknown	0.5	0.4	0.03	0.02

Marital Status

The Arabs, especially the Moslems, are fond of marrying and at an early age. There are many reasons for this. (1) From the religious point of view we find many verses of the Koran urging people to marry. Some sayings of the Prophet Mohammed strongly support marriage. (2) The climate of most of the Arab countries arouses the sexual impulses early, enticing them to marry at an early age. (3) The traditions of the Arabs cause the separation of the sexes rather than free mixing. This allows no sublimation of the sexual impulses; thus early marriages ensue. (4) The desire to have children is common among Arab men and women. The men like to have children, especially boys, to carry on their names and also to raise the earning power of the family. The women like to have children, especially boys, to feel secure with their husbands and safe from divorce. A great number of divorces are due to a barren wife or one who bears only girls. (5) The virginity of the girls and their morality are highly esteemed to the extent of being sacred. If the girl has any relations with a man, the family has been dishonored; this may be punishable by death to the girl. The family must not be disgraced. The family therefore encourages early marriage of the daughter, saving her honor and relieving much tension and anxiety. (6) The marriage of most Arab girls and the majority of the young men in some countries is arranged by their fathers or elders. These people feel very proud of having grandchildren. This is the tribe spirit of most of the Arab people.

Age of Marriage

Islam did not set a minimum age for marriage, and early marriages became the custom among the Arabs. Even now we find in some Arab countries children of ten and twelve getting married. Some Arab countries have legally set a minimum for the age of marriage as is shown below, considering only the countries which are members of the Arab League.

Table 4. MINIMUM LEGAL AGE OF MARRIAGE IN ARAB COUNTRIES

Country	Males	Females
Egypt	18	16
Iraq	none	none
Libya	18	16
Lebanon	18	18
Saudi Arabia	none	none
Syria	18	17
Transjordan	18	17
Yemen	none	none

Economic conditions and the spread of education have forced people to postpone marriage till they can afford supporting a home. We could not find any statistics related to ages of first marriages except in Egypt. The average ages in males and females are 26 and 20.7 years respectively. Among the educated married people in Iraq, on whom I made my research, I found the ages to be 25.1 and 21.8 years.

ARRANGEMENTS FOR MARRIAGE

Choice of Partners

The majority of the population of the Arab countries live in rural districts. We also find in nearly every Arab country some tribes adhering to the old traditions. In Iraq they form a good percentage of the whole population. In Saudi Arabia they form the majority. In Egypt and Lebanon they are a small majority.

The country people and the tribes vary from the urban population in the ways they choose their partners in marriage. First, they usually marry according to the choice of their parents. The girl, especially, has no say whatever in the matter of her marriage. Second, kinship marriage is common. A cousin has the first choice of marrying his female cousin. Unless he is reluctant, she cannot marry anybody else.

Among the urban population, there is more freedom of choice on the part of young men and women. However, they must usually have the consent of their partners. Lebanon is the most liberal country with regard to choice of partners. In cities most of the marriages are marriages of love. In the country they are also, though love grows secretly. The lovers cannot meet in the open as they do in cities and towns. The trend is toward freedom of choice on the part of young people. This is growing fast in some countries like Egypt, Iraq, Syria and of course Lebanon, where education is spreading and women's veils are disappearing rapidly, and the mixing of both sexes is going on. In other countries like Saudi Arabia and Yemen, the free choice will take a long time. In the research I made on educated married people in Iraq, I found that 63.1 per cent of the men and 61 per cent of the women married through becoming acquainted and falling in love with their partners.

Procedure of Marriage

In cases where the choice of partners is made by the couple themselves, they try to get the approval of their parents. This is very important for them. The steps for marriage after that are as follows: (1) A present is sent by the man to the girl, which is usually a piece of jewelry. This means they are engaged to each other. (2) After a duration of time, some weeks or months, the religious ceremony is performed by which the man and woman become husband and wife. A religious official is called to the bride's house. The father, or the head of the family acting as trustee of the girl, sits in front of him with the bridegroom and some witnesses and announces the approval of the marriage of both man and woman. The dowry, which usually is agreed upon before this ceremony, is announced and registered and paid by the groom to the trustee of the bride. The deferred dowry is also registered. This is a sum of money which should be paid to the wife in case of divorce or if the husband dies. It serves also, especially if it is a big sum, as a safeguard against easy divorce. The legal official agreement is signed by the groom, the trustee of the girl and the witnesses. After that, the bride's people prepare the furniture needed for the couple, and it is sent to the groom's house. Sometimes the husband buys the furniture. In both cases, it is considered the property of the wife. Then they get married in a joyful atmosphere of music and singing.

Types of Marriages

Monogamy and Polygyny ◆ The Moslem has the right to marry up to four wives. This right is not practiced much now in many Arab countries, because of (1) the spread of education, which makes more people conscious of the responsibility and sacredness of married life, and of the ill effects of polygyny, especially on the children; and (2) the hard economic conditions, which prevent men from supporting more than one wife and their children.

In Egypt, according to the census of 1947, those who are married to more than one wife are only 3.8 per cent of all married men. In Iraq this figure rises to 9 per cent, according to the census of 1947. In cities it is less. In Baghdad, for instance, it is only 5.3 per cent. Although we have no figures from Lebanon, we can say that polygyny is very scarce there. But in Saudi Arabia it is quite common.

Morganatic Marriage ◆ We described before the popular kind of marriage among Moslems. There is another kind of marriage which is approved by the Shiah.* It is called morganatic marriage. The man and the woman agree to marry for a certain period not exceeding six weeks, after which the marriage is considered over.

*The Shiah is a sect in Islam which became very strong and had many followers after the murder of Ali, the cousin of the Prophet. Some of its teachings are not recognized by the Sunnah [Orthodox Islam]. They are even denied. For example, the morganatic marriage is prohibited by the Sunnah. Nearly all the Moslems in Iran and half the Moslems in Iraq are Shiahs. In Saudi Arabia, there are none. In Egypt, they are very scarce and most of the Shiahs in this country come from Persian origin.

Civil Marriage ◆ In Islam, a religiously approved marriage can be arranged between the man, a trustee of the woman, and two witnesses. A dowry, however small, should be paid by the man, but to safeguard the interests of both parties and their children, the marriage should be legally registered. This is called civil marriage. The important reasons for this practice are (1) fear that the families of the two parties or the family of one would not consent to the marriage, especially the fear of one of them that his family might disinherit him. (2) The man might be married to a previous wife whom he does not want to lose or with whom he does not want any trouble, especially if she is a relative or they have children or if she is very rich. (3) The couple might have been lovers and begot a child. They contract the civil marriage so that the child would not be considered illegitimate. (4) In cases where there is a big difference between the social standards of the two parties, that is, man and his maid, or the woman and her servant.

Intermarriage ◆ The Moslems can marry any woman irrespective of her religion, but the Moslem woman cannot marry anyone but a Moslem. The Moslem is forbidden to marry any woman who has denied her religion or changed it to any other religion but Islam. Intermarriage is very scarce among the Arabs. Most of those who practice it are men who go to America or Europe and get married there to Christian women.

Medical Tests Before Marriage ◆ No Arab country except Egypt has established health centers for premarital examination and treatment without charge. The objective of these marriage health centers is to see if the person is medically fit for marriage or not, and to supply the necessary treatment. Whatever the case may be, the center has neither the authority to prevent him from getting married nor the power to compel him to be treated. These centers were started in 1941 and more centers are established every year.

Marriage Among the Non-Moslems ◆ The majority of the non-Moslem Arabs are Christians with varied faiths. Most of the Christians of Egypt and Syria are Coptic Orthodox. In Lebanon the majority are Catholic Maronites. There are agencies called Millet agencies (congregational councils) which deal with the problems of family relations: divorce, custody of children, alimony, etc. The members of these agencies are elected by the people of the faith. The Supreme President of the Congregation is the head of the church to which the members belong.

FAMILY

Size of the Family

The Arab family is usually of a large size for two reasons: (1) Arabs are fond of having many children, and (2) the prevalence of the patrilocal family among the Arabs, especially among the tribes and in the rural districts. The large-sized family is abundant in some countries like Saudi Arabia, Iraq, Transjordan and Yemen. In other countries like Egypt, Lebanon and Syria, we find it in *some parts* of the rural districts and among the tribes. But in the cities, the conjugal family is prevalent.

We have no figures denoting the size of the family in the Arab countries. My research on the Iraqi family, though an educated people, shows that 46 per cent of the married women and 54 per cent of the married men live with their parents, or the parents of their partners. Surely this percentage would rise if the uneducated are taken into consideration. This gives an idea of the size of the family in general in that country. In Egypt, according to the census of 1947, the average size of the family is 5.5 persons. This looks relatively small, but the Egyptians, even many of those who live in the country, are breaking away from the patrilocal system of family life.

Relationship Between Members of the Family

The head of the family is usually the most influential man. He may be the father, or the grandfather, or an uncle (father's brother). If the father is dead, he may be the eldest son. Usually other members of the family take his advice and follow it in almost everything of importance related to their living: marriage, divorce, business, schooling, etc. This is the usual thing among the tribes and most of the rural families, whether they are patrilocal or conjugal. The desire for independence of the new generation and the increasing education of women in some countries is beginning to limit this one-man authority. On the whole, the ties between the members of the family are quite strong.

Relation Between Husband and Wife

The husband usually has the upper hand over his wife. Islam morally supports him. In some countries where education and especially the education of women is still backward, and among the tribes and villagers of nearly all the Arab countries, the wife is subordinate and submissive to her husband. She can seldom protest against anything he does and yet she cannot do anything unless he approves of it. In the more progressive countries, education of women has changed this attitude. But both husband and wife suffer a terrible conflict. The man is trying to enjoy his traditional privileges and the educated woman is trying to break them. In doing so, she sometimes goes to the extreme, neglecting her husband and trying to lead an ultra-independent life. In trying to gain recognition of her own personality, she evades the spirit of cooperation and mutual understanding which are essential for the happiness of the family. This is just one phase of the long transitional period which is full of family trouble and disorganization, and yet which will lead in the near future to a better understanding between the two partners. The property of the wife is legally her own. But it is a common thing that the husband makes use of it without much protest on her part. Usually it is not the wife who stands in his way, but the wife's brothers, especially if the property is land.

Authority Over Children

In the majority of families, especially in the country, the father tends to be very dictatorial over his children. He is usually stern with them and sometimes harsh. He tries to make them feel small in front of him as a way of securing their obedience. The mother usually compensates by being lenient. However, if the mother is well educated, she shares the authority with the father over the children. Sometimes she becomes more authoritarian. This authority may be practiced by the head of the family, particularly whenever this head lives with the children and their parents are apart from them. If the father dies, the authority is usually transferred to the uncle or the elder son if he is mature enough.

Economic Activities of the Family

The whole family in the rural districts work together to earn their living. The father and sons work in the fields. The females run the house, look after the cattle, and try to increase the income of the family by rearing domestic birds, doing some manual work like weaving and knitting, and making dairy products such as butter and cheese. Sometimes, among the very poor, girls and boys work as servants or in factories, and thus increase the income of the family. In cities, the poor families may send some of their boys and girls to work as laborers or in shops. These children may go to work at an early age in Arab countries like Saudi Arabia and some parts of Iraq, where there is no compulsory education. But in countries where the education of the children is compulsory, they cannot start work until they finish with their primary education, usually at the age of twelve. Exchange of goods is very scarce. Usually all goods are purchased and sold.

Domicile

In Saudi Arabia, Iraq and Transjordan, where people stick to the old Arab traditions, the family, which is usually big, shares the same dwelling: grandfathers, their sons and their wives and children. We still find this common dwelling in most of the rural areas in other Arab countries, like Egypt, Syria and Lebanon. The educated people are inclined to live independently of their families in a dwelling of their own after marriage.

The homes of the rich people are large and convenient. If the family enlarges, more buildings are added. But most of the families are poor and we find that five or more people share one room. The domicile of large families is usually owned by the whole family, and seldom is an issue made of a share inheritance even if the part owner does not live in it.

Sexual Life

Premarital sex practice is common among men in those Arab countries where the veiling of women has vanished and the mixing of the sexes is allowed, especially in cities where men delay their marriage until they finish their education and can afford to get married. In countries where the veil is still prevalent and mixing of the two sexes is forbidden, these premarital sexual practices are scarce, but instead we find homosexuality among men and women to a certain extent. However, in these countries marriages are performed at an earlier age. In some countries like Iraq there are licensed places for prostitutes with medical supervision by the government. These are considered a safeguard against repression, sexual irregularities and venereal disease. The religious people in the Arab countries are against birth control; the people themselves are proud of large families. But in cities, especially among the educated people, some practice it for economic reasons. Abortion in most of the Arab countries is illegal. Though we have no figures to show its extent, we may say that its practice is scarce. Illegitimacy is also scarce in the Arab countries. In Egypt there were 610 illegitimate children in 1949, out of which 367 were found in Cairo and Alexandria.

Arabs are very sentimental toward their mates. Their sentiments are usually sexually toned. This is more egoistic than altruistic. Their sexual life is happy, as each partner tries to satisfy the other and feels proud in doing it. The husband looks at it as proof of his manhood. It gives the wife a sense of security and she hopes through it to keep her husband's love warm.

Protective Functions of the Family

In the Arab countries, the head of the family is usually responsible for the welfare and the protection of its members. If he fails in this duty, the law forces him or any other financially capable relative to help the needy and the disabled members. The government in Egypt started some four years ago what is called a Social Security Project, by which it helps by monthly payments the needy elderly, the completely disabled, the orphans and the widows. This project also helps temporarily some other classes of needy people: divorced women who have children, the family of prisoners, the family whose supporter is too ill to earn his living or is temporarily unemployed. The industrial renaissance will no doubt in time absorb many unemployed people. In many Arab countries the government pays monthly allowances to retired officials or their families in case they die.

The Arabian governments are doing their best to protect people from ill health by affording compulsory gratis vaccinations, establishing centers for the care of children and pregnant mothers, introducing pure water in villages, fighting against endemic diseases.

Education

Most of the Arab population is illiterate, especially in countries like Saudi Arabia and Iraq. Lebanon has the least illiteracy, about 30 per cent; Egypt, 70 per cent; Iraq, 89 per cent. There are government and private schools. The family in the Arab world does not usually supply any kind of education. Education of women is less than that of men in most of the Arab countries. In Egypt in 1954 illiteracy among women is 80 per cent, among men 60 per cent. In Iraq it is 80 per cent among men and 96 per cent among women according to the census of 1947.

Religious Training

Most Arabs are religious and they try to give their children religious training. The Moslem father teaches his children how to pray and cultivates this habit in them from the time they are six or seven years of age. He also teaches them some parts of the Koran. In villages and small towns this religious training of children within the home is more prevalent than in the larger cities.

Recreation

Recreation at home is very limited among the Arabs, except on a few occasions like weddings. The most highly educated people in countries which do not object to the mixing of the two sexes, e.g., Lebanon, Egypt, Syria, and Iraq, may have parties on occasions like birthdays. These people also exchange visits and go on picnics where men, women and children take part. Usually in cities, men visit men and women visit women, and the children are left to play in the house or outside. Clubs and cafe houses take a good deal of the time of men. They often spend their evenings there, chatting or playing indoor games. Occasionally the man might take his family to the cinema or to a public garden.

Marital Status and Family Disorganization

In Egypt, according to the census of 1947, the marital status is shown by the following table:

Table 5. MARITAL STATUS, EGYPT, 1947

Marital Status	Males	Per Cent	Females	Per Cent
Unmarried	1,514,320	27.6	662,533	11.5
Married	3,652,611	66.5	3,766,759	65.0
Divorced	69,620	1.3	127,609	2.2
Widowed	138,411	2.5	1,134,974	19.6
Undefined	116,467	2.1	95,262	1.7
Total	5,491,429		5,787,137	

The total shows that the per cent of married men and women is nearly equal (66.5 per cent and 65 per cent), and that the per cent of unmarried men is more than double that of women. This can be explained by the fact that the legal age of marriage for men is eighteen and for women sixteen. The figures in the table are taken on the basis of sixteen and over for men and women. Besides, the average age of marriage among men is always higher than that among women.

It is shown that the per cent of widowhood among women is nearly eight times that among men (19.6 per cent and 2.5 per cent). This also can be explained by the following facts: (1) The average age of men is lower than that of women. More women widows are left behind. (2) Men marry at an older age than women. (3) The widowed man in the Arab countries does not usually stay a widower. He can easily marry again and again. The chance for the widowed woman to remarry is rather small, especially if she has children.

According to the above census we find that 35.1 per cent of the married men have been married before and that 9.8 percent had one wife in their custody when being married. Later, most of these divorce the old wife after they marry the new one. In Egypt only 3.5 per cent of the married men keep more than one wife in their custody; 3.3 per cent have two; .2 per cent have three; and .03 per cent have four wives.

Polygyny in the other Arab countries is more abundant than it is in Egypt, with the exception of Lebanon. We have no figures from these countries except a rough estimate from Iraq which shows that 5.3 per cent of the married people in Baghdad have more than one wife. Surely the figure rises in smaller towns and villages. In Kadhemia, a suburb of Baghdad, about 8.6 per cent of married men have more than one wife. The percentage of those married to more than one wife in Saudi Arabia exceeds greatly the figure quoted above.

Divorce is easy among the Moslems; Islam allows it and the husband is not obliged to go to court for it. It is his religious and legal right. The wife can ask for divorce in the divine courts. She may be granted it if she has good reasons. This, however, is rather scarce. An outsider might think that divorce cases would be common, but this is not so. However, in the last few years, the Egyptian families have been suffering a comparatively high rate of divorce. This may be largely attributed to hard economic conditions and to some incompatibility between men and women resulting from the emancipation of women which started some years ago and which is exaggerated by some women's movements. These unintentionally unbalance family relations; by over-emphasizing the independence of women, they miss the idea of cooperation which is one of the most essential requirements of happy family relations. When men and women can conform to the changing traditions, and when women are better educated, their relations and their attitudes toward family living will improve.

The following shows the percentage of divorces to marriages in three Arab countries:

Table 6. NUMBER OF DIVORCES PER 100 MARRIAGES
IN THREE ARAB COUNTRIES

Country	1947	1950	1951	1952
Egypt	29	27.5	–	–
Iraq	8.5	8.2	–	–
Transjordan	–	–	16.9	17.3

We also find some significant figures in the 1947 census in Egypt related to divorce. Thirty-one per cent of all the divorces occurred within the first year of marriage and 79 per cent within the first five years.

Distinguishing Characteristics of the Arab Family

Usually the size of the family is big. The Arabs take pride in this. The wife and children are loyal to the head of the family, especially to the father. The wife is dependent on her husband socially and economically. The honor of women, especially unmarried women, is sacred to the family. Unfounded rumors or doubts about the honor of the girl may cost her her life. Married women are subordinate to their husbands. Since their childhood, they have been brought up to this. The husband may enjoy many liberties and yet deprive her of them. He can go out with friends or to any amusements or make visits at any time he likes and for any length of time, yet she must ask his permission if she wants to go out for a visit or shopping. In marriage, among the majority, relatives, especially cousins, have priority over a stranger, in spite of any advantages the stranger may have over the relative. The family is stable and has a strong sentiment toward the original home. Even if a member of a family emigrates he yearns for the family home, never loses touch with it, and cooperates in keeping it. Mixing of the two sexes is prohibited in some countries and is practiced in others only to a limited extent.

Trends

Education, especially education of women, has given rise to new attitudes and ideas. It has brought about mutual respect, mutual interests and mutual understanding between the two sexes. Subordination of women and their submissiveness to men are decreasing rapidly among educated people. Education of women has also afforded better care of children and better upbringing. This will reflect on society in general.

Old traditions which imprisoned women in towns and cities and put them behind doors and veils are breaking. Increasing numbers of women go to work in various fields, thus getting some experience of life and becoming more sophisticated. This gives them a feeling of independence which in turn makes them more self-confident and conscious of their personalities. Mixing of the two sexes is increasing and is bringing about mutual respect between them. The standards of morality are changing, allowing more freedom of behavior. More freedom is enjoyed by young people in choosing their partners in marriage. The elders are recognizing this freedom and giving way to it. A happier family life is expected. The new generation is moving toward freedom of thought and action. This will lead to a more democratic family and society. There is a tendency among educated people toward birth control. It is expected that this will prevail. This may take some time as education is still backward in many Arab countries and because many religious people oppose it.

Silwa is an Egyptian village in the province of Aswan, the southern-border province of Upper Egypt. The author, Hamed Ammar, was born and raised in this village, and his report is primarily a study of the social and psychological aspects of education in the community.

Few Arab writers, Muslim or other, in either medieval or modern times, have published studies of the Middle Eastern village. Ammar's study is a unique and important contribution toward a fuller understanding of the cultures of the region.

17

Adolescence and Marriage in an Egyptian Village

HAMED AMMAR

Adolescence as a stage of development in the individual's life assumes but little importance, and is unmarked by a ceremony or any other means of social recognition. By the age of thirteen or fourteen the child's maturing of sex organs is referred to as "bulough"—maturation (literally the stage when one reaches a peak). Adolescent boys are sometimes referred to as unmarried men (azab), or "he whose sweat has become odorous," or "he unto whom life has entered" (khashu al 'aish). For the parents, adolescent boys and girls do not present any specific problems, except for the fact that they are approaching the marriageable age.

From *Growing Up in an Egyptian Village* (1954), pp. 183–201; reprinted by permission of Routledge and Kegan Paul, Ltd.

In the villagers' view, adolescence and marriage are inextricably connected. It is not unusual for girls to get married by the age of twelve and thirteen, in spite of the law which stipulates that this may not be effected before the age of sixteen. This happens without official registration, and the reading of the "Fatiha" between the two parties is sufficient to sanction and validate the marriage. Nowadays, boys usually marry after eighteen, on finishing the requirements and examination connected with military conscription, and it is one of the youths' misgivings against conscription that it delays their marriage, or at least provides a pretext for their parents for such a delay.

According to our way of approach, it is appropriate here to discuss the dominant norms that are emphasized in the genetic development of the individual at this stage. Most of these norms are not new but they loom larger in this stage, while other norms are still imperceptibly reinforced.

The first of these social norms is the emphasis on industry and responsibility of the maturing boys and girls. By the age of twelve or thirteen, boys and girls are now, with few exceptions, out of school and Kuttab. They could be entrusted to work either in the fields or at home without parental supervision, thus becoming a decided economic asset. Participating in adult work, with full responsibility, provides the adolescents on their part with a secure position in the family.

With this increasing share of responsibility, boys enjoy a certain amount of freedom as compared with their period of childhood. They are not exposed to the physical punishment which is frequently administered during childhood, except, of course, for grave offenses such as stealing or neglect of their work. They are also entitled to move about freely and to mix with their age-mates without having to account for their absence at night to their parents. They can sleep outside the house in the open air in summer, or in the guest house in winter, or go to enjoy themselves at a wedding or any other ceremony.

Yet, while youths enjoy more freedom of movement concomitant with their assumed responsibilities, girls find their freedom more restricted and become more confined to the house and the neighbourhood. These restrictions are partly because their work is more concentrated in the house, and partly "because their breasts have grown," a sign of embarrassment and shame which the girls should not be encouraged to display.

Both boys and girls, however, are expected to give up their childish play and games. One can observe groups of adolescents at night sitting at a corner of the street or in an open space, talking or telling stories or riddles, while the group of younger boys are noisily at their games. If girls still make dolls at this stage, they are not those made of maize straw for play, but those to decorate their future houses, and are made of cloth.

Although the boys' freedom is in some ways less restricted than that of the girls, it does not mean that it is considerably increased. Both still have to maintain their social space and to observe the social norms of dominance-submission which govern the pattern of relationship between old and young; both have to adhere to rules governing sex behavior and sex dichotomy as will be shown later. On the whole the arc of growing up seems to be similar to that in Japan, represented as a curve with maximum freedom and indulgence allowed to babies and to the very old. Social disciplines are imposed after infancy, reaching the lowest point in the curve of freedom just before marriage, whereupon it gradually ascends. Marriage gives the individual a certain amount of freedom which gradually increases by having children, and later on by possessing property after the death of the father. On the other hand, old age, like infancy, is unhampered by some restrictions connected with etiquette, sexual shame, breaking wind, or covering the face—in the case of women. Old women, for instance, can go out wearing one black garment similar to children, and unlike adolescent girls, who usually wear two pieces. Old men are allowed to indulge in singing, which is different from that of the adolescents and which is called "nameem" or "wawat." Children are allowed to amuse themselves by mimicking or imitating old people and earn admiration from their parents or other boys for such imitation.[1]

Summing up the first dominant norm during the adolescent stage, one finds that boys and girls accept responsibility for active work and are characterized by the elimination of play elements compared with childhood and submission to parental authority as an ennobling virtue.

By the age of sixteen or seventeen the adolescent boys toe the line of adults, who reluctantly allow children to play their games or tell stories, provided they are assured of their victory in due course. The age-group of adolescents is interested in real issues and happenings of the village, e.g., disputes, ceremonies, neighbours' gossip, the new camel or bull that so-and-so bought, things that their families sell or buy in the market, the times of sowing and harvesting. Even in their interest in stories, it is the Jiha type of story with its realistic touch, and those of life or miraculous feats of saints rather than the fables that interest them.

The attitudes towards sex represent the second norm that becomes dominant in the individual's life at this stage. It is true that sex segregation of children in play, the boys' abandoning of their earrings (while girls keep them), starts earlier, at the age of nine and ten years, but it is almost fully established by the age of twelve and thirteen.[2]

Sex organs now become pudenda and adolescents become careful about the way they sit or what they wear. The notion of shame (Ar) is primarily a word connoting sex disgrace or sexual infidelity. This is the first association that arises in the villager's mind, and has been extended to comprise "every forbidden impropriety, from a trifling breach of etiquette to the most serious moral turpitude."[3] The first real emotional feeling of what it means to bring "ar" to one's family comes through the excessive shame connected with sex organs.   Adolescent boys urinate out of sight, while the girls make use of a private room inside the house.   Boys wear long pants, whereas girls wear a headcloth to cover part of their face and their breasts on passing by men.[4] For both, any conversation about sex is taboo, and they are forbidden to talk about it to their parents or to any grown-up. Chastity as a moral and religious ideal implies the avoidance of any stimulating pleasurable influence from the opposite sex, or talking about sex. Adolescent girls are not encouraged to look attractive for fear of tempting men.   One woman told me that a girl who beautifies herself will find difficulty in marriage and will have no "lamah" (halo) about her to please her husband when married.

During adolescence, however, the girl would be prepared for marriage by tattooing her lower lip and by a special mode of hair style, distinguishable from the loose hanging hair of childhood. For tattooing the lip, a special woman is invited to prick the lip with a pack of needles smeared in black soot mixed with animal bile.   The hair dressing of an adolescent girl and a woman is very much like that among the Sudanese women.[5] A special woman called "mashata" plaits the hair into small tresses tightly covering the head.   This style of hair makes a firm basis for fixing her ornaments on marriage, which are usually composed of three golden disks (dinar, pl. dananeer) that dangle over the forehead, and a silver chain connected to the ends of the hair at the back.

It is during adolescence also that boys show the greatest interest in singing, and for this purpose they form the so-called "circle of romance boys" (awlad al hawa).   In these circles, held usually in summer, on festive occasions, weddings and circumcision, youths give vent to their new interest in love.   They perform by standing in a circle with one taking the lead by singing a song while the other boys listen.   On finishing, they repeat in chorus the last line again and again, clapping their hands rhythmically till the first singer or another youth starts another song.   Some of these songs are composed extemporaneously, while others are old ones repeated.   The following three examples are typical of the songs sung:

> *Ya bit ya um ghawaish,*
> *khallaiti 'agli taish,*
> *nassaitini al ma'aish,*
>
> CHORUS: *Wi dmoui 'al'ashik 'al khaddain.*
>
> *O thou girl with bracelets,*
> *thou hast rendered my mind crazy,*
> *and hast made me neglect my work.*
>
> CHORUS: *And the tears of the lover are on the cheeks.*

> *Rakbah min foag wasil,*
> *tihki bil hasil,*
> *mafeesh adab wasil.*
> CHORUS: *'Ala annabi wahhid wi salli.*
>
> *She is on the top (on the roof),*
> *telling what has happened,*
> *she has no politeness at all.*
> CHORUS: *Say God is one and pray for the Prophet.*
>
> *Wana jayi mna al Mas'aeed,*
> *wi labis talat jalalaleeb,*
> *wi batgallab baihin gilleeb.*
> CHORUS: *Gol la abouy in kunt tahwani, gol la abouy.*
>
> *I was coming from al Masaeed*
>   *(a neighbouring village)*
> *wearing three garments*
> *in which I was rolling, rolling.*
> CHORUS: *Tell my father if you love me, tell my father.*

At this stage of adolescence, boys—especially those who have been to the Kuttab—begin to participate in mosque prayers and show intensified interest in religious practices. They go to Friday prayers, take part in the calling for prayers and the drawing of water from the mosque well for ablutions. A great number of youths also join the mystic order of "Nakshabandia"; they are called "Boys of the Path" (awlad attarik), and their headquarters is a room attached to the old mosque of the village. Members of the sect are expected to attend the night prayers ('isha) in the mosque, after which they congregate for reading and listening to mystic verses, followed by telling some of God's attributes silently several times. This is called "the mystic routine" (ratib). Moreover, on certain occasions, these youths perform collectively the "Zikr." The performance of this mystic ritual involves mainly the repetitive uttering of some of God's attributes aloud and in unison. The leader of the "Zikr," a blind man, stands in the middle of a circle, while youths, and sometimes with them a few married men, will be standing in a circle calling out together one of God's names, e.g., "Merciful" (Raheem), while swaying their bodies. This repetition may go on for about a quarter of an hour or so, to be stopped by the leader who will recite some verses of saints or some "mawwals." While the boys are listening to this, they express their approval and admiration, and they may ask for another "mawwal" from the reciter before they start chanting another of God's names. While those in the circle are repeatedly chanting a name of God, gradually getting into almost a state of ecstasy, the leader

in the centre would be clapping his hands and stimulating his boys to carry
on by more repetitive chanting.   The following are two examples of "mawwals" sung on such occasions:

> 'Ajaby 'ala welaid fi zikr al-Ilah zawwad,
> elif al-Jalalah, wib salaat annabi t'awwad,
> 'Ash gadr ma'ash la mal wa la hawwad,
> wa la umru jalas yoam ma'ally galbahum sawwad,
> lamma mat bayyan karamat la 'affan wa la dawwad.

*I admire the boy who has indulged in mentioning God's name,
and accustomed himself to His Glorious name and to prayers for the
    Prophet,
and lived all his time never deviating from the right path,
and never associating with those people whose hearts have been
    blackened.
When he died he showed signs of piety, and his body neither decayed,
    nor was attacked by worms.*

> Shams al giyama danat gum ya mureed safir,
> gum jahhiz azzad min gabl al-miaad safir,
> wi gabbad al-arwah daiman al-'ibad safir,
> as-shaib wiyya as-sigam ju lak ya fata mursal.
> wi lukul umnah ata liha nabi mursal,
> ata Jibril bil burag li annabi mursal.

*The sun of resurrection is approaching, a warning for departure.
Prepare yourself before the hour comes.
The seizer of souls is always apparent and about.
Grey hairs and sickness are messengers for you.
For every nation there has been a messenger,
and Gabriel delivered God's message to Muhammad.*

On some occasions these "Boys of the Path" go to visit their "brothers"
in another village. On their approaching that village, the heralding of which
would be by the visitors' chanting in unison popular verses and by beating
on a small drum, the latter would walk out to receive them before they
enter the village. They would offer them tea and dates and spend the rest
of the night reciting verses or holding a "Zikr."

Some of the adolescents and youths in the village do not take part in
either the singing or mystic activities, for they are not encouraged to do so
by their parents, and they are satisfied by only gathering in the neighbourhood for chanting. On asking some of these boys why they did not join in
such activities, they replied that they wanted to attend to their livelihood,
and as they usually felt tired through the day's work they could spare no
time or effort for such activities.

It must be pointed out that it is not maintained here that interest in religious matters is a psychological consequence of puberty and adolescence, or that the attitude towards sex is being learnt only at this stage. Such norms as mentioned earlier are being imbibed gradually from childhood.   With regard to religious matters, children start by learning about God's power at an early stage, even in their play and riddles.   On going to the Kuttab they know how to recite the major Islamic creed, "There is no God but Allah and Muhammad is his Phophet," learn the obligation of fasting through the adult practice and through their own attempts to fast half a day, a day or more according to their capacity in imitation of adults. As far as sex norms are concerned, they begin to express themselves in separate play as early as the age of eight and nine years.   But with the dawning of adolescence, the child finds himself awakened to the cumulative effect of social learning and to an intensified understanding of the social meaning of maturity.   Looking at adolescence as a stage of social development and social experience, it does not differ markedly from the stages of childhood.[6]   With the increase in the physical and mental capacities of the growing boy or girl, he or she is expected to have fully mastered the skills and faithfully observed the social norms and attitudes which he or she has hitherto been imbibing and practising.   What Fortes observed in the process of socialization in Taleland applies almost equally to this peasant community where the total pattern of behaviour is not built up bit by bit, through addition, but evolves from the embryonic form in an almost concentric pattern of development.[7]   In this way the norms of development are increasingly reinforced and intensified through institutional and social learning.   Moreover, with the comparatively slow pace of change, the adolescent develops a sense of cultural assurance since he sees others going through experiences culturally similar to his own.[8]

At this juncture it is appropriate to mention that in some communities characterized by continuity of social training combined with lax and even social disciplines, the period of adolescence does not witness emotional stress and turmoil which hitherto have been considered as inevitable characteristics of this phase of development.[9]   Moreover, recent investigations among adolescents in Western communities have shown that such symptoms of stress and ferment are absent amongst boys and girls who have been reared in favourable conditions; and the conclusion is that appearance of such traits is neither an inevitable accompaniment of the adolescent stage nor an inescapable consequence of the maturing of certain animal-like instincts.[10]

Some psychologists and especially Freudian analysts maintain that the biological changes in adolescence have a great impact on the individual's behaviour.[11] This is one extreme, while the other is to consider adolescence as purely a sociological phenomenon and merely a social experience involving new adjustments to social situations and relationships.   Here adolescence is to be considered as a bio-social phenomenon, dependent on the cultural

conditioning of the individual with regard to his maturing sex functions and
the impact of this standardization on the basic personality structure and social institutions.[12]   In the light of this statement, the social disciplines connected with sexuality are relevant data, and according to Kardiner, of great
significance in understanding the basic personality structure and in explaining partly the nature of primary institutions.

It seems that in Silwa the process of socialization is similar in many
points to that amongst the Tallensi and the Samoans, with regard to the
continuity of the inculcated social norms and the spheres of adult and child
activities.[13]   Unlike many Western societies, youth in Silwa do not express
in their attitudes that sense of being torn between youthful autonomy and
parental insistence on dependence. This problem does not seem to be disturbing to parents and would seem abhorrent to youth who like to demonstrate their allegiance to their family and clan. Even if such desire for
autonomy is occasionally expressed by boys, who on disagreement with
their parents desert them for some relatives in another village or go to town
to work, this is considered to be the exception, and of course such a desertion
can never be entertained by girls. The lack of such strong desire could be
explained by the security the youth derives from his status in his family and
his need to be married by his parents.

Psychologically, however, adolescent boys, and more so adolescent
girls, impressed the writer as being on the whole timid, apprehensive and
withdrawn. These traits stand out more clearly if compared with children's
groups. Attitudes of initiative, self-assertion and drive seem to be the exception in adolescent behaviour.[14]   In attempting to account for such general
characteristics, the writer does not claim them to be the negative phase of
the adolescent stage. He attributes their striking appearance to the cumulative effect of the severe social disciplines, and especially those connected
with sex. The maturing of sex functions at this stage is noted with great
embarrassment, shame and feeling of guilt by adolescents. As mentioned
before, complete hush and excessive secrecy prevails over sexual matters
among adolescents as well as adults. This seems to contrast sharply with
free bodily gratification given to the infants. There is no word for masturbation in the villagers' dialect. Sexual pleasure of any kind outside the
marriage tie is condemned by the text of the Koran, as mentioned earlier.

Manifestations of this excessive repression and fear of sex are obvious in
the veiling of adolescent girls and women and the hiding of the breast
contours with extra pieces of cloth, in the downcast look of boys when speaking to an adult, a well-known characteristic of this stage of development.
The writer also noticed on many occasions adolescent boys who were either
enraged or ashamed on seeing their mother sitting with relatives outside the
house at night, others who threw dust at their adolescent sisters and even
married sisters when looking outside the house without proper covering,

even when no man was passing by. When sisters become "a shame" in the matter of going out fetching water or running errands, adolescent boys do not object to taking over some of these duties. The writer also noticed an adolescent boy who, rebuked by his mother on the grounds of his "mature age" and "the smell of his pubic hair," flared up with rage and wept. This may be an extreme case, but it is indicative of the excessive shame and apprehension connected with sex. Obviously girls have not much scope for venting the pressures of sexual repressions, and they become more sullen and apprehensive than the boys, but not for long, as they are soon to get married. This excessively repressive and restrictive discipline over sex marks out the process of growing up in this community under study from Taleland and Samoa, where the attitude towards sex is much more permissive.

At this juncture it is appropriate to apply Kardiner's constructs concerning the effect on the basic personality structure of the way a culture satisfies the individual's dependency cravings, which are biologically determined. It seems that this excessive prohibition on sexuality at the stage of adolescence is a social discipline imposed to create and perpetuate the attitude of timidity and dependence of the growing individuals on their seniors. To obey such a discipline is a method of ingratiation, and of establishing conditions for being loved, protected and socially accepted. Thus it works as a lever which parental authority manipulates to make children acquiescent and dependent and as a social technique for minimizing initiative and ambitions.[15] These exaggerated cravings of dependency and their concomitant consequences of the inflation of the parental image and social conformity probably explain the psychological undercurrents lying behind the great indifference to social change in this village as well as in many other similar communities in Egypt.

To what extent do inordinate sibling rivalry and excessive shame and guilt, especially with regard to sex, produce the psychological disposition to sexual jealousy institutionalized in this community as well as in many other communities in rural Egypt? It is well known that in Egypt disputes over land, water and women rank as three of the most common causes of crime.[16] This does not mean that sibling rivalry and sex prohibitions are the only causes, but seem to provide the psychological field for the moral and religious values connected with fidelity and the propriety of sexual jealousy. A woman is identified not only with "shame" but also with "honour" and to preserve one's honour is tantamount to avoiding exposure to shame.[17]

These attitudes, according to Kardiner, would also help to understand the dichotomy of sexes and to prevent sexual jealousies from coming out to open hostilities. They also appear to be one of the weapons of social equilibrium and of preserving in-male and in-female solidarity.[18]

Here it is also possible to give some satisfactory answer to the connection between the nature of the community and its demands on individuals as represented by sexual regulations. The central and principal quality in a polite (muaddab) or virtuous person is his conformity to the norms governing sexual behavior; the flouting of which in any manner would condemn him as impolite and vicious irrespective of his other qualities. Morality and virtue are primarily connected with stringent sexual controls. The villagers, although envying the city dwellers their material comfort, deplore their moral laxity, e.g., women's emancipation in dress, love affairs, use of cosmetics, women's participation in men's work. In this community I heard of no cases of adultery or illegitimate children for the last thirty years, though cases of homosexuality and jokes about sexual pleasure from animals are not uncommon amongst the adolescents and young men. Stringent sexual controls are an essential agent for the maintenance of solidarity, the cohesion and the orderly living of a group with its puritanic religious code and its social organization based, among other things, on a clear-cut sex dichotomy.[19]

Whatever views may be held about the psychological problems connected with adolescence in Silwa, this stage is certainly the prologue to the full status of adulthood which is eventually attained by marriage. Marriage, after circumcision, marks the greatest ceremonial occasion in the individual's life. The best way of describing marriage conditions in Silwa is to give an account of a marriage ceremony which the writer witnessed, and which is typical as there is hardly any variation in the form it takes.

A is a boy who had recently been rejected for military conscription, on grounds of poor eyesight; he is known to be a good farmer, and a great help to his father. He was the eldest son in the family and felt that his father delayed his marriage unduly as "fathers usually get their first sons married as early as possible." After he was rejected for conscription, this boy could no longer bear any delay. As the custom is, he sent "messengers" to persuade his father to get him married, as "everybody was telling him that it was high time he got married." On the other hand, his father was reluctant; he was in a quandary whether or not to proceed with this project; he was apprehensive that the lad might not be so devoted to his work after marriage, yet he felt the time was ripe for getting his son married, otherwise the boy might at any time "bring disgrace" on the family. The lad's last appeal to the father was through a messenger who pointed out to the father that if the necessary steps for marriage were not instantly undertaken, the boy might think of leaving the village to find some work elsewhere. The father gave his consent, realizing that he would have to get his son married: "There will be more 'baraka' if it is done soon."[20] The actual preparations would start in a month's time, when the harvest was ready.

Now a dilemma of choice faced the parents, as there were two girls of marriageable age in the family; one was the daughter of the boy's maternal uncle and the other of the paternal uncle. It was partly because of the mother's influence, and partly because of the boy's personal inclinations that his parents decided to marry him to his maternal cousin. This affronted the boy's paternal uncle, as his daughter, according to custom, had precedence over that of the maternal uncle. This man asked the lad's father for an "Arab verdict" on the matter, and a formal gathering of relatives and some neighbours brought apparent reconciliation between the two brothers. They all agreed that "although the boy was to get married into his mother's family the oil was still preserved in the house (zaitakum fi baitakum) and that he was not marrying a stranger." Yet this slight was not forgotten and caused some tension and vituperation between some of the paternal and maternal relatives during the celebration of the ceremony.

The date of writing the marriage contract was then fixed. The father of the boy and his relatives and friends went to the house of the girl's father asking for her hand for their son in the usual phrase of "talbeen al gurb" (literally "we desire to get closer to you"). Neither the boy nor the girl was present during this gathering for writing the contract. Before the contract was written, the registrar (maazoon)[21] enunciated the following, which was repeated by the girl's father: "I have married my daughter X to A accepting the payment on which the people of the two sides concerned have agreed in the manner prescribed by the Holy Book and the Way of the Prophet." The contract was then signed by the two fathers as well as another witness for each side.[22] This was followed by the reading of the "Fatiha" and the giving of the marriage-payment (mahr) to the bride's father. In this case the amount was ten pounds paid in advance and two pounds to be paid later. According to the village practice, the payment always consists of two parts; the greater part (usually three-quarters of the total) is paid over after writing the contract and is called "mugaddam" (in advance), while the other, called "muakhar" (the delayed), is only payable in case of divorce. All these procedures in the ceremony described here were followed, as usual, by a specially prepared meal ending with the reading of the "Fatiha" and a prayer to God that He might help in making this marriage successful and fruitful. While all this was taking place, the girl's mother and her female relatives, but not the boy's mother or his female relatives, were singing and uttering their joy-cries now and again. The "maazoon" then left with his money gift from the bridegroom's father and sugar and corn from the bride's family. Thus the ceremony of "agreement" (tibah) ended.

The agreement between the two families was followed by their fixing the "night of marriage" (lailat addukhla), and this followed a fortnight later.[23] In the meanwhile, the bridegroom took his weekly presents to the girl's house on the market day. These presents usually consist of meat, sweets, fruit and similar delicacies. The girl's mother returned the handkerchief on the basket in which these gifts were sent with presents of pigeons

and flour. During his visits in this period, the boy, as expected, was not
allowed to see the girl, being usually met by the mother and father. During
this period also the girl's family were preparing her house and decorating
it. They had to build an extra room, and thus the newly-weds' apartment
consisted of two rooms, one with a completely covered roof with only two
small holes as windows, while the front room was half-covered. This is a
typical way of building a house in Silwa, making the inner room for use in
winter and the outer for summer. At the same time, the girl's family were
getting together her jewellery, by buying bits and borrowing others.

The boy's family bought an outfit for the girl composed of two black
outer garments (tobs) and two colourful patterned gallabiahs. Together
with the girl's outfit, a tob and a gallabiah were bought for the mother
and a gallabiah for each of the bride's younger brothers.

Two days before the actual night of marriage, the bridegroom and some
of his male relatives and friends who were unmarried went around distributing invitations to those the family wished to invite. Those invited would
be expected to contribute during the forthcoming ceremony of "haircutting"
as in the case of circumcision ceremonies.

The appointed day arrived, and began with the female celebration in
the bridegroom's house. Women came with corn on their trays as their
contribution to the mother who, in return, placed on the tray a loaf of
wheat bread or a part of it and a piece of meat according to the contribution received.[24] During this exchange of gifts which took place between the
late morning and the late afternoon, the boy's house looked very busy, but
with hardly any men about. Women were singing and calling out their joy-
cries and exchanging the good wishes.

In the late afternoon the girl invited her friends for the jar-filling ritual.
Accompanied by four other girls the bride took her jar to the Nile, and on
this occasion, as is the custom, she was allowed to linger as much as she
liked on her journey to the Nile, provided she came back before sunset.
On her arrival home she washed herself completely, was rubbed with henna
and perfume by her mother and was wrapped in a woman's cover (twada),
her face not being seen by anyone except her very close female relatives, e.g.,
mother, grandmother, maternal aunt.[25] She was then surrounded by a group
of girls of her age who began entertaining her by playing on the tambourine,
and singing the traditional songs of the occasion. The following is an example:

> How pretty is the one we are entertaining,
> How we are admiring her.
> The snake in his hole
> has spent a sleepless night.
> He kept one eye on her forehead,
> and the other on her anklets.[26]

In the bridegroom's house there was the preparation for the procession round the village to take place before the evening prayer. The procession was led by some religious men beating on their drums and tambourines while chanting hymns of praise to the Prophet. On the way, and on arriving at the mosque, dates and sweets were distributed and children usually find such occasions most exciting when they scramble for their booty. Behind this small gathering of men and a great crowd of children, followed the female procession crying out shrills and singing.

After the evening prayer the bridegroom offered a meal to those who were in the procession, as well as others who were invited, after which contributions from men began to be received in the "haircutting" ceremony. The details of announcement of contributions are exactly the same as those described earlier for the circumcision ceremony. While the bridegroom or "The Prince," as he is usually called on such an occasion, was having his hair cut, the circle of "the boys of romance" was in full swing outside the house; other adolescent boys were engaged in mock fighting with their staves.

As the contribution ceremony ended, the crowd of boys stopped their organised playing and singing and showed signs of excitement and anticipation for the next event, when the bridegroom in his best clothes, a dagger tied to his waist and a stick in hand, had to go to meet the bride. Immediately the bridegroom came out of the house, another procession was organised. The procession was led by a strong youth taking a camel-load of wheat, corn, lentils and beans which was to be the bridegroom's provisions for three months. The bridegroom himself was amidst a group of his friends, who were reciting the traditional song of: "O God, Praise our Prophet; our hearts love him because he will save us from Hell." At the very rear came the procession of women, and the whole procession moved towards the bride's house.

As the singing and beating of the drums were heard by the bride's people, they came out with her, face and body covered, and in the care of her mother and the midwife, with another girl walking beside them carrying candles and corn on a tray on her head. Other women and girls were following in a state of great excitement. When the two processions met, the midwife took the bride to the bridegroom. On her face being uncovered to see him, he was prepared to sprinkle her face with some milk which he had in his mouth and would expel with force.[27] At this moment the excitement reached its peak as the boys around the bridegroom sang at the top of their voices, "The roses are blossoming. She is rightfully thine, she is rightfully thine."[28]

The tension between the bridegroom's maternal and paternal relations reached its highest a short time later when the traditional mock fight began over the loaded camel. This fight usually takes place just in front of the bride's house, where some boys belonging to the bridegroom's family try to take the camel back to where it came from, while other boys from the bride's family try to prevent them from doing so and lead the camel to its destination. Each of the two sides call out, "The camel is ours, the camel is ours." On this occasion, the fight took on a serious note, the camel became frightened, and some grown-ups had to intervene to prevent further developments. After the camel had safely entered the homestead, the two processions, mostly of women and boys by now, proceeded to an elevated piece of ground to let the bride and bridegroom, who were still in their separate groups, see the Nile from a distance. All then returned to the bride's house. The bridegroom with his selected friends, mostly unmarried, retired to the house built for him, while the bride stayed with her mother and other female relatives. The bridegroom remained with his friends till the morning, for according to custom he does not sleep with his wife till the fourth night.

On his first breakfast, however, the bridegroom with his friends were served, as usual, with special wheat-cakes called in the villagers' language "kaak," with rice pudding and tea, for which the bridegroom paid a pound in return. After breakfast the "Prince" and his associates went to kiss the hands of his father, mother and greet other relatives in his patrilineal house. This was followed by a visit to the clan's guest house, where they received pots of tea from the father's house as well as from neighbours of the family. Meanwhile the bridegroom's mother received her breakfast from her in-laws to which her answer was a visit accompanied by other women taking back the trays full of corn.

For the next two days the bridegroom was still accompanied by his selected friends, who shared his meals and remained at night with him. On the fourth night he was left alone to see his wife after dinner. Before he retired with her he had to offer her a pound as a "placation" (ridwa) for her disrobing. On the following morning the boy brought a ram from his father's house for a special lunch to which this time only neighbours were invited; these also made gifts of money, sugar and tea, as their contributions.[29] Thus, through these elaborate procedures of exchanging food and gifts, the bridegroom establishes himself in his matrilocal residence amidst his neighbours and the new marriage is thus publicly declared and acknowledged.

At the end of the week, the bridegroom's mother with some of her friends went to visit her son's house, a ceremony called the "treading of the house," since she actually went to see the rooms prepared for her son for the first time. The other women who were invited or who were fulfilling their obligations carried their own contribution of wheat flour, pigeons and money to be given to the bride's mother. These contributions would be considered as part of the bridegroom's provisions and measured out by the mother-in-law.

The mother-in-law provided them with lunch and tea, thus marking the end of the wedding celebrations.

The end of the marriage celebrations marks the beginning of a formal avoidance between the bridegroom and his parents-in-law. Whatever might have been the relations between him and them before marriage, the newly created situation makes him no longer on familiar social terms with them. Traditionally, to remove this "avoidance" the bridegroom's family should send within the first two months of marriage a ram to the bride's family as a "reconciliation."[30]

This avoidance could be regarded as a recognition that, in the initial stages of marriage, much of the behavior of the married man to the family of his spouse has to be modified and reoriented. Even if he is married to his cousin, avoidance of her parents is required as a token of respect. Adoption of new phrases in reference to his in-laws, house habits of reserve, announcing his entrance into the house, manner of dress and similar items of etiquette must be observed by the newly married groom. In other words, previous informality and intimacy are replaced by a degree of formality to show consideration for the new ties of marriage.

This avoidance could also be considered as a manifestation that the husband, living in his matrilocal residence, feels uneasy and embarrassed in the home of a comparatively alien family; his ultimate home will be his patrilineal house to which he eventually takes his wife.[31] This custom also implies the psychological stresses involved in the new situation, where it is difficult to render the demands of consanguinity and affinity compatible, and where the support of the larger family unit has to be sustained for the maintenance of the newly created bonds of the individual family.[32]

Nadel explains such an avoidance in a similar manner. He maintains that in such a situation spontaneous shame and conventionalized sexual shame appear combined; for these cultural features express (and prevent) both the embarrassment between strangers (in a kinship sense) who are thrown together by marriage, and the embarrassment that springs from the awareness of the sexual occasion responsible for this new relationship.[33]

Such social procedures are implicit cultural solutions for smoothing transition from one state of life to another requiring concomitant adjustment and reorganization.

In Artas, the Palestinian village studied by Granqvist, the uneasiness in this stage of adjustment presents itself in a different way. As marriage in Artas is in the patrilocal residence, the bride, before leaving her family, would make demands on the bridegroom's family and make sure that her family's wishes have been fulfilled, before she is placed on the camel going to her bridegroom's house.[34]

As for the bride, she now starts her seclusion in the house till she brings forth a child and is never allowed to go out and never seen by a married man, even her husband's father and her married brothers. Her main job is to attend to her husband, to receive him when he knocks at the door, and to serve food to him. One of the main difficulties of newly married girls is their adjustment to the new situation, where they must break away from their previous life and assume a responsible role. The difficulties, however, are smoothed out in the matrilocal marriage period, where the bride's mother is really the one who, behind the scenes, provides her son-in-law with his requirements. This attention of the mother to her son-in-law usually makes her unmarried sons and daughters jealous, as epitomized in the common saying referred to earlier. Under her mother's supervision and instructions, the bride comes to learn the appropriate conduct of woman-hood. It is probably during this period that she receives sex information as the occasion arises. Moreover, her previous playmates do not sever their contacts with her; they still go to see her and "have a hand dip of henna" with her; but she is not allowed to join their games or play with "toys." Other women, especially relatives, come to see her, give her advice and praise her "halo" and jewellery. On the whole it seems that the girl comes under her mother's authority at this stage more than any other stage of her develop-ment. During this period of seclusion the direct influence of the mother is undoubtedly supreme, even much more than the husband. The latter, in fact, is not expected to linger in his bride's house. Except for his mealtimes, he should not remain in the house except when he comes in late at night after finishing his entertainments with his friends.

Indeed, the first year of marriage, for both the husband and wife, bristles with difficulties that may lead to divorce. According to my infor-mant, Mahmoud, marriages are more prone to break down during the first year than at any later period. This statement seems plausible, since during the first year especially, the economic, social and psychological ad-justments or maladjustments not only between the spouses, but also between their families, develop.[35] The amount of talk, gossip and vituperation, es-pecially amongst the womenfolk, might appear tragi-comic when they harp endlessly upon the shortcomings of the spouses, and their respective families. Complaints and gossip are heard about things such as the inability to provide the right amount of henna for the bride; or the bride's family's bad cooking of the groom's pigeons; the quality of the girl's jewellery and endless small things which reveal the difficulties of the adjustments of the individual family to an equally important wider circle of the joint family.

The following table shows that the percentages of divorce for the whole country reach their highest during the first two years of marriage.

Here a short note on divorce seems necessary. The right and power to

Table 1.   RELATION BETWEEN DIVORCE AND THE DURATION OF
MARRIAGE BETWEEN 1942 AND 1946 IN EGYPT[36]

Duration of Marriage	1942 %	1943 %	1944 %	1945 %	1946 %
Less than a month	4.20	4.31	4.46	3.88	3.99
One–six months	14.60	15.70	16.30	14.50	14.20
Six months–one year	12.50	13.10	14.40	14.60	13.05
One–two years	18.40	18.10	20.90	20.30	20.30
Two–three years	11.00	11.90	13.60	14.50	13.70
Three–four years	7.55	9.05	8.34	7.82	8.60
Four–five years	5.80	4.87	5.04	5.53	5.40
Five–ten years	15.30	13.10	13.70	12.30	11.90
Ten–fifteen years	5.42	5.23	5.10	4.63	4.74
Fifteen–twenty years	2.42	2.40	2.32	2.12	2.00
Twenty years and more	2.78	2.66	2.38	2.09	2.12

divorce one's wife is part of the male ethos in this community.   According to Moslem law (Sharia) a man can divorce his wife twice and on both occasions can take her back.   If he repeats any formula of divorce three times or says, "You are divorced threefold" (talga bi attalati), then the divorce is final; and husband and wife can only remarry on certain conditions.[37] Recently, in Egypt, the threefold formula of divorce has come to be regarded as one statement, and husband and wife can reunite immediately after its utterance if they wish.

The word "divorce" is also used as a conditional oath by men to convince others of the truth of a statement, or to force them to accept an offer or conform to a desire.[38]

The following table shows the percentages of monogamous and polygamous marriages among the Moslem population in the country as a whole.

Table 2.   PERCENTAGE OF MONOGAMOUS AND
POLYGAMOUS MARRIAGES[39]

Number of Wives	1927	1937
One wife	95.18	96.86
Two wives	4.49	2.95
Three wives	0.29	0.17
Four wives	0.04	0.02

What does it feel like to be a newly married bride, confined to her house, with the occasional temptations of stealing a peep through the holes of the door onto the outside world? What is her complex emotion on seeing her husband returning home or while serving him, washing his hands, watching him eat, etc.? Does she fear her first sexual experience? Does her husband show an affection towards the girl in sexual intercourse? Are other erogenous zones used in sex? What are the overtones of small talk, if any, between husband and wife in the midst of the recurrent experiences of sexual intercourse which is one of the great pleasures in such a culture?[40] Such issues are significant to a study of the factors influencing the interaction of culture and personality. The writer cannot claim to give any substantial answer to such questions as the whole issue is taboo and it would be impossible for a person who is normally part of this culture to raise such points without endangering his prestige.

By getting married, the bridegroom and bride have achieved the hallmark of adulthood; and this brings satisfaction to one's parents. The transfer of the wife to the patrilocal residence is usually thought of after she bears a child, and by then her mother prepares for her a special headcover (tawada) to enable her to go out. The wife's settlement in her husband's house does not end her connection with her family, as it is her father's home which is always opened for her as a safeguard against any maltreatment from her husband or other members of his family.[41]

NOTES

1. Talking about the "arc of life" in Japan, Ruth Benedict contrasts it with the "American arc of life." In the latter case, to secure the individual's energetic participation in life, the Americans rely on increasing his freedom of choice during adolescence, while the Japanese rely on maximizing the restraints upon him. *The Chrysanthemum and the Sword*, p. 254. This generalization applies, on the whole, to the methods of socialization in Silwa.

2. I noticed that some boys and girls in their free drawings used to draw a line between men and women in a wedding ceremony or a pilgrims' procession. In the Rorschach testing the contrast between the two sexes was expressed in phrases such as "These are women wearing black and these are men wearing white" although there was nothing in the blot to match statements like this.

3. W. Robertson Smith, *Lectures and Essays*, London, 1912, p. 156. This word "ar" is different from "L'ar" or "al'ard" as pronounced in Silwa which means "protection" and is said to invoke the help of another person. See E. Westermarck, "L'ar or the Transference of Conditional Curses in Morocco," in *Anthropological Essays presented to E. B. Tylor*, Oxford, 1907.

4. I was told that neither women nor adolescent girls wear any special clothes for menstruation.

5. Cf. Sophie Zenovsky, "Marriage Customs in Omdurman," in *Sudan Notes and Records*, Vol. XXVI, Part ii, 1945, p. 244.

6. M. Mead, *Coming of Age in Samoa*; Reuter, Foster and Mead, "Sociological Research in Adolescence," in *American Journal of Sociology*, Vol. XLII, 1936, 1937, pp. 81–94.

7. M. Fortes, *Social and Psychological Aspects of Education in Taleland*, pp. 42–3.

8. M. Mead, "Character Formation and Diachronic Theory," in *Social Structure —Essays Presented to Radcliffe Brown*, p. 22.

9. M. Fortes, *op. cit.*,—M. Mead, "Adolescence in Primitive and Modern Societies," in *Readings in Social Psychology*, ed. by T. M. Newcomb and E. L. Hartley, New York, 1947.

10. C. M. Fleming, *Adolescence*, London, 1949, pp. 240–2.

11. Wayne Dennis, "The Adolescent," in Carmichael, *Manual of Child Psychology*, pp. 636–7. He maintains that adolescence originally had a meaning which was biological, and not temporal or social. Hence studies concerning the psychology of adolescence must concern themselves with the effects of the biological process on the behaviour of the individual and their main aim therefore is an examination of a certain set of mental-physical correlations.

12. Richard T. Sollinberger, "The Concept of Adolescence," in *The Psychological Bulletin*, Vol. 36, 1939, pp. 600–1. A. Kardiner, *The Individual and His Society*.

13. For adolescence and puberty as treated in different societies, see also Ruth Benedict, *Patterns of Culture*, Chapter II.

14. This is the writer's general impression and could only be substantiated by comprehensive recording of the behaviour of adolescents. According to Fortes, however, "for most problems of social anthropology, variations are of minor importance as compared with the 'typical.' For problems of developmental psychology variations may be of the utmost importance." *Patterns of Culture*, p. 8.

15. This is based on Kardiner's explanation that restrictive sex discipline creates instead of a friendly attitude to the impulse, one of anxiety which is in "anticipation of danger." "Instead of the self-confidence and the idea 'I can get pleasure by and from myself,' there appears an exaggerated idea of the cruelty of the forbidding parent. Instead of the attitude of self-confidence, the opposite develops—a lack of it, together with an inordinate increase in dependency and timidity." He further maintains that interference with sexual development creates exaggerated dependency, the inflation of the parental image, an over-valuation of the boons of dependency, and the encouragement of secondary outlets for the repressed hostility to the interfering disciplinarian. *The Individual and His Society*, p. 28.

16. Doreen Warriner, *Land and Poverty in the Middle East*, London, 1948.

17. Cf. J. C. Flügel, *Men and their Motives*, London, 1943, and Ernest Jones, *Papers on Psycho-analysis*, where he writes: "The ultimate source of the fear and the guilt that lie behind all these reactions (of sexual jealousy) is the relationship to another potential man and it is derived from the boy's unconscious fixation on childish attitudes; it is hard for him to 'picture' a woman quite apart from another man to whom she secretly belongs," p. 483.

18. A. Kardiner, *op. cit.*, pp. 476–7.

19. See Margaret Read, "The Moral Code of the Ngoni and their Former Military State," in *Africa*, Vol. XI, 1938.

20. This remark of the father indicated his social obligation for the marriage of his son; its counterpart is for the son to accept his father's arrangement for his marriage.

21. The "maazoon" is a learned man who keeps the official register of marriage and divorce. He is officially appointed after an examination in the Koran and the Sharia; it is an unpaid job.

22. According to Islamic Law there must be two witnesses for each side to sanction the marriage. It must be noted here that the writing of the contract at this stage is not like an engagement; it is as religiously binding as if actual marriage had taken place. If the bride or the bridegroom happens to die immediately after the contract, the surviving partner is entitled to have a share in any property.

23. It literally means "the night on which the bridegroom enters into the bride." It must also be noted here that Moslems regard marriage as essentially a civil contract, the validity of which depends only on the agreement of both sides. See Westermarck, *Marriage Ceremonies in Morocco*, London, 1914.

24. It was here that the boy's paternal uncle's wife and some of her friends had a row with the boy's mother over what they ought to have received for their contribution.

25. Even the father himself is not supposed to see her face.

26. The snake is presumably the symbol of the husband, who has been admiring the girl from top to toe.

27. It is by no means the first time the bride and bridegroom saw each other, which might be inferred from such a ritual.

28. It is one of the signs of a "good man" not to show any signs of embarrassment, and to be able to aim the milk right at the bride's face, otherwise he would be chaffed about it. On this occasion, although the bridegroom did this job properly, he was not spared some criticism especially from those who were in favour of a marriage with his paternal cousin.

29. This meal takes place even if the bridegroom is married to a girl living across the road.

30. Although avoidance between bridegroom and parents-in-law is still strictly observed, the breaking away from it does not necessarily have to be achieved through a gift of a "slaughter," but occurs quite often nowadays through the exigencies of everyday life after the lapse of some time.

31. This is the ideal course to be taken, but, as mentioned earlier, other factors, e.g., lack of space in his father's house, the bride's parents' attachment to their daughter and her children, might keep the husband in his matrilocal residence for years.

32. This explanation is based on a similar situation referred to by R. Firth, *We, the Tikopia*, p. 343. This avoidance lends itself to psycho-analytical interpretation in terms of incestuous taboo. The uneasiness in the newly created situation could also be inferred from the "mock fight" which could be classified, according to Van Gennep, as one of the "rites de séparation," while exchange of gifts and the partaking of food would fall in the category of "rites d'agrégation." Cf. Van Gennep, *Les Rites de Passage*, p. 198.

33. S. F. Nadel, *Foundations of Social Anthropology*, p. 352. The psycho-analytical interpretation for such a taboo, according to Roheïm, is that in this way an attempt is made to separate the wife from the mother, genitality from orality, and infantile dependency. *Psycho-analysis and Anthropology*, p. 425.
34. Hilma Granqvist, *Marriage Conditions in a Palestinian Village*, Vol. II, Helsingfors, 1935, p. 72.
35. For a well-documented discussion on the economic, social and psychological factors curbing the Moslem's nominal freedom of divorce, see Hilma Granqvist, *op. cit.*, Chapter X. According to official statistics the ratio of divorce per thousand of the population of Egypt for the five years between 1942 and 1946 was 8.3, 9.2, 9.6, 8.9, 8.1 respectively. *Pocket Census of 1948*, Govt. Press, Cairo, 1950, p. 47 (in Arabic).
36. These percentages are worked out from the *Pocket Census of 1948*, Govt. Press, Cairo, 1950, p. 50 (in Arabic).
37. Cf. S. G. Fitzgerald, *Muhammadan Law*.
38. Hilma Granqvist, *Marriage Conditions in a Palestinian Village*, pp. 297–8.
39. *Pocket Census of 1948*, p. 12.
40. It is a well-known fact that some newly wed husbands become impotent during their first sexual experiences and are usually then called tied (marbout). In such cases, a religious man would be invited to read for him, or write a charm which he wears under his clothes. Sometimes when this fact is known, a friend of this married man would go and tell him that he has "tied" him; and for this the friend would invite the husband to a meal of pigeons.
41. When a wife forsakes her husband's home for her father's she is known as "hardani," and mediators or an Arab council would try to reconciliate the two sides. For a similar situation see Hilma Granqvist, *op. cit.*, pp. 225–32.

REFERENCES

Benedict, R., *Patterns of Culture*. London: Routledge, 1935.
———, *The Chrysanthemum and the Sword* (Patterns of Japanese Culture). Boston: Houghton Mifflin Company, 1946.
Dennis, W., "Does Culture Appreciably Affect Patterns of Infant Behavior?" *J. Soc. Psychol.*, 12, 1940.
———, "The Adolescent," in Carmichael, L., *Manual of Child Psychology*. New York: Wiley, 1946.
Firth, R., *We, the Tikopia*. London: Allen and Unwin, 1936.
———, *Elements of Social Organization*. London: Watts, 1950.
Fleming, C. M., *Adolescence*. London: Routledge & Kegan Paul, 1948.
Flügel, J. C., *The Psycho-analytical Study of the Family*. London: Hogarth Press, 1921.
Fortes, M., "Social and Psychological Aspects of Education in Taleland." Supplement to *Africa*, Vol. XI. London, 1938.

————, *The Dynamics of Clanship among the Tallensi*. London: Oxford University Press, 1945.

————, *The Web of Kinship among the Tallensi*. London: Oxford University Press, 1949.

————, (ed.), *On Social Structure: Studies Presented to A. R. Radcliffe-Brown*. Oxford: The Clarendon Press, 1949.

Granqvist, H., "Marriage Conditions in a Palestinian Village," in *Comm. Hum. Litt.*, Vol. 31. Helsingfors: Soc. Sci. Fenn., 1932. Vol. 4, 1935.

————, *Birth And Childhood Among the Arabs*. Helsingfors: Soderstrom & Co., 1947.

————, *Child Problems Among the Arabs*. Helsingfors: Soderstrom & Co., 1950.

Jones, E., *Papers on Psycho-analysis*. London: Baillière, Tindall and Cox (fourth edition), 1938.

Kardiner, A., *The Individual and His Society*. New York: Columbia University Press, 1939.

Mead, M., *Growing Up in New Guinea*. London: Kegan Paul, 1930.

————, *Coming of Age in Samoa*. London: J. Cape, 1928.

————, *Sex and Temperament in Three Primitive Societies*. London: Kegan Paul, 1935.

————, "Research on Primitive Children," in Carmichael (ed.), *Manual of Child Psychology*. New York: Wiley, 1946.

————, "The Use of Primitive Material in the Study of Personality." *Character and Personality*, 3, 1934.

————, "Our Educational Emphases in Primitive Perspective." *Amer. J. Sociol.*, 48, 1943.

————, "Adolescence in Primitive and Modern Societies," in Newcomb, T., and Hartley, E. (eds.), *Readings in Social Psychology*. New York: Holt & Co., 1947.

————, "Age Patterning in Personality Development." *Amer. J. Orthopsychiatry*, 17, 1947.

————, "The Primitive Child," in Murchison, *Handbook of Child Psychology*. Worcester, Mass., 1931.

Nadel, S. F., *The Foundations of Social Anthropology*. London: Cohen & West, 1951.

————, "A Field Experiment in Racial Psychology." *Brit. J. Psychol.*, 28, 1937.

————, "Nupe State and Community," *Africa*, 8, 1935.

————, "The Typological Approach to Culture." *Character and Personality*, 5, 1936–7.

————, "The Application of Intelligence Tests in the Anthropological Field," in Bartlett *et al.* (eds.), *The Study of Society*, 1937.

Read, M., *Native Standards of Living and African Culture Change*. London: Oxford University Press, 1938.

————, *Education and Cultural Tradition*. London: Evans, 1952.

————, "Cultural Contacts in Education." Typed copy of a paper read before the Education Section of the British Association, 1951.

————, "The Moral Code of the Ngoni and their Former Military State." *Africa*, 11, 1938.

————, Review of Childs, G. M., "Umbundi Kinship and Character." *Africa*, 21, 1951.

————, "Common Grounds in Community Development Experiments." *Community Development Bulletin*, 11, June, 1951.

Ròheim, G., *Psycho-analysis and Anthropology*. New York: International Universities Press, 1950.

Smith, W. R., *Lectures on the Religion of the Semites*. London: Adam & Charles Black, 1914.

Sollinberger, R., "The Concept of Adolescence." *Psychological Bulletin*, 36, 1939.

Sorokin, P., *Society, Culture and Personality: Their Structure and Dynamics*. New York and London: Harper, 1947.

Steward, J., *Area Research*. New York: Social Science Research Council, 1950.

Tannous, A., "Extension Work Among the Arab Fellahin," in Brunner, E., *et al.* (eds.), *Farmers of the World*. New York: Columbia University Press, 1947.

Tax, S., "World View and Social Relations in Guatemala." *Amer. Anthropologist*, 43, 1941.

Thompson, L., Joseph, A., *The Hopi Way*. Chicago: University of Chicago Press, 1944.

Thouless, R. H., "A Racial Difference in Perception." *J. Soc. Psychol.*, 4, 1933.

Warner, W., Lunt, P., *The Social Life of a Modern Community*. New Haven: Yale University Press, 1946.

————, *The Status System of a Modern Community*. New Haven: Yale University Press, 1947.

Warner, W., *et. al.*, *Who Shall be Educated?* London: Kegan Paul, 1946.

Westermarck, E. A., *Ritual and Belief in Morocco*, 2 vols. London: Macmillan, 1926.

————, *Wit and Wisdom in Morocco*. Routledge, 1930.

*In this study of child-rearing practices, 468 mothers were interviewed
and the five-year-old children of 397 of them were tested. The subjects
were drawn from three sects—Arab Sunni Muslims, Arab Greek
Orthodox Christians, and Armenian Gregorian Christians. The initial
phases of the study began in 1958 and interviewing was completed by
the summer of 1959.*

*Dr. Prothro deliberately modeled his study after selected American
studies in order that the results he obtained could be compared with
those of previous studies in the United States.*

*There is a dearth of data concerning this subject ("More is known
about the early development of obscure Arabian dialects than about the
early development of a contemporary Arab") and Prothro's work is a
most useful contribution.*

18

Child Rearing in the Lebanon

EDWIN TERRY PROTHRO

... We now turn to a socialization process which usually begins a little
later than ... (eating and bowel control) and continues for many years:
the training of the child in the handling of his aggressive impulses. Aggression is closely related to general questions of discipline, not only because
punishment may be thought of as a type of parental aggression, but also
because psychologists have often argued that parental discipline and child
aggression are interrelated. Yet parents do not exercise direct control at all
times, however strict they may be. In most families, it is expected that the
child will exercise some self-control from having internalized parental injunc-
tions. These internalized principles make up much of what is called
conscience, so the question of the child's conscience can be treated in con-

nection with the treatment of parental discipline and the socialization of aggression.

AGGRESSION

The mothers were questioned on their attitude toward the different sorts of aggression on the part of their little children: aggression toward the mother and father, aggression toward brothers and sisters, and aggression toward other children. In posing the question on parental aggression, an effort was made to make the behavior seem fairly normal: "A child sometimes gets angry and tries to hit his parents, or tries to shout at them and to insult them. To what extent should the parents just ignore this? What would you do when X behaved in that way?"

In spite of the phrasing of the question, more than 90 per cent of the mothers stated that no child should be allowed to aggress toward his parents. Even more revealing were the statements on how they would respond. Forty per cent of the mothers said they would "beat" (spank, slap, or the like) a child who did this and another 8 per cent said they would punish severely. About 20 per cent of the mothers would scold and threaten physical punishment. Another 23 per cent said that the child would never do such a thing, presumably because of previous training. Only 5 per cent said they would reason with the child or explain that such behavior was bad, and only 2 per cent would laugh or ignore the outburst. The various groups showed the same general pattern of taboo on aggression toward parents, so this attitude can be considered a general norm in Lebanon.

For mothers with more than one child, several questions were asked about the relationship of X with his brothers and sisters. . . . Nearly half the mothers said the children got along well, but one-fourth of the mothers described the relation as openly hostile: fighting, quarreling, teasing, etc. The remainder said the relations were sometimes good and sometimes bad. It is not exceptional to find many mothers describing sibling relations as good or mixed, but the fact that one-quarter would consider the relations as hostile does seem startling in a family-centered culture. Nevertheless, this datum is in agreement with the observations of anthropologists who have lived in Lebanese villages (Williams; V. Ayoub). They have noted that each child tends to resent the younger child who replaces him in the mother's affection, and who later comes to be a burden and a responsibility for him. A similar sibling rivalry exists in Egyptian families, according to one observer (Ammar) and is openly encouraged by the shaming of one child by comparing him with another. This shaming technique is also widely used in Lebanon. An Arabic proverb widely quoted in Lebanon says: "I against my brother, my brother and I against my cousin, my cousin and I against the stranger." This proverb stresses the defensive nature of family solidarity against outsiders, but assumes a hostility which erupts when external threats are absent.

The mothers' technique for coping with sibling aggression stresses control rather than training. They intervene when the quarreling takes place in the house, when it is loud enough to be a nuisance, or when there seems to be danger of serious physical harm. The most common device used in such cases is "beating," followed closely by scolding and threatening. Only one mother in six said she tried on such occasions to discuss with, or explain to, the child how he should treat his brothers and sisters. With respect to technique of handling, as with respect to frequency of occurrence, there were no significant group differences among Lebanese mothers.

Aggression toward other children in the neighborhood was also explored. . . . A majority of the mothers, 60 per cent of those replying, said the child got along fairly peaceably with the neighbors' children. Only 18 per cent of the mothers reported quarrels and fights with them. It would seem that conflicts at this age occur more often within the family than with neighboring children. It is possible, of course, that this impression is a function of the mothers' lack of knowledge of what happens outside the home. In addition, there is less contact of any sort with neighbors than there is with siblings. Only 5 per cent of the mothers said their child liked and enjoyed playing with the children of neighbors, and 18 per cent of them said that the child never played with anyone outside his own family. This impression of low contact is further confirmed by the mothers' statements of how they handled a conflict. The most common technique was to have the child come home, although beating and scolding were also common. Again we find little training and much control, for only 7 per cent of the mothers would check into the causes of the quarrel and only 9 per cent would employ reasoning or discussion.

At this point it might be well to see whether there is a general factor of child aggressiveness revealed by the data. That is, are there some children who quarrel both with siblings and with the neighbors, and some who quarrel with neither? If there were more such cases than might be expected by chance, then it might be possible to relate the generalized aggressiveness or lack of it to such variables as maternal warmth, social class, and the like. A check of the interviews, however, showed that there was no such general factor. The children described as having quarrels and fights with the neighbors' children were about evenly divided into those getting along well with siblings and those having difficulties. The children who had peaceable relations with the neighbors' children were likewise about evenly divided with respect to sibling relations, so our interviews do not reveal any general aggression factor. It is possible, of course, that some children are generally aggressive, while others are aggressive toward either siblings or neighbors, but not toward both. Our data do not permit us to say whether such may be the case.

Permissiveness for Aggression

How do the mothers feel about fighting? In our answer to this question we can speak with confidence. More than half of the mothers said that a child should never fight. As far as they were concerned, physical aggression was something that should be suppressed. About a third of the mothers believed that a child should fight in his own defense. Fewer than one mother in six thought that fighting should be learned by a child. Overt, physical aggression is not acceptable to most of our mothers.

There were some group differences among mothers on attitudes toward fighting. Only one group showed any tendency toward accepting fighting as necessary: the middle-class Orthodox mothers of the city. About a third of them believed it was necessary for a child to learn fighting. The Armenian mothers, in the valley and in the city, believed more than did Arab mothers that a child should be taught to fight in self-defense. As can be seen in Table 1, they gave this response significantly more frequently than did other

Table 1. OPINIONS OF MOTHERS ON FIGHTING AMONG CHILDREN

	Opinions Expressed by Mothers				
Sect	*Must Learn to Fight*	*Self-Defense Only*	*Sometimes Fight*	*Should Never Fight*	*Child Never Fights*
Gregorian	28	76	17	41	0
Orthodox	20	58	1	83	0
Sunni	5	25	1	101	12
All Lebanese	53	159	19	225	12

mothers. The Sunni mothers of both classes, in the city and in the valley, believed that a child should not be taught to fight—even in self-defense. This was the response of 70 per cent of the Sunni mothers, and another 8 per cent answered that the problem did not arise, because the child had learned not to fight. This Sunni rejection of fighting is considerably greater than could have occurred by chance. The most modern group, then, is more accepting of aggression, while the Gregorians stress defense, and the Sunnis oppose all fighting.

American mothers have been rated as somewhat more severe than most cultures in the socialization of aggression (Whiting and Child, p. 99), but they are considerably less severe than are Lebanese mothers. The mothers we interviewed were much less permissive of aggression toward parents and toward other children than were American mothers, and used much more severe techniques in their control of aggression (Sears *et al.*, pp. 245–248).

We have seen that the small group considered as least traditional was somewhat more permissive of aggression than were other mothers. Let us now consider some other factors related to attitude toward aggression. In examining these relationships we shall treat as "encouraging of aggression" those 53 mothers who stated that they believed that a child should learn to fight.

If we exclude the Beirut Orthodox middle-class mothers, we find no relationship between encouraging aggression and religion, social class, or place of residence. There was, however, a significant sex difference. Although nearly half of the children in our sample were girls, only 13 of the mothers encouraging aggression were the mothers of girls. In Lebanon, as in America, girls are less likely to be encouraged in aggression than are boys (Mussen and Conger, p. 279).

There were among mothers tolerant of aggression a few more high in warmth than there were among anti-aggressive mothers. Of the permissive mothers, 47 per cent were high in warmth, whereas only 40 per cent of all mothers were high in warmth. This difference is so small, however, that it could have occurred by chance alone. Moreover, the mothers of boys tend to be a little higher in warmth than do mothers of girls, so the disproportionate number of boys in the permissive group could easily explain the result obtained. As in the American study (Sears *et al.*, p. 255), it can be concluded that warmth is not a determiner of permissiveness for aggression.

Maternal belief in aggression did not produce more fighting in the child. Only 19 per cent of the permissive mothers reported that the child sometimes fought with the neighbors' children, and 18 per cent of the nonpermissive mothers reported such behavior.

Mothers who were permissive of aggression, who thought a child should learn to fight, were not more permissive in general than other mothers. On permissiveness for children to make noise around the house, or to mark on the walls, and the like, there was no difference between mothers who were permissive of aggression and those who were not. Nor were such mothers lenient toward the child's parental aggression. Indeed, mothers permissive of fighting were more likely than other mothers to beat the child for aggressing against the parent. Of the 53 mothers who thought a child should learn to fight, 57 per cent beat the child for aggression against the parents. Of the 225 mothers who thought a child should never fight, only 43 per cent beat the child for aggression against parents.

Perhaps the term "permissive of aggression" is not the most appropriate one for these mothers who encourage aggressive behavior. They believe a child should learn to fight, but this belief is not linked to general permissiveness. It is, rather, linked to the mother's own use of beating if the child aggresses toward her. It is also linked to the sex of the child. Perhaps, then, it is a tough-minded attitude, placing emphasis on the necessity for using force. Such an attitude is permissive of, or encouraging of, aggression only when it is directed outside the family. It should be stressed that these mothers are rare in Lebanon. The majority of Lebanese mothers do not endorse aggression in any form whatsoever.

Mothers' Expectations and Demands

The mothers require that their children suppress any aggressive impulses toward parents, and indeed they oppose aggression toward children as well. What else do they expect, or hope, to find in a child of five? One question called for opinions about the ideal child of this age: "People differ on the meaning of 'good boy' (or 'good girl'). In your opinion, what is a good boy (or girl) of five or six years of age?"

The mothers were allowed to answer this question in any way they chose. No list of terms was suggested, nor was any limit placed on the number of terms they could set forth. The replies showed a remarkable consistency. City mothers and valley mothers of both classes and all three sects replied most often that the good child was the obedient child. Other characteristics mentioned by more than half the mothers, and mentioned often by mothers in every group, were "polite" and "tidy" or "neat." Mothers in one group or another mentioned cleanliness, school work, and honesty fairly often. . . . At this point it is enough to note that mothers of all groups have as their ideal a child who is obedient, polite, neat, and not aggressive. The emphasis is on checking unruly impulses to produce docility, tractability.

Such expectations are not easily realized, however, as was shown by the mothers' replies to the question "What are the things about him that annoy you?" There were 78 mothers who could think of nothing annoying, but the great majority were able to mention one or more annoying traits. Leading the list of complaints was a term meaning willful, resistant, or stubborn, and next in order of frequency were fighting, noise, and destructiveness. As might be expected of any mothers, then, their aspirations for the child are balanced off against their annoyances as he fails to achieve that ideal.

One of the questions on the American schedule which we adopted and adapted asked how careful the child should be around the house, whether he could jump over the furniture or write on the walls, or do such things. The American students of child rearing were able to evolve a scale out of the answers to these questions, with some mothers rated high on restrictions, some rated moderate, and some rated low (Sears et al., p. 279). We were not able to construct any such scale, for more than 90 per cent of the mothers said they never allowed any such behavior. On play inside the house, as on aggression, the Lebanese mothers were quite non-permissive.

Another question aimed at the question of permissiveness from the standpoint of promptness: "Some parents require a child to obey immediately, as —for example—when told to stop making noise. Others do not attach much importance to how quickly a child obeys. What is your opinion about this? How does your husband feel about it?" Once again the mothers replied in a rather non-permissive fashion, with 318 out of 465 stating that they insisted on prompt obedience. There was, however, a difference between the Sunni mothers and the others. Nearly half the Sunni mothers said they would wait or forget it, at least sometimes, but less than a fourth of the other mothers were as permissive.

Permissiveness with respect to prompt obedience was not related to the warmth factor discussed earlier. The 147 mothers who stated that they would not insist on prompt and immediate obedience were no warmer on the average than were other mothers. Indeed, only 56 of them were rated as high in warmth, and this proportion is slightly, and insignificantly, lower than the proportion of other mothers rated high in warmth.

Permissiveness is only one aspect of the mothers' expectations of her children. There is also the positive side, her expectations regarding his constructive behavior. Having seen that the mothers hope to prevent the child from carrying out aggressive and destructive acts, let us now examine their expectations and demands for helpful acts. The question posed was: "Should children as old as X be requested to perform particular duties at home? Does X have certain duties to perform at home?" There were 459 mothers who replied to these questions, and 256 of them, 56 per cent, said the child had no regular tasks. For at least half the mothers, the child is expected to be obedient and polite, but not asked to do more. This proportion required to perform some tasks at age five is fairly similar to that in the suburbs of Boston (Sears *et al.*, p. 287). There were, however, differences among the three religious groups on this question, as can be seen in Table 2.

The proportion of Sunni mothers who assign jobs is about the average of the whole group. Only one-fourth of the Orthodox mothers assign tasks, but well over half the Armenian mothers make such demands. While all Lebanese mothers seem to agree that the ideal child is one whose aggressive

Table 2. DOES THE CHILD HAVE DUTIES TO PERFORM AT HOME?

Sect	Yes	No	Total
Orthodox	51	105	156
Gregorian	88	70	158
Sunni	64	81	145
Total	203	256	459

and disorderly impulses are restricted, only among the Armenians do a majority expect the child to perform certain constructive tasks as well.

TECHNIQUES OF CONTROL

The Lebanese mothers, according to their assertions, expect a child to measure up to rather rigid standards of conformity. How do they go about achieving this? Do they expect the child to learn to do right on his own, or do they expect to be forced to exercise close control over him? Do they rely on punishment to block negative behavior, or do they use reward to elicit positive behavior?

The ideal child of five is not only obedient and polite, he is also clean and neat. If the mothers hope for a high degree of neatness, how do they expect to bring it about? The interviewers asked the mothers what they expected of a child of five with regard to cleanliness. After the mothers had described their expectations, they were asked how they tried to achieve those goals. More than 60 per cent of the mothers said the child kept himself clean, but 24 per cent said they took care of this themselves, and another 14 per cent said they were too busy to do it so the child did not stay clean. Nearly four-tenths of the mothers, then, did not expect the child to meet the cleanliness standards by his own efforts. Those mothers expected to exercise direct control over the child's cleanliness.

In the similar survey of American mothers it was found that they expected the child by age five to exercise considerably more personal responsibility in these matters (Sears *et al.*, p. 286). Not all the groups of Lebanese mothers ranked below the Americans in child autonomy, however. There were no class or city-village differences, but there were sectarian differences. The percentage of each group placing responsibility on the child was as follows: Armenians, 85 per cent; Orthodox, 61 per cent; Sunnis, 47 per cent. The Sunni mothers exercise the most direct control over their children and the Armenians expect the greatest independent action. It should be noted that the Armenians are highest both in placing cleanliness responsibility on the child and in assigning regular home duties to the child.

The fact that one group of mothers encourages more responsibility than do the other groups raises the possibility that individual mothers vary with respect to the demands they make on their children. In order to examine this possibility, a tabulation was made of the mothers' responses to the question on cleanliness and the question on home duties. Of the 203 mothers who did expect the child to carry out certain tasks at home, 155 expected the child to take care of his own cleanliness and only 48 either looked after him themselves or let him stay dirty. Of the 256 mothers who did not have any regular home duties for the child, 145 expected the child to keep himself clean and 111 either looked after him themselves or gave up on the matter. There is, then, a definite association between self-care and executing household tasks, and the association is too great to be attributed to chance. The trend, as measured by the test of chi-square, is significant at the .01 level. We can therefore say that a demand for responsibility seems to run through the answers to these quite different questions. In a later chapter we shall see that this is related to the dependence and independence of the child.

Another question which inquired into techniques of training used by the mothers came as a follow-up to the question on home duties. The interviewers asked the mothers who said the child had regular tasks to perform how they went about getting the child to perform the task. Unfortunately, the meaning of the question was not clear enough, and most mothers answered by saying that their child was an obedient child, that he did as he was told, or the like. Many others answered that they did "nothing," and this too was uninformative. A few mothers talked about how they had gone about shaping the child's behavior, and they were about equally divided among those using reward, reasoning, and punishment.

Rewards

Psychologists often divide reinforcers, stimuli which influence the occurrence of certain behavior, into positive and negative ones. Mention has been made of the use of beatings or spankings by Lebanese mothers, but negative reinforcers are only a part of the total range of controls. Let us consider next the positive reinforcers that mothers may use to control the behavior of their children.

Two questions dealt with the mothers' attitudes toward praise and other rewards in general situations:

"Do you have any special arrangement to reward X when he behaves well?"

"Some parents praise their children so as to encourage them to behave well, and others consider that good behavior is simply to be expected. What is your opinion about this?"

In reply to the first question, 34 per cent of the mothers said they did not usually reward the child, 4 per cent said they "sometimes" reward him, and the others said they did use rewards. Of those who said they rewarded the child, nearly a third volunteered the statement that food was the reward. We have already seen that food carries in Lebanon the special significance of affection and acceptance. The rewards which the mothers described were largely of a spontaneous type. There was almost no indication of a system of rewards such as that used by many American mothers, with points, gold stars, or money (Sears et al., p. 320). The only important group difference was between the Sunni mothers and the other mothers. Sunni mothers of both classes in city and valley frequently stated that they did not systematically reward good behavior. Of the 157 Sunni mothers who replied, 57 per cent said that they did not reward the child. Of the 324 Christian mothers, 24 per cent said they did not reward. For the Sunnis, then, rewards for good behavior are significantly rarer than they are for other mothers.

The second question on positive reinforcement dealt with praise as the specific reward. Of the 465 mothers who replied, 65 per cent said they praised the child for good behavior, but 32 per cent said that good behavior was to be expected so they never praised a child for behaving well. This minority which does not believe in praise is much larger than the 7 per cent of Massachusetts mothers, described as seldom or never using praise (Sears *et al.*, p. 322). The Lebanese mothers have high expectations and demands, but they seem to feel oftener than do American mothers that their demands *should* be met, and that compliance merits no special recognition.

There were significant group differences in the use of praise. Armenian mothers, far more than Arab mothers, said that good behavior was to be expected, and merited no special praise. Indeed, only 25 per cent of the 159 Armenian mothers stated that they praised a child for good behavior. In contrast, 85 per cent of the 145 Sunni mothers said they used praise, and 86 per cent of the 159 Orthodox mothers did so. The belief of the Armenians that a child should behave well without praise is probably related to the greater autonomy they expect of the child. As we shall see, this belief does not prevent the Armenians from rewarding the child in specific situations.

Two other queries asked the mothers about the sorts of rewards used in specific situations:

> "Suppose he takes his meals easily for several days without any troubles. What would you do?"
> "Suppose you asked X to do a certain job, and he did it immediately. What would you do? Would you say anything to him?"

Although the first question seemed to imply that the mother would do something, 45 per cent of the mothers answering said that they would do nothing in such a situation. This matter-of-fact reaction to good behavior at meals was a little more common among lower-class than among middle-class mothers. Slightly more than half the lower-class mothers reported that they did nothing. The mothers who did reward the child for good behavior used praise in most instances, although they frequently also added a tangible reward. As might have been predicted, the most common of the tangible rewards was food. The Armenian mothers stated as often as did Arab mothers that they would praise a child in this situation. Only for good behavior in general do the Armenian mothers say the child should go unrewarded. In this specific case they praise as often as do Arab mothers. All Lebanese mothers, however, use positive sanctions for good eating much less often than do American mothers (Sears *et al.*, pp. 321–322). As we saw in the preceding chapter, Lebanese mothers are more casual about feeding than are American mothers.

The second question asked for the mothers' reactions to the prompt execution of some unspecified task. Nearly two-thirds of the mothers said they would praise a child for having done this. About one-sixth said they would reward the child, and food was mentioned as the reward in about half the cases. There remained, however, a core of one-sixth of the mothers who would not encourage the child in any way. Again there were no significant group differences, although a little higher proportion of the lower-class mothers than of the middle-class mothers said that they would do nothing.

In general, then, we find that positive reinforcement, through praise and other rewards, is used less often by Lebanese mothers than by American mothers. Sunni mothers had a practice of systematic rewarding less often than did the others, and Armenians expected good behavior without reward more than did the others. In response to questioning about specific situations, a majority of the mothers of all religions said they would praise or otherwise reward the child. Food was the most frequently mentioned tangible reward. There was a sizable minority, larger than that found in America, which never rewarded the child for good behavior.

Punishment

Several of the questions asked the mothers probed her responses to various types of wrongdoing on the part of the child. The most general of these was: "What do you do when he is intentionally disobedient?" The replies to this question were quite revealing. Only 10 per cent of the mothers said they would use reason, discussion, or explanation. A few mothers, roughly one per cent, would insist until the child obeyed. Thirteen per cent said they would not do anything, largely because they were too busy. The other mothers said they would punish the child in one way or another: 37 per cent would beat the child, 10 per cent would scold, 10 per cent would threaten, 15 per cent would "punish" in some unspecified fashion, and 2 per cent would withhold something the child wanted. The proportion of mothers who say they would use physical force on the child is considerably higher than the proportion of American mothers who say they would do this (Sears *et al.*, p. 328). For the Lebanese mothers, the use of physical punishment and verbal punishment are the principal techniques used in controlling the child. For a substantial minority, however, there was *no* technique of control.

Another question, occurring much earlier in the interview, gives us some check on the reliability of the mothers' replies on the subject of discipline: "Suppose he does something which you do not like. What do you do?" The replies were quite similar to those on the question just discussed. This time

12 per cent of the mothers said they would use reason, explanation, or discussion. Only one per cent said they would do nothing. The other mothers described various forms of appropriate punishment: beating, 45 per cent; scolding, 19 per cent; threatening, 8 per cent; unspecified punishment, 12 per cent; withholding favors, 2 per cent. This distribution of replies is quite similar to that of the previous question, except that there were fewer who would do nothing. The difference in the "do nothing" replies may possibly be due to the fact that this question posits a definite act on the part of the child, and not just a vague failure to obey.

Replies to several other questions bore out this same general pattern. As mentioned earlier, mothers were asked what they did when the child aggressed against a parent, against a sibling, or against other children. Punishment was far more likely when the aggression was against a parent, and doing nothing was more common when the aggression was against other children. When the parent did act, however, she was most likely to spank or beat, and next most likely to scold and threaten. A similar pattern was obtained in answer to the question of how the mother kept the child from being disorderly in the house (marking on the walls, jumping over furniture, or the like). Punishment, corporal or verbal, was the chief technique of control.

There were no class or city-valley differences in the use of punishment, but there were consistent differences among the religious groups on this matter. These are manifested in Table 3.

Table 3. SECTARIAN DIFFERENCES IN TYPE OF CHILD PUNISHMENT

Punishment Specified by Mothers*

Sect and Type of Offense	Beat	Scold	Punish	Explain, Reason	Withhold Favors	Threaten	Nothing
Gregorian							
Misbehavior	80	40	38	11	5	10	0
Disobedience	67	19	53	7	5	13	8
Orthodox							
Misbehavior	110	43	17	46	4	3	5
Disobedience	49	20	15	27	4	3	39
Sunni							
Misbehavior	73	32	16	16	2	35	3
Disobedience	62	7	5	14	2	31	19
All Mothers							
Misbehavior	263	115	71	73	11	48	8
Disobedience	178	46	73	48	11	47	66

* Only major categories are included in this table. When a mother mentioned more than one type of punishment, she was counted in each category.

The Gregorians generally used beating and scolding, and rather infrequently relied on threats or reasoning. The Orthodox mothers used discussion and reasoning, or did nothing at all, more often than did the other mothers. Only 35 per cent of the mothers interviewed were Orthodox. Yet, on the question about intentional disobedience, a majority of the mothers who said they would use reasoning were Orthodox mothers. On the same question, a majority of the mothers who said they would do nothing were Orthodox. On the question about the mother's response to the child's doing something she did not like, 46 of the 73 mothers who said they would use reasoning (63 per cent) were Orthodox. There is a definite tendency, not attributable to chance, for the mothers using reasoning, or being permissive of disobedience, to be in the Orthodox groups.

The Sunni mothers were more likely than others to threaten the child with some future punishment—either punishment from themselves or from the fathers. Only 31 per cent of the mothers replying to these questions were Sunnis. Yet, of the mothers who said they would rely on threatening when the child was intentionally disobedient, two-thirds were Sunnis. And of the mothers who would use threats when the child did something they disliked, more than two-thirds were Sunnis. An attempt to control the child by threats, then, was more characteristic of Sunni mothers than of other mothers.

There were several questions which dealt with the amount of physical punishment:

"Do you beat him very much?"

"Does your husband beat him very much?"

"As an example, how many times has he been beaten in the past two weeks?"

Some translation difficulty rendered the replies to the first two questions relatively useless. The term for "very much" in Arabic can mean either "very much" or "too much." The question could be interpreted by some mothers as asking whether the child was beaten a great deal, and by others as asking whether he was beaten excessively. The translation in Armenian asked "how much" the child was beaten or spanked, which is a different query altogether. For this reason the replies were not used to establish any generalizations.

The replies to the question regarding the number of times the child had been beaten or spanked in the preceding two weeks showed considerable uniformity from group to group. Most of the girls had been spanked not at all or only once in that period, and most of the boys had been spanked once or twice. Yet 47 mothers out of 425 replying said the five-year-old had been spanked five times or more during the past two weeks. Of these 47 mothers, 39 were lower class and only 8 were middle class. High frequency of punishment was more common in the lower than in the middle class in

Lebanon, just as it was in America (Sears *et al.*, p. 426). This class difference was the only significant group difference with respect to frequency of use of physical punishment.

Physical punishment seems to be the chief technique used by Lebanese mothers in their responses to disobedience. Do they believe that it is effective? When asked whether they thought that beating was useful in getting a child to behave properly, 47 per cent of the mothers said they did not think it was, 28 per cent said they thought it was sometimes useful, and only 21 per cent gave an unqualified affirmative response. When we compare these responses with those given by American mothers (Sears *et al.*, p. 356), who employ spanking far less, we find a little less faith in physical punishment among the Lebanese mothers! Apparently there are many Lebanese mothers who use such punishment as a device for immediate control even though they do not feel that it is of genuine use in training the child.

The Armenian mothers place faith in beating more often than do the Arab mothers. Fewer than half the Arab mothers were willing to say that beating was even sometimes useful, but 73 per cent of the 161 Armenian mothers replying said that they thought it was helpful. We have seen that the Armenian mothers rely on beatings and scoldings more than do Arab mothers, and we now find that they have more faith in physical punishment than do the Arabs. This suggests a relationship between belief and behavior or, more precisely, a relationship between statements of belief and statements of behavior. There were no class or city-valley differences with respect to belief in the use of physical punishment.

Was there a consistency between statement and behavior with respect to the child? Or did the mothers threaten the child with punishment which they later failed to carry out? Some mothers volunteered the statement that they used threats as a disciplinary device. Sunni mothers did this more often than did the Christian mothers. But this leaves the question of whether the threats were actually carried out. Did the mothers often threaten and then do nothing for some reason or other? This question was one of those the interviewers asked the mothers. Of the 460 mothers replying, 45 per cent said they did this often, and another 19 per cent said they did it sometimes. Nearly two-thirds of the mothers, then, admitted making empty threats. When the same question was asked American mothers, only 27 per cent admitted that they often made empty threats (Sears *et al.*, p. 356).

There were no consistent class differences in the number employing threats, but there were differences between the Sunni mothers and the others. The proportion of mothers in each community saying they often used threats which they failed to carry out was as follows: Beirut Sunnis, 52 per cent; Beirut Orthodox, 36 per cent; Beirut Gregorians, 35 per cent; Valley Sunnis, 88 per cent; Valley Orthodox, 28 per cent; Valley Gregorians, 16 per cent. The Sunnis used threats most often, and the Christians in the valley used them least often. The relationship between the use of this technique and the personality traits of individual mothers will be examined in the next section.

Another type of punishment is the withholding of favors, or the deprivation of privileges. Few of the mothers had volunteered the statement that they used this technique, but when asked whether they ever used this technique, 32 per cent said "yes," 33 per cent said "sometimes," and 35 per cent said "never." There were no large group differences, but more than half the middle-class Orthodox mothers said they did use such a technique regularly and more than half the lower-class Sunni mothers, in Beirut and in Baalbek, said they never used the technique. This difference suggests that the use of withholding may not be a traditional technique. It may be mentioned in this connection that a vast majority of American mothers said that they used deprivation of privileges in training. Only 15 per cent of the Massachusetts mothers said they "rarely" or "never" used deprivation (Sears *et al.*, p. 338). When Lebanese mothers punish their children, they seem to use more direct and immediate punishment than do Americans.

DISCIPLINE AND WARMTH

Are there traits of the mothers which are associated with the type of discipline used? This question was examined first for the mothers who used physical punishment. First a count was made to see whether the use of such punishment was consistent. There were 128 mothers who said they beat the child for aggression against a parent, for disobedience, and for doing something the mother did not like. The fact that such a large number of mothers answered all three questions by saying that they beat the child demonstrates that their answers, at least, are reliable. This proportion of mothers answering similarly is far greater than could have occurred by chance. These mothers, then, can be called a "punitive" group.

Of the punitive mothers, 45 per cent said they used empty threats. The same proportion of other mothers said they used threats, so there is no relationship between threatening a child and beating him. Some mothers do both, some do neither, and some do one without the other.

It has already been mentioned that 47 per cent of all mothers said that beating or spanking a child was of no value. Do the punitive mothers have more faith in the value of physical punishment? The answer is affirmative, as shown by the fact that only 36 per cent of the punitive mothers said that spanking was useless. This difference from non-punitive mothers, while small, is too great to have occurred by chance. We can conclude, as was concluded in the American study (Sears *et al.*, p. 331), that mothers who spank a great deal are a little less likely to say it is useless.

Is there a relationship between punitiveness and warmth? This question was investigated by comparing the warmth ratings of the punitive mothers with the ratings of other mothers. There were a few more "cold" mothers in the punitive group than in the non-punitive group, but the difference was so small that it may have been a merely chance occurrence. There is, then, little relationship between punitiveness and warmth. Some of the warm mothers use physical punishment and some do not, and the proportions are about the same for mothers low in warmth.

In the study of mothers living near Boston, it was found that punitive mothers who were high in warmth were more likely than punitive mothers low in warmth to believe that spanking was effective. That is, if a warm mother used spanking a great deal, she was more likely than other mothers to think it was effective. Indeed, for such cases, confidence in the efficacy of spanking was expressed in two-thirds of the replies (Sears et al., p. 335). This relationship did not hold with our mothers. Of the 45 mothers high in punitiveness and warmth, only 12 said they thought spanking helped. This number is not significantly greater than would have been expected by chance alone.

With respect to the use of physical punishment, we can only say that the mother who endorses it in one situation is more likely than other mothers to endorse it in another situation. We cannot say, however, that such a mother differs from others in the warmth she expresses for the child. The technique was widely used by Lebanese mothers, warm and cold alike.

There was a relationship between the warmth of the mothers and their use of reason, explanation, and discussion in response to the child's doing something they did not like. Of the 73 mothers who said they would use discussion, 48 were rated as high in warmth. This is a significantly larger number of warm mothers than would have been expected by chance. This relationship between warmth and the use of reason may be attributed in part to the fact that Orthodox mothers, who made up more than half of the group employing reason, are higher in warmth than are other mothers.

The relationships between positive sanctions and characteristics of the mothers are difficult to establish because of the many different sorts of rewards that the mothers gave the children. This problem was therefore approached by examining the mothers who used no rewards at all—no praise, or food, or special privileges for good behavior. There were 54 mothers who said they would do nothing at all if they asked the child to do a job and he responded immediately. And 39 of these 54 (72 per cent) said in response to a later question that they had no arrangement for rewarding good behavior, although less than a third of the other mothers said they had no such arrangement. Failure to reward appears to be a reliable response, showing consistency from one question to another. The 39 mothers who said they did not praise or otherwise reward their children will be considered to be "non-rewarding" mothers.

There was a relationship between punitiveness and failure to reward. Only 6 per cent of the 340 non-punitive mothers were non-rewarding, but 14 per cent of the 128 punitive mothers were non-rewarding. Punitive mothers were more than twice as likely to be non-rewarding as were other mothers.

Non-rewarding mothers were lower in warmth than were other mothers. Although less than 40 per cent of other mothers were low in warmth, 69 per cent of the non-rewarding mothers were rated low. In contrast, although more than 40 per cent of other mothers were rated high in warmth, only 15 per cent of non-rewarding mothers were rated high. There is then a definite relationship between low warmth and failure to reward. It should be pointed out, however, that the punishment and reward behavior of the mothers was one of the factors which entered into the total judgment of warmth. Hence the correlation found is between one facet of warmth and overall ratings of warmth.

Non-rewarding mothers did not differ from other mothers with respect to the assigning of tasks at home, nor did they differ from other mothers with respect to the encouraging of independence in their children. They did not differ from other mothers in general happiness at being a mother.

There were definite group differences in proportion of non-rewarding mothers. Mothers in the valley were much more often non-rewarding than were mothers in the city. Indeed, 34 of the 39 non-rewarding mothers were of the valley. There was also a marked class difference. Only 5 of the 39 non-rewarding mothers were middle class. There was no difference between Sunnis and Orthodox, but only 6 of the non-rewarding mothers were Gregorians. The non-rewarding mothers, then, were predominantly lower-class Arab mothers from the valley.

CONSCIENCE

In no culture can the parents exercise continuous direct control over the daily behavior of their children. When a child is not under immediate surveillance his parents must hope that he continues to behave properly through habit, fear of the consequences of wrongdoing, or through the guidance of conscience. Writers on Islamic culture in general and on Lebanese culture in particular have emphasized the role that shame, or loss of "honor," plays in controlling the behavior of Lebanese (Weulersse, p. 249; Williams, p. 31). But a concern for honor is a fear of consequences of an act, and not a self-condemnation of the act. Does self-condemnation through conscience, or a feeling of guilt, play a role in a culture where shame is of such influence? As a step toward answering this question, let us examine the mothers' descriptions of the behavior of their children.

The questions designed to ascertain the degree to which a child was influenced by conscience assumed that he had done something wrong when the mother was not watching him: "If while you are not around he does something wrong, what does he do when you return? Does he tell you about it without any questioning? Does he confess when you question him?"

An effort was made to estimate the extent to which the child showed signs of having a conscience. The descriptions were divided into three groups, according to the following criteria:

> *High Conscience:* Child confesses without the mother's asking, child feels unhappy when naughty, child actively seeks forgiveness, as through rendering service to the mother.
>
> *Intermediate or Indeterminate:* Child confesses if asked. Other cases, in which the description given by the mother was not clear or detailed enough for a judgment with confidence, were placed in this category.
>
> *Low Conscience:* Child does not seem unhappy over his naughtiness, denies the truth when asked directly by his mother.

There were 174 children who gave evidence of a high degree of conscience, and 59 children who gave evidence of having low conscience. The other children either could not be classified with any degree of certainty, or they seemed to show evidence of a conscience of intermediate degree. There were then 12 per cent of all children classified as "low" and 38 per cent classified as "high." While it is not possible to make accurate comparisons with American children, the evidence suggests that the five-year-old Lebanese shows at least as much evidence of conscience as does the American child. In 13 per cent of the cases studied in New England, the behavior of the child was clearly what we would call "low" conscience, and in only 12 per cent of the cases was the evidence clear that the child had "high" conscience (Sears *et al.*, p. 381). Among five-year-old Lebanese, then, the cultural importance of shame, "face," and honor as controls does not preclude the existence of guilt and conscience.

Conscience was not related in any consistent or significant way to social class, religious sect, or place of residence. It was not related to the amount of dependency the mother reported as characterizing the child. Nor was it related to sex. In the American study, a few more girls than boys were rated as having high conscience (Sears *et al.*, p. 384), but these trends did not hold among the Lebanese children.

There were several traits of the mothers, however, which seemed to be related to the degree of conscience reported in their description of the children's behavior. Warmer mothers were more likely than others to have children rated "high" in conscience, and "cold" mothers were more likely than others to have children rated "low" in conscience, as can be seen in Table 4. This relation between warmth of mother and reported degree of conscience in the child is significant at the .05 level of confidence as de-

termined by the chi-square test. In the study of Massachusetts mothers, it was
also found that there was a modest relationship between maternal warmth and
child conscience (Sears *et al.*, p. 382).

Table 4. RELATION BETWEEN WARMTH RATINGS OF MOTHERS AND CONSCIENCE RATINGS OF THEIR CHILDREN

	Low Warmth	Medium Warmth	High Warmth	Total
High conscience	57*	29	88	174
Low conscience	28	12	19	59
Total	85	41	107	233

* All numbers in the table refer to the number of mothers in the warmth categories whose child is in the conscience category.

The disciplinary techniques used by the mothers also seemed to have
some relation to the degree of conscience in the child, if we can judge from
the extreme cases. Mothers who relied chiefly on physical punishment, and
those who did not reward good behavior, were more likely than other mothers
to have children rated low in conscience. Mothers who used reasoning and
explaining, on the other hand, were more likely than other mothers to have
children rated high in conscience. As we have seen, there were in the entire
group three times as many children rated high in conscience as there were
rated low in conscience. Among the punitive mothers, however, there were
only 41 children rated as high conscience and 22 rated as low conscience.
Among non-rewarding mothers, there were 13 children rated as high conscience and 11 rated as low conscience. The mothers using discussion and
explanation when a child does something they do not like had children with
high conscience in twenty-two instances and low conscience in only two
cases. Similarly, the mothers who used reason with a disobedient child had
a child rated as high in conscience in twelve cases and as low in only one
case. In all of these examples but the last (where the sample is too small)
the proportion of highs and lows deviates from chance to a degree that
enables us to consider the results significant at the .05 level.

The relation between disciplinary technique used and the presence or
absence of conscience is particularly important because disciplinary techniques were one of the chief correlates of conscience in the Harvard study
(Sears *et al.*, p. 386). In America, too, they found that reasoning produced
high conscience and physical punishment produced low conscience more
often than would have been expected by chance.

To summarize, the Lebanese child was more likely to exhibit behavior
considered to show a strong degree of conscience if he had a warm mother
who used explanations and reasoning when he did wrong, who did not use a

great deal of physical punishment, and who did not ignore his positive achievements. In this sense the Lebanese child was similar to the American child. Conscience was not a product of sex, class, sect, or place of residence.

REFERENCES

Ammar, Hamed. *Growing Up in an Egyptian Village.* London: Routledge and Kegan Paul, 1954.

Ayoub, V. "Political Structure of a Middle East Community." Unpublished Ph.D. thesis, Harvard University, 1955.

Mussen, P. H., and Conger, J. J. *Child Development and Personality.* New York: Harper Brothers, 1956.

Sears, R. R., Maccoby, Eleanor E., and Levin, H. *Patterns of Child Rearing.* Evanston, Ill.: Row, Peterson and Co., 1957.

Weulersse, J. *Paysans de Syrie et du Proche-Orient.* 2nd ed. Paris: Gallimard, 1946.

Whiting, J. W. M., and Child, J. L. *Child Training and Personality: A Cross-cultural Study.* New Haven: Yale University Press, 1953.

Williams, H. H. "Some Aspects of Culture and Personality in a Lebanese Maronite Village." Unpublished Ph.D. dissertation, University of Pennsylvania, 1950.

Spiro's publications on the kibbutz, derived from his 1951–1952 field study, are outstanding contributions to the anthropological body of theory and knowledge, in addition to their being invaluable sources of data on certain of the peoples and cultures of the Middle East. Of particular value is Spiro's study of kibbutz child training and personality —designed to realize both descriptive and theoretical aims. At one level he attempted to provide an understanding of the unique socialization system characterizing the kibbutz, and at another level he attempted to test the predictive value of ontogenetic culture-and-personality theory by relating selected personality characteristics of the sabras of the kibbutz to selected aspects of the socialization system. The following selection indicates the high level of sophistication this approach entails.

19

Adolescent Personality in the Kibbutz

MELFORD E. SPIRO

TURMOIL

It is difficult to decide whether the now familiar *Sturm und Drang* experience of Western adolescence is found among kibbutz adolescents. Both teachers and parents attest to the fact that many students experience some type of adolescent emotional disturbance. Even parents, whose defenses were usually mobilized in answering the Questionnaire, were quite prepared to concede this point. Of the nine adults with adolescent children who answered the question, "Did your child undergo a 'crisis' during adolescence?," three answered, "definitely yes," three answered, "perhaps yes," and one did not respond; the remaining two answered, "no."

Teachers too report the existence of adolescent personality problems. In analyzing our teacher interviews the following conclusions emerged: at least 16 or 21 per cent of the students from Kiryat Yedidim were sufficiently disturbed to elicit the attention of their teachers and/or students. These included a girl who suffers from nightmares; two highly neurotic boys, who are characterized by extreme insecurity and lack of self-confidence; a neurotic girl who is a passive, dependent type without self-confidence, and with little ability to concentrate; a highly withdrawn girl who interacts with a minimum of affect; three enuretics—two boys and a girl—one of whom is also a thumbsucker; an aggressive, "cold" girl who is described by her teacher as having "no soul"; a boy with a serious emotional block to studying; five highly aggressive boys; and a boy who is probably schizophrenic.

Despite this incidence of disturbance—it is impossible to assess the significance of these figures, since there are no comparative data available—the question of adolescent *Sturm und Drang* remains an open one. We feel confident, however, that kibbutz adolescence—whatever the eventual evaluation of adolescent adjustment may be—is qualitatively different from the typical adolescent pattern described in professional journals and monographs.[1] This statement is based on an analysis of three areas which usually occasion or undergo some stress in our own culture during adolescence—aggression, sex, and relationship to parents.

AGGRESSION

Introduction

That the students in the Mosad are highly aggressive will be noted shortly. But it should be emphasized that there are no manifestations that correspond, even roughly, to what we term "juvenile delinquency." Nor is this surprising. Those kinds of juvenile delinquency that are motivated by such needs as social prestige, desire for material things, conspicuous consumption, the desire to belong (as well as to hurt those who prevent one from belonging), or by such cultural characteristics as invidious social class differences or poverty, are unlikely to be found in the kibbutz. None of these motives operates in the Mosad. They are effectively muted by the social structure of the kibbutz. All the students wear the same kind of clothes, which none of them own. All of them enjoy the same, relatively high, standard of living. The absence of social classes, in either an economic or social sense, means the absence of invidious comparisons and competitive prestige as a function of family background. No one, in other words, is excluded or made to feel inferior because of family or class affiliation. No one is left out because he lives "on the other side of the tracks," and no one feels inferior because his family is poor or dirty or immigrant or speaks with an accent. In short, there are few objective conditions that can give rise to feelings of deprivation, whether of material goods or of social prestige, and, hence, to that kind of juvenile delinquency which is motivated by desire for revenge or by the desire to bolster one's feelings of low self-esteem.

But self-esteem, though frequently a function of group-acceptance, is not always a function of social structure. Persons may be rejected by the group because of personal characteristics, and the unpopular adolescent, who feels that he does not belong and is not wanted, is generally miserable. This source of misery, too, is absent from the Mosad. Some students, to be sure, are unpopular; and they know it. But no student is ever left out, and therefore made to feel rejected, because of his unpopularity. And this is not because kibbutz adolescents are kinder than adolescents elsewhere, but because of the social structure of the Mosad. All activities encompass the entire group, so that everyone has an equal opportunity to participate in the group activities. There are no private parties from which certain students are excluded, nor are there other forms of exclusion. In short, there is no differential group participation. Students may, of course, form personal friendships, but such friendships are never the basis for exclusive group activities. These always comprise the entire kevutza, or the entire Mosad, or the entire branch of the Youth Movement.

Although aggression does not assume delinquent forms in the Mosad, it does exist, and it is expressed in many ways. Like most of our other categories, however, it is all but impossible to evaluate its significance for lack of comparative data. Although the opinions of the teachers are of little weight (for they too have no basis for comparisons) it should be noted that they were sufficiently disturbed by what they felt was an unusually high degree of aggression in the Mosad, to have devoted a number of faculty meetings to this problem. They were particularly disturbed, according to the report of one of the teachers, by the cruelty found among some of the students.

Despite the teachers' concern, I am confident that interpersonal aggression—at least in its physical form—is much less frequent in the Mosad than it is among the younger children. Whereas physical aggression is the most important cause for anger among the grammar school children—as revealed by the Emotional Response Test, at any rate—it is among the least important for the high school students. And, of the two possible hypotheses which could account for this downward shift—accommodation to aggression, or a diminution in aggression—our observations would support the latter.[2]

Interpersonal aggression is found in a number of forms other than physical attack—gossip, teasing, laughter, name-calling, and so on; and it is expressed against a number of persons—teachers and other adults, kevutza peers, students who fall into certain socially disliked categories, younger students, outside students, and refugees and other immigrants.

Racism

In general, students are aggressive toward strangers, that is, persons from outside the kibbutz. Hence, it is difficult to decide whether aggression against some of the teachers is a function of their status as teacher or as outsider;[3] or whether aggression against some of the city children is really instigated by their aggression, or is merely a function of their status as outsiders. On the other hand, there is no question but that the following incident is to be attributed to simple out-group aggression. When a group of students from a neighboring kibbutz first entered the Mosad, the students from Kiryat Yedidim were hostile toward them, particularly toward the girls. They teased them whenever they recited in class, so that to this day they are reluctant to speak up. There were several instances, moreover, in which the boys of Kiryat Yedidim physically beat the girls from this neighboring kibbutz.

The immigrant children bear the brunt of this out-group aggression. Many students, ideologically in favor of immigration, are hostile to the immigrants from the Middle East, whom they view as inferiors—they call them *shchorim*, "black ones." They are the constant butts of verbal aggression, taunting, and teasing. European immigrants may also be the objects of hostility. The Mosad authorities decided that, instead of remaining as a group apart, the Polish immigrant students should be integrated with the other children. But these refused to live with the kibbutz children (because of their aggression) and threatened to leave the Mosad if the proposed integration were pushed through.[4]

The immigrant children feel like pariahs as a result of this treatment. Describing their year's experience in an article in the student Annual, the members of this group wrote:

> We do not feel part of the Mosad. The other children laugh at us and do not accept us as friends and comrades . . . We feel lonely and lost.

This prejudice against immigrants extends beyond the immigrant students, for it includes the adult immigrants as well. A group of new immigrant workers was employed by the Mosad in its construction program and, of course, they were invited to eat their meals in the Mosad dining room. This created a serious problem, however, for some of the students refused to eat at the same tables with them. A girl in the seventh grade stood up and walked away when one of these workers sat at her table. It made her ill, she said, to sit at the same table with "them"—they didn't know any Hebrew, and besides they were "the new immigration."

Aggression Against Adults

Teachers are the primary adult victims of aggression. One expression of this type of aggression is to be found in the poor classroom discipline commented on previously. The following examples give some notion of the magnitude of the disorder. That such disorder is, among other things, an expression of aggression (disobedience) is indubitable. The students know that the teacher desires order, yet they refuse to comply with his request.

> The teacher (female) of the eighth grade and I enter the class, and she explains that I have come to observe. The children begin to shout and scream, and she cannot get their attention. When the geography lesson finally begins, each child talks at will, insisting that he be heard above the shouting of the others. She cannot discipline them . . . After the intermission, the children enter the classroom with great shouting. They cannot be calmed. Teacher asks questions, and they all answer at once. She refuses to continue until there is quiet, but there is no quiet. The children blurt out whatever idea they have as soon as it arises. . . . One boy becomes angry because the teacher calls on another when he —so he insists—had his hand up first. . . . Teacher reprimands boy for disturbing, and he laughs. Another boy beats a rhythm on the desk. Teacher shouts at children but cannot control them. (At least half of her time is spent trying to obtain order.)

> The ninth grade is discussing the Jewish community in ancient Alexandria. The class is in constant turmoil, and at times it is impossible to hear what is being said. The children walk in and out of the class, and move about the room to get books or paper. Some, instead of walking, slide across the desks to get what they want. To add to the confusion, children shout, "*sheket!*" (quiet!), to others.

> After writing their answers to a history questionnaire, the ninth-grade students are called upon by the teacher (male) to read their answers aloud. They say whatever comes to mind without waiting for teacher to call on them, interrupting another speaker if necessary . . . A boy does not want to answer a question and walks out of class, only to be called back by teacher . . . a boy is reading a paper, another is drawing a map, a girl is eating sunflower seeds. . . . A discussion ensues on plans for a program. The suggestion of the executive committee is presented. This creates such a furor that the class cannot be quieted for at least five minutes: all shout at one another, insisting that the suggestion is either good or bad; and teacher is helpless.

> (Early morning class in biology—male teacher, non-kibbutz member.) Only half the eleventh grade is present, but it is difficult to get order. Teacher begins lecture, but girls are looking at pictures, and will not listen. . . . They discuss the possibility of starting a project on "the Dead Sea." This leads to the mention of a hike they had taken to the Dead Sea the previous year. Teacher cannot get order. For twenty minutes there is talk and argument about this hike; emotions are high, voices strained, and all ignore teacher's plea to return to the subject at

hand. . . . Near the end of the lesson, two boys begin to wrestle in class, hitting and pinching one another. Girl shouts at them to stop. They ignore both her and teacher.

Class begins with two boys looking at ancient coins and talking together as teacher (male) of eleventh grade tries to begin. Teacher asks them a number of times to stop, but they continue to talk while he lectures. . . . Kibbutz electrician walks by classroom with wire for the new dormitory. Girl jumps up and down with joy. Other students ask her what she sees. Noise becomes teriffic, and teacher cannot continue . . .

(Early morning class in Marxism—male teacher.) Twenty minutes after class begins, two boys of the twelfth grade walk in, talking, laughing, stopping to talk to other students as they make their way to their desks . . . Some students are sleeping, some bored, some are talking, two are reading newspaper, some are catching flies, others are fighting, or laughing . . . Suddenly they all decide to participate in discussion. The result is bedlam, everyone shouting at once.

It should be noted that these disciplinary problems tend to diminish in grades eleven and twelve of the Mosad. It is not the youngest students, however, but those in the middle range—ninth- and tenth-graders—who present the greatest problems.

Students are not only disobedient; they are also insolent. A universal characteristic of the sabras, according to almost all observers of the kibbutz movement, is their *chutzpah* or insolence, a characteristic which we found in the grade school students as well. The sabras have little respect for authority, per se, and they have few compunctions about criticizing authority figures. It might be argued that there is a difference between a student who feels completely secure in his relationship with the teacher, and who, as a consequence, acts "fresh" in class, and a student who is insolent; I accept this distinction. Thus one might argue that it is the secure, not the insolent student, who retorts with *"lo nachon"*—that is incorrect—to some statement of the teacher. This student feels that the teacher is wrong, and says so without fear of punishment. Or, it might be claimed, it is the fresh, not the insolent student who, when the class suggests that they meet outside and the teacher insists that they meet in the classroom, retorts with *"maichpat lecha?,"* What difference does it make to you? The cases below, however, have an altogether different ring. They do not reflect a merely "brash" or "fresh" attitude. It is insolence, rather, which is their outstanding characteristic.

Girl is not listening, and teacher (male kibbutz member) of the ninth grade tells her to do what rest of class is doing. She says that she *is* doing what the rest of the class is doing—wasting time!

Some ninth-grade students come in late to class, singing. Teacher (non-kibbutz male) tells them to leave the room. They become hostile and argue with him, finally leave by jumping over the desks. . . . Later they pass the room, say something derisive to teacher, and pass on.

Girl is disturbing ninth-grade class in English, and teacher tells her to be still. Girl says, "What for? You haven't taught us a thing all year anyway."

Teacher (non-kibbutz male) asks how long Israel is. The tenth-grade students do not know, and become angry at him for asking such a question. "We never memorized it," says one boy in disdain.

Teacher (non-kibbutz male) of the tenth grade asks children to be quiet, to no avail. He calls on girl to read; she says, no. He says, "I told you, not asked you." She replies, "I told you, not asked you that I did not want to." . . . Class is in state of disorder . . . Teacher stops lesson, saying there is no point in continuing as no one is listening. They agree, saying it is very boring. He tries to discuss it with them, and they shout at him as if he were a fellow student.[5]

It is to be noted, in conclusion, that the students not only behave disrespectfully toward authority figures, but that respect for authority is an unimportant value for them. This conclusion may be inferred from the results of the Moral Ideology Test. Obedience to, or disobedience of, authority for the children of a Midwest American community, comprises 20 per cent of their responses to this test.[6] The corresponding figure for the kibbutz subjects is 4 per cent. Indeed proper respect for authority is the least important of all the values mentioned in the test.

Peer Aggression

There is some evidence to suggest that much of the hostility feelings that give rise to interpersonal aggression are evoked by peers. In the Emotional Response Test, to be specific, 70 per cent of all provocations to anger mentioned by the students are caused, whether wittingly or unwittingly, by peers. How much of this hostility is then expressed directly against them, and how much is expressed in some other way, we do not know.

Peer aggression may be classified into six categories. First, there is aggression against violators of group values. . . . The second category consists of generalized group gossip, which, according to the high school principal, is a favorite student pastime.

Derision is a third form of peer aggression. Typical examples follow.

Teacher returns a questionnaire to the members of his eighth-grade class, reading the names and the answers of those who did well and those who did poorly. When he reads the latter answers, the rest of the class laugh scornfully.

Teacher in ninth grade explains a grammatical construction for the fifth time, for the benefit of Ron, who does not understand it. Tamar calls Ron a "fool." Rivka laughs at him. Ron becomes angry, says, "What are you laughing at? You don't understand it either."

Teacher in tenth grade calls on Yael; she says she does not know the answer. Yehuda, sarcastically, says she "never listens to anything."

She says angrily, "Do you know that I was ill?"   He says with disdain, "So why didn't you tell him that?"

Derision often turns into simple name-calling, such as: *Nilavok,* Your father should die (this is not a Hebrew term); *mamzer,* bastard; *chamor,* ass; *tipesh,* fool; *menuval,* abomination.

While the above-mentioned names are reserved for special situations, the following phrases seem to punctuate any conversation, whether with peers or with adults.

Al tevalbel et ha-rosh (don't confuse the head): This is the invariable reply of the person whose statement has been contradicted or disagreed with, or who thinks that the other has raised an irrelevant matter.

Al tedaber shtuyot (don't speak foolish things): This is the response to a statement with which one disagrees.   Instead of refuting the statement with evidence, the student insults the person who makes it.

Hishtagata? (have you gone mad?): The ubiquitous retort to any idea, statement, proposal, with which one disagrees.   This is probably the most frequently heard phrase in the Mosad.

Ma ichpat lecha? (what concern is it of yours?): This, incidentally, is the favorite form of chutzpah that the students use against adults; and (because?) the latter become infuriated by it.   It is also employed, of course, in conversation with peers.   A teacher may tell a student to be quiet or not to interfere with someone else; he may ask him why he was late to class or why he did not go to work: and the response is "ma ichpat lecha?," that is, I don't see why this should concern you.   Or, what difference does it make to you?   Or, why should you butt into this?

A fourth form of peer aggression consists of generalized rudeness and ill-manners toward one's fellows.   Sabras seldom observe such simple amenities as greeting a fellow student with a "hello," or saying "thank you" when some courtesy has been extended them.   More important is their disruptive behavior during public performances.   Often they are so obstreperous during a mesiba, that it is all but impossible to hear what is being said from the platform.   The following excerpt is typical.

> The chairman calls for order, but he cannot obtain it.   Finally Ruth (the faculty advisor) tries to quiet them, and she is successful—for a few minutes.   This lack of order and of silence continues throughout the program.   At times the noise is so great that it is impossible to hear the students who are performing on the stage.[7]

This disrespect for peers finds other expressions as well.   The student magazine complained editorially, for example, that most articles submitted for publication are written in pencil, and on dirty scraps of paper, without punctuation.

A fifth form of aggression consists of mild forms of hazing, bullying, and practical jokes.   The favorite objects of such behavior are the younger students. That the older children bully the younger is well known; they dominate them and subject them to a kind of hazing. I was unable to discover the exact nature of this behavior. The students in the grade school are aware of this hazing, and express genuine anxiety about entering the Mosad. At the sixth-grade graduation party, for example, almost all the students said they were afraid to enter the Mosad. Although none articulated the reasons for this fear, one of the teachers feels that at least one of them was this fear of hazing. He also suggested that one of the causes of the perceptible change in the children once they enter the Mosad—from outgoing and poised, to shy and withdrawn children—is this hazing experience.

But the younger children are not the only victims of this type of behavior. The infinitive, *le-sader*, is a ubiquitous term in the Mosad. This term, which literally means "to fix," or "to put in order," has undergone a shift in connotation to one similar to the American slang expression, "to fix him good." If one says that he intends to *le-sader* someone, he means that he intends to play some practical joke on him, such as causing him to miss a bus, obtain the wrong book, attend the wrong class, and so on. Such behavior is practiced with sufficient frequency that the students frequently suspect their fellows of trying to "fix" them.

A final form of aggression is physical attack, which we have already indicated to be infrequent; and it is used almost exclusively as a technique of social control. There is one instance of fantasied physical aggression, however, which we feel merits mention here because of the social attitude, as well as the intensity of hostility, which it expresses. This case involves Avraham, the eleventh-grade boy who, we feel, is schizophrenic.

> When it became known that Avraham was to return to the kibbutz after having been away for a year, his kevutza had a long discussion, led by their mechanech, about how this might affect them. At least two of the students argued that he should not be readmitted to the group. In the biological world, they argued, an organism dies if it cannot adapt. Analogously, Avraham should be rejected. (They finally agreed to accept him.)

It should be noted that many students do not participate in these various forms of aggression, and some oppose them. Avraham, for example, had a protector—a fellow student (female) who would go out of her way to help him and to draw him into the group activities whenever possible. So, too, despite their use of derision, only rarely do students exploit the disabilities of their peers for aggressive ends. Avner, for example, is a sixteen-year-old enuretic. The entire kevutza knows of his difficulty, because every morning he hangs out his wet sheets and pajamas to dry. But no one has ever teased him about it.

It should be noted finally that though the students aggress against each other, they maintain their solidarity in the face of outside interference.

They may punish or taunt a fellow student, but they resent someone else who does it. Even in the case of Tamar—the most hated of all—this solidarity is maintained. When an English teacher (non-kibbutz member) chastised her in class, the students not only demanded that he "explain and clarify" his behavior, but they insisted that he be fired.

SEX

Sexual Conflict

The sexual conflicts that are frequently at the core of adolescent turmoil in our own society do not seem to be strong in the Mosad. When sexual problems occur, they do not seem to form the basis for morbid or obsessive thoughts or fantasies; nor are sex, sexual exploits, and sexual attractiveness the basis for much of social behavior. These findings are not unexpected in view of the culture of the kibbutz and the social structure of the Mosad.

To the extent that the sexual problem of adolescence involves more than glandular development, and is concerned, rather, with curiosity about the body and the "mystery" of sexuality, the formal structure of the Mosad, as well as the students' past experiences, would tend to preclude the development of sexual problems. From infancy through adolescence boys and girls are exposed to both the bodies and sexual anatomy of the opposite sex. They have, as youngsters, slept and bathed together, gone to the toilet together; and even now they sleep in the same rooms together. The obsession to *see* is probably absent. In addition, their sex education, which began at an early age, has been open, frank, and intelligent.[8] Hence, anxiety about anatomical and physiological changes is undoubtedly minimized, if not eliminated, and obsession with sex, which often results from viewing it as a great mystery or (as among certain groups in our own society) as sinful or dirty, does not occur among these students. They are taught that the sex drive is normal and natural, that it is neither sinful on the one hand, nor of overwhelming importance on the other.

Moreover, the host of sexual stimuli that evoke sexual fantasies in adolescents in our society—pictures, billboards, magazines, movies—are not found in the kibbutz; so too such artificial techniques as cosmetics and perfume for arousing sexual desire are taboo. The normal sex drives of these adolescents are, for the most part, effectively sublimated in their busy and exhausting round of classes, work, and extracurricular activities.

Finally, "dating," and all its attendant problems, is absent from the Mosad. All social activities are group- rather than couple-oriented; so that the student attends any social affair as a member of his kevutza (a group which includes both boys and girls) or as an individual. But he never attends as the partner of a person of the opposite sex. Though the couple phenomenon, in the form of "going steady," exists, the casual date is unheard of. A girl is not invited to a dance by one boy, to a swimming party by another, and to a movie by still another. Indeed, unless she is going steady, she is not invited to any affair by any boy. She (and he) goes alone, with her kevutza, or with certain members of it.

In short, a major sociological determinant of sexual maladjustment in our society is not to be found in the Mosad. For dating, with its values of competitive success, prestige, and the "dating and rating" complex; with its demands for clothes and the concern for style and fashion; with its demand for money (on the part of the male); with its implications of rejection and exclusion for those who are not "popular"—all these are absent in the kibbutz.

Moreover, no girl need worry lest she not be invited on a Saturday night date, and no boy need be alarmed because he is unable to obtain a date. No one need be anxious about his poor dancing, his inability to engage in small talk, his lack of a "line," and so forth. Since dating does and the whole host of anxieties and tensions that derive from it, are absent as well.

Adult Attitudes

Although sex is viewed by the Mosad (and by the kibbutz) authorities as a natural, rather than as an evil or sinful, appetite, and although the mixed dormitories (and formerly, mixed showers) are vigorously defended, they are (following the philosophy of The Movement) opposed to sexual intercourse among the students. This paradox must be explained.

The Mosad is an educational institution; its task, as it sees it, is to impart knowledge, skills, and values to its students. All three are imparted in the classroom, but many values and skills are also acquired through participation in the many extracurricular activities sponsored by the Mosad. Were sexual not exist in the Mosad, a major obsession of American adolescent culture, intercourse permitted or encouraged, it is felt, students' interests and energies would be withdrawn from their studies and from the many group activities which are such important preparation for their future lives. By discouraging sexual behavior, therefore, the authorities seek to channel adolescent energies in these culturally important activities. Nevertheless, should a couple be genuinely in love, the authorities will not interfere with their sexual activities. Such couples are left to themselves unless their relationship proves to be socially and/or emotionally disruptive. When the latter happens, students, as well as teachers, may take action, as the following example indicates.

The couple in question consisted of a fifteen-year-old girl and an eighteen-year-old boy. The Mosad authorities became concerned about this case because they felt that the girl was too young to be involved in such a relationship. Because she was with her boy friend almost every evening and did not return to her room until the early hours of the morning, she did not participate in Mosad activities, she did not have time to prepare her lessons, and she was too tired to be alert in class. Her kevutza, too, was concerned, because they felt that she had, in effect, broken away from them. The kevutza, probably at the instigation of its mechanech, called her to a beirur in which she was censured for her behavior. She apparently took their criticisms to heart, for she began to change her mode of living, at least to the extent of getting to sleep at an earlier hour, and fulfilling her academic responsibilities.

Unfortunately, we do not have direct data on parental attitudes toward sexual behavior among their adolescent children. The questions on the Questionnaire which were designed to measure parental attitudes toward sex refer to all premarital intercourse, and not merely in the period of adolescence. If we may assume, however, that parental attitudes regarding this age are less permissive than their attitudes toward post-high-school sexuality, we may perhaps draw some not invalid conclusions from the results of the Questionnaire. Dichotomizing their responses—by combining the responses of "definitely yes" and "perhaps yes" into one category, and their responses of "definitely no" and "perhaps no" into another—the results reveal that more than half the parents believe that they should attempt to ensure their children's virginity until marriage.[9]

Student Attitudes and Interests

Despite their sexually "enlightened" environment, certain aspects of sexual shame found in our own society are found among these students, as well. Its most instructive expression is to be found in the abolition of the mixed showers, an instance of paramount theoretical importance but one which, unfortunately, remains somewhat obscure.

Until a few years before this study, boys and girls showered together, and, according to the Mosad principal, they accepted this system without protest until the Mosad adopted the policy of admitting students from the city. The latter opposed the prevailing practice, and some viewed it as an opportunity for smutty and obscene behavior. These city students, with their typical Western attitude toward sex, were responsible for the abandonment of the mixed showers.

A teacher reports that it was the girls (of the kibbutz) who favored the abolition of the mixed showers, which they viewed as "a form of torture." The girls, he said, matured more rapidly than the boys, and their developed secondary sexual characteristics were the objects of taunts and teasing. It is not clear, however, whether it was the boys from the cities or from the kibbutz who were responsible for this teasing behavior.[10]

Granting that pressure for the abolition of mixed showers came primarily from the city children, they received no little assistance from many kibbutz parents. Many parents (as well as teachers) opposed the mixed showers from its very inception. Some parents informed us that sexual shame about nudity is "instinctive," and that it was wrong to expose the students to such an experience. Others thought that mixed showers caused sexual fears, and opposed them on this basis. Hence, the student opposition to mixed showers, said one parent, proves that "the children's instincts are superior to the educators' theories."

It is difficult to assess the degree to which student attitudes to mixed showers reflect those of their parents. Since the latter's attitudes, however, generally have considerable influence on their children, the opposition to, and the shame felt in, the mixed showers may well be a result (among other things) of parental influence, however subtly it may have been expressed.

In any event, the great majority of kibbutz students are opposed to the restoration of the mixed showers. In interviews with twenty-two students over the age of fourteen, only three said they favored the restoration of the mixed showers, and one was neutral. The reasons given by the opponents are identical with those suggested by the adults for its abolition. Eight of the eighteen opponents stressed the difficulty of maintaining mixed showers past pre-puberty or puberty, because of the differential rate of sexual maturation and the attendant discomfort for the girls caused by the curiosity and shaming behavior of the boys. Ten discounted this factor and stressed, instead, the embarrassment caused by showering with outsiders—either from the city or from other kibbutzim. Had their original kevutza remained intact, they said, they would have no opposition to the mixed showers.

Much of the sexual shame that led to the abolition of the mixed shower continues to characterize the attitude of some of the girls in their rooms as well. Most of the girls, for example, attempt to conceal their nudity from the boys. Even in the hot summers that are typical for Kiryat Yedidim, girls wear night clothes so that, should the sheets fall off the bed, they are not exposed. Boys and girls undress in the dark with their backs to each other to avoid exposure. At the same time there seems to be an unwritten code among them condemning voyeurism for, with but one exception, there have been no complaints about this. In spite of all these precautions, however, not one of the student interviewees preferred to live in unisexual dormitories. On the contrary, all of them stressed the importance of bisexual living because, they said, it is less boring; it reduces the sexual curiosity and sexual tensions that accompany the separation of the sexes; and it contributes to group solidarity.

Although, as we shall observe, there does not seem to be a great deal of overt sexual behavior among these students, their sexual interests and curiosity appear to be strong. Much of their gossip, for example, centers about boy-girl relationships, and especially about the couples. Their curiosity about the sexual activities of others is not necessarily confined to gossip. A recent graduate of the Mosad claimed that the girls, at least, always know about the sexual behavior of the couples because the girls tell each other what they do with their boy friends.

Equally strong is their interest in the sex life of the adults, whose sexual irregularities seem to be well known to them. The ninth-grade students, for example, like their parents, were well aware of the sexual exploits of the father of one of their classmates. Indeed, when his son criticized a girl in the classroom, she retorted with "You should be quiet, since your father has a concubine (*pilegesh*)." The students of another class were intrigued by the fact that the divorced father of one of them was having an affair with the divorced mother of another; and, when they were married, the girls in this class stayed up until two o'clock in the morning excitedly discussing the marriage.

Although the students have a strong interest in sexual matters, the teachers claim that theirs is a "healthy" interest, in contrast to the salacious interest of many non-kibbutz children. Kibbutz students, they claim, seldom, if ever, tell dirty stories, nor do they employ sexually obscene words. Moreover, though the younger students may giggle at the sexual passages in the Bible and are frequently embarrassed by them, this attitude seems to disappear after a year or two.

An important measure of healthy sexual attitudes is afforded by sexual fantasies, but, unfortunately, we have almost no data in this area. None of the students gave sexual responses to the Rorschach, but it is our impression that they suppressed any sexual percepts. One student, for example, told his teacher that one of the Rorschach plates was obviously that of a man and woman copulating, but that he was embarrassed to tell the ethnographer. Again, when the girls asked what the ethnographer did with the boys when he took them from class, this same student said that he undressed them in order to take their physical measurements.

The one spontaneous fantasy obtained in the Mosad was developed by the ninth-grade students. Shortly after the disappearance of one of the girls in this class while on a hiking trip near the Syrian border, her fellow students in the ninth grade asked their English teacher if he were going to the circumcision ceremony. When he asked to whose circumcision they were referring, they said, the circumcision of the son of Miryam (the girl who had disappeared) and Pasha (her putative abductor) which will occur in nine months. It seems that their sexual fantasies were stimulated by Miryam's disappearance, and they had visions of the Syrians' raping her.

The teachers also claim that, as a result of the positive attitude of the Mosad and of the instruction which they receive, the students have no sexual fears. In the absence of comparative data it is impossible to evaluate the validity of such claims. However, it should be noted that the nurses can recall only one instance of menstrual difficulties among the girls—and this involved a delay in the onset of menses.

On the other hand, the girls in the ninth grade developed a fear of childbirth, and their nurse discovered that they would frequently talk about the pain involved. When she discussed this matter with them it became apparent that they had acquired this notion from a few girls whose mothers had told them that they loved them very much because of the pain they had suffered in giving birth. The nurse was shocked by this, and devoted much time to explaining the nature of childbirth to the girls, discussions which she believes were effective.

Sexual Behavior

It is our impression that these students have less sexual experience than their counterparts in our own society. Homosexuality seems to be entirely nonexistent; the author observed no manifestations of it, nor did any respondent or informant report its existence. Masturbation exists—at least, so the teachers report—but we have no information on its incidence. The Mosad attitude toward masturbation is permissive, unless it is decided the student's behavior constitutes a problem either to himself or to others.

Heterosexual behavior does not begin in the Mosad, apparently, until the ninth grade; at least there are no reports of it, nor are any of the students for whom the author has information concerning heterosexual behavior in grades lower than the ninth. This means that heterosexual activity, if found at all, begins at about fifteen. At this age, an interest in sex, restricted almost exclusively to the girls, may be observed. Not directed toward the boys of their own kevutza whom they view as immature, hence, asexual, this interest is in the older students and the young unmarried males in the kibbutz. These girls, insists a recent graduate of the Mosad, are well aware of the attraction of their developing bodies, and are not unwilling to use them to attract males. In the heat of the day, for example, kibbutz field hands strip to the waist or, at least, to their undershirts. The Mosad girls who work in the fields remove their blouses, and work in undershirts. According to our informant, at least some of the girls remove their blouses with the specific intention of attracting the males.[11]

Although casual dating is nonexistent in the Mosad, "going steady" exists. Couples are known as *zugot* (sing. *zug*), the same term that is used in the kibbutz to refer to married couples. There is little question but that couples engage in the preliminaries of lovemaking, but it is only the rare couple that has a sexual affair. Indeed, according to all reports—from teachers, students, and former students—there seem to be almost no violations of the Mosad taboo on sexual intercourse. Two reasons, other than the simple motive to comply with Mosad norms, have been suggested for the observance of this taboo. A sophisticated graduate of the Mosad said that the girls while in the Mosad are opposed to sexual affairs as a kind of "instinctive self-preservation." Others say that its observance is a consequence of the absence of great sexual tension. As one former student put it, "We simply did not feel a need for it." It is my guess that most students are virgins when they graduate from high school.

The number of couples is small—with this statement everyone seems to agree—but the exact number is difficult to determine since only those that are publicly known came to our attention. These included a ninth-grade girl and a male senior, a male and female senior, a female senior and a recently graduated male, and a female senior and a young kibbutz male. An important characteristic is that the couple is never comprised of individuals who have grown up together in the kibbutz. Students who have always been members of the same kevutza have never been known to engage in sexual behavior with each other.

In general, couples are secretive about their relationship; according to some students, they are "ashamed" to have it known. The typical partners give few overt indications of their relationship; they never appear together in public as a couple, nor do they seek each other out informally, between classes or at work. It would be unthinkable to show any physical sign of affection in the presence of other people. As a result, their meetings are clandestine, and this gives rise to gossip and intrigue, and converts a typical case of "puppy love" into a minor *cause célèbre*. If the Mosad culture provided for dating, couples could interact publicly at dances and movies. But in the absence of a formal dating pattern, they must meet at night, a practice which surrounds the relationship with an aura of secrecy and danger and imparts an unhealthy air to a simple boy-girl relationship.

Interaction Between the Sexes

In general, boys and girls appear to interact as asexual peers rather than as potential sex objects. There seems to be no differential behavior between unisexual and bisexual groups, as there is in other societies. There is no special etiquette which governs specifically the interaction of members of opposite sex. Nor does one observe such typical Western manifestations as flirtatiousness, coquetry, and seductiveness.

Important age differences must be recorded, however. In the seventh and eighth grades male-female interaction is marked by social distance which is expressed in a number of ways. Boys and girls sit separately in the classroom, in the dining room, and at assemblies, and they seldom interact after class. What cliques or friendships exist are almost always unisexual in nature.[12] This social distance seems to be a continuation of a pattern which first develops in the last few years in the Grammar School where, it will be remembered, the children of the sixth grade break up into unisexual groups, in contrast to the younger grades in which the children's play is almost always bisexual. Sometimes, however, simple social distance between the sexes develops into aggression. The girls view the boys as immature, and treat them with disdain. The boys retaliate with aggression. Boys, for example, are highly critical of the girls in class, and they scoff at them whenever they make a mistake. The girls, though disdainful of the boys, usually remain passive in the face of this criticism. The eighth-grade teacher reports that he must frequently defend the girls against the hostile criticism of the boys, for which the latter accuse him of favoritism for the girls.

At times this hostility takes extreme forms. It has already been noted, for example, that some eighth-grade boys physically attacked some female students who came from outside the kibbutz. During this study another incident—one which shocked even the boys—occurred in the ninth grade. One of the boys disliked a girl in his kevutza and decided to make life difficult for her. He decided that she was to undress before her roommates; and to show her how easy this was he undressed before her, and strutted in the nude about the room.[13] A few days later he awakened just as the girl was getting dressed; he observed her carefully and then told what he had seen, in a coarse way, to the other members of the kevutza.

Hostility between the sexes diminishes with age, and by the ninth or tenth grades it is all but absent. All the students who reported that male-female relations were bad, were under fifteen years of age, as were those who reported that there were still some problems remaining. On the other hand, the seventeen students (out of a sample of twenty-six) who reported a good male-female relationship were over fifteen years of age.

Sex-linked Personality Differences

A number of sex differences may be noted at this age. First, the girls tend to be cleaner than the boys—at least they clean the rooms better and they complain that the latter leave the rooms dirty. Second, the girls—as measured by their interest in academic work—seem to be less intellectual than the boys. Over and over again our notes on classroom behavior include such statements as "The girls have little interest in the discussion," or "The girls don't participate in the discussion." This apathy is particularly characteristic of the seniors. After they had graduated from high school and were working in the kibbutz, the author asked them to compare the kibbutz with the Mosad. The unanimous response of the girls was that they much preferred the kibbutz because by their senior year they had become bored and disinterested with their studies and were just "marking time."

In general, the girls are more interested in humanistika than in realistika, for, they claim, the latter is much too difficult for them. In the senior class, for example, physics is an optional course, and at the time of our study, all but one of the girls registered instead for a discussion group in psychology. Even in the latter course, however, their performance was poor. Their teacher complained that the girls have less capacity for logical thought than the boys, and that only rarely can they think abstractly.[14]

Almost all teachers and nurses agree that the girls are much more mature emotionally than the boys. This is one of the reasons, it will be recalled, for the tensions that exist between them—the girls view the boys as infantile—as well as for the disturbances in the classroom. Finally, girls tend to retain closer ties to their parents than boys. They visit them more frequently, and they are more intimate with them.

RELATION TO PARENTS

Rebellion

The Mosad student is not exposed to conflicting values in either of the two senses—longitudinal and horizontal—in which American adolescents may experience such conflict. There are, that is, few conflicts between the values he had learned in childhood and those he must learn in adolescence; and there are few conflicts between the values he has learned in his family and other primary groups, and those which the school is trying to inculcate. The kibbutz is, so far as its values are concerned, a monistic community. The values of one's family are pretty much the same as those of all other families, and the values of these several families are the same as the values of the school. The student is rarely conflicted therefore by the problem of choice of values: my family's or another family's? my family's or the school's? the school's or the community's? These are all of one piece.

Related to this homogeneity in values is the absence in the students of rebellion against parental values—since the student does not have to choose competing values, he willy-nilly retains those of his parents. He could, of course, choose those values of the outside world, which are in conflict with kibbutz and parental values, but such a choice would be tantamount to leaving the kibbutz; and this, few, if any, students are willing to do. The kibbutz is their home and in the kibbutz they intend to remain.

Nor would one expect to find typical adolescent rebellion against parents. For all practical purposes the high school student is dependent upon his parents for nothing—except affection. His material, social, and intellectual needs are satisfied by the kibbutz and the Mosad. Unwilling conformity to parental desires or demands is not the price he must pay for either social privileges or economic goods. In short, subjected neither to his parents' control nor their authority, he has no need to rebel against them.   And this expectation is confirmed by the all but unanimous reports of the parents. Only nine of the respondents to the Questionnaire had adolescent children, but of the nine only one felt that his children had rebelled against him.

Estrangement

But the parent-child relationship is more complicated than the simple absence of value-conflict and adolescent rebellion might suggest.   For other types of strain are possible, and in the kibbutz this strain seems to be characterized by psychological distance between child and parent.   Indeed, a most important characteristic of the adolescent's relation to his parents is his psychological distance.   Although the high school is no farther than a five-minute walk from almost any parental room, only nine students, in a representative sample of thirty-one, said they visited their parents daily, and all but two of these were less than fifteen years old.[15]   The majority visited their parents less frequently, ranging from five and six times a week to once a week, the median being three or four times a week.   If we can assume that the rate of voluntary interaction is an adequate measure of psychological distance, we may then conclude from these data alone that psychological distance is a true description of the student attitude.

Some teachers, however, insist that the frequency with which students visit their parents is not a valid index of their feelings, and that, despite their irregular visits, the students do maintain an intimate relationship with their parents.   These claims, however, are generally ideological in nature, for, having made them, the teacher then usually points out that, since the child is not economically dependent upon his parents, he has no reason for not maintaining a good relationship with them.   The implications of the latter argument have been discussed elsewhere, and its merits have been noted.   No child, it is true, need feel bitter because his parents cannot provide him with the material goods which other parents give to their children; and no student need feel aggression toward his parents because he must acquiesce in their demands in order to retain their material support.   But this conclusion is not incompatible with our thesis concerning psychological distance.   The kibbutz adolescent does not rebel against his parents.   Instead he stops taking them into his confidence.   He becomes uncommunicative.

In order to obtain a more direct measure, the students were asked about the quality of their relationship with their parents.   Of the ten respondents (the sample is unfortunately small), only three claimed to be intimate with their parents.   The others said that they only sometimes took their parents into their confidence, or that they never did.

Parents feel even more strongly that their adolescent children have drifted away from them, and they complain bitterly about this.[16] The students, their parents say, tell them nothing, so that they never know what they are doing, thinking, or feeling. They are, their parents say, "closed" (*segurim*), and if the parents wish to know something about them they must, as one mother put it, "drag it out."

The following report by one mother is typical. Observing her son to be in a bad mood, she asked him what the matter was, and he "almost tore my head off." Since then she "never asked him anything." Another time, when her son was again in a bad mood, she went on a vacation. While she was away, he wrote her a wonderful letter, but he did not "even mention what was troubling him."

One father was particularly bitter. The students visit their parents, he said, only out of a sense of duty, but not out of desire. At best, they visit them because they feel that they still might need them for something. In general, however, "the parents are superfluous in their lives; they feel they can get along without them."

In view of the psychological distance that characterizes the child-parent relationship, it is not surprising that the students—the males at any rate—rarely express physical affection for them. An eighth-grade student will not permit his mother to kiss him for, he claims, it is not manly. An adult sabra responds with the exact words—"it is not manly"—when his mother wants to kiss him, although as a child he told her that she was the most beautiful woman in the world and that when he grew up he would marry her. So, too, a boy who has just entered the Mosad visits his parents infrequently and, when he does, he shows his mother no physical affection, although only two months previously he had spent all his spare time with her, wanted to sleep in the room with her, and had called her his "queen."

The parents not only complain bitterly about their relationship with their children,[17] but they are bewildered by it. "How can you explain it?" asked one of the teachers, herself a parent of two adolescents, "After all, it was necessary for us to conceal things from our parents, for we had to rebel in order to come to Palestine. But what do they have to conceal?"

Another parent said,

> I can understand why my generation was estranged from its parents. They had nothing in common. Take my own case. My parents were religious and I was not. My parents wanted me to enter business and I wanted to be a worker. I wanted to go to Israel and they wanted me to remain in Poland. But in the kibbutz what is the reason? Parents and children share the same values . . . I can only conclude that parent-child conflict is biological.

One interesting aspect of this estrangement is that it begins only after the child enters the Mosad, and in general it occurs regardless of the previous relationship between parents and children. Take Yaakov, for example.

While in grade school, he was probably the most deeply attached of any of the students to his parents, particularly to his mother. He was, what might be called in our culture, a "mamma's boy." While Yaakov was still in grade school I had occasion to discuss the problem of adolescent estrangement with his mother—an intelligent and sensitive woman. This would never happen between her and Yaakov, she said; their relationship would remain unimpaired. A few months later Yaakov graduated from Grammar School and entered the Mosad. When, a short time later, I asked Yaakov's mother how he was getting along, she said that she could not answer the question, for she never sees him. He is so busy, she continued, that he has no time to visit her; and that very week he even missed the usual Saturday afternoon tea with his parents. The previous night his parents had met him accidentally in front of the dining room, and when they asked him why he had not come to tea, he explained that his kevutza had recently obtained a new book which everyone wanted to read. He was fortunate to get the book on Saturday, and it proved to be so interesting that he had forgotten to visit his parents.

A short time later, the author again asked Yaakov's mother about her son. The answer was the same—she never sees him. She then volunteered an explanation. While in the grade school, he was repressed, he was "like a colt who wanted freedom." Now, suddenly, he has this freedom and he "doesn't know what to do with it." But she says nothing to him, she went on, because, "It is necessary to be a clever mother. He will return, you will see. Other sons, maybe not; but Yaakov will return."

The explanation of Yaakov's mother for his apparent estrangement is but one of many and conflicting parental interpretations of this phenomenon. Some say that their children visit them infrequently because of their very busy schedule. But this interpretation does not explain their psychological distance when they do visit them. Others, responding to this objection, say that, since their children love them very much, they do not wish to tell them their problems lest they hurt them. Still others maintain that the children's reticence springs from their feelings of superiority to their parents. The latter are the "generation of the desert"[18] and remain strangers, as it were, to the Israeli landscape. The children, on the other hand, are native Israelis; they are completely adjusted to the country which is their home. Feeling this difference, they feel superior to their parents, and are therefore "distant."

Another possible explanation may be found in the students' attitudes toward Judaism and the Jews of the Diaspora which is highly negative. It is not until the Mosad that the students become estranged from their parents, and it is in the Mosad that they acquire detailed knowledge of that East European Jewish culture (shtetl) to which they react with strong hostility. But, it must be remembered, their own parents originated in this culture; and, just as the sabras refuse even to read about the shtetl lest they be reminded of their own origins, so—it is our hypothesis—they are reluctant to see their parents, the living representatives and reminders of that hated past. In rejecting their Jewish past, the students reject their parents.

But the rejection of their parents may be related to the latter's European background in still another way. Although the sabras reject the shtetl, they do not reject Europe. On the contrary, there is reason to believe that European culture is highly admired by them, and that, by contrast, Israel is perceived as inferior. If their parents had not come to Israel, they might have been living in the superior cultures of Europe or the Soviet Union instead of in "our tiny country," as they refer to Israel.

The fundamental reason for parental estrangement, however, we believe to rest on a long history of insecure interpersonal relationships. . . .

Attachment

Despite their psychological distance, the students continue to view their parents, to some extent at least, as sources of authority and nurturance. When a problem arises in the Mosad, the students frequently support or oppose suggested solutions by an example from their home, or by an appeal to their parents' opinion. So, too, they are not loathe to fall back on their parents when they come into conflict with a teacher. Should the latter reprimand them, they may complain to their parents from whom they can expect support.

Moreover, although most sabras maintain a psychological reserve with their parents, there are a few who are deeply attached to them. Amir's parents, for example, are divorced, and fifteen-year-old Amir waits for his mother's bus (she lives outside the kibbutz) for hours before her expected arrival, so eager is he to see her. Rani (fourteen years old) is so attached to his mother, who works near the Mosad, that he follows her about in her various activities during all his free moments. Amnon (fifteen years old) is deeply devoted to his step-father, whom he thought from his earliest childhood to be his biological father; when informed of the truth, he rejected it in favor of his former belief.

In some cases student relationships to parents assume overtones that are usually associated with unresolved Oedipal difficulties. Meir (seventeen years old) dislikes his father intensely, and is deeply concerned lest he act like him; he is somber and serious unlike his gay and witty father. Moshe (fourteen years old) is, as his teacher puts it, "abnormally devoted" to his divorced mother. When she announced her intention of marrying a man notorious in the kibbutz for his many love affairs, he screamed at her, calling her a prostitute. Rena's parents are divorced. Sixteen-year-old

Rena is hostile to her mother, whom she rarely visits; but she adores her father, who lives in another kibbutz, and waits hours for the arrival of his bus. Recently, he has discontinued his visits to the Mosad, saying that Rena is a big girl and no longer needs him. She has responded to his absence by reverting to a habit she had always had difficulty in overcoming—enuresis.

Emotional Disturbance

The last example of enuresis illustrates another aspect of the parent-child relationship, and one which we observed among all preadolescent children as well—the crucial role of parents in the development of emotional disturbance in their children. Almost invariably the students with problems are those who have histories of disturbed family lives—that is, they did not get along with one or both parents and/or the latter did not get along with each other. It is these students, moreover, who either encounter intellectual difficulties with their school work or who become highly intellectual and/or intensely political.

To say that the emotionally disturbed children are products of a disturbed family relationship is only partially correct. As in the case of the preadolescent children, disturbed sibling relationships contribute heavily to the emotional disturbance of the child. Frequently the student who has great prestige needs and who, consequently, is extremely active in extracurricular activities, is one who suffers from intense sibling rivalry.

NOTES

1. One thing is evident—whatever its intensity or form, kibbutz adolescent turmoil is not somaticized. We did not observe a single instance of acne among the Mosad sabras. On the contrary, one is immediately struck, on meeting the students, by their clear complexions.
2. The evidence from the Emotional Response Test with respect to verbal aggression, however, is ambiguous. Though there is a diminution in the frequency of anger responses caused by aggression, there is an increase in the frequency of sadness responses.
3. In general the students are better disciplined in classes taught by kibbutz, than by non-kibbutz, teachers.
4. The racist attitude of the Mosad youth is shared by the adult sabras—as indeed it is shared by the older adults. "Things were good in the country," remarked a sabra, "until the shchorim came." A female sabra, referring to my previous research among "shchorim" (in Micronesia), said, sneeringly, that I approached the kibbutz as if it were a tribe of shchorim.

    This attitude may be seen in work activities as well. The sabra who supervises the work of the youth in the gardens is consistently more demanding of the oriental youth than of the Mosad students. When it was decided that the former could have an extra day for their vacation, the sabra supervisor became furious at their "indolence," although this extended their vacation to only ten days, whereas the Mosad students had three weeks.

5. Some teachers find it impossible to teach under such difficult psychological conditions and, if they are not members of the kibbutz, they resign. Just prior to our arrival, an English teacher resigned because of the continuous chutzpah to which he was exposed. The students consistently came to class late, laughed at his Hebrew, and criticized his teaching methods. Finally he quit—which was the original aim of the students.

6. Havighurst and Neugarten, *American Indian and White Children*, p. 106.

7. This expression of hostility toward peers is identical, of course, with their undisciplined behavior in the classroom, which we have interpreted as hostility toward the teachers. Such behavior characterizes attendance at kibbutz affairs as well. The following excerpt, recorded at a kibbutz mesiba attended by Mosad students, is representative.

    The students from the Mosad, and particularly the girls, made so much noise that it was difficult to hear the speakers on the stage. Their giggling and whispering in loud tones persisted during the speeches as well as the dramatic presentation.

8. It should be noted, however, that despite their sexual education a recent graduate of the Mosad said that, in her opinion, the girls in the Mosad are sexually naïve and should be given more sex education. A teacher, on the other hand, informed me that she was amazed to discover, when lecturing on sex to her seventh-grade class—she lectured separately to the boys and to the girls—that they already knew everything; indeed, she claimed, they knew more than she did about certain matters.

9. It is interesting to observe that, despite the sexual egalitarianism of the kibbutz, both male and female respondents show a slight tendency toward a double standard. Of eleven respondents, three believed that a mother should ensure her son's virginity until marriage, but five believed that she should ensure her daughter's virginity. Of sixteen respondents, five believed that a father should ensure his son's virginity, but six believed that he should ensure his daughter's virginity.

10. Both interpretations are consistent with the sequence of events that precipitated the mixed shower problem in the Grammar School.

11. In general, however, the students would poke fun at girls who attempted to enhance their attractiveness by wearing expensive or "sexy" dresses. A student from the city was the object of much criticism and teasing from her tenth-grade class because of her elaborate wardrobe and her great concern with her appearance. When the class was planning a trip to the Negev, some of the students predicted, jokingly, that this girl would not go because she did not have the proper undergarments for the *wadis*.

12. Apparently this is a characteristic found in all kibbutzim. An article in the educational journal states that in later childhood the kevutza often splits up into factions. "The boys become distant from the girls, they do not permit them to participate in their activities, they will not allow them to sit next to them in the dining room."

13. In stressing the aggressive aspects of this behavior, the exhibitionism and voyeurism should not be overlooked.

14. This sexual difference, for which I can suggest no plausible interpretation, is particularly interesting for it represents a reversal from what is observed among the younger children. Among the preschool children, the girls preponderate in artistic and intellectual activities. So, too, they contribute a greater share than the boys to the intellectual elite of the Grammar School.

15. Eight of the nine were females.

16. Our description of parental feeling is based on informal conversations with them. And though their responses to the Questionnaire are at variance with the sentiments expressed during conversations, we are inclined to accept the latter as a more valid expression of their true sentiments. Nine parents with adolescent children responded to the question of the schedule—"Do your older children confide in you?" Four checked "definitely yes," four, "perhaps yes," and one did not answer. Even from the Questionnaire, however, it is possible to deduce an attenuation in the child's overt affection for his parents. To the question "Do your *younger* children want to visit you?" thirteen of the sixteen respondents checked, "definitely yes," and three checked, "perhaps yes." To the same question concerning their *older* children, only three of the nine respondents checked, "definitely yes." Five checked, "perhaps yes," and one did not answer. It should be noted, finally, that five checked, "definitely yes," and three checked, "perhaps yes," to "Do your older children admire you?" One did not answer.

17. This bitterness is particularly poignant when it be remembered that an important motive for the establishment of collective education was to preclude parent-child estrangement.

18. This is a reference to the ancient Exodus from Egypt. According to the Biblical story, the emancipated slaves wandered in the Sinaitic wilderness for forty years, so that it was the second generation—those who had not experienced slavery—that entered the Promised Land.

PART IV

Culture Change and
Conservatism

*The bureaucratic phenomenon can operate as a strongly negative force,
defeating or stifling even the most energetic of rulers and programs.
For underdeveloped countries in the Middle East, this phenomenon
can be a critical and dangerous block.*

*One of the few really thorough studies of given aspects of this
problem has been Morroe Berger's 1953–1954 research interview of 249
higher civil servants of Egypt. His interview schedule was full and
detailed, his analysis was characterized by careful statistical
corroboration, and yet, as the following selection demonstrates, he was
able to present his material in a sensitive and lively manner.*

20

The Social Setting of the
Egyptian Civil Service

MORROE BERGER

In the spring of 1954 the world was thrilled by the discovery of a solar
ship, said to be 5,000 years old, near the great pyramid of Cheops a few
miles from Cairo. Insensitive to romance and mystery, this writer was less
interested in the description of the ship or in the drama of its discovery
than in the administrative byplay that followed. For, according to newspaper reports, the find precipitated a serious dispute between the young
discoverer and his superiors. The prime minister himself stepped into the
affair, it was reported, and, supporting the younger man against his chiefs,
warned that officials who were unfair to their subordinates would be taught

From *Bureaucracy and Society in Modern Egypt*, pp. 3–18; reprinted by permission of
Princeton University Press, Copyright 1957.

a lesson. A year later the discoverer was world-famous. He had lectured to large audiences in America. He was widely quoted by reporters for Western newspapers. Despite this acclaim and the public announcement of support by the prime minister, however, he found himself shorn of one responsibility after another by his chiefs until he was even denied access to the solar ship itself.

This administrative subplot to the main drama, appropriately played on the site of man's oldest recorded bureaucracy, carries several implications for the study of the public bureaucracy of Egypt today. The prime minister's support of the younger man exemplifies the effort to build a new relationship between the rulers of Egypt and the civil servants upon whom they must rely to realize the reforms they have promised the nation. As a result of the regime's intention to eradicate the spirit and the deeds of its royal predecessor, hundreds of high officials have been removed or have resigned or retired early, and younger subordinates have found easier access to responsible posts through ability and diligence. But the administrative eclipse of the discoverer of the solar ship, despite the prominence of his support, reveals the old bureaucracy's firm control over some aspects of day-to-day government business. It is significant, too, that the bureaucracy's resistance to the power-holders' intervention was confined to a question of relations between superior and subordinate in the hierarchy and did not touch matters of policy. For, as we shall see, the Egyptian civil service is more cohesive in the area of self-protection than in that of policy-making. It will challenge the political rulers less on public policy than on its own private interests.

This aspect of the Egyptian civil service—its place as a social group in the larger society—will concern us in this study, rather than its administrative functions. From the standpoints of both public administration and sociology the public bureaucracy of any country is an interesting subject of study. Especially in view of the myriad technical assistance programs, the prescriptions for industrializing the technologically retarded or the poor countries, and the innumerable plans adopted by these countries themselves, it is unnecessary to dwell at length upon the importance of the administrative task in such areas or upon that of the social groups who execute it.

Many countries that are primarily agricultural, including Egypt, are seeking to industrialize and thereby, they hope, to raise their living standards and to increase their national power in the international community. At the same time they want to avoid the social evils that accompanied industrialization in the West and which the West overcame only long after its economic growth. Such a combination of aims is laudably humane but to realize it a nation will require a high degree of expertise in public administration as well as in other arts and sciences. In Egypt and other countries where the state is likely to have to undertake a substantial part of the task of industrialization, the public bureaucracy, heretofore largely administrative, will have to add many more technicians in the sciences; this necessity is already felt in the Egyptian civil service and is soon bound to have its repercussions on the system of higher education. The role of public administration in easing the transition from rural-agricultural to urban-industrial society is given great importance by a prominent student of English industrialization, who says: "If the industrial revolution was not able to bring its rewards in full measure to the ordinary man and woman it is to the defects of administrative, and not of economic processes, that the failure must be ascribed."[1]

Even if this judgment is accepted only in part, the importance of the civil service would be considerable in societies seeking to industrialize. The civil servants themselves, thus, constitute a significant social group. In countries like Egypt they are a large proportion of the educated population and may comprise the main section of such a middle class as may be found in them. From what elements in the population do they come? What are their goals? How cohesive a group do they form? What administrative and technical capacities do they have? Such questions are of both sociological interest for the scholar and of practical consequence for the nation trying to industrialize.

Moreover, because it is one of the few outlets for the educated elite, the civil service has been a focus of much local political struggle and of nationalist agitation against the colonial powers. It is in this sense that the civil service of Egypt, for example, has been intimately involved in politics. It has been a weapon of partisanship among the Egyptian political parties and an articulate ally of all these parties in their struggle against British power. Yet in matters of public policy—as distinct from partisan politics—the Egyptian civil service has been a relatively pliant tool in the hands of any executive power rather than a rival seeking to exercise control over broad policy issues of government not directly affecting the exercise of political power itself. One reason for this pliability has been the fact that the group in power could bend the civil service to its will because of the absence of a strong system of job-tenure. Another is that the political parties themselves, except for some extremist groups, have not seriously divided on questions of public policy which were not connected with the issue of the British occupation or with the exercise of political power itself. The humdrum administration of day-to-day affairs is at least as important as larger political goals in the creation of public attitudes toward a regime and a system of government. In countries where new social classes are emerging and the distribution of power and prestige is shifting, the level of public administration affects the degree of confidence in orderly processes of government; a low level can destroy the promise and hope that people feel when they have gained political independence and embark upon programs of economic development.

The kind of public administration available to governments in technologically underdeveloped areas assumes added importance because of the intertwining of certain political and economic goals. The most dramatic recent example of this mingling is Egypt's nationalization of the Suez Canal company in July 1956, which embodied the political goal of obtaining greater Egyptian control over the waterway and the economic goal of bringing more revenue to Egypt. The political-economic ideology of many Near Eastern, Asiatic, and Latin American countries moves them in the direction of nationalization of foreign-owned, highly developed enterprises.

Egypt's nationalization of the Canal company brought it, for the first time as an independent state, into high international politics. It also posed the problem whether Egypt could operate the Canal. Both issues placed new responsibilities upon the higher civil service and put it to severe tests. Those who made the extraordinary decisions in July and August of 1956 must have needed expert technical advice of several kinds: political—the probable reaction of the Western powers and the Soviet Union; military— the strategic position of British and French forces and the capacity of Egypt to meet a threat from them; economic—the effect of a possible diversion of Western shipping from the Canal; technological—the ability of Egypt to operate the Canal as a national enterprise, and for how long.

Irrespective of the merits of the nationalization of the Canal from the standpoint of international law, Egyptian military and civil staff work seems to have been of a high order—higher, indeed, than had been expected in the West, considering Egypt's socio-economic and technological foundation. The capacities of the public bureaucracy in countries like Egypt are thus among the factors that are most likely to determine the success or failure of governmental plans not only to develop industry and agriculture but also to control and operate industrial enterprises of various kinds. We may, indeed, look upon the nature and capacities of the public bureaucracy as a mirror of a society in which are reflected, with varying degrees of clarity, its technological base, educational level, the kind of economic opportunities it affords, the fluidity of its class structure, the extent of its national unity, and the nature of the loyalties evoked in it.

The following chapters do not deal with all these subjects but they do examine some of them: the legacy of past Egyptian society and public administration to the present; the social origins of the higher civil servants today; the reasons for the attraction this career has for so many of the educated elite; the changing socio-economic status of the higher civil servants; their loyalties and the extent of their professionalization; and their attitudes toward such norms of bureaucratic behavior as impartiality, impersonality, subordination to one's superior, and the exercise of a permitted degree of personal initiative.

To throw light on these subjects, this book reports and analyzes data gathered in two ways: historical research, and the replies that 249 higher civil servants of Egypt gave in 1954 to a long questionnaire about their backgrounds, attitudes, and opinions. . . . In the remaining chapters the responses to the questionnaire are analyzed at length, and historical and documentary data are used to set forth the problems dealt with and to illuminate the replies given by the civil servants who were interviewed. We do not rely exclusively, then, upon one kind of research but try to combine the historical and the questionnaire-survey approaches in order to give our discussion depth in time as well as relevance to the present. The two approaches are complementary; each is used where it is best suited to the problem posed. If we are interested in the influences that have brought the higher civil service of Egypt to its present position, we must consider the Ottoman and British legacies. If we want to know the social origin of the present senior officials in Egypt, we can find out only by asking them the appropriate questions, for such information is nowhere available. There are, of course, limitations to the questionnaire method. We have tried to overcome as many of them as we could by judicious wording and spacing of questions, by the inclusion of items that can be checked against one another, and by setting up the most favorable interview-situation possible in the circumstances. Properly applied and interpreted, the questionnaire can be useful for some purposes. The newness of the method in Egypt was taken into account in planning the questions, and great effort was expended in developing several ways of increasing the probability that either the answers given were the respondents' true answers or that skillful interpretation of all the answers could reveal which were true and which were not true— and what significance should be placed upon the answers deemed to be conscious or unconscious evasions.

In analyzing the survey data, we shall have two tasks. First, we shall try to see the differences in the public bureaucracy of Egypt and that of most Western states. Second, we shall compare one group of Egyptian civil servants with another—the older with the younger, the administrative with the technical workers, those more exposed to Western influences with those less exposed, and so on. The first of these two kinds of comparisons will be the more difficult one, for there are few studies of the higher civil servants of Western states with whom we can compare the Egyptian officials we interviewed. Studies of the socio-economic background of senior officials in the United States, England, and France have been published in recent years, and these permit a few comparisons of social origin, age, and position. But there are no studies that would permit a comparison of the opinions and attitudes of Egyptian and Western higher civil servants. Such comparisons of this order as are found in the following pages, therefore, are based, on the Egyptian side, on the specific data collected in the questionnaire, and on the Western side only on what the author takes to be the generally accepted notions in the literature on its public bureaucracies.

One of the main themes we shall develop will be the degree to which the Egyptian higher civil service approaches Western norms of professionalization and bureaucratic behavior. This focus is not an ethnocentric weakness but, on the contrary, is dictated by Egypt's own goals and intentions as expressed in recent efforts to industrialize, in the long-term trend toward secularism in government, and in reforms in the civil service itself. Moreover, the goals announced by the leaders of regimes both before and since the end of the monarchy in 1952–1953 imply movement in the direction of a typically Western economy and polity (irrespective of the leadership's attitude toward the West at any given moment), although they see this process as one of "modernization," rather than of "Westernization." In the light of these Egyptian social changes and policies (and not as a reflection of Western bias) we are interested in learning how far the civil service, a social group essential to realization of these goals, has moved in a direction consistent with the kind of society the Egyptians want to create in their land.

Egypt is not the only country seeking to move in this direction. To what extent are our findings about Egypt applicable to other countries in the Near East, Asia, or even Latin America? The author prefers, in the absence of comparable studies, to leave the answer to readers familiar with the public bureaucracies of these areas. One could easily lump together all the "underdeveloped" lands and assume their civil service corps are like the Egyptian in many ways. But Egypt is far from being the "typical" "underdeveloped" area. Its civil service has a long tradition. Its population, unlike that of many non-industrial areas, is dense rather than sparse in settlement. Its efficient agriculture may indeed be said to be overdeveloped in some respects. It has, for a basically rural-agricultural economy, highly developed commercial and banking institutions. Its educational system is probably more advanced than that of most countries at the same level of economic development. Even within the Near East, Egypt can hardly be said to be typical; regarding our own focus of interest in this study, the Arab countries alone (not to mention Israel, Turkey, and Iran) have public bureaucracies ranging from those that are no more than personal advisers to the reigning family to the relatively modern civil service of the Egyptian republic.

Yet there are similarities among the "underdeveloped" countries, as a United Nations study group has pointed out: "The problems of underdeveloped countries that may be related to public administration are primarily problems of transition: transition from semi-feudal and traditional to more responsible and rational forms of administration; from an agricultural and extractive economy to an economy of industry and trade; from a colonial regime conducted by foreigners to a national government."[2]   Indeed, studies of other aspects of some Near Eastern countries, touching on public administration, mention characteristics similar to those we find in Egypt: the civil service as a social class, its peculiar status and prestige, and its special loyalties.   These studies (dealing only incidentally and briefly with what is our central concern here) cover Syria, Iraq, Turkey, Iran, and Afghanistan.[3] Other studies cover Mexico, Cuba, Guatemala, Nicaragua, Burma, Siam, and Malaya.[4]   Although such studies have been made, caution must be exercised in pointing to similarities, for we cannot know their significance until we know, through more detailed investigation than has thus far been made available, the full range of differences as well.

The Bureaucratic Atmosphere

To the reader interested in the "feel" or the "climate" of the Egyptian public bureaucracy all the statistics in the world are probably beside the point.   Even if the studies of other bureaucracies now lacking were to become available overnight and all the precise statistical comparisons made, such a reader would be hardly satisfied.   The bureaucratic "atmosphere" is a subject for the artist, a Daumier or a Balzac, not for the social scientist.   Moreover, the artist's evocation is likely to be so general in scope that it encompasses all bureaucratic systems and would hardly permit us to distinguish one national expression of this spirit from another.   Consider the following two descriptions by novelists:

> As government offices are at present constituted, four hours out of the nine which the clerks are supposed to give to the State are wasted, as will presently be seen, over talks, anecdotes, and squabbles, and, more than all, over office intrigues.   You do not know, unless you frequent government offices, how much the clerks' little world resembles the world of school; the similarity strikes you wherever men live together; and in the army or the law-courts you find the school again on a rather larger scale.   The body of clerks, thus pent up for eight hours at a stretch, looked upon the offices as classrooms in which a certain amount of lessons must be done.

> I scribbled at the bottom of the page: "To be filed with Report," and clasped my head in my hands, wondering what was to be done next in this case, and whom we could interrogate so as to bring our Report up to a minimum of twenty pages.   For I have never forgotten what a Public Prosecutor said to me one day when he received a ten-page Report.
> "What's all this?   A contravention or a misdemeanor?"

When I replied that it was a murder-case, he shouted at me in aston-
ishment:

"A Murder case investigated in ten pages! An assassination! The
murder of a human being! All in ten pages?"

When I replied that with those ten pages we had managed to get
the murderer, he paid no attention whatever, and went on weighing the
Report in his hand with careful accuracy.

"Who would ever have believed that this Report could be of a
murder case?"

I replied instantly: "Next time, God willing, we shall be more careful about the weight!"

However much we may admire the skill of these writers, we should have
to admit that they are depicting much the same kind of behavior, although
the first quotation is from Balzac's novel of early nineteenth-century France
and the second from Towfiq el Hakim's[5] novel of contemporary Egypt.[6] The
social scientist does not aim to communicate an "atmosphere" in this sense;
the artist does not have the social scientist's aim of developing precise statements of relations that fit into larger systems and can be compared with
statements about similar phenomena in other times and places.

Yet, below the level of things all bureaucracies have in common, there
are differences even in the intangible impressions they leave. These may
be only stereotypes, but they can nevertheless embody a core of truth. The
"typical" British civil servant, with bowler and tightly-rolled umbrella, is
reserved, aloof, and very correct. The "typical" French *fonctionnaire* sits
among his papers, inaccessible, and never permits the public business to
prevent him, every day at the same time, from reaching into the bottom
drawer of his desk for his lunch wrapped in brown paper. The "typical"
Egyptian clerical *muwazzaf*, for the author, is a man sitting at a desk in his
overcoat, his *tarbush* (or fez) hanging on a nail on the wall behind him, his
newspaper spread out, one hand holding his demitasse of Turkish coffee and
the other reaching for his buzzer to call in a messenger.

Such stereotypes, of course, are akin to the public image of any bureaucracy and are equally unflattering. Through the stereotypic lens all bureaucracies appear alike and unattractive. To the Western visitor, nevertheless,
the surface aspects of the Egyptian government office are considerably different from anything he has seen. The first thing he notices is the presence of
men, rather than women, in the reception rooms. Women are employed in
only a few ministries. The outer office presided over by a female secretary or
two, so familiar in the West, is never seen in Egypt. Nor can one usually see
the large office with scores of desks at which typists, clerks, and machine operators are working. Instead, there is a combination reception room and outer
office manned by one or two male secretaries who do no typing or stenography
but who handle appointments, pass and receive papers, and exercise much
more influence than do their closest counterparts in the West. Leading off

this room is a much larger one occupied by a superior official. Here the furnishings are more elegant. Serving both offices and others, along the corridor are a large number of servant-messengers, in uniforms of varying degrees of completeness, who usher in visitors, transmit papers, run errands, and bring Turkish coffee. Coffee-drinking (and, to an increasing extent, Coca-Cola drinking) is usually the first order of business when the official arrives and practically each time someone comes to see him. As a visitor enters, indeed, he usually finds many others there before him, most of them whispering to each other quietly, yet not in a conspiratorial air; this is simply the way things are done, for in Egyptian government offices the really private audience is almost unknown. The official simultaneously handles three or four items of business and converses with three or four visitors or colleagues who stand or sit around his desk. The number of such persons milling around an office gets to be considerable. Several years ago it reached a point where the Minister of Communications tried to forbid all "private" visits to officials in his ministry. At the same time he sought to end delays in work by requiring that every matter be studied for no more than twenty-four hours, after which, finished or not, it must yield its place to another item.[7] Perhaps the most striking thing to a Western visitor will occur at noon, when he may hear the Muslim call to prayer resound through the building. In a few minutes the faithful will form their ranks in the courtyard and corridors for the noon prayer. Those who join these ranks, however, are the messengers, porters, janitorial and kitchen workers—the clerks and senior officials remain at their desks.

Change is slow in the public bureaucracy of any country. Writing over a hundred years ago, in 1839, an Englishman described the conduct of business in Egyptian government offices in a way that anyone can still recognize despite the changes that have taken place. "The public business in Egypt," wrote John Bowring, "as generally in the East, is dispatched in a divan, presided over by a principal functionary. The correspondence is opened and read, and answers dictated to the surrounding scribes, who are almost invariably Copts. Sometimes there is a discussion, and the opinions of the different members of the divan are consulted; but a predominant weight is invariably given to that of the president. A sort of publicity pervades all these proceedings. There is a perpetual succession of auditors and spectators, many of whom have no interest in the matters under discussion."[8]

Egypt is, of course, not unique in the conservatism of its bureaucracy. Like that of France, for example, according to a recent interpretation by Herbert Lüthy, the government apparatus has supplied a continuity that the politicians have not been able to achieve, and has managed to keep all administrative authority centralized in its own hands. Lüthy says of France that the bureaucracy functions so automatically "that the only sphere of activity it concedes to politics is that of pure and irrelevant ideology."[9] The same cannot be said about the Egyptian government bureaucracy for, concerned as it has been with self-protection rather than public policy, the only major sphere of activity it has conceded to politics has been that of power. In other respects, however, the Egyptian public bureaucracy resembles the French even more than it does the British, despite the latter's greater political power in the area since the late nineteenth century. Other government institutions, as well as some features of all levels of the educational system, likewise owe much to French inspiration.[10]

The Public Bureaucracy in Egyptian Society

A public bureaucracy functions within a particular form of government and a particular kind of society. Differences between bureaucracies can be traced to the differences in the broader political, social, and economic spheres they serve. What are these broad differences between Egypt and the Western world? The following observations are not based on our questionnaire survey, but the results of the survey, reviewed in the remaining chapters, illustrate and in part substantiate them.

In Egypt, as in most of the Arab-Muslim world, the connection between economic and political power has been closer than in the West. Egypt is thus at a stage of development comparable to a much earlier era in the West, when these two types of power were less distinct in their exercise and in the groups of individuals who enjoyed their possession. The power of the upper economic classes in Egypt has not been private economic power as we know it in the West but, whether based on land or trade or industry, has been derived from their close relationship to the holders of political power. Government in the Near East is the major source of any organized social power, and no class wields much power outside it. Consequently government is respected and feared, for few persons have the economic independence to risk incurring its hostility. Owing to this close connection between economic and political power, and to the depressed state of the vast majority of the population, government posts have been largely a preserve of the upper and (more recently) the middle classes. Although the middle groups stand between the classes above and below them, they are much nearer the upper class in education, economic interest, goals and aspirations, and general attitude and taste. The prestige of the civil servant in the Near East is higher than in the West, for two reasons: first, because government and those who speak for it are more respected and feared; second, because the civil servant himself is likely to come from a higher socio-economic group. (A third but different sort of reason is that government in Egypt has been associated for thousands of years with foreign conquerors.)

When an Egyptian goes to the post office or police station or even to a railroad ticket office, he is almost certain to meet government officials who earn more than he does and who are better educated. In the West the situation is more likely to be just the opposite. Such contacts serve constantly to reinforce the prestige of the civil servant in the Near East. The mere fact that he can read and write places even the lowliest clerk above the vast mass of the illiterate population.

Egypt has been a society in which (irrespective of changing regimes) the relations between the people and their government are not so precisely articulated as they have become in the West. The state has for generations performed functions that lead to considerable contact between the people and the government; yet the rights and duties of both parties have not been so clearly defined as to permit much of this contact to become routine. Rather, there is still ignorance and uncertainty among the citizens, while among government officials there has always been a tendency to take advantage of such latitude as the law and public apathy allow. There are several reasons for this relatively vague structuring of relations between people and government. One is precisely the fact that Egypt has been ruled by a strong executive (at first foreign and then native, even during the constitutional regimes from 1923 to 1952), and has never known rulers responsible to a strong legislature representing an educated electorate. Second, the proliferation of government services and functions (often under Western influence) has been beyond the capacity of the public and the civil service to absorb quickly enough and probably even beyond the capacity of the largely rural nation to understand. It would be difficult to demonstrate fully, but it appears that the result of this lack of clarity is a disproportionately large number of personal contacts between citizen and government representative —disproportionate to the size and urbanization of the population and to the functions and services the state performs. One reason for this situation may be that the Near East has not yet developed the network of voluntary associations and interest-groups, known in the West, which can meet some individual needs directly or can represent individuals before the government. Moreover, where rights and responsibilities are vague (despite—perhaps because of—the presence of myriad laws and rulings), it is probably worth a trip to a government office to try to get a decision one wants even if it appears offhand that prospects are not good. Much more than in the West, people in the Near East seem to feel there is always a way to get around a regulation or to find one that helps instead of hurts your case. Such a situation, of course, adds to the power and prestige of the civil servant—and increases the temptation to act arbitrarily or upon the basis of irrelevant loyalties.

This vague structuring of relations between citizen and government exemplifies the fact that Egypt has not yet become a rational, secular state of the Western type, in spite of its efforts to do so. Much of what we may call a pre-bureaucratic character remains—that is, remnants of an older society in which the state was not clearly differentiated and government was personal instead of the impersonal, rational, uniform administration that is the goal (if not the performance) of modern bureaucracy. Egypt does not lack a long bureaucratic history. This history has been, most of the time, one of what Max Weber has called an administrative system based upon "traditional authority" rather than upon "legal authority." Both types of authority employ administrative staffs but Weber reserves for the staff of a "legal authority" the name of bureaucracy, with its now-familiar traits of impersonal obligation, hierarchical organization, legal jurisdiction, selection through technical qualification, remuneration and tenure governed by fixed principles, and so on. The administrative staff of a "traditional authority" lacks these features; instead, in it powers and duties shift with the decision of the chief, the staff is attached to the chief's household, functions are not permanently defined and assigned to certain posts, selection and promotion occur by grace of the chief, and so on.[11] It is immediately clear that Egypt's public bureaucracy has been moving from the model of "traditional authority" to that of "legal authority" and that vestiges of the older model persist to this day.

Another Egyptian (and perhaps Near Eastern) legacy is the tension between the local community and the central government. The village has fiercely resisted the advent of national or imperial authorities even where economic necessity has dictated it. Paralleling this tension has been a pervading difference in the pattern of social control between the periphery and the center. The village, especially in Egypt, is loosely structured, practically barren of formal controls, and those it has have been administered informally by the umda, the notable or mayor. The central government, in contrast, has been highly organized and has claimed control (on either secular or religious grounds) over the most minute and private aspects of life, although usually in effect it has scarcely touched the local community. Thus, in the village, authority has been wielded by the heads of the patriarchal families and by the notables. The absence of formal, political controls, however, has had a curious concomitant: a tendency to "politicize" interpersonal relations. Individuals tend to judge and assess one another in terms of social position and social power. The result is a pattern of ingratiation and manipulation which is political in motivation and effect but which proceeds on a level of interpersonal relations which virtually excludes concern with politics as a struggle for, and the exercise of, formal governmental controls.[12]

Any government of Egypt seeking to revamp its civil service has to contend with this broader and older legacy of society and government as well as with the more specific problems engendered by the system of public administration that it has inherited.

NOTES

1. T. S. Ashton, *Industrial Revolution 1760–1830*, Home University Library of Modern Knowledge, No. 204, Oxford University Press, London, 1948, pp. 139–141.

2. United Nations, Technical Assistance Administration, Report by the Special Committee on Public Administration Problems, *Standards and Techniques of Public Administration*, N.Y., 1951, par. 12, p. 5.

3. The International Bank for Reconstruction and Development has published reports on Syria, Iraq, and Turkey: *The Economic Development of Syria*, The Johns Hopkins Press, Baltimore, 1955, pp. 193–199; *The Economic Development of Iraq*, The Johns Hopkins Press, Baltimore, 1952, pp. 77–80; *The Economy of Turkey*, I.B.R.D., Wash., D.C., 1951, pp. 198–200. On Iran, see Arthur C. Millspaugh, *Americans in Persia*, The Brookings Institution, Wash., D.C., 1946, pp. 83–91. On Afghanistan, see Peter G. Franck, "Economic Planners," in Sydney N. Fisher, ed., *Social Forces in the Middle East*, Cornell University Press, Ithaca, 1955, pp. 149–153.

4. On Mexico, see Nathan L. Whetten, *Rural Mexico*, University of Chicago Press, 1948, pp. 545–554; and Luccio Mendieta y Nuñez, *La Administración Publica en Mexico*, Imprenta Universitaria, Mexico, 1942, pp. 293–303. On Cuba, Guatemala, and Nicaragua, see the volumes by the International Bank for Reconstruction and Development: *Report on Cuba*, I.B.R.D., Wash., D.C., 1951, pp. 453–455; *The Economic Development of Guatemala*, I.B.R.D., Wash., D.C., 1951, pp. 262–264; *The Economic Development of Nicaragua*, The Johns Hopkins Press, Baltimore, 1953, pp. 85–87. On Burma, Siam, and Malaya, see the series published by the Royal Institute of International Affairs: F. S. V. Donnison, *Public Administration in Burma*, London, 1953, pp. 81–86; W. D. Reeve, *Public Administration in Siam*, N.Y., 1951, pp. 31–39, 60–67, 80–82; S. W. Jones, *Public Administration in Malaya*, London, 1953, pp. 116, 124–125.

5. Transliteration of Arabic names and words in this book follows common usage rather than any linguistically consistent system.

6. The first quotation is from Balzac's *The Government Clerks* (*Les Employés*, 1836), tr. by James Waring, vol. 24 in *The Works of Honoré de Balzac*, The University Society, N.Y., n.d., pp. 260–261. The second is from Towfiq el Hakim, *Maze of Justice (Mudhakkirāt Nā'ib fi al-Aryāf*, 1937), tr. by A. S. Eban, The Harvill Press, London, 1947, pp. 11–12.

7. *The Egyptian Gazette* (Cairo), October 29, 1953, p. 5.

8. John Bowring, *Report on Egypt and Candia*, Sessional Papers 1840, Vol. XXXV, H.M.S.O., London, p. 48.

9. Herbert Lüthy, "Democracy and Its Discontents. II. France," *Encounter* (London). Vol. II, No. 5, May, 1954, pp. 23–24, and *France against Herself*, Praeger, N.Y., 1955, p. 18.

10. On the civil service, see especially Walter R. Sharp, *The French Civil Service*, Macmillan, N.Y., 1931, chapters I, II, XIV.

11. Max Weber, *The Theory of Social and Economic Organization*, ed. by Talcott Parsons, Oxford University Press, N.Y., 1947, pp. 333–336, 342–345.

12. See Hamed Ammar, *Growing Up in an Egyptian Village*, Routledge and Kegan Paul, London, 1954, especially chapters IV–VI; and El-Demerdash Abdel-Meguid Sarhan, *Interests and Culture. A Comparative Study of Interests, Concerns, Wishes, Likes, Dislikes, and Happiest Days of Egyptian and American Children*, Teachers College, Columbia University, Contributions to Education, No. 959, N.Y., 1950, especially chapter IX.

Numerous authorities have written on the dynamics of culture change in the Middle East, but it remained for Daniel Lerner to postulate a theoretical model, "The System of Modernity," and then go out and test it in five Middle Eastern countries—Turkey, Lebanon, Egypt, Jordan, and Iran. A decade of effort went into the studies that ultimately resulted in the volume from which the present selection is taken. This study of Iran was conducted in 1950, but the author's material on the politics and the "public emotion" of the country are both topical and significant.

21

◇◇◇

Iran in a Bipolar World

DANIEL LERNER

"Never did reformer take
Passion's way,
But that both worlds he must stake
In the play."
—Saadi

Geography set Iran's destiny as a gambit in contests among great nations —"Persia Among The Powers." Says one historian: "The modern era for Persia may be considered to have opened with the rise of Russia and the pursuing by Peter the Great of policies aimed at extending Russian rule to the Persian Gulf."[1] If one starts from the first Russian war in 1804, under the reign of Fath Ali Shah, the modern era in Iran is designed by the criss-cross of Russian ambitions and Western counterpoints.[2] Iran's internal evolution has been cut to the pattern of her external dependence, following the move-and-check sequence played across the Iranian plateau by the great

From *The Passing of Traditional Society*. Reprinted by permission of Free Press, Glencoe.

powers.   Iranian modernization today still follows the leads of external
power.

IRAN BETWEEN THE POWERS

The historic lines drawn in the contest between Imperial Russia and
Imperial Britain still shape the Iranian role.   But today the political arena
is global, Russia is Soviet, and the Western spearhead is in Washington.
The familiar stakes of Persian geography have been augmented by the flow
of Iranian oil.   This heightened interplay as subject and object of global
politics explains why Iran has so seldom, in the cold war era, been far outside
the spotlight of world attention.   The current interaction between external
stakes in Persian oil and geography with the internal process of social change
in Iran merits consideration.

Warm Waters and Crude Oil

Russia's historic search for warm waters inevitably took the southerly
direction.   Contained in the north by frozen Arctic seas, in the east by
Siberian wastes, in the west by the ramparts of modern Europe, the course
of Russian empire led southward to the Mediterranean or the Indian Ocean.
Effectively blocked from passage to the former through the Turkish Straits,
she only prized more highly the alternative route through the Persian Gulf.

Britain's interest in denying Russia access to the Mediterranean and the
Gulf followed from her permanent, almost obsessional, concern with the
imperial Lifeline.   The Gulf was used merely as a way-station between British
Channel and Indian Ocean, but it figured also as essential link in an alternate
Tigris-Euphrates route of egress from the Mediterranean—should Suez and
the Red Sea ever fall.   So powerfully did the Lifeline image work upon British
geopolitical thinking that inalienable control of the Persian Gulf became a
fixed condition of imperial policy.

A century of war and diplomacy aimed at Russia went to maintain
British primacy.   The main concession to Russian ambition was acquiescence
in the conversion of the Caspian Sea into a Russian lake.   But Soviet policy,
while welcoming the Caspian fisheries, never renounced the larger design
of Russian imperialism.   When the Soviets joined with the Nazis to carve
out a Eurasian "new order," Secret Protocol No. 1 of the Four-Power Agreement signed on November 26, 1940, began: "The Soviet Union declares
that its territorial aspirations center south of [its] national territory in the
direction of the Indian Ocean."[3]   The postwar Azerbaijan maneuver, the
tours of Bulganin-Khrushchev and Mikoyan-Saburov, signify that the USSR
has not renounced the traditional goals of Russian expansionism.   But the

old stakes have grown more weighty. Soviet presence in the Persian Gulf today endangers more than the British Lifeline. It gives the Soviets access to Asia Minor and North Africa; and therewith the posture for an envelopment action against the whole of Western Europe. That is why the American purse and power have now become available when British primacy has faltered.

Moreover, the modern West has become an oil civilization. Without the lubricants derived from petroleum, the wheels of Western life would grind to a halt. Mobility is the condition of modern enterprise and oil is prerequisite to movement. Some equivalent of a Berlin-to-Baghdad lifeline has become essential for every industrial nation of the modern West—e.g., the calamity which befell the Nazi *Luftwaffe* in World War II was not unrelated to the failure of the *Drang nach Osten*. This is not likely to change until some distant day when nuclear energy has replaced oil as the major means of mobility. Hence, there was consternation in the West when Dr. Mossadegh nationalized the Anglo-Iranian Oil Company (AIOC) in March 1951, forced its British operators from Iran, and thereby halted its daily flow of 700,000 barrels at a critical phase in Western rearmament. Domestic production in the U.S. and in Kuwait, Saudi Arabia, and Iraq was accelerated so rapidly that 1951 world production exceeded the previous year's by 460 million barrels. Thus the West reinsured itself against extreme dependence on Iranian oil.

But the West still needed the Iranian buffer to Soviet penetration of the Persian Gulf, which could compromise Western access to its other and possibly irreplaceable oil sources. Oil and geography thus conjoined as strategic necessities in a bipolar world. Stated concisely: "Any optimistic outlook for the free world rests on the availability to the NATO nations of adequate supplies of petroleum at all times and under any circumstances."[4] The oil image has become the nightmare of Free World policy as once the Lifeline image was of British policy. But there are genuinely new elements in the old game, which may prove decisive for social change in Iran.

New Bottles—New Wine?

It was a Persian poet who pointed out that old wine may be poured in new bottles. The old geopolitical stakes in Iran have received a new bipolar packaging. What effect have these external rearrangements upon the internal processes of Iranian life?

While Russian designs still supply a central theme of Iranian politics, Russian policy today is armed with the specifically Soviet instrument of a world Communist movement operating in each country according to Soviet requirements. The *Tudeh* Party is a genuinely new ingredient in Iran's world posture. Through its organization ancient grievances and new demands in the internal life of Iran can be channeled into a position of maximum leverage on issues of world policy. The collaboration of the *Tudeh* with Dr. Mossadegh in driving out the AIOC was a potent expression of this new force.

The classic counterpoint to fear of Russian ambitions has always been, for Iranian diplomacy, reliance upon some protector in the West. The usual big brother was Britain, but there was room for maneuver. In 1808, with Britain and Russia jointly engaged by Napoleonic maneuvers, Persia joined France in a campaign aimed at both—directly at Russia and also (with Napoleonic wile) at Britain in India. A century later, as Britain seemed ready to concede Tsarist supremacy in northern Iran for Russian support against the Triple Alliance, the diplomats at Tehran turned from "Perfidious Albion" to Berlin for protection against their ancient Russian enemy.

In the traditional game, then, "the West" was composed of highly competitive nations among whom, as one protector deserted her to seek Russian favor, Persia could choose another. The rules of the game have changed under the discipline of bipolarity. The Baghdad Pact raises Iranian balance-of-power politics to a global level. As the European nations no longer compete against each other with Russia as a balancing power, but rather form a Western bloc coordinated against a Soviet bloc, Tehran is likewise obliged to deal with "the West" as its protector. The terrain has expanded, while Iran's space for maneuver has shrunk. What changes of political style have accompanied this new structure of the world arena?

One type of change, under the rule of bipolarity, is the effort to eliminate the cruder forms of profiteering developed under the old imperialism. Before it was expropriated the AIOC provided the British government, which owned a 52% interest, with its greatest single source of revenue and was regarded as a pork barrel. The American government, deriving no part of its revenue from Iranian oil, regarded the issue as a powder keg. American intervention in the dispute led to an agreement which gave the Iranian government a far larger share in oil revenue than it had previously enjoyed. This represented a shift from colonial to cold war perspectives, from economic to political goals, from coercive to persuasive means.[5]

The impact of this new Great Power style is visible in recent Soviet practice as well. The Irano-Soviet Fisheries Company provided over the past quarter-century as rapacious a model of imperialist economics as the AIOC, with a measure of chicanery added. The Fisheries Convention of 1927 provided for equal shares of world proceeds from Soviet marketing of caviar bred by Caspian sturgeon in Iran's territorial waters. The USSR ignored its stipulation for a rotating director, chief accountant, and chief engineer. By keeping these posts in Russian hands, the USSR managed to keep the profits in the same place. Whereas Iranian sources computed the Company's annual earnings at about $2 million, the actual sums received by the Iranian government annually averaged about \$25,000 (1/40 of the amount due).[6] Recent negotiations sponsored by the USSR suggest that the Soviets too have reconsidered whether this game is worth the candle. As the primacy of politics over economics is acknowledged, \$1 million a year more or less comes to seem relatively trivial. The solicitude for genuine friendliness among the Iranian population, rather than mere acquiescence by its government, is quite new. As late as 1943, the allied Big Three felt free to hold their momentous conference in Tehran without the invitation, or indeed the prior knowledge, of Iranian officials.[7] Today such behavior might seem bad form.

Some new wine there doubtless is in these new bottles. The Baghdad Pact's MEDO—Middle East Defense Organization—is a case. Whatever its military value (and current depreciations may be as excessive as were earlier expectations), MEDO does possess psychic dignity. Unlike the regional security foreshadowed in the Sa'dabad Pact of 1937, it brings great powers of the West into reciprocally binding arrangements with the regional powers. Hence, whatever its impact upon Soviet designs or the Cairo calculus, the impulse underlying MEDO is likely to reshape the social structure of its participants. How much of the new wine of national autonomy can Iran take?

The Insecurity Elite

Aspirations toward autonomy are quickly raised, but the lifeways of dependence die hard. In a land habituated to defining itself in terms of those outside powers which, at any given moment, threaten or protect it, there develops a chronic instability. This diffuses certain traits of insecurity, which have cumulated in an Iran immobilized by a closed elite through many centuries. A recent monograph on the Iranian economy concludes:

> The background is insecurity: the insecurity of the landlord against the caprice of the government, insecurity in the face of attack by hostile elements, whether internal factions or foreign invasion, and the insecurity of the cultivator *vis-à-vis* the landowner and others. The law was not backed by a predominant and impartial force; effective power therefore rested with whoever wielded the greatest force and, in the absence of control by the law, the exercise of this force depended almost entirely on personal caprice. Insecurity is no less the keynote at the present day than in the past.[8]

Chronic insecurity breeds distrust. Government becomes a game of intrigue played by those who can pay the stakes. An elite forms with no claim to power but its purse—the machinery of Iranian politics being, according to Miss Lambton, "the relatively large sums of money which are at the disposal of the privileged classes."[9] Politics by bribery among the few usually implies politics by blackmail against the many. The Iranian peasantry, cowed by ignorance and fear, has traditionally maintained a stolid indifference regarding maneuvers in Tehran.

A frequent outcome, in nonparticipant social systems governed by a closed elite reliant upon intrigue and coercion, is the widespread diffusion of mendacity as an acceptable mode of self-defense against the mighty. Every army has some such phrase as "to lie like a trooper" and every autocracy has tended to produce a similar code among its subject peoples.[10] In the Ottoman Empire there flourished the code of *ketman*, whereby people spared themselves difficulties over their beliefs by simply disavowing them at appropriate moments.[11] The Persian Empire, home-based on Shi'ite Muslims in a non-Shi'ite world, long ago developed the comparable doctrine of *taqiyeh* or dissimulation. This permits a Shi'ite, in danger by reason of his religion, to pretend that he is a Sunni, a Christian, or a Jew as best serves his needs of self-defense. One American authority has moderately observed: "The ramifications of this practice extend beyond religion."[12] While Western discussions of *taqiyeh* have produced a net surplus of moral indignation over careful description, the pervasiveness of mendacity is acknowledged by Persians.[13] *Taqiyeh* has even been conventionalized to deal with superior force on the level of top policy negotiations:

> In view of Russian strength and Iranian weakness, the latter government . . . was compelled often to resort to almost every known form of evasion in dealing with issues, which originated in Moscow. Apparent naiveté, circumlocution, dilatoriness, specious argument, misunderstanding—these and numerous other techniques were employed by Iranian officials.[14]

Widespread mendacity as a mode of self-defense against a chronically insecure environment makes for a highly unstable self-system. Indeed the Persians are, according to Professor Frye, a "people of extremes" and a basic condition of modernization is to remedy "the Persian's lack of confidence in his fellow man."[15] Professor Hoskins notes the political relevance of "the character and behavior of the Iranian peoples, who are as given to extremes in temperament as their habitat is full of contrasts."[16] The extremist temperament leads to extremist politics, in which violence and the frenzy of mobs play a role. This makes conduct of a moderate policy exceedingly difficult, particularly within the limited margins for maneuver left by current world politics. No longer can Tehran, when Britain and Russia seem ready to lay Iran on the sacrificial altar of their joint convenience, counterpoint by *ad hoc* arrangements with France or Germany. "East" and "West" are now solid blocs. Tehran has been obliged to make a net choice between the two world constellations.

When domestic violence adjudicates world issues, the politics of the

mob requires systematic supervision. Certain social formations take over
the distinctive function of mediating messages, including calls to action, between elite and mass. Added to the traditional relay chains of bazaar merchants and itinerant peddlers are the modern message centers manned by the
new-style intelligentsia in government, education, mass communication.
Preoccupied with the play of power, they claim in return larger shares in the
process of decision than a closed elite in a non-growth economy can accommodate. Those deprived of what they consider their due, under the rule of
things-as-they-are, often turn from the course of moderation to stake their
chances (having nothing to lose but their claims) on extremist action.
Operating against the center from both extremes of the political spectrum,
these extremists limit the scope of moderate governance. By maintaining
mob rule in the streets, they can reduce any government to counter-violence
or impotence. One horn of this dilemma is Hajji Baba's ancient formula:
"Our kings must be drinkers of blood and slayers of men to be held in
estimation by their subjects and surrounding nations." The other horn is
surrender.

This cycle of Iranian politics was exhibited in the great postwar crisis
symbolized by Mossadegh. By coalescing the extremist factions around his
leadership, backing the slogans of radicalism with the techniques of assassination and mob violence, Dr. Mossadegh was able to destroy a moderate government, force the Shah into flight, and install himself in power. As the
inherent instability of governance by violence in turn undermined his own
controls, Iran tottered on the bipolar verge. The balance was restored only
by a vigorous coup organized by the army. Violence countered violence.
The rule of terror—not of principle or policy—decided the course of events.

The survey of Iranian attitudes was made at a propitious moment.
Iranian extremism had long focused on the AIOC. Passage of the oil
nationalization bill in March 1951, and the overt display of British resistance
to it, had raised to fever pitch the anti-British sentiment common to all
varieties of political extremism in Iran. The Nationalist interest in driving
out the foreign overlords was obvious; the Communist (*Tudeh*) interest
followed logically from its permanent alliance with the USSR. United behind
Mossadegh, who incorporated the stirring symbolism of independence in a
strategy of violence that released ancient hatreds and repressions, political
extremism took control of Iran. In the crucial months of this crisis—May
to July 1951—the interviews were collected. They provide a rare gallery of
political self-portraits, painted at a moment when cumulative tensions had
reached a critical phase.

THE STRUGGLE AT HOME

Underlying the chronic tensions of Iran, as of other Middle East lands, is the great gap between aspirations and capabilities. The desires for national independence, social justice, personal pride of place—these have been stirred among Iranians by the same gusts of ideology that have dispersed the symbols of modernity over all the lands of the earth. A "backward land" becomes an "underdeveloped country" when these winds of doctrine have inseminated a substantial portion of its population with the aspiration toward a modern style of life for themselves and their fellows.

Slow Starts and Extremist Goals

A modern society must know enough about itself to plan its probable future course in terms of trends from the past to the present—social science being, in this sense, a distinctive "feedback" mechanism required for modern governance. Iran does not know the distribution of its population, nor even its approximate total size. Population estimates range from 15 to 20 million—with a consensus around the median figure of 17 to 18 million.[17] This population occupies a total area of 628,000 square miles, a territory larger than all of western Europe. As no official census has even been taken, estimates of population density are partial and unreliable. But Iran clearly is not overpopulated, with density averaging about 27 per square mile over total area (excluding desert) and about 41 for inhabited areas. Density varies from a high 70–95 in the Caspian provinces to less than five in the southern regions.[18] Nor is there any early prospect of overpopulation. While actual rates of fertility, mortality, and morbidity are unknown, the birth rate has been estimated at 30/1000, which is low for the Middle East. With infant mortality estimated as high as 500/1000 live births, and average rural life expectancy at 27 years, net natural increase is relatively slow.[19]

Population distribution shows little regional mobility or urbanization. There are over 40,000 villages in Iran housing about 60% of the population, with another 10% living in migratory tribes. The 30% of townspeople are about equally divided between smaller towns, cities over 50,000 and Tehran. Rural resettlement during the past decade has been mainly toward larger cities. The population of Tehran alone doubled, in the period 1940–1950, to over one million.[20] These urban migrants, in Iran as in Egypt, encounter unemployment, undercompensation, and the miserable conditions of slum life. For there are few signs of a growth phase in the Iranian economy. Without industrial expansion, the movement of discontented and deprived thousands to cities augurs not economic growth but political instability.

The ecology of Iran provides optimum conditions for the prevalence of extremism. The population is dispersed around the vast desert, in villages isolated by inadequate or nonexistent communications. They remain locked in the ancient round of daily life, eking from their old soil with their antique tools (some antedating the Christian era) their immemorial produce. Regarding the new world stage, on which their national drama now unfolds, they are uninformed and uninvolved.

A striking result of the survey, made at fever pitch of the most profound crisis which has racked postwar Iran, is that a substantial proportion of the population was unaware and even uninterested. When the interviewers asked about the most important problem facing them and the nation, they responded in the manner of Traditionals in all places and times. Their concerns were not the nationalization of AIOC and expulsion of the British, nor the contest between Dr. Mossadegh and the Shah, nor the future alignment of Iran within the Soviet or Western worlds. Salient were the familiar concerns of the daily round—ranging from major problems of survival (health and livelihood) to trivial details of family life.

Sharply contrasted with this remote and inarticulate mass was the small group whose personal involvement with the national crisis was profound. These persons cared deeply about public affairs, vibrating to the day's headlines with the intense affectivity of a farmer hearing news of his sick calf or a mother of her soldier-son. When asked what were their main private and public problems, these Moderns could scarcely differentiate between them, so deeply had they incorporated the symbols of political identity. By contrast with the apathetic mass, these highly involved persons expressed an urgent need to impart to others their concern with public issues, a compulsion to "do something about it." This agitational disposition among a small frustrated corps is a distinctive mark of revolutionary extremism, just as the less intensive mode of "participation" by a massive contented electorate is a mark of democratic moderation. The mark of extremism is highly visible in Iran.

Non-Growth and Counter-Elite Formation

In each Middle Eastern land, we have seen, the political drama is played by a small cast of characters with the mass as chorus. As the wheel of social change turns, new aspirants come forward eager for a role downstage center. How the traditional elite will handle these aspiring young is a key question for the changing social structure: will they be incorporated in new sub-elites or alienated into counter-elite formation?

Incorporation is no easy task in a non-growth economy. Iran develops few of those constantly growing and changing occupational roles which embody young men in the elite structure. The clergy, the military, the bureaucracy—all these are charges on the public treasury, already overburdened and scarcely capable of expansion. The teaching corps is pitifully inadequate, but unlikely to multiply opportunities until Iran develops a modernizing economy in which literacy is an essential skill. Without an expanding business sector, there is little room for the lawyer and acountant, for the specialist in industrial management or labor relations, for the insurance broker or the investment manager, for the account executive or the public relations counsel. Advertising is stillborn and the mass media abortive. Where, in Iran, is "the man in the gray flannel suit"? Whatever his unpopularity among Westerners wearied by opinion brokers, in Iran he would be a more useful stimulus to modernization than the agitational intellectual in a hairshirt of vivid hue.

Given its limited absorptive capacity, Iran suffers from an overproduction of intellectuals. In a society about 90% illiterate, several thousand young persons go through the classical routines of higher education each year. Learning no skills that can be productively employed, these collegians seek outlets in the symbol-manipulating arts toward which their humanistic studies have oriented them. Their effort supplies a poignant instance of usable training rendered useless by its social environment—newspapers without readers that last a week or a month, film companies that never produce a film. The mass media, as a distinctive index of the Participant Society, flourish only where the mass has sufficient skill in literacy, sufficient motivation to share "borrowed experience," sufficient cash to consume the mediated product. In Iran the mass media are anemic and with them, annually, die a thousand hopes.

Meanwhile Iranian higher education continues to overproduce intellectuals as noted in this ironic comment:

> The existing school system has been relatively successful in accomplishing the aims of its founders three-quarters of a century ago, which were to produce a distinguished intellectual elite and to establish an instrument by which the thoughts and actions of the common people might be efficiently manipulated.[21]

A decade later, while "the secondary schools have produced graduates who apparently are not fitted for anything but to continue their schooling or to enter teaching," the collegiate population continues to rise. In the two-year period after 1946, a 50% increase brought the number of university students to 6,525. Adding to these another 2,000 abroad for higher education, one perceives that young intellectuals are being produced in quantities far exceeding Iran's capacity to consume.

Identifying the Extremists. ◆ All dressed up with no place to go, these frustrated young men go looking for excitement. It is they who form the hard core of political extremism in Iran today. This was indicated by the

1951 survey and confirmed by subsequent interviews which the author conducted in Tehran four years later. The political extremists were consistently the most Modern group in the Iranian sample. As in the other countries, so in Iran. The higher a respondent ranked on the scale of media behavior the more likely he was also urban, educated, well-off, and highly empathic. Controlled sampling had apportioned five men for each woman, three radio listeners for each non-listener, two urban for each rural resident; over half were relatively well-off by Iranian standards. But even among this preponderantly Modern sample, the Extremists differentiated themselves as a relatively homogeneous group.

The whole sample was classified along a continuum of political attitudes, located first by orientation as Left-Center-Right and then by intensity as low-moderate-extreme. Each person was classified by his response to these four questions:

1. What would you say is the biggest problem that Iran as a nation faces today?
2. What can people like yourself do to solve this problem?
3. Suppose you could suggest anything you wanted to our government— what are some of the things you would tell them?
4. What is the biggest problem that people in the same circumstances of life as you face? What can you do about solving it?

Responses were differentiated by the key symbols around which they were organized: Person, Class, Nation. Those responding in purely personal terms were classified as Apolitical. Respondents who defined problems in terms of Class—e.g., poverty, illiteracy, feudalism—and proposed solutions requiring social reform were classified as Left. Those preoccupied with problems of National aspiration requiring national action were classified as Right.

As in Syria, classification was based on the complete problem-solution sequence. Of two respondents naming "poverty" as the main problem, the one proposing to solve it by redistributing wealth was classified Left, the other solving it by "kicking out the foreigners" was classified Right. Similarly, if the problem was "disunity," the one proposing to solve it by "punishing the landlords" was sorted Left; if his solution was "strengthen the Army" he was marked Right. Attitudes toward the symbol NATION were usually consistent and decisive: the Left emphasized national obligations to the people, the Right individual responsibility to the nation.

Respondents both Left and Right were then sorted into three levels of intensity indexed by: (1) personal involvement in public problems; (2) violence of proposed solutions to these problems. All respondents had been asked whether they considered themselves happy or unhappy—and why.

Those who specified public problems as reasons for their unhappiness were classified as more involved, others who cited only family or other personal problems as less involved. Those who proposed such solutions as "hanging the landlords" or "overthrowing the government" were classified as more violent: others as less violent. The extremist Revolutionary Left was *both* involved and violent; the Middle Left was *either* involved or violent but not both; the Reform Left was *neither*.

To determine intensity among Right respondents, who were mainly preoccupied with National problems, a variant of this index was used. A respondent was considered involved if he expressed willingness to undergo personal deprivations for the achievement of national goals; if not he was considered less involved. Violence was indexed by the advocacy of aggressiveness against foreigners. A person who wanted to "destroy Britain" was classified as violent; one who merely wanted to "defend Iran against Britain" was not. The extreme Nationalistic Right was *both* involved and violent; the Middle Right was *either* but not both; the Conservative Right was *neither*. In this typology of political attitudes respondents distributed as shown in Table 1.

Table 1. DISTRIBUTION OF POLITICAL TYPES

Political Type	% of Respondents	No. of Cases
Revolutionary Left	12%	29
Middle Left	14	33
Reform Left	18	42
Apolitical	7	16
Conservative Right	29	69
Middle Right	10	22
Nationalistic Right	10	23
	100%	234

The Apolitical group represents the passive uninvolved mass of Iranians; the moderate groups on both sides include the traditional elite that has governed Iran over past decades; the extremists represent those newer formations that in Iran, as in the Arab lands, are using their access to the mass to challenge the traditional elites. The latter form those potential counter-elites whose influence upon the mass may be decisive for the duration, tempo, and balance of the modernizing processes at work in the area. This is why, despite their small numbers and lack of statistical significance, the data on extremism may clarify the interplay of communication and social change in shaping Iranian lifeways.

THE STRUCTURE OF
IRANIAN EXTREMISM*

The ideologies of Iranian extremists present themselves as sharply opposed. They espouse different causes, command different layers of loyalties, and appeal to different sets of sentiments. The *Tudeh* Party, a lightly camouflaged Communist movement which speaks for the Revolutionary Left, and the extremely nationalistic Pan-Iranian Party regard each other as mortal enemies. Underlying the symbolic divergence of the party ideologies, however, there is a remarkably similar sociology of party ideologists. The recruitment and composition of leadership at these schismatic extremes appear to follow the same process.

Sociology of Extremism

At both ends of the political continuum, Extremists register consistently higher on the sociological indices of the Participant style. Thus, while the sample was 20% female, the Extremists are exclusively male. Further, while the sample contained equal numbers over and under thirty years old, a disproportionate share of the younger persons are Extremists. It is no news that younger men tend more frequently than their elders of either sex toward extreme political positions. In Iran they move toward both extremes, and are mainly recruited from the same sociological environment as the ruling elite. A stable social structure, operating under a consensual elite, would absorb many of these vigorous young men into governance rather than alienate them into counter-elite extremism.

Consider urbanism, the index which makes the profound initial cleavage between elite and mass in Iran as elsewhere. By comparison with the Apoliticals, as in Table 2, both varieties of extremism are highly urban.

Table 2. URBANISM

	Extreme Left	Apolitical	Extreme Right
Those in *urban* areas now who were:			
raised in urban areas	73%	37%	73%
raised in rural areas	16	13	18
Those in *rural* areas now who were:			
raised in urban areas	0	13	0
raised in rural areas	11	37	9

* This section is based on the 1952 BASR report "The Political Extremes in Iran," by B. B. Ringer and D. L. Sills. See also their "Political Extremists in Iran," *Public Opinion Quarterly* (Winter 1952–53). (As 18 cases were added after these reports appeared, there are differences in percentages, usually minor.)

At both extremes three of every four were raised and still live in cities, as compared with one of three Apoliticals. Whereas 13% of the latter raised in a city have since moved to the country, not a single Extremist at either end has forsaken urban for rural pleasures. Clearly, the Extremists are urban.

Consider education, the next great cleaver between elite and mass in the Middle East. When differentiated at the point of effective literacy—the passage from elementary into secondary school—the results are shown in Table 3.

Table 3. EDUCATION

Education	Left			Apolitical	Right		
	Extreme	Middle	Moderate	Moderate	Middle	Extreme	
Elementary or less	39%	59%	53%	81%	56%	27%	25%
Secondary or higher	61	41	47	19	44	73	75

The Right is better educated than the Left. But the progression away from both sides of the Apolitical Center is more striking. What the Extremists have in common, compared with current elite as well as the mass, is that they are better educated. Consider, in Table 4, the index of socioeconomic status (SES).

Table 4. SES

SES	Left			Apolitical	Right		
	Extreme	Middle	Moderate	Moderate	Middle	Extreme	
Poor	6%	18%	12%	57%	17%	14%	9%
Moderate	78	65	55	36	68	71	82
Well-off	16	17	33	7	15	14	9

Poverty prevails only among the Apolitical mass. The politically involved respondents are better-off. Their lot improves as they move toward the extremes—up to a certain point. A lower proportion of Extremists than others is in the poor group, but the highest proportion is in the moderate (not wealthy) group. The data obviate the conventional assumption that the Extremists are simply the "have-nots," suggesting rather that they are the "want-mores." They oppose the current "system" not because they have no stake in it but because, on a range of social values, they want more than they get.

Illustrative are Extremist responses to the question whether they were happy about their lot in life. As unhappiness had been used to classify Left

Extremists, in this analysis the Extreme Left is unhappy by definition. Distribution of responses on the Right demonstrate, in Table 5, a comparable prevalence of unhappiness among the Extremists.

Table 5. HAPPINESS ON THE RIGHT

	Apolitical	Moderate Right	Middle Right	Extreme Right
Happy	61%	56%	57%	29%
Unhappy	39	44	43	71

What makes the Extremists so much unhappier than their fellows is that they "want more" and believe they deserve more—that is, that the society has not done as well by them as it should. While they have more education than the ruling group, for example, they have less money. Far from poverty themselves, they talk about the poor while their eyes are on the rich. This produces the phenomenon of "relative deprivation," whereby a person's discontent with his lot is set by the standard to which he aspires. His expectations determine whether a person feels that life has indulged or deprived him.

To check this attitude, each respondent's spontaneous references to economic matters were sorted into two categories: descriptive and deprivational. A doctor talking without affect about public health programs, a farmer about the relation of weather to crops, a business man about the costs of production—all such were classified as descriptive references. Counted as deprivational were statements reflecting the individual's dissatisfaction with his share of the national wealth. Included were general references to the economic status quo which indicated personal frustration— e.g., poverty, unemployment, economic insecurity. Where deprivational outnumbered descriptive statements by 5 to 1, the respondent was classified as highly deprivational, with results shown in Table 6.

Table 6. HIGH DEPRIVATION

Extreme Left	Middle Left	Moderate Left	Moderate Right	Middle Right	Extreme Right
80%	45%	29%	33%	36%	66%

While the saliency of deprivation is more frequent on the Left than the Right, there is a clear progression toward the extremes at both ends. This common attitude underlies their common posture toward the national community. This posture we call *alienation* and its widespread occurrence among Iranian Extremists on both sides merits consideration.

Psychology of Extremism—Alienation

Counter-elites typically dissociate themselves from the governing elite and its institutions. "We or they" is the classic rhetoric of dissociation. It symbolizes the counter-elite's partial or total transfer of participation from the current institutions of governance to competitive institutions under their own management—secret societies, clandestine networks of communication, illegal political parties (or legal parties controlled by a covert apparatus). If their withdrawal into covert institutions is successful, the counter-elite then uses these bases to reenter the arena of public participation for the purpose of subversion.

In Iran, the 1951 survey showed this subversion process in operation. While it is no part of our purpose to study political organization, the interviews do reveal pervasive dissociation from current institutional life among Extremists. In the next section we shall describe the ideological formulas invoked to justify their alienated posture. Here we note only the frequent occurrence of its psychic manifestation, namely dissociation from the major institutionalized orbits of social life. An Index of Social Dissociation, using the following items, provided the relevant data:

1. *Lack of family ties.* Those single at normal age-range for marriage; also those divorced, separated, or widowed, who have not remarried.
2. *Lack of religious ties.* Those who state that religion is of little or no importance, and rarely or never attend the mosque.
3. *Limitation of friendship ties.* Those who prefer to have few friends rather than many.
4. *Individualistic recreational patterns.* Those who prefer solitary rather than interactional recreations (e.g., visiting, conversation).

When respondents having more than two of these attributes were scored as highly dissociated, the distribution in Table 7 was obtained.

Table 7. HIGH DISSOCIATION

Left			Apolitical	Right		
Extreme	*Middle*	*Moderate*		*Moderate*	*Middle*	*Extreme*
75%	45%	38%	13%	28%	41%	51%

Dissociation from the institutional structure, among Extremists, paralleled its dissociation from the prevailing value-system. Very striking, for example, was the extent of Extremist withdrawal from religious participation. As Shi'ites, Iranian intellectuals historically have shown a special religious concern. Withdrawal from the community of religious practice and sentiment is a profound matter. Hence it is noteworthy that most Extremists score low on an index of religious involvement.   In their responses to the question how important they considered religion to be in their daily life, and the saliency of their spontaneous reference to religion, respondents showing high religious involvement are grouped in Table 8.

Table 8. HIGH RELIGIOUS INVOLVEMENT

Left			Apolitical	Right		
Extreme	*Middle*	*Moderate*		*Moderate*	*Middle*	*Extreme*
29%	37%	51%	44%	60%	33%	33%

A further test of alienation was made by constructing a general index of traditional reference. This classified and counted each respondent's spontaneous reference to traditional symbols—e.g., family, locale, religion, ethnic group—in discussing his views on public policy. Fully twice as many at both extremes, compared with the politicals, made *no* such traditional references whatsoever.

Extremist alienation from Iranian tradition is modulated by their acquisition of more expansive perspectives. An index of social horizons was constructed by noting the number and variety of "reference groups" which each respondent mentioned spontaneously. The assumption underlying this index is that a person who refers exclusively to a few familiar groups (family, community, nation) thereby exhibits narrower horizons of social contact than another whose discourse goes beyond these to include other, less traditional reference groups (class and mass, great powers and small, parties and politicians, etc.). Scoring the number and variety of their reference groups gave the distribution in Table 9 of respondents exhibiting broad social horizons.

Table 9. BROAD SOCIAL HORIZONS

Left			Apolitical	Right		
Extreme	*Middle*	*Moderate*		*Moderate*	*Middle*	*Extreme*
55%	33%	26%	0%	26%	38%	54%

This suggests that detachment from the governing institutions and dissociation from elite perspectives has not confined the Extremist within a narrow circle of purely personal activities and interests. On the contrary, withdrawal from the traditional governing symbolism has been accompanied by displacement of affect onto a new set of symbols. The outcome has been not privatization, but extreme politization—with the flow of political activity running in separatist counter-elite channels.

This was suggested by the broader social horizons among Extremists than their more moderate compatriots. But it was not conclusive, since social horizon so defined could be achieved by a social isolate, who might "interact" heavily in his fantasy life but experience few real contacts in his daily round. The question was whether Extremists really interacted so much more with others in their daily lives, as their broader social horizons indicated. To check the Participant Style in actual behavior, an index of social interaction was constructed on the basis of these three questions:

1.   Has anyone come to you for advice recently?
2.   Have you yourself gone to anyone for advice recently?
3.   Did you talk to anybody about this [news item]?

Persons answering yes to two of these questions were scored as socially active in Table 10.

Iranian Extremists, despite alienation from governing institutions and perspectives, are actively engaged with their fellows.

Table 10. SOCIAL INTERACTION

	Left			Apolitical	Right		
Extreme	Middle	Moderate		Moderate	Middle	Extreme
45%	33%	12%	6%	20%	34%	46%

Indeed, this appears to be closely related to their political commitment. To test whether this was so, respondents were divided by education, which provides skills and opportunities that foster contact among people. If only the better-educated persons in the sample scored high on interaction, then no new relationship had been established. Table 11 shows respondents scoring high on interaction.

Table 11. SOCIAL INTERACTION BY EDUCATION AND POLITICAL TYPE

High Interaction With	Left			Apolitical	Right		
	Extreme	Middle	Moderate		Moderate	Middle	Extreme
High Education	60%	36%	21%	0%	33%	46%	55%
Low Education	30	31	5	6	11	17	35

Two findings emerge from this distribution. First, as expected, well-educated people tend to be more interactive than poorly-educated people. Second, and more significant, the relationship between high interaction and political extremism exists *regardless of educational level*. Even among the poorly-educated, Extremists are more actively engaged with their fellows than

Moderates. It is not possible, from these data, to draw any chicken-or-egg conclusion: that interactivity breeds extremism or vice versa. We can conclude that the two "go together" and, whatever their psychogenetic relationship, tend to reinforce each other.

The importance of this finding is highlighted by a final test, designed to see whether high alienation (as scored on the earlier index of social dissociation) in fact occurred among the same persons as high interaction. If not, then we could not properly speak of an "extremist syndrome," but only of the high frequency of two special traits among different individuals who happened to share extremist political views. Cross-tabulating the two indices produced the distribution in Table 12. The association between the two traits, as we move toward the extremes, is very striking. There seems to emerge a clear "extremist syndrome"—an underlying psychic structure of political extremism in Iran which combines high dissociation from institutions and ideologies with a high degree of interaction among people.

This syndrome is important for public communication because it is the classic posture of the revolutionary agitator. Alienated from the governing system, he goes forth among his fellows to preach a new faith and gain loyalties for a new power. This mission is performed by persons who have mastered the New Word, and when political extremism enters this phase in any society it usually comes under the management of the alienated intelligentsia. In later phases of the quest for power the revolutionary movement is dominated by persons skilled in organizing techniques; but during the earlier phase of recruitment by propagation, leadership goes to those trained in the manipulation of symbols.

Table 12. DISSOCIATION AND INTERACTION

	Left			Apolitical	Right		
	Extreme	Middle	Moderate		Moderate	Middle	Extreme
Persons with *high* dissociation showing high interaction	67%	42%	6%	0%	26%	50%	57%
Persons with *low* dissociation showing high interaction	0	27	16	7	18	31	17

This requires a corps habituated to the skills and channels of the old elite—living and working in circumstances that provide the time and opportunities needed for agit-prop work; educated enough to formulate and diffuse the new ideologies. The Iranian Extremists, who are mainly urban, professional, moderately well-off, and well-educated, meet these sociological requirements. They manifest also the main psychological requirements—that they be sufficiently alienated from the old elite's perspectives and practices to develop their own code, and sufficiently interactive with their fellows to spread the new gospel through the society. The Extremists thus exhibit the characteristics that define radical opinion leaders. That a majority of Extremists appear to be potential leaders does not, of course, mean that a a majority of Iran's potential leaders are Extremists. But if such a leader is detached from existing institutions (alienation), is receptive to new ideas (rejects traditional for broader social horizons), is skilled in presenting these ideas to others (highly educated), and is in regular contact with his fellows (highly interactive)—then this type of leader is found most frequently, in Iran, among the political Extremists.

The survey reveals, then, the existence of a maturing Iranian counter-elite. As the sampling was originally controlled for other purposes, and the number of Extremists relatively small, the data permit neither inferences as to the present size of this revolutionary corps nor extrapolations as to its growth-potential. What the findings do show is that the logical structure of a revolutionary counter-elite is already in being, and that its internal struggle for power is inevitably linked to the bipolar external conflict between Communist and Free Worlds. At this point the Extremists diverge sharply in matters of ideology—the cleavage reflecting in miniature the bipolar division in the outer world, with the usual quota of qualifications imposed by local conditions.

In such a situation, where rival propagators of revolutionary symbols are locked in ideological conflict, the questions that interest students of communication concern content, technique, conditions of success. What are the rivals selling? With what sales technique? What market conditions favor the ones over the others? We examine these questions in turn, starting with the competing commodities—the rivalrous ideologies.

The Ideologies of Extremism

The function of ideologies is exceedingly complex. It requires clinical data of an order quite different from that obtained by survey methods to make a complete evaluation of the interaction between the public and private faces of any person. But our results do contain some findings of considerable suggestive value.

How ideology modifies perspective is illustrated by the divergent images of their own countrymen held by the two extremes of Iranian political sentiment. All respondents were asked what words they would use to describe the people of Iran. A composite description of an Iranian, as viewed by

Left Extremists, presents us with a poor, talented, intelligent, broad-minded, hospitable laborer. As perceived by Right Extremists, he is patriotic, brave, patient, faithful, chivalrous, intelligent, hospitable. Aside from the consensus on intelligence and hospitality, the Extremists are talking about two consistently different sorts of person. The differences recall our historical distinction between a traditional "courage culture" and a modernizing "ingenuity culture."

The main line of ideological cleavage ran along the axis of CLASS *versus* NATION symbolism. The nationalist Right, in the summer of 1951, was mainly preoccupied with expropriation of the AIOC, thereby putting the British in their place and restoring to Iran the glories of full national sovereignty. Their comments on this specific issue provide a profile of their posture. The greatest problem facing the nation is "the oil nationalization law," said one university teacher, and "to nationalize its oil, Iran will suffer death against any aggression."

The vocabulary of violent action against foreigners pervaded the solutions to this problem offered by the extremist Right. Some emphasized that the responsibility for such action rested with the government, which "should kick all foreigners from Iran," or "should oust the foreigners and cut their hands from Iran." Others stressed the need for popular action: "[We must] cut the English hands from Iran" and "get the pirates out of Iran." Still others invoked joint action by elite and mass—e.g., the government should "let all the people fight for oil nationalization."

Rightist attention was focused upon national aspiration and action, with no consideration of possible class deviations from the common goal. They simply assumed popular consensus behind the symbols of national will. One government employee sought direct action by the whole population: "All should be united and participate in demonstrations against the usurper oil company." Another civil servant, who considered himself a "holy warrior," said simply: "There is nothing above shedding blood for the nation, for which all Iranians are ready." He had no doubts about the universal readiness to struggle:

> All the people of Iran are of a single, united opinion. Fifteen million Iranians long for the day to sacrifice themselves for their country. The solution can be achieved merely by blood-letting.

This statement epitomizes the ideology of the Nationalistic Right. Expressed here is the supremacy of national goals, the mystique of national unity—an image of the big body politic in which no class-sentiment can compromise the universal desire to sacrifice oneself upon the altar of national aspiration. Furious indeed are these Right Extremists against all who permit personal or class desires to obstruct the course of national destiny. They call upon the government "to punish internal traitors"—for dissensus, in their eyes, can only be treason. And they would "hang all the country-sellers in one morning."

On the Rightist verdict, the trees of Iran would be well populated. For Leftist ideology, while enthusiastic about nationalization and expropriating the British, locates these items in a different battle order. On the Extreme Right, the goal is national sovereignty and the means is a unified national will; on the Extreme Left, the goal is a classless society and the instrument is class-struggle. Hence, even when the Extremists agree in identifying Iran's problems, they quickly diverge over appropriate solutions. The Left regarded nationalization of AIOC as but one step among several required to create a just society—and not necessarily the most important step. In discussing this issue, the Left quickly generalized its solution: "We should nationalize our industry, dividing the lands which rich people would turn over to the government."

The same divergence appears when Extremists discuss poverty, the other great commonly recognized problem. The Rightists perceive this as "the economic plight of Iran" and solve it by expropriating foreigners. The Leftists perceive it as "the suffering poor" due to class inequality and exploitation, and solve it with a class conception of Iranian society. "We should," they say:

"remove class discrimination by distributing the land among the peasants."

"give the right of every class to its own, so that the toilers would get their own, and the capitalists would not ask for more."

"take the idle money of the capitalists and exploit the mines in order to solve our problems."

From these different perspectives on such common problems as oil and poverty follow conflicting systems of loyalty, patterns of organization, courses of action. The Right seeks national unity in the struggle, to the point of bloodshed, directed primarily toward the expulsion of Britain. Says one Extremist physician: "I wish to see some day the British Isles completely overrun by water, and not an Englishman living on the earth." Says another Rightist, a civil servant: "If we could get the oil profits, we could solve all our problems."

The Leftists waste no affection on Britain, but they locate her on a different psychopolitical map of the world—not as personal enemy of all Iranians, but as political symbol of decadent imperialism: "Britain likes to have the whole world as her colonies; she has colonizing policies in Iran"; "She wants to perpetuate her colonizing policy in the world." The Leftists consider that colonialism maintains itself by alliance with the indigenous elite. Accordingly, they regard "national unity" against the British as a diversionary tactic (except, for the *Tudeh* Party, when this coincides with the requirements of Soviet foreign policy). Instead they urge a clean break with existing institutions, and advocate a struggle in which the blood that will be shed is Iranian blood.

Equally armed with their conflicting ideologies, equally equipped by temperament and training for public agitation, it remains for the Extremists on both sides to position their internal struggle with respect to the world bipolarity.

BIPOLARITY AND INTERNATIONAL COMMUNICATION

Most significant, for the general purpose of this study, is the manner in which international communication complicates or reinforces the bipolar postures inside Iran. One process is illustrated by a student, an articulate extremist of the Left, who dislikes certain Tehran newspapers because their editors "work for a group of parasites and are servants of obnoxious imperialism." He prefers to get his news from Radio Moscow which exposes "the ominous policies of stockholders, bankers, and brokers." These broadcasts reinforce the ideology of the Revolutionary Left: "It wakes the nation up, so we are not deceived by the pro-foreigners, parasites, and the subservient ruling class of Iran."

On the Right, the relationship between internal and external polarities is complicated by the special hostility toward Britain. Hence, the line of international communication from the West to the non-Communist population is less direct than that from Moscow to the Iranian Left. One government supervisor explains that he does not like BBC programs "because they emphasize the service which they believe they have rendered Iran, although in their 150 years of dominance they have done nothing except ruin the entire political, social, moral, and economic structure of the country."

An additional complication derives from the subtle differentiation in Rightest ideology between the beloved nation and the detested elite—between the abiding state and the current government. It is difficult to formulate this distinction clearly and persuasively, except in the name of some recognizable counter-elite formation. Thus, the Leftists can make clear, when they seek to subvert the ruling elite, that they propose to install their own governance in the form of the *Tudeh* Party or some other recognizable agency of revolution. The Right Extremists, on the other hand, oppose to the solid substance of the current elite mainly the incorporeal symbolism of the nation—its mission, primacy, unity. The Leftist advantage shows in their attitudes toward external communications.

Bipolarity and Extremism

Frequently respondents were unable to draw from their domestic political posture a definite choice between the bipolarized superpowers.* While
a substantial number of Leftists were not univocally pro-Russian, this was
more marked among Rightists who were not pro-American. But here an
extraordinarily interesting difference appeared: deviants from the American
side were mainly Right extremists; deviants from the Russian side were
mainly Left moderates.

This suggests a major modification of the conventional assumption that
pro-Americanism is Rightist and pro-Sovietism is Leftist. The more exact
formulation would be that pro-Sovietism goes with extremism, pro-Americanism with moderation. We shall examine the full implications of this
finding in [the epilogue] of this chapter. Here we present the data on which
it is based. The seven political types were regrouped according to the
intensity of their political convictions—respondents on the extreme Left
and Right combined as "extremists," middle Left and Right as "middle
range," Reform Left and Conservative Right as "moderates." These groups
were then cross-tabulated into the categories pro-Russian, pro-American,
Neutral. The distribution in Table 13 was obtained.

Table 13. BIPOLARITY BY POLITICAL INTENSITY

	Pro-Russian	Pro-American	Neutral
Extremists	40%	7%	4%
Middle Range	28	25	24
Moderates	28	66	55
Apoliticals	4	2	17
Totals	100% (28)	100% (94)	100% (75)

The pro-Russians are more likely to be Extremists, whereas two of every
three pro-Americans are Moderates. The more intense political involvement
of the pro-Russians goes with the fact that they are a younger, better-educated, more active group. Compared with the pro-Americans, 13% more
pro-Russians are under 30 years old, 23% more have had higher education,
and 8% more score higher on the index of social interaction.

By contrast, the pro-Americans are more numerous in the sample. Of
157 who expressed judgments on *both peoples*, 70% scored as pro-Americans
compared with 36% pro-Russians. On judgments of the *two governments*,
the margin was narrower but still substantial: of 110 respondents, 50% were
favorable to the U.S. government, only 29% to the Soviet government. (That

* This section is based on the 1952 BASR report "Partisanship and Communication Behavior in Iran" by B. B. Ringer.

the survey was American-sponsored, even though Iranians did all the interviewing, probably biased these results.)

But the most striking feature in the attitudinal map of Iranian bipolarity is the huge zone of nondifferentiation. Many Iranians assign equal-values to both poles. This finding emerged when the joint judgments of respondents on both American and Russian peoples and governments were crosstabulated in Table 14.

Table 14. THE ZONE OF NEUTRALIZATION (Equal Values)

Attitudes* Toward Americans	Attitudes* Toward Russians			
	Favorable	*Ambivalent*	*Indifferent*	*Unfavorable*
Favorable	3	15	2	23
Ambivalent	10	19	3	44
Indifferent	0	1	21	8
Unfavorable	10	5	2	35

* Respondents disapproving *neither* people nor governments are classified as favorable; those disapproving *both* are unfavorable; those disapproving *either but not both* are ambivalent; those expressing no judgment are indifferent.

We have given the actual numbers above, rather than percentages, for the persons in several of these categories may be regrouped with others to illustrate various points. For example, all 95 respondents (47% of sample) *above* the diagonal line were counted as pro-American on the view that each person in this position exhibits a less hostile view of the USA than of the USSR. On this view the 28 Iranians (14%) *below* the line are classed as pro-Russian; and the substantial 78 respondents (39%) *on* the diagonal are classed as Neutrals.

We note further that the process of equal-valuation does not lead to the theme "bless you all" but rather to "a plague on both houses." Only three respondents were equally favorable to both poles; over ten times as many were equally *unfavorable*. Moreover, hostility toward one pole does not imply a real preference for the other. Thus, 52 of the respondents unfavorable toward Russia are ambivalent (partially unfavorable) or merely indifferent toward America. If we consider these Iranians as effectively neutralized by the bipolarizing process, then the proportion of genuine Neutrals rises to 64% of the respondents—and this in a relatively dynamic and participant sample of the total Iranian population.

Why are they hostile toward Russia? Some see the cold war as a new name for the ancient geopolitical game: "Russia wants to lock us up behind the Iron Curtain. She wants to get to the Persian Gulf and develop her strategic position." Others still think of money rather than strategy: "Russia wants the whole world to become Communist. She has the same thought about Iran, besides she has some financial interests in Iran." Still others, recalling past cases where the Powers were quick to solve their differences over Iran by dividing the cake, see the current bipolarity as a new version of great-power conspiracy: "The Russians want to divide Iran between England and themselves."

Why are they hostile toward America? Here, be it noted, hostility is less widespread and more qualified—it is the U.S. policy, not the American nation, that draws fire. But the feeling is intense, and underpinned by a sense of deception. American performance has somehow not squared with Iranian expectations: "it has not fulfilled its promises"; "it has given many compliments [talked too much] but has not shown any effective action"; "she doesn't do what she says." Beyond this, America in a bipolar world has behaved just like every other Great Power—handling Iran as just another strategic pawn on her global chessboard. Thus: "America is thinking of its benefit all the time in any country. It wants to make Iran a military base, but it wasn't successful yet." Or, more generally: "America works for its own benefits. It pretends to be a friend of Iran, but its purpose is finding some influence in Iran."

The sense of deception became acute during the AIOC crisis: "Recently America has interfered against us and for the British in the oil dispute— that is why all the people dislike America." But its effects upon pro-American sentiment appear to be less profound than one might suppose. At the height of the crisis, the interviewees were asked: "Has your attitude changed any during the past year toward the U.S.?" Those who responded affirmatively were then asked: "Would you say you felt more or less favorable toward the U.S. today than you did a year ago? Why?" The same questions were asked regarding Russia, with results shown in Table 15.

Table 15. ATTITUDE CHANGES DURING OIL CRISIS

	Pro-Russians	Pro-Americans
More favorable to own side	68%	15%
Less favorable to own side	8	25
No change	24	60
	100% (25)	100% (70)

The most striking change was the proportion of pro-Russians who declared that they had become even more pro-Russian. Given the dialectical attitude of Communists toward public statements, the relatively low evaluation of objectivity among Iranians, and the difficulty anyone has in self-appraisal, this is a type of declaration that must be interpreted with considerable reserve. Even so, only one of four pro-Americans declared himself less favorable to America. Other evidence shows that American influence remained strong enough, through the crisis, to modify unfavorable attitudes toward the British. The reserve of good will which enabled pro-Americanism, though shaken, to survive even the oil crisis was formulated by one high school teacher:

> Americans in general are freedom-loving people and at the same time are prospered by conditions in their own country. Thus, their policies toward other countries, including Iran, are favorable. But I am worried that probably in a few cases they have joined Britain to take steps against foreign countries. This, however, is not proved to me yet.

The lesson of the oil crisis is significant for our study. Pro-Americanism did not founder, but it faltered and was slightly weakened. Pro-Sovietism, even with reserves made for purposeful mendacity, apparently gained a massive consolidation among its adherents. This was largely a communication process—for most Iranians had little direct knowledge of events, but judged the issue by "what they were told" through the mass media and through their informal networks of oral communication.

In these circumstances, it is important to understand why the bipolar allegiances of so many respondents were effectively neutralized. An important element is that the pro-Americans, while more numerous than the pro-Russians, are more Moderate. They take their political convictions more lightly, are more subject to the seizures of ambivalence, and are more likely to weaken in the presence of crisis. The pro-Russians, on the contrary, are Extremists whose personal involvement with their political ideology is very intense. In a crisis situation, they consolidate their gains. History, they feel, is on their side. And, sociologically, they are better equipped to act as the agents of a historical destiny. They are younger and better educated; they take a broader view of Iran's role in the world arena. Perhaps more important, they are more active among their fellows—giving and seeking advice, discussing the news. The pro-Russians, in short, have gained a superior position astride the Iranian communication networks, and this is likely to influence the future shape of Iranian society. Consider the facts.

The Bipolarization of Media Behavior

Each respondent was asked a set of questions about his radio-listening habits: (1) Did he listen at all? (2) How often? (3) By plan or at random? The answers are distributed in Table 16.

Table 16. RADIO-LISTENING BY BIPOLARITY[22]

	Pro-Russians	*Pro-Americans*	*Neutrals*
Radio listeners	93%	78%	56%
Daily listeners	87	79	29
Planned listeners	55	45	39

More pro-Russians listen at all; of the listeners more pro-Russians listen daily and more plan their listening.

What do they listen to? An important index is source: where messages come from, in the bipolar world, often determines their contents. Knowledge of international broadcasting indicates ideological sophistication—that is, awareness of the interplay of interests and ideologies in the world arena. The pro-Russians are way ahead in ability to identify international broadcasts that can be heard in Iran as shown in Table 17.

Table 17.   AWARENESS OF INTERNATIONAL BROADCASTS

	Pro-Russians	Pro-Americans	Neutrals
Russia	96%	55%	43%
England	88	61	40
India	84	71	40
Pakistan	76	46	35
United States	68	55	38
Arab Countries	24	15	11
France	16	7	5
Other	60	32	21
Don't know	4	25	54
Average per respondent	5.1	3.4	2.3

Many more pro-Russians know every major foreign station and all the minor stations grouped under "Other." Not only do more of them know Radio Moscow—but also BBC and VOA, broadcasts from India (voice of Asian Neutralism), from Pakistan (ally of MEDO), from Cairo (adversary of MEDO). Sophistication is not confined to a few pro-Russians but is spread uniformly among them. Whereas over half of the Neutrals and a fourth of the pro-Americans could identify no foreign stations, only one of 25 pro-Russians was so uninformed.

The pro-Russians match their extensive information with intensive partisanship. Asked which was their favorite foreign station, 83% named Radio Moscow and a few named India—that was all. By contrast, 71% of the low-intensity pro-Americans named India, while BBC and VOA were poor "also rans" for most of them. The non-differentiating Neutrals mainly preferred India, of course; while a few liked BBC and VOA, rather more liked Radio Moscow.

While the others listen apolitically and rather aimlessly, the pro-Russians put their superior knowledge of international broadcasting to the service of

their political bias. As in air warfare a priority mission is to knock out the
enemy's means of reprisal, so the pro-Russians have concentrated on "poison-
ing" rival sources of information in the war of the airwaves. Says one:
"The domestic radio is for a small portion of the people, but Moscow radio
is for everybody." Says another: "England broadcasts for propaganda
but the Russians want to acquaint Iranians with the world situation." Still
another says: "The United States broadcasts for propaganda purposes. But
the Russians," he adds with the privileged logic of the propagandist, *"only
for changing the people's ideas."* As with radio-listening, Table 18 shows,

Table 18. NEWSPAPER READING BY BIPOLARITY

	Pro-Russians	*Pro-Americans*	*Neutrals*
Reads newspaper at all	89%	78%	49%
Reads a paper daily	76	51	40
Reads three or more papers	78	48	44

so with newspaper reading. More pro-Russians read the newspapers at all.
Among those who do, more read their paper daily and they read more papers.
None reads only one paper and few read only two papers, whereas most of
the others are content with one or two papers. The pro-Russians also read
more types of news; they show more interest in *all* parts of the newspaper
and particularly political items (editorials, national and foreign news) as in
Table 19.

Table 19. PREFERRED PARTS OF NEWSPAPER

Most Interested in:	*Pro-Russians*	*Pro-Americans*	*Neutrals*
Foreign news	88%	73%	64%
Domestic news	88	84	85
Local news	12	10	9
Editorials	40	17	18
Culture	32	19	12
Other	56	51	45
Average per respondent	3.3	2.6	2.3

The centripetal tendency of media behavior that we have observed
throughout the Middle East is visible also in Iran. As the pro-Russians lead
in radio-listening and newspaper-reading, so Table 20 shows that they lead
in movie-going.

Table 20. MOVIE ATTENDANCE BY BIPOLARITY

Prefer films from:	Pro-Russians	Pro-Americans	Neutrals
America	35%	57%	58%
Russia	43	19	19
Britain	4	19	19
Don't know	4	19	19

This distribution is noteworthy. A practically universal result obtained by polling, in most of the movie-going world, is the substantial preference for American films. Even the Neutrals in the Iranian sample, whose other media preferences were as dispersed as their political ideas, give American films a solid majority vote. So, too, the hardly less diffuse pro-Americans. The preference for Soviet films expressed by the pro-Russians is a rare case. The political bias of this choice is obvious, but its full meaning is better understood in the context of general attitudes toward the movies.

The pro-Americans go to the movies "to relax," "to relax mentally," "for pleasure," "for pleasure and relaxation." This shows in the sorts of films they prefer: "love and dance movies"; "comedies, historical and technicolor movies"; "musical pictures with an interesting story"; "love, fighting and detective movies." Aesthetic and technical categories prevail among the reasons given for preferring American films: "the staging and acting," "clarity of lighting," "diversity of films and beautiful actresses," "skillful actors," "the technicolor." An unusually large number mention "the beautiful sceneries"—since, for inhabitants of the severe Iranian plateau, the sight of rolling country and greenery is a feast for the eyes. These clearly apolitical tastes sometimes become vigorously antipolitical. One pro-American moviegoer, who prefers "love and detective stories and sometimes sports," exploded: "I hate the political pictures. It is better to let the movies free from politics."

The context of movie-going is rather different among the pro-Russians. They go for "the real meaning of life," "moral purposes," "educational purposes," "scientific and ethical advantages." Those who go for pleasure do not "let themselves go" completely without a higher purpose: "to pass time and learn things," "for pleasure and to get their moral points," "to enjoy music and learn something." They prefer Russian movies, not for trivia of technique and aesthetic, but for reasons consonant with these high purposes. They have "more ethics than in any other country's productions"; they are "more realistic and more moralistic." There is little talk of "beautiful sceneries" here. The nuance is rather from the ethical to the ideological: "I go to the movies because they are the most powerful instruments to influence one's ideas." Good ideas should be shared and good ideologies propagated, hence Russian movies are best because they "teach lessons to

the masses of people." What do they teach? They "illustrate human struggle for peace and demonstrate equality for all mankind." No apolitical
nonsense here; art and life march forward together. A pro-Russian speaks
of his recent favorites:

> *The Real Man* was a masterpiece of perseverance, chivalry, self-
> sacrifice and all other good qualities which a real man should possess.
> In *The War of Stalingrad,* it was shown how the heroes of the Soviet
> Union cut the egoistic hands of Hitlerists. The result is this: that a
> nation with a strong theory and a doctrine of "the people" (everything
> for the people) shall never die. In that movie, we saw how Hitler was
> driven back to non-existence from behind the gates of Moscow.

Style and Stakes

Feelings about the media often exhibit very profoundly a person's general view of life, for the world is represented to him by the media—with the
greatest naturalism and impact by the movies. His responses often express
the interplay of reality and revery in his personal style. More than political
partisanship, as we understand it in the pluralist West, is implicated in the
divergent media tastes just reviewed.

There are important personality differences between those who regularly
shun political in favor of "lighter" films (which they admire for aesthetic
reasons) and others who regularly prefer "serious" films heavily freighted
with useful lessons of morality and ideology. The ones are using the media
as sublimational channels for vicarious experience of the lives of others.
This is what Aristotle called the cathartic function of art—a highly civilized
behavioral sequence. The others, meanwhile, are using the media as a
preparative rather than purgative—a more pragmatic behavioral sequence
akin to the war paint and dances by which certain tribes prepare warriors
for battle. These different modes of handling aesthetic experience produce
different results. The sublimational mode leads to contented quietism; the
inspirational mode elicits agitational activism.

When these divergent modes are regularly found among two distinct
groups of people, then we are dealing with a psychic gap of social consequence. Among groups which exhibit uniform sociological characteristics,
they spell class cleavage. When this is the most advanced class, such a split
elite tends to render the whole body politic schismatic. Wrapped in contrary ideologies and political organizations, the schismatic groups become
competing counter-elites. When affiliated to the rival poles of a bipolar
world arena, these competing elites tend to bipolarize the structure of internal politics as well. The strategic model of the two-player, zero-sum game
supplies the rules—no shifting coalitions, no mixed strategies, and winner
take all! Postwar Iran has moved in this sequence. Two extremist groups,
splitting away from their elite origins, have armed themselves with contrary

ideologies that instigate divergent behavioral styles leading to incompatible lifeways. Incorporating these ideologies into conflicting political movements, they have associated themselves with the rivalrous American and Russian poles of the bipolar world. Thereby they began to reshape Iran internally in the bipolar mold. But the internal bipolarization will not be completed until one of the players acquires the trump card—the Iranian mass.

The politically relevant segment of the masses is the big stake in the current phase of the game. Once it is clearly won by either side, the final coalitions will be fixed and the winner will take all. At the moment, the Moderates control the mass after surviving two major postwar crises over Azerbaijan and AIOC. Each of these was accompanied by a series of domestic crises—mass demonstrations in the streets, arrests and assassinations, interruption of parliamentary governance, flight of the Shah, overthrowing of governments. Recurrent crisis is a sign of sickness in any society; frequent and protracted crisis can be fatal. The Iranian elite survived its postwar crisis at a heavy cost, including alienation of potential recruits into both extremes of the political continuum. These counter-elites made important gains by effective manipulation of the personal insecurities which breed and multiply during public crises—manipulation accomplished through their influential positions in the national communication network.

Leftist success, in this phase of the struggle for mass support, is due to several factors:

1. They are *sociologically* better equipped for effective mass communication—that is, they are better educated, better informed, younger, and more active among those segments of the Iranian population that are ready to be politicized.

2. They are *psychologically* better equipped to incorporate propaganda successes in the recruitment and organization of a counter-elite—that is, whereas the Rightist ideology obliges people to judge issues one at a time, the Leftist ideology is a comprehensive way of life embodied in a Movement. Also, Leftist directives, cumulating in a "line" consistent with its own organizational growth, are administered by Extremists. The Rightists are restricted by the preponderance of Moderates on their side.

3. They are *politically* better equipped to exploit the limited margins of action permitted by the world bipolarity—that is, whereas ambivalence toward the West (Anglophobia plus apolitical pro-Americanism) among moderate Rightists weakens the bonds with their "natural pole" in the bipolar world and makes their public policy oscillate from one crisis to another, Leftist leadership, more homogeneous with respect to the Soviet center, maintains clear and consistent lines of communication between local operations and world communism in critical situations.

Under these conditions, new political energies tend to flow Leftward. The comprehensive ideology provides clear and simple solutions that attract restless souls; the monolithic organization channels their activity into a common program. Given the moderate character of the Rightist posture, extremist temperaments of variant persuasion find more outlets for vigorous action (oratory, assassination, mass demonstration, mob violence) on the Left.

The oil crisis was a case. While Right Extremists grew impatient with the moderate measures and compromise solutions sought by the governing group, the vigorous young propagandists on the Left were making their own nationalistic symbols resound and organizing the populace around themselves. The techniques of *shuluq* (commotion) and *tamasha* (show) were clearly paying off on the Left. Some Right Extremists, unable to restrain themselves, carried their colors into the rival camp and there made what seemed to be a common cause.

This *ad hoc* "united front" was finally routed (with a little Rightist *shuluq* led by Shaaban the Brainless) but the Left registered a significant gain. Not all the Rightists who had coalesced with the Left remained in the Leftist camp—but a substantial number doubtless did. More important, their defections deprived the Right of its own most vigorous and action-oriented elements. Rightist attrition while the Left consolidated meant that, in the next crisis, the extremist Left would be relatively and absolutely stronger. The symbol of this process was Dr. Mohammed Mossadegh.

THE MEANING OF MOSSADEGH

The political posture of Mossadegh derived from a combination of elements which, account taken of differences in their personal and national situations, we have described earlier as the "Nasser Syndrome." This difficult posture seeks to ride tandem on the two great currents of radical change surging through the Middle East—national independence and social democracy. The balance is delicate because the rider cannot control the velocity of the winds nor the height of the waves, but can only seek a steady course between these ungoverned elements. Mossadegh rode high to a fall; Nasser may do the same. Other riders will try the course after them. Each such player breaks the rules of the world political game by, more or less deliberately, overbidding his hand. This introduces a special type of chaos into the game.

Who was this aged Iranian that, for two long years, focused world attention upon his every word and deed? There is no mystery about the personality, for he gave ample public evidence of the self-dramatizing flair which identifies the propagandist-agitator type.[23] The fainting and weeping spells of "Mossy" were known throughout the newspaper-reading world, which was also permitted to share his active life in pajamas—his flight into hiding (before global cameras) from alleged assassins, his protest strikes against wicked adversaries at home and abroad.   The vanity associated with such exhibitionism was manifested by Mossadegh's celebration of his 69th birthday over five successive years; retirement from the Majlis being mandatory at 70 gave these demonstrations a simultaneous practical aspect.[24]

Mossadegh was prepared for his climactic years by the entire course of his career. Born in 1881 into the highest level of Iranian society, the world was his oyster. His father was a Minister of the Court, his maternal uncle a prince. After taking his diploma at the Ecole des Sciences Politiques in Paris, he was engaged at about age 17 in the Ministry of Finance, where he remained ten years. In good elite fashion, he then returned to Europe for advanced studies, first at the University of Liége in Belgium, then at the University of Neuchâtel in Switzerland.   Equipped with a Doctorate of Jurisprudence, he returned to a brilliant political career at home, climbing rapidly up the ladder of power:

1915–1917: Finance Committee, Third Majlis
1918–1919: Deputy Finance Minister, then Chief of General Accounts Department, then Minister of Justice (at 38)
   1920: Governor-General, Province of Fars
   1921: Minister of Finance (first year of Reza Shah regime)
   1922: Governor-General, Province of Azerbaijan
   1923: Minister of Foreign Affairs

From this height, at 42 head of Reza Shah's foreign ministry, Dr. Mossadegh suddenly toppled. During 1924–1928, as a simple member of the Majlis, he opposed the chief of state at every turn. According to one observer: "Dr. Mossadegh never supported anyone in the Majlis except himself and he never ceased to inveigh against foreign influence."[25] By 1928, Reza Shah had had enough. Mossadegh was imprisoned and finally banished from the capital to pastoral exile in Ahmadabad.[26]

The details of his fall from grace are obscure, for Iranian statesmen publish no memoirs.[27] But one root of the conflict was Mossadegh's opposition to the Shah's internationalizing-modernizing policies. Like many a young man before and since him, Mossadegh had returned from his European studies to a sense of shame about the dismal state of his homeland. (Recall the prominence of "shame" in the memoirs of both Naguib and Nasser.) His first book reformulated Muslim law according to the Shi'ite sect, using his advanced training in Western law for comparative purposes. Comparisons between Western and Iranian ways preoccupied much of his life; comparative studies of constitutional law, financial legislation, principles of finance came from his pen. He confronted the problem directly in *Iran and Capitulations,* and by a curious skirting maneuver in *The Principle of Non-Extradition for Political Crimes.*

Nationalism took on a xenophobic character when Mossadegh, throwing his fantasies in the face of facts, declared that Iran needed no financial assistance from abroad. He opposed American aid in any form and attacked, with equal bitterness, the Irano-Soviet commercial treaty. Mossadegh, some said, was one of the rare Iranians who had never asked a foreigner for a favor. This private and public style was destined for popularity. When Reza Shah was forced into exile, Mossadegh—remembered as the man who had dared to say "no" to the Shah—promptly resumed his political career. Elected deputy from Tehran in 1944, he soon sponsored a measure prohibiting further oil concessions to foil Russian designs against the subsoil of northern Iran. Six years later, he began his campaign against AIOC by drafting the nationalization law which precipitated the great oil crisis. This shook the world and split the Iranian ruling class that had nurtured him.

Dr. Mossadegh's deviation from the elite was primarily temperamental, not ideological. Rather Rightist than Leftist in his doctrines, he deviated by excessive zeal in seeking to activate these beliefs. The moderate ruling group sought to further the national interest by playing carefully with both poles of the world arena. The extremist Mossadegh would play with neither. Instead he aimed at driving them both from the native soil, though geopolitical destiny made this an all-but-impossible mission. Rebuffed by the practical men of his class, who gave higher priority to the effectiveness of their means than the sanctity of their ends, the agitational Dr. Mossadegh turned elsewhere for support. And with him, Iranian society took a turn.

For Dr. Mossadegh's illicit relationship with the Left restored the banned *Tudeh* Party to a position of public prominence, while splitting his own Rightist constituency at a vital point (by alienating the solid Moderates). This was a dangerous game in which, given the circumstances, Dr. Mossadegh could hardly win and the Leftists (whom he thought to use) could hardly lose. The ironic outcome was that this outraged product of the West nearly ceded Iran to the East, this extreme Nationalist made common cause that served the Communists. Never, according to informed consensus, was Iran pushed so close to the Iron Curtain.

The Mossadegh movement was stopped, but others will come to try again the hazardous course he designed. For the meaning of Mossadegh lies in the *style* of his politics. His daring effort to slip between the horns of bipolar dilemmas is bound to attract new impatient, extremist young men whose aspirations must find outlets in action. Mossadegh failed as a politician because his calculus of power was faulty—in a bipolar world one does not maximize gains by shouting "a plague on both your houses." Hence his place in history is likely to be small, for conventional history is not written in terms of political failure. But in any history of the mass media as an agency of social change in Iran, his place must be large. For Dr. Mossadegh, the political failure, was a magnificent success as a propagandist. He spoke with the weight of the ancient learned and mighty to the hearts of the newly aspiring. Hear the testimony of a minor government employee about the radio: "If there is Dr. Mossadegh . . . everybody will remain silent and listen. But there is no attention for others' speeches."

What Mossadegh did was to bring the mass media and their audiences into the arena of political conflict. Once there, they are a potential reserve of political activism which no future spokesman of extremist temperament is likely to overlook. The significance of this transformation in Iranian society—the initiation of the politically relevant mass into the bipolar game— was lost upon most reporters, caught up in the daily flow of events, but noted by one astute editorialist of *The New York Times*. Wrote Clifton Daniel, in an article headlined "Mossadegh Career Unique in Iran":

> Dr. Mossadegh was one of the first to discover that, after generations of illiteracy and political inertia, something like an informed public opinion is beginning to emerge in Iran, and he has made great use of it. It has been his custom, whenever he has any obstacle to surmount or new policy to propose, to speak to the people by radio and ask for their support.[28]

Small wonder that the first target in the *coup d'état* whereby General Zahedi overthrew Mossadegh, was Radio Tehran. "Without a microphone," said a learned Iranian observer, "Mossadegh was impotent." How, one may ask, in a land so inadequately equipped with mass media or mass audience, had Mossadegh applied so effectively the modern technique of governance through public opinion? What had changed in Iran by reason of the Mossadegh style?

EPILOGUE: THE FUTURE OF MEDIA AND MASS

In the spring of 1954, four years after the original survey, I returned to Iran with these questions in mind: What heritage of the Mossadegh method was still visible? How were his successors coping with this heritage? I interviewed leading Iranians at the Court, the Ministries, the Majlis; also, key Americans—the Ambassador, the head of Point Four, the chief of military mission, and specialists on their staffs. On the Mossadegh heritage these men, who had watched his operations from strategic observatories, were substantially agreed. On what to do about it, there was less clarity and less unanimity. I visited the modern media—radio stations, newspaper offices, cinemas. Also bazaars and teahouses—where messages are relayed into the mainstream of oral communication—in middle-sized towns and ancient villages. In a land where systematic social research is non-existent and statistics are treacherous, one sees what one can. I gained the impression that Iran today is balancing between two perspectives of governance. These were expressed in interviews with two responsible directors of Press and Propaganda—one before, the other after, Mossadegh.

General Farzanagan: "The People Need a Normal Quiet Life"

"What Mossadegh neglected to tell the people is that the world is larger than the city of Tehran. He encouraged people to believe they could decide issues that are beyond their real competence." So spoke General Farzanagan, director of Propaganda and Government Spokesman under Mossadegh's successor, General Zahedi. Intense, soft-spoken, obviously intelligent, Farzanagan is a modern type of military man. He received a complete civil education in the U.S.—from private schools through Harvard—and his two sons are now following the same course. No militarist or mandarin, Farzanagan prescribed social justice to cure social unrest. The Mossadegh technique, he said, was spurious: instead of solutions, he offered excitement. To unleash popular hatred of foreigners does not improve the well-being of Iranians and, deep down, people are aware of this. But the crowd enjoyed watching an Iranian leader who, instead of "negotiating endlessly" with foreigners, just "slapped them down."

"The Communists learned from Mossadegh, after having taught him, how to use these techniques of falsification, how to build true stones into a false mosaic. They raise constantly the same question: Is there social justice? Do people earn a fair living? Every one of us knows that the answer is 'No,' just as all of us know that the little peasant (*za'im*) really has no chance in the courts against his village-owner (*malik*). Over and over they ask: Is there not corruption in government? All of us know the answer to each question is 'Yes.' But do the questions go together? The falsity lies in stringing together true statements in a spurious syllogism, which leads to the false conclusion that Communism is the only and inevitable way out.

"These techniques have worked because there is a vacuum in the minds of the people, into which our enemy can pour what he wishes to be believed. The *Tudeh* preaches equality; Mossadegh preached nationalism. Both are fine ideals. What is false is that neither has any practice for his preachments. Meanwhile, by inciting people through hatred, they prepare them only for destruction and not construction. Under Mossadegh 'the sense of discipline was broken and irresponsible license was allowed to rule.' Of course our definition of 'the people' has to be different in this country: 17 of our 18 million people have not been involved in these excitements."

The mischief has been done among the other million, which is composed of three main groups. First, the intellectuals:

> In the poisoned atmosphere of our universities, people who should know better accept the Communist propaganda because it soothes some of their pains. This is to be expected when there are so few appropriate jobs for so many teachers, students, aspirants, and when those with jobs get such miserable wages. What would people in your university [M.I.T.] think of paying engineers $35 a month?

Second, the opportunists. "Their loyalties are for hire and they find ways to benefit from any disturbance. They helped Mossadegh and the *Tudeh* to create mass hysteria, which is not the same as an informed public opinion. The third and largest group were exploited by the first two—e.g., shopkeepers and artisans, unhappy with the way things are, and ready to believe what they are told and repeat it to others." These people have now recovered from the Mossadegh mischief. "The shopkeeper now tends his shop instead of spending his time orating in public."

The other 17 million are "nice, decent, kindly people who have been fooled too long by too many promises." The Mossadegh style of creating public clamor can be contained. What they need is deeds not words. "The people now must be *shown*, not simply told, the virtues of a normal quiet life."

"How are we going about this? Well, there is a National Orientation Committee whose mission is to tame people and to give them hope. Depolitizing the media is one technique: we now have a radio station broadcasting *only* music from 11 A.M. to 11 P.M. (an idea pretty popular in the States and very appreciated here). At the same time, we just signed a contract with the Varga firm in Sweden for delivery of radios, starting with 2,000 and gradually increasing to 5,000 per month, at one-third of their current price in Iran."

We left General Farzanagan wondering whether he could succeed in welding his two objectives—"to tame people" and "to give them hope"—into a single policy.

Professor Issa Sadiq: "Literacy Can Be Dangerous"

Professor Sadiq, now a member of the Senate, as Minister of Education under Reza Shah had created a department of Press and Propaganda in 1940–41. A thoughtful elder statesman, whose book *Modern Persia and Her Educational System* was published a quarter-century ago, he had long pondered the traditional structure of his society and its capacity for change. His evident interest in technical details, media relays, political relevance was located in a large context. The Iranian plateau, he pointed out, was an excellent receiving area for short-wave signals. The Russians used this condition to beam three powerful transmitters—from Moscow, Baku, and a secret place in South Caucasus—that are heard better in much of Iran than Radio Tehran. These are fully effective in jamming VOA and, somewhat less, BBC. Radio-listening, he continued, serves various purposes. Whereas Customs inspection estimated 350,000 receivers in Iran, Sadiq's independent estimate was closer to 500,000. Said he:

> Radios come in through other channels than Customs and often less
> as tax-evasion than as a military secret. I have never heard of a tribal
> chieftain without a radio. This is his surest means of always knowing
> the whereabouts of the Shah and the Chief of Staff, which at times is
> for him an important item of military intelligence.

His estimate of Mossadegh was qualified—an "expert publicist," certainly not a "great strategist." It seems difficult for Iranians to perceive, said Sadiq, that radio is not a national policy but one among several instruments of policy. The Zahedi government, being military men, are even less than Mossadegh used to thinking of "words and deeds as an ensemble." Mossadegh overvalued words; soldiers overvalue deeds. But since they are inevitably associated in daily life, "the political art consists in making them go together in the direction one has chosen."

Take the problem of illiteracy, said Sadiq. Teaching people to read and write is surely an admirable goal. But without a comprehensive social policy, literacy can be dangerous. My village (which Sadiq owns) became largely literate as the result of a school I created there years ago. But I left it at that. Result: Over 1,600 pamphlets in Persian, but printed in Russia, have been distributed by the *Tudeh* in my village. They have attacked every government in its turn, twisted the thinking of people without other sources of information, recruited supporters. How can they know that what is described to them as a great Peoples' Democracy is rather the blackest tyranny? How, having so little to lose themselves, shall they resist the idea that they could only gain by making others lose all? He who reads must run. "Without relation to earning a living, understanding the life of their society, and being prepared for citizenship, you see, literacy can be dangerous!"

Postscript

Returning from Iran by way of London, in May 1954, I consulted the files of letters from Iranian listeners in the BBC archives. One dated September 16, 1953, from a small town on the Persian Gulf, asked:

> Why is it that all the great capitalist countries, including Britain
> and the USA, are so afraid of the *Tudeh* Party and try to stop its growth
> with the most modern weapons? Is this party harmful to society?

This is a faithful Communist representation of the world, on the simple level of popular communication, and one may doubt that this writer is quite as naive as his questions are designed to suggest. But in scattered places around the vast Iranian area, people are asking similar questions, rhetorical in some measure, in these "loaded" formulae. And such spurious questions lead, as General Farzanagan pointed out, to a false choice.

For, in the curiously ahistorical process of social change now operating throughout the Middle East, psychic "participation" through opinion is spreading before genuine political and economic participation. People acquire a voice and even a vote before they acquire a "stake." They are stimulated to have opinions before achieving the lifeways historically regarded as requisite for people with opinions. This problem of timing underlies General Farzanagan's concern with the Communist techniques of deception and Professor Sadiq's caution that "literacy can be dangerous." Both are men of liberal stamp, but both confront a society still reeling from the impact of forces let loose by Dr. Mossadegh. Farzanagan wants social justice evolved within a "normal quiet life"; he wants "to tame people" while giving them hope. Sadiq, too, wants rising literacy but he has become wary of imbalanced social change—of spreading opinions without providing the context in which public opinion works efficiently.

The mark of Mossadegh is upon such men in Iran, as everywhere in the Middle East. How to develop a participant public without unleashing an unruly mob? Nasser has raised this problem in Egypt as have the extremist leaders in Syria and Jordan. A young Iranian professional man put it cogently: "There is no such thing as public opinion in Iran, there is only public emotion."[29] But public emotion has, since Mossadegh, been certified as an agency of social change.

NOTES

1. H. L. Hoskins, *The Middle East* (1954), p. 166.
2. G. Lenczowski, *Russia and the West in Iran, 1918–48* (1949).
3. Hoskins, *op. cit.*, p. 13.
4. *Ibid.*, p. 190.
5. H. F. Grady, "How The Iranian Crisis Began," *The New Leader* (April 27, 1953), pp. 3–4.
6. Hoskins, *op. cit.*, pp. 173–74.
7. *Ibid.*, p. 171.
8. A. K. S. Lambton, *Landlord and Peasant in Persia* (1953), p. 393.
9. *Ibid.*, p. 395.
10. J. A. Hobson, *Imperialism* (1954), p. 134. See pp. 206–22 for fuller analysis of the relationship between imperialism and dupery.

11. Czleslaw Milosz, *The Captive Mind* (1953).   Also review by D. Lerner in *American Sociological Review*, XIX (August 1954), pp. 488–89.

12. R. N. Frye (with L. V. Thomas), *The United States and Turkey and Iran* (1951), p. 209.

13. See: J. Morier, *The Adventures of Hajji Baba of Ispahan* (1949).

14. Hoskins, *op. cit.*, p. 175

15. Frye, *op. cit.*, pp. 183, 185.

16. Hoskins, *op. cit.*, p. 165.

17. As no census has ever been taken the following illustrates the range of authoritative estimates:

    14–16,000,000—*Statesman's Yearbook* (1955), p. 1289.

    15,000,000—R. N. Frye, *op. cit.*, p. 7.

    16,549,837—Overseas Economic Consultants, *Iran*, H.M.S.O. (1948), p. 49.

    17,750,000—Overseas Consultants, Inc., *Report on the Seven Year Development Plan* . . . (1949) II, p. 5.

    18,772,000—Europa Publications, Ltd., *The Middle East: 1953*, p. 249.

    19,139,563—estimate by Iranian Ministry of Interior in 1951, cited in *Statesman's Yearbook* (1955), p. 1289.

    19,798,000—U.N., *Population and Vital Statistics Reports* (January 1954) (official government estimate).

18. M. A. Djamalzadelh, "An Outline of the Social and Economic Structure of Iran," *International Labor Review*, LXIII (January 1951), p. 26.

19. On these demographic estimates, compare sources cited in Note 17.   A high figure of 2% net natural increase is given by L. P. Elwell-Sutton (personal letter).

20. U.N. Research Memorandum No. 11, p. 10.

21. Overseas Consultants, Inc., *op. cit.*, II, p. 82 and Exhibit B-17.

22. For small variations in the sample bases of Tables 16–20, see the BASR report by Ringer and Sills. (B. B. Ringer and D. L. Sills, "Political Extremists in Iran," *Public Opinion Quarterly*, 16, 1952–53.)

23. For clinical analysis of the personality type see H. D. Lasswell, *Psychopathology and Politics* (1930).   Also *Power and Personality* (1948) and *The Analysis of Political Behavior* (1948).

24. *The New York Times* (December 27, 1953).

25. M. Clarke, "New Iran Premier Foe of Foreigners," *The New York Times* (May 7, 1951), p. 11.

26. *Ibid.*, (May 7, 1951), p. 11.   Europa Publications, *op. cit.*, p. 405.

27. See R. N. Frye, *op. cit.*

28. C. Daniel, "Mossadegh Career Unique in Iran," *The New York Times* (March 1, 1953), IV, p. 5.

29. M. Panter-Downes, "Letter from Teheran," *The New Yorker* (April 21, 1956), p. 131.

The essential thesis of this paper is that the Middle East possesses a logical and coherent system of medicine—not a series of unrelated "superstitions" or "magical rites" practiced by "medicine men" or "witch doctors"—and the proper understanding and utilization of this system of medicine can allow for effective and economic positive interaction with the system of medicine of the West.

22

◇◇

The Interaction of the Middle Eastern and Western Systems of Medicine[1]

AILON SHILOH

The purpose of this paper is to explore the dynamics that can occur when the system of medicine of the Middle East interacts with the system of medicine of the West. The hypothesis to be considered is that, despite the apparent striking differences between the two medical systems, planned interaction can be positive in nature with only a limited area of possible culture conflict. This hypothesis will be considered first by analyzing the traditional system of medicine in the Middle East and then by structuring the interaction that can occur. Material from studies of interaction of other systems of medicine with that of the West will be utilized to amplify and support the hypothesis.

From *Social Science and Medicine*, pp. 235–248; reprinted by permission of Pergamon Press, Copyright 1968.

THE MIDDLE EAST SYSTEM OF MEDICINE

As has been detailed previously,[2] the essential philosophy underlying the system of medicine in the Middle East is that illnesses and injuries are subjective affairs arising out of commission (or omission) of certain personal acts or caused by someone or something possessed of a power. Illnesses or injuries do not simply happen—they befall a certain victim, at a given time, and in a definite manner through specific causal forces.

The two concepts necessary to apply this comprehensive medical philosophy are animism and animatism. In the Middle East the former is belief in the existence of evil spirits, and the latter is belief in the existence of the evil eye. These beliefs are basic to preventive and curative medicine in this area. An illness or injury is caused by a spirit that enters the body and creates difficulties or by a person or object with the power to influence the body negatively. Since this spirit or power causes the illness or injury, it is this spirit or power that must be exorcised or weakened. And it must constantly be placated, frightened away, or misled to prevent illness or injury. The spirit may be called "evil spirit," "jinn," "devil," or "Satan," or it may have a specific name like Lilith. The power to affect and influence the human body (and nature as well, in certain circumstances) is popularly attributed to individuals possessing the "evil eye," although specific objects may also have a power that can be used to attract or repel evil.

At this point we must distinguish between injuries affecting the "external body" and illnesses affecting the "internal body." The concepts of animism and animatism function in the former as well as in the latter but to a lesser degree. The emphasis in treatment of injuries to the external parts of the body is primarily upon remedying obvious, external, objective difficulties. Although the individual who falls from his rooftop or tree—or suffers a burn or scald in the home—may have been caused to suffer this affliction by an evil spirit or the evil eye, for example, the treatment of the afflicted limb or section of the body is prompt and based upon objective principles of bone setting, stopping blood, soothing flesh, and bandaging skin.

It is in dealing with illnesses of the inner body that beliefs in animism and animatism play their greatest role. Confronted by the mysterious unseen illness of the inner body, ignorance of an objective treatment and fears of the unknown encourage reliance on subjective beliefs in evil spirits and evil power.

This analysis may be carried a step further. In dealing with illnesses of the inner body, the primary emphasis is on prevention, whereas in accidents to the external body the primary emphasis is on treatment. It is realized very clearly and dispassionately that the techniques of curative medicine in illnesses of the inner body are not as successful as might be desired, whereas the results of preventive medicine are far more dramatic and fruitful. In dealing with illnesses of the inner body there is therefore a highly developed complex of permissible and taboo actions governing almost every moment in one's life.

Evil spirits, ready to pounce on the unsuspecting victim, abound in the environment. Strong, healthy, mature individuals are the least susceptible to such attacks; the most susceptible are infants and children, the weak, the ill, the aged, and normally healthy individuals under certain circumstances (women during menstruation, in pregnancy, or while giving birth). Evil spirits are always lurking ready to enter the body and, consequently, susceptible persons should never be left alone, lest solitude be interpreted by both patient and evil spirit as a sign of abandonment.

The presence of strong, healthy, mature individuals near the susceptible person is a strong deterrent to the evil spirit, but unfortunately such people cannot always be on duty. Therefore various inanimate objects possessing strong power to repel evil spirits are called into play. Common objects of this nature are images of the "hand of Fatimah" (beloved daughter of Muhammed), which may have inscribed on it holy words in Arabic or Hebrew and is generally worn around the neck (among Cochin Jews it may be found around the abdomen); of the "shield of David" (a six-pointed star and similar to the "hand of Fatimah" in function); blue beads, pieces of jewelry, or bits of cloth worn around the neck or attached to the clothing (blue is particularly repugnant to the evil spirits and the evil eye, and it is frequently used to paint around the doors and windows of a home or as the color of the dangling memento in the window of an automobile); a concoction of evil-smelling herbs placed in a bag and worn close to the body; or various religious phrases written on paper and sewn into the clothing or put into a bag and worn on the body.

A religious prayer or talisman tacked over the door is particularly efficacious in preventing evil spirits from entering a home. In the home where there is an infant, various additional measures are taken to protect the child from the evil spirits. Iron wards off the evil spirits, and therefore a mother may keep an iron knife or pair of scissors under the pillow of her baby. The Bible also possesses the power to repel the evil spirits, and thus some Jewish mothers place a copy of this book beneath the pillow. Another practice, less common, is to preserve the foreskin removed during the *brith millah* (the circumcision ceremony conducted for every Jewish male child when he is eight days old), dry it, powder it, sew it into a piece of cloth, and keep it under the pillow or among the blankets of the child's bed. A child's own foreskin is considered efficacious in repelling evil.

The evil spirits fear the name of Allah; it strikes terror into their hearts, weakens and forces them to withdraw, or repels them completely.

Consequently, people repeat his name constantly while engaging in the routines of life in the field or the kitchen and while eating, washing, or relaxing.

Otherwise healthy individuals must be particularly careful to invoke his name in susceptible circumstances. When a Muslim couple is about to engage in sexual intercourse the male must first say a prayer ("I seek refuge in Allah, from the accursed Satan, in the name of Allah, the Beneficent, the Merciful"). Otherwise, the evil spirit will enter the woman, and her child will be evil or even a devil, or she herself may fall ill. (A prayer to Allah also ensures conception—the mere physical act of intercourse is no guarantee.)

From the moment of conception until the last birth pang, the pregnant woman is especially susceptible to evil spirits. Each of her actions is carefully watched by them, and should she commit a transgression, omit a required performance, or fail to invoke the power of Allah constantly, retribution will follow as surely as night follows day. Through the actions of the pregnant woman, evil spirits may gain access to her body to cause abortion, difficult or fatal childbirth, or lasting detriment to the child.

During delivery a woman must constantly repeat "In the name of Allah," or the evil spirits will exchange her child for one of their own—a "changeling." (A changeling is not human, and therefore it is socially acceptable to let such a child die of neglect or malnutrition.)

The afterbirth contains a powerful protective force for the newborn child and must be saved. It may be left attached to the child for some hours or overnight, and it must then be preserved in or near the house. To cut off and dispose of the afterbirth immediately is callously to throw away a source of strength that the infant sorely needs.

Menstruating women are very dangerous because not only are they unclean but also they are, if not actually possessed by spirits, certainly facile transmitters of evil spirits. Accordingly, they must be separated from the healthy and, more important, from the susceptible (especially the ill and women in labor). As an extreme, a menstruating woman must leave home and live in a menstruation hut or tent for the entire period, returning only after she has been purified. (We might speculate on the salutary emotional, social, and physical effects of these monthly absences.) Or she may be permitted to remain at home subject to numerous restrictions. Among other things she must sleep on the floor or on a low bed, must have no sexual relations with her husband, must not even touch him or his bed, and should not prepare any meals or enter a home where there is an ill person or woman in labor. It is understood that this isolation or these restrictions function best within the society characterized by the extended family. The disintegration of the extended family forces abandonment of these practices, although not necessarily of the beliefs and fears of violating taboos.

The prevention of illness to the inner body caused by the evil eye, as distinct from the prevention of illness to the inner body caused by evil spirits, is based on the principle of misleading the evil eye, of deceiving it. The evil eye is a particularly feared thing, and more than half of all deaths are attributed to it. In contrast to the evil spirits, which are attracted to the ill, the weak, the aged, and children, the evil eye is attracted to the healthy, the beautiful, the happy, and children.

In the Middle East, possessors of the evil eye are most often women. I am unaware of any satisfactory explanation for this singular sex specialization. A clue to the theoretical foundation for research into this problem may be found in the writings of Sigmund Freud and Gèza Ròheim.[3] Freud wrote in 1919:

> Whoever possess something at once valuable and fragile is afraid of the envy of others, in that he projects on them the envy he would have felt in their place. A feeling like this betrays itself in a look even though it is not put into words; and when a man attracts the attention of others by noticeable, and particularly by unattractive attributes, they are ready to believe that his envy is rising to more than usual heights and that this intensity in it will convert it to effective action. What is feared is thus a secret intention of harming someone, and certain signs are taken to mean that such an intention is capable of becoming an act.

Ròhcim has amplified further the theory that the evil eye is really an envious eye, and it may not be incorrect to state that the entire corpus of preventive measures is based upon the principle of not attracting the attention of this envious or evil eye.

The young are a particular attraction to the evil eye, and thus children, who are esteemed as the greatest blessings, are kept dirty, ragged, and unkempt, particularly in public. The child may be addressed "Oh, dirty one," "Oh, evil one," and so on in order to disguise the true feelings of the parent. He may be given a false name and his true name kept secret, so that it cannot be overheard and used for negative purposes. The child is never praised in public or boasted about. On the contrary, he is constantly scolded and complained of. A boy may be dressed as a girl and referred to in the feminine, inasmuch as females have less status. All these practices are especially carefully followed if there have been previous infant deaths in the family or if there is only one child. To arouse disgust in the eye of the beholder is far healthier than to arouse admiration.

Praise, if given to anyone, must be met with denial or deprecation. Questions about personal or family health, business, or status should be answered with shaking heads and gloomy predictions. Boasting is considered a fool's way to court disaster, as is airing one's future plans. It is, however, possible to accept praise or note good looks, good health, or good fortune, if one is careful to invoke the name of Allah or deny the force of the evil eye.

Particularly valuable for defense against the evil eye are amulets. Blue beads are the most common type, and they may be found on one's person, in the house, or on a dog, horse, cart, or automobile.

These few examples should suffice to illustrate the workings of preventive medicine for illnesses of the inner body. If, by misfortune, evil spirits do gain access to the body or the evil eye does cast its dreadful influences so that illness or discomfort results, then curative medicine is brought to bear.

As indicated earlier, curative practices are recognized as ultimately less successful than preventive measures. Therefore, although the curative practices ostensibly assist in rejecting the evil spirit that has taken possession of the body or in ridding the body of the baleful influence of the evil eye, at a deeper level their purpose is to provide emotional comfort and security to the patient and his family. This function is clear in the techniques of the local practitioner at the patient's bedside.

First, he gives the family his undivided attention; he is there only in its interests, and he is clearly eager to listen to its members as long as they wish to speak.

Second, he identifies and names the disease—to do so is immediately to define it, circumscribe it, tame it, weaken it. The diagnosis provides the patient with a sense that the unknown pain has been mastered, and it influences the practitioner's choice of medical treatment.

Third, the practitioner then makes a positive prognosis—to pronounce a positive prognosis neutralizes or weakens the evil forces at work on the ill person and promotes and strengthens the assistance of strong or positive forces working on his behalf; the sick individual and his family know that only direct positive benefits can flow from such a pronouncement.

Fourth, he initiates certain measures to evict the evil spirits or draw away the evil eye. These measures include smoking, drinking, chanting, praying, burning, blood letting, emetics, purgatives, or massages. A burning blue rag may be snuffed and the smoke inhaled to weaken or frighten the evil spirits, especially during childbirth. Charms and holy phrases written on paper may be soaked in a liquid, which is then drunk in order to internalize the holy power. The spittle of a holy man may be applied to the disturbed organ of the body. The patient's name may be changed in order that the evil spirit may somehow be misled and lose the patient (or never find him in the first place). Drastic measures of a painful nature may be undertaken in order to force out the spirit. A red-hot nail may be pressed over and over against the abdomen of an infant to force out the evil causing dysentery; it may be pressed against other parts of the skin to evict the evil spirit causing smallpox or rheumatism, or it may be pressed against a "boil" under the tongue to enable the baby to take the breast. The entire family may be asked to chant special prayers, songs, or phrases. It may be called upon to fast or suffer other discomforts, the parents to abstain from sexual relations, or members of the family to make pilgrimages to a holy man, tomb, or town. The family may bargain with the spirit, sacrificing precious animals or objects to appease it. Vows of sacrifice, pilgrimage, servitude, deed, or dress may be sworn to Allah if only he will exert his power and save the patient.

Finally, the local practitioner leaves a token with the patient to serve as a tangible reminder of his visit and to symbolize the tremendous powers at work in defense of the patient.

The patient who is the recipient of this rich fund of strength is emotionally able to endure the physical discomfort of the prescribed course of treatment and is mentally prepared for possible death should the treatment not succeed. "Not succeeding" means not succeeding in the avowed purpose of ejecting the evil spirits or the evil eye. To succeed means literally to have ejected the evil eye or the spirit from the body. Should the patient die, it is because he or his family has, consciously or unconsciously, committed such offenses in attracting the evil eye or permitting evil spirits to enter the body that no power has been able to avert the evil or save the patient.

It is clear that both patient and practitioner operate within a cultural framework of knowledge, beliefs, and values that explain their respective actions. Within their terms of reference, the patient and his family search their thoughts and actions to ascertain how this misfortune could have occurred or by whom it could have been perpetrated; the practitioner formulates his diagnosis and treatment on the basis of their statements and the patient's complaint. Success in a certain number of these cases strengthens faith in the system. There are few cynics among the patients and few charlatans among the practitioners.

The type of medical practitioner called upon to render service depends primarily on the ailment and the sex of the patient. Within this medical system we may distinguish perhaps three or four types of local practitioners who specialize in areas and methods of treatment. These specialists vary in sex, role, status, and rewards.

The local practitioner who cures the external body possesses relatively little status and receives minimal material rewards. The treatment of scalds and burns and the setting of broken or fractured bones are frequently the tasks of the local barber or shepherd. By virtue of his experience with flocks of sheep and goats, the local shepherd has acquired extensive knowledge in this area of treatment. There is no particular status attached to this role; indeed, it is often regarded as one of the tasks of the local shepherd.

This kind of external treatment, as noted earlier, is based upon prompt application of objective remedies—stopping blood, setting bones, soothing flesh, and bandaging skin. The primary reward to the shepherd, both in his own eyes and those of the community, is the knowledge that "Allah knows what I did."

Gynecology, obstetrics, and pediatrics are under the authority of women who have first, ceased menstruation, and, second, acquired learning and experience on the subject and its problems. These female practitioners are responsible for the treatment of infertility, frigidity, conception, and abortion, for healthy pregnancies, successful births, and the initial years of infants' lives. In addition to concepts and practices based on animism and animatism, these women possess vast knowledge of the local pharmacopoeia and a shrewd grasp of the social and emotional factors in each case. The role of these women carries a unique status.[4]

The third type of specialist could be called a "pharmacologist." This person possesses an extensive knowledge and stock of lotions, potions, herbs, and drugs from plant, animal, and mineral sources considered efficacious in the treatment of assorted illnesses and injuries. The great majority of these remedies appear to be neutral or positive in effect. Few correspond to "Dreckopia" of Europe. All medical specialists possess knowledge of this subject, but the local population may have the size and resources to support a specialist in pharmacology.

The practitioner responsible for the preventive and curative medicine of the internal body has the highest status. He can secure the greatest immediate rewards in this world and the greatest potential rewards in the next world.

The medical specialist is generally a male of advanced years and of religious-medical standing. To perform his role he must be well versed in the concepts of animism and animatism. Such knowledge alone is not sufficient, however. He must also have a personality that inspires confidence so that he can elicit all relevant information from the patient and his family. In addition, he must understand the significance of a host of symptoms and complaints, some of which may not be described. He must possess sensitivity and intuition to a high degree, for many of his diagnoses will be based upon implicit understanding and tacit agreement. He must have the ability to analyze and to evaluate quickly the interrelations of his patient with his family and his community. Finally, he must have at his fingertips the knowledge of a vast store of diagnoses and treatments, any one of which he may need at any moment. In short, this medical specialist must be a model figure who radiates authority, prestige, and knowledge and possesses tappable resources of sympathy, identification, and assistance.

It is clear that very few persons are endowed with the abilities necessary to undertake this role or are able to acquire the vast knowledge necessary to fulfill it, particularly in a society in which the average life expectancy of the male does not exceed early adulthood. In addition, the intimate interrelationship of religion and medicine in this mysterious and dangerous problem—preventive and curative medicine to the internal body—tends to surround this role with an aura bordering on awe and even worship. As a result, the practitioner who specializes in preventive and curative medicine of the internal body possesses not only the highest status and prestige of all the medical specialists but also has elevated status within his community as a whole.

Finally, it must be noted that, although home care is the common procedure, there are also other treatment sites. Certain places are believed to be helpful in effecting successful cures of complex or chronic illnesses. Generally, these spots are believed to contain a positive power, which may be tapped through the correct procedure—entailing residence for purposes of prayer, sacrifice, or fulfillment of vows. These sites may be located where reputedly holy or powerful individuals have lived, visited, practiced, died, been buried, or made post-mortem appearances. They may boast unique or striking geographic features or other historical or cultural significance. They may be "general practitioners" effective with illness or difficulty or "specialists" primarily for specific ailments. The sites may be potent year-round or only during certain periods.

THE INTERACTION OF THE MIDDLE EASTERN AND WESTERN SYSTEMS OF MEDICINE

Despite the apparent striking differences between this system of medicine and that of the West, our hypothesis is that conflict in interaction between the two is neither natural nor inevitable. Given willingness among Western innovators to act rationally and appropriately, such interaction can be of a positive nature and the area of culture conflict quite limited.

Very frequently, those who have introduced Western medicine to other cultures have operated on the assumption that the success of their program depends upon destruction of the existing native program. They have dismissed some medical practices as "primitive customs," "superstitions," or "black magic rites" and the practitioners as "witch doctors" or "medicine men." They have launched frontal assaults on local medical practices and have unwittingly attacked medical systems that are intimately interwoven with the social structures, religions, and values of the local cultures. These Western practitioners have discovered, to their surprise and sorrow, that such assaults are expensive, time-consuming, and laden with potential failure and tragedy. Our hypothesis is that, at least in the Middle East, such assaults are also unnecessary.[5]

The interaction of Middle Eastern and Western medicine may even be so peaceful as to lead to blending of the two medical systems. The dynamics of interaction are dependent primarily upon the introducing agent, the Western figure.

First, there must be an awareness that in the Middle East, as in every culture of the world, there already exists a complex medical system of philosophy, concepts, and practices carried out by socially recognized medical practitioners in specific salubrious locations. Western-trained medical personnel must recognize that, when they attempt to introduce their medicine into another culture, they are not moving into a vacuum. On the contrary, all the entrenched knowledge and beliefs, values and personalities will be directly affected, and possibly threatened, by the new medicine. It is only logical, therefore, to predicate a degree of knowledge of the local system of medicine before, and not during or after, the intervention of Western medical practitioners and their programs.

Second, there must be searching analysis of the local medical system to locate areas of possible compatibility and conflict. A critical analysis of the Middle Eastern medical system suggests that blending can be achieved in both preventive and curative medicine for the external body and in curative medicine for the internal body.

As has been described previously, the system of medicine in the Middle East may be considered to possess a basic philosophy (Ph) expressed in concepts (C), which in turn give rise to a series of practices (Pr).

$$
Ph \quad \begin{cases} C & \begin{array}{l} Pr \\ Pr \\ Pr \\ Pr \end{array} \\ \\ C & \begin{array}{l} Pr \\ Pr \\ Pr \\ Pr \end{array} \end{cases}
$$

Whereas the practices are the most easily observed, they can easily be misinterpreted if the rationale of the whole system is not clearly grasped.

The system of medicine in the Middle East distinguishes between injuries affecting the external body (X) and illnesses affecting the internal body (N). The concepts of animism and animatism function far more importantly in treating the latter than the former.

The analysis should then be carried a step farther: In dealing with the internal body, the primary emphasis is on treatment, or curative medicine (c). Although there is preventive (p) and curative medicine for both the external and internal bodies, there is a distinct hierarchical ranking among the kinds of medicine:

It is not

$$
\begin{array}{cccc} \multicolumn{2}{c}{X} & \multicolumn{2}{c}{N} \\ p & c & p & c \end{array}
$$

but rather

> Np (internal body, preventive medicine)
> Nc (internal body, curative medicine)
> Xc (external body, curative medicine)
> Xp (external body, preventive medicine)

The highest importance is assigned to Np and the lowest to Xp.

For both the external and the internal bodies, the curative medicine in the West stands in marked contrast to the simplicity of that of the Middle East. The success of most Western surgery and pharmacy is generally obvious even to a suspicious Middle Easterner and, accordingly, given a rational approach on the part of the Western medical staff, he will voluntarily accept Western treatment of both internal and external ailments. Curative medicine for the internal body (Nc), which has a low status in the Middle Eastern system of medicine, may be particularly well accepted. This acceptance is often recognizable in numerous requests for injections and medications to cure ailments, for which the Western medical practitioner may not consider them medically justified. In fact, there may even be a very great demand for this type of service.

Preventive medicine for the external body (Xp)—that is, curbing the accident rate in the home and community—is an important but poorly developed area of medicine in both cultures. There is little scope and virtually no need for actual conflict.

The potentially serious problem arises in preventive medicine for the internal body (Np), and in this area the interaction of the two medical systems could be difficult, for in both the Middle East and the West they are rich and complex. The essential point, however, is that each medical system attacks different aspects of the problem.

Whereas Western medicine is very concerned with providing an accurate *diagnosis* of a complex of symptoms, based on the germ theory of disease, Middle Eastern medicine is essentially concerned with ascertaining the *cause* of a complex of symptoms, based on the concepts of the evil eye and evil spirits. Both cultures consider preventive medicine to the internal body important, both are equally concerned with the problem, but each attacks it from a different position.

The apparent locus of conflict can be eliminated by recognition that the two medical systems seek to prevent different phenomena, which are not necessarily mutually antagonistic. The Middle Eastern preoccupation with preventing the activities of the evil eye or the evil spirits is complemented by the Western preoccupation with preventing the activities of germs. A patient or practitioner anxious to maintain a given state of health sees, and should see, no necessary conflict in practices designed to prevent both evils.

There is little in the way of logic to prevent Western practitioners and

Middle Eastern patients from engaging in mutually beneficial health programs. The Western practitioner need not condemn or ban Middle Eastern practices designed to prevent the evil eye or evil spirits from operating on the body, and the Middle Eastern patient need experience no conflict in preventing another evil—germs—from entering the body. The essential reasoning is not too dissimilar.

Similar principles may operate in structuring the interaction between the Middle Eastern practitioners and their Western counterparts. The onus lies with the Western innovators. With rational behavior on their part, conflict can be avoided. Both systems of medicine contain, although in different quantities, elements of the natural and the supernatural, the rational and the irrational, the scientific and the pseudoscientific.[6] The reasoning here is that the principle of "integration" between the two medical systems is more logical and fruitful than is the principle of "displacement."

Such an interaction has already been structured[7] on a purely abstract level, and, although the idea has not been fully tested,[8] there is accumulating empirical evidence on a cross-cultural basis.

George Foster[9] has noted that, even though disease theories change very slowly, the pragmatic and essentially empirical attitude of many people enables them to alter rapidly or to accept certain medical practices or behavior. The striking impression that has emerged from recent studies of directed culture change is that people are practical to an unexpected degree. If they can see with their own eyes results they recognize as beneficial to them, then, regardless of whether or not they understand the reason and notwithstanding local tradition and belief, many people will supplement the old by accepting the new.

A most perceptive demonstration of this thesis was offered by Ozzie Simmons[10] in his analysis of popular and modern medicine of *mestizo* communities in coastal Peru and Chile. Dr. Simmons showed that, even though the people have tended to retain their own ideas about basic causes of disease, they have quite willingly accepted a number of Western curing techniques. After considering the local system of medicine, Simmons proposed that positive interactions between it and the Western system could best be achieved through gradual introduction of treatment of specific diseases, not by deliberate condemnation of traditional treatment.

Harold A. Gould[11] studied the medical behavior of peasant villagers in northern India to ascertain the degree of acceptance of Western medicine. He found, as did Simmons—and C. J. Erasmus[12] in Ecuador—that Western medicine was supplementing local medicine in quite definite selected patterns. The villagers went to the Western-based clinic for critical or incapacitating dysfunctions (appendicitis, burns), but they went to their village practitioner for such chronic, nonincapacitating dysfunctions as asthma, rheumatism, and headaches.

As one commentator on Erasmus' study has noted, "The villager is a pragmatist, not caring who is right but ready to use the method which seems to him to work, or to try both."[13]

Reports of medical behavior of the present-day Cherokee[14] and Navajo[15] Indians indicate that they also are making these practical accommodations.

A critical study of the cultural background of the Middle Eastern system of medicine, presently being prepared by this author, suggests that precisely such a process has been going on for a number of generations in the Middle East. Middle Easterners have pragmatically examined and rejected or accepted an integrated series of Western medical practices without necessarily understanding or accepting their rationale.

It is clear, of course, that studies are necessary to test the actual dynamics and patterning of this apparently one-sided conscious selective process (Rosenfeld,[16] Cameron,[17] and Pridan[18] have presented valuable material for such research) and that further investigations are necessary to document the validity of the reasoning presented here.

Even as research at these levels is being initiated, it is in order to suggest that Western-trained medical personnel acquaint themselves with indigenous systems of medicine; recognize that the interaction between these systems of medicine and that of the West must be reciprocal; and learn that the pragmatic reasoning of local populations can be used to influence positively the ensuing interaction.[19]

NOTES

1. Preliminary papers on this problem were read at the 57th annual meeting of the American Anthropological Association in November, 1958, and at a seminar on "Health and Illness in a Cross-cultural Perspective" at the Harvard School of Public Health in April, 1959. A Hebrew version of the paper was published in the Journal of the Israel Public Health Association, *Briut Hatsibor*, 1965, 8:60–69.

2. Ailon Shiloh: "Middle East Culture and Health," *Health Education Journal*, 1958, 16:232–243; "The System of Medicine in Middle East Culture," *The Middle East Journal*, 1961, 15:277–288.

3. Sigmund Freud: "The Uncanny," first published in *Imago*, Bd. V, 1919. Published in English in *Collected Papers* (London, 1950) 4:368–407; Gèza Ròheim: "The Evil Eye," *Yearbook of Psychoanalysis*, 1953, 9:283–291.

4. In this society with its traditional high death rate and low life expectancy rate, the individuals who live to an advanced age can be regarded with ambivalent feelings of envy and fear. It is felt that a person could have reached such an age only through collusion with evil spirits or possession of

the evil eye. To repudiate such beliefs, persons in this age category often attempt to achieve status and security through fulfilling educational, religious, or medical roles.

5. It is recognized that certain Middle Eastern medical practices may be considered unhygienic or dangerous, and that, from the Western medical point of view, there could be an undesirable time lag until they are called on to provide their medical services. The reasoning of this paper is that the potential gravity of such cases must be studied and dealt with on the individual and pragmatic level rather than by a massive and uncritical attack on the overall system.

6. Kingsley Davis, "Social Impediments to Health and Longevity," *Human Society* (New York, 1960), pp. 564–84; Talcott Parsons, "Social Structure and Dynamic Process: The Case of Modern Medical Practice," *The Social System* (New York, 1951), pp. 428–79.

7. Ailon Shiloh, "Conceptual Progress Toward Structuring the Universal Pattern of Medicine," *Health Education Journal*, 1963, 21:47–51.

8. Perhaps the single large-scale test of the planned integration of Western and traditional systems of medicine is that of mainland China. Although it is difficult to be clear on the details, it seems that an ambitious program has been embarked on whereby traditional Chinese medicine and Western medicine are deliberately being integrated. If the program has been correctly reported, then it may stand as a classic example of attempted cross-cultural medical systems' "integration" rather than "displacement." A concomitant of the hypothesis presented in this paper is that such a program is both theoretically and practically possible. It would be of definite value, accordingly, to consider the mechanics whereby China's integration is being planned and executed. T. F. Fox, "Medical Care in China Today," *American Journal of Public Health*, 1960, 50:28–35. Jane Phillips, "Red China: Integration of Western and Traditional Medicine," *Folk Healthways Newsletter*, pp. 8–11 (mimeographed report, no date). W. Penfield, "Oriental Renaissance in Education and Medicine," Ailon Shiloh, "Programming the Integration of Chinese Traditional and Modern Medicine," *The Health Education Journal*, 1967, 26:37–43.

9. George M. Foster, "Guidelines to Community Development Programs," *Public Health Reports*, 1955, 70:19–24.

10. Ozzie G. Simmons, "Popular and Modern Medicine in Mestizo Communities of Coastal Peru and Chile," *Journal of American Folklore*, 1955, 68:57–71.

11. Harold A. Gould, "The Implications of Technological Change for Folk and Scientific Medicine," *American Anthropologist*, 1957, 59:507–16.

12. Charles John Erasmus, "Changing Folk Beliefs and the Relativity of Empirical Knowledge," *Southwestern Journal of Anthropology*, 1952, 8:411–28.

13. Dorrian Apple, ed., *Sociological Studies of Health and Sickness: A Source Book for the Health Profession* (New York, 1960), pp. 7–8.

14. James Earl Somers, "Folk Medicine Meets Modern in an Isolated Mountain Community" (mimeographed report, no date).

15. Kurt W. Deuschle, "Cross-cultural Health Work Among the Navajo Indians," Part I: "Background and Medical Aspects" (mimeographed report, no date). Walsh McDermott *et al.*, "Introducing Modern Medicine in a Navajo Community," *Science*, 1960, 131:197–205, 280–7.

16. Henry Rosenfeld, "Tai'be: An Analysis of Its Patterns and Authority and an Investigation of Basic Health Conditions and Attitudes," *U.S. Operations Mission to Israel* (Tel Aviv, 1956).
17. Alick Cameron, "Folklore as a Problem Among Arab Refugees," *The Practitioner*, 1960, 185:347–53.
18. Daniel Pridan, "The Problem of Cultural Distances," *International Journal of Health Education*, 1962, 4:1–6.
19. The theoretical implications of this analysis as a test demonstration of my reasoning for a universal pattern of medicine (presented at the VIth International Congress of Anthropologists and Ethnologists, Paris, 1960, and published in the *Proceedings* of the Congress, as well as in *The Health Education Journal*, 1963) is developed more fully in my forthcoming work *Theory and Practice in Medical Anthropology*.

*Those Moroccan Jews who emigrated to Israel and were dispatched to
a newly established farming village in the Negev have been termed
by Weingrod the "reluctant pioneers." From 1957 until 1959 he studied
the people of this village utilizing the traditional anthropological
techniques of participant observation and key-informant intensive
interviewing. From 1959 to 1962 he was Director of Social Research
in the Jewish Agency Settlement Department and thus his data are an
excellent blend of village study and administrative perspective. The
following selection highlights, as few other studies have, the essential
two-way subtle process of culture change.*

23

<><><><><><><><><><><><><><><><><><><><><><><><><><><><><><><><><>

Reciprocal Change at Oren

ALEX WEINGROD

The dominant approach in the past few chapters has been chronological.
Before proceeding to the next phase in Oren's development, however, it will
be useful to draw some conclusions regarding one important dimension of
Oren's experience: the process and results of culture contact.

As we have seen, the settlers at Oren were predisposed to adopt new
behavioral patterns. Indeed, their new circumstances seemed to demand
changes in thought and action. A quick review of these circumstances—
immigration to Israel, settlement in a cooperative village, a farming career,
relationships with a different type of bureaucracy—indicates how truly different their conditions were and leads us to expect that the immigrants adopted
new forms of behavior.

This is the now familiar view of "culture change": we expect that immigrants, facing new conditions and in contact with a "receiving society," will adopt new techniques, wear new clothing, or enter into different social relations.[1] This conclusion seems commonplace, and it is supported by many studies of culture contact and change.[2] What is less well appreciated, however, is that culture contact may also provoke important changes within the receiving society. Not only were the immigrants themselves changed, immigration and settlement also generated changes within the veteran community. Both dimensions of the contact process—the reciprocal nature of culture contact—need to be analyzed and appreciated.

THE SETTLERS

Social change among the immigrants may be seen on a number of different levels. There have been changes in technology, in social relations, and in their political status. Although these are related developments, it is best to consider them separately.

The adoption by the settlers of farming materials and skills is a striking instance of change. There is a large gap indeed between peddling in a Moroccan market and raising tomatoes in a Negev village. While, as was earlier pointed out, not all of the settlers mastered the new skills, they all engaged in farming: seeds and fertilizers, irrigation and credits, cooperative marketing, and weeding were part of this new way of life. The villagers worked in the fields, using tools and techniques that were new and different from their previous experience. Although the farming role involved severe status conflicts and many became dissatisfied, all of the settlers used the same materials. The younger settlers might be more successful farmers and members of the kin groups have advantages, but the community as a whole was engaged in farming.

In addition to these specific farming skills, the settlers' contacts with Israeli society led to an expansion of their cultural inventory. They were prepared—and indeed eager—to accept technological innovations. For example, only the more affluent immigrants came to Israel with radios. Now each home boasted a radio. Many families purchased a gas plate, thereby replacing the older system of cooking on kerosene burners, and some also obtained a refrigerator and washing machine. One group of settlers purchased a tractor, and began to work their fields and the fields of others with the new machine. Most of those who had the financial resources made similar investments; they purchased mechanical equipment or household furnishings. It is important to recognize that the immigrants at Oren wanted what other Israelis had or wanted: they too wished to acquire a car or motor scooter, stylish clothing, and a better radio. Their desires included dairy cattle, a tractor, and other mechanized implements. They no longer took the old country for comparison, but rather looked to the new land for reference. The settlers did not compare their standard of living with Morocco so much as with Tel Aviv and Beersheba.

Obtaining accurate information regarding changes in diet and housing is made difficult by the lack of data on these conditions in Morocco. The settlers themselves related that their diet had not changed substantially: they continued to eat the same foods they ate in Morocco, though in different proportions. They now ate less meat and fish; these were not readily available, and meat was generally expensive. In Israel the villagers ate more *couscous* (a traditional doughy mixture) and more vegetables than previously, because they could not obtain other desired foods. As with farmers the world over, what was plentiful in the field was plentiful on the plate. Some women baked bread several times a week in earthen ovens built near the house; others raised vegetables familiar to their diet which were difficult to obtain in Israel. New foods, by and large, had not been adopted; for example, milk and cheese products, a basic part of the general Israeli diet, had not been widely accepted. The settlers' diet rather lacked variety and became more repetitive.

The village homes were different from the immigrants' former homes in Morocco. The concrete block houses, each of which included two rooms, were probably larger and airier than the dwellings most immigrants lived in in Morocco. The interior arrangements, however, did not easily permit the maintenance of the extended family. Households where parents lived with their married sons were therefore characterized by conflicts. In some cases this problem was partially solved by adding on a ramshackle frame room; the elder parents usually lived there, partly separated from the young couple. This arrangement was far from satisfactory, however, and the problem of joint residence remained a sore issue.

While village life led to the adoption of a new technology and to an expanded range of consumer goods, it had a constricting effect upon the settlers' style of life. The fact that the immigrants now lived in small rural villages had important consequences. It will be recalled that many settlers had previously migrated within Morocco itself; individuals and family groups left small towns and villages and moved to large urban centers. For these migrants, the urban traditions began to be influential, while village traditions became less binding. Many features of urban culture were desired and adopted: movies and the coffee house, the promenade, manufactured goods, and luxury items became part of the new culture complex. These things had important symbolic as well as intrinsic value: they represented the culture of the secular West and embodied a new, desired way of life.

It is ironic that in Israel this urbanizing group was settled in small, rural villages. The cycle of migration had been from Moroccan town or village to Moroccan city, and from there, once more, to village. The irony inheres in the fact that ruralization was based upon a model foreign to the settlers: the ideology of the veteran European pioneers. The founders of the *moshav* movement were city persons, urban intellectuals who self-consciously sought to transform themselves into a peasantry. The Moroccan immigrants were placed willy-nilly in their path: new city folk had been relocated into villages.

Ruralization resulted in a narrowing of the immigrants' forms of cultural expression. There were few opportunities for them to engage in the activities they had previously learned to value. There was no coffee house at Oren, no place for men to gather and chat. A movie arrived once a week, if at all, and the "theater" was a temporary building, barren of furnishings. There was no one to visit except the neighbors and "no place to go." The desires of urban life were present, but there were few opportunities for attaining them.

Turning next to social relations, there too one discovers extensive changes. In particular, a new system of social status grew dominant, and major changes also took place in primary group relations. How and why these changes occurred may best be seen in the context of Oren's brief history.

Immigration and settlement initiated two complementary processes: social leveling first took place, and new criteria of social differentiation then became effective. It will be recalled that, historically, wealth and ritual position were indices of social status in Morocco: privilege and power were associated with the rabbis and the rich. Age, too, was associated with deference and respect. At Oren, however, these criteria had little meaning. Few immigrants arrived with substantial resources, and those who had capital soon left the village. There was no eminent religious specialist within the group. Moreover, most of the immigrants were strangers, and consequently they had no easily available means of revealing their previous social status. At the same time, the settlement authorities themselves promoted a program of "equalization." The Department officials recognized none of the traditional social distinctions: each settler received the same-sized home, everyone was given the same tools and equipment, and all of the immigrants were expected to begin a new life of agricultural labor. An immigrant's previous position made little difference to the village instructors: old and young, the immigrant who had been an independent artisan as well as those who had been poor peddlars, all received equal treatment.

For a brief period, the old prestige symbols remained valid: the first village committee was dominated by older immigrants who had held higher status positions in Morocco. But these traditional symbols were soon brushed aside and replaced by different ones. Facility in Hebrew was the first new status mark. Soon, however, most of the immigrants gained some mastery of the new language. Two other bases of differentiation then grew in importance, and have remained major indices of social status: success in farming and a talent for leadership. Status was accorded to those settlers who successfully adapted to a life of physical labor, as well as those who were able to influence others and manage community affairs.

The emergence of these new prestige symbols resulted both from the demands of the situation and from the conscious efforts of the settlement authorities. The village instructors rewarded those farmers who showed promise: successful men were praised, they developed closer relations with the instructors, and they received greater financial rewards. In addition, those who prospered were admired, however grudgingly, by their fellow immigrants. The bewildering new life, with its strange ways and meanings, also opened avenues for settlers possessing ambition and talent for leadership. The more ambitious sought to gain the support of others. If they were moderate and cooperative, they also enjoyed the instructors' support. On the other hand, leadership might also be grasped by opposing the Department. This fluid situation often meant that the more aggressive settlers seized influential positions.

Social status was formally bestowed by membership on the village committee. When Sephardi and his followers resigned from the committee during Oren's first year, the new elections represented not only a change in leadership, but also validation of the new prestige symbols. The new committee members then elected were drawn from among the successful farmers and more aggressive leaders. These men were, moreover, younger persons: in contrast with the first committee, they were all between the ages of twenty-five and thirty-five, and several were even younger. The older settlers relinquished leadership posts and ambitions. The young, who were physically more able and who better understood the new world, have since dominated the committees.

The new *moshav* situation also affected relations within the family unit and between members of kinship groups. If, prior to immigration, the family was in the midst of a social crisis, then certainly these tensions grew in Israel. Better able to work and quicker to adopt the language and symbols of the new culture, youngsters challenged parental authority. Their enhanced prestige clashed with the traditional norms. The tragedies of immigrant generations were thus repeated: there were painful misunderstandings between father and son, mother and daughter, resulting in nagging tensions. There were also new problems of husband-wife relations, as some women demanded greater independence. The family unit thus experienced continuing tensions: this crisis was unresolved, and in fact became magnified under the immigration and *moshav* conditions.

Unlike the family unit, however, social bonds between kinsmen were often strengthened. The kinship group, a social form that had become disorganized in Morocco, reunited in Israel. In Morocco, migration and urbanization dispersed kinsmen throughout the land and generated social conditions in which kinship ties became lax. Israeli conditions changed this disintegrating trend: the kin group not only reconstituted itself, it also assumed new social functions.

Many new immigrants chose to live with kinsmen: in the new land, under unfamiliar conditions, they sought at least social familiarity. In many instances these were persons who had not previously lived together or who had been separated for many years. Oren, which had initially been a community of unrelated persons, soon became a village in which most persons had some kinsfolk in the community, and the two large kin groups composed nearly half the population.

This type of "chain migration" is a familiar feature of immigration.[3] More unusual, however, is the effect that the *moshav* system had upon the kinship bonds. Within the *moshav* community, kinsmen cooperated with one another: they lived along the same street, worked together in planting or harvesting, and sometimes made joint purchases. These activities forged new links between them. Even more important, kinship assumed a new political dimension; since political control of the village was advantageous, the kin groups became opposed units in the contest for power. The recurrent disputes intensified their interdependence, and these groups became increasingly solitary units. Thus, in effect, not only were kinship groups partially reconstituted, they adopted new social functions and became, in contrast to Moroccan life, more prominent social units.

This change had unanticipated consequences. One of the aims of the Department's directed change program was to build personal relationships upon criteria different from family ties. In a situation where kinship and power were so closely intertwined, however, family ties were decisive rather than relations based upon friendship or age. More universal types of social relations might have been nascent, but they could not prosper under the pressure of kinship obligations. The strengthening of kinship ties therefore restricted the growth of other types of social groups.

Thus far, changes in technology and social relations have been considered. Significant changes also took place in regard to the settlers' political status. Whereas, formerly, the immigrants were Jews in a Muslim-dominated society, in Israel they became members of the politically dominant Jewish majority. This shift brought a general feeling of security and satisfaction. "I never knew how to raise tomatoes," a settler once remarked. "I never worked in the sun. In Morocco I had a store, and we ate meat each day. But here I feel free. I'm no longer afraid." No matter how integral Jews were to the social system of old Morocco, and no matter how some sought and gained membership in the new Moroccan state, most Jews always lived in a shadow of fear. This was now gone: in their new circumstances they had a sense of security.

Not only did the settlers have a new sense of freedom, they also considered themselves to be participants: they were now Jews in a Jewish State, and consequently they were concerned with Israel's fate and felt themselves to be part of the state's future. The immigrants did not always fully understand national political developments, but they did identify with the state and its problems. Moreover, they developed new expectations regarding the state and the general society. Since the nation was Jewish, they expected its members to act "as Jews"—to behave toward them in a fashion that indicated warmth, sympathy, and assistance. These expectations, however, often led to conflict and disappointment, particularly in the settlers' relations with bureaucrats. For, instead of acting as "Jews," the officials tended to behave as "bureaucrats." Settler-bureaucrat ties were therefore usually tense and not infrequently explosive. In effect, the immigrants were drawn into the total society, but they also encountered some of its rigidities.

Immigration brought new symbols of social identity: if in Morocco the immigrant had been a "Jew," in Israel he became a "Moroccan." In the new society, ethnic origin was a fact of primary significance: every member of the society had an ethnic identity which distinguished him from others. An immigrant was recognized and known by this identity: for one to be Moroccan therefore made a difference. As was earlier pointed out, the Moroccan immigrants were strongly convinced that they were discriminated against because they were Moroccans. This identity was sometimes borne with shame, and it led to undertones of tension in social relations. On the other hand, their new identity made the immigrants part of an ethnic group and directed contacts to persons who were like themselves. For example, the immigrants often chose the company of fellow Moroccans; those who left Oren for a different *moshav* always chose another Moroccan community. All of the marriages contracted in Israel by members of the village were between Moroccans. "Being a Moroccan" thus bore overtones of communality and mutual sympathy: it distinguished the immigrants from others and drew them closer together.

These various levels of change indicate the scope of the revolution that transformed the settlers' lives. However, there were also many signs of cultural continuity. Although new farming methods had been successfully transferred, new cultural traditions were adopted more slowly. There are many examples of the gap between the settlers' way of life and the new Israeli traditions. Almost all of the male settlers spoke some Hebrew; they used the language, though they were not fully at ease with it. Most women, however, knew scarcely any Hebrew; this deficiency handicapped their contacts with other Israelis and limited their understanding of the new culture. Only three families received a daily Hebrew newspaper; the villagers were only vaguely aware of events in Israel and the world. While each home had a radio, the most popular programs were Arab-language broadcasts from the neighboring countries. None of the settlers felt themselves to be part of an Israeli movement or political party; these were largely unknown or considered with deep cynicism. Most holidays and family events (a birth or marriage) were celebrated in the traditional fashion rather than according to more secular Israeli traditions. As these examples suggest, while there were major technological and social changes, the immigrants' cultural traditions tended to persist. They undertook new acts with new equipment, but they did not yet adopt new ceremonies or different forms of thought.

Cultural continuity might also be seen in those areas where change appeared to be most marked—in the settlers' farm work. Some settlers, particularly the older ones, approached the farming tasks in a peddler-like fashion. The man who spread less than the required amount of fertilizer or who irrigated for shorter periods of time—all in an effort to save money—in effect approached the soil in a manner analogous to a peddler dealing with customers. He cheated the earth as a peddler might cheat a customer: he provided less than the required amount, since costs were thereby less, and who would know? One dealt with the soil as one dealt previously with clients and merchandise.

The private marketing practices indicated similar continuities. Most settlers, it will be recalled, cultivated small plots of vegetables which they marketed privately. Each Thursday they sold their produce in the weekly Beersheba market. This practice was strikingly reminiscent of peddling in Morocco. Many brought their sacks to town by wagon, thereby saving the cost of motor transportation; they left Oren late on Wednesday night, arrived in town before dawn, and arranged their wares in the vegetable market. There they rented a scale, and squatting behind their goods and calling out a price, sold their wares to the local Jewish and Bedouin customers. This practice was another instance of the continuation of the peddler tradition.

This type of response to changed circumstances extended to still other areas. The health clinic established near Oren was visited regularly by the settlers. Whenever the doctor arrived, long lines formed as persons waited for treatment. Vaccinations, medications, and hospitalization were familiar aspects of the treatment of disease. Yet, many settlers also availed themselves of the more traditional medical practitioners: the village rabbi and a local rabbi-healer. When a baby was ill he was brought to the clinic, but he wore an amulet around his neck. If a man had mysterious pains he consulted the doctor, but he was also likely to go to the local rabbi-healer, who found the cause and cure of disease in traditional cabalistic lore. Most persons said they were not superstitious and that the traditional techniques were old-fashioned. Yet these same people turned to the old practitioners for help and continued to understand disease in traditional terms. In this instance, the new techniques were readily accepted, but the older ones were maintained along with them.

While continuity in thought and tradition characterized the village as a whole, some settlers did adopt the new cultural patterns and took on Israeli traditions. This was particularly true of those young immigrants who underwent prolonged resocializing experiences in the army or other educational settings. These young men and women exhibited many signs of acculturation. The number of such cases at Oren was limited: two of the boys were in *aliyat noar* groups, and six served in the army. Yet the experience of this small group suggests a paradoxical conclusion: precisely those who changed most tended to leave the village. Four of the six who served in the army left, and only one of the two *aliyat noar* trainees remained. A youth who served in the army had difficulty readjusting to his family and village. To whatever degree he had taken on new attitudes and expectations, he was not well understood by his family and former friends: he had changed while the others had not. The returnee was not only under pressure at home, he also longingly recalled the life he experienced away from home. In the village he searched for others like himself, for friends who would understand him. If the returnee did not find support in the village, he was likely to leave; most often he went to the city, where he might find a more satisfying life. It was thus the least acculturated, the most traditional among the settlers, who remained in the village. Those persons whom the instructors and the Department considered most suitable candidates for leadership were therefore lost to the community. Paradoxically, success in the resocialization program did not necessarily lead to an acculturated village.

There are, of course, variations on this theme. Some returnees did accommodate themselves to the village. Back in the old familiar setting, among family and kin, they reverted to traditional norms of behavior. They lived between two cultural worlds: the old culture of their parents and family, and the new Israeli way of life. Within the village they moved between their parents' home and the home of the instructors. Generally speaking, they were ill at ease in both places: they might reject their home, but they were not fully accepted by the Israeli instructors. These young people were marginal persons, expressing all the classic tensions of marginality. Discontent and ill at ease, they became candidates for departure.

In summary, the settlers' Israeli experience surely resulted in far-ranging changes. The changes moved at different rates, however: a new technology was adopted, but older cultural traditions persisted. The settlers' patterns of social relations were altered, and their way of life shifted; yet they remained distinctively Moroccan. This identity seemed likely to persist for some time in the future. Further changes in social relations, or in consumer styles, might occur, but the settlers, living in a small, rural community, would probably retain their distinctively ethnic way of life.

THE VETERAN SOCIETY

Culture contact is a reciprocal process: all of the groups in contact may become changed. How then did the Moroccan immigrants influence the veterans?

Contact was selective, restrictive—only some of the members of the two groups interacted and then only in certain social contexts. The context of contact was the *moshav,* and although they established casual contacts with many persons, the settlers' most direct, abiding relations were with members of the Settlement Department. It was within these two spheres—the *moshav* and the settlement system—that reciprocal change can best be seen. The Oren experience illustrates how an immigrant group reshaped and induced changes within important institutions of a receiving society.

How did the Moroccan settlers respond to the *moshav?* This cooperative format was imposed upon them, *and yet they, in turn, reinterpreted the moshav system.* Reinterpretation—"the process by which old meanings are ascribed to new elements, or by which new values change the cultural significance of old forms"[4]—was well illustrated at Oren. Although the village instructors sought to cast the *moshav* ideals upon the settlers, quite the reverse process occurred: the settlers changed the *moshav* system to accord with their own ideals.

Different features of traditional *moshav* life were reinterpreted. For example, the villagers' translation of the *moshav* concept of equality differed significantly from the classic definition. For the founders of the *moshav,* equality meant equal opportunities—every member of the community was to receive the same chance. At Oren, however, equality was usually translated to mean equal shares and, in fact, tended to approach leveling. It was not so much that people were to have equal opportunities as that resources were to be divided into equal portions. To cite several instances of this ideal in practice, the settlers would insist upon an equal distribution of monthly loans regardless of the conditions of the crops. Their insistence upon equal distribution meant that the Settlement Department was often unable to fully implement its program of rewarding the more successful settlers: the villagers resisted programs that tended away from automatic, equal division. To take another example, when a teacher's helper was needed in the village nursery school, several teen-age girls submitted applications for the job. In order to appease the insistence on equality, pressure was exerted for a rotation system, in which each of the girls would work for several weeks (to the confusion of the children) and the remuneration would be equally divided.

A similar process of reinterpretation took place in regard to the *moshav* principle of cooperation. In theory, cooperation in the *moshav* was to be practiced among all of the village members. At Oren, however, cooperation did not join all men, but rather kinsmen. Each group of kin was a relatively closed unit, and mutual aid was restricted to the group itself. Primary group solidarity was dominant, and village-wide cooperation existed only on a formal level. The formal community cooperative structure was also changed. As was earlier pointed out, cooperative marketing only partially existed: the settlers did not have an ideology of cooperation, and they felt no twinge of conscience when they marketed their goods privately. Quite the opposite was in fact true: they looked forward to the weekly trip to market, where they sold their goods and made purchases in a traditional fashion. That this practice was considered illegal, or that it placed strain upon the *moshav* system, did not in any way deter the tendency toward individual marketing; the settlers continued to find private channels. Here again, the settlers' cultural ideals altered the *moshav* system.

Similar tendencies may be observed in relation to the traditional *moshav* antagonism to exploitation. There was no abhorrence of exploitation among the settlers at Oren: they had no ideological compunctions against hiring labor. On the contrary. Whenever possible, workers were hired to perform the more menial farm tasks. They were usually young boys or girls from a neighboring town who appeared each day in search of work. They were hired at low wage rates and assigned to pick or cultivate. Hiring labor had also become common practice in many older *moshavim*; yet in those communities it was not usually entered into so freely. (In the older villages, hired workers were usually paid a relatively high union salary.)

The settlers' values also led to a reorganization of the *moshav*'s political structure. In contrast with the original *moshavim*, the women at Oren never attended community meetings. There was, therefore, neither universal representation nor universal choice. The settlers' values in regard to male-female roles limited participation in community political life. Moreover, election and choice were not normally based upon universalistic criteria, but rather on particularistic affiliations. Voting tended to follow family lines: the settlers inevitably supported their kinsmen, and democracy in this instance meant that the largest bloc of kin dominated the political scene. It is not that merit and ability were not recognized, but rather that these qualities alone were insufficient and therefore had to be set within more familiar terms, the bonds of kinship. In place of open choice there were solidary factions, and instead of policy decision there were rival group jealousies.

Finally, the *moshav* stress upon independence was reinterpreted within Oren. The *moshav* way of life was designed to foster individual freedom: each member was to be independent, a man who thought and acted as a proud producer. Life at Oren, however, was intrinsically dependent, and the villagers' old sense of dependence became strengthened. Many awaited and indeed demanded outside guidance and decision; they were prepared to accept the exertions of others and even to demand more. This old cultural ideal was strengthened in the new situation, and the reinforcement in turn affected the entire settlement experiment. This far-reaching change sharply differentiated Oren and villages like it from the older, classic *moshavim*.

These examples indicate some of the areas in which reinterpretation took place. Set within the *moshav* organizational framework, required to function within a cooperative system, the settlers at Oren reacted to the new situation in terms of their own traditions. Oren was not a duplicate of the original *moshavim* upon which it was modeled. The settlers who were placed within a framework in order to be changed by it changed the framework instead. Oren resembled the classic *moshav* in plan and appearance but not in thought and deed.

Reinterpretation represented one type of change resulting from the contact situation—a change in the receiving society's social forms. There were additional dimensions to this reciprocal process. Culture contact led to organizational and behavioral changes within the Settlement Department bureaucracy. While this change was of a different order than the reinterpretation of the *moshav*, it too stemmed from the new conditions created by immigration and settlement.

Changes within the Settlement Department may be termed institutional adjustments. Institutional adjustment refers to the process by which members of formally organized groups consciously or unconsciously redefine their tasks and assume new roles in order to adjust to new social conditions. For example, contact conditions may result in new types of status and authority relations, as well as in new definitions and expressions of institutional tasks. Various forms of internal reorganization may also occur. This process is well illustrated in the Oren case: contact with immigrants led to redefinitions in the settlement system and thereby altered the status position and role behavior of the Department personnel.

Relations between the Department and its settler clients began changing with the advent of mass immigration. Historically, the Department's activity in directing settlement was restricted to loaning capital and extending expert agricultural advice to groups of pioneer farmers. The Department extended long-term capital loans, and the villages retained a large degree of autonomy in directing their own socioeconomic development. Department experts acted in an advisory capacity, but a village's investment program was primarily the settlers' own concern. At Oren, however, as well as in other immigrant villages, the Department's financial relationship with the settlers became completely reorganized. Rather than simply dispensing capital, the Department retained ownership and effective control over much of its capital investment. It no longer acted merely as a supply agency but planned and directed how its capital was to be used.

Loans or equipment were not granted to the settlers, but rather leased to them. Each individual settler was required to sign a contract to the effect that the equipment and installations he received were given on lease and that they remained the property of the Department. Settlement Department officials described this new relationship in the following terms:

> All the investments made by the Department in the villages are given for the utilization of the candidate for settlement (as licensee) until he reaches a position of consolidation and is ratified as a permanent settler in the village. The candidate will be entitled to utilize this property so long as permission has not been revoked by the Department. The status of the settler throughout his period of candidacy is that of a licensee, who is permitted to utilize Department property to cultivate and develop his farm in accordance with the plan determined by the Department.[5]

Thus, the horse and cart allotted by the Department was Department property; the settler might use the equipment, but he was not permitted to sell or exchange it. Were he to sell the horse he would be liable to prosecution in the courts. Similar contracts were entered into with regard to homes, farm buildings, agricultural equipment, and the like. (A settler who left the village was responsible for paying rent for the period during which he lived in the home allotted to him.) The "position of consolidation" described in the quoted passage refers to the period following completion of the investments planned by the Department: a village became "consolidated" when the villagers received the capital necessary for them to become self-sustaining. Neither Oren nor any of the other new *moshavim* in the Negev area had yet reached this stage. They continued to receive various forms of capital investment from the Department and were not yet responsible for repaying these loans.

This new type of contract completely changed the traditional Department-settler relationship. Whereas the village as a unit had formerly been the contracting agent, each individual settler now became directly responsible for the capital he received. The Department retained ownership over the capital; the villagers were licensees who might "utilize this property so long as permission has not been revoked by the Department." It is hardly surprising that the "owner" then became increasingly concerned with directing the efficient use of his capital: the settler "is permitted to utilize Department property to cultivate and develop his farm *in accordance with the plan determined by the Department.*" (Italics mine.) How each individual settler used the capital became the Department's main concern; each settler was required to follow the Settlement Department's instructions or face the threat of losing further support. As is apparent, no matter how benevolent its policies were, the Department increasingly assumed the position of landlord, and the settlers the position of tenants.

Why did this new relationship emerge? Until approximately 1952, the traditional Department-settler contract had been maintained: although instructors were attached to the new *moshavim* as management experts, in these villages the Department simply made allocations of funds and equipment to the community. Local village committees who received the capital directed its distribution. This program soon met with serious difficulties in the new villages. Since these communities were formed administratively, the settlers lacked any kind of ties to the *moshav* system and its ideology. It was therefore not uncommon for settlers to dispose of the materials allotted to them (by sale or trade), pocket the money, and later use it for private purposes. Department personnel found themselves in a position in which they were channeling large sums of money into the villages, only to have these sums rapidly vanish. Furthermore, the new villages could not carry the burden of debts incurred by individual settlers who borrowed large amounts and then could not, or would not, make repayment. Village debts often grew to astronomical sums without there being any real possibility of repayment. In order to guarantee its investment, the Department therefore adopted an individual contract-type program: since the village could not be responsible for its members, each individual settler would guarantee the capital leased to him. While the reasons for this shift may seem apparent, the implications were far-reaching: these contracts not only lent a formal, legalistic tone to villager-Department relations, they also redefined the relationship in a new and fundamentally different manner.

This new type of relationship was strengthened by the Department's policy of extending monthly loans. Since the settlers lacked funds for purchasing consumer goods, the Department lent the villagers small amounts each month. Collateral for the loans was the crops the settlers planted and tended. Once having extended these loans, the Department needed to devise procedures whereby it might protect its investment. Department workers were therefore concerned not only with how the settler maintained the original capital investment—homes, livestock, irrigation equipment, and the like—but also with each individual's daily work. A villager who farmed inefficiently or who marketed his produce privately was seen to be haphazardly or illegally utilizing the extended capital. In this fashion, the Department's range of interests and control became much wider: it saw its role as directing the settlers' daily work, thereby guaranteeing its agricultural investments. Crops growing in the settlers' fields were the Department's property: Department officials who inspected the rows of sugar beets or tomatoes were, in effect, inspecting crops that in large measure belonged to them. However reasonable they may seem, these policies only served to strengthen the landlord-tenant contract: the villagers became lessees, working the land and tending the crops.

These changes were further accompanied by shifts in status positions. Whereas high status had been traditionally accorded to the pioneer settlers, at Oren the officials rather than the farmers held the elite positions. There are various reasons for this change in status. For one thing, cultural differences between the groups lent the officials a higher position: Department workers were recognized and admired as models of the new and desirable Israeli way of life. Moreover, the Department personnel obviously had wide areas of direct authority. Village instructors or district executives were entrusted with making decisions that influenced the settlers' fate and future. The settlers' position also changed, since they had only limited means of influencing policy decisions. Groups of pioneer settlers had direct lines of communication to the highest levels of policy making. The immigrants, however, had no such contacts. They influenced plans by resistance and demonstrations, rather than by participating in the process of policy formation.

Another indication of change was the new kind of penalties employed by the settlement authorities. In disputes with pioneer-type settlers the Department normally coaxed, argued, and sought to convince the settlers of the validity of its programs. These efforts might be unsuccessful, and the villagers, who had other channels to authority, might proceed to develop their own plans and programs. At Oren, however, the Department brought severe economic pressure to bear upon uncooperative settlers. Those who did not follow Department crop programs were punished by not being granted full credits; uncooperative villagers often did not receive commodities that were generally distributed throughout the village. Those who acted in an illegal fashion were even prosecuted in court: the Department could bring suits against villagers who sold their produce privately and did not return loans granted to them, or who sold or otherwise disposed of capital goods distributed to them. Relations between the two groups thus assumed a formal, legalistic basis: while warm personal ties might develop between certain officials and the villagers, their contacts were framed within an increasingly formal system.

The mass settlement program initiated an entire new series of roles for Department personnel. "Village instructor" or "farm manager" were novel designations; an entirely new bureaucratic hierarchy was quickly developed. These were new positions, and their behavioral definitions were usually very imprecise. Village instructors were uncertain whether they were teachers or managers: should they be receptive to the villagers' demands or serve the Department's interests? Not only did ambiguity in role definition lead to uncertainty on the part of the Department personnel, but an instructor or District head was often thrust into a situation for which he was hardly prepared. Villagers sometimes turned to a young instructor and requested him to act as a judge in a family dispute. Agricultural instructors advised immigrants regarding their intimate personal problems, and farm managers began functioning as social workers. Thus it is fair to conclude that it was not only the immigrants who adopted new roles; the receiving personnel assumed equally novel roles.

What caused these changes to take place? Why did the Department reformulate its traditional policies, and why have the administrators and their clients adopted new roles? One interpretation might be to view these developments as stemming from internal bureaucratic forces: the tendency of the Department, in seeking to expand its scope of control, to reformulate and extend its usual policies. Such an interpretation would emphasize forces within the bureaucracy itself—a kind of Parkinson's Law—rather than the contact conditions. This interpretation is not, however, supported by an examination of Department relations with new, veteran settlements. That is, in its dealings with pioneer-type settlers—members of new *kibbutzim*, for example—the Department maintained its traditional relationships: although in recent years Department planners took a greater role in guiding these latter villages, higher status continued to be associated with the veteran settlers, and ties between administrators and clients were typically informal and highly personal. It would therefore appear that changes within the Department arose chiefly out of the new contact conditions. Faced with the problem of settling untrained, nonselected immigrants in cooperative farming villages, the Department adjusted its policies and entered into new types of relations. The new landlord role grew from the attempt to adapt to new social conditions —the attempt to settle Moroccan immigrants in a Negev *moshav*. Had the settlers at Oren been "pioneers," then the usual relations would have applied; but since they were "reluctant pioneers," their contacts with Department officials led to widespread changes in the normal policies and practices.

Changes similar to those described in this chapter took place within other veteran institutions. For example, the Jewish Agency Absorption Department and the Histadruth (the labor federation) also adopted new and different modes for dealing with their clients. In these and other cases the informal, personalized relationships were replaced by more rigid, bureaucratized procedures. As with the Department, new roles were adopted by administrators and officials of these groups. The processes of change that were described for the Department had therefore a general relevance throughout the veteran society as a whole.

What this analysis illustrates, then, is the reciprocal character of culture contact—the fact that different types of change derive from the contacts between diverse groups. It is important to emphasize that the types of change are different. The problem is not to see that while one group—in this case, the Moroccan settlers—adopted the veterans' technology, the veterans did not make similar adaptations. This is the familiar view, a view that concludes inevitably that culture change is a one-way process, since new materials do not flow equally in both directions. Rather, the advantage of the reciprocal view is precisely to see that contacts result in changes on different levels. For example, trait adoption is surely very different from institutional adjustment: the former is a type of change resulting from copying or modeling newly available forms, while the latter arises from decisions made due to new situations. Furthermore, institutional adjustment is a reversible kind of change: a group such as the Department may enter into different types of relations with its clients rather freely. Changes in primary group relations, on the other hand, are the products of much more complex historical factors and are not easily reversible. No matter how different these changes may be, however, they have in common the fact that they derive from the culture contact situation. Studying culture contact on different levels—viewing it as a reciprocal process—thus uncovers the varieties of change that contact provokes.

NOTES

1. This point is made repeatedly in the articles contained in W. D. Borrie, *The Cultural Absorption of Immigrants* (Paris, UNESCO, 1959).
2. "Culture contact" studies are legion. One sample of this kind is in E. Spicer, *Human Problems in Technological Change* (New York: Russell Sage Foundation, 1952).
3. C. A. Price, "Immigration and Group Settlement," in W. D. Borrie, *op. cit.*
4. M. Herskovits, *Cultural Anthropology* (New York: Knopf, 1955).
5. "The Agricultural Settlement Department," *Report of the 25th World Zionist Congress* (in Hebrew) (Jerusalem: Jewish Agency, 1955), p. 21.

Sea travel has been a common mode of population and culture transportation and communication dating back to perhaps the early Sumerian period. While the emphasis of movement has been across the landbridges and the "King's Highway," there exist archaeological and historical evidence indicating early, constant, and widespread sea utilization.

Unfortunately, there exist very few good studies of contemporary maritime utilization. As a descriptive report of one aspect of the contemporary maritime scene, and its problems of culture change, the study by Dr. Prins fills a critical need. Maritime culture is a major interest of Dr. Prins and the present material was derived from field studies in 1962 and 1963 on the coasts of Egypt, Syria and Lebanon, Greece and Turkey. Field methods included the participant-observer role, interviews, systematic observation, and the study of governmental records.

The present chapter is an edited version by Dr. Prins from his original publication.

24

◇◇

The Syrian Schooner: Problem Formulation in Maritime Culture Change

A. H. J. PRINS

This article aims to draw attention to the largely unexplored field of Arab maritime culture in the Levant, a field deserving to be explored for several reasons. One is because information on change in the eastern Mediterranean will be useful in a comparative study of the carrying trade in Arab schooners and Arab dhows, and, within that framework, on the problem of differential nautical modification. There is another reason, too. This sea is one of the few corners of the earth where sail was not driven out of the trades by the competition of steam and the changing conditions in the markets. If steam killed the big sailing ship, the oil engine prolonged the life of the

From *Human Organization,* 24 (1965), 32–42; reprinted by permission of the Society for Applied Anthropology.

small one.   Therefore, if the anthropologist (or, for that matter, the economist) wants to study maritime culture in the era of sail, and wants to do this on the spot, here is one of the few spots where he still can do it.   For the schooners there still is a lucrative trade worth competing for, mostly self-contained, but partly because they act as feeders to the great shipping lines.   This dual character of the trade must be mentioned, for it is not, as it was in Britain during the peak years of schooner trade (approximately from 1870 till 1920), in its very essence a small ship trade, where large quantities of some product lie awaiting collection at many obscure and inaccessible settlements on a shattered coast and where bulk cargoes are gathered at the heads of shallow creeks in countries deficient in road transport.   For the Persian Gulf this is largely true, but it is not in the Levant.

A third reason is, of course, that many studies on the terrestrial Middle East are available, but few on matters maritime.   This, then, is one small contribution toward remedying this deficiency.

The Levant is one of the two maritime provinces in the Middle East, the Indian Ocean shores forming another one.   It comprises four different shipping areas.   One is the Pontic or Black Sea coast of Turkey, characterized by a ship type called *taka*.   The next one is the Marmara area, north and south of Istanbul.   *Takas* are still to be seen here, but a heavier ship, called *tchektirmé* is more prevalent, with bluff, rounded bows and great sheer. South of the Dardanelles, in the Aegean area, a great variety of ships exists, mostly of Greek design.   Then, east of Rhodes, the Levant schooners begin to dominate.   This area includes South Turkey, Syria, Lebanon, Egypt (and Palestine until recently).   In this area, the Syrian schooner of *shakhtura* represents one sub-type, the Greek-Turkish schooner another one, the Egyptian schooner forming a variant of the *shakhtura*.   All sea-going ships in the Levant are, nowadays at least, fore-and-aft rigged.   They carry no square sails on yards.   The lateen rig is predominant elsewhere, around the Arabian peninsula and on the Nile.   Apart from the Persian Gulf, the Red Sea and southern Arabian waters (with extensions towards Zanzibar in one direction and Western India in another), which constitute the other major maritime province, mention should be made of the fluvial and lacustrian regions including the Caspian and the Nile, the lakes of Anatolia, Armenia and Galilee, as well as the Twin Rivers of Iraq.

I

As for the Syrian schooner, in her fully-rigged form she is a wooden fore-and-after, wide in the beam, with an overall length of up to 100 feet and of moderate draught.   Usually she has a full, flaring bow and concave, clipperlike stem, and (with two exceptions I know of) a transome stern, with the

sternpost outside. She measures from about 50 to 300 tons gross. Her rig
consists of two very long pole masts of about equal length, raking aft. For
correct rig description I follow the technical terminology (and sometimes the
exact wording) employed by Underhill,[2] although his description and interpretation are not based on direct observation. Both masts are supported by
four shrouds, a topmast backstay and a topgallant backstay per side. In
addition, the foremast has two running backstays to counteract the pull of the
headstays leading to the bowsprit. These lead from the hounds to well aft and
are set up with tackles to a point forward of where the shrouds of the mainmast come down. The single mainstay leads forward and is set up to the
deck midships aft of the foremast. There are no runners on the mainmast.
There is no further tophamper, and neither are there any spreaders aloft. All
standing rigging is wire, set up with dead-eyes and lanyards. The shrouds
carry wooden ratlines.

Formerly, gaff-rigged schooners, carrying gaff sails on both masts, could
be seen, along with the now normal jib-headed schooners carrying Bermuda
sails. With one or two exceptions, the Syrian schooners can therefore be said
to be two-masted, jib-headed staysail schooners, remarkable for their long,
raking bowsprits and their tall pole masts. The sails are very long at the
foot, the mainsail bent to a boom jutting far out over the stern. The main
staysail forward of the mainmast is also rigged to a boom, and so is the
schooner staysail forward of the foremast (or schooner mast). The foresail
abaft this mast is, however, loose-footed. There are three (sometimes four)
headsails rigged to a very long jib boom and bowsprit with a considerable
steeve.

The deck follows the beautiful sheer of the hull; only the foredeck is
raised. Of the small hatches, two are between the masts, one abaft the mainmast, and there is a penelled deckhouse farther aft. Steering gear is of the
screw-and-yoke type. There is no protection for the man at the wheel, except
for that provided by the planking of the bulwarks. To the casual observer,
it seems as if there might be a raised quarterdeck as well, but she is in fact
a flush-decker. The impression is caused by the turned wooden stanchions
supporting a rail, superimposed on the bulwark railcap and surrounding the
poop on three sides. The only other superstructures are the winch abaft the
foremast, working with pump-handle levers, and the gallows aft, supporting
the heavy boom. Finally there are the usual deck-fittings, such as belaying
pins, cleats, and so on.

II

Now, this beautiful schooner can be found nowhere today, for gone is the
fully-rigged ship, with one sole exception, as far as I know. Instead, there
is nowadays the modified schooner, either newly built to carry more goods

under reduced rig, or re-rigged and converted into a somewhat slower craft, also with a good carrying capacity and with a nice working rig. What exactly has changed and why? This is what I intended to find out, and although my answers are only partial, I will try to explain what can be observed.

My personal observation covers details on 22 schooners of the Syrian type and six or seven of the Turkish type. The first I studied in 1962, the second in 1963. My first, fleeting contact with Egyptian schooners was in 1948, before rig-reduction began. I will start with a summing-up of changes but before doing so I must say a few words about the way I suppose the schooner came into being. We can imagine a series of changes in which one line of development in the carrying trade runs: from earlier ships to fully-rigged schooners to trade with modified schooners.

III

The imputed original ship must have been a polacca brigantine with square rig on the foremast, if the multilinear evolution of sailing ships can be applied to the Levant—a hypothesis still to be proven.[3] Whether this brigantine had grown out of the brig, and how and when and why, falls outside the scope of this essay. Our interest is in the employing of schooners for seaborne traffic, and to embark on the genealogy of rig would indeed be looking for trouble.[4] However, one interesting question is whether the schooner might not have co-existed together with the brigantine (or even the brig), in which case she might even be a late and local evolution of a much earlier type of schooner under influence of the lateen rig, once widely employed in the Levant, although now almost gone—Egypt excepted. I raise this question because several details in the Syrian rig recall traits peculiar to American schooners. Also there is the rather curious but well-documented fact that the first two schooners introduced into the Mediterranean were built in the United States for the Dey of Algiers as far back as 1794,[5] and American cultural influence, particularly in Lebanon, goes well back into the nineteenth century.

The nature of the Mediterranean seems to me to be one factor which, when average speed began to count, caused the disappearance of the brig and also of the brigantine. For though these two are faster in a following wind, a schooner can beat to windward and keep up continuous speed better than any square-rigger. This is important in a sea with coastlines running in different directions. When quick despatch became imperative (as it did with perishable cargoes such as fresh fruit exported from the Levant), it was only natural that schooner rig was adopted, especially in the days when many small ports actually did offer small cargoes. On both sides of the Atlantic, it was in the seventies that the merchant schooners established themselves as economical and efficient vessels for all trades that offered small cargoes.[6]

When, in addition, steamer competition became heavier, certainly by

1890,[7] it must have been necessary to cut down running costs by cutting down rig. And here it must be considered how much cheaper fore-and-aft canvas is as compared with square sails, both in manpower and upkeep. Even if the wage factor is not of direct importance in a share economy (from the entrepreneurial point of view), the cost of victualling is less, and this is borne by the merchant. Since running rigging is much less in a schooner than in a brig or brigantine with the same sail area, this also must have been a factor in doing away with yards and square sails. Finally, greater overall speed must have enabled a vessel to make at least one more voyage each season, thus increasing the economy of running and probably converting loss into profit in many instances.

The fully rigged Syrian schooner as described thus does not seem to be much older than this century. The first mention of it by an authority on nautical matters dates back to 1911.[8] The only archaeological evidence I know of is at the Castle of Alanya (South Turkey), where a picture of a brig, a full-rigger and a gaff-schooner is scratched on a wall, but were they done simultaneously and if so, when? Positive earlier evidence must be available, but I have not yet found it. Many have been built since (and no doubt before) in Suez and Alexandria, in Ruad, and in many places in between and beyond.

I V

The picture of modification emerging from my observations is as follows. To begin with, the modern ships are bigger and have a greater carrying capacity obtained by widening the beam, and by making the hull more slabsided. The L–B ratio has thus diminished (3 to 8 in the one instance where I could measure). The hull often is still beautifully painted (white, yellow, reddish, green, blue, the colors always set off with white) and sometimes ornamented with scroll work, but dull grey hulls and lack of ornament also occur. Stanchions and rails on the quarter have gone in many cases. Hatches always kept as small as possible in wooden ships, are wider, sometimes two merging into one. The after hold is filled up by a diesel engine. More conspicuous is the introduction of a wheelhouse abaft the old deckhouse (and always much higher) to enable the helmsman to look forward. This wheelhouse encloses the steering-gear entirely. Since the wheelhouse (sometimes even amounting to a real bridge) is higher than the stern gallows, the latter lose their function of supporting the boom. In most cases, the gallows disappear, but sometimes are made higher or fitted on the wheelhouse roof. Forward of the deckhouse, but abaft the mainmast, a new, but lower, superstructure emerges, less conspicuous, but more vital to the newly styled ship. It contains the skylights for the engine room below. Protruding through its roofing a stovepipe exhaust juts out over either side of the ship. One or two funnels for the intake of air come through the deck abeam. Whalebacks on either side of the deck abeam the foremast shelter the companionway, and, still further forward a dolly winch has often replaced the old back-breaking winch of the "you-up-me-down" type. Occasionally there is a davit for the ship's boat, too. Finally, navigation lights at the required places, outlets for the cooling water of the engine, life belts, and fenders made of old tires should be mentioned.

There are many modifications in the schooner's rig, but, and this is interesting, they vary with individual ships. Ships, in whatever phase they are in a long process of change during their terms of life, always have personality. Two identical ships probably never existed, only ships of one type.

The process known as "cutting down rig," along with the installing of an auxiliary engine, has taken place without exception. But cutting down rig is a convenient blanket term only, and the same applies to "converting into an auxiliary." The latter process might best be expressed in terms of the horsepower of the various engines, but quantitative information is lacking. The process of re-rigging can more easily be described in terms of various relevant factors since these are open to inspection. In looking at present-day rigs, we see that some changes have been made in all ships, some in many ships and some only occasionally, as indicated in the following table.

Occasionally: a. schooner mast shortened, but mainmast removed (in six cases);

b. main boom and mainstay removed (where mainmast is still there);

c. schooner sail boom introduced;

d. runner forestay on mainmast introduced;

e. mainstay and mainstay sail removed;

f. boom on forestay sail removed.

Often: a. mast shortened considerably;

b. shrouds set up with bottle screws instead of deadeyes and lanyards;

c. jib boom removed, only bowsprit retained.

Almost always: a. masts shortened;

b. jib boom shortened and jib boom rigging reduced;

c. main boom shortened;

d. number of headstays reduced;

e. number of headsails reduced to two (in two cases to three);

f. area of both schooner sail and main sail reduced;

g. runner backstays on foremast removed (with one exception).

Some of these changes must go together. Change in one respect automatically causes another change. The simplest case is the removal of the mainmast which necessitates the removal of the corresponding shrouds, stays, booms and sails. Another one, which presupposes notions of efficiency and economy (which must hence be postulated for the culture as a whole) is the elimination of the runner backstays on the foremast after the foremast's headgear had been cut down. Similarly, shortening of the jib boom means that some of its intricate rigging becomes superfluous, although it can be retained if desired.

These are instances of what I believe to be explanations in the sense of Mill's inherent "active" principle being at work (here a nautical-mechanical one) and thus determining or causing. The explanatory principle, derived by reason, hence explains some of the observed changes. Other ways of explanation will be explored presently, but this requires some other independent, not inherent evidence. We must try to establish relations between observed facts (that is, changes), other than those of mechanical necessity, implication, or entailment, which form, in our opinion, meaningful connections.[9] This evidence concerns not the schooner but the schooner trade.

V

As far as schooner traffic is concerned, there is little doubt that Beirut is a climax area. Hence it is one of the best vantage points, even though it has very few (six, I believe) schooners of its own, and produces hardly any crews, the majority of seamen hailing from Ruad, a small island community of just over 3,000 people and a male working population of 900 or so. Of the total shipping movement in Beirut harbour, one quarter consists of schooners, although this represents only one percent of the total tonnage. Yet the schooners carry about ten percent of the export trade (against one and a half percent of the import), the lively beef and mutton trade not being counted. In Lattakieh, Syria, one other port on which I have information, comparable figures are 8 percent, 0.3 percent and 0.2 percent. Moreover, for every 100 schooners mooring in Beirut, only twenty trade with Lattakieh; and only ten trade with Tripoli which is the second port of Lebanon and has only one-tenth of the schooner movement of Beirut. Saida has even less, and Sur (Tyre) is, currently, a military area.

The Syrian schooners have the island of Ar-Ruad off the coast of Syria, or the mainland towns of Lattakieh, Tripoli, Beirut, Saida, Sur, Port Said, Damietta, and Alexandria as their home ports. They are manned by crews of four or five and carry general merchandise, timber, grain, vegetables, oil seed, fruit and cattle chiefly between ports in the Eastern Mediterranean. However, they also run as far as Constanza (in Rumania) and Jeddah, the

pilgrim port in the Hijaz. My estimate, based on various computations, is
that there are over one hundred Syrian schooners. About 15 are under
the Lebanese flag and about 70 under the Syrian; 25 or 30 fly Egyptian
colours. This is probably a conservative estimate, as it is based on evidence in the slack months. In fact, daily movement in Beirut fluctuates
between two (in winter) and five (in the peak month of summer). The
seasonal fluctuation in 1961 was very marked: November till May inclusive
were less than half as busy as the peak months of June and October (the Gaza
trade being exceptional, having an inverse season), but the months in between
were also marked by heavy traffic, all showing a movement of over 110.
January and February ranked lowest, with just over 40 sailing ships leaving
or entering. But the difference was less marked in some other years. Table
1 gives an impression of the traffic over the past ten years, showing a marked
increase in this type of business.

Table 1. SCHOONER MOVEMENT IN BEIRUT HARBOUR

Year	Number of Schooners	Tons Register (Net)	Average Tonnage per Schooner	Discharging (in 1,000 kg.)	Loading (Same)	Total Cargo Handled (Same)
1954	478	36,000	75	23	31	54
1955	534	38,000	72	28	33	61
1956	514	33,000	65	25	27	52
1957	769	49,000	63	35	41	76
1958	572	38,000	68	30	28	58
1959	792	52,000	66	53	25	58
1960	886	57,000	65	52	20	72
1961	1048	76,000	72	54	19	73
1962	1033	76,000	73	39	31	70
1963	1024	75,000	73	38	30	68

The table in this form hardly corroborates oral information as to the
increase in the size of schooners over recent years, unless the first two years
of the table are omitted. However, statistical information of seventy years
ago[10] is revealing. The average tonnage for Beirut was 30 tons in 1894 as
against 70 now. Sailing vessels calling at Saida, Sur and Tripoli were even
smaller, measuring less than 20 tons. However, the average tonnage of *all*
1894 sailing vessels (because of including big Dalmatian, Italian and Greek
vessels of several hundred tons) was appreciably higher than those under the
Ottoman flag, whose average size was between 19 and 29 tons. These Ottoman vessels probably included what would be Egyptian, Syrian or Lebanese
ones now. Incidentally, the number of schooners calling at Beirut was more

than twice as high then, but the total registered tonnage movement was about the same as compared with the last few years.

A first glance at the table suggests that the most profitable years for the schooners are over. Unless freights increase more in proportion to running costs, profits may well have become marginal, as the ratio between cargo and capacity fell from 1.5 (during 1954–1958) to 1 or 0.9 during more recent years. However, the port statistics do not include live animals under cargo, and the import of live cattle and beef for the meat market has risen rapidly over the past ten years. In 1963, more than 140,000 head were imported. But in the trade there is a marked difference between schooners under different flags, as is shown in Table 2.

Table 2. DIFFERENCES IN CARGO OVER 1963

Flag	Number of Schooners	Capacity in Tons (net)	General Cargo in Tons (inward and outward)	Animals per Head
Cypriot	14	408	145	–
Greek	58	1,679	920	–
Egyptian	152	17,189	19,173	4,105
Syrian	230	22,114	24,264	21,287
Lebanese	242	15,234	19,510	1,814
Turkish	328	19,091	3,819	115,700
	1024			

According to this table, the Syrians and Turks did most of the meat trade, whereas the Egyptians and Lebanese dealt mainly in general dry cargo. Each ton under Turkish flag transported six head of animals plus 200 kilograms of goods. For the Syrians, these figures were, respectively, one head and 1,000 kilograms, for the Lebanese, one eighth and 1200, and for the Egyptians one quarter and 1100 kilograms per ton. Not shown in this table is that the Turks found hardly any return cargo, and also that the Syrians went often more empty-handed than they arrived. The same holds true for the Egyptians, too. Only the Lebanese vessels showed something of a balance, taking away almost as much cargo as they brought. There are some fluctuations in the nationality of the schooners doing business in Beirut harbour, but there is not yet a marked trend of change. If we compare 1961 with 1963, years with similar totals, we get the differences in Table 3, counted in units in the harbour statistics, not in individual vessels.

This means roughly that in both years, of all Levant schooners, 60 percent were of the Syrian type, 40 percent of the Greek or Turkish type. This point must certainly be made, since it follows that we have here at least

Table 3. NUMBER OF SHIPS OF DIFFERENT NATIONALITY

	1961	*1963*
Syrians	316	230
Turks	260	328
Lebanese	212	242
Greeks	154	58
Egyptians	71	152
Cypriots	35	14

three, but maybe four, distinct types of vessels. This is confirmed by the fact that the average Greek vessel in 1961 measured about 30 tons, the Cypriot 40, the Lebanese and the Turkish both 60, but the Syrian and Egyptian 100 and 115 tons respectively. Subsuming this information in the form of Table 4, we get this picture.

Since then the Cypriote share has dwindled to insignificance and the Syrians have ceded place of precedence to the Turks (in numbers, not in cargo carried, although here too the gap has narrowed), Egyptians and Turks stepping in where Greeks and Syrians left. It should also be noted here that the Lebanese vessels show an increased tonnage, which has been confirmed by written information received since.

It is worthy of note that in Beirut two-thirds of all seaborne traffic with Cyprus and one-quarter of the trade with Turkey is by schooner. With the Gaza Strip it is a full hundred percent. Land communications with these countries (and with Egypt) are non-existent for all practical purposes. With

Table 4. AVERAGE CAPACITY OF SCHOONERS

Syrian schooners	under Egyptian flag—approx. 115 tons net
	under Syrian flag—approx. 100 tons net
	under Lebanese flag—approx. 60 tons net
Other Levant schooners	under Turkish flag—approx. 60 tons net
	under Cypriote flag—approx. 40 tons net
	under Greek flag—approx. 30 tons net

Syria, most traffic is overland, and the same applies to Lebanon itself. Even so, in the seaborne traffic with Syrian ports schooners play only a minor role (ten percent); but with Tripoli fifty percent of the maritime trade is carried on by schooners.

It is also interesting to see which ports are connected by the schooner trade, taking Beirut as a focal point.

Table 5 shows clearly the overall feature of Beirut as doing importing business in the main, although to a number of places export (often after transit) is more important. It also shows Port Said, Mersin, Iskenderun, Famagusta and Gaza to be by far the most important schooner ports at present (if Beirut is a proper measure for gauging, which I believe it is). Alexandria and Lattakieh come next. The importance of the other ports cannot be judged in this way. If this did not already follow from the rules of logic, it is clear from the empirical knowledge I have of Rhodos, Alanya, Antalya, Istanbul and Izmir and some of the minor Turkish ports.

Table 5. SCHOONER TRADE BETWEEN BEIRUT
(*Including Saida and Sur*) AND OTHER PORTS IN THE LEVANT (1961)

Port	Goods Exported to (*in 1000 kgs.*)	Goods Imported from (*in 1000 kgs.*)	Total (*same*)
Alexandria	1,657	–	1,657
Anamur	–	477	477
Antalya	–	355	355
Benghazi	12	–	12
Constanza	–	402	402
Damiette	–	421	421
Jeddah	8	–	8
Famagusta	6,350	4,136	10,486
Gaza	5,754	3,503	9,257
Iskenderun	228	12,826	13,054
Istanbul	–	360	360
Izmir	66	100	166
Larnaca	346	25	371
Lattakieh	833	211	1,044
Limassol	254	1,689	1,943
Mersin	247	13,849	14,096
Paphos	80	–	80
Pt. Said	4,131	13,686	18,517
Pt. Sudan	20	–	20
Rhodos	4	–	4
Tripoli	–	292	292
Yanbu	–	100	100

What is not shown in the table is the fact that Mersin is even more important as an export place for cattle, cattle not being measured in this table. Lebanon imports over 10,000 head each month from Turkey in the summer, against a few hundred in winter. Mersin then should rank highest with Beirut itself, and, possibly, with Alexandria.

VI

So far, observation has provided us with a certain amount of knowledge with respect to the state of affairs in the schooner trade, specifically to changes in the Syrian schooner trade over the past twenty years.   Explanation pre-supposes a problem, here of events occurring in some context of time and space, and it must show that the observed conjunction is in conformity with some order or law.[11]

We will first proceed by way of analogy and diagnosis and see whether the observed regularities of change are in accordance with a known order of things in shipping development.   We will see how fully things can be explained thus deductively, and how fully new and unexpected things cannot be explained that way, in which case we have to turn to induction based on analysis.   The explanation is meant to be non-historical.   Although I am pretty sure that the first modified schooners did not sail before 1948, I do not propose to try to find dates or historical sequences.   I only want to show that observed changes are thereby right, as Nadel put it.

We will first turn to hulls.   There is sufficient evidence elsewhere to war-rant the formulation of a law that clippers (that is, sharp ships, developing high speed and with restricted cargo capacity) must carry valuable goods paying high freights, assuming that they have to be operated economically. The same "law" can be stated inversely.   It says that packets, developing low speed, but with a good capacity, can only go with goods paying low freights. It can be said that the Levantine schooner, when she became slow, had to become wider.   Before her rig was cut down, she certainly must have made twelve to fifteen knots, whereas she only makes six now, six under sail alone, that is, and also six under power alone, but never more than eight or nine when both are combined.   Wider she is too, for her length-beam ratio is lower than in many schooners of similar size where values of 4.1, 4.2, and 4.3 are found.[12]   It is clear that a ship in a low freight market has to carry as big a cargo as she can, within the limits set by the quantities offered, the power available for propulsion (including the sail area), the number of crew required, safety margins, and accessibility of ports.   For low freights mean either economizing on the ship's expenses, which cannot be reduced beyond a certain minimum, or utilizing all available capacity within the technical possibilities inherent in the type.   Hull design emphasizes capacity at the expense of fine lines, but not at the expense of upkeep, for supervision is much stricter than before, especially in Egypt.   The change of hull form began prior to the conversion of the schooner into an auxiliary, for already the days of great haste were over.   The pre-war schooner already certainly was a schooner-rigged packet, whereas she must have started as a schooner-rigged clipper, as the clipper bow suggests.   Hence the somewhat incongruous appearance of the present-day schooner with rather full midship sections (some being almost slabsided) and with clipper bows. Explanation thus follows a chain pattern: Properties of trade (1) lead to specifications of the shipowners (2) and these to ship design (3). Changes in (3) are the results of changes in (1), or in other words, *the schooner trade conditions the design of the schooner.*

Similarly, regarding the last phase of the sailing ship in Britain, Greenhill remarks that the schooners decayed as their trades decayed.[13] But to return to the Levant.

The schooner as such is made for easy handling with relatively few men, thus showing a slightly better profit, by nature of her rig, than her postulated predecessors of the same burden. The auxiliary schooner must be considered as a more expensive ship. Even if the notion that the wind is free is very misleading, yet the installation of an engine entails costs. I believe that the installation of the engine necessarily meant that the schooners had to become still beamier (if post-war built) because of the loss of economical space taken up by engine and bunkers. Hence hulls can be explained deductively, but rigging, as we will see presently, through induction.

The introduction of the wheelhouse can be explained both by postulating an increased awareness of lack of safety at sea (people probably no longer accepting risk as easily as before) and by the technological necessity of housing engine controls as well as steering gear. Navigation lights, life belts, etc., have become necessary because of government regulations, just as nowadays a schooner skipper needs a master's certificate issued by the harbour master, and the vessel a registration number and her name painted on her quarter.

Other changes—such as the general practice of widening the hatches, the occasional substitution of the dolly winch (sometimes with power from the engine) for the "Armstrong Patent" windlass, or the exceptional introduction of a derrick boom (two instances were witnessed)—have always been explained in terms of efficiency, that is, the speeding up of handling cargo in addition to saving labour. This suggests the presence of such a theme in the culture, but I see no difficulty here. The explanation is provided by the "law" established on evidence from elsewhere, and I feel that it is adequate and not merely hypothetical.

The substitution of chain and wire for rope in the rigging, the deadeyes and lanyards often being replaced by bottle screws, can again be explained simply because they are lighter and last longer.

VII

The nature of the cargo, then, is one of the primary factors of change. Which cargoes formerly required high speed? First of all, the vessels of long ago were fruit carriers, bringing fresh fruit (citrus, grapes, figs and olives) to other ports in the Ottoman Empire, to Greece, and even to the Adriatic Sea. Vegetables were carried as far west as Malta. Quick dispatch was not so important for onions, oil seed, grain, or for live animals on the short run to Egypt.

All these were articles of export from Lebanon ports. Return cargoes did not, at the time (the 1890's), require speed. They included timber from the Adriatic and southern Turkey and building materials from various Mediterranean ports, as well as general merchandise. Presumably, ships were frequently ballasted, but this practice is obsolete, for the engines provide the necessary weight. As we have seen, Lebanon is now chiefly a country of import (implying transit for Syria and Jordan), and the schooners carry from Egypt (as they did before their conversion) onions, potatoes, and non-perishable vegetables; timber, as always from Turkey (but now also from Rumania), supplemented by cotton, wool and vegetables and animals for slaughter. Thus the trade in animals from Beirut to Egypt has been succeeded by one from Mersin to Beirut. None of these trades require speed. But there are two anomalies. Both are in the fruit-and-vegetable trade. The one is Gaza, offering watermelons and other perishable fruits as cargo, and yet the schooners are slow. But here a bottleneck condition comes in as Gaza is not accessible overland, and the port is too shallow for deep draft vessels. Also, the short run really reduces speed to an insignificant factor altogether. Here, then (as in the case of Anamur and Ruad and, to some extent Alanya), we have an instance of the schooner trade as a traditional small vessel trade, where explanation should be in terms of small quantities offered, shallow port entrances, and short time spent in loading small cargoes with only primitive gear being available.[14] It would certainly be interesting to know whether these trades are indeed out of the competition for the slowest ships.

Major changes appear often, then, to be interconnected. I had the occasion to refer to the extension of the trade to include both the Black and the Red Sea; to the closing of the overland route through Palestine; to increased capacity and the increase of the total schooner trade (entailing increased capital investment and a higher turn-over). We noticed the traits of comfort coupled with labour efficiency, and we saw a shift towards Turkish preponderance in the northern trade route, coupled with an overall increase in the Turco-Lebanese trade (with 60 percent during 1958–1959). Viewed backward, we can also see Egypt entering the trade (after 1894, when she had no sailing vessels on these routes at all and probably no schooners whatsoever). What remains to be done is to analyze the change caused by the installation of auxiliary engines, nautical and mercantile changes going hand in hand.

Let me begin with the last. Formerly, in pre-war days, it was common (as in many seafaring comunities, Eastern as well as Western) for many people to share one ship among them, one, the agent, acting as bookkeeper, legal owner and outfitter. This meant that maritime interests were shared by people not actively engaged in maritime pursuits, and, moreover, that risk was spread, people having invested in other branches of business as well. Two systems existed side by side in the Arab world (and still exist in small ports). In the one, the several nautical parts were owned by several separate owners, for example one owning (and receiving a share in the profit accordingly) the sail, another the mast, a third the hull, all elements which had mean specified costs, and, accordingly, part-investments when the ship was being built. In the other system the whole ship was owned in a number of equal shares, two, four, or more, and the net profit was divided accordingly. The first system is adhered to in several Persian Gulf ports, and, maybe, in a closely-knit community like Ruade. The other one was common in Lebanon, but has largely yielded place to concentration of all shares in one ownership, in most cases the agent's. This process went on simultaneously with the conversion of the schooners into auxiliaries, and the increased wealth of the agents and the rising cost of keeping an auxiliary afloat can certainly be thought of as being interconnected. But whether the obvious decline of maritime mindedness of the Lebanese merchants is among the causes, or among the effects, should be investigated. This seems to be a major theoretical issue in maritime anthropology, in fact.

As to the conversion itself, installing a diesel engine in a sailing ship can mean two things. Small marine oil engines began to appear before the first World War. They then were true auxiliary engines, helping the ship in certain conditions, nothing more. But the Syrian schooner entered the phase of conversion much later, when the choice of marine engines had become very wide indeed. And whereas the installation of the early engines did not lead to any change in sail plan, the schooners, on becoming auxiliaries, cut down rig to varying extents in individual vessels. The general process has been this, that a low-powered engine did not lead to any considerable alteration in rig because the ship would continue to depend mainly on sail. This initial phase has been followed by the fitting of more powerful engines, leading to the often total degeneration of the sail plan, because the sail had been reduced to an auxiliary of the engine.

It is possible to argue about the amount of power needed (too much reduces the ship's economy, too little often results in a breakdown), but the two principles I have mentioned stand apart. Whichever stand one takes, the auxiliary engine has drawbacks as well as advantages, and some entrepreneurs, in the past, have favoured plain sailing vessels, whereas many to-day favour investment in motorships proper (in Lebanon, Khayat's DEM-line is an example). But we are not concerned with these now. Among the drawbacks are increased wear and tear on the hull, the high initial cost, depreciation, and running expenses, these latter partly counterbalanced by the reduced expenses of reduced rig. This is a mercantile intervening factor which enables us to explain the casual nexus of engine installation and the cutting down of rig. But how exactly these two spheres of expenses relate to each other has not been investigated. What always has been mentioned as a factor, e.g., in Britain, is increased wages, because of the engineer on board. This does not hold for the Syrian schooner trade, since the wage factor operates in an entirely different manner, following the rules of a share economy. According to these rules, af'er each return voyage, the gross earnings less actual expenses (not equivalent to running expenses, depreciation not being calculated), including cost of victualing, are divided into two. One half goes to the owner(s), the other half is divided among the crew. Usually the skipper gets two, and the engineer one-and-a-half shares, the sailors one, and the boy half. This means that the number of shares, varying with the strength of the crew, does not affect the half of the owner, although it does affect the actual income of the seamen. The introduction of engines has altered the actual number of shares, through reducing the crew by one or two men, but also through raising the share of one member from one to one-and-a-half shares. All in all, the seamen fare better, other things being equal, in an auxiliary, whereas for the entrepreneur, equal profits mean less returns on a higher investment. For him it has become necessary to increase his profits during a season, either on each voyage, or by having his ship make more profitable trips per season. The advantage of being independent of wind implies a higher overall speed over a whole year, and this means a higher turnover. Thus there is, independent of speed as regards the customer, also speed as regards the capital-investing agent, which helps to make his ship competitive even if an auxiliary has less capacity per ton displacement as compared with a true sailing ship. Only too powerful engines, consuming fuel heavily and needing much room for bunkers may turn profit into loss, as they did in the big ocean-going auxiliary ships, sailing over long distances.

On both sides of the Atlantic the process of cutting down rig has consisted of several consecutive phases, almost in a historical sequence. It started with converting topmast schooners and brigantines into fore-and-afters by stripping the yards from the foremast. It went on by reducing pole length or by removing topmasts and by shortening main boom and bowsprit, and it ended up by the mainmast going. The sequence as such (which is well established, and which is at least an assured order if not a law) does not explain the observed change in the Syrian schooners. Here the empirically established state of affairs is one of simultaneousness rather than of sequence. And here we turn to induction and analysis.

The situation can be said to be as follows. Extensive canvas is no longer used when the schooners have to "work light airs." The low-powered engine can do this unaided, and therefore the sail area can be reduced. Costs involved in upkeep and maintenance do not yield any return insofar as flying jib or a jib boom or the elevated corners of the once-lofty principal sails are concerned. Cutting down to some degree is thus good practice, as it reduces costs in sail without sacrificing the speed of the ship. But, in the low-powered auxiliary, there is not enough engine power to warrant much reduction. This would place her outside competition in some trades, and thus jeopardize her economy. The sail area is reduced to the minimum the motor allows. To find the optimum relation between the two, in terms of combined costs and of the earning power they give under varying circumstances of trade, should be the main object of further investigation, just as it is the main goal of the merchant.

Thus, what we see are vessels with engines of sufficient power to drive the ship all the time and with sails greatly reduced, together with true auxiliaries going about their business under power alone only in calms or in narrow waters. Sails are set not for steadying, but for their driving power as soon as they enter the open sea, and if there is enough wind force (3 or 4 on the Beaufort scale). Having her go as a sailing ship is now both quicker and, presumably, cheaper, and her course is consequently adapted to the wind. When the wind and the destination allow, the schooner again becomes a true sailing ship, the engine being cut out, and she will make quite long passages quickly under sail alone.

Now the collected information suggests that in Syrian schooners with varying trade, the ratio between power installed and sail plan is optimal for any hull size. This sounds like a qualitative statement, and it should be so regarded. Our next problem therefore is, if we want to speak at all of co-variability, to rephrase it in such terms that quantitative treatment becomes possible. For if we want to arrive at the formulation of a proper law of maritime change, its elements must have been reduced to as few as possible. The reduction readily suggests itself. All the elements concerned (upkeep and maintenance, fuel consumption, carrying capacity, and a few more) can all be expressed in monetary units. The irreducible elements must be kept outside the formulation of the law. This consequence cannot be escaped if we truly want to investigate the covariability of rigging, engine power, hull capacity, and the type of trade. The reduction envisaged must be in terms of profit and loss, or, rather, in terms of gross earnings (Y) and costs (X), both of which can be represented graphically.   (See diagram.)

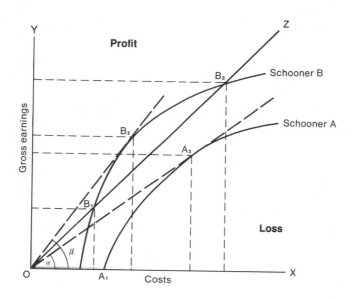

Fig. 1. *The tangential risk of schooner viability*

The graph represents, in its hypothetical form, the way in which further inductive, empirical information should be collected and in what way it can be profitably arranged and represented.   It furthermore suggests that the relation between type of trade and type of vessel is not merely one of causation as a one-way process, but rather is a reversible process of interdependency. Instead of saying that *the schooner trade conditions the design of the schooner,* we can now state that *changes in the total appearance of a vessel are co-variant with changes in the trade.*   This is not only because my treatment of the material expresses it as such, but also because it fits with reality. In other words: a ship operates in the type of trade in which it fits best—at least in a world of order and intelligibility.   As such, a vessel is the "architecture of sailing" as much as a mosque is the "architecture of prayer." Without this link they become either a ruin or a wreck—or a museum piece.

As I said, the graph shows the co-variability between the enumerated factors as reduced to costs and gross earnings.   The hull is considered as an invariable since the ship has been built as a hull.   The real variables thus are rigging, engine, and type of trade. What are subsumed are costs, in reality costs of upkeep, of sail and rig, of the engine, of fuel consumption, crew and port dues, depreciation, and repairs of hull. As the last two items can be treated as a constant (dues being payable on tonnage), their influence can be neglected to the extent of costs never reaching a zero point (0). The gross earnings indicated on the ordinate derive entirely from freights, and these depend on the type of trade. This again is a blanket term for distance covered, type of cargo forwarded, and the conditions of the freight market. Import or transit licenses, the closing of boundaries, the felling season for timber, the boom in building, and many other external factors, play a role in the conditions of the market.

The hypothetical law which must explain the maritime situation can now be formulated more precisely. It says that for any given hull there is an optimal relation (A_2, B_2) between running costs and gross earnings that varies with the type of trade and with the formula for rig and engine. This law (expressed in terms of angle α, B) might be called the "tangential rule of schooner viability." If this tangential relation is less than 1, the schooner works at a loss. To make a profit (that is, to move A so as to reach the OYZ triangle), she has two alternatives. In the first, she has to alter the formula, and to go on altering it until the optimum angle has reached the value $\alpha > 45°$, but staying in the trade. In the second, she has to enter a different trade, trying to find a freight market allowing her to reach the optimal point without altering the power formula.

The nautical facts indicate that both courses have been taken by the Levant entrepreneurs. If this were not so, then the empirical situation would remain unintelligible, unless one considers the Arab businessmen to be dull merchants, and this is contrary to established opinion.[15]

NOTES

1. A. H. J. Prins is Director of the Institute of Cultural Anthropology, Rijksuniversiteit, Groningen, Netherlands.
2. H. A. Underhill, *Deep-water Sail* (Glasgow, 1952), p. 19.
3. But compare the interesting evidence in Bartlett's engraving of the Ruad Foreshore in the 1830s in: J. Carne, *Syria, Holy Land and Asia Minor* (London, 1836–1838).
4. Underhill, *op. cit.*, p. 96.
5. H. I. Chapelle, *The History of the American Sailing Navy* (New York, 1949), pp. 135, 138, 150.
6. B. Greenhill, *The Merchant Schooners* (2 vols.; London, 1957) Vol. I, p. 17.

7. V. Cuinet, *Syrie, Liban et Palestine. Géographie administrative statistique, descriptive et raisonnée* (Paris, 1896), pp. 49, 66, 79, *et al.*

8. *The Mariner's Mirror, Quarterly Journal of the Society for Nautical Research* (London), IV, 221; XVII, 401; XX, 3; XXXIII, 54; XL, 314.

9. S. F. Nadel, *Foundations of Social Anthropology* (London, 1957), p. 230.

10. Cuinet, *op. cit.*, p. 66.

11. Nadel, *op. cit.*, pp. 194ff.

12. Underhill, *op. cit.*, pp. 20, 25, 31, 36.

13. Greenhill, *op. cit.*, Vol. I, p. 24; and Vol. II, pp. 42, 102.

14. *Ibid.*, Vol. I, p. 25.

15. C. Issawi, "Economic Development and Liberalism in Lebanon," *Middle East Journal*, XVIII (1964), 279–92. Also: *Le Commerce du Levant* (biweekly, Beirut).

PART V

The Schoolteacher as Anthropologist

Mahmut Makal, born in 1931 in a poverty-ridden village in central
Anatolia, makes no claims to being an anthropologist. He is the son of
a peasant and, benefiting from having grown up during Ataturk's period
of reforms, he was able to receive a secondary education at one of the
recently initiated Village Institute Schools. At the age of seventeen he
became the sole schoolteacher in a central Anatolian village near his
birthplace.

He wrote two books on his experiences—"probably the two most
controversial books to appear in Turkey in recent years." Shortly after
the publication of the first, which outsold any previous book in the
history of the Turkish press, Makal was jailed on suspicion of
subversion but subsequently released and rehabilitated.

According to Paul Stirling, "Mahmut Makal is the first genuine
villager, from the inarticulate millions of peasants all over the world,
to describe the village from within." As these selections demonstrate,
his writing is characterized by bitter emotion and dramatic clarity as he
describes, in no uncertain terms, the subculture of the Turkish peasant.

25

A Village in Anatolia

MAHMUT MAKAL

A FAMINE WINTER

[Eastern Turkey] has got a bad name. Here we are, supposed to be in
the very heart of Anatolia, but whenever I look at what we suffer, I shudder
to think that the people in the East could have it worse. For how is the
winter to be borne, unless one has a habitable house, clothing to protect one
against the cold, something with which to fill one's stomach, and just a
little fuel. With us, there's just nothing. Clothes are made once in five or
ten years, and what is made is of the coarsest kind, and of very little use
even in warm weather. Jackets are rarely worn; only waistcoats and trousers.
Some of the old men will adapt an ancient Army tunic, dye it, and pull it
on; and under the jacket a pair of trousers, at least ten years old, and a
smock, or simply a vest and pants alone. Most people wear clogs. In sum-

From *A Village in Anatolia* (1954), pp. 7–12, 27–34, 36–37, 109–112; reprinted by permission of Valentine, Mitchell & Co., Ltd.

mer, men wear sandals, and in winter mostly clogs. Few wear shoes, and you rarely find anyone wearing socks. In any case there's nothing much to do on a winter's day, except to walk from the house along to the village common-room, and then from there back again, so it's better to trail about in clogs than in shoes. As for the women, they wear even less, but for some reason they stand the cold better. It is they who work hard in winter. Such work as looking after the animals, watering them, and carrying water to the house, falls to them; whereas the men, having nothing to do, shiver through the winter. Many of them have nothing on their legs but a pair of the thinnest patched trousers.

People tell the villager who dries dung that "burning dry dung is a crazy thing to do," and that it is better to "spread it on the fields." You'll come across people who dash off "scientific" articles on the subject. My dear reader, we count ourselves lucky when we find any dung to dry; we treat it with all the respect in the world. And what do you suppose the villager is to burn, if he doesn't burn dried dung? Has he ever set eyes on a bit of wood or coal? I wonder how many villagers ever have! You go and ask them. Very often the dung, and the straw, and the other things will give out in the middle of winter. Then the village is in a pretty bad way. That is what happened this year. What a winter it was! May it plague our enemies! Everyone was waiting for the weather to clear; spring was on the way, and just as we were telling ourselves "It's over at last," it suddenly got worse, and we had a wind that blew incessantly, howling like a blizzard and as bitter as gall.

There are no stoves; and, unlike some of the local villages in the district, no *tandir*, but only an open fire. Around this you huddle together, getting covered with soot, so that you are roasted in front and your back is exposed. As the saying goes, "March looks in at the door, and pick and shovel go into the fire."

A little girl, with her hair all covered with straw-dust, hurried along, trembling with cold, her hands shielding her eyes, which smarted and watered from the smoke and could not face the glare of the snow. I looked at Sergeant Remzi as if to say: "What can one do about it?" He, thinking that I meant to ask him what she'd been doing, said, "Why, Efendi, that's peasant's gold she's wearing! I wish to goodness we had enough to burn plenty." He was quite right. We had come to the end of the straw; the dung fuel had run out. In many houses they were down to the bottom of their flour sacks. How the animals survived was a miracle; as it was, nothing was left of them but skin and bone. When the dung fuel runs out, the fire on the hearth can't be lit, and the children don't venture from under the bedclothes.

I had fifty to sixty pupils still able to attend school. We managed, with a great effort, to get along until the beginning of February, sometimes shivering, sometimes managing to get a little warmer. But at last, when

February came, and attacked us with all its venom, our knees gave way. Among all those pupils only one or two had a little dung fuel left in their homes. These were the children of the Agas, the more substantial villagers, who had more than two oxen. If I asked them to bring one piece of fuel every day, would their fathers and mothers agree, I wondered? And would they not soon run out of it themselves? So whenever I said something like "To-morrow will see the end of us—what can we do?" not a protest would be heard. People would simply bow their heads, meaning "How can we help it?" No doubt they would not spare their lives if there were something they could do about it. But what if God gives them nothing? ... And what can I do either, alone as I am, and at grips with this powerful, pitiless winter?

What would you have done in my place, I wonder? Anyway this is what I did. "Look here," I said to myself, "death is decreed for all, by Allah's will. This is a kind of warfare, too. If I die, I shall be a martyr; and if I survive, I shall be a hero." So I felt a certain sense of joy, of hope and energy. Sometimes, when I feel low-spirited, I go along to the common-room; there we are all friends together, bent on our game of shivering. My hands and my face grow purple, my hair stands on end; and if I stand up for a while, my knees give way. Each night when I go to bed I wrap myself up well; but what good are my thin blankets to keep out the cold? During the day it's a different matter. By walking and doing work of some kind or another one hasn't too much time to feel the cold. But when night comes—God help us! The cold pierces one's very marrow. At times I grow philosophical, and say to myself: "Well, I'm used to hardships. No amount of discomfort will break me now." And with thoughts of that kind, once I'm warm within, I'm not so anxious for the outside of my body.

During the whole of February and March, when we experienced the bitterest days of the severe winter, we never had more than twenty pieces of dung-fuel for the hearth. And these, too, I'd had to get from some of the Agas, in order to cook my meals. I used any number of my books and papers for setting light to such fuel. The villager does it by fanning the embers in the hearth. And when I can't find any matches, I have recourse to the same method, and even newspaper, which catches alight easily, is of some value. But even when one does get the stove going in this way for an hour or two, need I tell you that there's hardly any difference between indoors and out? Often, it's even warmer out than in.

On days when the children could stand the cold and come to school, we would give anything to go out when the interval came. Outside, with our lips and faces so frozen that we couldn't speak, we got some air, moved about a little, and got warmer. Like lizards crawling out of the ground, half dead, half alive, we reached the month of April. But let's consider what happened to the people in the meantime. It was Allah who gave the winter, and said "It's up to you to find what you need for it." That meant that if you can't, you must suffer the consequences. If you can save your ship, you can save your life; if not, you go under.

So it was that we grown-ups emerged from the winter with very little harm done; but the children! Ah, how the wretched children suffered! From the new-born to those a year old, not one survived. Pitiless children's diseases, profiting by the cold, swept the little creatures away. Ask any villager all the same, whether it was the cold that carried them off, or whether it was Allah's will!

I have a friend who is the health officer for the village and for thirteen others in the district. He may be called a reflective kind of man. Sometimes he drops in and we have a talk. Together we wrote a report for the Medical Officer of Health, by whom we'd been instructed "to let them know if there was any illness in the villages." So we did.

The day our report arrived, it seems, the doctor wasn't at his office, and the office door-keeper told our messenger to "come back to-morrow." But when he had delivered his note, our villager had no intention of waiting about, so he finished his business in town and returned to the village. In any case, it is rare that anyone goes to the town. Exactly thirty-five days later we wrote again, and expressed our anxiety at no notice having been taken of our first report. This time we got the following reply: "The winter is very severe, and as the roads are blocked, even if we got hold of a lorry, it couldn't manage the road. Nor could we do anything if we came. Tell the parents to keep their children warm, and make them stay in bed. Let them use medicine to stop the coughing, and tell them to make the children sweat. Also tell them to put hot towels on their chests, and to feed them well, and to give them plenty of milk. We are sending you a couple of pamphlets. Read them to the public; and if they act according to instructions, the number of deaths should go down."

Two pamphlets, published by the Ministry of Health, and printed on blue paper, with the headings "Pure Water Supply" and "Measles" respectively, were attached to the letter. I gave these to the children, who read them while I explained. Things like "permanganate and hypo-sulphate in the proportion of six centigrammes to one litre of water," and "charcoal"—these may not be expensive things for townsfolk, but where were we to find them here?

I read them during school hours. My friend the health officer read them out to the villagers in the village meeting-room, and he met with some sharp opposition.

"There's no sense in that!" he was told, "As though any doctor could oppose the will of God! It is Allah who gives and He who takes away. We should be thankful for the present day. We are alive, and what is the good of that? Day in, day out, it's our lot to curse our bad fortune—and that is a sin; as for these little innocents, leave them alone to join their mother angels in heaven!"

My friend the health official and I drew up and sent in a list of the dead—the "Death Paper," we called it. Our village has one hundred and thirty houses. The losses in February were much higher than they were in January or in March. In that month alone we inscribed the names of thirty-four children, not one of whom had lived to be one year old. There was a separate account of those who had been carried off by dysentery during July. Four of these died on the same day and at the same hour. They were all buried together.

Our village is the largest among those in my friend's district. There are villages of fifteen, twenty, and thirty houses. In these thirteen villages the number of children whom my colleague inscribed in the "Death Paper" during the month of February was one hundred and twenty. . . .

SHEPHERDING

I don't know whether it's the same thing all over this central Anatolia, but I can't help thinking that our land must be the driest and the most wretched of all. Sometimes I feel that green fields, abundance of fruit, and rich meadows must be a dream. But there must be some real places like that, just as this place is real.

The spring has come, and our crops have grown a little; but the grass —well! There's not enough to grind your teeth on. First and foremost our work is on the land, and of necessity we raise oxen and sheep, even if only a few. But just now our flocks are starving, miserable, breaking up. I find it harder to bear their suffering than I do the material loss involved. The way in which they die and are lost is heartrending. The 1,300 sheep belonging to the village of 350 houses have survived till spring. There were three herds. But in these last days their tongues have been hanging out. Side by side with the new-born lambs whose number is running out, the sheep have been reduced by about one-half. And these are in no condition to give any milk. Bone-dry skeletons, they wander about among the dry clods; and so they bring to an end the number of their days.

Of all the villagers, it's the shepherds who suffer the greatest hardships. But once they've got used to the work, village life bores them. They are only happy when they're following their flocks. It's difficult for grown-ups to get used to this work; but for those who start young, working on the land is not interesting. And they know the right way to tend flocks.

In winter, the flocks remain in Poyraz, in the underground caves. Bulgur is carried to the shepherds, who cook and eat it there. Owners of flocks take them flour if they have some, and those who have straw take a basket of straw to these caves. They try to keep their flocks alive till the spring; but even then, not half of the autumn's flock will come out again.

When the lambs are born, they're suckled there. Not a soul remains in the village. Women and girls and all the children go off every day, at noon, to get the lambs fed, and they return at about the hour of afternoon prayer. No one stays behind; while the village is deserted the roads are crowded with people. If one forgets about it and suddenly runs into the middle of the crowd as it sets off to feed the lambs, it's quite disconcerting.

One Sunday I, too, joined the crowd, and went along with the Agas to feed lambs. They told me: "You'll get there by the time you've smoked one cigarette." I should think they must have smoked a packet of cigarettes each, before we got there; it took us an hour and a half to reach the place. The flocks hadn't yet arrived, so we made a tour of the "sheep pens," as they are called. What they call "pens" are places dug in the ground, with the top closed over, in which the very young lambs are sheltered. Everybody has a pen. And when they've got the lambs fed, they pile them up inside and close the top; and there they stay till the next day at the same hour. Some die. All round us the streams are full of sheep's carcases. They fleece the dead animals, and then leave them there. Those which are in fair condition are taken home and eaten. The carcases, reddened by the sun, look like drums floating on the water; birds of all kinds gather round; I never knew there were so many birds in the world.

"What is all this, Sergeant Mehmet?" I asked.

"It's the will of God," he said.

We were thirsty. We had reached the well-head. Lord help us! All the filthy insects that God ever created were within it. A woman brought a milk-can. Several men took off their belts, joined them together, tied them to the can, and drew up the water in that way. But what water! It wouldn't have done for me to refuse it. Willy-nilly, I drank, muttering to myself, "This will certainly be the death of us." Just at this moment the flocks arrived. The lambs in the "pens" began to bleat, and the sheep "baa'd" forlornly in return. The shepherd's panniers were full of lambs. They distributed them to their owners and received two eggs as a reward. Although there was nothing to distinguish between the twenty to twenty-five lambs, the shepherds took them out of their panniers and gave each one to its owner.

The herdsman, seeing my surprise, told me: "We've grown grey at this job, Efendi." Sergeant Mehmet added: "That lamb with the black tip to his ear, for instance, belongs to the son of Bekir. Once a man's taken that in, he never forgets it."

Everyone stands by his pen, ready. The lambs are just about to be brought out, but must wait till the flocks have been watered. The children behind us are being lined up in front of the flocks. They stoop down awkwardly; there's a rotten old wooden trough there (a relic of the Prophet Noah, certainly!). Three flocks are to be watered from the well. At first I thought it impossible, but it was done. Again, they tied a few belts together, and tied three cans to one end. And if one got tired, another would take over the drawing; so they watered the three flocks of more than four hundred head each, in three hours.

When the lambs had been fed and petted, the "pens" were again filled up. Now the crowd started towards the village. As we were going, one of the shepherds asked: "How are things in the village? What news is there?"

"It's the same with us as it is with you," I said. "We don't see or hear much. How is it with you?"

"What is there, up here on the mountains, except me?" he said. "I've been here for six months. I've neither seen nor heard a thing. I've lost all count of myself even." He bared his chest: his shirt was like a piece of oilskin, the hairs on his chest black as pitch, and plastered with mud.

"Don't you ever wash your linen?" I inquired.

"What's that you're saying?" he retorted. "Linen? Washing? I know nothing of such things any more." . . .

AS FOR MYSELF . . .

I write these notes as we dig in the vegetable field. The sun wearies me, and makes me sweat. The crops are ripe now; my father is alone. It wouldn't do not to help him, but when I leave to go off to the fields I take with me books and paper. As I write these lines we are hoeing watermelons like everyone else—mother as well. The heat is overpowering; at last I can stand it no longer and look for a patch of shade. I stretch myself out in the shade of the maize, and as I write, my mother's voice reaches me. She is singing:

> *Were you cold in the snow that fell on the hills?*
> *You couldn't guess then how the heat would scorch.*

"Mother, when one comes to think of it, what good is it all?"

"Well, what do you expect? You shouldn't have left the house."

There's not a soul left in the village; everyone is occupied. And shall I be the only one to stay at home?

Away stretch the steppes, as bare as your hand. The flocks go off to the village to be milked, hungrily picking their way through the dry clods of earth—if, indeed, there can be anything worthy to be called milk in their udders. It is evening; we are back at home. To-morrow we shall go and gather vetch. I shall have to spend a bit of time there, too. So the wheel of fate grinds out our lives, turning and turning as it has done for the last thousand years. Ah, if only my pen had the power to tell these things as they should be told! Where are our artists? They should be witnesses of these scenes with their own eyes! Then, as fruit of all this toil and sweat, what masterpieces would result! Yakub Kadri has touched upon this village realism in his book "Yaban," which caused great stir. He was accused of giving a false picture of the Turkish village. People who think in terms of the poem "The herdsman plays his pipe, and leads a poet's life," do not really know this country of ours. Until we have become part and parcel of its stark realities, the least we can do is to give up claiming to know our villages or to speak for them. . . .

THE LICE PROBLEM

We ended the school year, 1947–48, in a semi-lousy condition. But I thought to myself: now, that was the first year, after all; after this things will go smoothly, our pupils will have no lice. But exactly the opposite occurred. It was quite unnecessary to open collars, or anything of that kind, to examine the children. In any case, as there were no means of dealing with the problem, why make an inspection? So I gave up the practice. But I had to listen to what they said. One day the funniest thing happened. It was a sunny day, and we were doing lessons out of doors. Eighteen hands were put up. The children announced the presence of one or two lice crawling on the necks of those next to them. (All children love giving away each other's secrets.) As always, I sent home those who were said to be lousy. And since there was nothing to be seen on the necks of the remainder, I didn't look at their underclothes.

This time they came back dressed in the same clothes. Their mothers or elder sisters had undressed them, and killed the lice they had found on their shirts, vests, and pants, by pinching them between thumb and forefinger. And then they dressed the children again and sent them back. "Come, let's see—what's been done?" I would say, and undo their collars to look. "I've been inspected," they would assure me. And there would be lice—dead and alive, all mixed up!

Now I have a pump. Several times I have taken my pupils indoors and given them a pumping, one by one! I used several bottles of D.D.T. Their hands, their faces, their clothing, their very bodies, began to smell of it. What I do is to undress them and spray them; but I have never seen any results. The lice were neither reduced in number nor in activity. The villagers, too, are aware of the use of the pump. They all know that I have a pump and come and ask for it. At first I used to give it to them empty; but the pity of it was, they used to bring it back without using it. I learnt afterwards that they had no insecticide; and they hesitated to ask me for some. And so now I ask those who come for it whether they have any insecticide, and put some in the pump, and give it to them. I think to myself, "If only I had a few lira, and could buy at least one bottle of insecticide for each house, and enough pumps for everyone!" But where is all that to come from?

A neighbour of mine comes in, and we sit together; there they are!—on his collar, on his trouser-legs. . . . Again, I may be talking with someone. He sees them himself, and catches one. "I collected one just as I was leaving Mollah Mehmed's," he'll say, "—you remember I was just talking to him. This must have come from there!"

My pupils and visitors were swarming with them; was I likely to go scot-free? What did I care? I would find myself wriggling about as if a scorpion had got into my clothes, and undress at once. There was the damned thing—as big as a young locust. The size of it! . . .

TOOTH DOCTORS

Among all forms of sickness, it is toothache that makes the villager most wretched. From the age of seven to seventy, men and women holding their jaws run to one of the many people who pass for Hojas, and set up as healers; or they seek out the village "dentist," or else sigh and groan with their chins in their hands at the foot of the wall—all presenting such a heart-breaking sight that it's enough to make one weep. As with all their troubles, after they've had to put up with toothache time after time, they finally try their own remedies. People who can't find good means don't hesitate to resort to bad ones.

In recent years I have learned what a merciless torture toothache can be; it attacks me when I am alone at night and gives me no peace, putting my body on the rack and bringing tears to my eyes. And then those neighbours of mine, who have suffered the same trouble—what tried measures haven't *they* suggested. As it was the first time I'd had toothache, and as I had never had one out before, this is what they recommended: to get the Hoja to say a prayer over a pinch of salt and drive a nail into a stake, and then to wrap up the salt with a charm in a piece of cloth and sew it inside my hat. As to whether that would get rid of the pain—"Well, prayer is prayer: for the rest it depends on God's Will. If He wishes, He can make it go away, and if He doesn't, He won't." That's their solution.

Bless them. Though I didn't give my consent they went on my behalf and got the nail and the salt prayed over, telling me: "You know nothing about it!" But I continued to have pain for two years, right up to the time when, at Istanbul, the well-known doctor Macit Yasaroglu put a stop to it. The Hojas say that no troubles come into the world which haven't got some cure; but not unnaturally, when a chap has been driven to banging his head on every stone because he cannot stand the agony, at the second attack he makes straight for the pincers. But it's these tooth doctors that I was really going to tell you about.

There are three such dentists in the village. When people come running to them, they grip their tooth with a pair of ordinary pliers, causing no end of trouble. Their patients bellow like oxen, and lose oceans of blood. Even the one tooth in a hundred that comes out cleanly is not exactly a success. Most of them break off, the root is left, and it gives rise to an everlasting agony—or else it won't come out at all, but, after it's been pushed and pulled and waggled about, it still clings to the jaw.

There is not much difference between our local town and the village. Although there is one uncertified dentist, most of the people, especially those who come from the village, run off to barbers' shops: I have seen with my own eyes people coming out of these shops with their mouths full of blood, fainting with pain, or else bending over a tin and spitting blood from their mouths. Much credit is due to these barbers' shops, for concerning themselves with the troubles of those who come from the villages. Everyone is, as it were, a guide to everybody else, asking them: "Have you been to Hakki Usta?" "Have you shown that to Mehmet Usta?" They have a look, and whether it's a headache or a pain in the backside that is the trouble, they rely on the needle, though no one really knows much about it.

But I was speaking of the village dentists. . . . Spring, with its first touch in March, seems to bring out people's ailments; perhaps bad teeth hurt more in March. Anyway, it was a lovely March day and the sun was warming our backs; we had been without this comfort for three months, and people came along to the sunny side of the walls feeling free and unrestrained. Towards noon, as I came from school, the women crowding in front of Deli Ali's shop attracted my attention. Deli Ali is one of the three dentists I have mentioned. I went over to him. The women stood there in a row waiting to get their teeth extracted; they all looked very miserable. (When Ali Usta makes them sit down on the stone and pulls, you should hear them scream!) Several people had gathered round the patient; some were holding her by the arms, some keeping her down by the shoulders. Some were holding teeth which had got broken in the course of extraction, looking on and staring at them. Some swayed their heads from side to side as they waited their turn. As I was surveying the clots of blood on the floor, the dentist saw me. There were some eggs in the corner, which the women had brought—five or six each; he thought I was looking at them, and raised his forceps. "I earned those eggs with this, Hoja!" he announced.

Although fairly skilled at his job, one of the other dentists seemed to take pleasure in hurting the people whose teeth he pulled out, and used to make a joke of it. Last year, while extracting a tooth from one of my colleagues, he broke it, so that my colleague was afraid of going again, though his tooth ached for days and his face swelled. There wasn't a trace of anything you could call mercy in that dentist. He would tie one end of a wire or strong string to the bottom of the tooth, and the other end to the anvil. (He himself was a blacksmith.) He then got a red-hot rod and put it near the man's mouth. The patient, with his tooth tied, and the fire close to his mouth, would suddenly start back, and the wire would pull the tooth out! Once he fastened the forceps on to the patient's tooth and made him chase round, bellowing, for a whole ten minutes, till the tooth was extracted. One colleague of mine must have been pretty bad, for at the risk of undergoing all these tortures, he got the blacksmith up one evening and had his tooth pulled out.

"What else can you expect, brother?" he said. "A drowning man clutches at a straw!"

BIBLIOGRAPHY

"More than forty thousand books in Western languages on subjects relating to the Near and Middle East have been published in the last century and a half. Many are mere travelogues; others are tracts of dubious value . . ."[1]

The purpose of this bibliography is to provide the reader with a range of relevant textual volumes on the peoples and cultures of the contemporary Middle East published since 1945. The listing is not intended to be exhaustive.

A historical foundation is absolutely essential for an adequate grasp of the contemporary scene and built into this bibliography are the references to five critical historical studies (Brockelmann, 1947; Fisher, 1959; Hitti, 1961, Kirk, 1957; and Lewis, 1956).

Volumes that have been regularly re-edited to be brought up to date and contain a wealth of material on the general features of the contemporary Middle East include the editions of the Royal Institute of International Affairs (Bullard, 1958), Europa Publications (1965), and W. B. Fisher (1954).

These three publications, in addition to the already cited historical studies, were of particular value in the preparation of the Introduction to this volume.

Finally, all serious students of the contemporary Middle East should have in their libraries well-printed translations of the Bible and the Koran.

Abdullah. *Memoirs of King Abdullah of Transjordan.* Translated by Philip P. Graves. New York, 1950.

Adams, D. G. *Iraq's People and Resources.* Berkeley, 1958.

Allen, Harold B. *Rural Education and Welfare in the Middle East.* London, 1946.

———. *Rural Reconstruction in Action: Experiences in the Near and Middle East.* Ithaca, 1953.

Ammar, Hamed. *Growing Up in an Egyptian Village.* London, 1954.

Anshen, Ruth N., ed. *Mid-East: World Center Yesterday, Today, and Tomorrow.* New York, 1955.

[1] S. N. Fisher, ed., *Social Forces in the Middle East* (Ithaca, 1955) ; p. 263.

Arasteh, Reza. *Educational and Social Awakening in Iran.* Leiden, 1962.
————. *Man and Society in Iran.* Leiden, 1964.
Atiyah, E. *An Arab Tells His Story.* London, 1946.
Baer, Gabriel. *Population and Society in the Arab East.* Translated by Hanna Szoke. New York, 1964.
Baratz, G., et al. *New Way of Life: The Collective Settlements of Israel.* London, 1949.
Barth, Fredrik. *Nomads of South Persia: The Basseri Tribe of the Khamseh Confederacy.* New York, 1961.
————. *Principles of Social Organization in Southern Kurdistan.* Oslo, 1953.
Ben Zvi, Yitzchak. *The Exiled and the Redeemed.* Philadelphia, 1957.
Berger, Morroe. *The Arab World Today.* New York, 1962.
————. *Bureaucracy and Society in Modern Egypt: A Study of the Higher Civil Service.* Princeton, 1957.
————, ed. *The New Metropolis in the Arab World.* New Delhi, 1963.
Bernstein, Marver H. *The Politics of Israel: The First Decade of Statehood.* Princeton, 1957.
Bisbee, Eleanor. *The New Turks.* Philadelphia, 1951.
————. *The People of Turkey.* New York, 1946.
Bonné, Alfred. *State and Economics in the Middle East: A Society in Transition.* 2nd ed. London, 1955.
Brockelmann, Carl. *History of the Islamic Peoples.* With a Review of Events, 1939–1947, by Moshe Perlmann. Translated by Joel Carmichael and Moshe Perlmann. New York, 1947.
Buber, Martin. *Israel and Palestine: The History of an Idea.* New York, 1952.
Bullard, Reader, ed. *The Middle East: A Political and Economic Survey.* 3rd ed. London, 1958.
Carmichael, Joel. *The Shaping of the Arabs.* New York, 1967.
Cohen, Abner. *Arab Border-Villages in Israel: A Study of Continuity and Change in Social Organization.* Manchester, 1965.
Cooke, Hedley V. *Challenge and Response in the Middle East.* New York, 1952.
Coon, Carleton S. *Caravan: The Story of the Middle East.* 6th printing. New York, 1956.
Dickson, H. R. P. *The Arab of the Desert: A Glimpse into Badawin Life in Kuwait and Saudi Arabia.* London, 1949.
————. *Kuwait and Her Neighbours.* London, 1956.
Dunner, Joseph. *The Republic of Israel.* New York, 1950.
Eaton, Joseph. *Prisons in Israel.* Pittsburgh, 1964.
Eisenstadt, S. N. *The Absorption of Immigrants.* London, 1954.
Eren, Nuri. *Turkey Today and Tomorrow.* New York, 1964.
Ettinghausen, Richard, ed. *A Selected and Annotated Bibliography of Books and Periodicals in Western Languages Dealing with the Near and Middle East with Special Emphasis on Medieval and Modern Times.* Washington, D.C., 1952. With Supplement (1954).
Europa Publications, Ltd. *The Middle East and North Africa.* London, 1965.

Field, Henry. *Ancient and Modern Man in Southwestern Asia.* Coral Gables, Fla., 1956.

————. *The Anthropolgy of Iraq.* Cambridge, Mass., 1952.

————. *Bibliography on Southwestern Asia.* 7 compilations. Coral Gables, Fla., 1953–62.

Fisher, Sidney N., ed. *Evolution in the Middle East: Reform, Revolt and Change.* Washington, 1953.

————. *The Middle East: A History.* New York, 1959.

————, ed. *Social Forces in the Middle East.* Ithaca, 1955.

Fisher, W. B. *The Middle East: A Physical, Social and Regional Geography.* 3rd ed. London, 1954.

Franck, Dorothy S., ed. *Islam in the Modern World.* Washington, 1951.

Frankenstein, Carl, ed. *Between Past and Future: Essays and Studies on Aspects of Immigrant Absorption in Israel.* Jerusalem, 1953.

Friedmann, Georges. *The End of the Jewish People?* New York, 1967.

Frye, Richard N., ed. *Iran.* New York, 1956.

Fuller, Anne H. *Buarij. Portrait of a Lebanese Muslim Village.* Cambridge, Mass., 1963.

Gibb, H. A. R. *Modern Trends in Islam.* Chicago, 1947.

————. *Mohammedism: An Historical Survey.* London, 1949.

————, and Kramers, J. H., eds. *Shorter Encyclopedia of Islam.* Ithaca, 1953.

Glubb, John B. *Britain and the Arabs: A Study of Fifty Years.* London, 1959.

————. *The Story of the Arab Legion.* London, 1948.

Goitein, S. D. *Jews and Arabs: Their Contacts Through the Ages.* New York, 1955.

Granqvist, Hilma. *Birth and Childhood Among the Arabs: Studies in a Muhammedan Village in Palestine.* Helsingfors, 1947.

————. *Child Problems Among the Arabs: Studies in a Muhammedan Village in Palestine.* Helsingfors, 1950.

Grunebaum, Gustave E. von. *Modern Islam: The Search for Cultural Identity.* London, 1962.

————. *Muhammedan Festivals.* New York, 1951.

————, ed. *Unity and Variety in Muslim Civilization.* Chicago, 1955.

Grunwald, K., and Ronall, J. O. *Industrialization in the Middle East.* New York, 1960.

Gulick, John. *Social Structure and Cultural Change in a Lebanese Village.* New York, 1955.

————. *Tripoli: A Modern Arab City.* Cambridge, Mass., 1967.

————, ed. *Dimensions of Cultural Change in the Middle East.* Special issue of *Human Organization*, 1965, 24:1.

Haas, William S. *Iran.* New York, 1946.

Habib-Ayrout, Henry. *The Fellaheen.* Cairo, 1945.

Hacker, Jane. *Modern Amman: A Social Study.* Durham, 1960.

Haddad, George. *Fifty Years of Modern Syria and Lebanon.* Beirut, 1950.

Halpern, Ben. *The Idea of a Jewish State.* Cambridge, Mass., 1961.

Halpern, Manfred. *The Politics of Social Change in the Middle East and North Africa.* Princeton, 1963.

Hamady, Sonia. *Temperament and Character of the Arabs.* New York, 1960.

Harris, George L., ed. *Egypt.* New Haven, 1957.

———, ed. *Jordan.* New Haven, 1958.

———, ed. *Iraq.* New Haven, 1958.

Hazard, Harry W. *Eastern Arabia.* New Haven, 1956.

———, ed. *Southern Arabia.* New Haven, 1956.

Hitti, Philip K. *History of the Arabs from the Earliest Times to the Present.* London, 1953.

———. *The Near East in History: A 5,000 Year Story.* New York, 1961.

Hottinger, Arnold. *The Arabs: Their History, Culture and Place in the Modern World.* London, 1963.

Hourani, A. H. *Minorities in the Arab World.* London, 1947.

Hurewitz, J. C. *The Struggle for Palestine.* New York, 1950.

Hussein, Taha. *The Stream of Days.* London, 1948.

Hyamson, Albert M. *Palestine under the Mandate, 1920–1948.* London, 1950.

Ingrams, Harold. *The Yemen.* London, 1963.

Issawi, C. *Egypt at Mid-century.* London, 1954.

Jackh, Earnest, ed. *Background of the Middle East.* Ithaca, 1952.

Janowsky, Oscar I. *Foundations of Israel.* Princeton, 1959.

Jurji, Edward J. *The Middle East: Its Religion and Culture.* Philadelphia, 1946.

Keen, B. A. *The Agricultural Development of the Middle East.* London, 1946.

Kerr, Malcolm. *Islamic Reforms: The Political Theories of Muhammed Abdullah and Rashid Rida.* Berkeley, Calif., 1966.

Khalaf, Samir. *Prostitution in a Changing Society; A Sociological Survey of Legal Prostitution in Beirut.* Beirut, 1965.

Kimche, Jon and David. *The Secret Roads.* New York, 1955.

Kirk, George E. *A Short History of the Middle East from the Rise of Islam to Modern Times.* 4th ed. New York, 1957.

Lacouture, Jean and Simonne. *Egypt in Transition.* Translated by Francis Scarfe. New York, 1958.

Lambton, Ann K. S. *Landlord and Peasant in Persia.* London, 1953.

Landau, Rom. *Islam and the Arabs.* London, 1958.

Laquer, Walter Z. *Communism and Nationalism in the Middle East.* New York, 1956.

———, ed. *The Middle East in Transition.* New York, 1958.

Lengyel, Emil. *The Changing Middle East.* New York, 1960.

Lerner, Daniel. *The Passing of Traditional Society: Modernizing the Middle East.* London, 1958.

Levy, Reuben. *The Social Structure of Islam.* (The 2nd ed. of *The Sociology of Islam.*) Cambridge, 1957.

Lewis, Bernard. *The Arabs in History.* 3rd ed. London, 1956.

———. *The Emergence of Modern Turkey.* London, 1961.

Lewis, G. L. *Turkey.* New York, 1955.

Lipsky, George A., ed. *Saudi Arabia.* New Haven, 1959.

Longrigg, Steven H. *Iraq, 1900–1950.* London, 1953.

———. *The Middle East: A Social Geography.* Chicago, 1963.

Lowdermilk, Walter C. *Palestine, Land of Promise.* New York, 1944.

Lutfiyya, Abdulla M. *Baytin, a Jordanian Village. A Study of Social Institutions and Social Change in a Folk Community.* London, 1966.

McFadden, Tom J. *Daily Journalism in the Arab States.* Columbus, 1953.

Makal, Mahmut. *A Village in Anatolia.* Translated by Wyndham Deedes and edited by Paul Stirling. London, 1954.

Marx, Emanuel. *Bedouin of the Negev.* New York, 1967.

Matras, Judah. *Social Change in Israel.* Chicago, 1965.

Matthews, Roderic D., and Akrawi, Matta. *Education in Arab Countries.* Washington, 1949.

Meyer, A. J. *Middle Eastern Capitalism.* Cambridge, Mass., 1959.

Morrison, S. A. *Middle East Survey: The Political, Social and Religious Problems.* London, 1954.

Nasser, Gamal Abdul. *Egypt's Liberation. The Philosophy of the Revolution.* Washington, 1955.

Nolte, Richard H., ed. *The Modern Middle East.* New York, 1963.

Parkes, James. *End of an Exile: The Jews and the Gentile World.* New York, 1954.

Patai, Raphael. *Cultures in Conflict: Three Lectures on the Socio-cultural Problems of Israel and Her Neighbors.* New York, 1958.

———. *Golden River to Golden Road.* Philadelphia, 1967.

———. *Israel Between East and West.* Philadelphia, 1953.

———. *Sex and Family in the Bible and the Middle East.* New York, 1959.

———, ed. *The Kingdom of Jordan.* New Haven, 1957.

———, ed. *The Republic of Lebanon.* 2 vols. New Haven, 1956.

———, ed. *The Republic of Syria.* 2 vols. New Haven, 1956.

Peake, F. G. *History of Jordan and Its Tribes.* Coral Gables, Fla., 1958.

Peretz, Don. *The Middle East Today.* New York, 1963.

Pearlman, Moshe. *The Army of Israel.* New York, 1950.

Prittie, Terence. *Israel: Miracle in the Desert.* London, 1966.

Phillips, Wendell. *Unknown Oman.* London, 1966.

Pierce, Joe E. *Life in a Turkish Village.* New York, 1964.

Prothro, Edwin Terry. *Child Rearing in the Lebanon.* Cambridge, Mass., 1961.

Rabin, A. I. *Growing Up in the Kibbutz.* New York, 1965.

Reinhold, Hanoch. *Youth Aliya: Trends and Developments.* Jerusalem, 1957.

Rivlin, Benjamin, and Szyliowicz, Joseph S., eds. *The Contemporary Middle East: Tradition and Innovation.* New York, 1965.

Ronart, Stephan and Nandy. *Concise Encyclopedia of Arabic Civilization.* Vol. I: *The Arab East.* New York, 1960.

Rosenfeld, Henry. *They Were Peasants: Social Anthropological Studies on the Arab Village in Israel.* Tel Aviv, 1964.

Sachar, Howard M. *The Course of Modern Jewish History.* Cleveland, 1958.

Sacher, Harry. *Israel: The Establishment of a State.* New York, 1952.

Salim, S. M. *Marsh Dwellers of the Euphrates Delta.* London, 1962.

Sanger, Richard H. *The Arabian Peninsula.* Ithaca, 1954.

———. *Where the Jordan Flows.* Washington, 1963.

Schechtman, Joseph B. *On Wings of Eagles.* New York, 1961.

Schwarz, Walter. *The Arabs in Israel.* London, 1959.

Seligman, Lester G. *Leadership in a New Nation.* New York, 1964.

Shumsky, Abraham. *The Clash of Cultures in Israel.* New York, 1955.

Shuval, Judith T. *Immigrants on the Threshold.* New York, 1963.

Sicron, Moshe. *Immigration to Israel, 1948–1953.* Jerusalem, 1957.

Spiro, Melford E. *Children of the Kibbutz.* New York, 1958.

Stern, Boris. *The Kibbutz That Was.* Washington, D.C., 1965.

Stewart, Desmond, and Haylock, John. *New Babylon: A Portrait of Iraq.* London, 1956.

Stewart-Robinson, J., ed. *The Traditional Near East.* New York, 1966.

Stirling, Paul. *Turkish Village.* London, 1965.

Sweet, Louise E. *Tell Toqaan: A Syrian Village.* Ann Arbor, 1960.

Thesiger, Wilfred. *Arabian Sands.* London, 1959.

———. *The Marsh Arabs.* London, 1964.

Thompson, J. H., and Reischauer, R. D., eds. *Modernization of the Arab World.* Princeton, 1966.

Tomlin, E. W. F. *Life in Modern Turkey.* New York, 1946.

Tritton, A. S. *Islam Beliefs and Practices.* London, 1951.

Van-Ess, J. *Meet the Arab.* London, 1947.

Vreeland, Herbert H., ed. *Iran.* New Haven, 1957.

Walz, Jay. *The Middle East.* New York, 1965.

Warriner, Doreen. *Land and Poverty in the Middle East.* London, 1948.

———. *Land Reform and Development in the Middle East.* 2nd ed. London, 1962.

Weingrod, Alex. *Israel: Group Relations in a New Society.* London, 1965.

———. *Reluctant Pioneers: Village Development in Israel.* New York, 1966.

Wheelock, Keith. *Nasser's New Egypt.* New York, 1960.

Wilber, Donald N. *Iran: Past and Present.* 3rd ed. Princeton, 1955.

———. *Contemporary Iran.* New York, 1963.

Yalman, Ahmed Emin. *Turkey in My Time.* Norman, Oklahoma, 1956.

Yaukey, David. *Fertility Differences in a Modernizing Country.* Princeton, 1960.

Young, T. Cuyler, ed. *Near Eastern Culture and Society: A Symposium on the Meeting of East and West.* Princeton, 1951.

Zeltzer, Moshe. *Aspects of Near East Society.* New York, 1962.

Ziadeh, Nicola. *Syria and Lebanon.* New York, 1957.

INDEX

Abbasid Empire, political reactions, xxviii
Abbasids, xxvii–xxix, xxxvi–xxxvii
Abdul-Aziz ibn Saud, xxxii
Abdullah of Jordan, xxxi, xxxii
Abu al-Abbas, xxvii
Abu Bakr, xxv
Abyssinia, xxiv, 72
Acre, xxviii
Aden, xxxiii
Afghanistan, 70–1
'Afrīn, 19, 27
Agha Khan, 34
aghas, Kurdish, 32
agriculture, xx, xxiv, xxxiii, xxxix–xl, 21, 27, 34, 54, 56, 60, 131, 388
Ahl Khayun, 208–15
Ahvaz, as a shrine, 61
Aisha, xxvi
ajaw̃d, 210
akh (brother), 128
al-Abbas, xxvii
al-'Asalī, 24
Alawis, xxxiv, 11, 21–6
Aleppo, 19, 22, 27, 29, 30, 38, 39, 40, 70
Alexandretta, 29
Alexandria 35
Algeria, 73
al'Halabī, 24
al-hay'a al-sha'biyya, 23
Ali, xxvi–xxvii, 21, 28, 33
Alī-Ilāhis, 20
Allah, xxv, 28, 374–5
Allat, xxv
almsgiving in Saudi Arabia, 219, 222

al-Pāchachī, 16
Alp Arslan, xxix
al Rab al-Khali, xix
Altneuland, 1
amīr, leader of the Baluchi tribes, 122
'Amir, 23
Amorites, 10
Amsar, xxvii
Anatolia, xxix, 427–37
Anglo-Iranian Oil Company (AIOC), 333–4, 337, 356
Antiochus, xxii
Anti-Taurus, xviii
ar (notion of shame), 249
Arab, xxiv–xxxiii, xxxv, 3–9, 58
Arab countries, 233
Arab League, xxxviii, 233
Arabia Felix, xxiv
Arabian American Oil Company (Aramco), 219–21, 225, 227, 230, 231
Arabian Peninsula, xviii–xix, xxiv–xxxiii
Arabic language, 23, 40, 63
Aramaic dialect, 35–6, 39
Aramean population of Syria, xxi
Arbil, 15
Aribi, 5
Armenian Church, xxiv, 23
Armenian Democratic League, 29
Armenian Patriarch, 42
Armenian Revolutionary Federation, 29
Armenians, xxx, 10–44, 60–1
arosi, 157
Ashkenazim, 75–6

'Asilīn, 126–9
assassins (hashashin), xxxvi, 33
Assyrian Church, xxiv
Assyrian Empire, xxii
Assyrians, xxi, 27, 36–8, 59–60
Aswan, 247–67
Ataturk, xxxi–xxxii
Atlas mountains, 73
Atrash, 23–4
awlad al hawa, 250
awlad attarik, 251
Ayyubids, xxiv
Azerbaijan, 14, 59, 60
Azeri, 59–60

Ba'adhrī, 27
baba, 28
Baba 'Ali, 20
Bābism, 28
Babylon, 70
Baghdad, xxviii, xxix, xlvii–xlviii, 35, 37, 39
Baghdad Pact, 335
Baha'i, 29, 61
Baha'is, 28–9
Bakhtiari, 55–7
Balad, 27
Balfour Declaration, xxxi, 1
Balkan Wars, xxix
Balkans, xxix
Baluchi, 58, 121–4, 134
Bani Hashim, xxv
Ba'qūba, 29, 36
Baradai, Jacob, 38
Barwar, 38
Barzan, 16
Barzani, 16–8
Basra, 37, 38, 205
Basseri, 153–68
Ba'th, 20
Battle of Hittim, xxviii
Battle of Karbala, 207
Bavlim, 76
Baybars, xxix
bedouin, xxvii, xxix, xxxiv, 24, 30, 121, 124–30, 136–52, 188, 220, 223–4
begs, 27
Beirut, xx, xlvi, xlvii, 35
Beni Isad, 208–15
Berber neo-Muslims, xxvii
Berbers, 73
Berlin-Baghdad railway, xxx

bigari, 107
Bilbas, 12
birth control, Arab family, 242, 246
Bnei Israel, 71
Bokhara, xxviii, 70
Brahui, 58, 64
British Declaration of 1924, xxxii
Buarij, 112–8
Byzantium, xxii–xxiv, xxvii, xxix, 11, 21

"Cadillac-camel" economy, xxxiii
Cairo, xvii, xix, 31, 39
California Arabian Standard Oil Company, 219
Caliphate, 6–7, 33
Canaan, xxi, 69
Canaanites, xxi–xxii
Carmel Ridge, xix
Caucasus, 36
Chachans, 30
Chahar Lang, 55
Chalabim, 76
Chaldeans, xxiv, 11, 35, 38
Charshambe, 156
child rearing in Lebanon, 270–89
Christian Assyrians, 60
Christian Gnosis, 11, 35
Christianity, early development of, xxiii–xxiv
"Christians of John the Baptist," 34
Church of the Orient, 35
Cilicia, 29
Circassians, xxxiv, xxxv, 11, 30–1
civil service in Arab countries, 181, 184–5
civil service in Egypt, 317–28
clans
   Druze, 23
   Iraqi Marsh Dwellers, 205–15
climate of the Middle East, xviii–xix
Cochin, 71
Constantine, xxiv
Constantinople, xxiv, xxix, xxx
Coptic Church, xxiv
Copts, xxxv, xxxvii–xxxviii
Council of Sovereignty in Iraq, 20
Crusades, xxviii, 8, 74
Cyprus, 38, 72
Cyrene, 72
Cyrus of Persia, xxii

Damascus, xxii, xxvii, xxviii, 19, 22, 24, 29, 35, 38–40
dar al-harb, xxvi
dar al Islam, xxvi
Darvesh, 154
Dazhmaks, 60
Dead Sea, xx
dervish brotherhoods, 18, 23, 28
Devil worshippers, 26
Deyr el-Zor, 27
dialects
    of Iran, 51, 54
    of Iraq and Syria, 35–6
    of Israel, 70
Diarbekr, 27
Diaspora, 1, 29, 69, 75
Diogenus, xxix
disease
    in Egypt, xliii–xliv
    in Saudi Arabia, 221–2, 225–31
divorce
    in Christian communities in Iraq and Syria, 41
    in Egypt, 262–3
    among the Muslims, 245–6
Diyāla liwā, 15, 28
Djerba, 73
Dravidian language, 58, 64
Druze, xxxiv, xxxvi, xxxviii, 11, 22–6

Eastern Christian communities, 42
ech Chibayish, 205–15
ecology of the Middle East, 119–35
education in Arab countries, 243
Egypt, xix, xx, xxi, xlix, 6, 9, 20, 31, 33, 38, 72, 175, 180, 181, 247–64, 317–28
Elburz Mountains, xviii
emancipation of women, 240–1, 245
emirs, 33
entrepreneurs, 178–80
Erzerum, 12
Esdraelon Valley, xix
État des Alaouites, 22
État du Jebel Druze, 22
Ethiopia, 72
Euphrates, xix
Euphrates Valley, 4
evil eye, 160–1, 373, 375, 376, 377, 378, 383, 384
evil spirits, 231, 373–86
extremism in Iran, 331–70

Falasha Jews, 72–3
family, Arab, 233–46
faqīran, 26
Fars, 58
Fatiha, 248, 257
Fatima, xxvi, 33, 205
Fatimid Caliphate, xxxvi
Fatimid dynasty, xxviii
Fatimis, 33
Faysal, 32, 86
fellah, xxxix–xli, xliii, 79–97, 112–8, 189
fellaheen, xxxiv, xxxix, xliii
fellihi, 39
Fertile Crescent, xvii, xix, xx, xxv
Five Pillars of Islam, xxvi
folk lore, 115–6
folk medicine; *see* medical treatment in the Middle East
forcible assimilation of the Kurds, 13–4
France, xxx, xxxi, xxxii
Franco-Turkish agreement of 1921, 30
French, 21, 22, 24, 25, 29, 30, 33, 37, 43–4, 73
French language, 64
"Frenchification," 73

Galilee highlands, xix
galut, 1
General Federation of Iraqi Labour Unions, 194
geography of the Middle East, xvii–xx
Georgia, 70
German language, 64
Germany, xxxi, xxxii
ghulāt, 28
Gilan, 54
Great Britain, xxx–xxxii, 16, 24, 32, 35, 36–7, 43–4
Greek Catholics, xxxviii, 11, 23, 40–2
Greek influence in the early Middle East, xxii–xxiv
Greek Orthodox Church, xiv, xxxviii, 11, 23, 40–2
Greek Patriarch, 42
Greeks, 40
Gregorians, 29
Gulf of Aqaba, xx

Haddād, 21

Hadhramut, 72
Haft Lang family, 55
Haganah, 1
Haifa, 29
Hajji Baba, 337
Hakkiari, 36
Halebja, 15
Hamā, 33, 40
Hamadan, 61
Hamidiyye calvary, 19
Hamites, xxi
hara, 73
Harki, 12, 15
Haroun al Rashid, xviii
Hasan, xxvii
hashar, 108
hashshāshin, 33
Hawrān, 40, 43
Hawrān plateau, 34
Haydarī, 21
Hebrew language, 32
Hebrews, xxi–xxii, 69
Hejaz, xxv
Hellenism, xxii–xxiv
Herod, xxiii
Herzl, Theodore, 1
Hijra, xxv
Hilwi, 79–97
Hittim, xxviii
Hittites, xxi
holy men, 205–8
Homs, 38–9
"House of Islam," 7
household, 136–51, 242
   in Iran, 56
   in Israel, 389
   in a Lebanese village, 83, 90
   in a Syrian peasant village, 99–104
Hoybun (National Committee), in
   Syria, 13
Huntchag Party, 29
Husayn, xxvii
Hussein, Sharif, xxxi, xxxii

Ibn Nusayr, 21
Ibn Saud, 222
Ibrāhīm al-Kinj, 25
Ihaggaren, 132–3
ikhtiyār, 26
il-khan, 55
illiteracy in Arab countries, 243
il-mujtahid, 207

imām, xxxv, 21, 33
Imam Husain, 207
Imami, xxxi
Imghad, 132–3
income in the Middle East, xxxiii,
   189–90, 192–3, 195–6
independent Arab state, 8
Indo-European language, 60, 62, 64
Indo-European peoples, xxi
inflation in Saudi Arabia, 221, 223
International Confederation of Arab
   Labour Unions, 194
International Sanitary Regulations,
   229
Iran, xviii, xxxii, 13–4, 20, 51–67, 331–
   370
   Anglophobia in, 362
   anti-British sentiment in, 337
   bipolarity and extremism in, 331–70
   geographical importance of, 331–3
   protection by Western powers, 334
   Tudeh Party in, 333–4, 337, 343, 365
Irano-Soviet Fisheries Company, 334–
   335
Iraq, xviii, xix, xxx, xxxii, xxxiii, xxxv,
   10–44
Iraqi, 57
   government, 17–8
   Marsh dwellers, 205–15
   parliament, 17
Islam, xxiv–xxxii, xxxvi, 6–7, 11, 21,
   26, 54, 154–5, 176, 182, 232–46
Islamic conquests, 9
Islamic Empire, 9
Ismā'īlis, 11, 21, 33–4
Israel, xix, xxxii, xlvi, xlvii, xlix–li,
   32, 68–76
   revitalization process in, 1
Israeli immigrants
   acculturation of, 387–403
   ethnic identity by, 393
   health practices of, 394–5
   status distinctions among, 390–1
is-sāda, 205–8
Isserles, Moshe, 76
Istanbul, xxiv
Istiqlāl, 20

Jabal, 24
Jabal al-Durūz, 22–3, 43
Jabal Ansāriyya, 21, 24, 43
Jabal Sinjār, 27

Jacobites, 19, 35, 38
Jaf, 12, 15
Jafar Quli Khan, 55
Jalali, 14
Janissaries, xxiv
Jarablus, 31
Jawlān, 30
Jazīra, 11, 19, 29, 30, 31, 35, 37–8
Jehova, xxii
Jenghis Kahn, xxviii
Jerusalem, xxii, xxiii, xxvi, xxviii, 38, 69
Jesuits, 11
Jewish history, xxi–xxii, xxiii, xxxii, xlix–li, 32–3, 68–76
Jews, xxii–xxiii, 7, 32–3, 36
  in China, 71
  in India, 71
  in Iraq, 32–3
  in Persia, 61
  in Spain, 74
jihad (holy war), xxvi, xxxi
jinn, 231, 373
Jordan, 30, 31
Jordan Rift, xx
Jordan Valley, xx
Judaism, xxiii–xxiv, xxvii
Judea, xxiii, 69
Judean Hills, xix–xx
juft, 107–9

Ka'aba, xxv
Kakā'iyya, 28
Kalbī, 21
Kalhur, 12
Karaim, 75
Karo, Joseph, 76
Kars, 12
Kauliyah, 173
kaum, 122
Kāzimayn, 28
Kemal Pasha, 36
Khabur, 37
Khadija, xxv
khan, 53, 55–6, 107
Khanāqīn, 14, 31
Khayyāt, 21
Khurasan, 57, 59
khushhali, 156
Khuzistan, 34
kibbutz, l, 290–314
  group acceptance in the, 291–2

  parent-child relationships in the, 307–12
  social structure of the, 291–2
  value system in the, 307
"King's Highway," xix, 404
Kirkuk, 14, 28, 31, 37
Kirkuk liwā, 14
Kirmanshah, 12, 57
Koran, xxvi, xxxvii, 115
küchaks, 26
Kurd Dag (Mountain of the Kurds), 19
Kurdim, 76
Kurdish-Arab confederation of Millī, 19
Kurdish *begs*, 27
Kurdish independence, 12–3
"Kurdish Republic," 57
Kurdish revolts, 13–4
Kurdish statehood, 13
Kurdistan, 70
Kurds, xxxv–xxxvii, xli, 10–44, 57, 59
Kūt, 14
Kuttab, 248, 251
Kuwait, xxxiii, xlvi, xlvii

Labour and Workman Regulations of Saudi Arabia, 199
Ladino, 75
landowners, xxxix–xl, 15, 21, 25, 30, 105, 176–80
land tenure system, xxxix–xl
Latakiya, 21, 23, 30, 40, 42
League of Nations, 15, 37
Lebanese Christians, xxxviii
Lebanese village, 79–97
"Lebano-Galilean" Massif, xix
Lebanon, xix, xxxviii, 12, 18, 22, 25, 29, 33, 37, 38, 39, 42, 70, 184, 270–89
leben (sour milk), 148
Levant, xvii, xix–xx, xxi–xxii, xxxi, 404–22
Libya, xvii, 72, 73
liwās, 14, 16, 31
Lurs, 20, 57

Maccabeans, xxii
Maccabees, 69
Ma'dan, 205
madhhab, 21

Mahabad, republic of, 14
mahr, 157
Maimonides, 72
majlis, xxv
Maku, 14
malik, 37
Mamluk Sultanate, xxix
Mamluks, xxix
Manat, xxv
Manbij, 30
Mandaean language, 35
Mandaeans, 11, 34–5, 213
Mandaeism, 26, 35
Mandalī, 12, 14
Mandate period, 68
Manichaeans, 11
Manichaeism, 35
Manzikart, xxix
Marash, 12
Ma'rib Dam, xxiv
Maronites, xxiv, 22–3, 42
marriage, 237–9, 244–5, 247–64
Marsh Arabs, 205
Marsh Dwellers of Iraq, 205–15
Masada, xxiii
Mawali, xxvii
Mazanderan, 54, 59
Mazuri, 12
McMahon, Sir Henry, xxxi
Mecca, xxv, xxvi, 18
Media, 34
medical treatment in the Middle East,
    227–32, 372–84
Medina, xxv
Melkites, 40
mellah, 73
merchants, 129, 177–9
Mesopotamia, xx–xxi, xxii, 4
Metāwira, 21
Middle East Defense Organization
    (MEDO), 335
migrations, 11–2, 73, 153–68
    in Iran, 56, 59
Mihirkan, 27
mijtahids, 28
Military Zone of the Middle East, xvii
millet, xxx, 35, 37, 42
Millet agencies, 239
Millī, 19
minorities in Iraq and Syria, 10–44
mir, amir al-umara', 27
miri land, xl
Mithridates, xxiii

Mizrachim Jews, 76
mob violence, xlviii
mobility of population in Iran, 338
Mongol invasions, xviii, xxix
monogamy, 238, 263
monotheism, xxiii
Morocco, xxviii, 9, 73
Mosad, 290–314
moshav, 391, 396–400
Mossadegh, Mohammed, and his influ-
    ence in Iran, 333, 337, 363–70
Mosul, 14, 20, 26–7, 31, 35–40, 70
Mount Herman, xix
Mount Hira, xxv
Mount Lebanon, xxxviii
"mountain Turks," 13
Muawiyah, xxvi
Mughrabim, 76
Muhammed, xxv–xxvi, 4, 6, 28, 205–7
Muḥarram, 207
mukhtārs, 210
mulk land, xl, 83
Mulla Mustafa, 16
mullah, 154
mūman, 207
Munīr al'Abbās, 25
muqaddam, 21
murabitīn, 133
murid (disciple), 26
Muslim, xxxv–xxxviii, 4, 7–9, 22, 27–8,
    36, 42–3, 73, 154–5, 221, 222, 225,
    229, 232, 235–6
Mustafa Barzani, 20
Mustafa Kemal Ataturk, xxxii
Mustansir, 33

Nabatean Empire, xxiii
Najaf, xxvii
"Nakshabandia," 251
nationalism, xxxvii, 13–20, 32, 44
Near East, xvii, 8
Negev, xix
Nejd, xviii
Neo-Babylonia, xxii
Nero, xxiii
Nestorian (Chaldean or Assyrian)
    Church, xxiv, 38
Nestorians, 11, 34–5, 60
Nile, xix
Nizār, 33
Nizāris, 33–4

nomads, xxv, xli–xlii, 4–7, 9, 15, 119–
    135, 153–68, 223–4, 226–7
North Africa, 9, 33, 72–3
North African Jews, 72–3
Nowruz, 155
Nūrī al'Sa'īd, 16, 20
Nusayries, xxxiv, xxxvi, 21

oil interests in Iran, 333
Oren, 387–403
"Oriental" Jews, 76
origin of "Arab," 3–9
Orontes, xx
Orthodox Caliphate of Islam, xxviii
Ottoman, 11–2, 38, 72
Ottoman Empire, xvii, xxix–xxx,
    xxxvii, 8

paganism, 26
Palestine, xx, xxii–xxiii, xxxi–xxxii,
    32; see Israel
Pan-Iranian Party, 343
pashalik, 18, 39
Pashas, 18
Patriarch of Antioch, 39
Patriarch of Babylon, 38
Peacock Angel, 26
peasant life in Middle East, xxxix–xl
peasants, xxxiii, 105–11, 112–8
People of the Veil, 130–5
Persia, xx, xxii, xxvii–xxviii, xxxv,
    xli, 6, 8, 11, 26, 28, 29, 33–5,
    51–67, 105–11; see Iran
Persian language, 53
Petra, xxiii
Pharaonic temple murals, xxxix
Philistines, xxi, xxii
Phonecians, xxii
pir, 26, 28, 124
Plain of Sharon, xx
political intrigue in Iran, 335–6
politics, 10–44, 55–6, 58, 180–1, 186–7,
    189, 199–200
polygamy, 263
polygyny, 238, 244–5
Pontic kingdom, xxiii
Popular Bloc, 24
Popular Force, 200
Popular Party, 24
population increase, xxxiii
Pravoslav Church, 40

Progressive Party, 29
protection of Iran by Western powers,
    334
Ptolemy, xxii, xxiii
public welfare programs in Saudi
    Arabia, 219–32
Pushdir, 15

Qajars, 59
Qamishli, 19, 29, 33
Qarmations, xxviii
Qashqa'i, 58
qat, 228
qewwāls, 26
Qizilbash tribe, 59
qrāyat ceremonies, 207

ra'īs, 21
Ramadan, xxvi
Ramgavar, 29
ratib, 251
ratna, 35
religion, 8, 11–2, 21, 22–3, 25, 26, 28–
    29, 35–44, 54, 60–1, 235, 243,
    251–2
religions of the Middle East, xxxiv–
    xxxviii
religious functionaries of Islam, 182–4
religious history of the early Middle
    East, xxii–xxvii
religious schisms of Islam, xxxv
riba, 178
Riddah, xxvii
role of women in a Arab Muslim vil-
    lage, 116–7
Roman Catholic Church, 11, 39, 42
Roman Empire, xxii, xxiii, xxiv
Roman Palestine, xxiii
rule of terror in Iran, 337
Russia; see Union of Soviet Socialist
    Republics
Ruwandiz, 15

Saadabad, 15
sabras, 290–312
sāda, 206–8
Sa'dabad Pact of 1937, 335
Sāfitā, 31
saha, 81, 83
Sahara, 130–5

Sahara caravan routes, 73
Said Muhammed, 154
Saladin, 12
Salah al Din, xxviii
Salamiya, 33
Sālim Namīq, 17
saluqi, 148
Samaritans, xxxv
Saracen, 5, 8
Sargon, xxi
sarifa, xlvii
Sassanid dynasty, 103
Saudi Arabia, xvii, 219–32
sayyid, xxv, 124, 154, 158, 161, 183, 206
schooling in an Arab Muslim village, 115
Sea of Galilee, xx
Second Temple, 69
Seleucids, xxiii
Seleucus, xxii
Seljuqs, xxix
Semitic language, 60, 63
Semitic traditions, xxiii
Sephardim, 75–6
Sephardis, 33
Sèvres, xxxi, 12–3
Shabak, 28
Shah Abbas, 60
Shah Savan tribe, 59
Shahbandar, 23
Shahbandariyya, 23
Shalmaneser V, xxii
Shammar, 31
share-cropping system, 22, 25
sharifs, 183
Shawaiya, 125
shaykh al Islam, xxx
Shaykhān, 27
sheikh, xxv, 26
Sheikh 'Adi, 27
Sheikh Mahmud, 60
Shepelah, xix
Shi'a, 54, 56, 58, 60
Shi'a Islam, 58, 60
Shi'a Muslim, xxxv–xxxvi, 56, 60, 154
Shi'i, 28, 31, 42–3
Shi'ism, 11, 21, 28
Shiites, xxvii, xxviii, 57, 58
Shim'ōn, 36
Shiraz, 63
shrines, xxvii, 61, 155–6
Shulchan Aruch, 76

Silwa, 247–64
şirkals, 210, 214–5
"Six-Day War," xlix
slaves, xxvii, xxviii–xxix, 23, 126, 127, 133, 134, 188, 211–3
social groups, 15, 21, 32
social mobility in Arab society, 176
social status, 41
social stratification, xlii, 124–35, 174–200
    in an Iraqi village, 205–15
social system, structure, 44
soureth, 36
Soviet Armenia, 16
spirits, 35
statehood of Kurds, 13
strikes by workers in the Arab East, 197–9
Şubba, 213–5
Suez Canal, 320
Sūfi, 27
Sulaba, 126, 127, 170–3
Sulaymān Murshid, 25
Sulaymāni, 14–5, 20
Suleiman the Magnificent, xxix
Sultan Abdul Hamid, xxx
Sultan Atrash, 24
Sumayl, 37
Sumerians, xxi
Sunna, xxv
Sunni, 22, 24, 28, 31, 42–3
Sunni Arab, 23
Sunni Islam, xxix, 12, 57
Sunni Muslim, xxxv–xxxviii
Sunni Muslim Kurds, xxxiv, xxxvi
Sunni Saldjuqs, 33
Syria, xix-xxix, 6, 8, 10–44, 70, 404–22
Syria-Arabian Desert, xxi, 5
Syria-Hejaz railroad, xxx
Syrian Catholics, 11, 35, 38–40
Syrian or Jacobite Church, xxiv
Syrian Orthodox, 11, 35, 38–9
Syrian Palmyra empire, xxiii
Syrian peasant household, 99–104
Syrian schooner, 404–23

targum, 32, 36
Taurus, xviii
Ta'ūs-é-Melek, 26
taviz, 161
taxes, xxix, 222
Teheran, xviii, 13, 61

Teheran dialect, 51–67
Tell Toqaan, 99–104
tent, Arab, 136–51
The Jewish State, 1
"Third Arab-Israel War," xlix
Tigris, xix
topography of the Middle East, 119,
    120, 121
trade, xxiv, xxix
trade unions in the Arab countries,
    193–201
tradition influencing village behavior,
    112–8
Trans-Arabian Pipe Line Company
    (Tapline), 220, 230
transhumants, 125
transitional period of the Middle East,
    xlv
Transjordan, xxxii, 24
tribe, xxv, 6–7, 12, 13, 14–8, 21, 23,
    25, 27, 28, 30, 31, 35, 52–3, 54–9,
    121–35, 170–3
Tuareg, 121, 131–5
Tunesia, 73
Turkestan, 11
Turkey, xviii, xxix–xxxvii, 9, 11–3, 15,
    17, 19, 23, 28, 29, 31, 36, 37, 38,
    39, 58–9, 72, 73
Turkic dialects, 63
Turkmenistan, 14
Turkomans, xxxiv, xxxv, 8, 11, 19, 28,
    31

'ulama, 182
ulema, xxx
Umar, xxv
Umayyad Caliphate, xxvii–xxviii
unemployment, 186, 189, 197
Uniate Eastern Church, 35
Union of Soviet Socialist Republics,
    xxxi–xxxii, 14, 29, 59
unions, 193–200
United Nations, xxxii
unskilled labor in Arab countries, 192–
    193
urbanization, xlv–xlix

Urfalim, 76
Uthman, xxv, xxix, xxvi
Uzrī, 17
Uzza, xxv

Vespasian, xxiii
villages
    Arab Muslim, 112–8
    Badawin (bedouin), 136–51
    Egyptian, 247–64
    Iraqi, 205–15
    Israeli, 387–403
    Lebanese, 79–97
    of the nomads, 119–35
    Persian, 105–11
    Syrian/Muslim Arab, 99–104
    Turkish/Anatolian, 427–37

wadis, 79, 120
Wafd, 196–7, 199
wejh, 128
welfare system in Saudi Arabia, 219–
    232
Westernization, xli, l–li, 181–2, 184,
    187
World Health Organization (WHO),
    222, 226, 227–31

Yazīdis, 11, 19, 26–8
Yemen, xviii–xix, xxxii, xxxvi, 33
Yerevan, 14
Yiddish, 75
Young Turks, 19

Za'faran, 39
Zagros Massi, xviii
Zagros mountains, 55
Zaydis, xxxvi
Zenobia, xxiii
Ziarat, 155
"Zikr," 251
Zionist nationalist movement, xxxi, 1
Zoroastrian faith, 54